Writing Exploratory Essays

Writing Exploratory Essays

STEVEN M. STRANG

Massachusetts Institute of Technology
and
Wheaton College

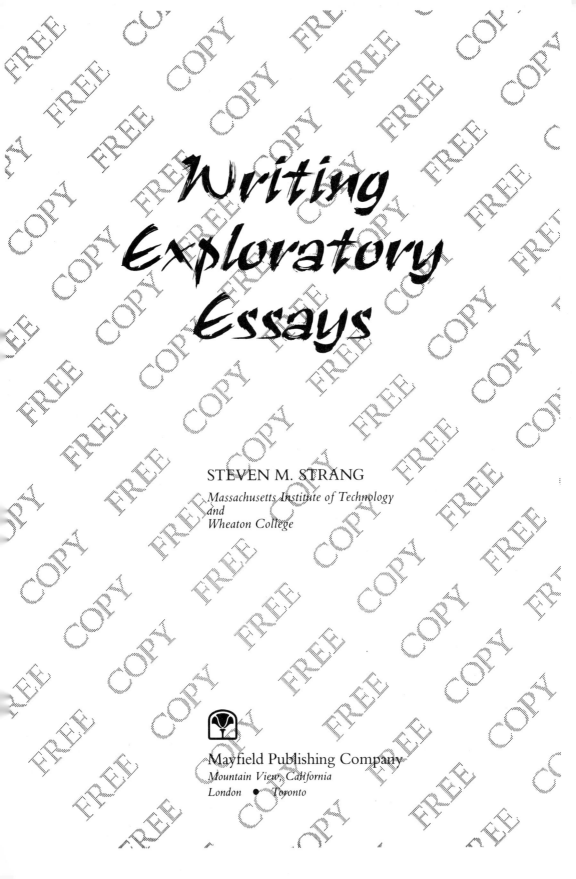

Mayfield Publishing Company
Mountain View, California
London • *Toronto*

LIBRARY OF CONGRESS CATALOGING-IN-PUBLICATION DATA
Strang, Steven M.
    Writing exploratory essays / Steven M. Strang.
        p.   cm.
    ISBN 1-55934-262-5
    1. English language—Rhetoric.   2. Exposition (Rhetoric)
3. Essay—Authorship.   4. Report writing.   I. Title.
PE1429.S76   1995
808'.042—dc20   94-41376
                                                                CIP

Manufactured in the United States of America

10   9   8   7   6   5   4   3   2   1

Mayfield Publishing Company
1280 Villa Street
Mountain View, California 94041

Sponsoring editor, Thomas V. Broadbent; production editor, April Wells-Hayes;
manuscript editor, Margaret Moore; art director, Jeanne M. Schreiber; text and
cover designer, Linda M. Robertson; manufacturing manager, Aimee Rutter.
The text was set in 10.5/12 Bembo by G&S Typesetters, Inc., and printed on
45# Restorecote by The Maple Vail Book Manufacturing Group.

Cover image: © Dovrat Ben Nahum; by permission.

Acknowledgments appear on pages A1–A4, which constitute an extension of
the copyright page.

 This book is printed on acid-free, recycled paper.

Preface

Too often, essay assignments are seen as merely something to be gotten through—students have to get through writing the essays and teachers have to get through reading them. This book tries to change that dreary perception by emphasizing the importance of the essays produced as well as the excitement of the process of writing.

Writing Exploratory Essays reflects the following beliefs: (1) self-knowledge is one of the main goals of education; (2) one of the best ways to learn about ourselves is by writing; (3) students care most about writing when they can connect to their subjects on a personal level; and (4) students revise more thoroughly and more carefully when they are revealing not only their academic insights but also themselves.

Given those beliefs, it is not surprising that all the suggested writing topics and all the selections in this book are intended to help students explore themselves by exploring some other subject at the same time. Students are invited to use their own experiences to shed light on the official subject (for example, a controversy or a literary text) and, conversely, to use the official subject to illuminate elements of their own inner selves. When students begin revising their drafts for their readers, they must make decisions about what aspects of themselves to reveal, how to link their insights into themselves to their insights into the subject, and how to make the resulting essays interesting and credible. Never is writing for an audience more charged with significance than when students have to decide how much of themselves they should reveal in their essays. At the same time, because self-revelation entails risks, this is a stage of the writing process in which students are especially vulnerable to that occasional foe of most writers, "writer's block." Accordingly, one key feature of this book is its straightforward advice about the causes of and remedies for students' hesitation or inability to write. Another helpful feature—introduced in Chapter 1—is an idea-generating technique I call "perspectives."

Because students are excited about the act of discovery and because this book emphasizes the desire of teachers to be informed and entertained by students' essays, the students begin to develop a sense of their own potential worth as writers, and writing becomes a means of communicating something both important and interesting.

THE STRUCTURE

Chapters 1–9 identify a general subject to be explored. For instance, Chapter 1 examines the reasons for writing. Chapter 2 discusses ways of viewing ourselves and of writing about ourselves. Chapter 3 moves outward into techniques for exploring events that are important to the writer. Chapter 4 discusses writing about other people, building on the fact that most events involve more people than just the writer and also looking at the types of people who can be significant in writers' lives. Chapter 5 builds on the previous chapters as it discusses ways to explore relationships of various kinds. In Chapter 6 students move beyond direct personal experience to include other sources—friends, experts, printed works—as they explore ideas and concepts. Chapter 7 moves them inward again as they explore the concepts that have become personal beliefs. Chapter 8 leads them outward to research as they explore controversies that involve their beliefs and assumptions about the world. Chapter 9 leads them further into analysis and interpretation as they explore texts (including literary texts such as stories, poems, and a short play). The last two chapters are devoted to the process of revision. Chapter 10 offers a particularly thorough explanation of how to revise and deepen content, while Chapter 11 offers techniques for revising style, moving far beyond mere correctness to show students how to analyze their own styles.

On the most obvious level this book starts with students looking inward at themselves and then helps them move progressively outward through events, relationships, controversies, and texts. On a more subtle level, however, the book engages students in a continual movement inward and outward. That is, students are encouraged first to look inward for their immediate reactions to whatever the chapter's topic may be, then to move outward by considering events and the ideas of other writers, then to carry that information inward to evaluate it, and finally to move outward again to communicate their insights to a reader.

Thus, each selection is preceded by a brief prereading assignment called "Inward Exploration." These assignments may be used for journal entries or for in-class writing at the end of the class before the essay is assigned. Such assignments encourage students to articulate their opinions about the issues or their expectations about the essay's subject before reading. As readers and thinkers, then, students become more active and engaged.

Each essay is followed by two sections. The first, "Outward Exploration: Discussion," poses questions intended to take the students deeper into the essays' ideas and techniques. The second, "Outward Exploration: Writing," suggests possible topics students might write about (in addition to the topics suggested at the end of each chapter).

For most of the essays in each chapter, there is a final section entitled "Style." Here, students' attention is directed to a sentence from the essay they have just read. Sometimes they are given a grammatical analysis (showing them all those dry terms in action); other times they are shown the effect of a particular technique such as parallelism. The students are then asked to use their own material to write a sentence imitating the one they have studied. Such brief exercises help students add to their stylistic repertoire and, at the same time, become more aware of how professional writers use language.

An extensive glossary of key terms and short biographies of all the writers are provided at the end of the book, just before the index.

In the Instructor's Manual I have tried to make useful suggestions both about the readings themselves and about the accompanying "apparatus."

THE READINGS

The book's eighty readings include many acknowledged masterpieces, as well as new selections that my students and I have found exciting. The writers range in time from Francis Bacon and Anne Bradstreet to Alice Walker and Grace Ming-Yee Wai. In addition to works by professional essayists, novelists, and poets, there are pieces by writers who are teachers, journalists, scientists, historians, doctors, and naturalists. Multicultural issues and writers from diverse backgrounds are abundantly represented.

The works in the book raise enduring themes and issues for students to ponder and explore, including art, beauty, education, family life, gender, identity, inspiration, language, love and hate, nature, parent-child relationships, personal epiphanies, morality, teachers and mentors, travel, and writing. These and other themes are highlighted in the alternate groupings—"Readings Arranged by Subject and Theme"—that follow the Table of Contents as a guide to some of the connections that can be made among the readings.

IN CONCLUSION

In over twenty years of teaching, I have observed that students do more revising and, in general, put more effort into exploratory essays than into any other kind of expository writing. A bonus for me has been that, in addition to receiving more interesting essays, I have come to know many students very well. Those exploratory essays reveal not only the events in their lives but also their beliefs and ways of thinking. Ultimately, this book encourages students to take chances with their writing and with themselves. It encourages them to stretch in order to expand their knowledge of themselves—and to communicate what they have learned.

ACKNOWLEDGMENTS

It is impossible to thank everyone who directly or indirectly influenced this book. Without question, however, this text would be something totally different and vastly inferior had it not been for the many wonderful, insightful, and challenging students at MIT and Wheaton College. Special thanks go to all the students in "Personal Essay" and "Writing and Reading the Essay" whose questions, comments, honesty, and interest forced me to refine—and sometimes change—my ideas. Also, many colleagues and friends at both colleges have been very supportive and helpful throughout.

Everyone at Mayfield Publishing Company deserves very special thanks. April Wells-Hayes skillfully guided this book through production and overcame several last-minute flurries of activity that no one should have to endure. Pamela Trainer helped me to obtain permissions. Margaret Moore's sensitive copyediting has made my prose better than it was. And I particularly want to thank Tom Broadbent, my editor, for his enthusiastic support for the concept from the beginning and for his advice and support throughout the process of writing.

I also thank all the members of my family, especially my grandmother and my parents, who encouraged my writing career in the first place with the gift of a manual typewriter when I was eleven years old.

Finally, I want to acknowledge the profound contribution made by my immediate family—my wife Ayni, my son Elly, and my daughter Marta. Without their comments, insights, thoughtful readings of chapters, patience, encouragement, and love, this project would still be only an idea waiting to be born. To them this book is dedicated.

Contents

Preface   *v*
Readings Arranged by Subject and Theme   *xix*

1 Introduction to Exploratory Writing   *1*

Writing: A Private Act Made Public   *2*
Personal versus Private Subject Matter   *2*
Writing to Readers   *4*
Types of Exploratory Essays   *5*
Thinking for Ourselves   *6*
Writing about Personal Experience   *7*
The Exploratory Essay Explained   *8*
   Montaigne's *Essais*   *8*
   Goals of the Exploratory Essay   *9*
   A Vehicle of Inquiry   *10*
   Implications of the Exploratory Essay   *11*
The Writing Process   *11*
   Prewriting   *11*
   Drafting   *11*
   Revising   *14*
   Editing   *15*
Prewriting: Generating Ideas and Planning   *16*
   Free Association   *16*
   Freewriting   *17*
   Directed Freewriting   *18*
   Listing   *18*
   Mind Mapping, or Ballooning   *20*
   Idea Trees   *21*
   Questioning   *21*
   Perspectives   *22*
   Planning   *25*
External Details versus Internal Details   *25*
The Illusion of Objectivity   *26*
Overview of This Book   *27*
Guidelines for Exploratory Essayists   *27*
Suggestions for Writing   *28*
Readings   *30*
   The Essayist and the Essay, E. B. WHITE   *30*
   Why I Write, JOAN DIDION   *33*
   The Singular First Person, SCOTT RUSSELL SANDERS   *40*
   Language and Literature from a Pueblo Indian Perspective,
     LESLIE MARMON SILKO   *52*
   Seeing, ANNIE DILLARD   *60*

2 Exploring the Self 75

Writer-Based Goals 75
Reader-Based Goals 76
Who Are You? 76
  Labeling Identities 76
  The Uses of Labeling Identities 78
Getting Personal 79
  Assume Complexity 79
  Ask Yourself Questions about Your Emotions and Ideas 79
  Ask Yourself Those Same Questions Again 80
  Locate the Sources of Your Emotions and Beliefs 80
  Consider Reactions Opposite Yours 81
  Explore Significant Relationships 82
Gaze Outward and Inward 82
A Vision of the Self 82
Using Vantage Points to Explore the Self 83
  Human Vantage Point 84
  Gender Vantage Point 84
  National Vantage Point 85
  Regional Vantage Point 85
  State Vantage Point 85
  Hometown Vantage Point 86
  Economic-Class Vantage Point 86
  Educational Vantage Point 87
  Family Vantage Point 87
  Religious or Philosophical Vantage Point 87
  Personal-Experience Vantage Point 87
Obstacles to Exploring the Self 88
  Embarrassment 89
  Fear That We Don't Have an Interesting Inner Self 89
  Fear of Revealing Too Much 90
How to Start 91
  Starting with a Mental Occurrence 91
  Starting with an Attitude 92
  Starting with External Information 92
Suggestions for Writing 93
Readings 94
  Growing Up Asian in America, KESAYA E. NODA 94
  How It Feels to Be Colored Me, ZORA NEALE HURSTON 102
  A Few Words about Breasts, NORA EPHRON 106
  On Being a Cripple, NANCY MAIRS 115
  Introduction to *Tuxedo Junction,* GERALD EARLY 127

3 Exploring Events   *141*

Writer-Based Goals   *142*
Reader-Based Goals   *143*
Selecting Events for Exploration   *143*
Three Potential Problems of Exploring Events   *147*
   Lack of Distance   *147*
   Lack of Focus   *148*
   Lack of a Point   *149*
Fulfilling Your Writer-Based and Reader-Based Goals   *150*
   Explore the External Nature of the Event   *150*
   Explore the Event's Personal Significance for You   *150*
      Emotional Significance   *151*
      Philosophical Significance   *152*
   Consider Your Split Perspective   *153*
   Explore the Event's Global Significance   *154*
   Use Vivid Description and Vivid Language   *155*
   Avoid Universality   *157*
   Be Alert to Symbolic Implications   *157*
   Sacrifice Facts for Emotional Truth   *157*
   Make Events Humorous   *158*
Our Dynamic Relationship to the Past   *159*
Suggestions for Writing   *159*
Readings   *161*
   On Being a Real Westerner, TOBIAS WOLFF   *161*
   A Hanging, GEORGE ORWELL   *165*
   The War of the Ants, HENRY DAVID THOREAU   *170*
   The Stone Horse, BARRY LOPEZ   *174*
   Once More to the Lake, E. B. WHITE   *183*
   Beauty: When the Other Dancer Is the Self,
      ALICE WALKER   *190*

4 Exploring Other People   *199*

Writer-Based Goals   *199*
Reader-Based Goals   *199*
Selecting Someone to Write About   *200*
   Someone You Know   *200*
   Public and Fictitious Figures   *200*
Understanding Other People   *201*
   Observing Someone You Know   *202*
   Observing Someone You Don't Know Personally   *205*
   Using Yourself as a Model   *205*
   Using the Techniques of Literary Analysis   *207*
      Physical Characteristics   *207*
      Background and Childhood Experiences   *207*

Dialogue *208*
Actions *208*
Contradictions *208*
Reactions to Situations *208*
Objects Associated with Characters *209*
Misperceptions *209*
Patterns of Behavior *209*
Applying the Techniques of Literary Analysis to
Real People *211*
Using Literary Characters in Another Way *211*
Exploring Complexities *213*
Exploring Groups *214*
Exploring Significance *214*
Suggestions for Writing *215*
Readings *216*
My Uncle Willie, MAYA ANGELOU *216*
Afterthoughts, JEAN ERVIN *220*
My Father's Life, RAYMOND CARVER *231*
Raymond Carver, Mentor, JAY MCINERNEY *240*
Notes of a Native Son, JAMES BALDWIN *247*

5 Exploring Relationships *267*

Writer–Based Goals *269*
Reader–Based Goals *270*
Selecting a Relationship *270*
Understanding the Relationship *271*
Sources of Our Assumptions *271*
Patterns *271*
Patterns within the Relationship *271*
Patterns among Relationships *272*
Obstacles to Exploring Relationships *272*
An Approach to Understanding Relationships *273*
Romantic Relationships *274*
Our Hopes for the Romantic Relationship *274*
Exercise 1 *276*
The Ideal Other Person in the Relationship *276*
Exercise 2 *277*
Our Fears about Romantic Relationships *277*
Exercise 3 *277*
Sources of Our Expectations about Relationships *277*
Exercise 4 *278*
Criteria for a Good Relationship *278*
Exercise 5 *278*
Exploring a Former Relationship *279*
My Criteria Then and Now *280*

Desirable Traits of My Ideal Partner Then and Now   *281*
Hopes for and Fears about the Relationship   *281*
Sources of These Expectations   *281*
Analyzing a Relationship   *282*
What Was the Context?   *282*
What Attracted Us to Each Other?   *282*
What Were the Good Times and the Bad Times?   *283*
What Was the Most Significant Event in the
Relationship?   *283*
Was There a Triggering Event?   *283*
Were There Other Causes?   *284*
What Was the Personal Significance of the Relationship?   *284*
What Is the Wider Significance of the Relationship?   *285*
Pitfalls of Writing about a Romantic Relationship   *285*
Exercise 6   *286*
Readings   *287*
Photographs of My Parents, MAXINE HONG KINGSTON   *287*
Like Mexicans, GARY SOTO   *291*
Students and Teachers, ALAN LIGHTMAN   *296*
My Horse and I, N. SCOTT MOMADAY   *302*
On Being Raised by a Daughter, NANCY MAIRS   *307*
Unlearning Romance, GLORIA STEINEM   *320*

6 Exploring Concepts   *337*

Writer-Based Goals   *337*
Reader-Based Goals   *338*
The Process for Exploring Concepts   *338*
Select an Idea That Interests You   *338*
Dictionary Seek-and-Write   *338*
Titles   *339*
Sample of Directed Freewriting   *339*
Discover What You Already Know about the Concept   *340*
Defining the Concept   *340*
One-Sentence Definitions   *341*
The *Mothering* Example   *342*
Exploring the Sources of Your Personal Definition   *343*
Examining Experiences That Illustrate the Concept   *343*
Gather Information from Outside Sources   *343*
Examining Outside Sources That Illustrate or Discuss the
Concept   *343*
Texts   *343*
People   *344*
Responding to Others' Visions of the Concept   *345*
Structure of an Essay Exploring a Concept   *345*
Possible Places to Expand Your Draft   *346*

Suggestions for Writing *346*

Readings *348*

"Mommy, What Does 'Nigger' Mean?" GLORIA NAYLOR *348*

Americanization Is Tough on "Macho," ROSE DEL CASTILLO GUILBAULT *352*

On the Decay of the Art of Lying, MARK TWAIN *356*

On Natural Death, LEWIS THOMAS *362*

Selections from *The Devil's Dictionary,* AMBROSE BIERCE *365*

The Ignored Lesson of Anne Frank, BRUNO BETTELHEIM *369*

7 Exploring Beliefs 383

What Is a Belief? *383*

Stating a Belief *384*

Considering the Implications of a Belief *385*

Considering the Sources of a Belief *385*

Writer–Based Goals *387*

Reader–Based Goals *387*

Structuring the Essay *387*

Beliefs in Action *388*

Looking for Complexity *388*

Avoiding Common Problems *390*

Exercise 1 *390*

Readings *394*

Was the World Made for Man? MARK TWAIN *394*

The Death of the Moth, VIRGINIA WOOLF *399*

The Perils and Pitfalls of Reporting in the Lone Star State, MOLLY IVINS *403*

Living Like Weasels, ANNIE DILLARD *414*

Where I Lived, and What I Lived For, HENRY DAVID THOREAU *419*

The Four Idols, FRANCIS BACON *430*

8 Exploring Controversies 441

Writing about Controversies *411*

Choosing a Controversy *443*

Writer–Based Goals *443*

Reader–Based Goals *444*

Types of Readers *444*

Developing Strategies to Explore Controversies *445*

Claims, Evidence, Warrants *447*

Claims *447*

Evidence *448*

Warrants *449*

Claims, Evidence, and Warrants in Action *450*

Suggestion for Writing *452*
Readings *453*
   Am I Blue? ALICE WALKER *453*
   Death and Justice: How Capital Punishment Affirms Life,
      EDWARD I. KOCH *458*
   Random Reflections of a Second-Rate Mind, WOODY
      ALLEN *464*
   Against Nature, JOYCE CAROL OATES *470*
   Save the Whales, Screw the Shrimp, JOY WILLIAMS *478*

9 Exploring Texts *491*

Writer–Based Goals *492*
Reader–Based Goals *492*
Responding to Literary Texts *492*
Exploratory Essays about Literary Texts *493*
   The First Step: Observe Your Own Responses *493*
   The Second Step: Write about Your Responses *494*
   The Third Step: Check the Responses of Others *494*
   The Fourth Step: Return to the Text *495*
   The Fifth Step: Write a Draft *495*
   The Sixth Step: Revise *495*
      Personalize the Exploration *495*
      Recreate Your Process *496*
Conditioned versus Real Responses *506*
Suggestions for Writing *508*
Readings *509*
   Désirée's Baby, KATE CHOPIN *509*
   Young Goodman Brown, NATHANIEL HAWTHORNE *515*
   The Dark Wood, JANETTE TURNER HOSPITAL *527*
   To Build a Fire, JACK LONDON *535*
   The Censors, LUISA VALENZUELA *549*
   Trifles, SUSAN GLASPELL *552*
   Poem for the Young White Man Who Asked Me How I, An
      Intelligent, Well-Read Person, Could Believe in the War
      Between Races, LORNA DEE CERVANTES *565*
   Five Short Poems, STEPHEN CRANE *568*
   The Woman Hanging from the Thirteenth Floor Window,
      JOY HARJO *571*
   Off from Swing Shift, GARRETT HONGO *574*
   Latero Story, TATO LAVIERA *576*
   The Weak Monk, STEVIE SMITH *579*
   The Youngest Daughter, CATHY SONG *580*
   Hopper's Women, SUE STANDING *582*
   Scene from the Movie *GIANT*, TINO VILLANUEVA *584*

10 Revising Content *587*

Why Revise? *587*
  Deleting Material *589*
  Adding Material *589*
    Adding Context and Background Information *590*
    Adding Details *591*
    Adding Dialogue *593*
    Adding Speculation about Motives and Meaning *594*
    Adding Personal Significance *595*
    Adding Global Significance *596*
Questioning *597*
Writing Introductions *597*
A Revision Checklist for Content *598*
The Tension Between Being Explicit and Being Implicit *601*

11 Revising Style *603*

What Is Style? *603*
Words *604*
  Choosing the Right Word *604*
    Exercise 1 605
  Avoiding Suitcase Words *605*
  Distancing Words *606*
  Avoiding Sexist Language *607*
Figurative Language *609*
  Simile *609*
  Metaphor *609*
  Symbol *612*
  Analogy *613*
Sentences *614*
  Sentence Length *615*
    Exercise 2 615
  Sentence Structure *616*
    Clauses *616*
      Exercise 3 617
    First Elements *618*
      Exercise 4 619
    Modifiers *619*
    Sentence Fragments *620*
Coherence *620*
Wordiness *623*
  Overuse of *I* *623*
  To Be or Not *to Be* *625*
Editing *628*

Final Advice about Revising Style   *629*
    Exercise 5   629
Checklist for Style   *630*

Further Readings   *633*

My Speech to the Graduates, WOODY ALLEN   *633*
Daze of Wine and Roses, DAVE BARRY   *637*
Proverbs of Hell, WILLIAM BLAKE   *641*
To My Dear Children, ANNE BRADSTREET   *644*
"You're Short, Besides!" SUCHENG CHAN   *650*
From *Narrative of the Life of Frederick Douglass, Written by Himself,*
    FREDERICK DOUGLASS   *658*
The Ghost Dance War, CHARLES ALEXANDER EASTMAN   *666*
Leaves from the Mental Portfolio of an Eurasian, EDITH MAUD
    EATON (SUI SIN FAR)   *674*
The Wretched of the Hearth, BARBARA EHRENREICH   *687*
Selections from *Poor Richard's Almanack,* BENJAMIN FRANKLIN   *690*
The Objects of My Invention, ABBY FRUCHT   *693*
Madonna: Plantation Mistress or Soul Sister? BELL HOOKS   *699*
From *Incidents in the Life of a Slave Girl,* HARRIET JACOBS   *707*
The Site of Memory, TONI MORRISON   *711*
Love Me or Leave Me, BHARATI MUKHERJEE   *720*
At Home in the Parliament of Whores, P. J. O'ROURKE   *728*
Shooting an Elephant, GEORGE ORWELL   *738*
Being a Jr., RAFAEL A. SUAREZ, JR.   *746*
A Modest Proposal, JONATHAN SWIFT   *749*
Fenimore Cooper's Literary Offenses, MARK TWAIN   *758*
Chinese Puzzle, GRACE MING-YEE WAI   *770*

Glossary   *777*
About the Authors   *789*
Acknowledgments   *A1*
Index of Authors and Titles   *I1*

Readings Arranged by Subject and Theme

Animals

Seeing, ANNIE DILLARD 60
On Being a Real Westerner, TOBIAS WOLFF 161
The War of the Ants, HENRY DAVID THOREAU 170
The Stone Horse, BARRY LOPEZ 174
Once More to the Lake, E. B. WHITE 183
My Horse and I, N. SCOTT MOMADAY 302
On Natural Death, LEWIS THOMAS 362
Was the World Made for Man? MARK TWAIN 394
The Death of the Moth, VIRGINIA WOOLF 399
Living Like Weasels, ANNIE DILLARD 414
Am I Blue? ALICE WALKER 453
Against Nature, JOYCE CAROL OATES 470
Save the Whales, Screw the Shrimp, JOY WILLIAMS 478
To Build a Fire [story], JACK LONDON 535
Trifles [play], SUSAN GLASPELL 552
Shooting an Elephant, GEORGE ORWELL 738

Arguments

Unlearning Romance, GLORIA STEINEM 320
The Ignored Lesson of Anne Frank, BRUNO BETTELHEIM 369
Was the World Made for Man? MARK TWAIN 394
The Perils and Pitfalls of Reporting in the Lone Star State, MOLLY
    IVINS 403
The Four Idols, FRANCIS BACON 430
Am I Blue? ALICE WALKER 453
Against Nature, JOYCE CAROL OATES 470
Save the Whales, Screw the Shrimp, JOY WILLIAMS 478
Poem for the Young White Man Who Asked Me How I, An
    Intelligent, Well-Read Person, Could Believe in the War Between
    the Races [poem], LORNA DEE CERVANTES 565
To My Dear Children, ANNE BRADSTREET 644
The Wretched of the Hearth, BARBARA EHRENREICH 687
Shooting an Elephant, GEORGE ORWELL 738
A Modest Proposal, JONATHAN SWIFT 749

The Arts

Language and Literature from a Pueblo Indian Perspective, LESLIE
    MARMON SILKO 52
How It Feels to Be Colored Me, ZORA NEALE HURSTON 102
Introduction to *Tuxedo Junction*, GERALD EARLY 127

The Stone Horse, BARRY LOPEZ   *174*
Beauty: When the Other Dancer Is the Self, ALICE WALKER   *190*
Raymond Carver, Mentor, JAY MCINERNEY   *240*
Photographs of My Parents, MAXINE HONG KINGSTON   *287*
Students and Teachers, ALAN LIGHTMAN   *296*
Unlearning Romance, GLORIA STEINEM   *320*
The Perils and Pitfalls of Reporting in the Lone Star State, MOLLY
   IVINS   *403*
Against Nature, JOYCE CAROL OATES   *470*
Hopper's Women [poem], SUE STANDING   *582*
Madonna: Plantation Mistress or Soul Sister? BELL HOOKS   *699*
Love Me or Leave Me, BHARATI MUKHERJEE   *720*

Biography and Portraiture

My Uncle Willie, MAYA ANGELOU   *216*
Afterthoughts, JEAN ERVIN   *220*
My Father's Life, RAYMOND CARVER   *231*
Raymond Carver, Mentor, JAY MCINERNEY   *240*
Notes of a Native Son, JAMES BALDWIN   *247*
Photographs of My Parents, MAXINE HONG KINGSTON   *287*
Students and Teachers, ALAN LIGHTMAN   *296*
My Horse and I, N. SCOTT MOMADAY   *302*
On Being Raised by a Daughter, NANCY MAIRS   *307*
The Ignored Lesson of Anne Frank, BRUNO BETTELHEIM   *369*
Désirée's Baby [story], KATE CHOPIN   *509*
Young Goodman Brown [story], NATHANIEL HAWTHORNE   *515*
To Build a Fire [story], JACK LONDON   *535*
The Censors [story], LUISA VALENZUELA   *549*
Trifles [play], SUSAN GLASPELL   *552*
Off from Swing Shift [poem], GARRETT HONGO   *574*
Latero Story [poem], TATO LAVIERA   *576*
The Weak Monk [poem], STEVIE SMITH   *579*
The Youngest Daughter [poem], CATHY SONG   *580*
Love Me or Leave Me, BHARATI MUKHERJEE   *720*
Chinese Puzzle, GRACE MING-YEE WAI   *770*

Childhood and Growing Up

Growing Up Asian in America, KESAYA E. NODA   *94*
How It Feels to Be Colored Me, ZORA NEALE HURSTON   *102*
A Few Words about Breasts, NORA EPHRON   *106*
On Being a Cripple, NANCY MAIRS   *115*
Introduction to *Tuxedo Junction,* GERALD EARLY   *127*
On Being a Real Westerner, TOBIAS WOLFF   *161*
Once More to the Lake, E. B. WHITE   *183*
Beauty: When the Other Dancer Is the Self, ALICE WALKER   *190*

My Uncle Willie, MAYA ANGELOU   *216*
Afterthoughts, JEAN ERVIN   *220*
My Father's Life, RAYMOND CARVER   *231*
Notes of a Native Son, JAMES BALDWIN   *247*
Photographs of My Parents, MAXINE HONG KINGSTON   *287*
Like Mexicans, GARY SOTO   *291*
My Horse and I, N. SCOTT MOMADAY   *302*
On Being Raised by a Daughter, NANCY MAIRS   *307*
Unlearning Romance, GLORIA STEINEM   *320*
"Mommy, What Does 'Nigger' Mean?" GLORIA NAYLOR   *348*
The Ignored Lesson of Anne Frank, BRUNO BETTELHEIM   *369*
Random Reflections of a Second-Rate Mind, WOODY ALLEN   *464*
Off from Swing Shift **[poem]**, GARRETT HONGO   *574*
The Youngest Daughter **[poem]**, CATHY SONG   *580*
Scene from the Movie *GIANT* **[poem]**, TINO VILLANUEVA   *584*
To My Dear Children, ANNE BRADSTREET   *644*
"You're Short, Besides!" SUCHENG CHAN   *650*
From *Incidents in the Life of a Slave Girl*, HARRIET JACOBS   *707*
Love Me or Leave Me, BHARATI MUKHERJEE   *720*
Chinese Puzzle, GRACE MING-YEE WAI   *770*

Crime and Punishment

On Being a Real Westerner, TOBIAS WOLFF   *161*
A Hanging, GEORGE ORWELL   *165*
Beauty: When the Other Dancer Is the Self, ALICE WALKER   *190*
Notes of a Native Son, JAMES BALDWIN   *247*
Death and Justice: How Capital Punishment Affirms Life,
    EDWARD I. KOCH   *458*
Young Goodman Brown **[story]**, NATHANIEL HAWTHORNE   *515*
The Censors **[story]**, LUISA VALENZUELA   *549*
Trifles **[play]**, SUSAN GLASPELL   *552*

Cultures

Language and Literature from a Pueblo Indian Perspective, LESLIE
    MARMON SILKO   *52*
Growing Up Asian in America, KESAYA E. NODA   *94*
How It Feels to Be Colored Me, ZORA NEALE HURSTON   *102*
A Few Words about Breasts, NORA EPHRON   *106*
On Being a Cripple, NANCY MAIRS   *115*
Introduction to *Tuxedo Junction*, GERALD EARLY   *127*
On Being a Real Westerner, TOBIAS WOLFF   *161*
A Hanging, GEORGE ORWELL   *165*
The Stone Horse, BARRY LOPEZ   *174*
Beauty: When the Other Dancer Is the Self, ALICE WALKER   *190*
My Uncle Willie, MAYA ANGELOU   *216*

Afterthoughts, JEAN ERVIN   *220*
Notes of a Native Son, JAMES BALDWIN   *247*
Like Mexicans, GARY SOTO   *291*
My Horse and I, N. SCOTT MOMADAY   *302*
"Mommy, What Does 'Nigger' Mean?" GLORIA NAYLOR   *348*
Americanization Is Tough on "Macho," ROSE DEL CASTILLO
   GUILBAULT   *352*
The Ignored Lesson of Anne Frank, BRUNO BETTELHEIM   *369*
Random Reflections of a Second-Rate Mind, WOODY ALLEN   *464*
Désirée's Baby [story], KATE CHOPIN   *509*
The Woman Hanging from the Thirteenth Floor Window [poem],
   JOY HARJO   *571*
Off from Swing Shift [poem], GARRETT HONGO   *574*
Daze of Wine and Roses, DAVE BARRY   *637*
To My Dear Children, ANNE BRADSTREET   *644*
The Ghost Dance War, CHARLES ALEXANDER EASTMAN   *666*
Leaves from the Mental Portfolio of an Eurasian, EDITH MAUD
   EATON (SUI SIN FAR)   *674*
The Wretched of the Hearth, BARBARA EHRENREICH   *687*
Love Me or Leave Me, BHARATI MUKHERJEE   *720*
Shooting an Elephant, GEORGE ORWELL   *738*
Chinese Puzzle, GRACE MING-YEE WAI   *770*

Death

On Being a Real Westerner, TOBIAS WOLFF   *161*
A Hanging, GEORGE ORWELL   *165*
The War of the Ants, HENRY DAVID THOREAU   *170*
Once More to the Lake, E. B. WHITE   *183*
On Natural Death, LEWIS THOMAS   *362*
Selections from *The Devil's Dictionary,* AMBROSE BIERCE   *365*
The Ignored Lesson of Anne Frank, BRUNO BETTELHEIM   *369*
The Death of the Moth, VIRGINIA WOOLF   *399*
Death and Justice: How Capital Punishment Affirms Life,
   EDWARD I. KOCH   *458*
Against Nature, JOYCE CAROL OATES   *470*
Save the Whales, Screw the Shrimp, JOY WILLIAMS   *478*
To Build a Fire [story], JACK LONDON   *535*
Trifles [play], SUSAN GLASPELL   *552*
To My Dear Children, ANNE BRADSTREET   *644*
Chinese Puzzle, GRACE MING-YEE WAI   *770*

Education

The Singular First Person, SCOTT RUSSELL SANDERS   *40*
Growing Up Asian in America, KESAYA E. NODA   *94*
How It Feels to Be Colored Me, ZORA NEALE HURSTON   *102*

Introduction to *Tuxedo Junction,* GERALD EARLY *127*
Once More to the Lake, E. B. WHITE *183*
Beauty: When the Other Dancer Is the Self, ALICE WALKER *190*
Afterthoughts, JEAN ERVIN *220*
Raymond Carver, Mentor, JAY MCINERNEY *240*
Notes of a Native Son, JAMES BALDWIN *247*
Students and Teachers, ALAN LIGHTMAN *296*
On Being Raised by a Daughter, NANCY MAIRS *307*
"Mommy, What Does 'Nigger' Mean?" GLORIA NAYLOR *348*
Selections from *The Devil's Dictionary,* AMBROSE BIERCE *365*
The Ignored Lesson of Anne Frank, BRUNO BETTELHEIM *369*
The Perils and Pitfalls of Reporting in the Lone Star State, MOLLY
  IVINS *403*
The Four Idols, FRANCIS BACON *430*
My Speech to the Graduates, WOODY ALLEN *633*
To My Dear Children, ANNE BRADSTREET *644*
From *Narrative of the Life of Frederick Douglass, Written by Himself,*
  FREDERICK DOUGLASS *658*
The Ghost Dance War, CHARLES ALEXANDER EASTMAN *666*
Chinese Puzzle, GRACE MING-YEE WAI *770*

Ethics and Morality

On Being a Real Westerner, TOBIAS WOLFF *161*
A Hanging, GEORGE ORWELL *165*
On the Decay of the Art of Lying, MARK TWAIN *356*
Selections from *The Devil's Dictionary,* AMBROSE BIERCE *365*
The Ignored Lesson of Anne Frank, BRUNO BETTELHEIM *369*
The Perils and Pitfalls of Reporting in the Lone Star State, MOLLY
  IVINS *403*
Living Like Weasels, ANNIE DILLARD *414*
Where I Lived, and What I Lived For, HENRY DAVID THOREAU *419*
Am I Blue? ALICE WALKER *453*
Death and Justice: How Capital Punishment Affirms Life,
  EDWARD I. KOCH *458*
Random Reflections of a Second-Rate Mind, WOODY ALLEN *464*
Against Nature, JOYCE CAROL OATES *470*
Save the Whales, Screw the Shrimp, JOY WILLIAMS *478*
Désirée's Baby **[story]**, KATE CHOPIN *509*
Young Goodman Brown **[story]**, NATHANIEL HAWTHORNE *515*
The Censors **[story]**, LUISA VALENZUELA *549*
Trifles **[play]**, SUSAN GLASPELL *552*
Five Short Poems **[poems]**, STEPHEN CRANE *568*
The Weak Monk **[poem]**, STEVIE SMITH *579*
My Speech to the Graduates, WOODY ALLEN *633*
To My Dear Children, ANNE BRADSTREET *644*

The Ghost Dance War, CHARLES ALEXANDER EASTMAN   *666*
From *Incidents in the Life of a Slave Girl*, HARRIET JACOBS   *707*
A Modest Proposal, JONATHAN SWIFT   *749*

Family and Friends

Growing Up Asian in America, KESAYA E. NODA   *94*
How It Feels to Be Colored Me, ZORA NEALE HURSTON   *102*
A Few Words about Breasts, NORA EPHRON   *106*
On Being a Cripple, NANCY MAIRS   *115*
On Being a Real Westerner, TOBIAS WOLFF   *161*
Once More to the Lake, E. B. WHITE   *183*
Beauty: When the Other Dancer Is the Self, ALICE WALKER   *190*
My Uncle Willie, MAYA ANGELOU   *216*
Afterthoughts, JEAN ERVIN   *220*
My Father's Life, RAYMOND CARVER   *231*
Raymond Carver, Mentor, JAY MCINERNEY   *240*
Notes of a Native Son, JAMES BALDWIN   *247*
Photographs of My Parents, MAXINE HONG KINGSTON   *287*
Like Mexicans, GARY SOTO   *291*
Students and Teachers, ALAN LIGHTMAN   *296*
My Horse and I, N. SCOTT MOMADAY   *302*
On Being Raised by a Daughter, NANCY MAIRS   *307*
Unlearning Romance, GLORIA STEINEM   *320*
"Mommy, What Does 'Nigger' Mean?" GLORIA NAYLOR   *348*
Americanization Is Tough on "Macho," ROSE DEL CASTILLO
   GUILBAULT   *352*
Selections from *The Devil's Dictionary,* AMBROSE BIERCE   *365*
The Ignored Lesson of Anne Frank, BRUNO BETTELHEIM   *369*
Désirée's Baby **[story]**, KATE CHOPIN   *509*
The Dark Wood **[story]**, JANETTE TURNER HOSPITAL   *527*
Trifles **[play]**, SUSAN GLASPELL   *552*
The Woman Hanging from the Thirteenth Floor Window **[poem]**,
   JOY HARJO   *571*
Off from Swing Shift **[poem]**, GARRETT HONGO   *574*
The Youngest Daughter **[poem]**, CATHY SONG   *580*
To My Dear Children, ANNE BRADSTREET   *644*
Leaves from the Mental Portfolio of an Eurasian, EDITH MAUD
   EATON (SUI SIN FAR)   *674*
The Wretched of the Hearth, BARBARA EHRENREICH   *687*
Being a Jr., RAFAEL A. SUAREZ, JR.   *746*
Chinese Puzzle, GRACE MING-YEE WAI   *770*

Formats and Unusual Approaches

Selections from *The Devil's Dictionary,* AMBROSE BIERCE   *365*
Save the Whales, Screw the Shrimp, JOY WILLIAMS   *478*
My Speech to the Graduates, WOODY ALLEN   *633*

Proverbs of Hell, WILLIAM BLAKE *641*
To My Dear Children, ANNE BRADSTREET *644*
Selections from *Poor Richard's Almanack,* BENJAMIN FRANKLIN *690*

Gender: Men's Experiences

The Singular First Person, SCOTT RUSSELL SANDERS *40*
Introduction to *Tuxedo Junction,* GERALD EARLY *127*
On Being a Real Westerner, TOBIAS WOLFF *161*
A Hanging, GEORGE ORWELL *165*
Once More to the Lake, E. B. WHITE *183*
My Uncle Willie, MAYA ANGELOU *216*
My Father's Life, RAYMOND CARVER *231*
Raymond Carver, Mentor, JAY MCINERNEY *240*
Notes of a Native Son, JAMES BALDWIN *247*
Like Mexicans, GARY SOTO *291*
Students and Teachers, ALAN LIGHTMAN *296*
My Horse and I, N. SCOTT MOMADAY *302*
Unlearning Romance, GLORIA STEINEM *320*
Americanization Is Tough on "Macho," ROSE DEL CASTILLO
   GUILBAULT *352*
The Ignored Lesson of Anne Frank, BRUNO BETTELHEIM *369*
To Build a Fire **[story]**, JACK LONDON *535*
Off from Swing Shift **[poem]**, GARRETT HONGO *574*
Latero Story **[poem]**, TATO LAVIERA *576*
From *Narrative of the Life of Frederick Douglass, Written by Himself,*
   FREDERICK DOUGLASS *658*
The Ghost Dance War, CHARLES ALEXANDER EASTMAN *666*
Love Me or Leave Me, BHARATI MUKHERJEE *720*
Being a Jr., RAFAEL A. SUAREZ, JR. *746*

Gender: Women's Experiences

Growing Up Asian in America, KESAYA E. NODA *94*
How It Feels to Be Colored Me, ZORA NEALE HURSTON *102*
A Few Words about Breasts, NORA EPHRON *106*
On Being a Cripple, NANCY MAIRS *115*
Beauty: When the Other Dancer Is the Self, ALICE WALKER *190*
My Uncle Willie, MAYA ANGELOU *216*
Afterthoughts, JEAN ERVIN *220*
Photographs of My Parents, MAXINE HONG KINGSTON *287*
On Being Raised by a Daughter, NANCY MAIRS *307*
Unlearning Romance, GLORIA STEINEM *320*
"Mommy, What Does 'Nigger' Mean?" GLORIA NAYLOR *348*
Americanization Is Tough on "Macho," ROSE DEL CASTILLO
   GUILBAULT *352*
The Ignored Lesson of Anne Frank, BRUNO BETTELHEIM *369*
Désirée's Baby **[story]**, KATE CHOPIN *509*

The Dark Wood **[story]**, JANETTE TURNER HOSPITAL   *527*

Trifles **[play]**, SUSAN GLASPELL   *552*

Poem for the Young White Man Who Asked Me How I, An Intelligent, Well-Read Person, Could Believe in the War Between the Races **[poem]**, LORNA DEE CERVANTES   *565*

The Woman Hanging from the Thirteenth Floor Window **[poem]**, JOY HARJO   *571*

The Youngest Daughter **[poem]**, CATHY SONG   *580*

Hopper's Women **[poem]**, SUE STANDING   *582*

To My Dear Children, ANNE BRADSTREET   *644*

"You're Short, Besides!" SUCHENG CHAN   *650*

Leaves from the Mental Portfolio of an Eurasian, EDITH MAUD EATON (SUI SIN FAR)   *674*

The Wretched of the Hearth, BARBARA EHRENREICH   *687*

From *Incidents in the Life of a Slave Girl*, HARRIET JACOBS   *707*

The Site of Memory, TONI MORRISON   *711*

Love Me or Leave Me, BHARATI MUKHERJEE   *720*

Chinese Puzzle, GRACE MING-YEE WAI   *770*

History

How It Feels to Be Colored Me, ZORA NEALE HURSTON   *102*

A Hanging, GEORGE ORWELL   *165*

The War of the Ants, HENRY DAVID THOREAU   *170*

The Stone Horse, BARRY LOPEZ   *174*

The Ignored Lesson of Anne Frank, BRUNO BETTELHEIM   *369*

To My Dear Children, ANNE BRADSTREET   *644*

From *Narrative of the Life of Frederick Douglass, Written by Himself,* FREDERICK DOUGLASS   *658*

The Ghost Dance War, CHARLES ALEXANDER EASTMAN   *666*

Leaves from the Mental Portfolio of an Eurasian, EDITH MAUD EATON (SUI SIN FAR)   *674*

From *Incidents in the Life of a Slave Girl*, HARRIET JACOBS   *707*

The Site of Memory, TONI MORRISON   *711*

A Modest Proposal, JONATHAN SWIFT   *749*

Language, Literature, and Writing

The Essayist and the Essay, E. B. WHITE   *30*

Why I Write, JOAN DIDION   *33*

The Singular First Person, SCOTT RUSSELL SANDERS   *40*

Language and Literature from a Pueblo Indian Perspective, LESLIE MARMON SILKO   *52*

Introduction to *Tuxedo Junction*, GERALD EARLY   *127*

Beauty: When the Other Dancer Is the Self, ALICE WALKER   *190*

Raymond Carver, Mentor, JAY MCINERNEY   *240*

Unlearning Romance, GLORIA STEINEM   *320*

Americanization Is Tough on "Macho," ROSE DEL CASTILLO
   GUILBAULT *352*
The Ignored Lesson of Anne Frank, BRUNO BETTELHEIM *369*
The Perils and Pitfalls of Reporting in the Lone Star State, MOLLY
   IVINS *403*
The Objects of My Invention, ABBY FRUCHT *693*

Love and Marriage

A Few Words about Breasts, NORA EPHRON *106*
Beauty: When the Other Dancer Is the Self, ALICE WALKER *190*
Afterthoughts, JEAN ERVIN *220*
My Father's Life, RAYMOND CARVER *231*
Like Mexicans, GARY SOTO *291*
On Being Raised by a Daughter, NANCY MAIRS *307*
Unlearning Romance, GLORIA STEINEM *320*
Désirée's Baby [story], KATE CHOPIN *509*
Young Goodman Brown [story], NATHANIEL HAWTHORNE *515*
The Dark Wood [story], JANETTE TURNER HOSPITAL *527*
Trifles [play], SUSAN GLASPELL *552*
The Woman Hanging from the Thirteenth Floor Window [poem],
   JOY HARJO *571*
The Wretched of the Hearth, BARBARA EHRENREICH *687*

Nature

Seeing, ANNIE DILLARD *60*
On Being a Real Westerner, TOBIAS WOLFF *161*
The War of the Ants, HENRY DAVID THOREAU *170*
Once More to the Lake, E. B. WHITE *183*
Beauty: When the Other Dancer Is the Self, ALICE WALKER *190*
My Horse and I, N. SCOTT MOMADAY *302*
On Natural Death, LEWIS THOMAS *362*
Was the World Made for Man? MARK TWAIN *394*
The Death of the Moth, VIRGINIA WOOLF *399*
Living Like Weasels, ANNIE DILLARD *414*
Where I Lived, and What I Lived For, HENRY DAVID THOREAU *419*
Am I Blue? ALICE WALKER *453*
Against Nature, JOYCE CAROL OATES *470*
Save the Whales, Screw the Shrimp, JOY WILLIAMS *478*
To Build a Fire [story], JACK LONDON *535*

Observation and Perception

The Singular First Person, SCOTT RUSSELL SANDERS *40*
Language and Literature from a Pueblo Indian Perspective, LESLIE
   MARMON SILKO *52*

Seeing, ANNIE DILLARD   *60*

Growing Up Asian in America, KESAYA E. NODA   *94*

How It Feels to Be Colored Me, ZORA NEALE HURSTON   *102*

Introduction to *Tuxedo Junction,* GERALD EARLY   *127*

On Being a Real Westerner, TOBIAS WOLFF   *161*

A Hanging, GEORGE ORWELL   *165*

The War of the Ants, HENRY DAVID THOREAU   *170*

Once More to the Lake, E. B. WHITE   *183*

Beauty: When the Other Dancer Is the Self, ALICE WALKER   *190*

My Uncle Willie, MAYA ANGELOU   *216*

My Father's Life, RAYMOND CARVER   *231*

Raymond Carver, Mentor, JAY MCINERNEY   *240*

Students and Teachers, ALAN LIGHTMAN   *296*

On Being Raised by a Daughter, NANCY MAIRS   *307*

On Natural Death, LEWIS THOMAS   *362*

The Ignored Lesson of Anne Frank, BRUNO BETTELHEIM   *369*

The Death of the Moth, VIRGINIA WOOLF   *399*

The Perils and Pitfalls of Reporting in the Lone Star State, MOLLY
    IVINS   *403*

Living Like Weasels, ANNIE DILLARD   *414*

Where I Lived, and What I Lived For, HENRY DAVID THOREAU   *419*

The Four Idols, FRANCIS BACON   *430*

Am I Blue? ALICE WALKER   *453*

Random Reflections of a Second-Rate Mind, WOODY ALLEN   *464*

Young Goodman Brown **[story]**, NATHANIEL HAWTHORNE   *515*

The Dark Wood **[story]**, JANETTE TURNER HOSPITAL   *527*

To Build a Fire **[story]**, JACK LONDON   *535*

Trifles **[play]**, SUSAN GLASPELL   *552*

Five Short Poems **[poems]**, STEPHEN CRANE   *568*

Love Me or Leave Me, BHARATI MUKHERJEE   *720*

Philosophy, Religion, and Belief

On Being a Real Westerner, TOBIAS WOLFF   *161*

On Natural Death, LEWIS THOMAS   *362*

The Ignored Lesson of Anne Frank, BRUNO BETTELHEIM   *369*

Was the World Made for Man? MARK TWAIN   *394*

The Death of the Moth, VIRGINIA WOOLF   *399*

The Perils and Pitfalls of Reporting in the Lone Star State, MOLLY
    IVINS   *403*

Living Like Weasels, ANNIE DILLARD   *414*

Where I Lived, and What I Lived For, HENRY DAVID THOREAU   *419*

Am I Blue? ALICE WALKER   *453*

Random Reflections of a Second-Rate Mind, WOODY ALLEN   *464*

Against Nature, JOYCE CAROL OATES   *470*

Young Goodman Brown [story], NATHANIEL HAWTHORNE   *515*
Five Short Poems [poems], STEPHEN CRANE   *568*
The Weak Monk [poem], STEVIE SMITH   *579*
My Speech to the Graduates, WOODY ALLEN   *633*
Proverbs of Hell, WILLIAM BLAKE   *641*
To My Dear Children, ANNE BRADSTREET   *644*
The Ghost Dance War, CHARLES ALEXANDER EASTMAN   *666*

Politics

A Hanging, GEORGE ORWELL   *165*
The War of the Ants, HENRY DAVID THOREAU   *170*
The Ignored Lesson of Anne Frank, BRUNO BETTELHEIM   *369*
The Perils and Pitfalls of Reporting in the Lone Star State, MOLLY IVINS   *403*
Where I Lived, and What I Lived For, HENRY DAVID THOREAU   *419*
Am I Blue? ALICE WALKER   *453*
Random Reflections of a Second-Rate Mind, WOODY ALLEN   *464*
Save the Whales, Screw the Shrimp, JOY WILLIAMS   *478*
The Censors [story], LUISA VALENZUELA   *549*
My Speech to the Graduates, WOODY ALLEN   *633*
At Home in the Parliament of Whores, P. J. O'ROURKE   *728*
Shooting an Elephant, GEORGE ORWELL   *738*
A Modest Proposal, JONATHAN SWIFT   *749*

Psychology and Human Behavior

Seeing, ANNIE DILLARD   *60*
Growing Up Asian in America, KESAYA E. NODA   *94*
How It Feels to Be Colored Me, ZORA NEALE HURSTON   *102*
A Few Words about Breasts, NORA EPHRON   *106*
On Being a Cripple, NANCY MAIRS   *115*
Introduction to *Tuxedo Junction,* GERALD EARLY   *127*
On Being a Real Westerner, TOBIAS WOLFF   *161*
A Hanging, GEORGE ORWELL   *165*
The War of the Ants, HENRY DAVID THOREAU   *170*
Once More to the Lake, E. B. WHITE   *183*
Beauty: When the Other Dancer Is the Self, ALICE WALKER   *190*
My Uncle Willie, MAYA ANGELOU   *216*
Afterthoughts, JEAN ERVIN   *220*
My Father's Life, RAYMOND CARVER   *231*
Raymond Carver, Mentor, JAY MCINERNEY   *240*
Notes of a Native Son, JAMES BALDWIN   *247*
Photographs of My Parents, MAXINE HONG KINGSTON   *287*
Like Mexicans, GARY SOTO   *291*
My Horse and I, N. SCOTT MOMADAY   *302*

On Being Raised by a Daughter, NANCY MAIRS   *307*

Unlearning Romance, GLORIA STEINEM   *320*

"Mommy, What Does 'Nigger' Mean?" GLORIA NAYLOR   *348*

On Natural Death, LEWIS THOMAS   *362*

Selections from *The Devil's Dictionary,* AMBROSE BIERCE   *365*

The Ignored Lesson of Anne Frank, BRUNO BETTELHEIM   *369*

Was the World Made for Man? MARK TWAIN   *394*

The Death of the Moth, VIRGINIA WOOLF   *399*

The Perils and Pitfalls of Reporting in the Lone Star State, MOLLY
   IVINS   *403*

Where I Lived, and What I Lived For, HENRY DAVID
   THOREAU   *419*

The Four Idols, FRANCIS BACON   *430*

Death and Justice: How Capital Punishment Affirms Life,
   EDWARD I. KOCH   *458*

Random Reflections of a Second-Rate Mind, WOODY ALLEN   *464*

Against Nature, JOYCE CAROL OATES   *470*

Save the Whales, Screw the Shrimp, JOY WILLIAMS   *478*

Désirée's Baby **[story]**, KATE CHOPIN   *509*

Young Goodman Brown **[story]**, NATHANIEL HAWTHORNE   *515*

The Dark Wood **[story]**, JANETTE TURNER HOSPITAL   *527*

To Build a Fire **[story]**, JACK LONDON   *535*

The Censors **[story]**, LUISA VALENZUELA   *549*

Trifles **[play]**, SUSAN GLASPELL   *552*

Five Short Poems **[poems]**, STEPHEN CRANE   *568*

The Woman Hanging from the Thirteenth Floor Window **[poem]**,
   JOY HARJO   *571*

Off from Swing Shift **[poem]**, GARRETT HONGO   *574*

Latero Story **[poem]**, TATO LAVIERA   *576*

The Weak Monk **[poem]**, STEVIE SMITH   *579*

The Youngest Daughter **[poem]**, CATHY SONG   *580*

My Speech to the Graduates, WOODY ALLEN   *633*

Proverbs of Hell, WILLIAM BLAKE   *641*

"You're Short, Besides!" SUCHENG CHAN   *650*

The Ghost Dance War, CHARLES ALEXANDER EASTMAN   *666*

The Wretched of the Hearth, BARBARA EHRENREICH   *687*

Selections from *Poor Richard's Almanack,* BENJAMIN FRANKLIN   *690*

Love Me or Leave Me, BHARATI MUKHERJEE   *720*

Shooting an Elephant, GEORGE ORWELL   *738*

Race and Racism

Language and Literature from a Pueblo Indian Perspective, LESLIE
   MARMON SILKO   *52*

Growing Up Asian in America, KESAYA E. NODA   *94*

How It Feels to Be Colored Me, ZORA NEALE HURSTON   *102*

Introduction to *Tuxedo Junction*, GERALD EARLY   127
A Hanging, GEORGE ORWELL   165
Beauty: When the Other Dancer Is the Self, ALICE WALKER   190
My Uncle Willie, MAYA ANGELOU   216
Notes of a Native Son, JAMES BALDWIN   247
Photographs of My Parents, MAXINE HONG KINGSTON   287
Like Mexicans, GARY SOTO   291
My Horse and I, N. SCOTT MOMADAY   302
"Mommy, What Does 'Nigger' Mean?" GLORIA NAYLOR   348
The Ignored Lesson of Anne Frank, BRUNO BETTELHEIM   369
Am I Blue? ALICE WALKER   453
Désirée's Baby [story], KATE CHOPIN   509
Poem for the Young White Man Who Asked Me How I, An
    Intelligent, Well-Read Person, Could Believe in the War Between
    the Races [poem], LORNA DEE CERVANTES   565
The Woman Hanging from the Thirteenth Floor Window [poem],
    JOY HARJO   571
Latero Story [poem], TATO LAVIERA   576
The Youngest Daughter [poem], CATHY SONG   580
Scene from the Movie *GIANT* [poem], TINO VILLANUEVA   584
"You're Short, Besides!" SUCHENG CHAN   650
From *Narrative of the Life of Frederick Douglass, Written by Himself,*
    FREDERICK DOUGLASS   658
The Ghost Dance War, CHARLES ALEXANDER EASTMAN   666
Leaves from the Mental Portfolio of an Eurasian, EDITH MAUD
    EATON (SUI SIN FAR)   674
Madonna: Plantation Mistress or Soul Sister? BELL HOOKS   699
From *Incidents in the Life of a Slave Girl*, HARRIET JACOBS   707
The Site of Memory, TONI MORRISON   711
Love Me or Leave Me, BHARATI MUKHERJEE   720
Chinese Puzzle, GRACE MING-YEE WAI   770

Satire and Humor

A Few Words about Breasts, NORA EPHRON   106
On the Decay of the Art of Lying, MARK TWAIN   356
Was the World Made for Man? MARK TWAIN   394
The Perils and Pitfalls of Reporting in the Lone Star State, MOLLY
    IVINS   403
The Censors [story], LUISA VALENZUELA   549
My Speech to the Graduates, WOODY ALLEN   633
Daze of Wine and Roses, DAVE BARRY   637
At Home in the Parliament of Whores, P. J. O'ROURKE   728
A Modest Proposal, JONATHAN SWIFT   749
Fenimore Cooper's Literary Offenses, MARK TWAIN   758

Science and Technology

Students and Teachers, ALAN LIGHTMAN   *296*
On Natural Death, LEWIS THOMAS   *362*
Was the World Made for Man? MARK TWAIN   *394*
My Speech to the Graduates, WOODY ALLEN   *633*

Texts

Language and Literature from a Pueblo Indian Perspective, LESLIE
   MARMON SILKO   *52*
Introduction to *Tuxedo Junction,* GERALD EARLY   *127*
The War of the Ants, HENRY DAVID THOREAU   *170*
On Being Raised by a Daughter, NANCY MAIRS   *307*
Unlearning Romance, GLORIA STEINEM   *320*
Americanization Is Tough on "Macho," ROSE DEL CASTILLO
   GUILBAULT   *352*
The Ignored Lesson of Anne Frank, BRUNO BETTELHEIM   *369*
Was the World Made for Man? MARK TWAIN   *394*
Living Like Weasels, ANNIE DILLARD   *414*
Hopper's Women **[poem]**, SUE STANDING   *582*
The Wretched of the Hearth, BARBARA EHRENREICH   *687*
The Objects of My Invention, ABBY FRUCHT   *693*
Madonna: Plantation Mistress or Soul Sister? BELL HOOKS   *699*
The Site of Memory, TONI MORRISON   *711*
Love Me or Leave Me, BHARATI MUKHERJEE   *720*
Fenimore Cooper's Literary Offenses, MARK TWAIN   *758*

Violence and War

On Being a Real Westerner, TOBIAS WOLFF   *161*
A Hanging, GEORGE ORWELL   *165*
The War of the Ants, HENRY DAVID THOREAU   *170*
Beauty: When the Other Dancer Is the Self, ALICE WALKER   *190*
Notes of a Native Son, JAMES BALDWIN   *247*
The Ignored Lesson of Anne Frank, BRUNO BETTELHEIM   *369*
Living Like Weasels, ANNIE DILLARD   *414*
Am I Blue? ALICE WALKER   *453*
Death and Justice: How Capital Punishment Affirms Life,
   EDWARD I. KOCH   *458*
Random Reflections of a Second-Rate Mind, WOODY ALLEN   *464*
Against Nature, JOYCE CAROL OATES   *470*
Save the Whales, Screw the Shrimp, JOY WILLIAMS   *478*
Trifles **[play]**, SUSAN GLASPELL   *552*
Scene from the Movie *GIANT* **[poem]**, TINO VILLANUEVA   *584*
The Ghost Dance War, CHARLES ALEXANDER EASTMAN   *666*
A Modest Proposal, JONATHAN SWIFT   *749*

Writing Exploratory Essays

1

Introduction to Exploratory Writing

The unexamined life is not worth living.

—SOCRATES

I write entirely to find out what I'm thinking, what I'm looking at, what I see and what it means. What I want and what I fear.

—JOAN DIDION

Those are the underlying tenets of this book—the beliefs that the process of examining our own lives is crucial to education and to our personal development and that one of the best ways to examine our-selves is through writing. In short, that is the definition of exploratory writing—to use the act of writing to examine your life, your thoughts, your beliefs, your feelings, to use writing to discover more about your inner self as well as to discover more about the outside world and how you connect to it. Exploratory essays tell readers about the "official sub-ject" such as an event, a text, an idea, a controversy; they also tell readers something important about the writer. In fact, one of the major reasons people read exploratory essays is to meet the writer. Not surprising, scientific reports and news articles are rarely exploratory essays because they focus only on the official subject—the experiment, the automobile accident at Dead Man's Curve. Their readers want and expect only in-formation about the official subject.

This is not the case, however, for exploratory essays. Their readers always ask the following kinds of questions: "What does the official subject mean to you, the writer?" "What does it mean to be you?" "How are you like and unlike other people?" "What ideas, beliefs, and feelings motivate you?" "In what ways do you connect with the outside world?" Answering such questions includes writing about your past, your associates, your environment (work, college, home, places where you spend time), your goals and beliefs, your actions, your patterns of behavior, your reactions to texts and to controversial issues.

Ultimately, it is impossible to write without revealing part of yourself. As I'll discuss later in this chapter, objectivity in writing is an illusion. In exploratory essays, however, writers consciously try to reveal parts of their personalities. Often, in fact, they consciously shape the aspects of their personalities which they reveal.

WRITING: A PRIVATE ACT MADE PUBLIC

Writing is probably the most private act you'll ever do for the public. Seated at your desk or on your bed or in the library, fingers gripping a pen or poised above the keyboard, you are alone with your thoughts, your fears, your beliefs, your knowledge, your past. Regardless of how often you ask your friends, teachers, or editors for advice, ultimately the act of writing is a solitary affair: you and words trying to form some sort of union that will reveal your thoughts or emotions.

Despite the privacy of the creative act, much of what you write will eventually be read by someone else—by friends and relatives, by your teachers, and perhaps by classmates and peers—in short, by readers.

Writing, then, is a private act often made public.

And in that paradox lies the essence of writing: a private act made public. When we write only for ourselves as in a journal, we frequently experience a kind of freedom. The private act frees us. Since no one else will read our words and hence no one else will judge us by what we say or how we say it, we are free to play with unorthodox ideas and to use language that we might not use in more formal writing.

In such journal writing we often don't bother to express our ideas fully or to provide all the relevant details of the event we describe or of the thought process we followed. After all, we are the only audience and we assume that we'll always remember all the important details.

Just as the privacy of writing sets us free, so its public nature might seem to limit us. Most of us don't want to be judged on the basis of *all* our ideas or fantasies or experiences. Fortunately, no one expects us to detail everything. Let's explore this issue of what exactly your subject matter should be when you write for readers.

PERSONAL VERSUS PRIVATE SUBJECT MATTER

Any subject is appropriate for an exploratory essay if it reveals you, your experiences, your beliefs, your mind working with ideas. Most exploratory essays have two subjects: the "official subject" (for example, your father, your definitions of success, your first date) and you. The act of exploring yourself is one of the goals of every exploratory essay. No subject matter or topic is inappropriate *if you are comfortable with the idea of writing about it*. Over the years, students have written about everything: for example, conflicts with their parents, conflicts within themselves, the horror of being raped, the struggle with being anorexic, the process of overcoming their fear of speaking in public, the impact of alcoholism on a family member or on themselves, drug addiction, homosexuality, their agony about stuttering, the impact of being abused as children, their fears of commitment, deciding to have or not have an abortion, their *real* hopes for the future (rather than those which society programmed into them), successful and unsuccessful relationships.

So no subject matter or topic is inappropriate *if you are comfortable enough to write about it*. The key here is your degree of comfort. Let's draw a distinction between personal and private subjects. **Personal subjects** are those which you can bring yourself to write about in order to reveal something about your personality, your thoughts, your beliefs, your life experiences. They are the subjects you might discuss with acquaintances, friends, religious leaders, or therapists. You might find that you have a psychological or emotional resistance to writing about some of these personal subjects (revealing ourselves to others is often difficult), but often that resistance fades as you discover the excitement of exploration and of the act of writing itself. If the resistance or discomfort doesn't fade as you write, abandon the subject—perhaps it really is a private subject for you. **Private subjects** are those which you cannot bring yourself to write about for readers. For your whole life, such subjects can stay where they are, hidden and safe. They may be too private to explore in front of an audience. As the semester progresses, however, some subjects that seemed to be private might turn out to be merely personal. Nothing is automatically or irrevocably private or personal. In other words, the distinction here is based entirely on your perception, and perceptions sometimes change.

How can you tell whether the subject you've selected is personal, private, or a personal subject that only seems private? Here are some guidelines:

> If you feel a little nervous about the subject as you write, you are probably breaking new ground for yourself as a writer and as a person. Keep writing; it is probably a personal subject.

> If, however, you are having a strong negative reaction as you write (or as you think about writing), it is probably a private subject. Stop writing and select a different topic.

> If you have physical symptoms (sweaty palms, shaking hands, tears) as you write or think about the subject, stop. It is a private subject.

If you find yourself procrastinating more than usual about beginning the paper, or, paradoxically, if you find you have no feelings or ideas about the topic at all, then your subject is probably private. Select a new one.

Each subject has its own time to be explored. Ultimately, we should probably write about all personal and private subjects because the very act of writing somehow frees us from their power over us. The act of putting the experience or feeling into words demystifies it and makes it somehow manageable.

But some subjects require time. Remember that exploratory writing doesn't end with the semester. You can continue such writing for the rest of your life. If there's a subject you want to write about but can't bring yourself to do it now, you can do it later.

In addition, some of the published essays included in this text deal with subjects that you might have originally believed were private. Seeing such topics in print might free you to write about similar topics. At the least, such published essays reveal how similar we are to other thoughtful people.

WRITING TO READERS

Let's assume, then, that at least some subjects are ready to be explored. Although revealing anything about ourselves can seem unnerving, the benefits of writing exploratory essays far outweigh the "danger" of revelation.

On the practical level, knowing that we are writing to readers other than ourselves can improve our memory and style. Knowing that other people will read our essays forces us to fill in the details, each of which might lead us to a new and deeper understanding of ourselves and our lives. Once we have deepened our understanding and developed the details, we have an essay we can truly value. In order to make our readers value it too, we refine its style, looking for just the right word or phrase that will have an emotional impact on them or which will clarify our thoughts for them.

Frankly, we ourselves don't fully understand an event in our lives or a facet of our personality until we try to write about it for someone else. The very act of trying to explain it deepens our own understanding of it. Trying to explain (perhaps for the first time) the assumptions that underlay a particular action or attitude of ours can be very revealing because our readers (unlike ourselves) might ask, "Why would you think *that?*" Often we don't know why we thought *that* until we try to explain it to them and thus explain it to ourselves at the same time.

Writing to readers, then, is an effective way to push ourselves deeper into our topics. In our early drafts, we are actually writing to ourselves, discovering what we know and think about the topic. In other words, our early drafts are **self-expression** just as writing in a journal is self-expression. If our only audience is ourselves, the chances are that we won't care much about craft or even about exactness since we assume our memories will always be able to fill in whatever gaps we've left in the text. With readers other than ourselves, however, we are forced to do more. We must clarify thoughts, give examples, explain our assumptions. We are forced to structure the information in a way that is most accessible to other people. We must work to create effects—making something dramatic or humorous or climactic. We begin to be concerned about the *effect* of our words and ideas on someone else, about ways to appeal to readers' emotions, senses, and intellect. Although we might not be able to duplicate exactly our feelings or the process of our thought, we can create prose that approximates them. In short, we are forced to turn self-expression into **communication,** prose that is crafted and polished to meet the needs of our readers. In exploratory essays, we should be as concerned with the craft of the essay as we are with its content.

Such exploratory essays communicate important insights to our readers. As poet May Sarton says,

> I believe one has to stop holding back for fear of alienating some imaginary reader or real relative or friend, and come out with personal truth. If we are to understand the human condition, and if we are to accept ourselves in all the complexity, self-doubt, extravagance of feeling, guilt, joy, the slow freeing of the self to its full capacity for action and creation, both as human being and as artist, we have to know all we can about each other, and we have to be willing to go naked.

In this wonderful brief passage, Sarton highlights the fear most writers have of revealing too much and thus hurting someone they love. Her response to that is to ignore the fear and write. Even more important, however, Sarton says we must "go naked" (metaphorically) in order to communicate our personal truth so that we all can understand humankind more fully.

TYPES OF EXPLORATORY ESSAYS

The process that begins with exploratory writing has several end products, all covered by the term "exploratory essay." More specifically, exploratory essays include the personal essay, the familiar essay, and the literary essay. Although each type focuses on a particular element of what we can generically call "the exploratory essay," all share the freedom to use the resources of language to explore a wide range of subjects. The term *personal essay,* for example, suggests the revelation of the writer's self—opinions, emotions, beliefs, life experiences. *Familiar essay* suggests the writer's friendly attitude and tone toward the reader, the essay's "commonplace" subject matter, and its informal and at times almost conversational mode of expression. *Literary essay* suggests the greater emphasis on the essay itself as a crafted artifact rather than as a simple deliverer of messages, as well as on the greater use of "literary" devices such as dialogue, description of scene, dramatic heightening, and figurative language. As critic Robert Scholes notes,

> Essays are not necessarily literary but become so to the extent
> that they adopt the dominant qualities of any of the three major
> forms of literature. The more an essay alludes or fictionalizes,
> the more the author adopts a role or suggests one for the reader,
> the more the language becomes sonorous or figured, the more
> literary the essay (or the letter, the prayer, the speech, etc.)
> becomes.

In short, exploratory essays reveal the art and craft of the essay form. All forms of the exploratory essay allow us to explore ourselves in terms of other subjects such as experiences we have had, important events and people, **texts** (such as books, articles, films, photographs, and advertisements), ideas, beliefs, controversies. And they encourage us to do so artfully.

THINKING FOR OURSELVES

College is a place for questing and questioning, a place where each solution raises more problems. That is what makes learning so exciting—the delving deeper and deeper into the question, discovering new depths just when an answer has been devised. For the true learner, doubt is the only certainty. No fact is so true that it cannot be questioned. No truth is so sure that such questioning does not illuminate it. In fact, the purpose of education is to teach us to question everything.

We call this process "thinking for ourselves."

Thinking for ourselves—that means we must learn to interact with the ideas we encounter, to test them against our own experiences. When an idea proves to be sound, it articulates what we have felt or sensed or suspected but couldn't quite pin down for ourselves because we lacked the necessary concepts or terminology.

When an idea doesn't ring true, we question it; the idea might seem to account for something we've observed, but it doesn't leap out at us as the truth. We think about it, perhaps even write about it in a journal. We read an article or a book to gain more context. Or we talk to someone who's interested in that topic. We do all of this in order to resolve the issue to our satisfaction. At times, we will disagree with the idea because it is not congruent with our experiences. Sometimes, of course, concepts are wrong. At other times, concepts are difficult to comprehend and we may not have enough experience or information to judge them. Ultimately, we need a critical mass of information to make us confident enough to interact with the texts, to question their assumptions, to carry on a dialogue with texts. In any event, we continue to test the ideas against our own knowledge and experience.

That is what exploratory writing helps us to do.

WRITING ABOUT PERSONAL EXPERIENCE

Perhaps the advice most often given to writers has been "write about what you know." Common sense tells us that selecting a subject about which we know nothing will make our essay a disastrous hodge-podge of generalizations (unless we do a great deal of research before we begin writing). Obviously, then, it is prudent to write about something we know. In many ways, that is the advice this text gives: Write about what you know. That the events you have experienced are potential subjects for exploratory essays is obvious by now. Usually the first thing that occurs to us as personal subject matter is what we've done or experienced.

Yet those events are but the beginning. Anything that you have ever experienced or reacted to in any way is part of your **personal experience:** every book you've read, everything you've seen on television and in the movies, every song lyric you've listened to, every conversation you've overheard, every family story ever told to you, every adventure recounted to you by family or friends or strangers. More: every thought you've ever had, every attitude you've ever held, every observation you've ever made, every fantasy you've ever had, every dream that you remember—all are part of your personal experience. All are fair game for exploratory essays.

Personal experience, then, can be broken down into five categories:

events you have participated in

events you have witnessed

mental occurrences such as thoughts or fantasies

attitudes such as assumptions or beliefs

any external information (facts or opinions) that you have acquired from any source including television, movies, conversations, books, songs, lectures

The value of personal experiences for exploratory essays cannot be overstated. After all, you are the primary subject of exploratory essays, and in many ways you are the sum of your personal experiences.

THE EXPLORATORY ESSAY EXPLAINED

You have probably had the following experience: You are reading a book, either for pleasure or for class. Suddenly you realize that your thoughts have strayed away from the book, following some tangent. You may not even remember the last page or two that you know your eyes traveled over. Sometimes this straying occurs because the book bores you (or frustrates you if you are cramming for an exam); at other times, the words have triggered a line of thought that you start pursuing beyond the confines of the book's page. Such straying can be an enjoyable experience if you are reading for pleasure. Overall, this interaction with the book is highly desirable; it is part of the process of learning. Further, these wanderings are not restricted to reading. Your mind can start exploring while you are in the midst of activity—for example, while you walk across campus, take an exam, listen to a lecture, or hang-glide.

Montaigne's *Essais*

In the sixteenth century, a French diplomat named Michel de Montaigne had such experiences. Unlike most of us, however, he began recording the ideas which came to mind as he read. He realized that such strayings from the act of reading or from other activities were valuable—in fact, that they were the essence of thought and education. His "records" became the source of a new literary form—the essay. With tongue in cheek, he explained why he started writing down these "strayings":

> When I lately retired to my own house, determined as far as possible to concern myself with nothing else than spending in privacy and repose the little remainder of time I have to live, I fancied I could not more oblige my mind than to permit it a full leisure to entertain itself and come to rest in itself, which I hoped it might now the more easily do, having with time become more settled and mature; but I find . . . that, quite the contrary, like a runaway horse it gives itself a hundred times more trouble than it used to take for others, and creates me so many chimeras and fantastic monsters, one upon another, without order or design, that, the better at leisure to contemplate their strangeness and absurdity, I have begun to record them, hoping in time to make it [his mind] ashamed of them.
>
> —("OF IDLENESS," 9)

Montaigne's self-deprecating humor here does not disguise his intentions: First, he's writing in order to discover all the "fantastic monsters" his mind can conjure; second, he's recording his thoughts for himself and others to examine.

In 1580, with the publication of the first volume of these short pieces, titled *Essais* ("Attempts"), the essay form was born. Montaigne was clear that his "attempts" were tentative compared to the ordinary philosophical writings of his day; in other words, he did not adopt the tone his peers used in their philosophical essays—a tone of certainty and of intellectual confidence. Instead, his tone was conversational, friendly, open to suggestions. In his "personal essays," Montaigne wrote not so much to prove a point or to convince his readers as to explore the implications of an idea and to discover how true it was.

In the quotation from Montaigne just given, we have several characteristics of the exploratory essay. First, it is *personal in subject matter,* finding its topic in a subject which is of deep interest to the writer. Second, it is *personal in approach,* revealing aspects of the writer as they are illuminated by the subject at hand. The justification for this personal approach rests in part on the assumption that all people are similar; Montaigne implies that if we look honestly and deeply into any person we will find truths appropriate to all people. Each of us is humankind in miniature. Third, notice *the extended use of figurative language* (in this case the simile comparing his mind to a runaway horse). Such language is also characteristic of the exploratory essay.

Goals of the Exploratory Essay

In many ways, the exploratory essay carries on the essay tradition begun by Montaigne, who used the essay to explore his ideas and observations. That is what the exploratory essay encourages you to do—to explore the world, to test limits, to juggle concepts, to push language to its creative limits. These goals are what made the essay such a valuable form for the Renaissance: It offered writers a chance to try out ideas, to bounce them against one another. These are the goals that make it valuable today, for you as a student and as a person.

In practical academic terms, the exploratory essay fulfills at least two useful functions. First, it is the best way to discover what original notions you have about any subject. Second, it is an exciting way to see how bits of knowledge from various fields can fit together in interesting and revealing ways. Often information from each course seems to be compartmentalized: An insight drawn from a poem by Keats goes in the drawer marked "Literature"; a fact about cell reproduction goes into the drawer labeled "Biology." To see the connections among ideas in all disciplines is one of the goals of exploratory writing. Further, writing exploratory essays can help you identify what is important to you in any field—from art to zoology—and to see how those fields connect. In addition, such essays can help you to discover the "truths" that you believe and those you don't, to define the problems that interest you and those that don't.

Put a slightly different way, exploratory writing tries to engage your whole self in each essay you write: all the information, observations, and insights you have accumulated since the doctor first got your attention with a slap on your bottom. And such discovery, connection, and involvement are some of the major goals of education.

A Vehicle of Inquiry

The exploratory essay, then, is a vehicle of inquiry. Think of this image literally: The exploratory essay is a vehicle—a bicycle, a car, a Concorde jet—that carries you through an investigation. That vehicle might be hijacked by a more interesting idea, and its announced route might thus be changed to follow a tangent suggested by that more interesting idea. Although you might end up at a different place from the one you intended—just as a hijacked plane ends up in an unscheduled airport—you do end up somewhere, and every place is interesting.

Notice here that the hijack analogy is not a completely fortunate one. The idea of a hijack nicely captures the concept that I want to express, namely, that writers are surprised and their essays veer off course and end up somewhere other than where the writers originally intended. But the image breaks down after this. For example, hijackers rarely take the passengers to resort areas, and the experience of being hijacked is in itself terrifying—invoking a kind of terror that rarely enters into essay writing. Although the first time an idea changes course may be disconcerting, ultimately the exploration should be an interesting and exciting event, not a terrifying one. Only if the tangents take you into an area of your experience that you are not ready to deal with—only then will exploratory writing make you uncomfortable. Even then, however, the experience is not terrifying. Unlike the passengers on the hijacked plane, for example, you can always stop the experience by taking your fingers off the keys or by capping your pen.

The preceding two paragraphs are an example of a tangent taking over. When I first created the hijack image, those two paragraphs didn't exist. Each time I rewrote the image paragraph, however, the hijack image bothered me a bit more. I wasn't sure at first what was wrong with it. In fact, I was pleased that the image had come so readily to mind. When I could no longer ignore the discomfort the image was causing me, I asked myself where the image had come from. The word *jet* no doubt sparked it, and that spark reminded me of a newspaper column about hijacking which I wrote years ago.

Then I stopped thinking about my pleasure at developing an apt image and thought about you, the reader. Perhaps you have been hijacked or know someone who went through that experience. At the least, simply reading about the experiences of people who have been hijacked would be more than enough to make the image disturbing. I began to see that the image wasn't totally accurate (in point of fact, no analogy is perfect). Thus these two paragraphs were added to prevent your rejecting the idea of exploratory writing in case my hijack image called up unpleasant associations. And I also wrote them to demonstrate my process of writing and thinking.

Implications of the Exploratory Essay

Such focusing on yourself is not to suggest that you don't have to read, or listen in class, or do research in order to make your writing interesting and informative. Learning is a lifetime occupation. Every day in college you are required to read, to think about what you've read and heard, to assimilate it in some way. Exploratory writing helps you relate the new information and insights to yourself and to other pieces of information you've acquired. It helps you grow intellectually, and it helps you monitor that growth. By making the learning process conscious, exploratory writing makes the learning deeper and more relevant to you.

We should not forget the example of Montaigne here. He always sought out interesting facts and ideas by reading everything he could lay his hands on and by talking with anyone who had something to say. Then Montaigne wrote about what he had read and heard to explore those ideas and to play with them intellectually.

THE WRITING PROCESS

Writing is a process. Although the process is usually not as linear as the following explanation may imply, we can say that writing involves four steps or stages: prewriting, drafting, revising, editing.

Prewriting

Anything that you do before writing a complete first draft is called **prewriting.** It includes such activities as talking about the topic with your friends, doing research, making notes, and planning. It includes all the idea-generating techniques discussed later in this chapter: free association, freewriting, directed freewriting, listing, mind mapping or ballooning, idea trees, questioning, and perspectives.

Drafting

Once the ideas seem somewhat in place, you should write a complete draft of the essay. This will not be the final draft of your essay; in fact, that final essay may be several drafts away and might look almost nothing like this first draft. I call this first draft a **fast-write** because you should write it quickly, not stopping to worry about the finer points of style or punctuation or spelling. The fast-write's purpose is to let you get all the ideas into words, the words into sentences, the sentences into paragraphs, the paragraphs into a coherent organization. If a tangent occurs to you as you fast-write, follow it. Tangents can become the main point or topic of your eventual final essay. Indeed, the act of phrasing an idea in words can alter the idea and can raise new issues that you hadn't considered. The very words you choose carry implications and associations that can lead you to deeper insights. It may be helpful to think of the fast-write as self-expression, an act in which you tell yourself about the topic in the essay, an act in which you discover what you have to say about it.

As part of their prewriting, some writers, particularly professional writers, seriously consider the rhetorical situation. The **rhetorical situation** includes three major questions: What is your purpose for writing this particular essay? Who are your readers? What are their expectations and levels of knowledge about your topic?

Your purpose for writing may be the only element that is not significantly altered by the nature of your readers, although even it can be influenced in certain circumstances. In exploratory writing, you have a dual purpose: to say something about the official subject (for example, an event or a text or a relationship) and to reveal something about yourself. Most often, your purposes remain constant, and consciously knowing those purposes helps you see how to develop your ideas and what content needs to be added to or deleted from your fast-write. For example, if your purpose is to demonstrate the complexity of your motives for selecting a particular college, that purpose will require you to give readers many details about the thoughts and feelings you had as you evaluated various colleges. If, instead, your purpose is to reveal the complex emotions you felt once you were on campus, your motives for selecting the college in the first place might be reduced to a mere sentence ("After an agonizing process of selection, I found myself on campus . . .") or eliminated entirely. Devoting paragraphs to your evaluation process would hinder communication because it would prevent readers from having a clear sense of the essay's point.

Occasionally, who your readers are might cause a change in purpose. By the end of your fast-write, for instance, you might discover that what you intended to say about the official subject is inappropriate for your particular audience (for example, perhaps it reveals too much about a friend's or relative's life). Or you might find that the fast-write says more about you than you feel comfortable revealing to an audience. In such cases, then, even your purpose is altered by the nature of your readers. Most often, however, it is not.

But *who your readers are* should influence almost every other aspect of the final essay you produce, including what content you include, the kinds of language you use, and the kinds of references and allusions you make. Consider this example. You are writing an essay about a family wedding you attended last summer. Your purpose is to show how unusual the wedding was and to reveal your mixed emotions about weddings in general and about this wedding in particular. If your readers are your classmates, then you can assume the following about them before they read your essay: (1) Your readers don't know members of your family, (2) they don't know your attitude toward various family members, (3) they don't know the idiosyncrasies of your various family members, (4) they don't know your family's particular traditions and beliefs, (5) they don't know that Aunt Rose predicted divorce for the newlyweds within their first year, (6) they don't know that Aunt Rose is psychic and hasn't been wrong about a family wedding in 25 years, (7) they don't know what point you are planning to make. For such readers, you are going to have to provide a lot of background information, physical descriptions of the major participants, and a detailed explanation of how you fit into all of this activity. Part of your communication task will be to give readers the "big picture" as well as to reveal your own thoughts and emotions. Since they don't know any of the people involved, you might allow yourself to be satiric, perhaps even mocking or sarcastic.

If, on the other hand, your readers will be primarily family members and people who also attended the wedding, the content of your essay will change even though your purpose will remain the same. For instance, you need not waste a lot of paper filling in the "big picture" since your readers were all at the wedding. You won't have to explain that Uncle Phil is Aunt Martha's eighth husband since everyone already knows that fact (although you might say something like "Aunt Martha seemed confused about what she was supposed to do at a wedding that wasn't her own"). In this case, you might focus on two or three small events that those who attended the wedding might not have noticed. Certainly you might still sketch people's personalities since no one can know your particular vision of them, but you'll probably be less sarcastic since your readers are the people in the essay (or you might be particularly vicious, depending on how you feel about them, I suppose). If you think Aunt Rose is crazy in general but amazingly lucky in her predictions, and if you know she will read the essay, and if you don't want to hurt her feelings, then you might mention her prediction but avoid commenting on her sanity (a comment you would hasten to make if your readers didn't know anyone at the wedding).

In addition to content, the types of language you use will be determined in large part by who your readers are. If you were writing an essay for a chess magazine about winning an important chess tournament, for example, you would not hesitate to use a technical term like "the Nimzo-Indian defense." If you were writing that same essay for readers whose interest in and knowledge of chess could not be assumed, you would have to consider seriously the advisability of using that term. At the least, you would need to define the term if you used it. More likely, however, you would decide that your essay would gain little from defining the defense since your readers probably wouldn't appreciate such detail anyway.

The same is true for references and allusions. If you were writing a literary analysis of a poem by Ralph Waldo Emerson for an advanced course in American literature, you wouldn't hesitate to make a passing allusion to James Russell Lowell. If you were analyzing that same Emerson poem for a writing class that included people from a variety of majors, you should explain just who Lowell was.

In short, your purpose for writing and the nature of your readers seriously influence the essay you produce. For many writers, considering the rhetorical situation is the first step in the revision process rather than part of their prewriting activity.

Revising

Once the fast-write is completed, give yourself some time away from it (at least a few hours, preferably a few days). This hiatus allows your subconscious mind to continue working on the essay while your conscious mind deals with assignments from other courses and with life in general. When we try to revise immediately after writing a draft, it is almost impossible to see the essay on the screen or piece of paper before us; instead, we see the essay that is in our mind. We can't see accurately *what we wrote* because we are still seeing *what we intended to write*. We overlook information gaps and misleading statements. We see only with the writer's eyes, not with a reader's eyes. So we should take a break after the draft is finished. While our conscious mind is busy with other tasks, the essay in our mind fades so that when we return to the essay we actually wrote, our vision is not as clouded by our assumptions (and hopes) about what we really produced. We see it with a reader's eyes as well as with those of a writer. Then we are ready to revise.

To revise is to add and elaborate on ideas, to add examples and details, to fine-tune the style. Here's some general advice: Always look at your fast-write with the *assumption* that you can say more. Never ask yourself, "Does anything need to be changed or added to this essay?"—this phrasing invites a "No" response. Instead, tell yourself, "A lot has to be changed in the essay." A good way to start revising ideas is to ask yourself "Why?" after every statement in the essay. Then ask, "How do I know this?" And then, "What does this fact or statement reveal about my inner self, about the way I see the world?" Writing responses to each question (each time you ask it) will automatically deepen your insights and your essay. The responses might range from one sentence to several paragraphs.

For any kind of revising, it is most efficient to focus on only one area as you go through the essay. If you try to focus on adding evidence and ideas and fixing verb tenses and changing the essay's structure, you will inevitably miss areas that require attention and will feel overwhelmed by the whole revision process. Therefore, it is a good idea to go through the essay several times, each time concentrating on one type of improvement. For instance, you might go through the essay the first time concentrating on filling in background information for readers. Your second pass through the essay might focus on elaborating on your feelings or thoughts. The third time you might focus on adding evidence or quotations where appropriate. Once the ideas are in place, look at the style, trying to sharpen and refine your prose. If you have problems making explicit connections between ideas, for example, make one pass through the essay looking only at such connections. Then make a second pass through the essay looking at verb tenses.

It is helpful to think of revision as the beginning of your dialogue with your readers. In the revision process, you play two roles: You "speak" the essay but you also imagine what your readers would ask to have clarified and developed more fully. Revision is the process by which you fashion your material for your readers. Here you add details the readers "request" and explain concepts or events or people that they might not understand. Here you use imagery to suggest the unexplainable. In short, revision is the stage at which the art and craft of writing come most fully into play.

Editing

This final stage involves finding and correcting grammatical, spelling, punctuation, and other mechanical errors. Sloppiness in such areas annoys your readers and thus impedes the act of communication. In fact, for many readers errors obscure everything: If readers see errors, they are blinded to everything else, including the essay's ideas. They believe, rightly or wrongly, that error-laden writing signals inexact thinking. If you do not care enough to perfect your prose, they feel, then they do not have to care enough to pay close attention to what your essay says. In other words, everyone loses. Readers miss out on what you have to tell them, and all your hard work and good ideas accomplish nothing. Remember that you are writing about something important—yourself—and that topic deserves the best prose you can create.

For more details about editing, see Chapter 11, "Revising Style."

Then you fine-tune your thoughts and your prose. You find just the right word that names the thought, or you adjust the nuance of the thought and its name pops onto your page. Always keep in mind that when you revise an essay you are doing more than simply working on an essay: You are also refining and deepening your understanding of yourself.

This whole writing process is a moving inward and then outward in a potentially never-ending spiral. In other words, you explore both your inner world and the outer world, using each to illustrate and clarify the other. In prewriting and drafting, you go inward to discover your thoughts and feelings, then you move outward to see if they coincide with the real world, then you carry new real-world information back inward to see how it alters or adds nuances to your inner world, then outward to discover the opinions of others, then back inward to weigh their ideas against yours. Back and forth. Inward and outward. Then you revise, often going outward again to find new sources. Your final move outward occurs when you share the results of your exploration with your readers after revising and crafting the final draft especially for them.

PREWRITING: GENERATING IDEAS AND PLANNING

Contrary to some popular notions, most of us don't have full-blown ideas popping out of our heads like Athena, fully armored in elegant prose and equipped with examples and arguments. For most of us, ideas need nurturing and time to reach maturity. Even a great idea needs time to develop, to stretch out the fingers of its implications, to reveal its true worth and its true limitations.

You have probably developed some techniques that help you get started when you must write an essay, techniques which help you find the idea within you and wrap it up in words so that you can see it. Whatever techniques work for you are great. I'm not advocating that you abandon them. Unfortunately, idea-generation methods come with no guarantees. A method that works miracles for you one time might fail you the next. Your state of mind, the topic itself, your attitude (both conscious and unconscious) toward the assignment or the teacher, even the way your left hand happens to feel—all kinds of factors influence what technique will work at any given time. Here, however, are some methods that have been proven to work, some techniques that are particularly useful for exploratory writing, so that if your old reliable technique fails, you'll have several others available. The beauty of knowing several strategies is that if Old Reliable fails you, other techniques are waiting backstage for just this moment: With the star technique out of action, the understudy leaps on the stage to perform impressively. After all, like the show, the writing must go on.

Free Association

This technique requires no writing at all. Simply let your mind wander. Talking aloud often helps me find a topic, particularly when whatever I want to explore is hiding inside me (it is hiding because exploration is always a bit scary as well as very exciting). By talking to myself (or to someone else I trust), I allow that topic to slip out and be seen. Using a tape recorder helps.

Free association also works well if you have a particular assignment, such as "write a narrative about an important event" or "describe a person who has been significant in your life." Begin by free-associating to the words *event* or *person*. As you talk or think, the event or person you really want to explore may stand discretely in the background or may pop out and startle you.

Freewriting

Like free association, freewriting is a way of letting ideas slip from your subconscious into your conscious mind, but this time you write instead of talk. It is a particularly fruitful technique for the exploratory essay because it gets you in a frame of mind that allows free exploration. It is also particularly useful when you can't think of anything to write about.

The technique is simple. Start with a blank sheet of paper or a blank computer screen. Relax. Then write *nonstop* for 10 minutes. Never raise the pen from the paper or your fingers from the keyboard. Just write. Don't worry about punctuation or spelling. In fact, don't even worry about making sense. You want to "numb" all the built-in inhibitions and restrictions which block the free flow of ideas. Never stop, and never reread what you just wrote. If you are working on a computer, try turning off the monitor or blanking out the image on the screen. You're not writing an essay here; you're letting ideas slide pell-mell out of your fingers. Later you can worry about craft.

In other words, do not censor yourself.

When 10 minutes are up, read what you've written (and save it if you're using a computer). Find the words, phrases, or lines that strike you (you don't have to know *why* they strike you). Create a coherent sentence for each word or phrase, and select the most promising one to write at the top of a new sheet of paper or at the top of a blank screen and write for another 10 minutes. Make no conscious effort to direct your thoughts or to stick to the sentence you've written at the top. Just write nonstop again.

Repeat the process two or three times. By then you should have some ideas about what topic you want to deal with. Then you'll probably employ another of the methods below to develop more insight into the topic.

Here is a 90-second sample of my freewriting:

> My room is cold and I feel like a machine gun in a 1940s movie with lots of ammo and no target and fill up the cup and run it over the top you mop and sing a song and think a thought and find me a cabbage patch doll for Xmas with or without an X pal

> buddy friend amigo and all that good stuff stuff stuff is what
> we're made of buddy good buddy sidekick I get a kick out of
> my sidekick that's all folks and that's the beginning and horror
> movies with "the beginning?" at the end instead of "the end"
> and doesn't anything ever end and is this or that and then some
> more and road maps are tumbling down the falls of life what-
> ever that is fat cat mat bat and all the ships at sea.

Note the word games that the subconscious likes to play (the rhymes
such as *top/mop* and the puns such as "I get a kick out of my sidekick").
The triple repetition of the word *stuff* shows my mind trying to shift
tracks—I just kept writing the same word until another idea appeared.
It is very difficult to read this passage aloud because the logical connections are missing. But some of the ideas are connected by the process of
association (for example, "sing a song" inspires "think a thought" and
the "X" in "Xmas" seems to suggest "ex" as in "ex-friend").

After rereading this bit of freewriting, I might compose one or more
of the following sentences:

> Although I consider myself to be a peaceful person, I often de-
> scribe myself in violent terms, comparing myself to such things
> as *machine guns*.

> A lot of different words describe a *friend,* but each suggests an
> element of friendship rather than a total friend.

> All the bad stuff in life just seems *to never end.*

Any one of these three sentences could be the topic of an exploratory
essay.

Directed Freewriting

Directed freewriting is a variation of freewriting which writers use
when they have a topic but don't have any ideas about it. In this case,
write the topic at the top of a blank sheet of paper. Then follow the
directions in the "Freewriting" section. For example, after finding the
three center-of-gravity sentences above, I could write "The violent me"
(or "Friends" or "Never-ending bad stuff in life") at the top of the sheet
or screen and then do directed freewriting. Don't try to force your freewriting to deal with the topic you've written, but allow the topic to
guide you.

Listing

Like freewriting, this is a way of allowing your mind free range,
permitting all sorts of associations to pop up. Once again, write your
topic at the top of the page. Then, in single words or short phrases, list
everything that comes to mind about the topic. Don't worry about connection or relevance; simply jot down everything that occurs to you.

Once that is finished, look at the list carefully. If some items seem to belong together, group them and try to assign a name to that group. Feel free to add to the list at any time and eliminate any items that don't fit. Then try to write a sentence that asserts something about each group. As you can see, this technique is a powerful tool for generating ideas and for seeing connections between them once you know what your topic is.

Some writers work better in the opposite direction: They begin with the categories and then list to find information to put into them. You should use whichever method works for you.

For example, if the topic were "love," the list might be:

Romeo and Juliet

passion

parental love

romance

dancing on a pier

beautiful eyes

my best friend

sex

friendship

parents

Elizabeth and Darcy (*Pride and Prejudice*)

nervousness

dating

Humbert and Lolita

"Looking for Love in All the Wrong Places"

singles bars

fraternity parties

flowers and candy

sharing

Looking over that list, I see that most of the items fit into three categories:

types of love (passionate, romantic, parental, friendship)

fictional lovers (Elizabeth and Darcy, Romeo and Juliet)

dating (singles bars, fraternity parties, nervousness, flowers and candy)

Having established my categories, I would write a sentence asserting something about each grouping:

Romantic love can sometimes include the other three major types of love—passionate, paternal, and friendship.

In fiction as in life, romantic love sometimes works out happily as in the case of Elizabeth and Darcy and sometimes ends in tragedy as in the case of Romeo and Juliet.

Although dating can take many forms such as meeting people at singles bars and at fraternity parties, it always has one constant factor for me—nervousness.

Once I had written those assertions, I would start deciding what idea(s) I wanted to explore. For example, I might try to use all three categories as my major ideas. More likely, however, I would focus on one and try to develop more secondary ideas to go with it.

Mind Mapping, or Ballooning

Much like listing, this technique allows you to put ideas in writing with no limiting structure. If you are like me, every time I start a list, I end up jamming in all kinds of oversights into tiny margins. The mind-mapping technique was invented for crowders like me.

Begin by turning a sheet of paper sideways; in the middle write your subject. One advantage of this technique is that it is nonlinear; you don't have to decide about order or importance of items. So starting in the middle of the paper is helpful. For example, Carl had to describe his relationship with a pitcher in a Little League game, a former friend who used his knowledge of Carl to defeat him at the plate. Carl began with the mind map in Figure 1.1, writing "pitcher" in the middle of a page

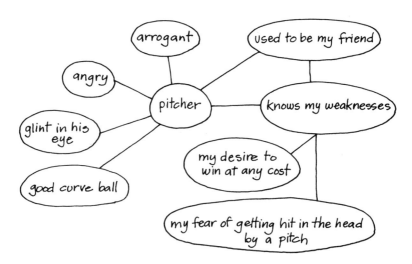

Figure 1.1 Example of a Mind Map

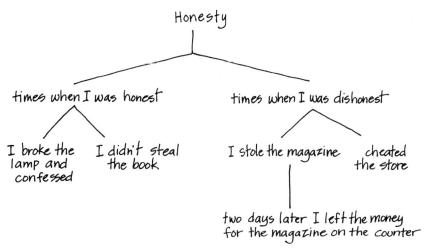

Figure 1.2 An Idea Tree for an Essay about Honesty

and circling it. Then he wrote words or phrases that occurred to him about that pitcher. He drew a circle or balloon around each word or phrase. Where it seemed appropriate, he drew a line (or spoke) between circles, indicating a connection between the circles that he would explore in his fast-write. Each spoke radiates from the center. As you can see, Carl saw significant connections between the pitcher's emotions (anger and arrogance) and the glint in his eye (hence the lines connecting their circles). The line between "used to be my friend" and "knows my weaknesses" reveals how the pitcher got the knowledge of Carl's weaknesses; they were revealed in friendly discussions.

Idea Trees

Similar to mind maps are idea trees. The major difference between the two techniques is that idea trees allow you to see or impose an order on your material more easily than mind maps do. Write the key concept near the top of a page (or top of the screen), then make branches below it for major ideas. Figure 1.2 shows the beginning of an idea tree for an exploratory essay about honesty. If this were a fully developed idea tree, the branches could continue and each episode on the third level would have details branching from it on the fourth level. Often it is a good idea to turn the paper horizontally to allow more space for branching to the left and right.

Questioning

Like listing, mind mapping, and creating idea trees, questioning is a good technique to use when you already have a topic in mind. *Topics* can be loosely classified as *objects* (anything with a physical presence including people, places, and things), *concepts* (such as truth and beauty), *propositions* (for example, "Abortions should be allowed on demand for three reasons"), and *events*.

Write your topic at the top of a blank sheet of paper. Try to write at least a one-paragraph response to each of the following questions which is appropriate for your topic. Do not try to write good prose; do not stop to correct. The point here is to get some ideas down on paper about the topic.

What is it (the topic)? If it is an object, describe it fully.

What is it similar to and why?

What else is associated with it? Explain the connection.

How is it made or formed?

Who makes it or supports it?

For what purpose is it made?

How is it used and by whom and for what purposes?

Why is it good or bad, useful or useless, effective or ineffective?

Perspectives

Because no one sees any of your prewriting except you, part of the excitement of idea generation is the chance to explore something from different perspectives, to gamble, to make a fool of yourself and perhaps to thus discover something particularly interesting about your subject or yourself. That is what this technique is all about—*making a constructive fool out of yourself.* It uses role-playing. Once you know what your topic will be, assume one of the following perspectives and write notes or even a full paragraph about your subject (and then try one or two perspectives that don't seem as though they could possibly be helpful):

1. Assume the *observer perspective.* Study the physical nature of your subject. If your subject is an object, a person, a place— describe it; if it is a text (for example, a book, poem, movie, painting), consider its physical layout (for instance, a poem's shape or arrangement of lines is often crucial, the order of scenes is important in books and movies); if it is an event, imagine the scene of that event (the sights, sounds, smells, texture).

2. Assume the *insider perspective.* What is it like *to be* that subject? What does it feel like to be a rock, a poem, your mother, your room? What does the world look like to you? Describe it through the senses or imagination of the subject you've become. If your subject is a poem or a piece of writing, imagine events in your life as lived through the ideas or concepts of the poem/book/historical event.

3. Assume the *shallow perspective*. You are someone who just can't see the value of your subject, who doubts its worth. Refuse to see its merits; prove that it has no real value.

4. Assume the *depth perspective*. You are still outside your subject, but now you care a great deal about it. Look for its essence. What makes it unique? What makes it valuable to you? To others?

5. Assume the *conservationist perspective*. How would the world be diminished or deprived if this subject were extinct? If it had never been? What can we do to better serve its needs or to help preserve it?

6. Assume the *consumer perspective*. How can we use this subject? Are there new, unthought-of ways to use it, to exploit it, to derive some benefit (no matter how small or selfish) from it? For example, someone might use the poem "She Walks in Beauty Like the Night" to impress a girlfriend.

7. Assume the *god perspective*. Look down from so high above that you can see the grand scheme, you can see how all the pieces fit. Where does this subject fit in that grand scheme? How big a grand scheme can you devise? Start small and then work your way up the scale—for example, how does your mother fit into the family unit? the neighborhood? the city? the state? the country? womankind in general? humankind in general? the animal kingdom? the earth's ecological system? the universe?

8. Assume the *flea perspective*. You can't see any big schemes (or at least, no schemes humans would call "big"). In this case, how does your subject appear to the "little guy?" To your younger brother or sister? To your pet goldfish? To your father's car keys? Concentrate on a small piece of your subject (if it is a poem, concentrate on a stanza; if your room, on the desk or your bed; if a philosophical argument, on the definition of one key term; if your mother, on her face or her typical morning's activity).

9. Assume the *joker perspective*. Make fun of your subject. Try to invent a pun about it. Make a joke about its name; mock it, parody it, caricature it. Imagine it in an absurd situation, acting absurdly (but in character, of course). Imagine it in an embarrassing situation (what would be an embarrassing situation for a rock? for the concept of existentialism?)

10. Assume the *advocate perspective*. Make a case for the continuation of your subject, for increasing it or its power or number.

11. Assume the *skeptic perspective*. Begin by listing every idea or assumption you have made about the topic/subject. Then attack each one, argue that the opposite idea is better.

12. Assume the *perspective of the person you most admire*. Try to put yourself in that person's mind, look at the subject through his or her eyes. Even try to imitate his or her style of writing or speech. For example, if you admire Thomas Jefferson, how would he view your subject (computers)? As inventor of the "seeing-eye" door, he would probably enjoy the inventiveness a great deal. As a Renaissance man, he might be highly impressed and enthusiastic about the computer's potential to increase learning and the absorption of information. As a writer, he might be pleased by the speed of composition, although he might have reservations that such a machine could encourage some people he could name to run off at the mouth a bit. Write in his style. Or, if you admire Ben Franklin or Oscar Wilde, try writing some pithy epigrams about the computer.

13. Assume the *perspective of the person you dislike or least admire*. Try to put yourself in that person's mind; look at the subject through his or her eyes. Again, total honesty here is crucial. Assume you dislike Ben Franklin but you really like computers. Write some pithy epigrams attacking the computer—its impersonality, perhaps, its time-consuming games.

14. Assume a *politician's perspective*. Argue that your subject is vital to national security; then argue that it is a waste of taxpayers' money or time or whatever.

15. Assume the *poet's perspective*. Compare your subject to something with which it seems to have nothing in common. Create an *extended analogy* which shows connections between your subject and some dissimilar thing (for example, your brother to a door, a rock to a telephone, your father to a car, justice to a television set).

16. Assume the *novelist's perspective*. Create a narrative about your subject (your first encounter with a computer; an argument with your best friend; your attempt to apply utilitarianism's "the greatest good for the greatest number" in a real situation).

Writing paragraphs in response to some of these perspectives gives you a chance to get outside your usual assumptions and beliefs, a chance to try out other voices.

Nothing is too bizarre, too far out.

Remember, though, that all of these exercises are *prewriting*. You can't string a series of such paragraphs together and assume you have a complete exploratory essay. The techniques exist to help you see your topic/subject from different angles and in different lights. One (or more) of them might give you key insights into your connection to the topic/subject. Then the planning and drafting begin.

Planning

After all the idea generation is completed, you are ready for the final stage of prewriting: planning. Here you begin the process of arranging your material, seeing which ideas lead to other ideas, which require more idea generation. For some writers, this is the time to prepare an outline, whether a formal outline (with roman numerals and capital letters) or an informal scratch outline (a list of ideas in the order they should follow in the essay). For others, idea trees might be the schematic used to make the organization visual. Still others might simply plan where they will start in their minds and move right into the drafting stage. The point is that somewhere in the writing process you will need to consider the arrangement of your ideas.

EXTERNAL DETAILS VERSUS INTERNAL DETAILS

External details can be taken in by the five senses. Internal details, on the other hand, are your feelings and thoughts. In exploratory essays, both the external and internal details of your life are important, but in different ways. For example, external details are important in setting the context of a particular event, for setting the scene, and for making the event and the people involved in that event "real" for your readers. Such details are part of the craft of writing, of putting your readers "into the picture" rather than simply telling them about it.

But if you merely give the external details, you have not written an exploratory essay. Certainly you may have revealed a great deal about *your external life;* but you have not revealed much about *your inner self.* To change a superficial "this is my life" essay into a true exploratory essay, you must describe and analyze your reactions, thoughts, and feelings.

For example, it might be incredibly wonderful for you to win $50 million in the lottery. But that external fact is not the stuff that exploratory essays are made of. The "stuff" would be the complex emotions accompanying that event—for example, you'd probably discuss the joy about winning, but also the fear about the inevitable changes in your life that would follow, the doubts about whom you could trust. Or suppose that your family moved to ten different states in five years—that would be an interesting external detail. How you felt about each of those moves, what those moves did to your self-esteem, to your ability to interact with other children, to your sense of permanence—that would be good material for an exploratory essay.

THE ILLUSION OF OBJECTIVITY

While in some ways exploratory writing is "unscientific," in other ways, it is profoundly scientific. The scientific method, after all, is one of exploration: observe, hypothesize, experiment. We could say that the exploratory essay is a way of observing ourselves. Prewriting is the observing step. The hypothesizing comes next when we express our ideas in sentences and paragraphs in a draft. Then we test the ideas about ourselves and the world in progressively refined prose. Ultimately we write the final draft that takes into account readers other than ourselves.

Of course, such writing is not and cannot be objective. Fortunately. Exploratory writing revels in subjectivity. That is its raison d'être.

If this subjectivity seems dangerous or anti-intellectual, it isn't. The truth is, we can't ever escape our subjectivity completely, so why not ride that subjectivity as far as it will take us? Each of us filters reality through our assumptions, prejudices, and beliefs. Some scientists now suggest that the only unfiltered experience we can have is the act of smelling. Data from all the senses except (perhaps) smell get "processed" first. This is one explanation of why a smell can trigger a vivid and profound memory from many years ago whereas other sense data get us involved in the *act* of remembering instead of the *experience* of remembering.

One goal of exploratory writing is to make us more aware of the extent of that filtering. Even everyday language suggests that this filtering occurs. When people want to suggest that you are overly optimistic, for example, they often say, "You're looking at the world through rose-colored glasses." In actuality, we all wear metaphorical glasses; only the hues of their lenses differ, not the fact of our wearing glasses. They distort, bend, twist, and cast a tinge over all we see. It is the nature of the beast called *human:* We are not objective receivers with perfect reception.

Distortions can be interesting, even beautiful. If you don't believe it, look at a painting by any impressionist (or by any artist, for that matter). If the artist's "distortion" matches yours, the painting will seem "realistic." But no painting can give us reality; at the least, it reduces a three-dimensional object or person to two dimensions. Beyond that, the artist has painted his or her vision of that person or that landscape, not the real person or the real landscape. The artist's subjectivity and distortions are in play. They have to be; all of our distortions are always in play, because we humans *are* our distortions.

This is a profound philosophical issue, the intricacies of which are beyond the scope of this book. Yet it is important that you recognize the subjective nature of *all* your perceptions. For that recognition is one of the cornerstones on which exploratory writing is built. Since distortions inevitably (and, I might add, gloriously) exist, it is of great interest and practical benefit to discover what our particular distortions are. We can do that by writing to report not only what we think we see or understand, but also why we think and understand it in just that particular way.

Is there a contradiction here? Sure. Since we are incurably subjective, even our examination of our own subjectivity will be subjective. Yet becoming aware of our own subjectivity opens up numerous ideas and approaches that we might otherwise reject if we believed we were simply accurate recorders of reality; knowing that we don't automatically have the truth about anything makes us more willing to hear what other people have to say about everything.

One of the most interesting aspects of any exploratory essay, then, is the writer who is revealed in it. But there is likely to be other interesting material too: information (consider the way Annie Dillard tells us so much about wildlife while still revealing so much about herself); the opinions of others (that is, quotations from primary and secondary sources); insights into events or people; interesting images and language. Each of those pieces of information is enhanced, not ruined, by revelations about the writer.

In short, as an essayist observing yourself engaging with a topic, you discover insights into both yourself and the topic. And both are interesting.

OVERVIEW OF THIS BOOK

In the rest of this book, each chapter will give advice about how to explore a particular type of official subject. In Chapter 2, the official subject is you; in Chapter 3, events; in Chapter 4, other people; in Chapter 5, relationships; in Chapter 6, concepts; in Chapter 7, beliefs; in Chapter 8, controversies; in Chapter 9, texts. Chapter 10 gives advice about deepening and revising the content of your essays, and Chapter 11 gives advice about revising your style in those essays. Chapters 2–9 offer some writer-based goals and some reader-based goals for your writing. *Writer-based goals* suggest what you should be trying to accomplish for yourself as a writer and person; *reader-based goals* suggest what you should be trying to accomplish for your readers.

GUIDELINES FOR EXPLORATORY ESSAYISTS

Here are some basic guidelines that many exploratory essayists follow:

1. Be *truthful* in what you say, *adventurous* in how you write, and *thoughtful* in how you revise.

2. Write *modern edited English* to aid in communication. Occasional slang words or specialized language may be used to give

the sense of people's real speech, but such terms should be "translated" for your readers if you are not sure they will understand them.

3. Push yourself and your ideas in every essay; never settle for the easy essay. Select topics which interest you, and then try to dig into them and into yourself.

4. Never forget that the only constant subject in exploratory writing is your inner self.

SUGGESTIONS FOR WRITING

1. Write paragraphs about yourself from at least three of the perspectives described on pages 22–24. Obviously there may be a little overlap, but if you find yourself saying the same thing over and over, try thinking of your subject as being upside down (or viewed through your legs as you bend over), or force yourself to use the vocabulary of a six-year-old (the "see Spot run" approach). Or try writing sentences about it using words that begin only with the letters *a* through *o*. Most of all, loosen up.

2. Symbols are powerful. Select one *public symbol* (for instance, the American flag, red roses, a BMW) and one *private symbol* (anything that has symbolic value for you but not necessarily for the person in the street). For each symbol write about: (a) their meanings for others and (b) their meanings for you.

3. Sum up what you know about yourself so far by doing at least one of the following as a form of prewriting:
   a. Briefly explain your personal history: for example, where you were born, who your parents are, the number of siblings you have, schools you attended, the major things you learned there. Then explain which of those facts you'd like to change (for instance, maybe you wish you had been born in a big city instead of in a small town) and why. If you don't want to change any of them, why not? Then go one step further: What is the significance of each of these facts to you?
   b. Using vivid words and details, describe your personality. List at least four key personality traits (for example, honest, thoughtful, timid, concerned about my appearance, concerned about animals).
   c. What makes you different from everyone else in the class? What makes you similar to everyone else in class? Make each list as long as you can.

d. What was the best thing you ever did? Explain why it was the best and in what sense it was the best (for instance, the most honorable? the most effective? the most fun?).

e. Describe the way you study and learn. What kind of environment do you like? Why?

The Essayist and the Essay

E. B. WHITE

☐ *Inward Exploration*

Write at least a paragraph describing what an essayist *is, not only what an essayist does ("write essays"), but also the personality traits he or she probably needs in order to be a successful essayist.*

The essayist is a self-liberated man, sustained by the childish belief 1
that everything he thinks about, everything that happens to him, is of
general interest. He is a fellow who thoroughly enjoys his work, just as
people who take bird walks enjoy theirs. Each new excursion of the
essayist, each new "attempt," differs from the last and takes him into
new country. This delights him. Only a person who is congenitally self-
centered has the effrontery and the stamina to write essays.

There are as many kinds of essays as there are human attitudes or
poses, as many essay flavors as there are Howard Johnson ice creams.
The essayist arises in the morning and, if he has work to do, selects
his garb from an unusually extensive wardrobe: He can pull on any sort
of shirt, be any sort of person, according to his mood or his subject
matter—philosopher, scold, jester, raconteur, confidant, pundit, devil's
advocate, enthusiast. I like the essay, have always liked it, and even as
a child was at work, attempting to inflict my young thoughts and experiences on others by putting them on paper. I early broke into print
in the pages of *St. Nicholas.* I tend still to fall back on the essay form
(or lack of form) when an idea strikes me, but I am not fooled about
the place of the essay in twentieth-century American letters—it stands
a short distance down the line. The essayist, unlike the novelist, the
poet, and the playwright, must be content in his self-imposed role of
second-class citizen. A writer who has his sights trained on the Nobel
Prize or other earthly triumphs had best write a novel, a poem, or a
play, and leave the essayist to ramble about, content with living a free
life and enjoying the satisfactions of a somewhat undisciplined existence. (Dr. Johnson called the essay "an irregular, undigested piece";
this happy practitioner has no wish to quarrel with the good doctor's
characterization.)

There is one thing the essayist cannot do, though—he cannot indulge himself in deceit or in concealment, for he will be found out in no
time. Desmond MacCarthy, in his introductory remarks to the 1928

E. P. Dutton & Company edition of Montaigne, observes that Montaigne "had the gift of natural candour. . . ." It is the basic ingredient. And even the essayist's escape from discipline is only a partial escape: The essay, although a relaxed form, imposes its own disciplines, raises its own problems, and these disciplines and problems soon become apparent and (we all hope) act as a deterrent to anyone wielding a pen merely because he entertains random thoughts or is in a happy or wandering mood.

I think some people find the essay the last resort of the egoist, a much too self-conscious and self-serving form for their taste; they feel that it is presumptuous of a writer to assume that his little excursions or his small observations will interest the reader. There is some justice in their complaint. I have always been aware that I am by nature self-absorbed and egoistical; to write of myself to the extent I have done indicates a too great attention to my own life, not enough to the lives of others. I have worn many shirts, and not all of them have been a good fit. But when I am discouraged or downcast I need only fling open the door of my closet, and there, hidden behind everything else, hangs the mantle of Michel de Montaigne, smelling slightly of camphor.

🔲 *Outward Exploration: Discussion and Writing*

1. According to White, what personality traits does an essayist have?
2. According to White, what roles might an essayist play? Are these roles consistent with the roles played by essayists you encountered before? Do any of these roles conflict with Joan Didion's vision of the writer as revealed in "Why I Write" (page 33)?
3. What is the tone of this essay?
4. What standing in American letters does White believe the essay has? Why? Do you agree? How often do you read essays compared to how often you read other kinds of material?
5. According to White, what one thing can an essayist not do? Why not? What are this idea's implications for you as an essayist?
6. In paragraph 3, White seems to switch from happy to serious. In that paragraph, does he contradict his comment in paragraph 1?

🔲 *Style*

Consider this sentence from White's essay:

The essayist is a self-liberated man, sustained by the childish belief that everything he thinks about, everything that happens to him, is of general interest. (paragraph 1)

The structure of the sentence is as follows:

subject ("The essayist")

predicate verb ("is")

predicate nominative ("a self-liberated man")

comma separating free modifier (participial phrase) from the independent clause

past participle ("sustained")

prepositional phrase ("by belief")

relative pronoun beginning a long dependent clause ("that")

subject of the long dependent clause ("everything")

an implied relative pronoun ("that")

a short dependent clause modifying "everything" ("he thinks about")

comma

repeated subject of the dependent clause ("everything")

dependent clause modifying the second "everything" ("that . . . him")

verb of the dependent clause ("is")

prepositional phrase ending the large dependent clause and the sentence ("of . . . interest")

period.

The most important feature of this sentence is its use of the free modifier, which begins at the comma with a past participle ("sustained") and continues to the end of the sentence, even though it contains several other parts such as prepositional phrases and dependent clauses. The second most important feature—and the one that gives the sentence its rhythm—is the repetition of the word *everything* and its own small dependent *that* clause.

Write a sentence of your own that replicates this structure (the free modifier following the sentence's independent clause, the repetition of the subject of a dependent clause contained within that free modifier) but which uses your own information.

Why I Write

JOAN DIDION

☐ *Inward Exploration*

Write at least one paragraph on your reasons for writing. Go beyond "I have assignments."

Of course I stole the title for this talk from George Orwell. One   1
reason I stole it was that I like the sound of the words: *Why I Write*.
There you have three short unambiguous words that share a sound, and
the sound they share is this:

I

I

I

In many ways writing is the act of saying *I,* of imposing oneself
upon other people, of saying *listen to me, see it my way, change your mind.*
It's an aggressive, even a hostile act. You can disguise its aggressiveness
all you want with veils of subordinate clauses and qualifiers and tentative subjunctives, with ellipses and evasions—with the whole manner of
intimating rather than claiming, of alluding rather than stating—but
there's no getting around the fact that setting words on paper is the tactic
of a secret bully, an invasion, an imposition of the writer's sensibility on
the reader's most private space.

I stole the title not only because the words sounded right but because
they seemed to sum up, in a no-nonsense way, all I have to tell you. Like
many writers I have only this one "subject," this one "area": the act of
writing. I can bring you no reports from any other front. I may have
other interests: I am "interested," for example, in marine biology, but
I don't flatter myself that you would come out to hear me talk about
it. I am not a scholar. I am not in the least an intellectual, which is not
to say that when I hear the word "intellectual" I reach for my gun, but
only to say that I do not think in abstracts. During the years when I
was an undergraduate at Berkeley I tried, with a kind of hopeless late-
adolescent energy, to buy some temporary visa into the world of ideas,
to forge for myself a mind that could deal with the abstract.

In short I tried to think. I failed. My attention veered inexorably
back to the specific, to the tangible, to what was generally considered,
by everyone I knew then and for that matter have known since, the

peripheral. I would try to contemplate the Hegelian dialectic and would find myself concentrating instead on a flowering pear tree outside my window and the particular way the petals fell on my floor. I would try to read linguistic theory and would find myself wondering instead if the lights were on in the bevatron up the hill. When I say that I was wondering if the lights were on in the bevatron you might immediately suspect, if you deal in ideas at all, that I was registering the bevatron as a political symbol, thinking in shorthand about the military-industrial complex and its role in the university community, but you would be wrong. I was only wondering if the lights were on in the bevatron, and how they looked. A physical fact.

I had trouble graduating from Berkeley, not because of this inability   5
to deal with ideas—I was majoring in English, and I could locate the house-and-garden imagery in *The Portrait of a Lady* as well as the next person, "imagery" being by definition the kind of specific that got my attention—but simply because I had neglected to take a course in Milton. For reasons which now sound baroque I needed a degree by the end of that summer, and the English department finally agreed, if I would come down from Sacramento every Friday and talk about the cosmology of *Paradise Lost,* to certify me proficient in Milton. I did this. Some Fridays I took the Greyhound bus, other Fridays I caught the Southern Pacific's City of San Francisco on the last leg of its transcontinental trip. I can no longer tell you whether Milton put the sun or the earth at the center of his universe in *Paradise Lost,* the central question of at least one century and a topic about which I wrote 10,000 words that summer, but I can still recall the exact rancidity of the butter in the City of San Francisco's dining car, and the way the tinted windows on the Greyhound bus cast the oil refineries around Carquinez Straits into a grayed and obscurely sinister light. In short my attention was always on the periphery, on what I would see and taste and touch, on the butter, and the Greyhound bus. During those years I was traveling on what I knew to be a very shaky passport, forged papers: I knew that I was no legitimate resident in any world of ideas. I knew I couldn't think. All I knew then was what I couldn't do. All I knew then was what I wasn't, and it took me some years to discover what I was.

Which was a writer.

By which I mean not a "good" writer or a "bad" writer but simply a writer, a person whose most absorbed and passionate hours are spent arranging words on pieces of paper. Had my credentials been in order I would never have become a writer. Had I been blessed with even limited access to my own mind there would have been no reason to write. I write entirely to find out what I'm thinking, what I'm looking at, what I see and what it means. What I want and what I fear. Why did the oil refineries around Carquinez Straits seem sinister to me in the summer of 1956? Why have the night lights in the bevatron burned in my mind for twenty years? *What is going on in these pictures in my mind?*

When I talk about pictures in my mind I am talking, quite specifically, about images that shimmer around the edges. There used to be an illustration in every elementary psychology book showing a cat drawn by a patient in varying stages of schizophrenia. This cat had a shimmer around it. You could see the molecular structure breaking down at the very edges of the cat: The cat became the background and the background the cat, everything interacting, exchanging ions. People on hallucinogens describe the same perception of objects. I'm not a schizophrenic, nor do I take hallucinogens, but certain images do shimmer for me. Look hard enough, and you can't miss the shimmer. It's there. You can't think too much about these pictures that shimmer. You just lie low and let them develop. You stay quiet. You don't talk to many people and you keep your nervous system from shorting out and try to locate the cat in the shimmer, the grammar in the picture.

Just as I meant "shimmer" literally I mean "grammar" literally. Grammar is a piano I play by ear, since I seem to have been out of school the year the rules were mentioned. All I know about grammar is its infinite power. To shift the structure of a sentence alters the meaning of that sentence, as definitely and inflexibly as the position of a camera alters the meaning of the object photographed. Many people know about camera angles now, but not so many know about sentences. The arrangement of the words matters, and the arrangement you want can be found in the picture in your mind. The picture dictates the arrangement. The picture dictates whether this will be a sentence with or without clauses, a sentence that ends hard or a dying-fall sentence, long or short, active or passive. The picture tells you how to arrange the words and the arrangement of the words tells you, or tells me, what's going on in the picture. *Nota bene:*

It tells you.

You don't tell it.

Let me show you what I mean by pictures in the mind. I began *Play It as It Lays* just as I have begun each of my novels, with no notion of "character" or "plot" or even "incident." I had only two pictures in my mind, more about which later, and a technical intention, which was to write a novel so elliptical and fast that it would be over before you noticed it, a novel so fast that it would scarcely exist on the page at all. About the pictures: The first was of white space. Empty space. This was clearly the picture that dictated the narrative intention of the book—a book in which anything that happened would happen off the page, a "white" book to which the reader would have to bring his or her own bad dreams—and yet this picture told me no "story," suggested no situation. The second picture did. This second picture was of something actually witnessed. A young woman with long hair and a short white halter dress walks through the casino at the Riviera in Las Vegas at one in the morning. She crosses the casino alone and picks up a house telephone. I watch her because I have heard her paged, and recognize her

10

name: She is a minor actress I see around Los Angeles from time to time, in places like Jax and once in a gynecologist's office in the Beverly Hills Clinic, but have never met. I know nothing about her. Who is paging her? Why is she here to be paged? How exactly did she come to this? It was precisely this moment in Las Vegas that made *Play It as It Lays* begin to tell itself to me, but the moment appears in the novel only obliquely, in a chapter which begins:

> Maria made a list of things she would never do. She would never: walk through the Sands or Caesar's alone after midnight. She would never: ball at a party, do S-M unless she wanted to, borrow furs from Abe Lipsey, deal. She would never: carry a Yorkshire in Beverly Hills.

That is the beginning of the chapter and that is also the end of the chapter, which may suggest what I meant by "white space."

I recall having a number of pictures in my mind when I began the novel I just finished, *A Book of Common Prayer.* As a matter of fact one of these pictures was of that bevatron I mentioned, although I would be hard put to tell you a story in which nuclear energy figured. Another was a newspaper photograph of a hijacked 707 burning on the desert in the Middle East. Another was the night view from a room in which I once spent a week with paratyphoid, a hotel room on the Colombian coast. My husband and I seemed to be on the Colombian coast representing the United States of America at a film festival (I recall invoking the name "Jack Valenti" a lot, as if its reiteration could make me well), and it was a bad place to have fever, not only because my indisposition offended our hosts but because every night in this hotel the generator failed. The lights went out. The elevator stopped. My husband would go to the event of the evening and make excuses for me and I would stay alone in this hotel room, in the dark. I remember standing at the window trying to call Bogotá (the telephone seemed to work on the same principle as the generator) and watching the night wind come up and wondering what I was doing eleven degrees off the equator with a fever of 103. The view from that window definitely figures in *A Book of Common Prayer,* as does the burning 707, and yet none of these pictures told me the story I needed.

The picture that did, the picture that shimmered and made these other images coalesce, was the Panama airport at 6 A.M. I was in this airport only once, on a plane to Bogotá that stopped for an hour to refuel, but the way it looked that morning remained superimposed on everything I saw until the day I finished *A Book of Common Prayer.* I lived in that airport for several years. I can still feel the hot air when I step off the plane, can see the heat already rising off the tarmac at 6 A.M. I can feel my skirt damp and wrinkled on my legs. I can feel the asphalt stick to my sandals. I remember the big tail of a Pan American plane floating motionless down at the end of the tarmac. I remember the sound of a slot machine in the waiting room. I could tell you that I remember a particular woman in the airport, an American woman, a *norteamericana,* a thin *norteamericana* about 40 who wore a big square emerald in lieu of a wedding ring, but there was no such woman there.

I put this woman in the airport later. I made this woman up, just as I later made up a country to put the airport in, and a family to run the country. This woman in the airport is neither catching a plane nor meeting one. She is ordering tea in the airport coffee shop. In fact she is not simply "ordering" tea but insisting that the water be boiled, in front of her, for twenty minutes. Why is this woman in this airport? Why is she going nowhere, where has she been? Where did she get that big emerald? What derangement, or disassociation, makes her believe that her will to see the water boiled can possibly prevail?

> She had been going to one airport or another for four months, one could see it, looking at the visas on her passport. All those airports where Charlotte Douglas's passport had been stamped would have looked alike. Sometimes the sign on the tower would say "Bienvenidos" and sometimes the sign on the tower would say "Bienvenue," some places were wet and hot and others dry and hot, but at each of these airports the pastel concrete walls would rust and stain and the swamp off the runway would be littered with the fuselages of cannibalized Fairchild F-227's and the water would need boiling.
> I knew why Charlotte went to the airport even if Victor did not.
> I knew about airports.

These lines appear about halfway through *A Book of Common Prayer,* but I wrote them during the second week I worked on the book, long before I had any idea where Charlotte Douglas had been or why she went to airports. Until I wrote these lines I had no character called "Victor" in mind: the necessity for mentioning a name, and the name "Victor," occurred to me as I wrote the sentence. *I knew why Charlotte went to the airport* sounded incomplete. *I knew why Charlotte went to the airport even if Victor did not* carried a little more narrative drive. Most important of all, until I wrote these lines I did not know who "I" was, who was telling the story. I had intended until that moment that the "I" be no more than the voice of the author, a 19th-century omniscient narrator. But there it was:

> I knew why Charlotte went to the airport even if Victor did not.
> I knew about airports.

This "I" was the voice of no author in my house. This "I" was someone who not only knew why Charlotte went to the airport but also knew someone called "Victor." Who was Victor? Who was this narrator? Why was this narrator telling me this story? Let me tell you one thing about why writers write: Had I known the answer to any of these questions I would never have needed to write a novel.

□ *Outward Exploration: Discussion and Writing*

1. According to Didion, how is the act of saying *I* an act of aggression (paragraph 2)?

2. What are some strategies for disguising this act of aggression? Can you find any examples of such disguising in this essay?

3. What is Didion's definition of an *intellectual?* Do you agree with her definition? Why does she consider herself not an intellectual? What is her definition of a *writer?*

4. In paragraph 5, Didion raises an interesting distinction between being a *thinker* and being a *writer.* Explain that distinction. Do you agree with it? Why or why not?

5. According to Didion, what is her major motivation for writing?

6. What images does she use to describe grammar?

7. Didion is explaining how she writes a novel. How could her explanation help you as you write essays?

□ *Style*

Consider the following sentence from Didion's essay:

To shift the structure of a sentence alters the meaning of that sentence, as definitely and inflexibly as the position of a camera alters the meaning of the object photographed. (paragraph 9)

Here is the structure:

> subject (an infinitive phrase: "To shift . . . sentence")
> predicate verb ("alters")
> direct object ("the meaning of that sentence")
> **comma**
> adverbs ("as . . . inflexibly")
> conjunction ("as")
> subject of dependent clause ("the position")
> verb ("alters")
> direct object ("the meaning . . . photographed")
> **period.**

There are two nice touches here: first, the infinitive phrase used as the sentence's subject and, second, the *as . . . as* construction leading into a dependent clause. Write a sentence of your own that replicates this structure (in other words, that uses an infinitive phrase as the sentence's subject and which uses the *as . . . as* construction) but which uses your own information.

The Singular First Person

SCOTT RUSSELL SANDERS

◻ *Inward Exploration*

Write at least one paragraph about what you've been taught about what should be included in an essay (and what should be excluded). For example, what have you been told about the organization of essays? About the use of the first person in essays? About who the audience is for your essays? About what your audience expects and wants from your essays?

Write at least one paragraph exploring your thoughts and feelings about self-revelation in essays. For example, are there topics that should not be explored in essays which others will read? How do you feel when you encounter an essayist discussing a topic you think is too personal for print?

The first soapbox orator I ever saw was haranguing a crowd beside   *1* the Greyhound Station in Providence, Rhode Island, about the evils of fluoridated water. What the man stood on was actually an upturned milk crate, all the genuine soapboxes presumably having been snapped up by antique dealers. He wore an orange plaid sports coat and matching bow tie and held aloft a bottle filled with mossy green liquid. I don't remember the details of his spiel, except his warning that fluoride was an invention of the Communists designed to weaken our bones and thereby make us pushovers for a Red invasion. What amazed me, as a tongue-tied kid of seventeen newly arrived in the city from the boondocks, was not his message but his courage in delivering it to a mob of strangers. I figured it would have been easier for me to jump straight over the Greyhound Station than to stand there on that milk crate and utter my thoughts.

To this day, when I read or when I compose one of those curious monologues we call the personal essay, I often think of that soapbox orator. Nobody had asked him for his two cents' worth, but there he was declaring it with all the eloquence he could muster. The essay, although enacted in private, is no less arrogant a performance. Unlike novelists and playwrights, who lurk behind the scenes while distracting our attention with the puppet show of imaginary characters, unlike scholars and journalists, who quote the opinions of others and shelter behind the hedges of neutrality, the essayist has nowhere to hide. While the poet can lean back on a several-thousand-year-old legacy of ecstatic speech, the essayist inherits a much briefer and skimpier tradition. The poet is allowed to quit after a few lines, but the essayist must hold our attention over pages and pages. It is a brash and foolhardy form, this one-man or one-woman circus, which relies on the tricks of anecdote, conjecture, memory, and wit to enthrall us.

Addressing a monologue to the world seems all the more brazen or preposterous an act when you consider what a tiny fraction of the human chorus any single voice is. At the Boston Museum of Science an electronic meter records with flashing lights the population of the United States. Figuring in the rate of births, deaths, emigrants leaving the country and immigrants arriving, the meter calculates that we add one fellow citizen every twenty-one seconds. When I looked at it recently, the count stood at 249,958,483. As I wrote that figure in my notebook, the final number jumped from three to four. Another mouth, another set of ears and eyes, another brain. A counter for the earth's population would stand somewhere past five billion at the moment, and would be rising in a blur of digits. Amid this avalanche of selves, it is a wonder that anyone finds the gumption to sit down and write one of those naked, lonely, quixotic letters-to-the-world.

A surprising number do find the gumption. In fact, I have the impression there are more essayists at work in America today, and more gifted ones, than at any time in recent decades. Whom do I have in mind? Here is a sampler: Wendell Berry, Carol Bly, Joan Didion, Annie Dillard, Stephen Jay Gould, Elizabeth Hardwick, Edward Hoagland, Phillip Lopate, Barry Lopez, Peter Matthiessen, John McPhee, Cynthia Ozick, Paul Theroux, Lewis Thomas, Tom Wolfe. No doubt you could make up a list of your own—with a greater ethnic range, perhaps, or fewer nature enthusiasts—a list that would provide equally convincing support for the view that we are blessed right now with an abundance of essayists. We do not have anyone to rival Emerson or Thoreau, but in sheer quantity of first-rate work our time stands comparison with any period since the heyday of the form in the mid-nineteenth century.

Why are so many writers taking up this risky form, and why are so 5 many readers—to judge by the statistics of book and magazine publication—seeking it out? In this era of prepackaged thought, the essay is the closest thing we have, on paper, to a record of the individual mind at work and play. It is an amateur's raid in a world of specialists. Feeling overwhelmed by data, random information, the flotsam and jetsam of mass culture, we relish the spectacle of a single consciousness making sense of a portion of the chaos. We are grateful to Lewis Thomas for shining his light into the dark corners of biology, to John McPhee for laying bare the geology beneath our landscape, to Annie Dillard for showing us the universal fire blazing in the branches of a cedar, to Peter Matthiessen for chasing after snow leopards and mystical insights in the Himalayas. No matter if they are sketchy, these maps of meaning are still welcome. As Joan Didion observes in her own collection of essays, *The White Album,* "We live entirely, especially if we are writers, by the imposition of a narrative line upon disparate images, by the 'ideas' with which we have learned to freeze the shifting phantasmagoria which is our actual experience." Dizzy from a dance that seems to accelerate hour by hour, we cling to the narrative line, even though it may be as pure an invention as the shapes drawn by Greeks to identify the constellations.

The essay is a haven for the private, idiosyncratic voice in an era of anonymous babble. Like the blandburgers served in their millions along our highways, most language served up in public these days is texture-less, tasteless mush. On television, over the phone, in the newspaper, wherever humans bandy words about, we encounter more and more abstractions, more empty formulas. Think of the pablum ladled out by politicians. Think of the fluffy white bread of advertising. Think, lord help us, of committee reports. By contrast, the essay remains stub-bornly concrete and particular: It confronts you with an oil-smeared toilet at the Sunoco station, a red vinyl purse shaped like a valentine heart, a bow-legged dentist hunting deer with an elephant gun. As Or-well forcefully argued, and as dictators seem to agree, such a bypassing of abstractions, such an insistence on the concrete, is a politically sub-versive act. Clinging to this door, that child, this grief, following the zigzag motions of an inquisitive mind, the essay renews language and clears trash from the springs of thought. A century and a half ago, in the rousing manifesto entitled *Nature,* Emerson called on a new genera-tion of writers to cast off the hand-me-down rhetoric of the day, to "pierce this rotten diction and fasten words again to visible things." The essayist aspires to do just that.

As if all these virtues were not enough to account for a renaissance of this protean genre, the essay has also taken over some of the territory abdicated by contemporary fiction. Whittled down to the bare bones of plot, camouflaged with irony, muttering in brief sentences and grade-school vocabulary, peopled with characters who stumble like sleepwalk-ers through numb lives, today's fashionable fiction avoids disclosing where the author stands on anything. In the essay, you had better speak from a region pretty close to the heart or the reader will detect the wind of phoniness whistling through your hollow phrases. In the essay you may be caught with your pants down, your ignorance and sentimen-tality showing, while you trot recklessly about on one of your hobby-horses. You cannot stand back from the action, as Joyce instructed us to do, and pare your fingernails. You cannot palm off your cockamamie notions on some hapless character.

To our list of the essay's contemporary attractions we should add the perennial ones of verbal play, mental adventure, and sheer anarchic high spirits. To see how the capricious mind can be led astray, consider the foregoing paragraph, which drags in metaphors from the realms of toys, clothing, weather, and biology, among others. That is bad enough; but it could have been worse. For example, I began to draft a sentence in that paragraph with the following words: "More than once, in sitting down to beaver away at a narrative, felling trees of memory and hauling brush to build a dam that might slow down the waters of time. . . ." I had set out to make some innocent remark, and here I was gnawing down trees and building dams, all because I had let that *beaver* slip in. On this occasion I had the good sense to throw out the unruly word. I don't always, as no doubt you will have noticed. Whatever its more visible subject, an essay is also about the way a mind moves, the links and leaps and jigs of thought. I might as well drag in another metaphor—and another unoffending animal—by saying that each doggy sentence, as it noses forward into the underbrush of thought, scatters a bunch of rabbits that go bounding off in all directions. The essayist can afford to chase more of those rabbits than the fiction writer can, but fewer than the poet. If you refuse to chase any of them, and keep plodding along in a straight line, you and your reader will have a dull outing. If you chase too many, you will soon wind up lost in a thicket of confusion with your tongue hanging out.

The pursuit of mental rabbits was strictly forbidden by the teachers who instructed me in English composition. For that matter, nearly all the qualities of the personal essay, as I have been sketching them, violate the rules that many of us were taught in school. You recall we were supposed to begin with an outline and stick by it faithfully, like a train riding its rails, avoiding sidetracks. Each paragraph was to have a topic sentence pasted near the front, and these orderly paragraphs were to be coupled end-to-end like so many boxcars. Every item in those boxcars was to bear the stamp of some external authority, preferably a footnote referring to a thick book, although appeals to magazines and newspapers would do in a pinch. Our diction was to be formal, dignified, shunning the vernacular. Polysyllabic words derived from Latin were preferable to the blunt lingo of the streets. Metaphors were to be used only in emergencies, and no two of them were to be mixed. And even in emergencies we could not speak in the first person singular.

Already as a schoolboy, I chafed against those rules. Now I break *10* them shamelessly, in particular the taboo against using the lonely capital *I*. Just look at what I'm doing right now. My speculations about the state of the essay arise, needless to say, from my own practice as reader and writer, and they reflect my own tastes, no matter how I may pretend to gaze dispassionately down on the question from a hot-air balloon. As Thoreau declares in his cocky manner on the opening page of *Walden:* "In most books the *I,* or first person, is omitted; in this it will be retained; that, in respect to egotism, is the main difference. We commonly do not remember that it is, after all, always the first person that is speaking. I should not talk so much about myself if there were anybody else whom I knew as well." True for the personal essay, it is doubly true for an essay about the essay: One speaks always and inescapably in the first person singular.

We could sort out essays along a spectrum according to the degree to which the writer's ego is on display—with John McPhee, perhaps, at the extreme of self-effacement, and Norman Mailer at the opposite extreme of self-dramatization. Brassy or shy, center stage or hanging back in the wings, the author's persona commands our attention. For the length of an essay, or a book of essays, we respond to that persona as we would to a friend caught up in a rapturous monologue. When the monologue is finished, we may not be able to say precisely what it was about, any more than we can draw conclusions from a piece of music. "Essays don't usually boil down to a summary, as articles do," notes Edward Hoagland, one of the least summarizable of companions, "and the style of the writer has a 'nap' to it, a combination of personality and originality and energetic loose ends that stand up like the nap of a piece of wool and can't be brushed flat" ("What I Think, What I Am"). We make assumptions about that speaking voice, assumptions we cannot validly make about the narrators in fiction. Only a sophomore is permitted to ask if Huckleberry Finn ever had any children; but even literary sophisticates wonder in print about Thoreau's love life, Montaigne's domestic arrangements, De Quincey's opium habit, Virginia Woolf's depression.

Montaigne, who not only invented the form but nearly perfected it as well, announced from the start that his true subject was himself. In his note "To the Reader" at the beginning of the *Essays,* he slyly proclaimed:

> I want to be seen here in my simple, natural, ordinary fashion, without straining or artifice; for it is myself that I portray. My defects will here be read to the life, and also my natural form, as far as respect for the public has allowed. Had I been placed among those nations which are said to live still in the sweet freedom of nature's first laws, I assure you I should very gladly have portrayed myself here entire and wholly naked.

A few pages after this disarming introduction, we are told of the Emperor Maximilian, who was so prudish about exposing his private parts that he would not let a servant dress him or see him in the bath. The Emperor went so far as to give orders that he be buried in his underdrawers. Having let us in on this intimacy about Maximilian, Montaigne then confessed that he himself, although "bold-mouthed," was equally prudish, and that "except under great stress of necessity or voluptuousness," he never allowed anyone to see him naked. Such modesty, he feared, was unbecoming in a soldier. But such honesty is quite becoming in an essayist. The very confession of his prudery is a far more revealing gesture than any doffing of clothes.

A curious reader will soon find out that the word *essay,* as adapted by Montaigne, means a trial or attempt. The Latin root carries the more vivid sense of a weighing out. In the days when that root was alive and green, merchants discovered the value of goods and alchemists discovered the composition of unknown metals by the use of scales. Just so the essay, as Montaigne was the first to show, is a weighing out, an inquiry into the value, meaning, and true nature of experience; it is a private experiment carried out in public. In each of three successive editions, Montaigne inserted new material into his essays without revising the old material. Often the new statements contradicted the original ones, but Montaigne let them stand, since he believed that the only consistent fact about human beings is their inconsistency. In a celebration called "Why Montaigne Is Not a Bore," Lewis Thomas has remarked of him that "He [was] fond of his mind, and affectionately entertained by everything in his head." Whatever Montaigne wrote about—and he wrote about everything under the sun: fears, smells, growing old, the pleasures of scratching—he weighed on the scales of his own character.

It is the *singularity* of the first person—its warts and crotchets and turn of voice—that lures many of us into reading essays, and that lingers with us after we finish. Consider the lonely, melancholy persona of Loren Eiseley, forever wandering, forever brooding on our dim and bestial past, his lips frosty with the chill of the Ice Age. Consider the volatile, Dionysian persona of D. H. Lawrence, with his incandescent gaze, his habit of turning peasants into gods and trees into flames, his quick hatred and quicker love. Consider that philosophical farmer, Wendell Berry, who speaks with a countryman's knowledge and a deacon's severity. Consider E. B. White, with his cheery affection for brown eggs and dachshunds, his unflappable way of herding geese while the radio warns of an approaching hurricane.

E. B. White, that engaging master of the genre, a champion of idiosyncrasy, introduced his own volume of *Essays* by admitting the danger of narcissism: *15*

> I think some people find the essay the last resort of the egoist, a much too self-conscious and self-serving form for their taste; they feel that it is presumptuous of a writer to assume that his little excursions or his small observations will interest the reader. There is some justice in their complaint. I have always been aware that I am by nature self-absorbed and egoistical; to write of myself to the extent I have done indicates a too great attention to my own life, not enough to the lives of others.

Yet the self-absorbed Mr. White was in fact a delighted observer of the world, and shared that delight with us. Thus, after describing memorably how a circus girl practiced her bareback riding in the leisure moments between shows ("The Ring of Time"), he confessed: "As a writing man, or secretary, I have always felt charged with the safekeeping of all unexpected items of worldly or unworldly enchantment, as though I might be held personally responsible if even a small one were to be lost." That may still be presumptuous, but it is a presumption turned outward on the creation.

This looking outward helps distinguish the essay from pure autobiography, which dwells more complacently on the self. Mass murderers, movie stars, sports heroes, Wall Street crooks, and defrocked politicians may blather on about whatever high jinks or low jinks made them temporarily famous, may chronicle their exploits, their diets, their hobbies, in perfect confidence that the public is eager to gobble up every least gossipy scrap. And the public, according to sales figures, generally is. On the other hand, I assume the public does not give a hoot about my private life. If I write of hiking up a mountain with my one-year-old boy riding like a papoose on my back, and of what he babbled to me while we gazed down from the summit onto the scudding clouds, it is not because I am deluded into believing that my baby, like the offspring of Prince Charles, matters to the great world. It is because I know the great world produces babies of its own and watches them change cloud-fast before its doting eyes. To make that climb up the mountain vividly present for readers is harder work than the climb itself. I choose to write about my experience not because it is mine, but because it seems to me a door through which others might pass.

On that cocky first page of *Walden,* Thoreau justified his own seeming self-absorption by saying that he wrote the book for the sake of his fellow citizens, who kept asking him to account for his peculiar experiment by the pond. There is at least a sliver of truth to this, since Thoreau, a town character, had been invited more than once to speak his mind at the public lectern. Most of us, however, cannot honestly say the townspeople have been clamoring for our words. I suspect that all writers of the essay, even Norman Mailer and Gore Vidal, must occasionally wonder if they are egomaniacs. For the essayist, in other words, the problem of authority is inescapable. By what right does one speak? Why should anyone listen? The traditional sources of authority no longer serve. You cannot justify your words by appealing to the Bible or some other holy text, you cannot merely stitch together a patchwork of quotations from classical authors, you cannot lean on a podium at the Atheneum and deliver your wisdom to a rapt audience.

In searching for your own soapbox, a sturdy platform from which to deliver your opinionated monologues, it helps if you have already distinguished yourself at some other, less fishy form. When Yeats describes his longing for Maud Gonne or muses on Ireland's misty lore, everything he says is charged with the prior strength of his poetry. When Virginia Woolf, in *A Room of One's Own,* reflects on the status of women and the conditions necessary for making art, she speaks as the author of *Mrs. Dalloway* and *To the Lighthouse.* The essayist may also lay claim to our attention by having lived through events or traveled through terrains that already bear a richness of meaning. When James Baldwin writes his *Notes of a Native Son,* he does not have to convince us that racism is a troubling reality. When Barry Lopez takes us on a meditative tour of the far north in *Arctic Dreams,* he can rely on our curiosity about that fabled and forbidding place. When Paul Theroux climbs aboard a train and invites us on a journey to some exotic destination, he can count on the romance of railroads and the allure of remote cities to bear us along.

Most essayists, however, cannot draw on any source of authority from beyond the page to lend force to the page itself. They can only use language to put themselves on display and to gesture at the world. When Annie Dillard tells us in the opening lines of *Pilgrim at Tinker Creek* about the tomcat with bloody paws who jumps through the window onto her chest, why should we listen? Well, because of the voice that goes on to say: "And some mornings I'd wake in daylight to find my body covered with paw prints in blood; I looked as though I'd been painted with roses." Listen to her explaining a few pages later what she is up to in this book, this broody, zestful record of her stay in the Roanoke Valley: "I propose to keep here what Thoreau called 'a meteorological journal of the mind,' telling some tales and describing some of the sights of this rather tamed valley, and exploring, in fear and trembling, some of the unmapped dim reaches and unholy fastnesses to which those tales and sights so dizzyingly lead." The sentence not only describes the method of her literary search, but also exhibits the breathless, often giddy, always eloquent and spiritually hungry soul who will do the searching. If you enjoy her company, you will relish Annie Dillard's essays; if you don't, you won't.

Listen to another voice which readers tend to find either captivating *20* or insufferable:

> That summer I began to see, however dimly, that one of my ambitions, perhaps my governing ambition, was to belong fully to this place, to belong as the thrushes and the herons and the muskrats belonged, to be altogether at home here. That is still my ambition. But now I have come to see that it proposes an enormous labor. It is a spiritual ambition, like goodness. The wild creatures belong to the place by nature, but as a man I can belong to it only by understanding and by virtue. It is an ambition I cannot hope to succeed in wholly, but I have come to believe that it is the most worthy of all.

That is Wendell Berry in "The Long-Legged House" writing about his patch of Kentucky. Once you have heard that stately, moralizing, cherishing voice, laced through with references to the land, you will not mistake it for anyone else's. Berry's themes are profound and arresting ones. But it is his voice, more than anything he speaks about, that either seizes us or drives us away.

Even so distinct a persona as Wendell Berry's or Annie Dillard's is still only a literary fabrication, of course. The first person singular is too narrow a gate for the whole writer to squeeze through. What we meet on the page is not the flesh-and-blood author, but a simulacrum, a character who wears the label *I*. Introducing the lectures that became *A Room of One's Own,* Virginia Woolf reminded her listeners that "'I' is only a convenient term for somebody who has no real being. Lies will flow from my lips, but there may perhaps be some truth mixed up with them; it is for you to seek out this truth and to decide whether any part of it is worth keeping." Here is a part I consider worth keeping: "Women have served all these centuries as looking-glasses possessing the magic and delicious power of reflecting the figure of man at twice its natural size." It is from such elegant, revelatory sentences that we build up our notion of the "I" who speaks to us under the name of Virginia Woolf.

What the essay tells us may not be true in any sense that would satisfy a court of law. As an example, think of Orwell's brief narrative, "A Hanging," which describes an execution in Burma. Anyone who has read it remembers how the condemned man as he walked to the gallows stepped aside to avoid a puddle. That is the sort of haunting detail only an eyewitness should be able to report. Alas, biographers, those zealous debunkers, have recently claimed that Orwell never saw such a hanging, that he reconstructed it from hearsay. What then do we make of his essay? Or has it become the sort of barefaced lie we prefer to call a story?

Frankly, I don't much care what label we put on "A Hanging"— fiction or nonfiction, it is a powerful statement either way—but Orwell might have cared a great deal. I say this because not long ago I was bemused and then vexed to find one of my own essays treated in a scholarly article as a work of fiction. Here was my earnest report about growing up on a military base, my heartfelt rendering of indelible memories, being confused with the airy figments of novelists! To be sure, in writing the piece I had used dialogue, scenes, settings, character descriptions, the whole fictional bag of tricks; sure, I picked and chose among a thousand beckoning details; sure, I downplayed some facts and highlighted others; but I was writing about the actual, not the invented. I shaped the matter, but I did not make it up.

To explain my vexation, I must break another taboo, which is to speak of the author's intent. My teachers warned me strenuously to avoid the intentional fallacy. They told me to regard poems and plays and stories as objects washed up on the page from some unknown and unknowable shores. Now that I am on the other side of the page, so to speak, I think quite recklessly of intention all the time. I believe that if we allow the question of intent in the case of murder, we should allow it in literature. The essay is distinguished from the short story, not by the presence or absence of literary devices, not by tone or theme or subject, but by the writer's stance toward the material. In composing an essay about what it was like to grow up on that military base, I *meant* something quite different from what I mean when concocting a story. I meant to preserve and record and help give voice to a reality that existed independently of me. I meant to pay my respects to a minor passage of history in an out-of-the-way place. I felt responsible to the truth as known by other people. I wanted to speak directly out of my own life into the lives of others.

You can see I am teetering on the brink of metaphysics. One step   *25* farther and I will plunge into the void, wondering as I fall how to prove there is any external truth for the essayist to pay homage to. I draw back from the brink and simply declare that I believe one writes, in essays, with a regard for the actual world, with a respect for the shared substance of history, the autonomy of other lives, the being of nature, the mystery and majesty of a creation we have not made.

When it comes to speculating about the creation, I feel more at ease with physics than with metaphysics. According to certain bold and lyrical cosmologists, there is at the center of black holes a geometrical point, the tiniest conceivable speck, where all the matter of a collapsed star has been concentrated, and where everyday notions of time, space, and force break down. That point is called a singularity. The boldest and most poetic theories suggest that anything sucked into a singularity might be flung back out again, utterly changed, somewhere else in the universe. The lonely first person, the essayist's microcosmic "I," may be thought of as a verbal singularity at the center of the mind's black hole. The raw matter of experience, torn away from the axes of time and space, falls in constantly from all sides, undergoes the mind's inscrutable alchemy, and reemerges in the quirky, unprecedented shape of an essay.

Now it is time for me to step down, before another metaphor seizes hold of me, before you notice that I am standing, not on a soapbox, but on the purest air.

☐ *Outward Exploration: Discussion*

1. What are the implications of Sanders's image of a personal essay as a "monologue" (paragraph 2)? Are there ways in which the image is too limiting?

2. What other images does he use for the essay?

3. According to Sanders, what separates essays from other nonfiction forms of our era?

4. In paragraph 8, Sanders says that an essayist can chase more "mental rabbits" than a short-story writer can but fewer than a poet can. What rabbits does he chase in this essay?

5. According to Sanders, what draws readers to essays?

6. According to Sanders, what separates essays from "pure autobiography"? What is the effect of all the references to other writers and quotations from them?

7. What is the effect of Sanders's referring to the soapbox again in paragraphs 18 and 27?

8. What is the effect of his use of such words as *gumption* (paragraph 4) and *fishy* (paragraph 18)?

9. In paragraph 21, Sanders suggests that even distinct persona are fabrications. Why?

10. How does Sanders establish and "prove" his authority to speak about the topic of essay writing, particularly since he begins and ends by saying that essayists often lack "normal" kinds of ready-made authority?

11. Ultimately, how well does Sanders run his "one-man circus" (paragraph 2)? Find examples of his use of "anecdote, conjecture, memory, and wit." Did they keep you "enthralled," or at least did they keep you reading?

🗋 *Outward Exploration: Writing*

1. Write an essay in which you consciously create a persona. This persona should be a reflection of your interests and attitudes, but try to highlight certain elements (for example, your logical thinking, your sense of humor, your interest in puns and word plays, your attention to small details, or your concern about ethical thinking).

2. Write an essay about something you know well. This could be an activity (for example, writing a poem, programming a computer, playing a particular position in a sport, building birdhouses, playing a musical instrument) or an area of interest (for example, trends in horror novels or movies, development in the music of a particular performer or group, advantages of one type of computer over another). Regardless of the topic, your task is to develop an authentic persona who speaks with authority (along the lines of Sanders's persona in this essay). The essay should be personal but also informative. Above all, it should be a one-man or one-woman circus that keeps readers interested.

🗋 *Style*

Consider the following sentence by Sanders:

Unlike novelists and playwrights, who lurk behind the scenes while distracting our attention with the puppet show of imaginary characters, unlike scholars and journalists, who quote the opinions of others and shelter behind the hedges of neutrality, the essayist has nowhere to hide. (paragraph 2)

The structure of this sentence is as follows:

prepositional phrase ("Unlike . . . playwrights")

comma separating a long introductory prepositional phrase

relative clause explaining the significance of that preposition's objects ("who . . . characters")

comma

parallel prepositional phrase ("unlike . . . journalists")

comma

parallel relative clause ("who . . . neutrality")

comma

subject ("the essayist")

predicate verb ("has")

infinitive ("to hide")

period.

The most elegant element of this sentence is its *parallelism,* which is further reinforced by the repetition of the key first words ("unlike" and "who"). Notice as well the fact that the sentence's subject is the 38th word in the sentence (an unusual occurrence), yet the clear parallelism and the clear connections between the opening ideas (and the context provided by the whole paragraph) leave us readers confident that the sentence will make perfect sense by the time we reach the period. Further, such parallelism reassures us subconsciously that we are in the hands of a skilled writer, so we don't panic when we don't find the subject in the first part of the sentence. A more subtle parallelism is the use of nouns—all names of types of writers ("novelists," "playwrights," "scholars," "journalists"). Imagine the sentence if we substituted "people who write plays" for "playwright"—both the parallelism and the *rhythm* of the sentence would be broken.

Beginning the sentence with a prepositional phrase (or in this case, two prepositional phrases) also adds *structural variety* to Sanders's prose (the previous two sentences began with the subject). Doing so also emphasizes the idea of the *differences* ("unlike") between the other kinds of writers and the essayist (1) because an unexpected sentence element (prepositional phrase) occurs out of order and (2) because it is placed in one of the sentence's most emphatic spots (the beginning). In other words, the form of the sentence helps reinforce the meaning of the sentence's content. Write a sentence of your own that replicates this structure but which uses your own ideas and information.

Language and Literature from a Pueblo Indian Perspective

LESLIE MARMON SILKO

☐ *Inward Exploration*

Write at least one paragraph about the rules or conventions which you feel govern academic writing in English. Make a list of family stories that were told to you.

Where I come from, the words that are most highly valued are those which are spoken from the heart, unpremeditated and unrehearsed. Among the Pueblo people, a written speech or statement is highly suspect because the true feelings of the speaker remain hidden as he reads words that are detached from the occasion and the audience. I have intentionally not written a formal paper to read to this session because of this and because I want you to hear and to experience English in a non traditional structure, a structure that follows patterns from the oral tradition. For those of you accustomed to a structure that moves from point A to point B to point C, this presentation may be somewhat difficult to follow because the structure of Pueblo expression resembles something like a spider's web—with many little threads radiating from a center, crisscrossing each other. As with the web, the structure will emerge as it is made and you must simply listen and trust, as the Pueblo people do, that meaning will be made.

I suppose the task that I have today is a formidable one because basically I come here to ask you, at least for a while, to set aside a number of basic approaches that you have been using and probably will continue to use in approaching the study of English or the study of language; first of all, I come to ask you to see language from the Pueblo perspective, which is a perspective that is very much concerned with including the whole of creation and the whole of history and time. And so we very seldom talk about breaking language down into words. As I will continue to relate to you, even the use of a specific language is less important than the one thing—which is the "telling," or the storytelling. And so, as Simon Ortiz has written, if you approach a Pueblo person and want to talk words or, worse than that, to break down an individual word into its components, ofttimes you will just get a blank stare, because we don't think of words as being isolated from the speaker, which, of course, is one element of the oral tradition.

Moreover, we don't think of words as being alone: Words are always with other words, and the other words are almost always in a story of some sort.

Today I have brought a number of examples of stories in English because I would like to get around to the question that has been raised, or the topic that has come along here, which is what changes we Pueblo writers might make with English as a language for literature. But at the same time I would like to explain the importance of storytelling and how it relates to a Pueblo theory of language.

So first I would like to go back to the Pueblo Creation story. The reason I go back to that story is because it is an all-inclusive story of creation and how life began. Tséitsínako, Thought Woman, by thinking of her sisters, and together with her sisters, thought of everything which is, and this world was created. And the belief was that everything in this world was a part of the original creation, and that the people at home realized that far away there were others—other human beings. There is even a section of the story which is a prophesy—which describes the origin of the European race, the African, and also remembers the Asian origins.

Starting out with this story, with this attitude which includes all things, I would like to point out that the reason the people are more concerned with story and communication and less with a particular language is in part an outgrowth of the area [pointing to a map] where we find ourselves. Among the twenty Pueblos there are at least six distinct languages, and possibly seven. Some of the linguists argue—and I don't set myself up to be a linguist at all—about the number of distinct languages. But certainly Zuni is all alone, and Hopi is all alone, and from mesa to mesa there are subtle differences in language—very great differences. I think that this might be the reason that what particular language was being used wasn't as important as what a speaker was trying to say. And this, I think, is reflected and stems or grows out of a particular view of the story—that is, that language *is* story. At Laguna many words have stories which make them. So when one is telling a story, and one is using words to tell the story, each word that one is speaking has a story of its own too. Often the speakers or tellers go into the stories of the words they are using to tell one story so that you get stories within stories, so to speak. This structure becomes very apparent in the storytelling, and what I would like to show you later on by reading some pieces that I brought is that this structure also informs the writing and the stories which are currently coming from Pueblo people. I think what is essential is this sense of story, and story within story, and the idea that one story is only the beginning of many stories, and the sense that stories never truly end. I would like to propose that these views of structure and the dynamics of storytelling are some of the contributions which Native American cultures bring to the English language or at least to literature in the English language.

First of all, a lot of people think of storytelling as something that is done at bedtime—that it is something that is done for small children. When I use the term "storytelling," I include a far wider range of telling activity. I also do not limit storytelling to simply old stories, but to again go back to the original view of creation, which sees that it is all part of a whole; we do not differentiate or fragment stories and experiences. In the beginning, Tséitsínako, Thought Woman, thought of all these things, and all of these things are held together as one holds many things together in a single thought.

So in the telling (and today you will hear a few of the dimensions of this telling) first of all, as was pointed out earlier, the storytelling always includes the audience and the listeners, and, in fact, a great deal of the story is believed to be inside the listener, and the storyteller's role is to draw the story out of the listeners. This kind of shared experience grows out of a strong community base. The storytelling goes on and continues from generation to generation.

The Origin story functions basically as a maker of our identity— with the story we know who we are. We are the Lagunas. This is where we came from. We came this way. We came by this place. And so from the time you are very young, you hear these stories, so that when you go out into the wider world, when one asks who you are, or where are you from, you immediately know: We are the people who came down from the north. We are the people of these stories. It continues down into clans so that you are not just talking about Laguna Pueblo people, you are talking about your own clan. Within the clans there are stories which identify the clan.

In the Creation story, Antelope says that he will help knock a hole in the earth so that the people can come up, out into the next world. Antelope tries and tries, and he uses his hooves and is unable to break through; and it is then that Badger says, "Let me help you." And Badger very patiently uses his claws and digs a way through, bringing the people into the world. When the Badger clan people think of themselves, or when the Antelope people think of themselves, it is as people who are of *this* story, and this is *our* place, and we fit into the very beginning when the people first came, before we began our journey south.

So you can move, then, from the idea of one's identity as a tribal 10 person into clan identity. Then we begin to get to the extended family, and this is where we begin to get a kind of story coming into play which some people might see as a different kind of story, though Pueblo people do not. Anthropologists and ethnologists have, for a long time, differentiated the types of oral language they find in the Pueblos. They tended to rule out all but the old and sacred and traditional stories and were not interested in family stories and the family's account of itself. But these family stories are just as important as the other stories—the older stories. These family stories are given equal recognition. There is no definite, pre-set pattern for the way one will hear the stories of one's own family, but it is a very critical part of one's childhood, and it continues on throughout one's life. You will hear stories of importance to the family—sometimes wonderful stories—stories about the time a maternal uncle got the biggest deer that was ever seen and brought back from the mountains. And so one's sense of who the family is, and who you are, will then extend from that—"I am from the family of my uncle who brought in this wonderful deer, and it was a wonderful hunt"—so you have this sort of building or sense of identity.

There are also other stories, stories about the time when another uncle, perhaps, did something that wasn't really acceptable. In other words, this process of keeping track, of telling, is an all-inclusive process which begins to create a total picture. So it is very important that you know all of the stories—both positive and not so positive—about one's own family. The reason that it is very important to keep track of all the stories in one's own family is because you are liable to hear a story from somebody else who is perhaps an enemy of the family, and you are liable to hear a version which has been changed, a version which makes your family sound disreputable—something that will taint the honor of the family. But if you have already heard the story, you know your family's version of what *really* happened that night, so when somebody else is mentioning it, you will have a version of the story to counterbalance it. Even when there is no way around it—old Uncle Pete did a terrible thing—by knowing the stories that come out of other families, by keeping very close watch, listening constantly to learn the stories about other families, one is in a sense able to deal with terrible sorts of things that might happen within one's own family. When a member of one's own family does something that cannot be excused, one always knows stories about similar things which happened in other families. And it is not done maliciously. I think it is very important to realize this. Keeping track of all the stories within the community gives a certain distance, a useful perspective which brings incidents down to a level we can deal with. If others have done it before, it cannot be so terrible. If others have endured, so can we.

The stories are always bringing us together, keeping this whole together, keeping this family together, keeping this clan together. "Don't go away, don't isolate yourself, but come here, because we have all had these kinds of experiences"—this is what the people are saying to you when they tell you these other stories. And so there is this constant pulling together to resist what seems to me to be a basic part of human nature: When some violent emotional experience takes place, people get the urge to run off and hide or separate themselves from others. And of course, if we do that, we are not only talking about endangering the group, we are also talking about the individual or the individual family never being able to recover or to survive. Inherent in this belief is the feeling that one does not recover or get well by one's self, but it is together that we look after each other and take care of each other.

In the storytelling, then, we see this process of bringing people together, and it works not only on the family level, but also on the level of the individual. Of course, the whole Pueblo concept of the individual is a little bit different from the usual Western concept of the individual. But one of the beauties of the storytelling is that when something happens to an individual, many people will come to you and take you aside, or maybe a couple of people will come and talk to you. These are occasions of storytelling. These occasions of storytelling are continuous; they are a way of life.

Storytelling lies at the heart of the Pueblo people, and so when someone comes in and says, "When did they tell the stories, or what time of day does the storytelling take place?" that is a ridiculous question. The storytelling goes on constantly—as some old grandmother puts on the shoes of a little child and tells the child the story of a little girl who didn't wear her shoes. At the same time somebody comes into the house for coffee to talk with an adolescent boy who has just been into a lot of trouble, to reassure him that *he* got into that kind of trouble, or somebody else's son got into that kind of trouble too. You have this constant ongoing process, working on many different levels.

One of the stories I like to bring up about helping the individual in   15
crisis is a recent story, and I want to remind you that we make no distinctions between the stories—whether they are history, whether they are fact, whether they are gossip—these distinctions are not useful when we are talking about this particular experience with language. Anyway, there was a young man who, when he came back from the war in Vietnam, had saved up his Army pay and bought a beautiful red Volkswagen Beetle. He was very proud of it, and one night drove up to a place right across the reservation line. It is a very notorious place for many reasons, but one of the more notorious things about the place is a deep arroyo behind the place. This is the King's Bar. So he ran in to pick up a cold six-pack to take home, but he didn't put on his emergency brake. And his little red Volkswagen rolled back into the arroyo and was all smashed up. He feld very bad about it, but within a few days everybody had come to him and told him stories about other people who had lost cars to that arroyo. And probably the story that made him feel the best was about the time that George Day's station wagon, with his mother-in-law and kids in the back, rolled into that arroyo. So everybody was saying, "Well, at least your mother-in-law and kids weren't in the car when it rolled in," and you can't argue with that kind of story. He felt better then because he wasn't alone anymore. He and his smashed-up Volkswagen were now joined with all the other stories of cars that fell into that arroyo.

There are a great many parallels between Pueblo experiences and the remarks that have been made about South Africa and the Caribbean countries—similarities in experiences so far as language is concerned. More specifically, with the experience of English being imposed upon the people. The Pueblo people, of course, have seen intruders come and intruders go. The first they watched come were the Spaniards; while the Spaniards were there, things had to be conducted in Spanish. But as the old stories say, if you wait long enough, they'll go. And sure enough, they went. Then another bunch came in. And old stories say, well, if you wait around long enough, not so much that they'll go, but at least their ways will go. One wonders now, when you see what's happening to technocratic-industrial culture, now that we've used up most of the sources of energy, you think perhaps the old people are right.

But anyhow, our experience with English has been different because the Bureau of Indian Affairs schools were so terrible that we never heard of Shakespeare. There was Dick and Jane, and I can remember reading that the robins were heading south for winter, but I knew that all winter the robins were around Laguna. It took me a long time to figure out what was going on. I worried for quite a while about the robins because they didn't leave in the winter, not realizing that the textbooks were written in Boston. The big textbook companies are up here in Boston and *their* robins do go south in the winter. But this freed us and encouraged us to stay with our narratives. Whatever literature we received at school (which was damn little), at home the storytelling, the special regard for telling and bringing together through the telling, was going on constantly. It has continued, and so we have a great body of classical oral literature, both in the narratives and in the chants and songs.

As the old people say, "If you can remember the stories, you will be all right. Just remember the stories." And, of course, usually when they say that to you, when you are young, you wonder what in the world they mean. But when I returned—I had been away from Laguna Pueblo for a couple of years, well more than a couple of years after college and so forth—I returned to Laguna and I went to Laguna-Acoma high school to visit an English class, and I was wondering how the telling was continuing, because Laguna Pueblo, as the anthropologists have said, is one of the more acculturated pueblos. So I walked into this high school English class and there they were sitting, these very beautiful Laguna and Acoma kids. But I knew that out in their lockers they had cassette tape recorders, and I knew that at home they had stereos, and they were listening to Kiss and Led Zeppelin and all those other things. I was almost afraid, but I had to ask—I had with me a book of short fiction (it's called *The Man to Send Rain Clouds* [New York: Viking Press, 1974]), and among the stories of other Native American writers, it has stories that I have written and Simon Ortiz has written. And there is one particular story in the book about the killing of a state policeman in New Mexico by three Acoma Pueblo men. It was an act that was committed in the early fifties. I was afraid to ask, but I had to. I looked at the class and I said, "How many of you heard this story before you read it in the book?" And I was prepared to hear this crushing truth that indeed the anthropologists were right about the old traditions dying out. But it was amazing, you know, almost all but one or two students raised their hands. They had heard that story, just as Simon and I had heard it, when we were young. That was my first indication that storytelling continues on. About half of them had heard it in English, about half of them had heard it in Laguna. I think again, getting back to one of the original statements, that if you begin to look at the core of the importance of the language and how it fits in with the culture, it is the *story* and the feeling of the story which matters more than what language it's told in.

📖 *Outward Exploration: Discussion*

1. From her opening paragraph, Silko undermines some of the "principles and conventions" of academic writing that may have been presented to you in the past as hard-and-fast rules. List the ones she undermines. Find evidence throughout the essay of the ways she uses the Pueblo principles.

2. Explain the "Pueblo perspective."

3. In paragraph 5, Silko says that, for the Pueblo, "what particular language was being used wasn't as important as what a speaker was trying to say." What are the implications of this statement if we pretend for a moment that her description is a prescription (in other words, that she is giving advice to focus on the content that we are trying to convey and to ignore the language we use to do that conveying)? What are the strengths of that approach? What are its weaknesses?

📖 *Outward Exploration: Writing*

1. In paragraphs 9–12, Silko explains the role and value of family stories in the creation of an individual's identity If you have heard some family stories that have helped you see yourself in certain ways, write an essay about those stories and that process.

2. Write an essay about yourself or about a topic you know well, an essay that follows Silko's organizational scheme rather than the more traditional academic scheme.

3. Write an essay illustrating and exploring Silko's belief that the process of telling family stories helps us recover or get well because the stories encourage us to look after each other and to take care of each other (paragraph 12).

4. For the Pueblo, storytelling is a way of life. If it has been a way of life for you and your family, write an essay about that fact.

□ *Style*

Consider the following sentence from Silko's essay:

Inherent in this belief is the feeling that one does not recover or get well by one's self, but it is together that we look after each other and take care of each other. (paragraph 12)

What is interesting about this sentence is its structure: "Inherent in this *X* is the *Y* that *W*, but *Z*." Using your own information to substitute for *X, Y, W,* and *Z*, write a sentence of your own.

Seeing

ANNIE DILLARD

📖 *Inward Exploration*

Write at least one paragraph on the concept of seeing. For example, you might consider what seeing really is. Are there things that we can't see? How does the process of seeing work? What would it mean to have never been able to see?

When I was six or seven years old, growing up in Pittsburgh, I used   1
to take a precious penny of my own and hide it for someone else to find. It was a curious compulsion; sadly, I've never been seized by it since. For some reason I always "hid" the penny along the same stretch of sidewalk up the street. I would cradle it at the roots of a sycamore, say, or in a hole left by a chipped-off piece of sidewalk. Then I would take a piece of chalk, and, starting at either end of the block, draw huge arrows leading up to the penny from both directions. After I learned to write I labeled the arrows: SURPRISE AHEAD or MONEY THIS WAY. I was greatly excited, during all this arrow-drawing, at the thought of the first lucky passer-by who would receive in this way, regardless of merit, a free gift from the universe. But I never lurked about. I would go straight home and not give the matter another thought, until, some months later, I would be gripped again by the impulse to hide another penny.

It is still the first week in January, and I've got great plans. I've been thinking about seeing. There are lots of things to see, unwrapped gifts and free surprises. The world is fairly studded and strewn with pennies cast broadside from a generous hand. But—and this is the point—who gets excited by a mere penny? If you follow one arrow, if you crouch motionless on a bank to watch a tremulous ripple thrill on the water and are rewarded by the sight of a muskrat kit paddling from its den, will you count that sight a chip of copper only, and go your rueful way? It is dire poverty indeed when a man is so malnourished and fatigued that he won't stoop to pick up a penny. But if you cultivate a healthy poverty and simplicity, so that finding a penny will literally make your day, then, since the world is in fact planted in pennies, you have with your poverty bought a lifetime of days. It is that simple. What you see is what you get.

I used to be able to see flying insects in the air. I'd look ahead and see, not the row of hemlocks across the road, but the air in front of it.

My eyes would focus along that column of air, picking out flying insects. But I lost interest, I guess, for I dropped the habit. Now I can see birds. Probably some people can look at the grass at their feet and discover all the crawling creatures. I would like to know grasses and sedges—and care. Then my least journey into the world would be a field trip, a series of happy recognitions. Thoreau, in an expansive mood, exulted, "What a rich book might be made about buds, including, perhaps, sprouts!" It would be nice to think so. I cherish mental images I have of three perfectly happy people. One collects stones. Another—an Englishman, say—watches clouds. The third lives on a coast and collects drops of seawater which he examines microscopically and mounts. But I don't see what the specialist sees, and so I cut myself off, not only from the total picture, but from the various forms of happiness.

Unfortunately, nature is very much a now-you-see-it, now-you-don't affair. A fish flashes, then dissolves in the water before my eyes like so much salt. Deer apparently ascend bodily into heaven; the brightest oriole fades into leaves. These disappearances stun me into stillness and concentration; they say of nature that it conceals with a grand nonchalance, and they say of vision that it is a deliberate gift, the revelation of a dancer who for my eyes only flings away her seven veils. For nature does reveal as well as conceal: now-you-don't-see-it, now-you-do. For a week last September migrating red-winged blackbirds were feeding heavily down by the creek at the back of the house. One day I went out to investigate the racket; I walked up to a tree, an Osage orange, and a hundred birds flew away. They simply materialized out of the tree. I saw a tree, then a whisk of color, then a tree again. I walked closer and another hundred blackbirds took flight. Not a branch, not a twig budged: The birds were apparently weightless as well as invisible. Or, it was as if the leaves of the Osage orange had been freed from a spell in the form of red-winged blackbirds; they flew from the tree, caught my eye in the sky, and vanished. When I looked again at the tree the leaves had reassembled as if nothing had happened. Finally I walked directly to the trunk of the tree and a final hundred, the real diehards, appeared, spread, and vanished. How could so many hide in the tree without my seeing them? The Osage orange, unruffled, looked just as it had looked from the house, when three hundred red-winged blackbirds cried from its crown. I looked downstream where they flew, and they were gone. Searching, I couldn't spot one. I wandered downstream to force them to play their hand, but they'd crossed the creek and scattered. One show to a customer. These appearances catch at my throat; they are the free gifts, the bright coppers at the roots of trees.

It's all a matter of keeping my eyes open. Nature is like one of those 5 line drawings of a tree that are puzzles for children: Can you find hidden in the leaves a duck, a house, a boy, a bucket, a zebra, and a boot? Specialists can find the most incredibly well-hidden things. A book I read when I was young recommended an easy way to find caterpillars to rear: You simply find some fresh caterpillar droppings, look up, and there's your caterpillar. More recently an author advised me to set my mind at ease about those piles of cut stems on the ground in grassy fields. Field mice make them; they cut the grass down by degrees to reach the seeds at the head. It seems that when the grass is tightly packed, as in a field of ripe grain, the blade won't topple at a single cut through the stem; instead, the cut stem simply drops vertically, held in the crush of grain. The mouse severs the bottom again and again, the stem keeps dropping an inch at a time, and finally the head is low enough for the mouse to reach the seeds. Meanwhile, the mouse is positively littering the field with its little piles of cut stems into which, presumably, the author of the book is constantly stumbling.

If I can't see these minutiae, I still try to keep my eyes open. I'm always on the lookout for antlion traps in sandy soil, monarch pupae near milkweed, skipper larvae in locust leaves. These things are utterly common, and I've not seen one. I bang on hollow trees near water, but so far no flying squirrels have appeared. In flat country I watch every sunset in hopes of seeing the green ray. The green ray is a seldom-seen streak of light that rises from the sun like a spurting fountain at the moment of sunset; it throbs into the sky for two seconds and disappears. One more reason to keep my eyes open. A photography professor at the University of Florida just happened to see a bird die in midflight; it jerked, died, dropped, and smashed on the ground. I squint at the wind because I read Stewart Edward White: "I have always maintained that if you looked closely enough you could *see* the wind—the dim, hardly-made-out, fine débris fleeing high in the air." White was an excellent observer, and devoted an entire chapter of *The Mountains* to the subject of seeing deer: "As soon as you can forget the naturally obvious and construct an artificial obvious, then you too will see deer."

But the artificial obvious is hard to see. My eyes account for less than one percent of the weight of my head; I'm bony and dense; I see what I expect. I once spent a full three minutes looking at a bullfrog that was so unexpectedly large I couldn't see it even though a dozen enthusiastic campers were shouting directions. Finally I asked, "What color am I looking for?" and a fellow said, "Green." When at last I picked out the frog, I saw what painters are up against: The thing wasn't green at all, but the color of wet hickory bark.

The lover can see, and the knowledgeable. I visited an aunt and uncle at a quarter-horse ranch in Cody, Wyoming. I couldn't do much of anything useful, but I could, I thought, draw. So, as we all sat around the kitchen table after supper, I produced a sheet of paper and drew a horse. "That's one lame horse," my aunt volunteered. The rest of the family joined in: "Only place to saddle that one is his neck"; "Looks like we better shoot the poor thing, on account of those terrible growths." Meekly, I slid the pencil and paper down the table. Everyone in that family, including my three young cousins, could draw a horse.

Beautifully. When the paper came back it looked as though five shining, real quarter horses had been corraled by mistake with a papier-mâché moose; the real horses seemed to gaze at the monster with a steady, puzzled air. I stay away from horses now, but I can do a creditable gold-fish. The point is that I just don't know what the lover knows; I just can't see the artificial obvious that those in the know construct. The herpetologist asks the native, "Are there snakes in that ravine?" "No-sir." And the herpetologist comes home with, yessir, three bags full. Are there butterflies on that mountain? Are the bluets in bloom, are there arrowheads here, or fossil shells in the shale?

Peeping through my keyhole I see within the range of only about thirty percent of the light that comes from the sun; the rest is infrared and some little ultraviolet, perfectly apparent to many animals, but in-visible to me. A nightmare network of ganglia, charged and firing with-out my knowledge, cuts and splices what I do see, editing it for my brain. Donald E. Carr points out that the sense impressions of one-celled animals are *not* edited for the brain: "This is philosophically inter-esting in a rather mournful way, since it means that only the simplest animals perceive the universe as it is."

A fog that won't burn away drifts and flows across my field of vi-sion. When you see fog move against a backdrop of deep pines, you don't see the fog itself, but streaks of clearness floating across the air in dark shreds. So I see only tatters of clearness through a pervading ob-scurity. I can't distinguish the fog from the overcast sky; I can't be sure if the light is direct or reflected. Everywhere darkness and the presence of the unseen appalls. We estimate now that only one atom dances alone in every cubic meter of intergalactic space. I blink and squint. What planet or power yanks Halley's Comet out of orbit? We haven't seen that force yet; it's a question of distance, density, and the pallor of reflected light. We rock, cradled in the swaddling band of darkness. Even the simple darkness of night whispers suggestions to the mind. Last sum-mer, in August, I stayed at the creek too late. *10*

Where Tinker Creek flows under the sycamore log bridge to the tear-shaped island, it is slow and shallow, fringed thinly in cattail marsh. At this spot an astonishing bloom of life supports vast breeding popu-lations of insects, fish, reptiles, birds, and mammals. On windless sum-mer evenings I stalk along the creek bank or straddle the sycamore log in absolute stillness, watching for muskrats. The night I stayed too late I was hunched on the log staring spellbound at spreading, reflected stains of lilac on the water. A cloud in the sky suddenly lighted as if turned on by a switch; its reflection just as suddenly materialized on the water upstream, flat and floating, so that I couldn't see the creek bottom, or life in the water under the cloud. Downstream, away from the cloud on the water, water turtles smooth as beans were gliding down with the current in a series of easy, weightless push-offs, as men bound on the moon. I didn't know whether to trace the progress of one turtle I was sure of, risking sticking my face in one of the bridge's spider webs made invisible by the gathering dark, or take a chance on seeing the carp, or scan the mudbank in hope of seeing a muskrat, or follow the last of the swallows who caught at my heart and trailed it after them like streamers as they appeared from directly below, under the log, flying upstream with their tails forked, so fast.

But shadows spread, and deepened, and stayed. After thousands of years we're still strangers to darkness, fearful aliens in an enemy camp with our arms crossed over our chests. I stirred. A land turtle on the bank, startled, hissed the air from its lungs and withdrew into its shell. An uneasy pink here, an unfathomable blue there, gave great suggestion of lurking beings. Things were going on. I couldn't see whether that sere rustle I heard was a distant rattlesnake, slit-eyed, or a nearby sparrow kicking in the dry flood debris slung at the foot of a willow. Tremendous action roiled the water everywhere I looked, big action, inexplicable. A tremor welled up beside a gaping muskrat burrow in the bank and I caught my breath, but no muskrat appeared. The ripples continued to fan upstream with a steady, powerful thrust. Night was knitting over my face an eyeless mask, and I still sat transfixed. A distant airplane, a delta wing out of nightmare, made a gliding shadow on the creek's bottom that looked like a stingray cruising upstream. At once a black fin slit the pink cloud on the water, shearing it in two. The two halves merged together and seemed to dissolve before my eyes. Darkness pooled in the cleft of the creek and rose, as water collects in a well. Untamed, dreaming lights flickered over the sky. I saw hints of hulking underwater shadows, two pale splashes out of the water, and round ripples rolling close together from a blackened center.

At last I stared upstream where only the deepest violet remained of the cloud, a cloud so high its underbelly still glowed feeble color reflected from a hidden sky lighted in turn by a sun halfway to China. And out of that violet, a sudden enormous black body arced over the water. I saw only a cylindrical sleekness. Head and tail, if there was a head and tail, were both submerged in cloud. I saw only one ebony fling, a headlong dive to darkness; then the waters closed, and the lights went out.

I walked home in a shivering daze, up hill and down. Later I lay open-mouthed in bed, my arms flung wide at my sides to steady the whirling darkness. At this latitude I'm spinning 836 miles an hour round the earth's axis; I often fancy I feel my sweeping fall as a breakneck arc like the dive of dolphins, and the hollow rushing of wind raises hair on my neck and the side of my face. In orbit around the sun I'm moving 64,800 miles an hour. The solar system as a whole, like a merry-go-round unhinged, spins, bobs, and blinks at the speed of 43,200 miles an hour along a course set east of Hercules. Someone has piped, and we are dancing a tarantella until the sweat pours. I open my eyes and I see dark, muscled forms curl out of water, with flapping gills and flattened eyes. I close my eyes and I see stars, deep stars giving way to deeper stars, deeper stars bowing to deepest stars at the crown of an infinite cone.

"Still," wrote van Gogh in a letter, "a great deal of light falls on   *15* everything." If we are blinded by darkness, we are also blinded by light. When too much light falls on everything, a special terror results. Peter Freuchen describes the notorious kayak sickness to which Greenland Eskimos are prone. "The Greenland fjords are peculiar for the spells of completely quiet weather, when there is not enough wind to blow out a match and the water is like a sheet of glass. The kayak hunter must sit in his boat without stirring a finger so as not to scare the shy seals away. . . . The sun, low in the sky, sends a glare into his eyes, and the landscape around moves into the realm of the unreal. The reflex from the mirrorlike water hypnotizes him, he seems to be unable to move, and all of a sudden it is as if he were floating in a bottomless void, sinking, sinking, and sinking. . . . Horror-stricken, he tries to stir, to cry out, but he cannot, he is completely paralyzed, he just falls and falls." Some hunters are especially cursed with this panic, and bring ruin and sometimes starvation to their families.

Sometimes here in Virginia at sunset low clouds on the southern or northern horizon are completely invisible in the lighted sky. I only know one is there because I can see its reflection in still water. The first time I discovered this mystery I looked from cloud to no-cloud in bewilderment, checking my bearings over and over, thinking maybe the ark of the covenant was just passing by south of Dead Man Mountain. Only much later did I read the explanation: Polarized light from the sky is very much weakened by reflection, but the light in clouds isn't polarized. So invisible clouds pass among visible clouds, till all slide over the mountains; so a greater light extinguishes a lesser as though it didn't exist.

In the great meteor shower of August, the Perseid, I wail all day for the shooting stars I miss. They're out there showering down, committing hara-kiri in a flame of fatal attraction, and hissing perhaps at last into the ocean. But at dawn what looks like a blue dome clamps down over me like a lid on a pot. The stars and planets could smash and I'd never know. Only a piece of ashen moon occasionally climbs up or down the inside of the dome, and our local star without surcease explodes on our heads. We have really only that one light, one source for all power, and yet we must turn away from it by universal decree. Nobody here on the planet seems aware of this strange, powerful taboo, that we all walk about carefully averting our faces, this way and that, lest our eyes be blasted forever.

Darkness appalls and light dazzles; the scrap of visible light that doesn't hurt my eyes hurts my brain. What I see sets me swaying. Size and distance and the sudden swelling of meanings confuse me, bowl me over. I straddle the sycamore log bridge over Tinker Creek in the summer. I look at the lighted creek bottom: snail tracks tunnel the mud in quavering curves. A crayfish jerks, but by the time I absorb what has happened, he's gone in a billowing smokescreen of silt. I look at the water: minnows and shiners. If I'm thinking minnows, a carp will fill my brain till I scream. I look at the water's surface: skaters, bubbles, and leaves sliding down. Suddenly, my own face, reflected, startles me witless. Those snails have been tracking my face! Finally, with a shuddering wrench of the will, I see clouds, cirrus clouds. I'm dizzy, I fall in. This looking business is risky.

Once I stood on a humped rock on nearby Purgatory Mountain, watching through binoculars the great autumn hawk migration below, until I discovered that I was in danger of joining the hawks on a vertical migration of my own. I was used to binoculars, but not, apparently, to balancing on humped rocks while looking through them. I staggered. Everything advanced and receded by turns; the world was full of unexplained foreshortenings and depths. A distant huge tan object, a hawk the size of an elephant, turned out to be the browned bough of a nearby loblolly pine. I followed a sharp-shinned hawk against a featureless sky, rotating my head unawares as it flew, and when I lowered the glass a glimpse of my own looming shoulder sent me staggering. What prevents the men on Palomar from falling, voiceless and blinded, from their tiny, vaulted chairs?

I reel in confusion; I don't understand what I see. With the naked eye I can see two million light-years to the Andromeda galaxy. Often I slop some creek water in a jar and when I get home I dump it in a white china bowl. After the silt settles I return and see tracings of minute snails on the bottom, a planarian or two winding round the rim of water, roundworms shimmying frantically, and finally, when my eyes have adjusted to these dimensions, amoebae. At first the amoebae look like muscae volitantes, those curled moving spots you seem to see in your eyes when you stare at a distant wall. Then I see the amoebae as drops of water congealed, bluish, translucent, like chips of sky in the bowl. At length I choose one individual and give myself over to its idea of an evening. I see it dribble a grainy foot before it on its wet, unfathomable way. Do its unedited sense impressions include the fierce focus of my eyes? Shall I take it outside and show it Andromeda, and blow its little endoplasm? I stir the water with a finger, in case it's running out of oxygen. Maybe I should get a tropical aquarium with motorized bubblers and lights, and keep this one for a pet. Yes, it would tell its fissioned descendants, the universe is two feet by five, and if you listen closely you can hear the buzzing music of the spheres.

Oh, it's mysterious lamplit evenings, here in the galaxy, one after the other. It's one of those nights when I wander from window to window, looking for a sign. But I can't see. Terror and a beauty insoluble

20

are a ribband of blue woven into the fringes of garments of things both great and small. No culture explains, no bivouac offers real haven or rest. But it could be that we are not seeing something. Galileo thought comets were an optical illusion. This is fertile ground: since we are certain that they're not, we can look at what our scientists have been saying with fresh hope. What if there are *really* gleaming, castellated cities hung upside-down over the desert sand? What limpid lakes and cool date palms have our caravans always passed untried? Until, one by one, by the blindest of leaps, we light on the road to these places, we must stumble in darkness and hunger. I turn from the window. I'm blind as a bat, sensing only from every direction the echo of my own thin cries.

I chanced on a wonderful book by Marius von Senden, called *Space and Sight*. When Western surgeons discovered how to perform safe cataract operations, they ranged across Europe and America operating on dozens of men and women of all ages who had been blinded by cataracts since birth. Von Senden collected accounts of such cases; the histories are fascinating. Many doctors had tested their patients' sense perceptions and ideas of space both before and after the operations. The vast majority of patients, of both sexes and all ages, had, in von Senden's opinion, no idea of space whatsoever. Form, distance, and size were so many meaningless syllables. A patient "had no idea of depth, confusing it with roundness." Before the operation a doctor would give a blind patient a cube and a sphere; the patient would tongue it or feel it with his hands, and name it correctly. After the operation the doctor would show the same objects to the patient without letting him touch them; now he had no clue whatsoever what he was seeing. One patient called lemonade "square" because it pricked on his tongue as a square shape pricked on the touch of his hands. Of another postoperative patient, the doctor writes, "I have found in her no notion of size, for example, not even within the narrow limits which she might have encompassed with the aid of touch. Thus when I asked her to show me how big her mother was, she did not stretch out her hands, but set her two index-fingers a few inches apart." Other doctors reported their patients' own statements to similar effect. "The room he was in . . . he knew to be but part of the house, yet he could not conceive that the whole house could look bigger"; "Those who are blind from birth . . . have no real conception of height or distance. A house that is a mile away is thought of as nearby, but requiring the taking of a lot of steps. . . . The elevator that whizzes him up and down gives no more sense of vertical distance than does the train of horizontal."

For the newly sighted, vision is pure sensation unencumbered by meaning: "The girl went through the experience that we all go through and forget, the moment we are born. She saw, but it did not mean anything but a lot of different kinds of brightness." Again, "I asked the patient what he could see; he answered that he saw an extensive field of light, in which everything appeared dull, confused, and in motion. He could not distinguish objects." Another patient saw "nothing but a confusion of forms and colours." When a newly sighted girl saw photographs and paintings, she asked, "'Why do they put those dark marks all over them?' 'Those aren't dark marks,' her mother explained, 'those are shadows. That is one of the ways the eye knows that things have shape. If it were not for shadows many things would look flat.' 'Well, that's how things do look,' Joan answered. 'Everything looks flat with dark patches.'"

But it is the patients' concepts of space that are most revealing. One patient, according to his doctor, "practiced his vision in a strange fashion; thus he takes off one of his boots, throws it some way off in front of him, and then attempts to gauge the distance at which it lies; he takes a few steps towards the boot and tries to grasp it; on failing to reach it, he moves on a step or two and gropes for the boot until he finally gets hold of it." "But even at this stage, after three weeks' experience of seeing," von Senden goes on, "'space,' as he conceives it, ends with visual space, i.e. with colour-patches that happen to bound his view. He does not yet have the notion that a larger object (a chair) can mask a smaller one (a dog), or that the latter can still be present even though it is not directly seen."

In general the newly sighted see the world as a dazzle of color-patches. They are pleased by the sensation of color, and learn quickly to name the colors, but the rest of seeing is tormentingly difficult. Soon after his operation a patient "generally bumps into one of these colour-patches and observes them to be substantial, since they resist him as tactual objects do. In walking about it also strikes him—or can if he pays attention—that he is continually passing in between the colours he sees, that he can go past a visual object, that a part of it then steadily disappears from view; and that in spite of this, however he twists and turns—whether entering the room from the door, for example, or returning back to it—he always has a visual space in front of him. Thus he gradually comes to realize that there is also a space behind him, which he does not see." *25*

The mental effort involved in these reasonings proves overwhelming for many patients. It oppresses them to realize, if they ever do at all, the tremendous size of the world, which they had previously conceived of as something touchingly manageable. It oppresses them to realize that they have been visible to people all along, perhaps unattractively so, without their knowledge or consent. A disheartening number of them refuse to use their new vision, continuing to go over objects with their tongues, and lapsing into apathy and despair. "The child can see, but will not make use of his sight. Only when pressed can he with difficulty be brought to look at objects in his neighborhood; but more than a foot away it is impossible to bestir him to the necessary effort." Of a twenty-one-year-old girl, the doctor relates, "Her unfortunate father, who had hoped for so much from this operation, wrote that his daughter carefully shuts her eyes whenever she wishes to go about the house, especially when she comes to a staircase, and that she is never happier or more at ease than when, by closing her eyelids, she relapses into her former state of total blindness." A fifteen-year-old boy, who was also in love with a girl at the asylum for the blind, finally blurted out, "No, really, I can't stand it any more; I want to be sent back to the asylum again. If things aren't altered, I'll tear my eyes out."

Some do learn to see, especially the young ones. But it changes their lives. One doctor comments on "the rapid and complete loss of that striking and wonderful serenity which is characteristic only of those who have never yet seen." A blind man who learns to see is ashamed of his old habits. He dresses up, grooms himself, and tries to make a good impression. While he was blind he was indifferent to objects unless they were edible; now, "a sifting of values sets in . . . his thoughts and wishes are mightily stirred and some few of the patients are thereby led into dissimulation, envy, theft and fraud."

On the other hand, many newly sighted people speak well of the world, and teach us how dull is our own vision. To one patient, a human hand, unrecognized, is "something bright and then holes." Shown a bunch of grapes, a boy calls out, "It is dark, blue and shiny. . . . It isn't smooth, it has bumps and hollows." A little girl visits a garden. "She is greatly astonished, and can scarcely be persuaded to answer, stands speechless in front of the tree, which she only names on taking hold of it, and then as 'the tree with the lights in it.'" Some delight in their sight and give themselves over to the visual world. Of a patient just after her bandages were removed, her doctor writes, "The first things to attract her attention were her own hands; she looked at them very closely, moved them repeatedly to and fro, bent and stretched the fingers, and seemed greatly astonished at the sight." One girl was eager to tell her blind friend that "men do not really look like trees at all," and astounded to discover that her every visitor had an utterly different face. Finally, a twenty-two-year-old girl was dazzled by the world's brightness and kept her eyes shut for two weeks. When at the end of that time she opened her eyes again, she did not recognize any objects, but, "the more she now directed her gaze upon everything about her, the more it could be seen how an expression of gratification and astonishment overspread her features; she repeatedly exclaimed: 'Oh God! How beautiful!'"

I saw color-patches for weeks after I read this wonderful book. It was summer; the peaches were ripe in the valley orchards. When I woke in the morning, color-patches wrapped round my eyes, intricately, leaving not one unfilled spot. All day long I walked among shifting color-patches that parted before me like the Red Sea and closed again in silence, transfigured, wherever I looked back. Some patches swelled and loomed, while others vanished utterly, and dark marks flitted at random over the whole dazzling sweep. But I couldn't sustain the illusion of flatness. I've been around for too long. Form is condemned to an eternal danse macabre with meaning: I couldn't unpeach the peaches. Nor can I remember ever having seen without understanding; the color-patches of infancy are lost. My brain then must have been smooth as any balloon. I'm told I reached for the moon; many babies do. But the color-patches of infancy swelled as meaning filled them; they arrayed themselves in solemn ranks down distance which unrolled and stretched before me like a plain. The moon rocketed away. I live now in a world of shadows that shape and distance color, a world where space makes a kind of terrible sense. What gnosticism is this, and what physics? The fluttering patch I saw in my nursery window—silver and green and shape-shifting blue—is gone; a row of Lombardy poplars takes its place, mute, across the distant lawn. That humming oblong creature pale as light that stole along the walls of my room at night, stretching exhilaratingly around the corners, is gone, too, gone the night I ate of the bittersweet fruit, put two and two together and puckered forever my brain. Martin Buber tells this tale: "Rabbi Mendel once boasted to his teacher Rabbi Elimelekh that evenings he saw the angel who rolls away the light before the darkness, and mornings the angel who rolls away the darkness before the light. 'Yes,' said Rabbi Elimelekh, 'in my youth I saw that too. Later on you don't see these things any more.'"

Why didn't someone hand those newly sighted people paints and   *30* brushes from the start, when they still didn't know what anything was? Then maybe we all could see color-patches too, the world unraveled from reason, Eden before Adam gave names. The scales would drop from my eyes; I'd see trees like men walking; I'd run down the road against all orders, hallooing and leaping.

Seeing is of course very much a matter of verbalization. Unless I call my attention to what passes before my eyes, I simply won't see it. It is, as Ruskin says, "not merely unnoticed, but in the full, clear sense of the word, unseen." My eyes alone can't solve analogy tests using figures, the ones which show, with increasing elaborations, a big square, then a small square in a big square, then a big triangle, and expect me to find a small triangle in a big triangle. I have to say the words, describe what I'm seeing. If Tinker Mountain erupted, I'd be likely to notice. But if I want to notice the lesser cataclysms of valley life, I have to maintain in my head a running description of the present. It's not that I'm observant; it's just that I talk too much. Otherwise, especially in a strange place, I'll never know what's happening. Like a blind man at the ball game, I need a radio.

When I see this way I analyze and pry. I hurl over logs and roll away stones; I study the bank a square foot at a time, probing and tilting my head. Some days when a mist covers the mountains, when the muskrats won't show and the microscope's mirror shatters, I want to climb up the blank blue dome as a man would storm the inside of a circus tent, wildly, dangling, and with a steel knife claw a rent in the top, peep, and, if I must, fall.

But there is another kind of seeing that involves a letting go. When I see this way I sway transfixed and emptied. The difference between the two ways of seeing is the difference between walking with and without a camera. When I walk with a camera I walk from shot to shot, reading the light on a calibrated meter. When I walk without a camera, my own shutter opens, and the moment's light prints on my own silver gut. When I see this second way I am above all an unscrupulous observer.

It was sunny one evening last summer at Tinker Creek; the sun was low in the sky, upstream. I was sitting on the sycamore log bridge with the sunset at my back, watching the shiners the size of minnows who were feeding over the muddy sand in skittery schools. Again and again, one fish, then another, turned for a split second across the current and flash! the sun shot out from its silver side. I couldn't watch for it. It was always just happening somewhere else, and it drew my vision just as it disappeared: flash, like a sudden dazzle of the thinnest blade, a sparking over a dun and olive ground at chance intervals from every direction. Then I noticed white specks, some sort of pale petals, small, floating from under my feet on the creek's surface, very slow and steady. So I blurred my eyes and gazed towards the brim of my hat and saw a new world. I saw the pale white circles roll up, roll up, like the world's turning, mute and perfect, and I saw the linear flashes, gleaming silver, like stars being born at random down a rolling scroll of time. Something broke and something opened. I filled up like a new wineskin. I breathed an air like light; I saw a light like water. I was the lip of a fountain the creek filled forever; I was ether, the leaf in the zephyr; I was flesh-flake, feather, bone.

When I see this way I see truly. As Thoreau says, I return to my [35] senses. I am the man who watches the baseball game in silence in an empty stadium. I see the game purely; I'm abstracted and dazed. When it's all over and the white-suited players lope off the green field to their shadowed dugouts, I leap to my feet; I cheer and cheer.

But I can't go out and try to see this way. I'll fail, I'll go mad. All I can do is try to gag the commentator, to hush the noise of useless interior babble that keeps me from seeing just as surely as a newspaper dangled before my eyes. The effort is really a discipline requiring a lifetime of dedicated struggle; it marks the literature of saints and monks of every order East and West, under every rule and no rule, discalced and shod. The world's spiritual geniuses seem to discover universally that the mind's muddy river, this ceaseless flow of trivia and trash, cannot be dammed, and that trying to dam it is a waste of effort that might lead to madness. Instead you must allow the muddy river to flow unheeded in the dim channels of consciousness; you raise your sights; you look along it, mildly, acknowledging its presence without interest and gazing beyond it into the realm of the real where subjects and objects act and rest purely, without utterance. "Launch into the deep," says Jacques Ellul, "and you shall see."

The secret of seeing is, then, the pearl of great price. If I thought he could teach me to find it and keep it forever I would stagger barefoot across a hundred deserts after any lunatic at all. But although the pearl may be found, it may not be sought. The literature of illumination reveals this above all: Although it comes to those who wait for it, it is always, even to the most practiced and adept, a gift and a total surprise. I return from one walk knowing where the killdeer nests in the field by the creek and the hour the laurel blooms. I return from the same walk a day later scarcely knowing my own name. Litanies hum in my ears; my tongue flaps in my mouth Ailinon, alleluia! I cannot cause light; the most I can do is try to put myself in the path of its beam. It is possible, in deep space, to sail on solar wind. Light, be it particle or wave, has force: You rig a giant sail and go. The secret of seeing is to sail on solar wind. Hone and spread your spirit till you yourself are a sail, whetted, translucent, broadside to the merest puff.

When her doctor took her bandages off and led her into the garden, the girl who was no longer blind saw "the tree with the lights in it." It was for this tree I searched through the peach orchards of summer, in the forests of fall and down winter and spring for years. Then one day I was walking along Tinker Creek thinking of nothing at all and I saw the tree with the lights in it. I saw the backyard cedar where the mourning doves roost charged and transfigured, each cell buzzing with flame. I stood on the grass with the lights in it, grass that was wholly fire, utterly focused and utterly dreamed. It was less like seeing than like being for the first time seen, knocked breathless by a powerful glance. The flood of fire abated, but I'm still spending the power. Gradually the lights went out in the cedar, the colors died, the cells unflamed and disappeared. I was still ringing. I had been my whole life a bell, and never knew it until at that moment I was lifted and struck. I have since only very rarely seen the tree with the lights in it. The vision comes and goes, mostly goes, but I live for it, for the moment when the mountains open and a new light roars in spate through the crack, and the mountains slam.

❑ *Outward Exploration: Discussion*

1. In the second paragraph, why does Dillard wonder whether we will value a penny enough so that "finding a penny will literally make your day"? What experiences does she equate with finding a penny?

2. Throughout the essay she returns again and again to the issue of seeing. What points does she make about seeing?

3. Discuss her use of particular examples drawn from Nature to illustrate ways of seeing.

4. How would this essay have been different if Dillard's orientation were not that of a naturalist? For example, what if she were a satirist? Or a historian? Or a painter? Or a revolutionary political theorist? What would be left out of the essay, and what new material would probably be added?

❑ *Outward Exploration: Writing*

1. Dillard provides her readers with interesting information about seeing and raises several interesting issues about seeing and perception. Write an essay in which you do something similar for one of the other senses—smelling, touching, tasting, or hearing.

2. It might be argued that Dillard has the orientation and perception of a naturalist. In other words, she has trained herself to notice and remember the minutiae of the natural world and to be open to experiencing natural events that are too small or too big for most of us to notice. Similarly, Lewis Thomas ("On Natural Death") has the perception of a biochemist, Bruno Bettelheim ("The Ignored Lesson of Anne Frank") has the perception of a psychoanalyst, and P. J. O'Rourke ("At Home in the Parliament of Whores") has the perception of a satirist. Consider your own orientation and perception—these might grow from your college major (biology, history, psychology), or from your hobby (hunting, playing chess, painting), or from your personality traits (humorous, angry, impetuous, careful), or from some aspect of childhood such as religious or educational training, or from some combination of any of these. Observe some phenomenon and carefully record what you see and your interpretation. Then write an essay that records and interprets the data that you gathered and which then analyzes the sources of your style of perception.

2

Exploring the Self

Discovering and revealing aspects of yourself is one of the major reasons for exploratory writing. In the prewriting and drafting stages, you should probe as deeply as possible into your experiences, your ideas, your past, your hopes, your fears, your beliefs, your personality traits, your relationships with family members and friends, the details of your inner self. The point of this probing is to discover something new about yourself. When it comes time to craft those materials into a polished essay for your readers, you decide how much of what you've discovered you want to reveal to them. Throughout the final draft, you should keep referring back to yourself, to the feelings and ideas that you feel comfortable revealing.

WRITER-BASED GOALS

There are three writer-based goals. The primary one is deceptively simple: to get to know yourself better on a profound level by practicing introspection in writing, by scrutinizing your inner self, and by verbalizing your feelings and beliefs. All other writer-based goals grow from this one.

The second writer-based goal concerns your relationship to your readers: to discover how much of yourself you are willing to reveal to them. On some level, of course, any act of writing is also an act of self-revelation. Even a biology lab report reveals some things about you: for example, your possible interest in a particular biological question, your way of approaching a problem, your skill in manipulating and interpreting data, your verbal skills.

Here, though, I'm speaking about revealing your thoughts and beliefs, your past and your relationships, your vision of yourself and of others. Revealing these to readers can seem difficult at first, and there will be some insights you do not want to share. That is fine—none of us wants to reveal everything. But discovering what you feel comfortable revealing, what you can bring yourself to reveal, and what you cannot bring yourself to reveal—those discoveries not only increase your knowledge of yourself but also help you discover how you relate to your readers.

The third writer-based goal is to explore and enhance the connection between your self-revelation and the other, official subjects which your essays will inevitably include such as events, people, concepts, and texts.

READER-BASED GOALS

There are two reader-based goals: (1) to reveal something of significance about yourself to your readers and (2) to explain that revelation fully (its sources, its significance, its implications, its expression in your life, its global significance for the readers themselves).

WHO ARE YOU?

"Who are you?" is a question that each of your essays will attempt to answer in part. Conventional wisdom says that we are the sum of our past experiences, our thoughts, hopes, fears, beliefs, and physical characteristics, and the environmental influences upon us. One place to start answering this question is to label your various identities.

Labeling Identities

The following sentences come from essayist Nancy Mairs's introduction to *Carnal Acts:*

> I'm a white, middle-aged, middle-class, heterosexual, crippled feminist of a reclusive and rather bookish temperament, turned from New England Congregationalist to Roman Catholic social activist in the desert Southwest. Because I write as directly as possible out of my own experience, these traits inevitably shape my work.

At least 13 different defining traits are crammed into that amazing sentence. Let's look more closely at the various criteria that Mairs employs:

her *racial identity*—white

her *age identity*—middle aged

her *economic class identity*—middle class

her *sexual identity*—heterosexual

her *physical identity*—crippled

her *social identity*—reclusive

her *temperamental identity*—bookish

her *former regional identity*—New England

her *former religious identity*—Congregationalist

her *current religious identity*—Roman Catholic

her *political identity*—social activist

her *current regional identity*—desert Southwest

Other categories might exist that are not included here because they are inappropriate for her purpose at the moment, but they might be very appropriate for your purpose.

Notice, too, that many of these are only partial identities. For example, more than just "social activist," her political identity would include at least her political party affiliation, and her temperamental identity would include such things as her depressions and her tendency to self-mockery when alone. Mairs could (and often does) explore each one of those identities in separate essays.

Another way to think about our identities is to consider the roles we play: For example, I am a father, a teacher, a husband, a son, a cousin, a nephew, a fiction writer, a textbook writer, a poet, a driver, a passenger, a consumer, a letter writer, a piano player (bad), a guitar player (worse), a singer (even worse), a collector of books, a computer user, a Celtics fan, a New York Giants fan, a walker, a chess player, a tennis player, a cross-country skier, a reader. And that is hardly an exhaustive list.

We all play many roles, and each role has profound implications. For example, why do we choose one particular role rather than another? What do we derive psychologically from that role? Here's a brief example. Since boyhood, I've been a Yankees fan in New England, a region dedicated to the Red Sox. Why did I choose that role and what did I derive from it, particularly when circumstances dictated against it? For instance, fewer opportunities existed to see the Yankees play (in my home state of Maine, the Yankees were televised only when they were featured in the "Game of the Week" or when they played the Red Sox—all of whose games were aired). All of my friends were Red Sox fans. Every day the local newspaper carried in-depth stories about the Red Sox players, never about the Yankees. So why did I decide to play the role of Yankees fan? Even in childhood, I valued being independent, being the one who made up his own mind. I liked feeling different, probably because *different* suggested *special* to me. For reasons I would need to explore in a whole essay, I enjoyed the competition and friendly conflict that being a Yankees fan afforded. In those years, too, the

Yankees were the winningest team in baseball. Although I hate to admit it, I probably liked being identified with a winner too. So even a somewhat silly role like baseball fan can lead to important insights into the complexities of our personalities.

In short, identifying ourselves as members of particular groups or as playing particular roles can help us think about ourselves in new ways.

The Uses of Labeling Identities

The previous section encourages you to classify yourself, to label yourself as having particular identities and playing particular roles. That is an effective strategy for helping you to see yourself in ways you might not have considered before. But the labels are the beginning of the exploratory process, not its end product. Labels carry suggestions and connotations that are often not applicable to individuals within that group. The trick is to explore the implications of those labels, accepting the ones that fit, rejecting those that don't fit, and explaining why.

Here is a simple example. I am an *only child*. We all know the cultural stereotype of the only child—spoiled, selfish, egotistical. Fortunately, I have none of those characteristics (at least, according to me). Yet my two children insist that my sense of "this is mine, that is yours" is the product of my being an only child and therefore of my never having learned to share. They're right that I am very reluctant to share my "stuff" with others. They are wrong, I think, about the source of this reluctance. It comes, I think, from the fact that I've always felt I could live with the fact that I broke one of my things (a toy, my typewriter, my car)—a just punishment for irresponsible behavior, I suppose. But if someone else broke one of my things, I'd feel both (1) stupid for having lent it in the first place and (2) upset about what to do about it.

Two aspects of my personality combine in that second element. First, I don't "do confrontation" very well, so the idea of demanding that the other person (child or adult) replace the broken item feels impossible. Second, I pride myself on being able to imagine what the other person is feeling. Part (or all) of this might be mere projection of my feelings onto the other person. But whether it is true sensitivity or neurotic projection, the point is that I believe that I know what the other person feels. If I broke something belonging to someone else, I would be overwhelmed with guilt and embarrassment. I would feel that I had violated some "sacred trust," that people could never trust or respect me again. I could write essays exploring the origins of each of these feelings, of course, but the point here is that the combination of feelings and thoughts individualizes the standard stereotypical only-child attitude of mine. So my apparent only-child emphasis on property rights comes not (I think) from only-child selfishness but rather from a dislike of confrontation and from a crippling sense of guilt when I do anything "wrong."

Of course, such causes are not true for all only children, and that is my point entirely. Each response by anyone stems from more than what society assumes is the cause (the group we belong to, the label we wear). Exploring those causes in ourselves (and in our vision of other people) helps us understand ourselves and others even better.

GETTING PERSONAL

Writing to explore yourself requires serious thought and a willingness to revise again and again as you write. Here are some techniques for exploring yourself:

Assume there's more complexity in you than you think.

Ask yourself questions about your emotions and ideas.

Ask yourself those same questions again.

Locate the sources of your emotions and beliefs.

Consider reactions opposite to yours.

Explore significant relationships.

Assume Complexity

The real key to exploring ourselves is to assume that there's more complexity within us than first meets the eye. We are all made up of many layers, and our motivation has much greater depth than most of us are aware of (and perhaps want to acknowledge). For example, let's assume that David refuses to let Mary copy his history homework. It comforts David to believe that he refused because he is honest. Period. Forcing himself to dig into his motives, however, he might find that he also refused because Mary already owed him a favor and he wanted to be paid back first. Deeper, David might find that he fears his homework is not very good and he doesn't want to be embarrassed by letting Mary see it. Deeper still, he may fear being caught cheating, a feeling that comes from confrontation with an authority figure in his past. Deeper again, he might find that he resents Mary because she indicated a romantic interest in John instead of in him. And so on.

In short, we all have complex motives for every act that we do; exploring those motives helps us learn about ourselves and also teaches our readers something significant about the way the world works since we are, as Montaigne might say, "representative humans."

Ask Yourself Questions about Your Emotions and Ideas

After every statement or question, ask:

Why?

How do I know this is true?

What's the significance of this for me emotionally and intellectually?

Write sentences or whole paragraphs answering these questions. These answers will move you deeper into yourself and will enrich your essay.

Ask Yourself Those Same Questions Again

Often we ask those questions only once. Yet often the answers we find are not the most profound insights into ourselves that we can discover. By asking the same questions again (this time asking them of the answers we just wrote), we often find even more interesting and revealing insights. Like "double jeopardy" on the quiz show *Jeopardy,* the second round of questioning pays bigger dividends; in other words, you will find yourself burrowing even deeper into your emotions, motivation, and beliefs.

Locate the Sources of Your Emotions and Beliefs

The immediate source of an emotion is often highly visible in the event itself. Getting a job, for example, would probably give you a sense of relief (you don't have to keep trying to sell yourself to other employers) and joy (satisfaction that you did something well, a sense of being accepted as a person). Those emotions, however, have sources. For example, why do you hate to "sell yourself" to employers? Perhaps you are shy. But where did that shyness come from? Are you always shy, or only with strangers, or only with authority figures? If you feel insecure, why? Are you poorly trained for this particular job? If so, what is the source of your audacity in applying for it in the first place? Perhaps circumstances are a factor (you have to pay for college), but more complex explanations always exist. Does your shyness hide a deep-seated overconfidence? If you're shy, what did you do to psyche yourself into going to the interview? Who taught you those techniques?

The immediate source of a belief or an idea might be some code of behavior or some system of beliefs. Consciously or unconsciously, we have all answered the philosophical question "What is a good and moral person?" Often, though, our answers to that question are makeshift, jerry-built for particular situations. Exploratory writing will help you answer that question more cogently. At times, that answer might conflict with another answer to a question you value more highly—for example, "What is a successful person?" or "What is a happy person?" Discovering your most profound answers to such questions will teach you much about yourself.

Once you know the answers to such questions, the next task is to explore the more hidden sources of your beliefs and ideas. Some obvious answers are parents, family, friends, books, TV and movies, songs, and society in general. But dig deeper than that. Most parents try to instill a lot of moral principles in their children; some principles take seed and grow, others don't. Why did the ones that grew in you survive and the others not? Perhaps the ones that stayed with you were the ones you saw your parents (or friends or family) actually living. Or perhaps the opposite is true—the principles you saw in action turned you off.

At times, many of us experience a conflict between the principles we think we should follow and the expedient actions we have to take in order to achieve some goal. Exploring such conflicts always leads to interesting essays.

Consider Reactions Opposite Yours

Another way to discover more about yourself is to consider the ways other people have reacted or might react to similar situations. You might find such reactions in literature and in visual texts such as television shows and movies. Or you might role-play, considering reasons why someone would react differently from you. Or you might discuss the situation with your friends to learn their reactions and their reasons for those reactions.

In the earlier example of David's refusing to lend his homework to Mary, David decides to discuss the situation with his friends. All three friends recommend that he lend her the homework. Nnenna explains that most of the homework for that particular class is repetitious and so Mary will learn almost as much by copying his as by doing it on her own. Carlos asserts that doing Mary the favor costs David nothing and gains him Mary's appreciation. Nicola believes that Mary will never develop romantic feelings for David if he gives her grief over such an issue.

Having amassed those reactions, David reassesses his own position and motives. He sees that all of his friends make pragmatic points. For example, Nnenna makes an argument about the practical impact on Mary's learning the material, while Carlos and Nicola consider the practical impact on his continuing relationship with Mary. Seeing their emphasis on pragmatic considerations, David realizes that resentment, not morality, is one of his core reasons for refusing, an insight he had not developed before. He decides to eliminate resentment as one of the factors influencing his decision. This decision is based on another element in his own moral code that he had not considered earlier. He states that element as follows: "Decide moral questions by appeals to logic and morals, not by appeals to emotions." Of course, he still has his own pragmatic arguments—the fear of being caught cheating and his fear of being embarrassed by the quality of his homework. Whether he finally decides that his friends' arguments or his own are most convincing, he has learned more about himself through this process of looking at opposite reactions.

Explore Significant Relationships

Closely related to beliefs about the world are our ideas about relationships. Consider how many relationships you have right now: At the least, you probably have separate relationships with each member of your family, with friends, acquaintances, a spouse or significant other, classmates, your professors, some members of the college's administration, perhaps an employer and co-workers. Each of those relationships might be a source of some of your beliefs and emotions.

Explore a relationship as it is now, considering other elements as well, such as the relationship's history and your expectations about the relationship when it started and now. How would you like the relationship to be in the future (a year from now, five years from now)? What are the sources of those expectations and hopes?

GAZE OUTWARD AND INWARD

British novelist and philosopher Iris Murdoch makes an important distinction between seeing and gazing. *Seeing* is the act of looking at superficial details of life and at the masks that all people wear. *Gazing,* on the other hand, is the act of giving complete attention to another person, of trying to deal honestly with the intricate complexities that make up each human being. Seeing is not always bad, of course. It would be impossible for us to operate in the world if we tried to gaze into the soul of every person we came into incidental contact with. For example, the guest lecturer in a class, the chef in a restaurant, the pilot of the plane—each of these people deserves to be truly understood, but it is not necessarily *our* task to do the understanding.

We can adapt this concept to exploratory writing. For the people and events that you write about, try gazing instead of merely seeing. Look always for the complexity in the person, in the event, in the concept, in the text. Because you are always one of the subjects of your essay, there will be another kind of gazing—gazing inward to understand your own complexity.

A VISION OF THE SELF

Psychological theory divides the mind into three parts: (1) the conscious, (2) the preconscious, and (3) the unconscious. The *conscious* includes all the activity that we are immediately aware of and which we can control. The *preconscious* includes memories and feelings that we are not immediately aware of but which we can gain access to with some effort. The *unconscious* contains elements that influence our feelings and behavior but which can never be recalled or controlled by the conscious mind. Although this geography of the mind is simplistic, it serves to illustrate an important point for exploratory writing.

We all have experienced moments of insights into ourselves, suddenly realizing secondary motives for our actions. And all of us certainly have perceived other people's "hidden agendas" and "secret motives." The term *hidden agenda* has a negative connotation in our society (in part because it usually suggests a *consciously* hidden agenda), but we all have motives which are secret, sometimes even from our conscious mind.

Intense discussions with family and friends, professional guidance (for instance, by counselors and therapists), and—especially for our purposes in this book—the serious introspection involved in writing can often lead us into the preconscious layer. Here we discover some of the early experiences that establish our patterns of behavior. Here we find some of the sources of those awkward impulses and beliefs that we have such trouble explaining to ourselves and others.

As you prepare to write, tunneling into your history and hidden motives, imagine yourself as the miner. You chip off a piece of rock, think it might be gold, and go back to the surface to evaluate the fragment in the clear light of day. Perhaps you discover that it really is gold, in which case you return to the end of the tunnel and keep digging in the same direction. Perhaps the light reveals only fool's gold, in which case you return to the tunnel and begin digging a branch off to the left or right. When you find something that seems potentially interesting (the bit of ore might be an event you've remembered, a text you respond to in an unusual way, an idea from a lecture), take it into the daylight (that is, write about it in prewriting or a first draft), turn it this way and that in the light, consider it from a number of perspectives. Unless it comes directly from the surface (which we will assume are the external details of your life), chances are whatever you've found is worth writing about, although you may have to go back into the tunnel to look for related treasures.

USING VANTAGE POINTS TO EXPLORE THE SELF

Here are some **vantage points** from which you can consider yourself. They are based in part on the idea expressed in Nancy Mairs's sentence quoted earlier. Notice that the following list goes from the most general category to the most specific. For each vantage point, you might list all the characteristics (for example, personality traits, needs, drives, desires, attitudes, and assumptions) that you think are caused wholly or in part by your belonging to that category. Each vantage point encourages you to develop a **stereotype,** a generalization about some group (for example, human beings, Americans, Democrats, mothers-in-law) based perhaps on observations of a few individuals within that group that are expanded to include all members of the group. Thus a stereo-type is always a simplification (and often can be totally incorrect for all but the one or two individuals within the group who were originally observed). Nevertheless, stereotypes can be useful *as a starting place* when you consider yourself or a concept (for instance, *fathering*).

Human Vantage Point

Consider yourself as a representative human. Avoid any elements that seem to come from anything but basic human nature. Consider first the elements that unite all humans. For instance, what are the basic needs that all humans must have satisfied in order to survive? Food and shelter come quickly to mind. What about physical activity, companionship, solitude, or beauty—are they also basic human needs? Why or why not? If they are, how much of each is necessary? How much is desirable?

What are basic human traits? This is a very complex area, one that might require you to consult some sources. For instance, are humans naturally aggressive and combative? Is it basic human nature to fight? Is it basic human nature to be greedy and to look out for "Number 1" first? Or is it basic human nature to be generous and altruistic? How do you know?

Once you have established your vision of what is basic for humans, consider what needs or traits individualize you. What basic human elements would you like to eliminate if you could? Why?

Gender Vantage Point

Consider yourself as a representative of your gender. You will need to think about the traits commonly associated with your gender and the stereotypes as well. For example, men are often seen as favoring logic over emotions, as preferring aggression and physical expression to con-ciliation and conversation. Women, on the other hand, are seen as valu-ing relationships and emotions. They are perceived as nurturers. These are obvious stereotypes; you must add your own insights and observa-tions. You might consider a hypothetical situation—for example, per-son A has just discovered that person B has been unfaithful. Person B doesn't want the relationship to end. If person A were a man, how would he probably react to the news? What (if anything) could convince him to forgive person B? Why would that be effective? If person B were a woman, how would she tell person A about the act of unfaithfulness? How would she try to convince him that she still loves him and doesn't want the relationship to end? Then reverse the roles. If person A were a woman, how would she probably react to the news? What (if anything) could convince her to forgive person B? Why would that be effective? If person A were a man, how would he tell person B about the act of unfaithfulness? How would he try to convince her that he still loves her and doesn't want the relationship to end? Such hypothetical situations help you discover your own versions of stereotypes.

Once you've established the traits and attitudes of the typical representative of your gender, then examine yourself. What differentiates you from the "typical" members of your gender? Why? What characteristics (if any) would you eliminate from your gender if you could? Why? Which would you include from the other gender? Why?

National Vantage Point

For many people, their homeland is a place to love and honor. When political oppression occurs, they might flee the country, but most still love the country while hating the oppressive government. In other words, they separate the government from the land itself. Further, many people accept certain tenets or values of their homeland as obvious truths. For example, I was born in the United States and believe that such things as freedom of speech and the opportunity to develop all talents are rights of every person in the world. People born under different political, philosophical, or national assumptions might disagree. Consider yourself as a representative of your nation. What tenets or values would you change if you could? Why?

Regional Vantage Point

A particular region of your homeland may also contribute elements to your personality. For instance, I come from New England and was taught to value education (New England's long heritage of education). I also picked up the Yankee keep-to-yourself mentality. Coupled with my natural shyness, this mentality kept me a bit aloof from strangers for several years. Consider yourself as a representative of your region. What elements of your personality would you change? Why?

State Vantage Point

Naturally this blends in with the regional vantage point, but differences exist. I come from Maine, a nonindustrial, sparsely populated state, and was soon taught to value rugged individualism, to do for myself, to have a provincial vision of the world. I often heard the adage "As Maine goes, so goes the nation" and was amazed to discover at age 12 that people from other states had apparently never even heard the saying (and, needless to say, didn't believe it when I informed them of it). While I was growing up, there was a "feud" between Wisconsin and Maine about who could claim Paul Bunyan as a native son. Obviously, Maine's claim to the mythical logger was more valid, I thought. Bangor even has a statue of Paul to prove he was a Maine boy. Consider yourself as a representative of your home state. What elements of your personality might have been contributed by your growing up there? If you've lived in several different states, what elements did each state contribute to your personality?

It is also important to think about the consequences if you had been born somewhere else. If I had been born in some other New England state, would I have turned out differently? Let's say I was born in Massachusetts, which is much more heavily populated than Maine and whose people tend to be more highly educated. Further, Maine has traditionally been Republican and conservative whereas Massachusetts has been Democrat and liberal. I might have avoided several of the struggles of conscience I went through in high school and college if I had been born and raised in Massachusetts. Or perhaps I would have had the same struggles but ended up with views and values opposite those I now have.

Hometown Vantage Point

It is not hard to imagine the differences that might have occurred had I been born and raised in a big city rather than in a town with a population of 10,000. Even my cousins who were raised in Springfield, Massachusetts, had moral values and outlooks on life significantly different from mine. Some of those differences, of course, were the result of our natural tendencies, but not all. Many were caused by the environment. Consider yourself as a representative of your hometown. Then speculate about how different (or not) you would have been if you had been raised in an environment that was its opposite.

Economic-Class Vantage Point

Each economic class has certain ideas, assumptions, and values that distinguish it from the others. For example, the middle class is often depicted as valuing material goods more than anything else. Members of the middle class are blamed for being consumers first and environmentalists second. Their values are supposed to include working hard, making a better life for their children than they themselves had, and "keeping up with the Joneses." They supposedly assume that all people in America have an equal chance to better themselves. This is a stereotype, so some or all of these traits may be erroneously assigned to the middle class. Yet it is a prevalent stereotype, so it is one that you could begin your exploration with if you come from the middle class. Of course, there are more refinements to the class structure than simply *upper, middle,* and *lower* class. For instance, there are *upper-lower* class, *lower-middle* class, *upper-middle* class, and the like. The definitions of these class distinctions seem vague, so you might consult some sources to clarify exactly what you mean when you use the terms. Do you know of other ways of breaking down economic classes? If so, use them.

Consider yourself as a representative of your economic class. What aspects of your personality resulted from being a member of that class? Which would you change?

Educational Vantage Point

The fact that you are in college suggests several things about you. Why exactly are you in college? What was its allure? What expectations and assumptions about education does your family have? How have they influenced you and your expectations and assumptions? What are your assumptions about life, and how have your education and your assumptions about your future education influenced them?

Consider yourself as a representative student from your college. What assumptions and personality traits do you share with others on campus? Why? Which traits and assumptions of yours separate you from the other students on your campus? Explain.

Family Vantage Point

In addition to educational expectations, what assumptions and values do the members of your family have? How have those assumptions and values influenced you? Some of us accept most of our family's values. Others reject those values. What are the reasons that you either accepted or rejected them? Consider yourself as a representative of your family. In what ways do you fulfill that role? In what ways do you not fulfill that role? Why?

Religious or Philosophical Vantage Point

Often religious and philosophical ideas come first from families, but they soon are influenced profoundly by other sources such as friends, teachers, mentors, writers, and politicians. Consider yourself as a representative of a religious or philosophical group. How has being a member of that group influenced you? Remember to define the terms you use (for example, what exactly do you mean by *liberal* or *conservative* or *existentialist?*).

Personal-Experience Vantage Point

Perhaps the most individualizing vantage point is personal experience—that unique combination of occurrences that have happened only to you in that particular way. For example, everyone has a different combination of reasons for being in college, on a particular campus, in a specific class this semester. Perhaps you decided to attend college because you are fascinated by medieval history, yet the person sitting next to you is attending college because she does not want to end up with the same lifestyle that her parents have; perhaps the person sitting in front of you is attending college because he hopes to be drafted to play professional sports and college is his "training ground." Perhaps you selected your particular college because it is far away from your hometown, while someone else chose it because it was close to home. It may be that you are here because this college offered you the best financial deal, while someone else is here in spite of having to pay his own way. One person may be in this class merely to fulfill a college requirement, while another hopes this course will be part of the process of becoming a professional writer. In short, there are a multitude of reasons and combinations of reasons why someone is a college student at this particular college.

In addition to providing motivation, personal experiences alter the way we understand the world, and they help us discover what does and what does not interest us. Which of your personal experiences have changed the way you act, the way you understand people, your vision of yourself?

Consider yourself as a complete individual, different from everyone else. What makes you different? Be as specific as you can. For instance, perhaps spending time at a wilderness camp was the final factor needed to convince you to become a vegetarian. Yet a similar experience might convince someone else to become a veterinarian or to avoid living anywhere except in a big city.

Feel free to add other vantage points to your list.

How important is it to think about yourself from all of these perspectives? Frankly, I want to believe that each of us is unique, that no one could predict what any of us thinks about a given topic or how any of us would react to a particular situation. If that were true, then thinking about yourself in terms of the preceding vantage points would not accomplish much. But media coverage of presidential elections has shaken my belief in the existence of total individuality. I'm still unnerved by how quickly and accurately pollsters can predict winners in elections from a very small sample of voters. When I first voted in college, I was dismayed to discover that a staggering majority of college students from New England had voted exactly the way I had. If anything, the accuracy of pollsters' predictions has improved since then. If I were a unique individual, how could pollsters anticipate my votes so easily? Apparently all the factors those pollsters considered really did influence me and did help shape my personality as well as my politics.

So, being able to see yourself from these various perspectives has got to be useful in the exploration of yourself.

OBSTACLES TO EXPLORING THE SELF

At times, most of us have difficulty talking or writing about ourselves. Oh, sure, we don't mind telling (and retelling) how we won the big game for our high school or how we wowed them at the prom (if we did such things). But those are only the superficial details of our lives. They may be crucial in terms of our external lives, but exploratory essays are about your **inner self.** The inner self is our essence as a person. It is the collection of hopes, fears, and beliefs that gives us a sense of our identity and our self-image. The inner self is our sense of who we are after all the role-playing is over and after all pretense has been removed. The inner self is what we see when we remove the masks we have worn to meet the day. It is the naked soul. It is our core identity.

Occasionally the fact that exploratory writing is about the inner self can create some obstacles, particularly when we write our first exploratory essays. Looking squarely at possible obstacles is the easiest way to overcome them and get on with our writing.

Embarrassment

Let's face it—some of the most interesting things that have happened to us (and which have the potential of sparking introspection) are embarrassing. At some time, for example, most of us have been rejected by someone we're attracted to, or have done something we are ashamed of, or have felt ourselves to be total jerks. We have all experienced "the worst moment in our lives," the moment we knew we could never live down, the rejection from which we'd never recover, the Guiness gaffe of the century. Not surprising, most of us don't want to dwell on those moments.

Yet those experiences are the ones that test us and push us to explore our resources and our abilities. Such experiences teach us about ourselves if we're willing to learn, and telling others about them can exorcise the ghosts that haunt us. Finally, when we can write about and explore such events, they become truly ours; until then, they are merely something that *happened to us.*

In other words, writing about the pratfalls as well as the pinnacles of our lives helps us to learn about ourselves and helps us overcome our negative emotions. When we contemplate how we can present a moment to our readers, we are also considering other ways to present that moment to ourselves. By writing we come to understand.

We tame the moment and it is ours.

Fear That We Don't Have an Interesting Inner Self

Although some of us assume that we don't have an inner self, we all have an essence, an inner self. Exploratory writing can help us perceive it, and perhaps such writing can even influence its development.

But even after we acknowledge that we have an inner self, we might still doubt that anyone cares to read about it. We mistakenly believe that to be interesting on paper we need to have lived adventure-filled lives or to have profound insights into life. You don't have to be Indiana Jones or Aristotle to have a life filled with fascinating events and profound ideas and observations. Any event or aspect of our personality can be interesting if we reveal enough of our inner self.

Writing thoughts and observations in journals not only gives us glimpses of our inner self but also can help us overcome the feeling that we have nothing interesting to write about. As journals grow, we begin to be conscious of just how complex, complicated, and downright interesting we are. We begin to see that *our experience* of events in our life is unique, even if the events themselves are not exotic. We begin to record and to consider our reactions to people, places, and events. In fact, a good journal exercise is to write a page about one particular idea or event. The events might have just happened or might be plucked from the past.

In addition, once the ideas of our inner self are on paper, they don't seem such horrible things to reveal to others. Again, journals encourage us to play with those revelations. We get a handle on them, tame them, and mock them. If we wish, we can talk about them from the perspective of someone else, adopting that person's assumptions and beliefs to give us new insights. In short, we make them ours to do with as we please.

Fear of Revealing Too Much

Most of us fear that we will reveal too much in our writing. Ideally, every exploratory essay should reveal something to you about yourself that you didn't know before. As you work on revisions, you may discover that you feel surprisingly comfortable about sharing that revelation with your readers. If you do, great. That revelation may become the core of your essay. If not, that is fine too. *You* are the writer; *you* are in control. *You* decide what to include in your final essay and what to leave out.

The key point is this: Explore the topic as deeply as you can without serious emotional distress, reveal only the parts that you feel comfortable disclosing, and leave yourself open to the possibility of revealing more if it feels comfortable to do so in the future.

One of the most crucial pieces of advice in this book is this: *If pursuing a particular topic becomes emotionally distressful, stop writing about that topic.* Topics are like flowers: They don't all bloom at the same time. Some topics are ready for exploration now; some will be ready later on in the semester; some will be ready next year; and some might not be ready for five years. If trying to think about or write about a topic causes you severe discomfort, stop! Move on to another topic that causes less distress.

Almost every personal topic is going to feel a bit embarrassing or "too private" to reveal at first. The idea of writing anything personal at all will probably raise the questions "Should I reveal this or not?" and "What will people think of me if they read this?" Such uneasy feelings about addressing any topic of significance are to be expected. In fact, a little discomfort is a good sign—it suggests that you are exploring and revealing parts of your inner self.

In short, never reveal more than you feel comfortable revealing, but always keep testing yourself to see what "comfortable" really is.

HOW TO START

Because all exploratory writing is about revealing you, each of this book's chapters suggests starting places and techniques. This chapter focuses briefly on three starting places: mental occurrences, attitudes, and external information.

Starting with a Mental Occurrence

A mental occurrence is any thought, question, dream, or fantasy you've had. To begin, record that mental occurrence quickly. Don't worry about your style—simply try to get as many details into words as possible. For example, you might wonder, "Does God exist?" Write the question on the top of a blank sheet of paper (or in your journal or at the top of your computer screen), and then write whatever comes into your mind. When you've exhausted the topic (or yourself), take a break. Then start exploring. What caused you to ask the question in the first place? What in your family background, education, or life experience has made this question an issue for you? What did you believe before you asked yourself that question? Where did that belief come from? Where might you go to find some cogent arguments about or discussions of this issue?

Mental occurrences can often turn into research papers, and that is fine. The God question, for example, might lead you to read some theology or philosophy and to discuss the issue with someone on campus (for example, a college chaplain, a philosopher, a sociologist, a psychologist, a teacher of comparative religion). The more you learn, the better. The point of the essay will *not* be to prove conclusively that there is or isn't a God; the point will be to show your thought processes, to follow your investigation, to see what questions have been raised and answered (or simply raised) by your quest.

The structure of the final essay, of course, need not be a chronological record of your investigation. Very likely, it will not be. Instead, it might begin with a quotation that captures the essence of your thought at this moment or one that sums up an opinion with which you profoundly agree or disagree. Or it might begin with an event that caused you to ask the question about God in the first place. The essay might be a narrative, an analysis, or an argument. It might be a comparison and contrast between two views of God that you've encountered, between your views before and after doing the research, between your view and your family's. In short, when you are ready to put your materials together as a coherent essay for readers, you should consciously consider what content, what purpose, and what structure will be most effective.

The same process is true for any mental occurrence. If you have a dream, for example, record the dream as accurately as you can (and as quickly as you can, for dreams fade fast). Then explore, focusing first on your feelings about the dream. How did you feel during the dream itself? What are your feelings now, as you look back on the dream? Then focus on your bodily sensations as you think about the dream. Is there a tightness in your chest? Does your stomach feel queasy? Do your legs feel like moving, like running? What do you think those bodily sensations suggest? Finally, does the dream remind you of any experience you've had while awake? of any other dreams? of any experiences you've read about?

Equipped with this information, you might then start to write about the dream's meaning. Of course, by this time you might have tumbled onto another (and probably somehow) related topic. The final essay might not even mention the dream that spawned it.

Starting with an Attitude

If mental occurrences don't spark your writing, try starting with an attitude. You might begin with a current attitude you hold—perhaps you've decided that your older sister is not such a total jerk as you used to believe. Okay. What changed your mind? Exactly when did you start to doubt your original assessment of her personality? For that matter, what caused that original unfavorable belief about her? Or when did you discover what a best friend really is? Or when did you decide you wanted to be a best friend to someone? Any attitude or belief that has been called into question recently will make a great topic to consider. The very process of exploring why you questioned that attitude will reveal something about you to yourself and to your readers.

Starting with External Information

The external world is teeming with topics for exploratory writing. Keep your five senses attuned to the world around you and you'll find subjects everywhere.

For example, you might begin by recounting a conversation you overheard which sparked your interest and raised issues about yourself in similar circumstances. A fact from a textbook or newspaper might start your speculation. You might observe your own reaction to something—the way birds fly or a teacher lectures, or perhaps a piece of information from a course that you found particularly enlightening.

And then you might try to discover the roots of your reactions, or try to argue yourself into the opposite attitude, or examine the implications of your reactions. That is the beauty of the exploratory essay: You are free to write about whatever captures your attention.

SUGGESTIONS FOR WRITING

1. Following Mairs's sentence structure (page 76), write a sentence about yourself, plugging in the truth about you for each one of the identities she lists or substituting others more pertinent for you. Try to get as close-to-the-bone as you can. For example, don't settle for saying you are a "noncripple." Think about which physical characteristic most defines you *in your own mind*—for example, it could be height, weight, hair color, or body type.

2. List as many of your personality traits as possible. Answer the following questions, but don't limit your list to the questions. Range far and wide.

   Are you a leader or a follower? a "doer" or a "thinker"? a laugher or a crier? a practical joker or a victim?

   Do you have an active or a passive temperament? a warm or cool temperament? a happy or sad temperament?

   Are you primarily honest or dishonest? reliable or unreliable? thoughtful or impulsive? brave or timid? talkative or quiet? aggressive or passive? self-sacrificing or self-serving? calm or temperamental? never angry or always angry? logical or emotional? physical or not physical?

   Do you usually reveal your feelings or hide them?

   Do you usually trust everyone or doubt everyone?

3. Using one or more of the traits or identities from the sentence or list you wrote in #1 and #2, write an essay that explores that trait or identity. First, define the trait or identity in your own words. Then give examples of times when you exhibited it—give enough details so that we understand the context of each event. Were other traits or identities also involved? Would your life be better if you didn't have that trait/identity or if it were more or less dominant in your life?

Growing Up Asian in America

KESAYA E. NODA

☐ *Inward Exploration*

Write at least one paragraph exploring your attitudes toward Asian Americans.

Sometimes when I was growing up, my identity seemed to hurtle   *1*
toward me and paste itself right to my face. I felt that way, encountering
the stereotypes of my race perpetuated by non-Japanese people (primarily white) who may or may not have had contact with other Japanese
in America. "You don't like cheese, do you?" someone would ask. "I
know your people don't like cheese." Sometimes questions came making allusions to history. That was another aspect of the identity. Events
that had happened quite apart from the me who stood silent in that
moment connected my face with an imcomprehensible past. "Your parents were in California? Were they in those camps during the war?" And
sometimes there were phrases or nicknames: "Lotus Blossom." I was
sometimes addressed or referred to as racially Japanese, sometimes as
Japanese-American, and sometimes as an Asian woman. Confusions and
distortions abounded.

How is one to know and define oneself? From the inside—within a
context that is self-defined, from a grounding in community and a connection with culture and history that are comfortably accepted? Or from
the outside—in terms of messages received from the media and people
who are often ignorant? Even as an adult I can still see two sides of my
face and past. I can see from the inside out, in freedom. And I can see
from the outside in, driven by the old voices of childhood and lost in
anger and fear.

I Am Racially Japanese

A voice from my childhood says: "You are other. You are less than.
You are unalterably alien." This voice has its own history. We have indeed been seen as other and alien since the early years of our arrival in
the United States. The very first immigrants were welcomed and sought
as laborers to replace the dwindling numbers of Chinese, whose influx
had been cut off by the Chinese Exclusion Act of 1882. The Japanese fell
natural heir to the same anti-Asian prejudice that had arisen against the

Chinese. As soon as they began striking for better wages, they were no longer welcomed.

I can see myself today as a person historically defined by law and custom as being forever alien. Being neither "free white," nor "African," our people in California were deemed "aliens, ineligible for citizenship," no matter how long they intended to stay here. Aliens ineligible for citizenship were prohibited from owning, buying, or leasing land. They did not and could not belong here. The voice in me remembers that I am always a *Japanese*-American in the eyes of many. A third-generation German-American is an American. A third-generation Japanese-American is a Japanese-American. Being Japanese means being a danger to the country during the war and knowing how to use chopsticks. I wear this history on my face.

I move to the other side. I see a different light and claim a different   5 context. My race is a line that stretches across ocean and time to link me to the shrine where my grandmother was raised. Two high, white banners lift in the wind at the top of the stone steps leading to the shrine. It is time for the summer festival. Black characters are written against the sky as boldly as the clouds, as lightly as kites, as sharply as the big black crows I used to see above the fields in New Hampshire. At festival time there is liquor and food, ritual, discipline, and abandonment. There is music and drunkenness and invocation. There is hope. Another season has come. Another season has gone.

I am racially Japanese. I have a certain claim to this crazy place where the prayers intoned by a neighboring Shinto priest (standing in for my grandmother's nephew who is sick) are drowned out by the rehearsals for the pop singing contest in which most of the villagers will compete later that night. The village elders, the priest, and I stand respectfully upon the immaculate, shining wooden floor of the outer shrine, bowing our heads before the hidden powers. During the patchy intervals when I can hear him, I notice the priest has a stutter. His voice flutters up to my ears only occasionally because two men and a woman are singing gustily into a microphone in the compound, testing the sound system. A prerecorded tape of guitars, samisens, and drums accompanies them. Rock music and Shinto prayers. That night, to loud applause and cheers, a young man is given the award for the most *netsuretsu*—passionate, burning—rendition of a song. We roar our approval of the reward. Never mind that his voice had wandered and slid, now slightly above, now slightly below the given line of the melody. Netsuretsu. Netsuretsu.

In the morning, my grandmother's sister kneels at the foot of the stone stairs to offer her morning prayers. She is too crippled to climb the stairs, so each morning she kneels here upon the path. She shuts her eyes for a few seconds, her motions as matter of fact as when she washes rice. I linger longer than she does, so reluctant to leave, savoring the connection I feel with my grandmother in America, the past, and the power that lives and shines in the morning sun.

Our family has served this shrine for generations. The family's need to protect this claim to identity and place outweighs any individual claim to any individual hope. I am Japanese.

I Am a Japanese-American

"Weak." I hear the voice from my childhood years. "Passive," I hear. Our parents and grandparents were the ones who were put into those camps. They went without resistance; they offered cooperation as proof of loyalty to America. "Victim," I hear. And, "Silent."

Our parents are painted as hard workers who were socially uncom- *10* fortable and had difficulty expressing even the smallest opinion. Clean, quiet, motivated, and determined to match the American way; that is us, and that is the story of our time here.

"Why did you go into those camps?" I raged at my parents, frightened by my own inner silence and timidity. "Why didn't you do anything to resist? Why didn't you name it the injustice it was?" Couldn't our parents even think? Couldn't they? Why were we so passive?

I shift my vision and my stance. I am in California. My uncle is in the midst of the sweet potato harvest. He is pressed, trying to get the harvesting crews onto the field as quickly as possible, worried about the flow of equipment and people. His big pickup is pulled off to the side, motor running, door ajar. I see two tractors in the yard in front of an old shed; the flatbed harvesting platform on which the workers will stand has already been brought over from the other field. It's early morning. The workers stand loosely grouped and at ease, but my uncle looks as harried and tense as a police officer trying to unsnarl a New York City traffic jam. Driving toward the shed, I pull my car off the road to make way for an approaching tractor. The front wheels of the car sink luxuriously into the soft, white sand by the roadside and the car slides to a dreamy halt, tail still on the road. I try to move forward. I try to move back. The front bites contentedly into the sand, the back lifts itself at a jaunty angle. My uncle sees me and storms down the road, running. He is shouting before he is even near me.

"What's the matter with you?" he screams. "What the hell are you doing?" In his frenzy, he grabs his hat off his head and slashes it through the air across his knee. He is beside himself. "Don't you know how to drive in sand? What's the matter with you? You've blocked the whole roadway. How am I supposed to get my tractors out of here? Can't you use your head? You've cut off the whole roadway, and we've got to get out of here."

I stand on the road before him helplessly thinking, "No, I don't know how to drive in sand. I've never driven in sand."

"I'm sorry, uncle," I say, burying a smile beneath a look of sincere   15
apology. I notice my deep amusement and my affection for him with
great curiosity. I am usually devastated by anger. Not this time.

During the several years that follow I learn about the people and the
place, and much more about what has happened in this California village where my parents grew up. The issei, our grandparents, made this
settlement in the desert. Their first crops were eaten by rabbits and rav-
aged by insects. The land was so barren that men walking from house
to house sometimes got lost. Women came here too. They bore children
in 114-degree heat, then carried the babies with them into the fields to
nurse when they reached the end of each row of grapes or other truck-
farm crops.

I had had no idea what it meant to buy this kind of land and make
it grow green. Or how, when the war came, there was no space at all
for the subtlety of being who we were—Japanese-Americans. Either/or
was the way. I hadn't understood that people were literally afraid for
their lives then, that their money had been frozen in banks; that there
was a five-mile travel limit; that when the early evening curfew came
and they were inside their houses, some of them watched helplessly as
people they knew went into their barns to steal their belongings. The
police were patrolling the road, interested only in violators of curfew.
There was no help for them in the face of thievery. I had not been able
to imagine before what it must have felt like to be an American—to
know absolutely that one is an American—and yet to have almost everyone else deny it. Not only deny it, but challenge that identity with
machine guns and troops of white American soldiers. In those circumstances it was difficult to say, "I'm a Japanese-American." "American"
had to do.

But now I can say that I am a Japanese-American. It means I have a
place here in this country, too. I have a place here on the East Coast,
where our neighbor is so much a part of our family that my mother
never passes her house at night without glancing at the lights to see if
she is home and safe; where my parents have hauled hundreds of pounds
of rocks from fields and arduously planted Christmas trees and blue-
berries, lilacs, asparagus, and crab apples; where my father still dreams
of angling a stream to a new bed so that he can dig a pond in the field
and fill it with water and fish. "The neighbors already came for their
Christmas tree?" he asks in December. "Did they like it? Did they
like it?"

I have a place on the West Coast where my relatives still farm, where
I heard the stories of feuds and backbiting, and where I saw that people
survived and flourished because fundamentally they trusted and relied
upon one another. A death in the family is not just a death in a family;
it is a death in the community. I saw people help each other with money,
materials, labor, attention, and time. I saw men gather once a year,

without fail, to clean the grounds of a ninety-year-old woman who had helped the community before, during, and after the war. I saw her remembering them with birthday cards sent to each of their children.

I come from a people with a long memory and a distinctive grace. *20*
We live our thanks. And we are Americans. Japanese-Americans.

I Am a Japanese-American Woman

Woman. The past piece of my identity. It has been easier by far for me to know myself in Japan and to see my place in America than it has been to accept my line of connection with my own mother. She was my dark self, a figure in whom I thought I saw all that I feared most in myself. Growing into womanhood and looking for some model of strength, I turned away from her. Of course, I could not find what I sought. I was looking for a black feminist or a white feminist. My mother is neither white nor black.

My mother is a woman who speaks with her life as much as with her tongue. I think of her with her own mother. Grandmother had Parkinson's disease and it had frozen her gait and set her fingers, tongue, and feet jerking and trembling in a terrible dance. My aunts and uncles wanted her to be able to live in her own home. They fed her, bathed her, dressed her, awoke at night to take her for one last trip to the bathroom. My aunts (her daughters-in-law) did most of the care, but my mother went from New Hampshire to California each summer to spend a month living with Grandmother, because she wanted to and because she wanted to give my aunts at least a small rest. During those hot summer days, mother lay on the couch watching the television or reading, cooking foods that Grandmother liked, and speaking little. Grandmother thrived under her care.

The time finally came when it was too dangerous for Grandmother to live alone. My relatives kept finding her on the floor beside her bed when they went to wake her in the mornings. My mother flew to California to help clean the house and make arrangements for Grandmother to enter a local nursing home. On her last day at home, while Grandmother was sitting in her big, overstuffed armchair, hair combed and wearing a green summer dress, my mother went to her and knelt at her feet. "Here, Mamma," she said. "I've polished your shoes." She lifted Grandmother's legs and helped her into the shiny black shoes. My Grandmother looked down and smiled slightly. She left her house walking, supported by her children, carrying her pocket book, and wearing her polished black shoes. "Look, Mamma," my mom had said, kneeling. "I've polished your shoes."

Just the other day, my mother came to Boston to visit. She had recently lost a lot of weight and was pleased with her new shape and her feeling of good health. "Look at me, Kes," she exclaimed, turning toward me, front and back, as naked as the day she was born. I saw her small breasts and the wide, brown scar, belly button to pubic hair, that marked her because my brother and I were both born Caesarean section. Her hips were small. I was not a large baby, but there was so little room for me in her that when she was carrying me she could not even begin to bend over toward the floor. She hated it, she said.

"Don't I look good? Don't you think I look good?"   *25*

I looked at my mother, smiling and as happy as she, thinking of all the times I have seen her naked. I have seen both my parents naked throughout my life, as they have seen me. From childhood through adulthood we've had our naked moments, sharing baths, idle conversations picked up as we moved between showers and closets, hurried moments at the beginning of days, quiet moments at the end of days.

I know this to be Japanese, this ease with the physical, and it makes me think of an old Japanese folk song. A young nursemaid, a fifteen-year-old girl, is singing a lullaby to a baby who is strapped to her back. The nursemaid has been sent as a servant to a place far from her own home. "We're the beggars," she says, "and they are the nice people. Nice people wear fine sashes. Nice clothes."

> If I should drop dead,
> bury me by the roadside!
> I'll give a flower
> to everyone who passes.

> What kind of flower?
> The cam-cam-camellia [tsun-tsun-tsubaki]
> watered by Heaven:
> alms water.

The nursemaid is the intersection of heaven and earth, the intersection of the human, the natural world, the body, and the soul. In this song, with clear eyes, she looks steadily at life, which is sometimes so very terrible and sad. I think of her while looking at my mother, who is standing on the red and purple carpet before me, laughing, without any clothes.

I am my mother's daughter. And I am myself.

I am a Japanese-American woman.   *30*

Epilogue

I recently heard a man from West Africa share some memories of his childhood. He was raised Muslim, but when he was a young man, he found himself deeply drawn to Christianity. He struggled against his inner impulse for years, trying to avoid the church yet feeling pushed to return to it again and again. "I would have done *anything* to avoid the change," he said. At last, he became Christian. Afterwards he was afraid to go home, fearing that he would not be accepted. The fear was groundless, he discovered, when at last he returned—he had separated

himself, but his family and friends (all Muslim) had not separated themselves from him.

The man, who is now a professor of religion, said that in the Africa
he knew as a child and a young man, pluralism was embraced rather
than feared. There was "a kind of tolerance that did not deny your par-
ticularity," he said. He alluded to zestful, spontaneous debates that
would sometimes loudly erupt between Muslims and Christians in the
village's public spaces. His memories of an atheist who harangued the
villagers when he came to visit them once a week moved me deeply.
Perhaps the man was an agricultural advisor or inspector. He harassed
the women. He would say: "Don't go to the fields! Don't even bother to
go to the fields. Let God take care of you. He'll send you the food. If
you believe in God, why do you need to work? You don't need to work!
Let God put the seeds in the ground. Stay home."

The professor said, "The women laughed, you know? They just
laughed. Their attitude was, 'Here is a child of God. When will he come
home?'"

The storyteller, the professor of religion, smiled a most fantastic
tender smile as he told this story. "In my country, there is a deep affirmation of the oneness of God," he said. "The atheist and the women
were having quite different experiences in their encounter, though the
atheist did not know this. He saw himself as quite separate from the
women. But the women did not see themselves as being separate from
him. 'Here is a child of God,' they said. 'When will he come home?'"

❏ *Outward Exploration: Discussion*

1. What does Noda mean when she says her identity pasted itself to her
   face (paragraph 1)?
2. What does she mean when she says that she can see two sides of her
   face and past?
3. Why does Noda use so many passive verbs in paragraph 3?
4. What is the connection between her raging at her parents (paragraph
   11) and her uncle's raging at her (paragraphs 13–15)?
5. In paragraph 23, why does Noda repeat what her mother said twice?
   Why is the second version somewhat different from the first?
6. What is the effect of the four headings?
7. What solution does Noda find to the divided self caused by belonging
   to two cultures? Does it work? Why or why not?

❏ *Outward Exploration: Writing*

1. Write an essay in which you give your own answer to Noda's question: "How is one to know and define oneself?" (paragraph 2).

2. Have you ever felt as though you had a divided self or that two cultures were wrestling within you? If so, write an essay exploring that struggle. Try to find episodes or stories that illustrate your ideas in the way that Noda does.

3. If you belong to a group to which society has assigned particular characteristics and traits (either flattering or not), explore your thoughts and feelings about such stereotypes in an essay. Speculate about the sources of the stereotype. What are your feelings about being labeled thusly?

❏ *Style*

Consider the following sentence from Noda's essay:

I come from a people with a long memory and a distinctive grace. (paragraph 20)

The structure of this sentence is as follows:

subject ("I")

predicate verb ("come")

prepositional phrase ("from a people")

preposition ("with")

two 3-word objects of that preposition ("a long memory and a distinctive grace")

period.

What is noticeable about this sentence is its ending with one preposition ("with") that has two 3-word objects.

Using your own information, write a sentence that replicates this structure (a preposition that has two multiword objects).

How It Feels to Be Colored Me

ZORA NEALE HURSTON

I am colored but I offer nothing in the way of extenuating circum-   1
stances except the fact that I am the only Negro in the United States
whose grandfather on the mother's side was *not* an Indian chief.

I remember the very day that I became colored. Up to my thirteenth
year I lived in the little Negro town of Eatonville, Florida. It is exclusively a colored town. The only white people I knew passed through the
town going to or coming from Orlando. The native whites rode dusty
horses, the Northern tourists chugged down the sandy village road in
automobiles. The town knew the Southerners and never stopped cane
chewing when they passed. But the Northerners were something else
again. They were peered at cautiously from behind curtains by the
timid. The more venturesome would come out on the porch to watch
them go past and got just as much pleasure out of the tourists as the
tourists got out of the village.

The front porch might seem a daring place for the rest of the town,
but it was a gallery seat to me. My favorite place was atop the gate-post.
Proscenium box for a born first-nighter. Not only did I enjoy the show,
but I didn't mind the actors knowing that I liked it. I usually spoke to
them in passing. I'd wave at them and when they returned my salute, I
would say something like this: "Howdy-do-well-I-thank-you-where-
you-goin'?" Usually the automobile or the horse paused at this, and
after a queer exchange of compliments, I would probably "go a piece of
the way" with them, as we say in farthest Florida. If one of my family
happened to come to the front in time to see me, of course negotiations
would be rudely broken off. But even so, it is clear that I was the first
"welcome-to-our-state" Floridian, and I hope the Miami Chamber of
Commerce will please take notice.

During this period, white people differed from colored to me only
in that they rode through town and never lived there. They liked to hear
me "speak pieces" and sing and wanted to see me dance the parse-
me-la, and gave me generously of their small silver for doing these
things, which seemed strange to me for I wanted to do them so much
that I needed bribing to stop. Only they didn't know it. The colored

people gave no dimes. They deplored any joyful tendencies in me, but I was their Zora nevertheless. I belonged to them, to the nearby hotels, to the county—everybody's Zora.

But changes came in the family when I was thirteen, and I was sent   5 to school in Jacksonville. I left Eatonville, the town of the oleanders, as Zora. When I disembarked from the river-boat at Jacksonville, she was no more. It seemed that I had suffered a sea change. I was not Zora of Orange County any more, I was now a little colored girl. I found it out in certain ways. In my heart as well as in the mirror, I became a fast brown—warranted not to rub nor run.

But I am not tragically colored. There is no great sorrow dammed up in my soul, nor lurking behind my eyes. I do not mind at all. I do not belong to the sobbing school of Negrohood who hold that nature somehow has given them a lowdown dirty deal and whose feelings are all hurt about it. Even in the helter-skelter skirmish that is my life, I have seen that the world is to the strong regardless of a little pigmentation more or less. No, I do not weep at the world—I am too busy sharpening my oyster knife.

Someone is always at my elbow reminding me that I am the granddaughter of slaves. It fails to register depression with me. Slavery is sixty years in the past. The operation was successful and the patient is doing well, thank you. The terrible struggle that made me an American out of a potential slave said "On the line!" The Reconstruction said "Get set!" and the generation before said "Go!" I am off to a flying start and I must not halt in the stretch to look behind and weep. Slavery is the price I paid for civilization, and the choice was not with me. It is a bully adventure and worth all that I have paid through my ancestors for it. No one on earth ever had a greater chance for glory. The world to be won and nothing to be lost. It is thrilling to think— to know that for any act of mine, I shall get twice as much praise or twice as much blame. It is quite exciting to hold the center of the national stage, with the spectators not knowing whether to laugh or to weep.

The position of my white neighbor is much more difficult. No brown specter pulls up a chair beside me when I sit down to eat. No dark ghost thrusts its leg against mine in bed. The game of keeping what one has is never so exciting as the game of getting.

I do not always feel colored. Even now I often achieve the unconscious Zora of Eatonville before the Hegira. I feel most colored when I am thrown against a sharp white background.

For instance at Barnard. "Beside the waters of the Hudson" I feel   10 my race. Among the thousand white persons, I am a dark rock surged upon, overswept by a creamy sea. I am surged upon and overswept, but through it all, I remain myself. When covered by the waters, I am; and the ebb but reveals me again.

Sometimes it is the other way around. A white person is set down in our midst, but the contrast is just as sharp for me. For instance, when I sit in the drafty basement that is The New World Cabaret with a white person, my color comes. We enter chatting about any little nothing that we have in common and are seated by the jazz waiters. In the abrupt way that jazz orchestras have, this one plunges into a number. It loses no time in circumlocutions, but gets right down to business. It constricts the thorax and splits the heart with its tempo and narcotic harmonies. This orchestra grows rambunctious, rears on its hind legs and attacks the tonal veil with primitive fury, rending it, clawing it until it breaks through to the jungle beyond. I follow those heathen—follow them exultingly. I dance wildly inside myself; I yell within, I whoop; I shake my assegai above my head, I hurl it true to the mark *yeeeeooww!* I am in the jungle and living in the jungle way. My face is painted red and yellow and my body is painted blue. My pulse is throbbing like a war drum. I want to slaughter something—give pain, give death to what, I do not know. But the piece ends. The men of the orchestra wipe their lips and rest their fingers. I creep back slowly to the veneer we call civilization with the last tone and find the white friend sitting motionless in his seat, smoking calmly.

"Good music they have here," he remarks, drumming the table with his fingertips.

Music! The great blobs of purple and red emotion have not touched him. He has only heard what I felt. He is far away and I see him but dimly across the ocean and the continent that have fallen between us. He is so pale with his whiteness then and I am *so* colored.

At certain times I have no race, I am *me*. When I set my hat at a certain angle and saunter down Seventh Avenue, Harlem City, feeling as snooty as the lions in front of the Forty-Second Street Library, for instance. So far as my feelings are concerned, Peggy Hopkins Joyce on the Boule Mich with her gorgeous raiment, stately carriage, knees knocking together in a most aristocratic manner, has nothing on me. The cosmic Zora emerges. I belong to no race nor time. I am the eternal feminine with its string of beads.

I have no separate feeling about being an American citizen and colored. I am merely a fragment of the Great Soul that surges within the boundaries. My country, right or wrong.   15

Sometimes, I feel discriminated against, but it does not make me angry. It merely astonishes me. How *can* any deny themselves the pleasure of my company! It's beyond me.

But in the main, I feel like a brown bag of miscellany propped against a wall. Against a wall in company with other bags, white, red and yellow. Pour out the contents, and there is discovered a jumble of small things priceless and worthless. A first-water diamond, an empty spool, bits of broken glass, lengths of string, a key to a door long since crumbled away, a rusty knifeblade, old shoes saved for a road that never was and never will be, a nail bent under the weight of things too heavy for any nail, a dried flower or two, still a little fragrant. In your hand is the brown bag. On the ground before you is the jumble it held—so much like the jumble in the bags, could they be emptied, that all might be dumped in a single heap and the bags refilled without altering the content of any greatly. A bit of colored glass more or less would not matter. Perhaps that is how the Great Stuffer of Bags filled them in the first place—who knows?

❑ *Outward Exploration: Discussion*

1. What impact does living in the all-black Eatonville have on Zora as a child?
2. When does Hurston feel most colored?
3. What is the difference between the way she experiences jazz and the way her white friends experience it?
4. What does she mean by the term "the cosmic Zora"?
5. What is her strategy for discussing racism in this essay?
6. What is the point of her final paragraph?
7. Why are there four sections in the essay?

❑ *Outward Exploration: Writing*

1. Write an essay titled "How It Feels to Be X Me" with you supplying the adjective to replace the X. Explore as deeply as you can. Hurston looks at being black from four different perspectives; try to do the same about X.
2. This is one of several essays that explore what it means to be African American in the United States (for example, Gerald Early's "Introduction," James Baldwin's "Notes of a Native Son," and Alice Walker's "Beauty: When the Other Dancer Is the Self"). Write an essay exploring the similarities and differences of the writers' experiences and feelings and thoughts about the issue of race in the United States.

A Few Words about Breasts

NORA EPHRON

Write at least one paragraph about body images. Most of us don't like some-thing about ourselves (our weight, height, nose, earlobes, whatever). In your paragraph, explain what you like or what you don't like about your own body. These paragraphs will not *be shared with the class, so feel free to be honest. Think about what first made you satisfied or dissatisfied with that aspect of your body; in other words, what were the sources of your dissatisfaction—for ex-ample, friends, advertisements, relatives?*

I have to begin with a few words about androgyny. In grammar *1* school, in the fifth and sixth grades, we were all tyrannized by a rigid set of rules that supposedly determined whether we were boys or girls. The episode in *Huckleberry Finn* where Huck is disguised as a girl and gives himself away by the way he threads a needle and catches a ball— that kind of thing. We learned that the way you sat, crossed your legs, held a cigarette, and looked at your nails—the way you did these things instinctively was absolute proof of your sex. Now obviously most chil-dren did not take this literally, but I did. I thought that just one slip, just one incorrect cross of my legs or flick of an imaginary cigarette ash would turn me from whatever I was into the other thing; that would be all it took, really. Even though I was outwardly a girl and had many of the trappings generally associated with girldom—a girl's name, for ex-ample, and dresses, my own telephone, an autograph book—I spent the early years of my adolescence absolutely certain that I might at any point gum it up. I did not feel at all like a girl. I was boyish. I was athletic, ambitious, outspoken, competitive, noisy, rambunctious. I had scabs on my knees and my socks slid into my loafers and I could throw a football. I wanted desperately not to be that way, not to be a mixture of both things, but instead just one, a girl, a definite indisputable girl. As soft and as pink as a nursery. And nothing would do that for me, I felt, but breasts.

I was about six months younger than everyone else in my class, and so for about six months after it began, for six months after my friends had begun to develop (that was the word we used, develop), I was not particularly worried. I would sit in the bathtub and look down at my breasts and know that any day now, any second now, they would start growing like everyone else's. They didn't. "I want to buy a bra," I said to my mother one night. "What for?" she said. My mother was really hateful about bras, and by the time my third sister had gotten to the point where she was ready to want one, my mother had worked the whole business into a comedy routine. "Why not use a Band-Aid instead?" she would say. It was a source of great pride to my mother that she had never even had to wear a brassiere until she had her fourth child, and then only because her gynecologist made her. It was incomprehensible to me that anyone could ever be proud of something like that. It was the 1950s, for God's sake. Jane Russell. Cashmere sweaters. Couldn't my mother see that? "*I am too old to wear an undershirt.*" Screaming. Weeping. Shouting. "Then don't wear an undershirt," said my mother. "But I want to buy a bra." "What for?"

I suppose that for most girls, breasts, brassieres, that entire thing, has more trauma, more to do with the coming of adolescence, with becoming a woman, than anything else. Certainly more than getting your period, although that, too, was traumatic, symbolic. But you could see breasts; they were there; they were visible. Whereas a girl could claim to have her period for months before she actually got it and nobody would ever know the difference. Which is exactly what I did. All you had to do was make a great fuss over having enough nickels for the Kotex machine and walk around clutching your stomach and moaning for three to five days a month about The Curse and you could convince anybody. There is a school of thought somewhere in the women's lib/women's mag/gynecology establishment that claims that menstrual cramps are purely psychological, and I lean toward it. Not that I didn't have them finally. Agonizing cramps, heating-pad cramps, go-down-to-the-school-nurse-and-lie-on-the-cot cramps. But unlike any pain I had ever suffered, I adored the pain of cramps, welcomed it, wallowed in it, bragged about it. "I can't go. I have cramps." "I can't do that. I have cramps." And most of all, gigglingly, blushingly: "I can't swim. I have cramps." Nobody ever used the hard-core word. Menstruation. God, what an awful word. Never that. "I have cramps."

The morning I first got my period, I went into my mother's bedroom to tell her. And my mother, my utterly-hateful-about-bras mother, burst into tears. It was really a lovely moment, and I remember it so clearly not just because it was one of the two times I ever saw my mother cry on my account (the other was when I was caught being a six-year-old kleptomaniac), but also because the incident did not mean to me what it meant to her. Her little girl, her firstborn, had finally become a woman. That was what she was crying about. My reaction to the event, however, was that I might well be a woman in some scientific, textbook sense (and could at least stop faking every month and stop wasting all those nickels). But in another sense—in a visible sense—I was as androgynous and as liable to tip over into boyhood as ever.

I started with a 28 AA bra. I don't think they made them any smaller in those days, although I gather that now you can buy bras for five-year-olds that don't have any cups whatsoever in them; trainer bras they are called. My first brassiere came from Robinson's Department Store in Beverly Hills. I went there alone, shaking, positive they would look me over and smile and tell me to come back next year. An actual fitter took me into the dressing room and stood over me while I took off my blouse and tried the first one on. The little puffs stood out on my chest. "Lean over," said the fitter. (To this day, I am not sure what fitters in bra departments do except to tell you to lean over.) I leaned over, with the fleeting hope that my breasts would miraculously fall out of my body and into the puffs. Nothing.

"Don't worry about it," said my friend Libby some months later, when things had not improved. "You'll get them after you're married."

"What are you talking about?" I said.

"When you get married," Libby explained, "your husband will touch your breasts and rub them and kiss them and they'll grow."

That was the killer. Necking I could deal with. Intercourse I could deal with. But it had never crossed my mind that a man was going to touch my breasts, that breasts had something to do with all that, petting, my God, they never mentioned petting in my little sex manual about the fertilization of the ovum. I became dizzy. For I knew instantly—as naïve as I had been only a moment before—that only part of what she was saying was true: the touching, rubbing, kissing part, not the growing part. And I knew that no one would ever want to marry me. I had no breasts. I would never have breasts.

My best friend in school was Diana Raskob. She lived a block from   10 me in a house full of wonders. English muffins, for instance. The Raskobs were the first people in Beverly Hills to have English muffins for breakfast. They also had an apricot tree in the back, and a badminton court, and a subscription to *Seventeen* magazine, and hundreds of games, like Sorry and Parcheesi and Treasure Hunt and Anagrams. Diana and I spent three or four afternoons a week in their den reading and playing and eating. Diana's mother's kitchen was full of the most colossal assortment of junk food I have ever been exposed to. My house was full of apples and peaches and milk and homemade chocolate-chip cookies— which were nice, and good for you, but-not-right-before-dinner-or-you'll-spoil-your-appetite. Diana's house had nothing in it that was good for you, and what's more, you could stuff it in right up until dinner and nobody cared. Bar-B-Q potato chips (they were the first in them, too), giant bottles of ginger ale, fresh popcorn with melted butter, hot fudge sauce on Baskin-Robbins jamoca ice cream, powdered-sugar doughnuts from Van de Kamp's. Diana and I had been best friends since we were seven; we were about equally popular in school (which is to say, not particularly), we had about the same success with boys (extremely intermittent), and we looked pretty much the same. Dark. Tall. Gangly.

It is September, just before school begins. I am eleven years old, about to enter the seventh grade, and Diana and I have not seen each other all summer. I have been to camp and she has been somewhere like Banff with her parents. We are meeting, as we often do, on the street midway between our two houses, and we will walk back to Diana's and eat junk and talk about what has happened to each of us that summer. I am walking down Walden Drive in my jeans and my father's shirt hanging out and my old red loafers with the socks falling into them and coming toward me is . . . I take a deep breath . . . a young woman. Diana. Her hair is curled and she has a waist and hips and a bust and she is wearing a straight skirt, an article of clothing I have been repeatedly told I will be unable to wear until I have the hips to hold it up. My jaw drops, and suddenly I am crying, crying hysterically, can't catch my breath sobbing. My best friend has betrayed me. She has gone ahead without me and done it. She has shaped up.

Here are some things I did to help:
Bought a Mark Eden Bust Developer.
Slept on my back for four years.
Splashed cold water on them every night because some French   15
actress said in *Life* magazine that was what *she* did for her perfect bustline.
Ultimately, I resigned myself to a bad toss and began to wear padded bras. I think about them now, think about all those years in high school and I went around in them, my three padded bras, every single one of them with different-sized breasts. Each time I changed bras I changed sizes: one week nice perky but not too obtrusive breasts, the next medium-sized slightly pointy ones, the next week knockers, true knockers; all the time, whatever size I was, carrying around this rubber-ized appendage on my chest that occasionally crashed into a wall and was poked inward and had to be poked outward—I think about all that and wonder how anyone kept a straight face through it. My parents, who normally had no restraints about needling me—why did they say nothing as they watched my chest go up and down? My friends, who would periodically inspect my breasts for signs of growth and reassure me—why didn't they at least counsel consistency?
And the bathing suits. I die when I think about the bathing suits. That was the era when you could lay an uninhabited bathing suit on the beach and someone would make a pass at it. I would put one on, an absurd swimsuit with its enormous bust built into it, the bones from the suit stabbing me in the rib cage and leaving little red welts on my body, and there I would be, my chest plunging straight downward ab-solutely vertically from my collarbone to the top of my suit and then suddenly, wham, out came all that padding and material and wiring absolutely horizontally.
Buster Klepper was the first boy who ever touched them. He was

my boyfriend my senior year of high school. There is a picture of him in my high-school yearbook that makes him look quite attractive in a Jewish, horn-rimmed–glasses sort of way, but the picture does not show the pimples, which were air-brushed out, or the dumbness. Well, that isn't really fair. He wasn't dumb. He just wasn't terribly bright. His mother refused to accept it, refused to accept the relentlessly average report cards, refused to deal with her son's inevitable destiny in some junior college or other. "He was tested," she would say to me, apropos of nothing, "and it came out a hundred and forty-five. That's near-genius." Had the word "underachiever" been coined, she probably would have lobbed that one at me, too. Anyway, Buster was really very sweet—which is, I know, damning with faint praise, but there it is. I was the editor of the front page of the high-school newspaper and he was editor of the back page; we had to work together, side by side, in the print shop, and that was how it started. On our first date, we went to see *April Love,* starring Pat Boone. Then we started going together. Buster had a green coupe, a 1950 Ford with an engine he had hand-chromed until it shone, dazzled, reflected the image of anyone who looked into it, anyone usually being Buster polishing it or the gas-station attendants he constantly asked to check the oil in order for them to be overwhelmed by the sparkle on the valves. The car also had a boot stretched over the back seat for reasons I never understood; hanging from the rearview mirror, as was the custom, was a pair of angora dice. A previous girlfriend named Solange, who was famous throughout Beverly Hills High School for having no pigment in her right eyebrow, had knitted them for him. Buster and I would ride around town, the two of us seated to the left of the steering wheel. I would shift gears. It was nice.

There was necking. Terrific necking. First in the car, overlooking Los Angeles from what is now the Trousdale Estates. Then on the bed of his parents' cabana at Ocean House. Incredibly wonderful, frustrating necking, I loved it, really, but no further than necking, please don't, please, because there I was absolutely terrified of the general implications of going-a-step-further with a near-dummy and also terrified of his finding out there was next to nothing there (which he knew, of course; he wasn't that dumb).

I broke up with him at one point. I think we were apart for about two weeks. At the end of that time, I drove down to see a friend at a boarding school in Palos Verdes Estates and a disc jockey played "April Love" on the radio four times during the trip. I took it as a sign. I drove straight back to Griffith Park to a golf tournament Buster was playing in (he was the sixth-seeded teenage golf player in southern California) and presented myself back to him on the green of the eighteenth hole. It was all very dramatic. That night we went to a drive-in and I let him get his hand under my protuberances and onto my breasts. He really didn't seem to mind at all.

20

"Do you want to marry my son?" the woman asked me.

"Yes," I said.

I was nineteen years old, a virgin, going with this woman's son, this big strange woman who was married to a Lutheran minister in New Hampshire and pretended she was gentile and had this son, by her first husband, this total fool of a son who ran the hero-sandwich concession at Harvard Business School and whom for one moment one December in New Hampshire I said—as much out of politeness as anything else—that I wanted to marry.

"Fine," she said. "Now, here's what you do. Always make sure you're on top of him so you won't seem so small. My bust is very large, you see, so I always lie on my back to make it look smaller, but you'll have to be on top most of the time."

I nodded. "Thank you," I said.

"I have a book for you to read," she went on. "Take it with you when you leave. Keep it." She went to the bookshelf, found it, and gave it to me. It was a book on frigidity.

"Thank you," I said.

That is a true story. Everything in this article is a true story, but I feel I have to point out that that story in particular is true. It happened on December 30, 1960. I think about it often. When it first happened, I naturally assumed that the woman's son, my boyfriend, was responsible. I invented a scenario where he had had a little heart-to-heart with his mother and had confessed that his only objection to me was that my breasts were small; his mother then took it upon herself to help out. Now I think I was wrong about the incident. The mother was acting on her own, I think: That was her way of being cruel and competitive under the guise of being helpful and maternal. You have small breasts, she was saying; therefore you will never make him as happy as I have. Or you have small breasts; therefore you will doubtless have sexual problems. Or you have small breasts; therefore you are less woman than I am. She was, as it happens, only the first of what seems to me to be a never-ending string of women who have made competitive remarks to me about breast size. "I would love to wear a dress like that," my friend Emily says to me, "but my bust is too big." Like that. Why do women say these things to me? Do I attract these remarks the way other women attract married men or alcoholics or homosexuals? This summer, for example. I am at a party in East Hampton and I am introduced to a woman from Washington. She is a minor celebrity, very pretty and Southern and blond and outspoken, and I am flattered because she has read something I have written. We are talking animatedly, we have been talking no more than five minutes, when a man comes up to join us. "Look at the two of us," the woman says to the man, indicating me and her. "The two of us together couldn't fill an A cup." Why does she say that? It isn't even true, dammit, so why? Is she even more addled than I am on this subject? Does she honestly believe there is something wrong with her size breasts, which, it seems to me, now that I look hard at them, are just right? Do I unconsciously bring out competitiveness in women? In that form? What did I do to deserve it?

As for men.

There were men who minded and let me know that they minded. There were men who did not mind. In any case, *I* always minded.

And even now, now that I have been countlessly reassured that my figure is a good one, now that I am grown-up enough to understand that most of my feelings have very little to do with the reality of my shape, I am nonetheless obsessed by breasts. I cannot help it. I grew up in the terrible fifties—with rigid stereotypical sex roles, the insistence that men be men and dress like men and women be women and dress like women, the intolerance of androgyny—and I cannot shake it, cannot shake my feelings of inadequacy. Well, that time is gone, right? All those exaggerated examples of breast worship are gone, right? Those women were freaks, right? I know all that. And yet here I am, stuck with the psychological remains of it all, stuck with my own peculiar version of breast worship. You probably think I am crazy to go on like this: Here I have set out to write a confession that is meant to hit you with the shock of recognition, and instead you are sitting there thinking I am thoroughly warped. Well, what can I tell you? If I had had them, I would have been a completely different person. I honestly believe that.

After I went into therapy, a process that made it possible for me to   *25* tell total strangers at cocktail parties that breasts were the hang-up of my life, I was often told that I was insane to have been bothered by my condition. I was also frequently told, by close friends, that I was extremely boring on the subject. And my girlfriends, the ones with nice big breasts, would go on endlessly about how their lives had been far more miserable than mine. Their bra straps were snapped in class. They couldn't sleep on their stomachs. They were stared at whenever the word "mountain" cropped up in geography. And *Evangeline,* good God what they went through every time someone had to stand up and recite the Prologue to Longfellow's *Evangeline:* ". . . stand like druids of eld . . . / With beards that rest on their bosoms." It was much worse for them, they tell me. They had a terrible time of it, they assure me. I don't know how lucky I was, they say.

I have thought about their remarks, tried to put myself in their place, considered their point of view. I think they are full of shit.

📖 *Outward Exploration: Discussion*

1. Why does Ephron start her essay talking about androgyny instead of talking about breasts, the topic announced in her title?

2. Explore reasons why Ephron's mother was "really hateful about bras" (paragraph 2).

3. How does Ephron convince us of the differences between her home and Diana Raskob's in paragraph 10?

4. What effect is Ephron trying to achieve by switching to present tense in paragraph 11?

5. Based on this essay, what do you think Ephron's attitude toward mothers in general is? Why do you think so?

6. Why does Ephron spend so little time talking directly about men's attitude toward her breast size?

7. What is the overall tone of this essay? Are there places where that tone varies? Why? What is the tone of the last sentence?

8. What is the effect of Ephron's directly addressing us readers in paragraph 24?

9. What is the ultimate effect of paragraphs 25 and 26 on you? Are you left thinking that Ephron is right and her big-breasted girlfriends are wrong? Or that Ephron is wrong? Or some other idea? Why?

❑ *Outward Exploration: Writing*

1. Write a personal response to Ephron's essay. You might agree with her major points (in which case you will use your personal experiences to provide further documentation of her claims); you might disagree with her major points (in which case you will use your personal experiences as counterexamples); you might say "yes, but . . ." (in which case you will qualify some of her points, using your personal experiences as evidence).

2. Write an essay about self-image, using your own self-image as evidence. Investigate and explore the sources of your self-image and of society's "preferred images" as well.

3. Ephron grew up in the early 1950s, a time notorious for sexual stereotyping. Perhaps your childhood put less (or more) emphasis on not being androgynous, on being male or being female in very prescribed ways. Write an essay exploring the forces pushing you toward your gender identity. Feel free to make overt comparisons and contrasts with Ephron's childhood and with any other childhoods from other eras.

4. If you had a friend like Diana Raskob (paragraph 10) whose house and parental attitudes were very different from yours, write an essay exploring those differences and their sources, remembering to focus primarily on your home and your parents' attitudes and the ultimate impact they had on you as you grew up.

❑ *Style*

Consider the following fragment from Ephron's essay:

Agonizing cramps, heating-pad cramps, go-down-to-the-school-nurse-and-lie-on-the-cot cramps. (paragraph 3)

The structure of the fragment is as follows:

adjective ("agonizing")

noun ("cramps")

comma

two-word hyphenated adjective ("heating-pad")

repeated noun ("cramps")

comma

12-word hyphenated adjective ("go-down-to-the-school-nurse-and-lie-on-the-cot")

repeated noun ("cramps")

period.

Three aspects are particularly worthy of note here. First, notice the increasing length of the adjectives—the longer the string of hyphenated words, the more effect it seems to have. Second, notice the repetition of the word *cramps,* which drills it into the reader's mind. Third, lists tend to build to the most important element, which comes last. Here, Ephron shows us that, contrary to what we might suppose, the physical agony is not as important as the fact that she could legitimately go to the nurse's office and lie down. Thus the order of the list reinforces what she has been saying throughout the first part of the essay—namely, the appearance of having "womanly traits" was still more important to her (even after she legitimately had them and didn't have to fake anymore) than the pain.

Try to replicate this structure using your own information. Emphasize one key noun by repeating it three times as Ephron does. Make the list build to the most important aspect of that noun. Give the first noun one adjective, the second noun a hyphenated two- or three-word string, and the final noun at least a four-word hyphenated adjective string (you don't need a 12-word hyphenated adjective string, simply a longer string than the previous one).

On Being a Cripple

NANCY MAIRS

☐ *Inward Exploration*

Write at least one paragraph about whether or not it makes a difference what terms we use to describe a person or thing. Write at least one other paragraph on what the word cripple *suggests to you.*

To escape is nothing. Not to escape is nothing.

—LOUISE BOGAN

The other day I was thinking of writing an essay on being a cripple. I was thinking hard in one of the stalls of the women's room in my office building, as I was shoving my shirt into my jeans and tugging up my zipper. Preoccupied, I flushed, picked up my book bag, took my cane down from the hook, and unlatched the door. So many movements unbalanced me, and as I pulled the door open I fell over backward, landing fully clothed on the toilet seat with my legs splayed in front of me: the old beetle-on-its-back routine. Saturday afternoon, the building deserted, I was free to laugh aloud as I wriggled back to my feet, my voice bouncing off the yellowish tiles from all directions. Had anyone been there with me, I'd have been still and faint and hot with chagrin. I decided that it was high time to write the essay.

First, the matter of semantics. I am a cripple. I choose this word to name me. I choose from among several possibilities, the most common of which are "handicapped" and "disabled." I made the choice a number of years ago, without thinking, unaware of my motives for doing so. Even now, I'm not sure what those motives are, but I recognize that they are complex and not entirely flattering. People—crippled or not—wince at the word "cripple," as they do not at "handicapped" or "disabled." Perhaps I want them to wince. I want them to see me as a tough customer, one to whom the fates/gods/viruses have not been kind, but who can face the brutal truth of her existence squarely. As a cripple, I swagger.

But, to be fair to myself, a certain amount of honesty underlies my choice. "Cripple" seems to me a clean word, straightforward and precise. It has an honorable history, having made its first appearance in the Lindisfarne Gospel in the tenth century. As a lover of words, I like the accuracy with which it describes my condition: I have lost the full use of my limbs. "Disabled," by contrast, suggests any incapacity, physical

1

or mental. And I certainly don't like "handicapped," which implies that I have deliberately been put at a disadvantage, by whom I can't imagine (my God is not a Handicapper General), in order to equalize chances in the great race of life. These words seem to me to be moving away from my condition, to be widening the gap between word and reality. Most remote is the recently coined euphemism "differently abled," which partakes of the same semantic hopefulness that transformed countries from "undeveloped" to "underdeveloped," then to "less developed," and finally to "developing" nations. People have continued to starve in those countries during the shift. Some realities do not obey the dictates of language.

Mine is one of them. Whatever you call me, I remain crippled. But I don't care what you call me, so long as it isn't "differently abled," which strikes me as pure verbal garbage designed, by its ability to describe anyone, to describe no one. I subscribe to George Orwell's thesis that "the slovenliness of our language makes it easier for us to have foolish thoughts." And I refuse to participate in the degeneration of the language to the extent that I deny that I have lost anything in the course of this calamitous disease; I refuse to pretend that the only differences between you and me are the various ordinary ones that distinguish any one person from another. But call me "disabled" or "handicapped" if you like. I have long since grown accustomed to them; and if they are vague, at least they hint at the truth. Moreover, I use them myself. Society is no readier to accept crippledness than to accept death, war, sex, sweat, or wrinkles. I would never refer to another person as a cripple. It is the word I use to name only myself.

I haven't always been crippled, a fact for which I am soundly grateful. To be whole of limb is, I know from experience, infinitely more pleasant and useful than to be crippled; and if that knowledge leaves me open to bitterness at my loss, the physical soundness I once enjoyed (though I did not enjoy it half enough) is well worth the occasional stab of regret. Though never any good at sports, I was a normally active child and young adult. I climbed trees, played hopscotch, jumped rope, skated, swam, rode my bicycle, sailed. I despised team sports, spending some of the wretchedest afternoons of my life, sweaty and humiliated, behind a field-hockey stick and under a basketball hoop. I tramped alone for miles along the bridle paths that webbed the woods behind the house I grew up in. I swayed through countless dim hours in the arms of one man or another under the scattered shot of light from mirrored balls, and gyrated through countless more as Tab Hunter and Johnny Mathis gave way to the Rolling Stones, Creedence Clearwater Revival, Cream. I walked down the aisle. I pushed baby carriages, changed tires in the rain, marched for peace.

When I was twenty-eight I started to trip and drop things. What at first seemed my natural clumsiness soon became too pronounced to

5

shrug off. I consulted a neurologist, who told me that I had a brain tumor. A battery of tests, increasingly disagreeable, revealed no tumor. About a year and a half later I developed a blurred spot in one eye. I had, at last, the episodes "disseminated in space and time" requisite for a diagnosis: multiple sclerosis. I have never been sorry for the doctor's initial misdiagnosis, however. For almost a week, until the negative results of the tests were in, I thought that I was going to die right away. Every day for the past nearly ten years, then, has been a kind of gift. I accept all gifts.

Multiple sclerosis is a chronic degenerative disease of the central nervous system, in which the myelin that sheathes the nerves is somehow eaten away and scar tissue forms in its place, interrupting the nerves' signals. During its course, which is unpredictable and uncontrollable, one may lose vision, hearing, speech, the ability to walk, control of bladder and/or bowels, strength in any or all extremities, sensitivity to touch, vibration, and/or pain, potency, coordination of movements—the list of possibilities is lengthy and, yes, horrifying. One may also lose one's sense of humor. That's the easiest to lose and the hardest to survive without.

In the past ten years, I have sustained some of these losses. Characteristic of MS are sudden attacks, called exacerbations, followed by remissions, and these I have not had. Instead, my disease has been slowly progressive. My left leg is now so weak that I walk with the aid of a brace and a cane; and for distances I use an Amigo, a variation on the electric wheelchair that looks rather like an electrified kiddie car. I no longer have much use of my left hand. Now my right side is weakening as well. I still have the blurred spot in my right eye. Overall, though, I've been lucky so far. My world has, of necessity, been circumscribed by my losses, but the terrain left me has been ample enough for me to continue many of the activities that absorb me: writing, teaching, raising children and cats and plants and snakes, reading, speaking publicly about MS and depression, even playing bridge with people patient and honorable enough to let me scatter cards every which way without sneaking a peek.

Lest I begin to sound like Pollyanna, however, let me say that I don't like having MS. I hate it. My life holds realities—harsh ones, some of them—that no right-minded human being ought to accept without grumbling. One of them is fatigue. I know of no one with MS who does not complain of bone-weariness; in a disease that presents an astonishing variety of symptoms, fatigue seems to be a common factor. I wake up in the morning feeling the way most people do at the end of a bad day, and I take it from there. As a result, I spend a lot of time *in extremis* and, impatient with limitation, I tend to ignore my fatigue until my body breaks down in some way and forces rest. Then I miss picnics, dinner parties, poetry readings, the brief visits of old friends from out of town. The offspring of a puritanical tradition of exceptional venerability, I cannot view these lapses without shame. My life often seems a series of small failures to do as I ought.

I lead, on the whole, an ordinary life, probably rather like the one   *10* I would have led had I not had MS. I am lucky that my predilections were already solitary, sedentary, and bookish—unlike the world-famous French cellist I have read about, or the young woman I talked with one long afternoon who wanted only to be a jockey. I had just begun graduate school when I found out something was wrong with me, and I have remained, interminably, a graduate student. Perhaps I would not have if I'd thought I had the stamina to return to a full-time job as a technical editor; but I've enjoyed my studies.

In addition to studying, I teach writing courses. I also teach medical students how to give neurological examinations. I pick up freelance editing jobs here and there. I have raised a foster son and sent him into the world, where he has made me two grandbabies, and I am still escorting my daughter and son through adolescence. I go to Mass every Saturday. I am a superb, if messy, cook. I am also an enthusiastic laundress, capable of sorting a hamper full of clothes into five subtly differentiated piles, but a terrible housekeeper. I can do italic writing and, in an emergency, bathe an oil-soaked cat. I play a fiendish game of Scrabble. When I have the time and the money, I like to sit on my front steps with my husband, drinking Amaretto and smoking a cigar, as we imagine our counterparts in Leningrad and make sure that the sun gets down once more behind the sharp childish scrawl of the Tucson Mountains.

This lively plenty has its bleak complement, of course, in all the things I can no longer do. I will never run again, except in dreams, and one day I may have to write that I will never walk again. I like to go camping, but I can't follow George and the children along the trails that wander out of a campsite through the desert or into the mountains. In fact, even on the level I've learned never to check the weather or try to hold a coherent conversation: I need all my attention for my wayward feet. Of late, I have begun to catch myself wondering how people can propel themselves without canes. With only one usable hand, I have to select my clothing with care not so much for style as for ease of ingress and egress, and even so, dressing can be laborious. I can no longer do fine stitchery, pick up babies, play the piano, braid my hair. I am immobilized by acute attacks of depression, which may or may not be physiologically related to MS but are certainly its logical concomitant.

These two elements, the plenty and the privation, are never pure, nor are the delight and wretchedness that accompany them. Almost every pickle that I get into as a result of my weakness and clumsiness—and I get into plenty—is funny as well as maddening and sometimes painful. I recall one May afternoon when a friend and I were going out for a drink after finishing up at school. As we were climbing into opposite sides of my car, chatting, I tripped and fell, flat and hard, onto the asphalt parking lot, my abrupt departure interrupting him in mid-sentence. "Where'd you go?" he called as he came around the back of the car to find me hauling myself up by the door frame. "Are you all right?" Yes, I told him, I was fine, just a bit rattly, and we drove off to find a shady patio and some beer. When I got home an hour or so later, my daughter greeted me with "What have you done to yourself?" I looked down. One elbow of my white turtleneck with the green froggies, one knee of my white trousers, one white kneesock were blood-soaked. We peeled off the clothes and inspected the damage, which was nasty enough but not alarming. That part wasn't funny: The abrasions took a long time to heal, and one got a little infected. Even so, when I think of my friend talking earnestly, suddenly, to the hot thin air while I dropped from his view as though through a trap door, I find the image as silly as something from a Marx Brothers movie.

I may find it easier than other cripples to amuse myself because I live propped by the acceptance and the assistance and, sometimes, the amusement of those around me. Grocery clerks tear my checks out of my checkbook for me, and sales clerks find chairs to put into dressing rooms when I want to try on clothes. The people I work with make sure I teach at times when I am least likely to be fatigued, in places I can get to, with the materials I need. My students, with one anonymous exception (in an end-of-the-semester evaluation), have been unperturbed by my disability. Some even like it. One was immensely cheered by the information that I paint my own fingernails; she decided, she told me, that if I could go to such trouble over fine details, she could keep on writing essays. I suppose I became some sort of bright-fingered muse. She wrote good essays, too.

The most important struts in the framework of my existence, of course, are my husband and children. Dismayingly few marriages survive the MS test, and why should they? Most twenty-two- and nineteen-year-olds, like George and me, can vow in clear conscience, after a childhood of chicken pox and summer colds, to keep one another in sickness and in health so long as they both shall live. Not many are equipped for catastrophe: the dismay, the depression, the extra work, the boredom that a degenerative disease can insinuate into a relationship. And our society, with its emphasis on fun and its association of fun with physical performance, offers little encouragement for a whole spouse to stay with a crippled partner. Children experience similar stresses when faced with a crippled parent, and they are more helpless, since parents and children can't usually get divorced. They hate, of course, to be different from their peers, and the child whose mother is tacking down the aisle of a school auditorium packed with proud parents like a Cape Cod dinghy in a stiff breeze jolly well stands out in a crowd. Deprived of legal divorce, the child can at least deny the mother's disability, even her

15

existence, forgetting to tell her about recitals and PTA meetings, refusing to accompany her to stores or church or the movies, never inviting friends to the house. Many do.

But I've been limping along for ten years now, and so far George and the children are still at my left elbow, holding tight. Anne and Matthew vacuum floors and dust furniture and haul trash and rake up dog droppings and button my cuffs and bake lasagna and Toll House cookies with just enough grumbling so I know that they don't have brain fever. And far from hiding me, they're forever dragging me by racks of fancy clothes or through teeming school corridors, or welcoming gaggles of friends while I'm wandering through the house in Anne's filmy pink babydoll pajamas. George generally calls before he brings someone home, but he does just as many dumb thankless chores as the children. And they all yell at me, laugh at some of my jokes, write me funny letters when we're apart—in short, treat me as an ordinary human being for whom they have some use. I think they like me. Unless they're faking. . . .

Faking. There's the rub. Tugging at the fringes of my consciousness always is the terror that people are kind to me only because I'm a cripple. My mother almost shattered me once, with that instinct mothers have—blind, I think, in this case, but unerring nonetheless—for striking blows along the fault-lines of their children's hearts, by telling me, in an attack on my selfishness, "We all have to make allowances for you, of course, because of the way you are." From the distance of a couple of years, I have to admit that I haven't any idea just what she meant, and I'm not sure that she knew either. She was awfully angry. But at the time, as the words thudded home, I felt my worst fear, suddenly realized. I could bear being called selfish: I am. But I couldn't bear the corroboration that those around me were doing in fact what I'd always suspected them of doing, professing fondness while silently putting up with me because of the way I am. A cripple. I've been a little cracked ever since.

Along with this fear that people are secretly accepting shoddy goods comes a relentless pressure to please—to prove myself worth the burdens I impose, I guess, or to build a substantial account of good will against which I may write drafts in times of need. Part of the pressure arises from social expectations. In our society, anyone who deviates from the norm had better find some way to compensate. Like fat people, who are expected to be jolly, cripples must bear their lot meekly and cheerfully. A grumpy cripple isn't playing by the rules. And much of the pressure is self-generated. Early on I vowed that, if I had to have MS, by God I was going to do it well. This is a class act, ladies and gentlemen. No tears, no recriminations, no faint-heartedness.

One way and another, then, I wind up feeling like Tiny Tim, peering over the edge of the table at the Christmas goose, waving my crutch, piping down God's blessing on us all. Only sometimes I don't want to play Tiny Tim. I'd rather be Caliban, a most scurvy monster. Fortunately, at home no one much cares whether I'm a good cripple or a bad cripple as long as I make vichyssoise with fair regularity. One evening several years ago, Anne was reading at the dining-room table while I cooked dinner. As I opened a can of tomatoes, the can slipped in my left hand and juice spattered me and the counter with bloody spots. Fatigued and infuriated, I bellowed, "I'm so sick of being crippled!" Anne glanced at me over the top of her book. "There now," she said, "do you feel better?" "Yes," I said, "yes, I do." She went back to her reading. I felt better. That's about all the attention my scurviness ever gets.

Because I hate being crippled, I sometimes hate myself for being a *20* cripple. Over the years I have come to expect—even accept—attacks of violent self-loathing. Luckily, in general our society no longer connects deformity and disease directly with evil (though a charismatic once told me that I have MS because a devil is in me) and so I'm allowed to move largely at will, even among small children. But I'm not sure that this revision of attitude has been particularly helpful. Physical imperfection, even freed of moral disapprobation, still defies and violates the ideal, especially for women, whose confinement in their bodies as objects of desire is far from over. Each age, of course, has its ideal, and I doubt that ours is any better or worse than any other. Today's ideal woman, who lives on the glossy pages of dozens of magazines, seems to be between the ages of eighteen and twenty-five; her hair has body, her teeth flash white, her breath smells minty, her underarms are dry; she has a career but is still a fabulous cook, especially of meals that take less than twenty minutes to prepare; she does not ordinarily appear to have a husband or children; she is trim and deeply tanned; she jogs, swims, plays tennis, rides a bicycle, sails, but does not bowl; she travels widely, even to out-of-the-way places like Finland and Samoa, always in the company of the ideal man, who possesses a nearly identical set of characteristics. There are a few exceptions. Though usually white and often blond, she may be black, Hispanic, Asian, or Native American, so long as she is unusually sleek. She may be old, provided she is selling a laxative or is Lauren Bacall. If she is selling a detergent, she may be married and have a flock of strikingly messy children. But she is never a cripple.

Like many women I know, I have always had an uneasy relationship with my body. I was not a popular child, largely, I think now, because I was peculiar: intelligent, intense, moody, shy, given to unexpected actions and inexplicable notions and emotions. But as I entered adolescence, I believed myself unpopular because I was homely: my breasts too flat, my mouth too wide, my hips too narrow, my clothing never quite right in fit or style. I was not, in fact, particularly ugly, old photographs inform me, though I was well off the ideal; but I carried this sense of self-alienation with me into adulthood, where it regenerated in response to the depredations of MS. Even with my brace I walk with a limp so pronounced that, seeing myself on the videotape of a television program on the disabled, I couldn't believe that anything but an inchworm could make progress humping along like that. My shoulders droop and my pelvis thrusts forward as I try to balance myself upright, throwing my frame into a bony S. As a result of contractures, one shoulder is higher than the other and I carry one arm bent in front of me, the fingers curled into a claw. My left arm and leg have wasted into pipe-stems, and I try always to keep them covered. When I think about how my body must look to others, especially to men, to whom I have been trained to display myself, I feel ludicrous, even loathsome.

At my age, however, I don't spend much time thinking about my appearance. The burning egocentricity of adolescence, which assures one that all the world is looking all the time, has passed, thank God, and I'm generally too caught up in what I'm doing to step back, as I used to, and watch myself as though upon a stage. I'm also too old to believe in the accuracy of self-image. I know that I'm not a hideous crone, that in fact, when I'm rested, well dressed, and well made up, I look fine. The self-loathing I feel is neither physically nor intellectually substantial. What I hate is not me but a disease.

I am not a disease.

And a disease is not—at least not singlehandedly—going to determine who I am, though at first it seemed to be going to. Adjusting to a chronic incurable illness, I have moved through a process similar to that outlined by Elizabeth Kübler-Ross in *On Death and Dying*. The major difference—and it is far more significant than most people recognize— is that I can't be sure of the outcome, as the terminally ill cancer patient can. Research studies indicate that, with proper medical care, I may achieve a "normal" life span. And in our society, with its vision of death as the ultimate evil, worse even than decrepitude, the response to such news is, "Oh well, at least you're not going to *die*." Are there worse things than dying? I think that there may be.

I think of two women I know, both with MS, both enough older than I to have served me as models. One took to her bed several years ago and has been there ever since. Although she can sit in a high-backed wheelchair, because she is incontinent she refuses to go out at all, even though incontinence pants, which are readily available at any pharmacy, could protect her from embarrassment. Instead, she stays at home and insists that her husband, a small quiet man, a retired civil servant, stay there with her except for a quick weekly foray to the supermarket. The other woman, whose illness was diagnosed when she was eighteen, a nursing student engaged to a young doctor, finished her training, married her doctor, accompanied him to Germany when he was in the service, bore three sons and a daughter, now grown and gone. When she can, she travels with her husband; she plays bridge, embroiders, swims regularly; she works, like me, as a symptomatic-patient instructor of medical students in neurology. Guess which woman I hope to be.

At the beginning, I thought about having MS almost incessantly. And because of the unpredictable course of the disease, my thoughts were always terrified. Each night I'd get into bed wondering whether I'd get out again the next morning, whether I'd be able to see, to speak, to hold a pen between my fingers. Knowing that the day might come when I'd be physically incapable of killing myself, I thought perhaps I ought to do so right away, while I still had the strength. Gradually I came to understand that the Nancy who might one day lie inert under a bedsheet, arms and legs paralyzed, unable to feed or bathe herself, unable to reach out for a gun, a bottle of pills, was not the Nancy I was at present, and that I could not presume to make decisions for that future Nancy, who might well not want in the least to die. Now the only provision I've made for the future Nancy is that when the time comes—and it is likely to come in the form of pneumonia, friend to the weak and the old—I am not to be treated with machines and medications. If she is unable to communicate by then, I hope she will be satisfied with these terms.

Thinking all the time about having MS grew tiresome and intrusive, especially in the large and tragic mode in which I was accustomed to considering my plight. Months and even years went by without catastrophe (at least without one related to MS), and really I was awfully busy, what with George and children and snakes and students and poems, and I hadn't the time, let alone the inclination, to devote myself to being a disease. Too, the richer my life became, the funnier it seemed, as though there were some connection between largesse and laughter, and so my tragic stance began to waver until, even with the aid of a brace and a cane, I couldn't hold it for very long at a time.

After several years I was satisfied with my adjustment. I had suffered my grief and fury and terror, I thought, but now I was at ease with my lot. Then one summer day I set out with George and the children across the desert for a vacation in California. Part way to Yuma I became aware that my right leg felt funny. "I think I've had an exacerbation," I told George. "What shall we do?" he asked. "I think we'd better get the hell to California," I said, "because I don't know whether I'll ever make it again." So we went on to San Diego and then to Orange, up the Pacific Coast Highway to Santa Cruz, across to Yosemite, down to Sequoia and Joshua Tree, and so back over the desert to home. It was a fine two-week trip, filled with friends and fair weather, and I wouldn't have missed it for the world, though I did in fact make it back to California two years later. Nor would there have been any point in missing it, since in MS, once the symptoms have appeared, the neurological damage has been done, and there's no way to predict or prevent that damage.

The incident spoiled my self-satisfaction, however. It renewed my grief and fury and terror, and I learned that one never finishes adjusting to MS. I don't know now why I thought one would. One does not, after all, finish adjusting to life, and MS is simply a fact of my life—not my favorite fact, of course—but as ordinary as my nose and my tropical fish and my yellow Mazda station wagon. It may at any time get worse, but no amount of worry or anticipation can prepare me for a new loss. My life is a lesson in losses. I learn one at a time.

And I had best be patient in the learning, since I'll have to do it like   *30* it or not. As any rock fan knows, you can't always get what you want. Particularly when you have MS. You can't, for example, get cured. In recent years researchers and the organizations that fund research have started to pay MS some attention even though it isn't fatal; perhaps they have begun to see that life is something other than a quantitative phenomenon, that one may be very much alive for a very long time in a life that isn't worth living. The researchers have made some progress toward understanding the mechanism of the disease: It may well be an autoimmune reaction triggered by a slow-acting virus. But they are nowhere near its prevention, control, or cure. And most of us want to be cured. Some, unable to accept incurability, grasp at one treatment after another, no matter how bizarre: megavitamin therapy, gluten-free diet, injections of cobra venom, hypothermal suits, lymphocytopharesis, hyperbaric chambers. Many treatments are probably harmless enough, but none are curative.

The absence of a cure often makes MS patients bitter toward their doctors. Doctors are, after all, the priests of modern society, the new shamans, whose business is to heal, and many an MS patient roves from one to another, searching for the "good" doctor who will make him well. Doctors too think of themselves as healers, and for this reason many have trouble dealing with MS patients, whose disease in its intransigence defeats their aims and mocks their skills. Too few doctors, it is true, treat their patients as whole human beings, but the reverse is also true. I have always tried to be gentle with my doctors, who often have more at stake in terms of ego than I do. I may be frustrated, maddened, depressed by the incurability of my disease, but I am not diminished by it, and they are. When I push myself up from my seat in the waiting room and stumble toward them, I incarnate the limitation of their powers. The least I can do is refuse to press on their tenderest spots.

This gentleness is part of the reason that I'm not sorry to be a cripple. I didn't have it before. Perhaps I'd have developed it anyway— how could I know such a thing?—and I wish I had more of it, but I'm glad of what I have. It has opened and enriched my life enormously, this sense that my frailty and need must be mirrored in others, that in searching for and shaping a stable core in a life wrenched by change and loss, change and loss, I must recognize the same process, under individual conditions, in the lives around me. I do not deprecate such knowledge, however I've come by it.

All the same, if a cure were found, would I take it? In a minute. I may be a cripple, but I'm only occasionally a loony and never a saint. Anyway, in my brand of theology God doesn't give bonus points for a limp. I'd take a cure; I just don't need one. A friend who also has MS startled me once by asking, "Do you ever say to yourself, 'Why me,

Lord?'" "No, Michael, I don't," I told him, "because whenever I try, the only response I can think of is 'Why not?'" If I could make a cosmic deal, who would I put in my place? What in my life would I give up in exchange for sound limbs and a thrilling rush of energy? No one. Nothing. I might as well do the job myself. Now that I'm getting the hang of it.

☐ *Outward Exploration: Discussion*

1. In paragraph 2, Mairs says that she consciously chose to describe herself as a cripple. What words do you choose to describe yourself?
2. Explain her concept of "the plenty and the privation" (paragraph 13).
3. List some of the stylistic devices that Mairs uses in the essay.
4. According to Mairs, what is American society's ideal for women? How does she know?
5. What is the effect of the one-sentence paragraph 23?
6. How does Mairs keep you from seeing her as a saint? How do you come to see her by the end of the essay?
7. What is the overall effect of this essay?

☐ *Outward Exploration: Writing*

1. Use Mairs's concept of "the plenty and the privation" to write an essay about your own life and its limitations.
2. Most people are "crippled"—for example, they may be crippled physically, socially, psychologically, spiritually, or emotionally. If you see an example of disability in yourself, write an essay exploring that disability, its sources, its implications for your life, the attitudes it has helped develop in you.

☐ *Style*

Consider the following sentence from Mairs's essay:

Saturday afternoon, the building deserted, I was free to laugh aloud as I wriggled back to my feet, my voice bouncing off the yellowish tiles from all directions. (paragraph 1)

The structure of the sentence is as follows:

time marker ("Saturday afternoon")

comma

noun ("the building")

past participle ("deserted")

comma

sentence's subject ("I")

sentence's verb ("was")

adjective ("free")

infinitive phrase ("to laugh aloud")

dependent clause ("as . . . feet")

comma

participial phrase ("my voice . . . directions")

period.

Two things are noteworthy about this structure: First, it opens with a time marker and a statement of the prevailing conditions before we get to the subject ("I"); second, it ends with a participial phrase.

Using your own information, write a sentence that replicates this structure (in other words, it should start with a time marker and a statement of the prevailing conditions before the sentence's subject, and it should end with a participial phrase).

Introduction to *Tuxedo Junction*

Gerald Early

☐ *Inward Exploration*

Write at least one paragraph on what an essay is and what its purposes are. Write at least one additional paragraph explaining what specific tasks a book's introduction should accomplish.

But then who can ever figure anyone else out?
— Cornell Woolrich, *Night Has a Thousand Eyes*

I. Anthropology

It is a daunting matter for any writer, and especially for those who   *1*
do not write fiction (because that means they must write something
called nonfiction, which means they shall be known by a kind of negative capability), to find himself in the position of having to explain or
more precisely justify his work. I am aware that my job here may be
more on the order of descriptive rather than analytical, more a simple
act of previewing than the more comprehensive one of evaluating, and
finally akin to the sort of thing some writers of liner notes for jazz albums do, telling whether a tune is fast or slow, pretty or raucous, all
with the aplomb of a salesman selling soft and subtle. I suppose I am
attempting to set a mood for the reader, to place or perhaps ease him or
her into a state of mind suitable for what comes next. Creating moods
is dangerous, for one can hardly tell if, in the end, one has succeeded in
creating a hypnotic tamburalike drone or has simply been trying stu-
pidly to attract flies with his tongue. Of course, any description signifies
analysis on some even rudimentary level and preview does become
evaluation, just as mood-setting is a form of salesmanship: "I feel this
way sometimes. Don't you feel that way too?" It is the old snake-oil
charm that confidence men and women have used for years to fool
people, something called instant and faked intimacy. But I do wish to
give my readers pleasure, to make see, to make know, to make understand; not simply to perceive a personality behind the words but a voice
resonating both within the words and within themselves as readers. But
the pleasure of which I speak is not a desire to be liked as a *personality* or
as a *critic,* but to serve my readers as a *writer* by giving them a substan-
tiality that provokes.

Let us begin by assuming that no writer can really explain, justify, or describe a collection of his words simply by offering more of his own words. He can neither plead for his own work nor can he judge it—or at least he cannot plead for it very convincingly or judge it very well. Suffice it to say that this is not the book I really wanted to write. Like most writers, I produced the only book I *could* write when pushed up against the necessity of having to write *something,* and a writer is always pushed up against that necessity for a variety of reasons ranging from raging ambition, to feeding the kids, to a fear that he or she will never write again. I wanted to write another book altogether, not a better one but simply one that would have been, to use Gertrude Stein's phrase, "older and different." I think writers might always be wishing that their present or latest work were older and different. When I was younger and was told, quite to my misfortune, that I could do such a thing, I wanted to write novels. After fifteen years of various efforts at long, short, and medium novels, I discovered that I cannot write novels or even fiction. When one is young, novel-writing is always the dream because all one does is novel-reading and the novel, to the youthful mind, seems a perfect author-centered or author-ized literary work. (As a boy I thought of novels, quite incorrectly, as the only kind of literature, aside from "classics," that people read because of who wrote them rather than for what they say.) It does not matter that I lost time wishing that I could write novels and that I could have written this book when I was younger. In truth, I could not have done so. Like many, I have tried to learn from a kind of negative realization, from understanding what I could not do so that I might better understand what I could do. (As a boy I used to think that if I dropped a quarter on a sidewalk on a very hot summer day it would shrink, raisinlike, into a penny. And now I believe that if thick novels lie fallow they become longish essays.) Writing essays, for me, is not simply a realization of being *unable* to write fiction, it is a clear acknowledgment of being *able* to do something else. Negative capability is essentially an enabling function meant to generate a kind of myth of accomplishment through irony.

I understand this book to be one very long essay made up of essays that are made up of parts that might rightly be called chapters, recitations, or movements—not an anthology, not the best of Gerald Early (a phrase that is meant to be as parodic as it sounds.) Which isn't to say this book is not a fabrication—conventional, certainly, in that it tends, in its parts, to signify a total intelligibility that others might call accessibility or transparency. The book is a fabrication about the mythology of making fabrications.

The essays that make up this volume, pieces written over the last eight years, from 1981 to 1989 (the earliest essay being "Hot Spicks Versus Cool Spades: Three Notes Toward a Cultural Definition of Prizefighting," and the latest, "Jesse Jackson's Black Bottom, or, Crossing the Roads at Tuxedo Junction"), are meant to speak for themselves quite plainly in the expression of their purpose and meaning. And their thematic relatedness, the essence of their fabricating possibilities, lies in the insistent strain of speaking about African-American culture within the wider contexts of both American intellectual/high-brow culture and American popular culture—that should be obvious. (Incidentally, I might add that these essays discuss the reverse proposition: namely, American culture within the wider context of African-American culture.) Little can be said about blacks in this country, their role, their impact, their myth, their drama, without talking at some great length about popular culture, the great basin (or sink, if you will) that exists to commodify and absorb the marginal in American society. (The cultural margins, we Americans have discovered, are fine sources to reinvent and reinvigorate the language; they also provide the necessary background noise for people to buy booze, sex, and a number of other things.) Indeed, it is far from being an overstatement to assert that large components that comprise American popular and youth cultures are to a great extent the inventions of blacks. But there is more to say about the book than merely that.

In illustrating a point, I am reminded of how Frederick Douglass in   5
his second autobiography, 1855's *My Bondage and My Freedom,* described the plantation as "a little nation of its own, having its own language, its own rules, regulations, and customs." In effect, in describing and analyzing where he grew up, the various prison-houses of language and myth—indeed, not a prison-house culture but the prison-house *of* culture—Douglass became something of an anthropologist, the standard field ethnographer (who better for such a job than a *field* hand). Any decent black essayist, and Douglass was often as essayistic as fictional in his autobiography (indeed, I posit that the peculiarly black literary form of the essay grew from Douglass's autobiographies and from black autobiography generally, although it is certainly related to the black sermonic tradition as Martin Luther King's "Letter from a Birmingham Jail" and Baldwin's *The Fire Next Time,* two of the famous black essays of the last thirty years, attest), is not, in effect, literary, or trying to be literary merely, but is trying quite self-consciously to be anthropological. He (or she, as the case may be) cannot help but be anthropological, as there can be no mistaking that for the African-Americans, the place where they live never ceases to be a prison-house of culture (not necessarily a bad prison as prisons go, and sometimes confinement can be strengthening), and in prison one is forced constantly to think about writing as theater. All black essayists, ultimately, with either resolution or resignation, write, as Douglass stated he did, "from sound." It is through sound, uncertain though it may be, that the anthropologist understands his work. The essays in this volume are filled with sound. They talk of little else. They try to replicate nothing so much as the sound of other things, of language bouncing off the prison-house walls. But, for the black essayist, sound must always try to be subversion, the

slave's language is always undermining the master's tongue even as it imperfectly replicates it, even as it aspires to be the master's tongue. The perfect image of the black writer is Jim trapped in his prison that is not really a prison in the last chapters of Mark Twain's novel while Huck and Tom cover the walls with language and invent signs for Jim's white captors, all of which has no meaning except that the language and signs refer to novels, romances, literary conventions—that verisimilitude, in this instance and perhaps in all instances, is not a term describing how art is related to life but how life is related to books (and artistic vision), which are, in effect, more real than life. Nothing is more real than our fantasies, Twain's novel tells us. Jim, through his displays of common sense, rebels against being an instrumentality of white consciousness while succumbing to it for lack of anything better to do. I hope this singular dilemma becomes clearer as I go along. But how can one distinguish, in the case of Jim, for instance, subversion from simulation in this vastness of verisimilitude?

Consider how Douglass, in *My Bondage and My Freedom,* appropriates the terms "Nature" and "Nurture" from mid-1850s American pop-scientific, anthropological discourse and uses them to illustrate the slave's humanity, in direct opposition to their contemporary use in the hermeneutical language of the nineteenth-century white intellectual as absences of both a civilizing environment and proper genetic properties (ah, the slave, being property in a world where property was the touchstone of reality, was completely without property, and so was not only completely unreal himself but was forced to see the world as unreality). Douglass achieves this without ever using the words themselves but by appropriating the cultural symbol that compresses and decomposes both terms: mother. Douglass tells two elaborate stories of his mother, who was largely absent from his life: first, how she rescued him from a cruel black "Auntie" and gave him bread, and second, how his literary turn of mind was directly inherited from his maternal (black) side (Douglass always believed his father to be white). So, with Douglass, the absent mother (not "Mammy" or "Auntie," that lover and rearer of white sons and daughters and beloved of them) becomes the presence that repudiates the cultural absences that have been assigned the black. There is a lesson in that bit of fabrication by Douglass (literal fabrication because he could not possibly have remembered the bread incident and how does anyone know, in most instances, which source of genes produced what talents, especially in the case of someone who did not know his father as Douglass did not); a lesson that would stand any black essayist in good stead about playing with language in the prison-house of culture. For Douglass, after all, bread, the staff of life, becomes both nature and nurture and, in effect, Douglass proves the two terms are essentially interchangeable and absolutely meaningless as they both signify "mother," and everyone has one of those, as Douglass demonstrates—you can make of her whatever you wish.

But in the matters of anthropology and language on and reverber-
ating within the prison-house walls no black writer can be more instructive than Zora Neale Hurston, a trained anthropologist/ethnographer in
her own right and a novelist of some distinction. In her 1942 autobiography, *Dust Tracks on a Road,* a marvelously and shrewdly fabricated
book, she tells of three successive incidents concerning language that
occur when she joins a white theater company as a teenager:

> In the first place, I was a Southerner, and had the map of Dixie
> on my tongue. They [the theater company] were all Northerners
> except the orchestra leader, who came from Pensacola. It was
> not that my grammar was bad, it was the idioms. They did not
> know of the way an average Southern child, white or black, is
> raised on simile and invective. They know how to call names. It
> is an everyday affair to hear somebody called a mullet-headed,
> mule-eared, wall-eyed, hog-nosed, 'gator-faced, shad-mouthed,
> screw-necked, goat-bellied, puzzle-gutted, camel-backed, butt-
> sprung, battle-hammed, knocked-kneed, razor-legged, box-
> ankled, shovel-footed, unmated so-and-so! . . . Since that stratum
> of the Southern population is not given to book-reading, they
> take their comparisons right out of the barnyard and the woods.
> When they get through with you, you and your whole family
> look like an acre of totempoles.

As much as the white company liked young Hurston's own colorful
language, they enjoyed even more having her saying things which she
did not understand:

> Another sly trick they played on my ignorance was that some of
> the men would call me and with a very serious face send me to
> some of the girls to ask about the welfare and condition of cher-
> ries and spangles. They would give me a tip and tell me to hurry
> back with the answer. Some of the girls would send back word
> that the men need not worry their heads at all. They would
> never know the first thing about the condition of their cherries
> and spangles. Some of the girls sent answers full of double talk
> which went over my head.

Finally, this incident with written discourse:

> I got a scrapbook, and everybody gave me a picture to put in it.
> I pasted each one on a separate page and wrote comments under
> each picture. This created a great deal of interest, because some
> of the comments were quite pert. They egged me on to elaborate.
> Then I got another idea. I would comment on daily doings and
> post the sheets on the call-board. This took on right away. The
> results stayed strictly mine less than a week because members of
> the cast began to call aside and tell me things to put in about

others. It got to be so general that everybody was writing it. It was just my handwriting, mostly. Then it got beyond that. Most of the cast ceased to wait for me. They would take a pencil to the board and set down their own item. Answers to the wise-cracks would appear promptly and often cause uproarious laughter. They always started off with either "Zora says" or "The observant reporter of the Call-board asserts"—Lord, Zora said more things! I was continually astonished, but always amused.

The passages, taken together, constitute a highly complex rendering of the political realities of blacks and language in the prison-house of culture, explicating and dramatizing all the various issues that a black essayist might think about in relation to what he or she does—for here, to borrow a Roland Barthes phrase, language literally becomes theater. First, there is a political reversal occurring here as Hurston moves from being mascot to becoming something like a scribe to, in fact, something like an anthropologist; moving from being a totem of animal imagery and ritual insult language to serving as a liaison for double entendres about cherries and heads to being a headmistress of a kind of school for scandal or a gossip exchange. Literally, once she controls the call board, the actual script of the lives of the company, she becomes the one who has not only recorded the dialect but actually shaped its creation. That a black should become the central controlling figure for the discourse of whites is, ironically, both a remarkable political feat of assertion-subversion and something genuinely ignominious if we remember Jim as the central and "controlling" figure of the whites at the end of Twain's novel. The method of ritual insulting, which she describes at first as being Southern, she describes later in the book as being particularly female and Negro and refers to it as "specifying." The shift is extremely important because specifying occurs when she is in the all-black southern towns collecting data (folk stories, i.e., oral language) for her books. Among the blacks, she is purely the scientist (the objective subject), evacuating and saving a culture. Among the whites, she is purely the exhibitionist (the subjective object) signifying the tricks and trumps of language. In effect, among the whites, Hurston makes the transition from taboo to totem (which is exactly what Jim does in *Huckleberry Finn*); for Hurston, the writer is the totem who enables the language of others ("the Other") to have meaning. That Hurston should be able to write about this in such a way that she so disguises her seizing the essential instrumentality of an acting company (its language and its script), becoming not simply its conduit for discourse but its source as well while seemingly remaining an instrumentality of the whites themselves (in essence, while still remaining a creation of the white imagination: a folksy innocent) is a masterful stroke of the trickster (although it is the very strength of her trickster dissimulation that is her final undoing—

because as the folksy innocent she can do nothing more than either be an exhibitionist or an observer, wavering between the anthropologist as actor to the anthropologist scribe). It is simply the problem of both being there (author) and being here (participant) that black nonfiction writers face as a kind of peculiar hazard of their game. In very stunning ways, the black nonfiction writer as anthropologist exemplifies the point of Clifford Geertz's essay "Being There: Anthropology and the Scene of Writing" better than any academic anthropologist ever could. For Hurston and Douglass—and, by extension, for most black nonfiction writers—"being there" is an ontological conundrum.

The black essayist is caught between acting and writing, between seizing the instrumentality and being trapped by the fact that he is inescapably an instrumentality; as he uses language he becomes both mascot and scribe, an odd, ambivalent coupling of the purloined and the purposeful. Hazrat Inayat Khan, Sufi philosopher and musician, spoke wisely when he said, "The nature of creation is the doubling of one." Perhaps, stated in a different context, it would read, "The predicament of racial politics is the doubling of one." Surely, when Du Bois described in that classic passage from *The Souls of Black Folk* the two-ness of the black, his being torn between his Americanness and his blackness, he did not simply restate a variation of the postmodern divided self. This book aspires to comprehend certain complexities of consciousness that exist among a group of people by considering the very simple idea of "being there" while "being here." I chose the title *Tuxedo Junction* because it is the name of a song by the great black band leader, Erskine Hawkins, recorded July 1939 and a hit with black dancers that became a much bigger hit with whites when Glenn Miller's orchestra "covered" it in 1940. (Tuxedo Junction was the streetcar terminal near a dance hall where the trumpet-playing Hawkins played as a youth.) "Tuxedo Junction" was, to use today's parlance, a crossover hit (although never recognized as such because whites do not "cross over," only blacks do), exemplifying the doubleness of our American culture, the sense of something being there and being here, of being for "them" and for "us" and for all. Those systems of doubleness in our culture are what generates the vital syncretism that makes it function. America's major myth is that of crossing over (ironically signifying both a pure rebirth and a mongrelized synergism), from crossing the ocean (the immigrants and the slaves) to crossing the street or crossing the tracks (social and class mobility or going from uptown to downtown) to crossing the Rubicon (irrevocable commitment). But for blacks it has always been the weight of one's previous location bearing down on where you are now, the doubleness best exemplified by the current craze for the self-determining term "African-American" (not the first time blacks have opted for a hyphenated name; in the 1850s the race term shifted from "Anglo-African" to "Afro-American"). Or, as Paule Marshall put it about one of her black characters, crazy Aunt Cuney, in the novel *Praisesong for the Widow,* when Aunt Cuney, as a girl, imagined seeing slaves walking on water back to Africa: "Her body she always usta say might be in Tatem but her mind, her mind was long gone with the Ibos." Alas, the fantasy of the doubleness of being here and being there, of being both an expansive soul while holding earnestly to a specifically located identity, of being pure yet united with an Other. And, paradoxically, American blacks have always measured their ideological and biological purity by how much they approached and resembled the idealized, fantasized Other: the African. Crossing over has long been a myth in African-American thought, closely associated with Christian theology, crossing the river Jordan, for instance, Zora Neale Hurston, in her 1939 novel, *Moses, Man of the Mountain,* captures both the racial and the theological aspects of being here and being there, the ontological nature of the black American's consciousness, when she describes Moses's crossing the Red Sea and leaving Egypt in exile:

> Moses had crossed over. He was not in Egypt. He had crossed over and now he was not an Egyptian. He had crossed over. The short sword at his thigh had a jewelled hilt but he had crossed over and so it was no longer the sign of high birth and power. He had crossed over, so he sat down on a rock near the seashore to rest himself. He had crossed over so he was not of the house of Pharaoh. He did not own a palace because he had crossed over. He did not have an Ethiopian Princess for a wife. He had crossed over. He did not have friends to sustain him. He had crossed over. He did not have enemies to strain against his strength and power. He had crossed over. He was subject to no law except the laws of tooth and talon. He had crossed over. The sun who was his friend and ancestor in Egypt was arrogant and bitter in Asia. He had crossed over. He felt as empty as a post for he was none of the things he once had been. He was a man sitting on a rock. He had crossed over.

The myth of fabrication in American culture is crossing over and that is what in essence, this book is about: the explication of that myth.

II. Autobiography

> Never to be yourself and yet always—that is the problem.
> —VIRGINIA WOOLF

It is, perhaps, not so odd that I should write a book of essays and that probably all the books I write shall be books of essays. Although when I was young, in high school and college, I wanted to write novels, doubtless the book that impressed me most during those years was a collection of essays: Amiri Baraka's (LeRoi Jones's) *Home: Social Essays.* Between the ages of eighteen and twenty-two I must have read that book no fewer than eight or nine times. (I cannot recall, either before or since, reading any other book so persistently.) I found the writing to be enormously engaging, both adventuresome and elegant, and I remember after the first reading to have been, to paraphrase Fitzgerald, p-p-paralyzed with enlightenment. No one seemed to say as well or as forcefully the sorts of things that Baraka said in that book (although I don't remember everything he said). I do remember the book stressed the doctrine of cultural nationalism, which enormously appealed to my puritan instincts of renovating the world through a covenant with one's own strength of character and one's sense of election (American millennialism served on the racial half-shell). Muhammad Ali, at this time, was a walking proof of that. Baraka's book was out around the time of Eldridge Cleaver's *Soul on Ice,* and I recall preferring Baraka to Cleaver, a preference that has been subsequently justified, not by the mutability of the political views of either man, but by the fact that overall, regardless of their views, Baraka was the better, and undoubtedly more significant and honest, writer. I am not likely to think so highly of Baraka's book now (and I have not opened it in roughly eight or nine years), but I am sure that this is the work that made me want to write essays.

I mention this, first, because several readers have noted the influence 10 of James Baldwin upon my work, an influence, an impact, if you will, that I would be the last to deny. Indeed, both "Waiting for Miss America" and "*The Color Purple* as Everybody's Protest Art" are self-consciously constructed tributes to Baldwin. But Baldwin did not really inspire me to write essays. I do not recall in high school or college ever imitating Baldwin, although I remember quite well mimicking or outright plagiarizing passages from Baraka. I think partly this particular form of the anxiety of influence occurred because of the times: I came of age in the late 1960s and the early 1970s, when Baraka was in, at least for part of that time, and Baldwin was, more or less, out. I also think that despite my having read *Notes of a Native Son* when I was thirteen, I do not think I appreciated it. I am sure I really did not understand it until I was in my late twenties, or not until I had read a great deal of Henry James and more than a little G. K. Chesterton, the two writers whose styles, I assume, most influenced and inspired Baldwin. (I am certain about James; I am merely guessing about the old Catholic conservative whose views Baldwin would have disliked intensely.) Also, I was not reared in a black charismatic church (I am an Episcopalian and grew up in an all-black Episcopal church), therefore the black sermonic roots of Baldwin's work not only never impressed me; like lost figures in a carpet, they simply never appeared to me. If anything, the appearance of this element in Baldwin's work probably alienated and annoyed me, disturbed and distressed me, and I am sure I gravitated to Baraka because that element was absent. Although I am deeply flattered when critics mention me and Baldwin in the same breath, I have been no more influenced by Baldwin than I have been by George Orwell, Chesterton, Aldous Huxley, Albert Camus (in French and English), Norman Mailer (under whose spell I fell around the time I discovered Baraka; it was fairly short-lived), or Virginia Woolf. If I pay a particular homage to Baldwin it is because his best work made him easily the best American essayist of his time and one ought to place flowers on certain altars. But context is everything: in the late sixties I saw both Baldwin and Baraka on television; I think Baldwin was being interviewed by William F. Buckley and Baraka was featured on a show hosted by David Frost. Baraka struck me far more favorably at the time; he not only seemed more assertive, he seemed a great deal more intellectual. Baraka did not preach; he argued, and quite effectively at that. It was the broad intellectual and literary reaches of Baraka's essays that I wanted, secretly, to match, to attain; I wanted, when I first started writing essays in earnest, to make the language zoom (Baraka's phrase) and to p-p-paralyze my readers with enlightenment, with how much I knew. Of course, actual practice of the art has made me a great deal more humble than I was in my salad days. I might add that I have never forgotten the look of pain and anguish on the face of Baldwin when he was interviewed on television those many years ago and have learned over time to understand that gallant grief, and to hold that picture in my mind may have taught me more about writing essays than anything else—to wish to have such a face as that, a dissipated and despairing face, a gem of a writer's face because it was a face filled with conscience.

The second reason I mention Baraka's collection is that he presented it in his introduction as a kind of intellectual autobiography. I suppose my essays are much the same, unavoidably so, although, despite some autobiographical passages, I am not—nor do I ever imagine myself being—terribly interested in writing autobiography. It is not the primary thrust or purpose of these essays to serve as autobiography. The strictly autobiographical portions are to be approached with caution. This is not to suggest that they are not true, but veracity is hardly the issue or the point. The autobiographical parts often serve the same purpose as notes in a symphony or passage of music: simply to get from one place to another. The personage I am in some of the essays, to borrow Henry Adams's metaphor, is simply a manikin on which I model some suitable clothes for the occasion. Sometimes autobiographical passages are used as authenticating devices, providing me with some authority to say the things I say; at other times, the reader is simply being guided through a particular terrain by these passages; at still other moments, they are meant to serve as a thematic, stylistic, or literary counterpoint to more discursive matters. I am a critic and it is best for the reader never to forget that, even if at times I appear to be playing other roles. All roles are subordinated to the critic; he manipulates all other personages in these pieces to his ends.

But I have spoken of this book as a long essay composed of essays, yet I have not said what I think an essay is. What is it that I write? Before I try to answer, I should say that I learned to write essays, or began the practice of them (my apprenticeship, if you will), by writing for a newspaper, my college newspaper, *The Daily Pennsylvanian*. Starting with personal pieces on the street-gang murder of my cousin in West Philadelphia, I proceeded week by week to crank out a column for more than a year. That what started out with energy and excitement should dull with fatigue and stress goes without saying. But this was very good training indeed (and every good essayist owes more than a little to H. L. Mencken, who has always been one of my heroes; journalism is the essence of the mastering of the art even if it is not the essence of the art itself); first, because I had to write to provoke people to read me in order to continue doing it (I cannot think of a more superfluous writer than someone who is doing op-ed pieces on a college newspaper. I was not simply speaking from rank ignorance, but in almost the basest contempt for knowledge—most students who think they have something to say are too arrogant to be humble). Second, I could write only four to five pages of copy; and third, I had to write even when I did not want to. As Virginia Woolf wrote, "a novel has story, a poem rhyme . . ." but an essay has nothing but its sheer insistence that the writer knows how to write well enough to make you read something that could attempt to be anything and threatens at any moment to be nothing at all. The essay is, thus, doubly damned; it is a negative function (a nonfiction and a non-poem but literature of some sort nevertheless) and it is an amorphous beast, serpentine, as Chesterton expressed "elusive, evasive, impressionistic, and shading away from tint to tint." Yet the very best place to learn to write them is at a newspaper, where one learns the three virtues of the essay: to so intensify some aspect of life for someone whose attention is distracted (newspaper readers are always distracted and distractable) as to make that person read with intensified interest; to learn the right number of pages for the subject; and to write persistently. Aldous Huxley spoke of essays being classified in one of three categories: autobiographical; factual, objective/observer; and abstract/philosophical; but after years of thinking and writing essays I find that they are, finally, prose, the common language, stating with clarity and consciousness the startlingly human triumph of forthright conviction without story as its aim.

It would be pleasing to know one day that I had written an American Common Reader. This book is certainly meant to be a continuation of that particularly deeply rooted branch of black letters of political engagement, of the Orwellian branch of humanist letters humanely considered, of the Woolfian art of common reading. And that is that.

❏ *Outward Exploration: Discussion*

1. What does Early see as the purpose of this essay (which is also an introduction to a volume of his essays)?

2. What does Early see as his role as an essayist? How does this concept compare to those of such writers as Joan Didion, E. B. White, and Scott Russell Sanders?

3. What reasons underlie Early's assertion (in paragraph 2) that no writer can really explain or justify or judge his own works? Do you ever feel that way?

4. Why does Early make such a point in paragraph 2 about being a failed novelist? What did he gain from that realization?

5. Drawing from your own experience, in what ways does America's dominant culture use the cultural margins (for example, ethnic and racial minorities) to "reinvent and reinvigorate the language" (paragraph 4)? Give as many examples as you can.

6. What does Early mean when he says that Frederick Douglass grew up in "various prison–houses of language and myth" (paragraph 5)? In what ways might language function as a prison, restricting freedom and movement and perception? What myths about African Americans in the first half of the nineteenth century and in our own era act as prisons? Do members of the United States's dominant groups (whites, males) also find themselves imprisoned in language and myth, even though they might realize as clearly that they are prisons? Explore and explain.

7. How does Frederick Douglass's use of the two stories about his mother (in paragraph 6) undercut the "Nature–Nurture" controversy? Why does Early believe these two stories are "fabricated"?

8. Does Early view such fabrication as a violation of the essayist's responsibility to tell the truth? Why or why not?

9. What is the "ontological conundrum" that the "black nonfiction writer as anthropologist" (paragraph 7) faces?

10. Why did Early name his volume *Tuxedo Junction?*

11. What does Early mean by the term *crossing over* (paragraph 8)?

12. Why does Early break his essay into two sections?

13. According to Early, how does he use the autobiographical passages in his essays?

14. According to Early, which of his roles supersedes all the others?

15. According to Early, what "negative" traits characterize the essay form?

16. According to Early, why is a newspaper the best place to learn how to write essays?

17. What are the three virtues that essayists can learn from writing for newspapers?

18. Ultimately, how does Early see the essays in his book—what are they?

☐ *Outward Exploration: Writing*

1. In paragraph 2, Early says he learned an important lesson when he realized that he wasn't a novelist. Have you ever had the experience of learning from a negative realization—in other words, understanding what you could not do helped you better understand what you could do? Explore and explain.

2. If you have read Mark Twain's *Huckleberry Finn,* comment on Early's analysis (in paragraph 5) of its last chapters. Explain your response to those chapters before you read Early. Has that response changed since reading Early's analysis? Are there scenes from other novels or plays or poems that you might subject to the same kind of cultural analysis?

3. Frederick Douglass says that where he grew up (the plantation) was "a little nation of its own, having its own language, its own rules, regulations, and customs" (paragraph 5). Explore that concept as applied to wherever you grew up; try to be an anthropologist looking at your own hometown.

4. In paragraph 9, Early talks about being "p-p-paralyzed with enlightenment" after reading Amiri Baraka's *Homes: Social Essays.* If you have ever had a similar experience with any text (for example, a book, poem, play, song), explain and explore that experience in an essay.

☐ *Style*

Consider the following sentence from Early's essay:

Sometimes autobiographical passages are used as authenticating devices, providing me with some authority to say the things I say; at other times, the reader is simply being guided through a particular terrain by these passages; at still other moments, they are meant to serve as thematic, stylistic, or literary counterpoint to more discursive matters. (paragraph 11)

The structure of this sentence is as follows:

adverb ("Sometimes")

subject of first independent clause ("autobiographical passages")

verb of first independent clause ("are used")

prepositional phrase ("as . . . devices")

comma separating the participial phrase acting as a free modifier from the previous independent clause

participial phrase ("providing . . . say")

semicolon joining two independent clauses

prepositional phrase ("at . . . times")

comma

subject of second independent clause ("the reader")

verb of second independent clause ("is . . . being guided")

prepositional phrase ("through . . . terrain")

prepositional phrase ("by . . . passages")

semicolon joining two independent clauses

prepositional phrase ("at . . . moments")

comma

subject of third independent clause ("they")

verb of third independent clause ("are meant")

infinitive phrase ("to serve . . . matters")

period.

This sentence offers several interesting points. First, notice that this is a compound sentence with *three* independent clauses. Second, notice the subtle variety created by the sandwiching of the second independent clause's subject ("the reader") between clauses with the same subject ("passages" and "they"). Third, notice the judicious use of the singular form of "reader" to avoid any confusion about the referent of "they" in the third clause.

Using your own information, write a sentence that replicates this structure.

3

Exploring Events

For many of us, the most obvious way of exploring ourselves is to explore a significant event from our past. Often we begin exploring events by telling the story of that event, by **narrating** it. This narrative impulse seems universal. We all have had experiences that "need" to be told, that we wish to share with others. Perhaps we want to amuse our friends by telling of a humorous run-in we had with the infamous Professor Absentminded. Or we want to warn others about the dangers we experienced while riding a bicycle across campus at night without a headlight. Or we want to impress them with our heroism. Or we want to dazzle them with our wit.

Whatever the reason, this narrative impulse is responsible for much of our literature: fiction, plays, movies, and epic poems—and many narrative exploratory essays.

What makes narration interesting and exciting? Details. Specific details. Details and **dramatized** events. This advice to use details and to dramatize is the same advice that fiction writers have been receiving for years—"Show, don't tell." To **show** means to dramatize, to let your readers see what happened rather than merely read a report about it. To **tell** means to report to readers what happened; the readers seem to get a secondhand account. You've probably had a friend recommend a particular movie by recounting the whole plot. Later, despite this detailed recital, you do indeed see the movie. Which experience was more "real," more enjoyable, more fulfilling—seeing the movie unfold before your eyes or hearing your friend *tell* you the plot? No doubt, seeing the movie was the more satisfying experience.

The same applies to writing for readers. Only if you *show* **how** funny Hector was will your essay be effective. Your readers must hear a sampling of his jokes about physics and "see" his comical expressions. Only then will they be amused. If you find yourself starting to say, "You had to be there" or "Well, it struck me funny," you know you're in trouble because you have merely *told* readers Uncle George was funny instead of *showing* them; instead of making your readers laugh, you have merely *told* them that they would have laughed had they been present.

This is not to say that you should always show and never tell. In most exploratory essays, you should combine showing with telling in order to reveal emotions and thoughts. For instance, you can explicitly *tell* the name of your feelings—"I was angry," "I felt anger." But you should augment that naming with vivid details ("I was so angry that my fingernails sliced into my palms"; "the anger blazed on my face"). Such combinations are very effective: The showing deepens our understanding of the telling and vice versa. Some writers do the naming in early drafts, then add the details later. Other writers give the details in early drafts and then deduce from those details the name of the emotions they felt. Either method is fine; do whatever works for you. This is one place where fiction and essays might differ because modern fiction writers have the option of being only suggestive and never *have to* explicitly name their character's emotions; exploratory essayists usually do.

There are some occasions, however, when essayists may not have to be explicit. Although most exploratory essays have both suggestive and explicit elements, some essays eliminate most of the telling and emphasize the showing, thus forcing readers to do more analysis. For example, such essays force readers to examine the details the writer provides and create their own names for the emotions depicted. They must visualize and consider the situation and then create their own statement of the event's significance rather than relying on the essayist's explicit statement. In short, readers must **interpret** such essays. Woody Allen's "Random Reflections of a Second-Rate Mind" is an example. Check with your professor about the desirability of your writing such essays.

In any case, the most satisfying and effective narrative exploratory essays are often those which sharply convey the details of what happened, explain the event's significance in some way, and explicitly explore the writer's thoughts, feelings, actions, reactions, and motivations.

WRITER-BASED GOALS

There are three writer-based goals in exploring an event: (1) to recreate vividly that event and the people involved; (2) to discover something that you didn't know or fully understand before about your role in that event—perhaps something about your own personality, about your motivation, about your perception of the event, about your perception of the people involved, about your understanding of interpersonal relationships; (3) to discover and verbalize the personal **internal significance** the event holds for you. Internal significance includes the psychological, spiritual, emotional, or intellectual importance or meaning of anything (such as an event, concept, or belief) for you the writer.

READER-BASED GOALS

There are four reader-based goals: (1) to dramatize an event vividly—that is, to tell an interesting and revealing story; (2) to answer the "journalist's questions" about the event—who was involved, what happened, when it happened, where it happened, why it happened, what other events were connected to it, and how it happened; (3) to reveal the event's internal significance to you; (4) to point out the event's global significance—how your internal experiences connect to those of other people.

SELECTING EVENTS FOR EXPLORATION

Choose an event from your personal experience. Personal experience is any trip you've ever taken, every visit to every relative you've made, every ball game or chess match you've participated in. It is every run down every ski trail, every date you've been on, your "first" anything (kiss, birthday party, solo drive in a car, encounter with your roommate or a fellow employee). Every story you've read or heard is also part of your experience.

Clearly, then, if you were involved in a car accident, being in a car accident would be part of your personal experience. But what if you were standing on the street corner and saw a car accident occur? Then we'd have to say that *the witnessing* of a car accident was part of your personal experience. Although you couldn't know from your spot on the corner what an occupant of the car experienced, you certainly would know what an observer saw and felt and thought.

However, this issue is more complicated and subtle than I've just suggested. One possibility for exploratory writing, in fact, is imagining yourself in another role; thus you could imagine what you would feel as the car's occupant even if, in reality, you were only a witness. In that case, you would indicate the "what-if" nature of the essay, and you would draw on other experiences of yours which would supply the emotions and thoughts. For instance, you might assume that someone in an accident would feel frightened and confused as the event occurred. So you would remember a time when you felt frightened and confused, and you'd transfer your sense of those feelings to the accident scene. Often, explaining the process by which you imagine yourself in the accident can be as interesting to your readers as what you say about the accident itself. Such "what-if" essays are, however, a limited and specialized group. For this chapter, we'll focus on events that happened directly to you.

Using an event that seems important to you is a good method for exploring yourself. But I can't stress enough that *the event, in and of itself, is not the important thing.* No matter how upsetting it was to fail the French test, no matter how funny Uncle George was at the dinner table last Christmas, no matter how embarrassing it was to spill tea on your grandmother's heirloom tablecloth—ultimately your readers won't care about the event per se. After all, your readers' lives are equally filled with crisis, comedy, and calamity. There is nothing *inherent* in the events to make your readers interested. What will interest them, however, is how the events affected you—the "human connection." The key is to use the event to reveal yourself.

If the event fulfills the following three criteria, it is probably a fine potential topic for a narrative exploratory essay.

1. *The event should interest you.* Most of us have some "set stories" that we trot out whenever we meet someone new. Yet many of the events that make up your repertoire of stories probably don't interest you any longer. Sure, they're guaranteed to make new acquaintances laugh or feel sympathy for you, but the events themselves seem set in concrete; you may even use the same words and phrases when you retell the event. Probably your "set stories" will be the first events that come to mind when you start searching for a personal topic. Give them their due before abandoning them. Each one probably has potential for an exploratory essay, but only if you can get beyond your standard approach to it, only if you can approach the event from a new perspective.

If you can't seem to get beyond the standardized version of those events, put them aside temporarily. They might be subject matter for later, after you've sharpened your exploratory skills. Jot down each of those events so that you won't forget them (and so that they won't keep interfering with your thoughts); then let your mind wander back over your past. Any event that catches your attention, any event that seems to have an aura or glow about it, even if you can't imagine why it appeals to you—*that* event should be explored.

2. *The event should encourage you to say* I. Often we have trouble being personal in essays. Even on the most basic level, we have trouble saying *I* in papers. Part of this comes from bad advice most of us received in high school—"Never use *I* in a paper." If we were writing lab reports exclusively, that advice might be tenable. For exploratory writing, though, that advice is downright dangerous. The point of exploratory essays is to use the first-person singular: how *I* reacted, how *I* felt, what *I* thought.

Keep in mind, however, that anyone can overuse *I* in a paper (see Chapter 11, "Revising Style," for more about the use of first-person singular). But *I* is an inevitable ingredient of exploratory writing.

3. *The event should feature your thoughts and feelings.* An event which features complex or conflicting thoughts and emotions is the most challenging and the most rewarding for exploratory writing. So pick an event in which your feelings and thoughts are prominent. Notice that I did not say, "an event *in which you played* a prominent part." *It is your thoughts and feelings about the event—not your prominence in the event—that are important.* Often we get so focused on *what* we did that it is difficult to get beyond that to our feelings and thoughts. The very fact that we accomplished "X" makes it almost impossible to see the internal significance of that event for us, to remember or to discover our complex emotions and thoughts. We are left saying only "I felt proud" or "I felt happy." And such superficiality makes boring essays. Often you may do better by selecting an event in which you did not figure prominently as a participant. Consider the following examples. The first, written by a basketball player, has numerous details, an effective structure, and it builds nicely to a climax. But as a narrative exploratory essay it falls short. It simply doesn't reveal very much about Billy or his view of the world:

> We had no time-outs left. There were only four seconds on the clock, and we were down by one point. I wasn't sure what the coach wanted me to do when I got the in-bounds pass because the crowd drowned out his instructions. Craig tossed the ball in-bounds to me, and I spun with my first dribble. I had to get up court fast. But one of the opponents was standing in my way. I had to detour around him as precious seconds ticked off the clock.
>
> Then I heard someone yell, "Shoot it! Shoot it!"
>
> Who yelled? My coach? My teammates? The opponents? I never found out. All I know is that I threw the ball towards the basket with all my might. I was at half-court, and it was a desperation shot. But it worked!
>
> Suddenly everyone was all around me—teammates, cheerleaders, the coach. Everyone thumped me on the back and said what a great clutch player I was. They lifted me on their shoulders and carried me to the locker room. Hey, I felt proud.
>
> —BILLY KROGH, "THE SHOT"

The potential is here: the writer's confusion about the coach's instructions and about who yelled for him to shoot the ball, his own sense of inadequacy about long-range shooting. Yet there is no exploration. *To the writer,* the event is fascinating—and it is probably interesting for most of us to read (particularly because it is also relatively brief). But we have no clue about the event's significance: Maybe this was Billy's one moment of glory, or perhaps it was simply one of many such glory moments; maybe Billy gained confidence in himself as a person because of this event, or maybe his overall game fell apart after this event because he got a swelled head and stopped taking practice seriously. From the essay we can't know.

Here is the same event written about by a spectator rather than by the player:

The game is over. Once again Billy is the star. An impossible   1
desperation shot from half court that even Larry Bird would be
embarrassed to acknowledge and the stupid ball goes "swish." I
bet Billy had his eyes closed.

Why does he get everything? I'm sitting up here in the
stands, alone, watching him be carried off the court. The star.
If that's not enough, his father just bought a new RX7 and lets
him drive it everywhere. On dates. And he's dating Sherry, the
head cheerleader. Me, I've got a ten-speed bike and I'm alone in
the stands. If only I had an RX7, then I'd have some foxy babe
on my arm too.

But is that the only reason I'm alone—no wheels? Other
guys with no cars and poor fathers make out okay. So there
must be something wrong with me. Or maybe not. Who knows?
If there is a limited amount of luck in the world, and if some
guys like Billy have a lot more than they deserve, well . . . I
guess it all has to balance out. He gets both his luck and my
luck, and I get nothing.

All I need is some of my own luck back; let Billy keep his
share but let me have what I deserve.

Is Billy really lucky, though? After all, his parents are di-   5
vorced and he took that really hard. In fact, that's when his
game started getting into overdrive, as though he were compen-
sating for having nothing at home. At least my parents are hanging together. Not rich, but not dirt poor either. Their priorities
are just not in the right place—insurance and home repairs before an RX7.

Now that I think about it, Billy is probably heading for a
fall. There has been so much written about him in the newspapers lately that he really believes he'll be a college basketball
star. He even thinks he'll be a star in the NBA. No way. Sure
he's 7-feet tall, but he's really not very well coordinated. He
dominates local high school ball okay because no other team in
the state has anyone as tall as he. But his vertical leap is about
three inches, and he is very slow running up and down the
court. In the pros, speed is crucial, even for a big man. In the
pros, there are several 7-foot basketball players who sit on the
bench, and there are others who are cut before training camp is
even over.

If he doesn't make it in the pros, what's he going to do? How does a 7-footer fit into everyday life if he doesn't have star status to carry him? Maybe Billy has not been given both his luck and my luck. Maybe he's only getting his whole life's worth of luck in one big dose. Here, the gods say, have all your luck between the ages of 15 and 22. After that, Pit City. Maybe they're saving up all my luck for college or afterwards, when I'm launched in my career. Maybe it will be me rather than my father who owns the RX7.

Then again, maybe I'm trying to keep from crying by fantasizing. Luck or no luck, I sure wish it was me and not Billy who was taking Sherry out after the game tonight.

—James Osmanski, "Luck"

Clearly this essay uses the event to reveal the thoughts and feelings of the writer. He doesn't get sidetracked by the event itself; his eyes are on his reactions, thoughts, and feelings. Because the "hero" was Billy, James was able to keep focused on his inner world. And he was able to keep exploring. Billy's essay *could* become as emotionally revealing as James's, but Billy was so caught up in his external role in the event that he could never really explore his thoughts and emotions.

THREE POTENTIAL PROBLEMS OF EXPLORING EVENTS

Three problems often arise in selecting an event to explore: lack of distance, lack of focus, and lack of a point.

Lack of Distance

You might be tempted to write about very recent events (for example, getting stuck on the highway last night, the party last weekend). They seem particularly attractive topics for narrative exploratory essays, in part because the details are still fresh in your mind. But at times the freshness of an event is its biggest drawback. Consider the humble oyster. A piece of grit gets inside its shell. Over time, it surrounds that piece of grit with layer after layer after layer until a pearl is produced. Events are often like that. If we write about them too soon after they happen, we end up with a slimy piece of grit rather than with a pearl. We need to let the event sit inside us long enough for its layers to develop, for its implications and ramifications to manifest themselves.

Another, totally different metaphor for this phenomenon is physical distance. If you are standing right in the middle of an accident scene, for instance, you see the details very clearly—the skid marks, the wrecked cars. Perhaps you even saw car A come around the bend in the wrong lane and cause the accident with car B. But you need to get some distance from the scene; you must stand on the hill over there in order to get the big picture—to see the injured dog lying in the road around the bend, the dog that caused car A to swerve in the first place. In the act of swerving, the driver lost control and couldn't get back in the correct lane before turning the corner and running into car B. Although the fault is the same—car A, after all, was on the wrong side of the road—some assumptions you might have made (the driver of car A was drunk or had fallen asleep at the wheel) need modification and, perhaps, your attitude toward driver A will become more sympathetic. The big picture.

In other words, to write effectively about any event, we require **distance.** At times that distance is in time, but such temporal distance usually involves a more important type of distance, namely, emotional distance. Without emotional distance from an event, you probably won't be able to write effectively about it. As long as you're "seeing red," you're going to be "writing red," too, and that emotion gets in the way of the analytical elements that should be in exploratory essays. If you discover you've picked such an event, switch to another. Let the hot topic cool down to a simmer on your mind's back burner for a while; then write about it later on.

Still, some writers are able to gain almost instantaneous distance. If you're such a writer, then the previous hour's events may be a rich source of inspiration. For most of us, however, at least a few days' distance helps us see beyond our immediate emotional response and into an event's significance. There is no easy formula for telling whether or not the event is too recent—sometimes an event that happened five years ago is still too recent (perhaps you are not emotionally or analytically or philosophically ready to explore it yet), whereas an event from five hours ago is primed and ready for exploration. A good rule of thumb is the following: If you can't identify the issues involved in the event, you are still too close to it to write an effective essay.

Once the proper amount of distance is obtained, the task you face is straightforward. You need to select an event that sets up reverberations in you—they may be tiny reverberations, but you'll feel them. Once you find the event, dramatize it (in other words, give specific details that make vivid the scene, the action, and the people) and look for its significance.

Lack of Focus

Sometimes it is difficult to separate the key event from a series of events. Since life's events often seem so interconnected, you may have trouble knowing what to dramatize and what not to dramatize or what to include and what to leave out. One major danger here is summarizing (telling) everything and dramatizing (showing) nothing.

One solution is to write about *all* the seemingly connected events in your prewriting and in your first drafts. As you do so, you will probably start to see that one particular period (an hour, a day, a week) was the crucial time. Within that period will be the key event, the "turning point," the moment when you recognized X (about yourself, about relationships, about the world). That turning point or moment of recognition will probably be the event that you dramatize.

Here's an example. Carlotta wrote a first draft about "the worst nightmare evening of my life." In brief, the evening began when her best friend decided not to accompany Carlotta to a fraternity party at another campus across town. Desiring to meet an "older frat man," Carlotta decided to go to the party with several "mere acquaintances." The drive to the party was filled with small talk and minor ego clashes. Once there, Carlotta had a terrible time—people were "obnoxious," her acquaintances abandoned her for other people, she developed a throbbing headache, and she argued with several women from the host campus. She left the party at 10:30 p.m. and ended up waiting for a taxi with three drunk men who might or might not have been from campus. Finally she got a taxi and headed back to her own campus dorm.

This early draft lacked focus. Carlotta never really dramatized any event(s). Her writing dilemma came from her assumption that the whole evening was "the event," but, in actuality, that evening was made up of numerous events. She needed to select one, dramatize it completely, and then use the other events as background. Any of the events might have been the key one, and which event she ultimately selected would dictate the point of the essay and the issue(s) she explored: for instance, her friend's letting her down (the issue might be the nature of friendship or Carlotta's dependence on others), or the ego clashes in the car (competition on campus, the difference between friends and acquaintances), or the obnoxious behavior (parties and Carlotta's expectations versus reality), or the arguments with the women from the other campus (the importance of being on your own turf or Carlotta's tendency to be confrontational), or the "humiliation" of leaving the party early (Carlotta's seeing herself through other people's eyes or her tendency to avoid confrontations), or waiting with the drunks (Carlotta's fears about being verbally assaulted, mugged, or raped).

Lack of a Point

The third pitfall in selecting an event is stringing together a series of events that have no deeper connection than the fact that they occurred one after the other. For example, Flora wrote a draft about visiting her dying grandmother in Taiwan, returning to Boston, and encountering a search dog in the airport, a dog which terrified her so much, she ran and hid. No significant whole was formed by the three events. Seeing all the events together didn't reveal anything deeper to her readers, but it should have. For example, if Flora's grandmother had instilled the fear of dogs in her and if she had remembered that fact when she saw the dog in the airport, there would have been some deeper connection than chronology between events. If the dog somehow came to symbolize death, Flora might have speculated about the dog as symbol of her grandmother's impending death. If the flight to Boston had increased her sense of isolation from most of her family, that would have explained her increased susceptibility to her childhood fear of dogs. Without question, Flora *felt* a connection, but she needed to make that connection explicit and analyze it in order to write a successful exploratory essay. Finding the issue that united the events would have given the essay significance.

FULFILLING YOUR WRITER-BASED AND READER-BASED GOALS

Several techniques will help you fulfill your writer-based and reader-based goals as you explore an event.

Explore the External Nature of the Event

The first task is to understand more fully the external nature of the event, including the details of the location and what happened. To make the event as vivid as possible for yourself and your readers, provide specific details by appealing to the reader's five senses in the same way fiction writers do and by dramatizing the event, perhaps even giving dialogue. You should "put the readers in the scene," not just tell them about it. Ultimately, the details you give and the objects and settings you describe will create a dominant impression or mood. You might not be aware of what that dominant impression *should be* or *might be* as you write your early drafts, so simply describe as much as you can. The greatest danger here is not showing your readers enough, dashing on when you should pause. Dramatizing forces you as writer (and later, your readers) to "dwell in the moment"—lingering to hear the dialogue, to see the scene, to touch the objects. Such lingering gives you many more opportunities to discover your subtle, less visible feelings and thoughts, your reactions as well as your later ruminations on the event. Consider, for example, the details George Orwell gives us in "The Hanging" (page 165)—the way the prisoner avoids the puddle of water and the antics of the dog.

Explore the Event's Personal Significance for You

Events have both external and internal significance. **External significance** refers to the impact an event has on your "visible," external life. It includes changes in your lifestyle and in your circumstances.

Internal significance refers to your "inner world" and how the external events change you the person.

Consider, for example, the day you forced yourself to interview for a desirable job and got it. That event has external significance: The salary raised your income, the on-the-job training improved your job skills, and the job added depth to your résumé. Such an event might change the nature of your lifestyle (for example, you might buy a car or eat in restaurants every night). In short, such an event would have a profound external significance.

Yet such external significance is not the point of exploratory essays. Readers certainly need to know the external significance since it is important background information. Ultimately, though, readers care most about the internal significance of events.

To explore internal significance, always begin by asking, "What aspect(s) of my personality does this event reveal?" and "How did this event change me as a person?" If the event neither reveals something significant about your inner world nor changed you, why bother to write about it?

To clarify the event's internal significance for you, you need to give details and to comment on them. If the event reveals something significant about your personality, for example, you need to name and detail the implications of that trait as revealed in the event. If the event changed you in some significant way, you should explain what you were like before the event, what you were like after the event, why and how this particular event caused the change. For convenience, we can break internal significance into two parts—emotional and philosophical.

EMOTIONAL SIGNIFICANCE   Almost any meaningful event has an emotional content for us—it affected (and perhaps still affects) our emotions in some way. So you should always ask, "How were my emotions revealed or changed by this event?"

Let's return to the example of the job interview. If, as I suggested, even going in for the job interview required an act of courage, your first question might be, *Why* did it require an act of courage? Then: What were you like *before* the interview? Did you doubt your ability to *do* the job? Why? Had you never done such work before? Were you afraid of having that much responsibility? Did you believe you could do the job but doubt your ability to *get* the job? Why? Did you believe that you never made a good impression in interviews? Did you believe that you had to "know someone" in order to get such a good job? If so, why did you believe that? Did you feel insecure about yourself in some other way? Did you lack self-confidence because your parents or teachers or friends tended to devalue you?

Then consider how your emotions changed because of the event. Some change might have been immediate—perhaps relief and joy that you got the job. Maybe your self-confidence soared; maybe you felt like thumbing your nose at someone who had told you that you never could do anything right. Even here, though, there may be surprises. Maybe you also felt fear that you were not as skilled as your résumé and interview suggested. Remember, emotions are always more complex than we at first believe them to be.

Once you've explored the immediate emotions, do not neglect the emotions that you felt later that day and later that week, or which you feel now as you look back on the event. All of those emotions are worth exploring.

PHILOSOPHICAL SIGNIFICANCE   Most experiences have more than an emotional component; they also have an intellectual or philosophical side. Consider the job interview example again. Assume that you believed an "old boy network" was the only way to get a job, and then you got the job on your own merit. Such evidence ("I got the job without knowing anyone important") should affect your world view. Old boy networks certainly might still exist, but at least not everywhere. In other words, your philosophical vision of the world has changed slightly based on the experience of getting the job. In addition, your intellectual understanding of yourself, of your abilities, of your personality may also have changed. With the job in hand, you might change your idea that you don't present yourself well in interviews. Or you might develop yet another negative self-image (for example, "She gave me the job out of pity" or "She gave me the job because her brother went to my college"). Then you should ask, "Why can't I believe that I got the job because I'm skillful?"

Once you've established the internal significance of the event, ask yourself, "What was the source of the original belief or feeling that the event changed?" Some possible sources include family, friends, peers, cultural background, society in general. The more accurately and precisely you locate the source(s) of that belief or idea for you, the greater your insight into yourself.

In early drafts, you need to probe further and further into yourself to discover all the internal personal significance of the event. When you prepare to write the final draft, however, think about how much of that significance you are comfortable sharing with your readers. Once you've made that decision, give them enough background information to be able to understand what you say (this might include explaining your personality or philosophy or attitude before the event and the sources of your ideas and assumptions). Also ask yourself *what* your readers need to know (about you, about others involved in the event, about the event itself) and *when* in the essay they need to know it.

The greatest pitfall here is assuming that, without your help, your readers will simply know exactly what you felt or thought. They won't. The same event can cause very different feelings in different people. It is your task as a writer to be very explicit, detailed, and vivid about what your particular feelings and thoughts were.

Another possible pitfall is the mistaken belief that an exploratory essay is an outburst of raw feelings. It isn't. It is the *re-creation* of and the exploration of your feelings—some analysis and some distance must be involved as well as the strong feelings themselves. And, as with all exploratory essays, the prose should demonstrate careful craft.

Consider Your Split Perspective

By now it should be clear that for the purposes of the exploratory essay, events in and of themselves are not important; your thoughts and feelings are. A moment's reflection will suggest, however, that you have at least two sets of thoughts and feelings about any event: those you had while the event was occurring, and those you have now as you look back on that event and on those previous thoughts and feelings. This **split perspective**—*you-then* and *you-now*—can provide a great deal of insight into how you and your attitudes have changed over a period of time—an interesting topic for an exploratory essay.

Often, changing which perspective you take (for instance, you–then to you–now) can turn a serious essay into a humorous one. Events that seemed tragic when they occurred might seem comic now; you might now think of your former self as naive instead of smart, intelligent instead of dumb, brave instead of cowardly. Essayist Thomas Simmons suggests a similar point:

> Two years ago I felt buried in a sense of conventionality, as if my life and love and career had brought me simply to a point of stasis. The sense of emptiness which comes with such an intuition of conventionality, however, may also be a sign that what one calls one's life remains largely unexamined: the surface is all one has. To smash through that surface is to endure pain, to raise old angers and hatreds, to confront one's own stupidity and stubbornness and unfulfilled hope. But, I think, it is also to see the new patterns which form in one's own personal history. History is never a single truth, but a study of vantage points.

Simmons is talking about split perspectives, about the different ways we connect to our past. As we move away from an event emotionally and temporally and perhaps even geographically, we gain perspective. In Simmons's words, we change "vantage points." Patterns that we weren't aware of when the event occurred are now clearer. Perhaps the event can now be seen as the first in a series that ultimately formed a pattern. Perhaps we've gained new insights into ourselves and others which, in turn, cast new light on the feelings and emotions involved in the event.

The key point here, however, is not that seeing the event from one vantage point gives us the "right" version of the event or the truth about the event. Rather, each vantage point has value in and of itself—it reveals something about us as we were at that point. Our personal identity keeps changing and evolving. Seeing what we were like at different times reveals much about us as we are now.

When you use the split perspective, signal switches between you-then and you-now by the careful use of verb tenses and by transitional phrases such as "Now I see that . . . ," "Looking back, I realize that . . . ," "Then I felt . . . ." In other words, remember your readers' need for clarity.

Explore the Event's Global Significance

When we say that an event has **global significance,** it means that the insights you've gained into the event and into yourself are significant for others. Most often, global significance resides in the issues involved in the event. For example, many events involve relationships. Name the relationships involved (friendship, sibling rivalry, love) and you have a solid clue about global significance. Similarly, events often include actions, and actions almost always raise questions of morality. Name the action (cheating, rescuing, believing) and you again have a clue about global significance.

Once you know the issues, consider the following: Is there some way in which your experiences parallel or approximate or differ from those of other people? Global significance can often be suggested by references to the works of other writers, by references to famous people, and by allusions to fictional characters. Quotations from experts can also help. For example, you might compare your thoughts and feelings about some physical impairment to those of Alice Walker in "Beauty: When the Other Dancer Is the Self" (page 190) or to those of Nancy Mairs in "On Being a Cripple" (page 115). Ask yourself, "In what ways are their experiences like mine?" Don't focus primarily on external similarities; look for the emotional and internal connections. If you can find no connection between your reactions, thoughts, and feelings and those of other people, then look deeper into yourself and into them. Perhaps you have not yet identified the key issues at play in the event.

Remember, however, that as individuals we differ from each other in various ways. So don't expect your reactions to mirror exactly those of other people. Besides differences that result from physical characteristics, we come from different cultural backgrounds and environments, we've learned to make different assumptions about ourselves and our world, and our own life experiences have made us highly individualistic. Resist the temptation to force your reactions to fit those of other people. Your reactions are as true and as valuable as anyone else's, so point out the differences as well as the similarities.

For a final example, assume that when you were five or six, your parents came home with your new baby sister. This event has a lot of potential significance because you probably felt several conflicting emotions and had several disturbing thoughts. For instance, while you were excited about the idea of having a baby in the house, you were feeling a bit left out of things. Although you loved the baby immediately, you might have felt jealous of her too. You may have hidden that jealousy from others and perhaps even from yourself. It might have revealed itself in a number of indirect ways—too much solicitude for the baby or rebellious acts against your parents. You might have consciously thought, "What great training having a baby around the house will be for me when I grow up." But you might have also wondered, "Why did Mom and Dad need another child? Aren't I good enough?"

Looking for the conflicts ("I loved the new baby but . . ."), the discrepancies ("I wanted the baby out of the house even though I was very attentive to her every sound and movement"), and the surprises ("I thought she'd obey me") reveals internal personal significance. Thinking about similar experiences undergone by other people leads to the global significance of the event. For instance, whole books have been written on the issue of sibling rivalry. Essays galore—both humorous and serious—detail individuals' reactions to a new sibling. How do they compare to your reactions? Can you find a pattern of behavior, of feeling, of thought? How do you account for the differences between your reactions, thoughts, and feelings and those of others? Individual traits? Cultural background? Environmental influences?

Use Vivid Description and Vivid Language

Exploratory narratives require description, but not simply description for description's sake. Study published essays to see how and when description becomes effective. Remember, the more specific the detail, the better the chance that it will trigger interesting memories, associations, emotions, or speculations.

Specific details require vivid language. Consider this vividly detailed passage:

> It [covering cucumber and tomato plants with burlap sacks] was a hated, cold-handed job which had to be done every evening. I daydreamed along in a halfhearted, distracted way, flopping the sacks onto the plants, sorry for myself and angry because I was alone at my boring work. No doubt my younger brother and sister were in the house and warm. Eating cookies.
>
> But then a great strutting bird appeared out from the dry remnants of our corn, black tail feathers flaring and a monstrous yellow-orange sac pulsating from its white breast, its throat croaking with popping sounds like rust in a joint.
>
> The bird looked to be stalking me with grave slow intensity, coming after me from a place I could not understand as real, and yet quite recognizable, the sort of terrifying creature which would sometimes spawn in the incoherent world of my night

dreams. In my story, it looked like death, come to say hello. Then, it was simply an apparition.

—WILLIAM KITTREDGE, "HOME"

Notice how Kittredge turns a physical sensation—cold hands—into a vivid adjective ("cold-handed job"). Note, too, that he reveals his thoughts—his envy of his siblings and their warm happiness that contrasts with his cold hands. And notice the bird. Most of us would simply say: "A big bird came at me from out of the corn." Kittredge chooses instead to elaborate on its approach and on his own state of mind before seeing the bird. By connecting the bird with the creatures from his dreams, he reveals his own concern with death.

Here's another example:

Sometimes a strong wind tossed and lowered a tree branch against the skylight. In fine weather, that tree pulsed with small golden birds, finches that must have eaten food touched by Midas—even their excrement was liquid gold. I loved skying into weather just developing: clouds rapidly changing to mist, swirling apart until suddenly the skylight framed shades of blue; blurs and blots of clouds, a vast calligraphy that kept erasing, then rewriting itself in an excess, an exuberance of alphabets, or into a patois of bruises, a jargon of violet streakings, thick squid ink that seemed the very opacity of language and desire.

—SUSAN MITCHELL, "DREAMING IN PUBLIC"

I like most the whimsy in Mitchell's passage, the idea that golden birds have eaten food touched by Midas. But notice as well the visual verbs Mitchell uses and the breathtaking imagery—the clouds are like writing in calligraphy, a writing which is constantly erased and written again using the letters from many alphabets. Consider, too, her bold comparison of that cloud lettering with violet jargon written in squid ink.

Here's a third example:

Spring jitterbugs inside me. Spring is wind, symphonic and billowing. A dark cloud pops like a blood blister over me, letting hail down.

—GRETEL EHRLICH, "SPRING"

Here the verb *jitterbugs* is an example of a perfect choice of a vivid verb: It calls forth a picture of a couple bouncing and spinning in dance, their arms flapping and their hands waving. Imagine such a couple dancing inside of you—doesn't that image approximate the jumpy, twitchy, don't-know-what-to-do-with-myself feeling that spring evokes in us? And the cloud like a blood blister shocks and surprises us, making us reexamine our experience of hailstorms.

The point here is that vivid details and memorable language are compelling and should be used whenever possible (see Chapter 11, "Revising Style," for more detail about language).

Avoid Universality

The desire to be universal has ruined many potentially good exploratory essays because many people assume that *universal* means "general." It doesn't. Literary texts gain their universality by giving very specific details; texts become general when they eliminate specific details and try to include only what everybody has experienced. Try to reflect accurately *your own experiences and feelings,* not anyone else's. The appeal of your essay will come from the color of the specifics, not from the monochrome hue of "general experience."

Be Alert to Symbolic Implications

For our purposes, a symbol is anything which, within the context of your writing, suggests more than itself—that is, it hints at deeper implications.

Here's an example. Whenever my family went on picnics (just about every summer weekend) during my childhood, my grandmother would hunt for and find four-leaf clovers, supposedly good luck symbols. We kids would play, our parents would talk, and my grandmother would hunt for four-leaf clovers. Her quest for four-leaf clovers symbolically suggests an important insight. Although my grandmother was very religious, she spent a lot of time seeking four-leaf clovers. What does such an interest suggest about her religion? Was it augmented by the good luck symbols? Replaced by them? With research I found that four-leaf clovers were originally considered good luck because they represent the Christian cross. Is there irony here? My grandmother augments her religious belief with good-luck charms which turn out to derive their "good luck quality" from her religion. Thinking she was invoking two sources of good luck to help her through her difficult life, she was ironically invoking only one.

Don't consciously worry about symbols as you work through your early drafts. If you notice something with symbolic value as you write, explore it. Treat it like another tangent. When you've exhausted its possibilities, go back to the events. When you get ready to write the final draft, though, seek out those suggestive elements in your manuscript and see which ones connect with your purpose and which do not. Allow yourself to consider the symbolic aspects of your narration. Then play with those aspects to see where they lead.

Sacrifice Facts for Emotional Truth

Yes, essays are about real events that happened to real people. But exploratory essays are not sworn testimony in a court of law. At times, you might create a more effective essay by sacrificing some *mere facts* for the sake of the *emotional truth* you are exploring. In such a case, you might eliminate some people who were extraneous to the event's significance and who would merely crowd the essay needlessly. Or you might take two events that occurred at different times and blend them into one experience.

Consider again the story of my grandmother's looking for four-leaf clovers. In real life, my grandmother, my parents, one or two sets of aunts and uncles, numerous cousins, and I were usually at the picnics—a lot of people for one exploratory essay. If I'm focusing on my grandmother and my reactions to her four-leaf clovers, do I need to mention those aunts and uncles? Maybe I need to mention one cousin because we were playing (and I might discover some parallel between playing and hunting for clovers), but the aunts and uncles and at least three of the cousins are dispensable for my purpose in the essay. For the sake of focus, I'd eliminate them.

In addition to such focusing, I might blend two events together. During one picnic, for example, my grandmother found five four-leaf clovers in one hour. During a different picnic, she clowned around by looking through the wrong end of a pair of binoculars, changing her perception of reality. For the sake of reinforcing the truth about her attempts to change her reality and about her blending religion and superstition, I would merge the binoculars episode with the episode of her finding five four-leaf clovers. In other words, I would have both events occur at the same picnic—a sacrifice of mere fact for emotional truth, and emotional truth should always be our goal. Notice, by the way, that I did not *invent* episodes to reveal the truth. I simply blended two true events together and eliminated some people who, in this version of the event, were not important.

Make Events Humorous

Many family stories are funny. Although people might occasionally tell stories about tragedies in their lives, they often tell and retell humorous stories about themselves and others. It would not be surprising, then, if a humorous event pops into your mind as a possible subject.

That is fine. Remember, though, that no event is *inherently* funny or sad to your readers. Writers make events humorous or sad by the way they write about them. In other words, *it is possible to write humorously about any topic,* no matter how painful and frightening that topic is. Probably no one writer could write humorously about everything. But every topic could be written about humorously by someone.

If the event per se is not inherently funny, what makes an essay humorous? Humor is very subjective, so you should read humorous essays by, for example, Dave Barry or Woody Allen and observe which of their techniques and approaches make you laugh. Humorous techniques include (but are not limited to) exaggerated details, unusual word choices, puns, an irreverent attitude toward an event or toward the writer's younger self. Such techniques make reading the essay a humorous experience for the readers. Notice what I just said: not that the *episode* is humorous, but that *reading the essay* becomes a humorous experience. Once again, the key point is this: *The episode is never funny to readers; only the essay can be funny.*

OUR DYNAMIC RELATIONSHIP
TO THE PAST

Experiences in our life are not static. Since we can never know the whole truth about an event, each return to that event could reveal something new; for example, we might remember some detail that was forgotten or repressed. Further, each time we examine an event from our past, we ourselves are different; our greater experience in the world and with people changes how we view ourselves, life, and even that particular past event. Changes in the consequences of that event in our present life also change our vision of it (for example, the romantic breakup in January that seemed to doom us to tragic loneliness might later seem the happy moment that freed us to find true love in February). Even *what* we see in that event can change because the concepts and assumptions we bring to the exploration constantly change too.

In other words, we do not passively view the past; we actively engage with it. As poet Charles Simic says in "Reading Philosophy at Night," "I am in dialogue with certain decisive events in my life as much as I am with the ideas on the page."

Our dynamic relationship to our past is the underlying theory of narrative exploratory essays. To understand ourselves and our past more fully, we must be "in dialogue" with the past events of our lives. We must constantly ask questions of those events, and then we must re-question and ask for clarification of whatever answers we receive.

The past is fluid, and it is filled with many surprises. Narrative exploratory essays are an effective means of rediscovering and deepening our sense of our personal past and of finding those surprises and revelations.

SUGGESTIONS FOR WRITING

1. Select an event which has internal significance for you. Write an essay in which you narrate that event vividly, dramatizing the key scene(s) by letting us hear dialogue, see the setting and the people involved, smell the smells, taste the tastes, and feel the textures of the setting and its objects. Be explicit about what the event's significance is.

Also, be sure that the whole essay is shaped to reflect that significance (in other words, choose details that suggest that significance and eliminate those which are superfluous). Many events in our lives have built-in symbolic significance; the following is merely a list of suggestions:

"Official" important days: Holidays, anniversaries, birthdays (on your 18th birthday the United States considers you officially an adult, for example, and on your 65th many people will consider you officially old).

First times: Any "first" can be highly significant (for instance, the first time you kissed someone romantically, the first time you purchased college textbooks, the first time you wrote a check).

Decisions: Every time you have to make a decision, there's the possibility of that decision's having profound internal significance.

Memorable events: Events can be memorable for many reasons. For example, an event can reveal your beliefs, your values, your way of viewing the world, perhaps even a personality trait (for example, you discover that you are fearful or brave, timid or bold, happy or sad). Or an event can change some belief, vision, or personality trait. Or an event can reveal strong emotions that you didn't believe you had.

Humorous or embarrassing events: Such events can reveal a lot about you, since often what is perceived as humorous or embarrassing now might not have seemed so then, so your split perspective comes into play.

"Obscure" events: Often an event whose symbolic significance is not perceived can actually be filled with internal significance (for example, your *second* date, the *twenty-third* dance you attended, the *tenth* check you wrote).

2. Select any family story that has been told to you (it might involve you or it might not). Write down all the details you remember. Then write down all the details you might have remembered if you had a perfect memory (or which you can add to it from other similar events). Then think about why you decided to write about this particular family story. What importance does the story have for you? Does it reveal something about your personality or about relationships in your family? Was the actual hearing of the story the important thing—for example, telling you that story was the first time your grandfather ever really paid attention to you? Did hearing the story make you angry or happy or sad? Why?

On Being a Real Westerner

TOBIAS WOLFF

◻ *Inward Exploration*

Write at least one paragraph about some object that has great significance for you now or which had great significance for you when you were younger. What was that object's appeal to you? What was its significance?

Just after Easter Roy gave me the Winchester .22 rifle I'd learned to shoot with. It was a light, pump-action, beautifully balanced piece with a walnut stock black from all its oilings. Roy had carried it when he was a boy and it was still as good as new. Better than new. The action was silky from long use, and the wood of a quality no longer to be found. 1

The gift did not come as a surprise. Roy was stingy, and slow to take a hint, but I'd put him under siege. I had my heart set on that rifle. A weapon was the first condition of self-sufficiency, and of being a real Westerner, and of all acceptable employment—trapping, riding herd, soldiering, law enforcement, and outlawry. I needed that rifle, for itself and for the way it completed me when I held it.

My mother said I couldn't have it. Absolutely not. Roy took the rifle back but promised me he'd bring her around. He could not imagine anyone refusing him anything and treated the refusals he did encounter as perverse and insincere. Normally mute, he became at these times a relentless whiner. He would follow my mother from room to room, emitting one ceaseless note of complaint that was pitched perfectly to jelly her nerves and bring her to a state where she would agree to anything to make it stop.

After a few days of this my mother caved in. She said I could have the rifle, if, and only if, I promised never to take it out or even touch it except when she and Roy were with me. Okay, I said. Sure. Naturally. But even then she wasn't satisfied. She plain didn't like the fact of me owning a rifle. Roy said he had owned several rifles by the time he was my age, but this did not reassure her. She didn't think I could be trusted with it. Roy said now was the time to find out.

For a week or so I kept my promises. But now that the weather had turned warm Roy was usually off somewhere and eventually, in the dead hours after school when I found myself alone in the apartment, I decided that there couldn't be any harm in taking the rifle out to clean it. Only to clean it, nothing more. I was sure it would be enough just to break it down, oil it, rub linseed into the stock, polish the octagonal barrel and 5 then hold it up to the light to confirm the perfection of the bore. But it wasn't enough. From cleaning the rifle I went to marching around the apartment with it, and then to striking brave poses in front of the mirror. Roy had saved one of his army uniforms and I sometimes dressed up in this, together with martial-looking articles of hunting gear: fur trooper's hat, camouflage coat, boots that reached nearly to my knees.

The camouflage coat made me feel like a sniper, and before long I began to act like one. I set up a nest on the couch by the front window. I drew the shades to darken the apartment, and took up my position. Nudging the shade aside with the rifle barrel, I followed people in my sights as they walked or drove along the street. At first I made shooting sounds—kyoo! kyoo! Then I started cocking the hammer and letting it snap down.

Roy stored his ammunition in a metal box he kept hidden in the closet. As with everything else hidden in the apartment, I knew exactly where to find it. There was a layer of loose .22 rounds on the bottom of the box under shells of bigger caliber, dropped there by the handful the way men drop pennies on their dressers at night. I took some and put them in a hiding place of my own. With these I started loading up the rifle. Hammer cocked, a round in the chamber, finger resting lightly on the trigger, I drew a bead on whoever walked by—women pushing strollers, children, garbage collectors laughing and calling to each other, anyone—and as they passed under my window I sometimes had to bite my lip to keep from laughing in the ecstasy of my power over them, and at their absurd and innocent belief that they were safe.

But over time the innocence I laughed at began to irritate me. It was a peculiar kind of irritation. I saw it years later in men I served with, and felt it myself, when unarmed Vietnamese civilians talked back to us while we were herding them around. Power can be enjoyed only when it is recognized and feared. Fearlessness in those without power is maddening to those who have it.

One afternoon I pulled the trigger. I had been aiming at two old people, a man and a woman, who walked so slowly that by the time they turned the corner at the bottom of the hill my little store of self-control was exhausted. I had to shoot. I looked up and down the street. It was empty. Nothing moved but a pair of squirrels chasing each other back and forth on the telephone wires. I followed one in my sights. Finally it stopped for a moment and I fired. The squirrel dropped straight into the road. I pulled back into the shadows and waited for something to happen, sure that someone must have heard the shot or seen the squirrel fall. But the sound that was so loud to me probably seemed to our neighbors no more than the bang of a cupboard slammed shut. After a while I sneaked a glance into the street. The squirrel hadn't moved. It looked like a scarf someone had dropped.

When my mother got home from work I told her there was a dead squirrel in the street. Like me, she was an animal lover. She took a cel- *10* lophane bag off a loaf of bread and we went outside and looked at the squirrel. "Poor little thing," she said. She stuck her hand in the wrapper and picked up the squirrel, then pulled the bag inside out away from her hand. We buried it behind our building under a cross made of popsicle sticks, and I blubbered the whole time.

I blubbered again in bed that night. At last I got out of bed and knelt down and did an imitation of somebody praying, and then I did an imitation of somebody receiving divine reassurance and inspiration. I stopped crying. I smiled to myself and forced a feeling of warmth into my chest. Then I climbed back in bed and looked up at the ceiling with a blissful expression until I went to sleep.

For several days I stayed away from the apartment at times when I knew I'd be alone there.

Though I avoided the apartment, I could not shake the idea that sooner or later I would get the rifle out again. All my images of myself as I wished to be were images of myself armed. Because I did not know who I was, any image of myself, no matter how grotesque, had power over me. This much I understand now. But the man can give no help to the boy, not in this matter nor in those that follow. The boy moves always out of reach.

❑ *Outward Exploration: Discussion*

1. What is the effect of the details which Wolff gives about the rifle?
2. Why did Wolff want the rifle in the first place?
3. Why is Wolff's statement that he is an "animal lover" both ironic and frightening?
4. In paragraph 11, do you think that the boy (Wolff then) knew he was pretending to have a religious experience, or is that the insight of the adult (Wolff now)?

❑ *Outward Exploration: Writing*

1. On one level, Wolff's essay is about fitting into stereotypical male behavior. Write an essay about an event in which you conformed to or rebelled against your gender's stereotypes. Consider the sources of your conformity or rebellion. Make the event as vivid and detailed as Wolff makes his.
2. On one level, this is an essay about power. Write an essay about an event in which you had power over others. Make the event as vivid and detailed as Wolff makes his.
3. Wolff suggests that we are all compelled by our images of ourselves. Write an essay about an event which revealed or enacted some image

of yourself that seemed compelling. Make the event as vivid and detailed as Wolff makes his.

□ *Style*

Consider the following sentence–fragment combination from Wolff's essay:

> I decided that there couldn't be any harm in taking the rifle out to clean it. Only to clean it, nothing more. (paragraph 5)

What's notable about this combination is the way Wolff repeats the phrase "to clean it" in order to emphasize it in the fragment.

Write a sentence–fragment combination of your own in which you replicate this structure—taking a key word or phrase from the end of the sentence and emphasizing it in the fragment. If possible, replicate as well the "nothing more" emphasis.

A Hanging

GEORGE ORWELL

☐ *Inward Exploration*

Make a list of events which revealed something about someone to you. Select one event and write at least one paragraph about it, giving details and explaining what exactly the event revealed about that person.

It was in Burma, a sodden morning of the rains. A sickly light, like   1
yellow tinfoil, was slanting over the high walls into the jail yard. We
were waiting outside the condemned cells, a row of sheds fronted with
double bars, like small animal cages. Each cell measured about ten feet
by ten and was quite bare within except for a plank bed and a pot for
drinking water. In some of them brown, silent men were squatting at
the inner bars, with their blankets draped round them. These were the
condemned men, due to be hanged within the next week or two.

One prisoner had been brought out of his cell. He was a Hindu, a
puny wisp of a man, with a shaven head and vague liquid eyes. He had
a thick, sprouting moustache, absurdly too big for his body, rather like
the moustache of a comic man on the films. Six tall Indian warders were
guarding him and getting him ready for the gallows. Two of them stood
by with rifles and fixed bayonets, while the others handcuffed him,
passed a chain through his handcuffs and fixed it to their belts, and
lashed his arms tight to his sides. They crowded very close about him,
with their hands always on him in a careful, caressing grip, as though
all the while feeling him to make sure he was there. It was like men
handling a fish which is still alive and may jump back into the water.
But he stood quite unresisting, yielding his arms limply to the ropes, as
though he hardly noticed what was happening.

Eight o'clock struck and a bugle call, desolately thin in the wet air,
floated from the distant barracks. The superintendent of the jail, who
was standing apart from the rest of us, moodily prodding the gravel
with his stick, raised his head at the sound. He was an army doctor,
with a grey toothbrush moustache and a gruff voice. "For God's sake
hurry up, Francis," he said irritably. "The man ought to have been dead
by this time. Aren't you ready yet?"

Francis, the head jailer, a fat Dravidian in a white drill suit and gold
spectacles, waved his black hand. "Yes sir, yes sir," he bubbled. "All iss
satisfactorily prepared. The hangman iss waiting. We shall proceed."

"Well, quick march, then. The prisoners can't get their breakfast till this job's over." 5

We set out for the gallows. Two warders marched on either side of the prisoner, with their rifles at the slope; two others marched close against him, gripping him by arm and shoulder, as though at once pushing and supporting him. The rest of us, magistrates and the like, followed behind. Suddenly, when we had gone ten yards, the procession stopped short without any order or warning. A dreadful thing had happened—a dog, come goodness knows whence, had appeared in the yard. It came bounding among us with a loud volley of barks and leapt round us wagging its whole body, wild with glee at finding so many human beings together. It was a large woolly dog, half Airedale, half pariah. For a moment it pranced round us, and then, before anyone could stop it, it had made a dash for the prisoner, and jumping up tried to lick his face. Everybody stood aghast, too taken aback even to grab the dog.

"Who let that bloody brute in here?" said the superintendent angrily. "Catch it, someone!"

A warder detached from the escort, charged clumsily after the dog, but it danced and gambolled just out of his reach, taking everything as part of the game. A young Eurasian jailer picked up a handful of gravel and tried to stone the dog away, but it dodged the stones and came after us again. Its yaps echoed from the jail walls. The prisoner, in the grasp of the two warders, looked on incuriously, as though this was another formality of the hanging. It was several minutes before someone managed to catch the dog. Then we put my handkerchief through its collar and moved off once more, with the dog still straining and whimpering.

It was about forty yards to the gallows. I watched the bare brown back of the prisoner marching in front of me. He walked clumsily with his bound arms, but quite steadily, with that bobbing gait of the Indian who never straightens his knees. At each step his muscles slid neatly into place, the lock of hair on his scalp danced up and down, his feet printed themselves on the wet gravel. And once, in spite of the men who gripped him by each shoulder, he stepped slightly aside to avoid a puddle on the path.

It is curious, but till that moment I had never realized what it means 10
to destroy a healthy, conscious man. When I saw the prisoner step aside to avoid the puddle I saw the mystery, the unspeakable wrongness, of cutting a life short when it is in full tide. This man was not dying, he was alive just as we are alive. All the organs of his body were working—bowels digesting food, skin renewing itself, nails growing, tissues forming—all toiling away in solemn foolery. His nails would still be growing when he stood on the drop, when he was falling through the air with a tenth-of-a-second to live. His eyes saw the yellow gravel and the grey walls, and his brain still remembered, foresaw, reasoned—even

about puddles. He and we were a party of men walking together, seeing, hearing, feeling, understanding the same world; and in two minutes, with a sudden snap, one of us would be gone—one mind less, one world less.

The gallows stood in a small yard, separate from the main grounds of the prison, and overgrown with tall prickly weeds. It was a brick erection like three sides of a shed, with planking on top, and above that two beams and a crossbar with the rope dangling. The hangman, a grey-haired convict in the white uniform of the prison, was waiting beside his machine. He greeted us with a servile crouch as we entered. At a word from Francis the two warders, gripping the prisoner more closely than ever, half led, half pushed him to the gallows and helped him clumsily up the ladder. Then the hangman climbed up and fixed the rope round the prisoner's neck.

We stood waiting, five yards away. The warders had formed in a rough circle round the gallows. And then, when the noose was fixed, the prisoner began crying out to his god. It was a high, reiterated cry of "Ram! Ram! Ram! Ram!" not urgent and fearful like a prayer or cry for help, but steady, rhythmical, almost like the tolling of a bell. The dog answered the sound with a whine. The hangman, still standing on the gallows, produced a small cotton bag like a flour bag and drew it down over the prisoner's face. But the sound, muffled by the cloth, still persisted, over and over again: "Ram! Ram! Ram! Ram! Ram!"

The hangman climbed down and stood ready, holding the lever. Minutes seemed to pass. The steady, muffled crying from the prisoner went on and on, "Ram! Ram! Ram!" never faltering for an instant. The superintendent, his head on his chest, was slowly poking the ground with his stick; perhaps he was counting the cries, allowing the prisoner a fixed number—fifty, perhaps, or a hundred. Everyone had changed colour. The Indians had gone grey like bad coffee, and one or two of the bayonets were wavering. We looked at the lashed, hooded man on the drop, and listened to his cries—each cry another second of life; the same thought was in all our minds: oh, kill him quickly, get it over, stop that abominable noise!

Suddenly the superintendent made up his mind. Throwing up his head he made a swift motion with his stick. "Chalo!" he shouted almost fiercely.

There was a clanking noise, and then dead silence. The prisoner had 15 vanished, and the rope was twisting on itself. I let go of the dog, and it galloped immediately to the back of the gallows; but when it got there it stopped short, barked, and then retreated into a corner of the yard, where it stood among the weeds, looking timorously out at us. We went round the gallows to inspect the prisoner's body. He was dangling with his toes pointed straight downwards, very slowly revolving, as dead as a stone.

The superintendent reached out with his stick and poked the bare brown body; it oscillated slightly. "*He's* all right," said the superintendent. He backed out from under the gallows, and blew out a deep breath. The moody look had gone out of his face quite suddenly. He glanced at his wrist-watch. "Eight minutes past eight. Well, that's all for this morning, thank God."

The warders unfixed bayonets and marched away. The dog, sobered and conscious of having misbehaved itself, slipped after them. We walked out of the gallows yard, past the condemned cells with their waiting prisoners, into the big central yard of the prison. The convicts, under the command of warders armed with lathis, were already receiving their breakfast. They squatted in long rows, each man holding a tin pannikin, while two warders with buckets marched round ladling out rice; it seemed quite a homely, jolly scene, after the hanging. An enormous relief had come upon us now that the job was done. One felt an impulse to sing, to break into a run, to snigger. All at once everyone began chattering gaily.

The Eurasian boy walking beside me nodded towards the way we had come, with a knowing smile: "Do you know, sir, our friend (he meant the dead man), when he heard his appeal had been dismissed, he pissed on the floor of his cell. From fright. Kindly take one of my cigarettes, sir. Do you not admire my new silver case, sir? From the box-wallah, two rupees eight annas. Classy European style."

Several people laughed—at what, nobody seemed certain.

Francis was walking by the superintendent, talking garrulously: "Well, sir, all hass passed off with the utmost satisfactoriness. It was all finished—flick! like that. It iss not always so—oah, no! I have known cases where the doctor wass obliged to go beneath the gallows and pull the prissoner's legs to ensure decease. Most disagreeable!"   20

"Wriggling about, eh? That's bad," said the superintendent.

"Ach, sir, it iss worse when they become refractory! One man, I recall, clung to the bars of hiss cage when we went to take him out. You will scarcely credit, sir, that it took six warders to dislodge him, three pulling at each leg. We reasoned with him. 'My dear fellow,' we said, 'think of all the pain and trouble you are causing to us!' But no, he would not listen! Ach, he wass very troublesome!"

I found that I was laughing quite loudly. Everyone was laughing. Even the superintendent grinned in a tolerant way. "You'd better all come out and have a drink," he said quite genially. "I've got a bottle of whisky in the car. We could do with it."

We went through the big double gates of the prison into the road. "Pulling at his legs!" exclaimed a Burmese magistrate suddenly, and burst into a loud chuckling. We all began laughing again. At that moment Francis' anecdote seemed extraordinarily funny. We all had a drink together, native and European alike, quite amicably. The dead man was a hundred yards away.

❑ *Outward Exploration: Discussion*

1. Make a list of vivid details in the essay that particularly strike you.
2. What was Orwell's attitude toward the prisoner at first?
3. What makes Orwell change his mind?
4. What thematic purposes does the dog serve?
5. Why does everyone laugh at Francis's anecdote after the execution?

❑ *Outward Exploration: Writing*

1. If you have ever been in a situation where you felt subtly pressured by your duty or by your peers to do something you suddenly realized you didn't believe in doing, write an essay exploring the event and your feelings and thoughts, then and now. Make the event as vivid and detailed as Orwell makes his.
2. Recreate a significant event from your life, exploring its implications for you then and now. Make the event as vivid and detailed as Orwell makes his.

❑ *Style*

Consider the following sentence from Orwell's essay:

He had a thick, sprouting moustache, absurdly too big for his body, rather like the moustache of a comic man on the films. (paragraph 2)

This sentence's independent clause ("He had a thick, sprouting moustache") is followed by the two pieces of additional description ("absurdly too big for his body" and "rather like the moustache of a comic man on the films") which are joined by a comma.

Write your own sentence replicating this effect. Following the independent clause, put a comma and a multiword descriptive detail followed by another comma and another multiword detail (using the word *rather* to introduce this second descriptive element might be helpful).

The War of the Ants

HENRY DAVID THOREAU

☐ *Inward Exploration*

First, make a list of events you have witnessed occurring in Nature. Second, write at least one paragraph about a type of human behavior of which you strongly disapprove or approve.

One day when I went out to my wood-pile, or rather my pile of stumps, I observed two large ants, the one red, the other much larger, nearly half an inch long, and black, fiercely contending with one another. Having once got hold they never let go, but struggled and wrestled and rolled on the chips incessantly. Looking farther, I was surprised to find that the chips were covered with such combatants, that it was not a *duellum,* but a *bellum,* a war between two races of ants, the red always pitted against the black, and frequently two red ones to one black. The legions of these Myrmidons covered all the hills and vales in my wood-yard, and the ground was already strewn with the dead and dying, both red and black. It was the only battle which I have ever witnessed, the only battle-field I ever trod while the battle was raging; internecine war; the red republicans on the one hand, and the black imperialists on the other. On every side they were engaged in deadly combat, yet without any noise that I could hear, and human soldiers never fought so resolutely. I watched a couple that were fast locked in each other's embraces, in a little sunny valley amid the chips, now at noonday prepared to fight till the sun went down, or life went out. The smaller red champion had fastened himself like a vise to his adversary's front, and through all the tumblings on that field never for an instant ceased to gnaw at one of his feelers near the root, having already caused the other to go by the board; while the stronger black one dashed him from side to side, and, as I saw on looking nearer, had already divested him of several of his members. They fought with more pertinacity than bulldogs. Neither manifested the least disposition to retreat. It was evident that their battle-cry was "Conquer or die." In the meanwhile there came along a single red ant on the hillside of this valley, evidently full of excitement, who either had despatched his foe, or had not yet taken part in the battle; probably the latter, for he had lost none of his limbs; whose mother had charged him to return with his shield or upon it. Or perchance he was some Achilles, who had nourished his wrath apart, and

1

had now come to avenge or rescue his Patroclus. He saw this unequal combat from afar,—for the blacks were nearly twice the size of the red,—he drew near with rapid pace till he stood on his guard within half an inch of the combatants; then, watching his opportunity, he sprang upon the black warrior, and commenced his operations near the root of his right fore leg, leaving the foe to select among his own members; so there were three united for life, as if a new kind of attraction had been invented which put all other locks and cements to shame. I should not have wondered by this time to find that they had their respective musical bands stationed on some eminent chip, and playing their national airs the while, to excite the slow and cheer the dying combatants. I was myself excited somewhat even as if they had been men. The more you think of it, the less the difference. And certainly there is not the fight recorded in Concord history, at least, if in the history of America, that will bear a moment's comparison with this, whether for the numbers engaged in it, or for the patriotism and heroism displayed. For numbers and for carnage it was an Austerlitz or Dresden. Concord fight! Two killed on the patriots' side, and Luther Blanchard wounded! Why here every ant was a Buttrick,—"Fire! for God's sake fire!"—and thousands shared the fate of Davis and Hosmer. There was not one hireling there. I have no doubt that it was a principle they fought for, as much as our ancestors, and not to avoid a three-penny tax on their tea; and the results of this battle will be as important and memorable to those whom it concerns as those of the battle of Bunker Hill, at least.

I took up the chip on which the three I have particularly described were struggling, carried it into my house, and placed it under a tumbler on my window-sill, in order to see the issue. Holding a microscope to the first-mentioned red ant, I saw that, though he was assiduously gnawing at the near fore leg of his enemy, having severed his remaining feeler, his own breast was all torn away, exposing what vitals he had there to the jaws of the black warrior, whose breastplate was apparently too thick for his to pierce; and the dark carbuncles of the sufferer's eyes shone with ferocity such as war only could excite. They struggled half an hour longer under the tumbler, and when I looked again the black soldier had severed the heads of his foes from their bodies, and the still living heads were hanging on either side off him like ghastly trophies at his saddle-bow, still apparently as firmly fastened as ever, and he was endeavoring with feeble struggles, being without feelers, and with only the remnant of a leg, and I know not how many other wounds, to divest himself of them; which at length, after half an hour or more, he accomplished. I raised the glass, and he went off over the window-sill in that crippled state. Whether he finally survived that combat, and spent the remainder of his days in some Hôtel des Invalides, I do not know; but I thought that his industry would not be worth much thereafter. I never learned which party was victorious, nor the cause of the war; but I felt for the rest of that day as if I had had my feelings excited and harrowed by witnessing the struggle, the ferocity and carnage, of a human battle before my door.

Kirby and Spence tell us that the battles of ants have long been celebrated and the date of them recorded, though they say that Huber is the only modern author who appears to have witnessed them. "Æneas Sylvius," say they, "after giving a very circumstantial account of one contested with great obstinacy by a great and small species on the trunk of a pear tree," adds that "'this action was fought in the pontificate of Eugenius the Fourth, in the presence of Nicholas Pistoriensis, an eminent lawyer, who related the whole history of the battle with the greatest fidelity.' A similar engagement between great and small ants is recorded by Olaus Magnus, in which the small ones, being victorious, are said to have buried the bodies of their own soldiers, but left those of their giant enemies a prey to the birds. This event happened previous to the expulsion of the tyrant Christiern the Second from Sweden." The battle which I witnessed took place in the Presidency of Polk, five years before the passage of Webster's Fugitive-Slave Bill.

❏ *Outward Exploration: Discussion*

1. Why does Thoreau use words such as *combatants, bellum, internecine war, adversary, champion*?
2. How does he know that the red ants are "republicans" and the black ones are "imperialists"?
3. Discuss the irony in this essay.
4. What is the point of the essay's last paragraph?

❏ *Outward Exploration: Writing*

1. Write an essay about an event that you observed.
2. After closely observing an event that occurs in Nature, write an essay in which you describe and comment on the event in a manner similar to Thoreau's; in other words, draw parallels between the event and human behavior in such a way that your attitude toward that human behavior is strongly implied throughout your essay.

❏ *Style*

Consider the following sentence from Thoreau's essay:

I took up the chip on which the three I have particularly described were struggling, carried it into my house, and placed it under a tumbler on my window-sill, in order to see the issue. (paragraph 2)

One interesting element of this sentence is Thoreau's use of three compound verbs (*took, carried, placed*) all governed by the sentence's subject (*I*). Notice that each verb is followed by direct objects (*the chip, it, it*) and that commas separate the verb phrases from each other. Using your own information, create a sentence that uses three verbs governed by your sentence's subject.

The Stone Horse

BARRY LOPEZ

❑ *Inward Exploration*

Write at least one paragraph defining the term art.

The deserts of southern California, the high, relatively cooler and   *1*
wetter Mojave and the hotter, dryer Sonoran to the south of it, carry the
signatures of many cultures. Prehistoric rock drawings in the Mojave's
Coso Range, probably the greatest concentration of petroglyphs in
North America, are at least three thousand years old. Big game hunting
cultures that flourished six or seven thousand years before that are
known from broken spear tips, choppers, and burins left scattered along
the shores of great Pleistocene lakes, long since evaporated. Weapons
and tools discovered at China Lake may be thirty thousand years old;
and worked stone from a quarry in the Calico Mountains is, some argue, evidence that human beings were here more than two hundred
thousand years ago.

Because of the long-term stability of such arid environments, much
of this prehistoric stone evidence still lies exposed on the ground, accessible to anyone who passes by—the studious, the acquisitive, the indifferent, the merely curious. Archaeologists do not agree on the sequence
of cultural history beyond about twelve thousand years ago, but it is
clear that these broken bits of chalcedony, chert, and obsidian, like
the animal drawings and geometric designs etched on walls of basalt
throughout the desert, anchor the earliest threads of human history, the
first record of human endeavor here.

Western man did not enter the California desert until the end of the
eighteenth century, 250 years after Coronado brought his soldiers into
the Zuni pueblos in a bewildered search for the cities of Cibola. The
earliest appraisals of the land were cursory, hurried. People traveled
through it, en route to Santa Fe or the California coastal settlements.
Only miners tarried. In 1823 what had been Spain's became Mexico's
and in 1848 what had been Mexico's became America's; but the bare,
jagged mountains and dry lake beds, the vast and uniform plains of
creosote bush and yucca plants, remained as obscure as the northern
Sudan until the end of the nineteenth century.

Before 1940 the tangible evidence of twentieth-century man's passage here consisted of very little—the hard tracery of travel corridors;
the widely scattered, relatively insignificant evidence of mining opera-

tions; and the fair expanse of irrigated fields at the desert's periphery. In the space of a hundred years or so the wagon roads were paved, railroads were laid down, and canals and high-tension lines were built to bring water and electricity across the desert to Los Angeles from the Colorado River. The dark mouths of gold, talc, and tin mines yawned from the bony flanks of desert ranges. Dust-encrusted chemical plants stood at work on the lonely edges of dry lake beds. And crops of grapes, lettuce, dates, alfalfa, and cotton covered the Coachella and Imperial valleys, north and south of the Salton Sea, and the Palo Verde Valley along the Colorado.

These developments proceeded with little or no awareness of earlier   5
human occupations by cultures that preceded those of the historic Indians—the Mohave, the Chemehuevi, the Quechan. (Extensive irrigation began to actually change the climate of the Sonoran Desert, and human settlements, the railroads, and farming introduced many new, successful plants and animals into the region.)

During World War II, the American military moved into the desert in great force, to train troops and to test equipment. They found the clear weather conducive to year-round flying, the dry air, and isolation very attractive. After the war, a complex of training grounds, storage facilities, and gunnery and test ranges was permanently settled on more than three million acres of military reservations. Few perceived the extent or significance of the destruction of aboriginal sites that took place during tank maneuvers and bombing runs or in the laying out of highways, railroads, mining districts, and irrigated fields. The few who intuited that something like an American Dordogne Valley lay exposed here were (only) amateur archaeologists; even they reasoned that the desert was too vast for any of this to matter.

After World War II, people began moving out of the crowded Los Angeles basin into homes in Lucerne, Apple, and Antelope valleys in the western Mojave. They emigrated as well to a stretch of resort land at the foot of the San Jacinto Mountains that included Palm Springs, and farther out to old railroad and military towns like Twentynine Palms and Barstow. People also began exploring the desert, at first in military-surplus jeeps and then with a variety of all-terrain and off-road vehicles that became available in the 1960s. By the mid-1970s, the number of people using such vehicles for desert recreation had increased exponentially. Most came and went in innocent curiosity; the few who didn't wreaked a havoc all out of proportion to their numbers. The disturbance of previously isolated archaeological sites increased by an order of magnitude. Many sites were vandalized before archaeologists, themselves late to the desert, had any firm grasp of the bounds of human history in the desert. It was as though in the same moment an Aztec library had been discovered intact various lacunae had begun to appear.

The vandalism was of three sorts: the general disturbance usually caused by souvenir hunters and by the curious and the oblivious; the wholesale stripping of a place by professional thieves for black-market sale and trade; and outright destruction, in which vehicles were actually used to ram and trench an area. By 1980, the Bureau of Land Management estimated that probably thirty-five percent of the archaeological sites in the desert had been vandalized. The destruction at some places by rifles and shotguns, or by power winches mounted on vehicles, was, if one cared for history, demoralizing to behold.

In spite of public education, land closures, and stricter law enforcement in recent years, the BLM estimates that, annually, about one percent of the archaeological record in the desert continues to be destroyed or stolen.

2

A BLM archaeologist told me, with understandable reluctance, where to find the intaglio. I spread my Automobile Club of Southern California map of Imperial County out on his desk, and he traced the route with a pink felt-tip pen. The line crossed Interstate 8 and then turned west along the Mexican border.

"You can't drive any farther than about here," he said, marking a small *x*. "There's boulders in the wash. You walk up past them."

On a separate piece of paper he drew a route in a smaller scale that would take me up the arroyo to a certain point where I was to cross back east, to another arroyo. At its head, on higher ground just to the north, I would find the horse.

"It's tough to spot unless you know it's there. Once you pick it up . . ." He shook his head slowly, in a gesture of wonder at its existence.

I waited until I held his eye. I assured him I would not tell anyone else how to get there. He looked at me with stoical despair, like a man who had been robbed twice, whose belief in human beings was offered without conviction.

I did not go until the following day because I wanted to see it at dawn. I ate breakfast at 4 a.m. in El Centro and then drove south. The route was easy to follow, though the last section of road proved difficult, broken and drifted over with sand in some spots. I came to the barricade of boulders and parked. It was light enough by then to find my way over the ground with little trouble. The contours of the landscape were stark, without any masking vegetation. I worried only about rattlesnakes.

I traversed the stone plain as directed, but, in spite of the frankness of the land, I came on the horse unawares. In the first moment of recognition I was without feeling. I recalled later being startled, and that I held my breath. It was laid out on the ground with its head to the east, three times life size. As I took in its outline I felt a growing concentration of all my senses, as though my attentiveness to the pale rose color of the morning sky and other peripheral images had now ceased to be important. I was aware that I was straining for sound in the windless air and I felt the uneven pressure of the earth hard against my feet. The horse, outlined in a standing profile on the dark ground, was as vivid before me as a bed of tulips.

I've come upon animals suddenly before, and felt a similar tension, a precipitate heightening of the senses. And I have felt the inexplicable but sharply boosted intensity of a wild moment in the bush, where it is not until some minutes later that you discover the source of electricity—the warm remains of a grizzly bear kill, or the still moist tracks of a wolverine.

But this was slightly different. I felt I had stepped into an unoccupied corridor. I had no familiar sense of history, the temporal structure in which to think: This horse was made by Quechan people three hundred years ago. I felt instead a headlong rush of images: people hunting wild horses with spears on the Pleistocene veld of southern California; Cortés riding across the causeway into Montezuma's Tenochtitlán; a short-legged Comanche, astride his horse like some sort of ferret, slashing through cavalry lines of young men who rode like farmers. A hoof exploding past my face one morning in a corral in Wyoming. These images had the weight and silence of stone.

When I released my breath, the images softened. My initial feeling, of facing a wild animal in a remote region, was replaced with a calm sense of antiquity. It was then that I became conscious, like an ordinary tourist, of what was before me, and thought: This horse was probably laid out by Quechan people. But when, I wondered? The first horses they saw, I knew, might have been those that came north from Mexico in 1692 with Father Eusebio Kino. But Cocopa people, I recalled, also came this far north on occasion, to fight with their neighbors, the Quechan. And *they* could have seen horses with Melchior Díaz, at the mouth of the Colorado River in the fall of 1540. So, it could be four hundred years old. (No one in fact knows.)

I still had not moved. I took my eyes off the horse for a moment to 　*20* look south over the desert plain into Mexico, to look east past its head at the brightening sunrise, to situate myself. Then, finally, I brought my trailing foot slowly forward and stood erect. Sunlight was running like a thin sheet of water over the stony ground and it threw the horse into relief. It looked as though no hand had ever disturbed the stones that gave it its form.

The horse had been brought to life on ground called desert pavement, a tight, flat matrix of small cobbles blasted smooth by sand-laden winds. The uniform, monochromatic blackness of the stones, a patina of iron and magnesium oxides called desert varnish, is caused by long-term exposure to the sun. To make this type of low-relief ground glyph, or intaglio, the artist either selectively turns individual stones over to their lighter side or removes areas of stone to expose the lighter soil underneath, creating a negative image. This horse, about eighteen feet from brow to rump and eight feet from withers to hoof, had been made in the latter way, and its outline was bermed at certain points with low ridges of stone a few inches high to enhance its three-dimensional qualities. (The left side of the horse was in full profile; each leg was extended at 90 degrees to the body and fully visible, as though seen in three-quarter profile.)

I was not eager to move. The moment I did I would be back in the flow of time, the horse no longer quivering in the same way before me. I did not want to feel again the sequence of quotidian events—to be drawn off into deliberation and analysis. A human being, a four-footed animal, the open land. That was all that was present—and a "thoughtless" understanding of the very old desires bearing on this particular animal: to hunt it, to render it, to fathom it, to subjugate it, to honor it, to take it as a companion.

What finally made me move was the light. The sun now filled the shallow basin of the horse's body. The weighted line of the stone berm created the illusion of a mane and the distinctive roundness of an equine belly. The change in definition impelled me. I moved to the left, circling past its rump, to see how the light might flesh the horse out from various points of view. I circled it completely before squatting on my haunches. Ten or fifteen minutes later I chose another view. The third time I moved, to a point near the rear hooves, I spotted a stone tool at my feet. I stared at it a long while, more in awe than disbelief, before reaching out to pick it up. I turned it over in my left palm and took it between my fingers to feel its cutting edge. It is always difficult, especially with something so portable, to rechannel the desire to steal.

I spent several hours with the horse. As I changed positions and as the angle of the light continued to change I noticed a number of things. The angle at which the pastern carried the hoof away from the ankle was perfect. Also, stones had been placed within the image to suggest, at precisely the right spot, the left shoulder above the foreleg. The line that joined thigh and hock was similarly accurate. The muzzle alone seemed distorted—but perhaps these stones had been moved by a later hand. It was an admirably accurate representation, but not what a breeder would call perfect conformation. There was the suggestion of a bowed neck and an undershot jaw, and the tail, as full as a winter coyote's, did not appear to be precisely to scale.

The more I thought about it, the more I felt I was looking at an individual horse, a unique combination of generic and specific detail. It was easy to imagine one of Kino's horses as a model, or a horse that ran off from one of Coronado's columns. What kind of horses would these have been, I wondered? In the sixteenth century the most sought-after horses in Europe were Spanish, the offspring of Arabian stock and Barbary horses that the Moors brought to Iberia and bred to the older, eastern European strains brought in by the Romans. The model for this horse, I speculated, could easily have been a palomino, or a descendant of horses trained for lion-hunting in North Africa.

A few generations ago, cowboys, cavalry quartermasters, and draymen would have taken this horse before me under consideration and not let up their scrutiny until they had its heritage fixed to their satisfaction. Today, the distinction between draft and harness horses is arcane knowledge, and no image may come to mind for a blue roan or a claybank horse. The loss of such refinement in everyday conversation leaves me unsettled. People praise the Eskimo's ability to distinguish among forty types of snow but forget the skill of others who routinely differentiate between overo and tobiano pintos. Such distinctions are made for the same reason. You have to do it to be able to talk clearly about the world.

For parts of two years I worked as a horse wrangler and packer in Wyoming. It is dim knowledge now; I would have to think to remember if a buckskin was a kind of dun horse. And I couldn't throw a double-diamond hitch over a set of panniers—the packer's basic tie-down—without guidance. As I squatted there in the desert, however, these more personal memories seemed tenuous in comparison with the sweep of this animal in human time. My memories had no depth. I thought of the Hittite cavalry riding against the Syrians 3500 years ago. And the first of the Chinese emperors, Ch'in Shih Huang, buried in Shensi Province in 210 B.C. with thousands of life-size horses and soldiers, a terra-cotta guardian army. What could I know of what was in the mind of whoever made this horse? Was there some racial memory of it as an animal that had once fed the artist's ancestors and then disappeared from North America? And then returned in this strange alliance with another race of men?

Certainly, whoever it was, the artist had observed the animal very closely. Certainly the animal's speed had impressed him. Among the first things the Quechan would have learned from an encounter with Kino's horses was that their own long-distance runners—men who could run down mule deer—were no match for this animal.

From where I squatted I could look far out over the Mexican plain. Juan Bautista de Anza passed this way in 1774, extending El Camino Real into Alta California from Sinaloa. He was followed by others, all of them astride the magical horse; *gente de razón,* the people of reason, coming into the country of *los primitivos.* The horse, like the stone animals of Egypt, urged these memories upon me. And as I drew them up from some forgotten corner of my mind—huge horses carved in the white chalk downs of southern England by an Iron Age people; Spanish horses rearing and wheeling in fear before alligators in Florida—the images seemed tethered before me. With this sense of proportion, a memory of my own—the morning I almost lost my face to a horse's hoof—now had somewhere to fit.

I rose up and began to walk slowly around the horse again. I had *30* taken the first long measure of it and was looking now for a way to depart, a new angle of light, a fading of the image itself before the rising sun, that would break its hold on me. As I circled, feeling both heady and serene at the encounter, I realized again how strangely vivid it was. It had been created on a barren bajada between two arroyos, as nondescript a place as one could imagine. The only plant life here was a few wands of ocotillo cactus. The ground beneath my shoes was so hard it wouldn't take the print of a heavy animal even after a rain. The only sounds I had heard here were the voices of quail.

The archaeologist had been correct. For all its forcefulness, the horse is inconspicuous. If you don't care to see it you can walk right past it. That pleases him, I think. Unmarked on this bleak shoulder of the plain, the site signals to no one; so he wants no protective fences here, no informative plaque, to act as beacons. He would rather take a chance that no motorcyclist, no aimless wanderer with a flair for violence and a depth of ignorance, will ever find his way here.

The archaeologist had given me something before I left his office that now seemed peculiar—an aerial photograph of the horse. It is widely believed that an aerial view of an intaglio provides a fair and accurate description. It does not. In the photograph the horse looks somewhat crudely constructed; from the ground it appears far more deftly rendered. The photograph is of a single moment, and in that split second the horse seems vaguely impotent. I watched light pool in the intaglio at dawn; I imagine you could watch it withdraw at dusk and sense the same animation I did. In those prolonged moments its shape and so, too, its general character changed—noticeably. The living quality of the image, its immediacy to the eye, was brought out by the light-in-time, not, at least here, in the camera's frozen instant.

Intaglios, I thought, were never meant to be seen by gods in the sky above. They were meant to be seen by people on the ground, over a long period of shifting light. This could even be true of the huge figures on the Plain of Nazca in Peru, where people could walk for the length of a day beside them. It is our own impatience that leads us to think otherwise.

This process of abstraction, almost unintentional, drew me gradually away from the horse. I came to a position of attention at the edge of the sphere of its influence. With a slight bow I paid my respects to the horse, its maker, and the history of us all, and departed.

3

A short distance away I stopped the car in the middle of the road to   *35* make a few notes. I had not been able to write down what I was thinking when I was with the horse. It would have seemed disrespectful, and it would have required another kind of attention. So now I patiently drained my memory of the details it had fastened itself upon. The road I'd stopped on was adjacent to the All American Canal, the major source of water for the Imperial and Coachella valleys. The water flowed west placidly. A disjointed flock of coots, small, dark birds with white bills, was paddling against the current, foraging in the rushes.

I was peripherally aware of the birds as I wrote, the only movement in the desert; and of a series of sounds from a village a half-mile away. The first sounds from this collection of ramshackle houses in a grove of cottonwoods were the distracted dawn voices of dogs. I heard them intermingled with the cries of a rooster. Later, the high-pitched voices of children calling out to each other came disembodied through the dry desert air. Now, a little after seven, I could hear someone practicing on the trumpet, the same rough phrases played over and over. I suddenly remembered how as children we had tried to get the rhythm of a galloping horse with hands against our thighs, or by fluttering our tongues against the roofs of our mouths.

After the trumpet, the impatient calls of adults, summoning children. Sunday morning. Wood smoke hung like a lens in the trees. The first car starts—a cold, eight-cylinder engine, of Chrysler extraction perhaps, goosed to life, then throttled back to murmur through dual mufflers, the obbligato music of a shade-tree mechanic. The rote bark of mongrel dogs at dawn, the jagged outcries of men and women, an engine coming to life. Like a thousand villages from West Virginia to Guadalajara.

I finished my notes—where was I going to find a description of the horses that came north with the conquistadors? Did their manes come forward prominently over the brow, like this one's, like the forelocks of Blackfeet and Assiniboine men in nineteeth-century paintings? I set the notes on the seat beside me.

The road followed the canal for a while and then arced north, toward Interstate 8. It was slow driving and I fell to thinking how the desert had changed since Anza had come through. New plants and animals—the MacDougall cottonwood, the English house sparrow, the chukar from India—have about them now the air of the native-born. Of the native species, some—no one knows how many—are extinct. The populations of many others, especially the animals, have been sharply reduced. The idea of a desert impoverished by agricultural poisons and varmint hunters, by off-road vehicles and military operations, did not seem as disturbing to me, however, as this other horror, now that I had been those hours with the horse. The vandals, the few who crowbar rock art off the desert's walls, who dig up graves, who punish the ground that holds intaglios, are people who devour history. Their self-centered scorn, their disrespect for ideas and images beyond their ken, create the awful atmosphere of loose ends in which totalitarianism thrives, in which the past is merely curious or wrong.

I thought about the horse sitting out there on the unprotected plain. 40
I enumerated its qualities in my mind until a sense of its vulnerability receded and it became an anchor for something else. I remembered that

history, a history like this one, which ran deeper than Mexico, deeper than the Spanish, was a kind of medicine. It permitted the great breadth of human expression to reverberate, and it did not urge you to locate its apotheosis in the present.

Each of us, individuals and civilizations, has been held upside down like Achilles in the River Styx. The artist mixing his colors in the dim light of Altamira; an Egyptian ruler lying still now, wrapped in his byssus, stored against time in a pyramid; the faded Dorset culture of the Arctic; the Hmong and Samburu and Walbiri of historic time; the modern nations. This great, imperfect stretch of human expression is the clarification and encouragement, the urging and the reminder, we call history. And it is inscribed everywhere in the face of the land, from the mountain passes of the Himalayas to a nameless bajada in the California desert.

Small birds rose up in the road ahead, startled, and flew off. I prayed no infidel would ever find that horse.

☐ *Outward Exploration: Discussion*

1. What is the purpose of the essay's first section?
2. What types of vandalism occurred?
3. What can we learn from the detailed description of the horse?
4. Why does Lopez's first sight of the horse bring "a headlong rush of images"?
5. Why does Lopez keep changing his position?
6. What does he discover about the horse?
7. According to Lopez, why do people distinguish between types of pinto horses or types of snow?
8. What does he discover about the aerial photograph?
9. What are his feelings toward vandals who destroy records of the past?

☐ *Outward Exploration: Writing*

1. If you have ever "lost yourself" in the contemplation of a work of art, write an essay exploring the experience.
2. Several essays in this book have dealt with horses, including Alice Walker's "Am I Blue?" and N. Scott Momaday's "My Horse and I." Write an essay exploring the horse's significance to these writers and Lopez. You might consult some sources to broaden your essay's topic to "horses in the American imagination."
3. Write an essay exploring a significant experience of a place. Describe the place vividly, and explore your feelings and thoughts both then and now.

Once More to the Lake

E. B. WHITE

☐ *Inward Exploration*

Why are certain places important to us? Make a list of places which have been significant in your life. Select one place and write at least one paragraph about it. Perhaps it was once meaningful to you, or perhaps it continues to be meaningful. Perhaps it is a place to which you returned after an extended absence. In any event, describe the place and list some significant events that occurred there.

One summer, along about 1904, my father rented a camp on a lake   1
in Maine and took us all there for the month of August. We all got
ringworm from some kittens and had to rub Pond's Extract on our arms
and legs at night and morning, and my father rolled over in a canoe
with all his clothes on; but outside of that the vacation was a success and
from then on none of us ever thought there was any place in the world
like that lake in Maine. We returned summer after summer—always on
August 1 for one month. I have since become a salt-water man, but
sometimes in summer there are days when the restlessness of the tides
and the fearful cold of the sea water and the incessant wind that blows
across the afternoon and into the evening make me wish for the placidity
of a lake in the woods. A few weeks ago this feeling got so strong I
bought myself a couple of bass hooks and a spinner and returned to the
lake where we used to go, for a week's fishing and to revisit old haunts.

I took along my son, who had never had any fresh water up his nose
and who had seen lily pads only from train windows. On the journey
over to the lake I began to wonder what it would be like. I wondered
how time would have marred this unique, this holy spot—the coves and
streams, the hills that the sun set behind, the camps and the paths behind
the camps. I was sure that the tarred road would have found it out, and
I wondered in what other ways it would be desolated. It is strange how
much you can remember about places like that once you allow your
mind to return into the grooves that lead back. You remember one
thing, and that suddenly reminds you of another thing. I guess I remembered clearest of all the early mornings, when the lake was cool and
motionless, remembered how the bedroom smelled of the lumber it was
made of and of the wet woods whose scent entered through the screen.
The partitions in the camp were thin and did not extend clear to the top
of the rooms, and as I was always the first up I would dress softly so as

not to wake the others, and sneak out into the sweet outdoors and start out in the canoe, keeping close along the shore in the long shadows of the pines. I remembered being very careful never to rub my paddle against the gunwale for fear of disturbing the stillness of the cathedral.

The lake had never been what you would call a wild lake. There were cottages sprinkled around the shores, and it was in farming country although the shores of the lake were quite heavily wooded. Some of the cottages were owned by nearby farmers, and you would live at the shore and eat your meals at the farmhouse. That's what our family did. But although it wasn't wild, it was a fairly large and undisturbed lake and there were places in it that, to a child at least, seemed infinitely remote and primeval.

I was right about the tar: it led to within half a mile of the shore. But when I got back there, with my boy, and we settled into a camp near a farmhouse and into the kind of summertime I had known, I could tell that it was going to be pretty much the same as it had been before—I knew it, lying in bed the first morning, smelling the bedroom and hearing the boy sneak quietly out and go off along the shore in a boat. I began to sustain the illusion that he was I, and therefore, by simple transposition, that I was my father. This sensation persisted, kept cropping up all the time we were there. It was not an entirely new feeling, but in this setting it grew much stronger. I seemed to be living a dual existence. I would be in the middle of some simple act, I would be picking up a bait box or laying down a table fork, or I would be saying something, and suddenly it would be not I but my father who was saying the words or making the gesture. It gave me a creepy sensation.

We went fishing the first morning. I felt the same damp moss covering the worms in the bait can, and saw the dragonfly alight on the tip of my rod as it hovered a few inches from the surface of the water. It was the arrival of this fly that convinced me beyond any doubt that everything was as it always had been, that the years were a mirage and that there had been no years. The small waves were the same, chucking the rowboat under the chin as we fished at anchor, and the boat was the same boat, the same color green and the ribs broken in the same places, and under the floorboards the same fresh-water leavings and débris—the dead helgramite, the wisps of moss, the rusty discarded fishhook, the dried blood from yesterday's catch. We stared silently at the tips of our rods, at the dragonflies that came and went. I lowered the tip of mine into the water, tentatively, pensively dislodging the fly, which darted two feet away, poised, darted two feet back, and came to rest again a little farther up the rod. There had been no years between the ducking of this dragonfly and the other one—the one that was part of memory. I looked at the boy, who was silently watching his fly, and it was my hands that held his rod, my eyes watching. I felt dizzy and didn't know which rod I was at the end of.

5

We caught two bass, hauling them in briskly as though they were mackerel, pulling them over the side of the boat in a businesslike manner without any landing net, and stunning them with a blow on the back of the head. When we got back for a swim before lunch, the lake was exactly where we had left it, the same number of inches from the dock, and there was only the merest suggestion of a breeze. This seemed an utterly enchanted sea, this lake you could leave to its own devices for a few hours and come back to, and find that it had not stirred, this constant and trustworthy body of water. In the shallows, the dark, water-soaked sticks and twigs, smooth and old, were undulating in clusters on the bottom against the clean ribbed sand, and the track of the mussel was plain. A school of minnows swam by, each minnow with its small individual shadow, doubling the attendance, so clear and sharp in the sunlight. Some of the other campers were in swimming, along the shore, one of them with a cake of soap, and the water felt thin and clear and unsubstantial. Over the years there had been this person with the cake of soap, this cultist, and here he was. There had been no years.

Up to the farmhouse to dinner through the teeming, dusty field, the road under our sneakers was only a two-track road. The middle track was missing, the one with the marks of the hooves and the splotches of dried, flaky manure. There had been three tracks to choose from in choosing which track to walk in; now the choice was narrowed down to two. For a moment I missed terribly the middle alternative. But the way led past the tennis court, and something about the way it lay there in the sun reassured me; the tape had loosened along the backline, the alleys were green with plantains and other weeds, and the net (installed in June and removed in September) sagged in the dry noon, and the whole place steamed with midday heat and hunger and emptiness. There was a choice of pie for dessert, and one was blueberry and one was apple, and the waitresses were the same country girls, there having been no passage of time, only the illusion of it as in a dropped curtain—the waitresses were still fifteen; their hair had been washed, that was the only difference—they had been to the movies and seen the pretty girls with clean hair.

Summertime, oh, summertime, pattern of life indelible, the fadeproof lake, the woods unshatterable, the pasture with the sweetfern and the juniper forever and ever, summer without end; this was the background, and the life along the shore was the design, the cottagers with their innocent and tranquil design, their tiny docks with the flagpole and the American flag floating against the white clouds in the blue sky, the little paths over the roots of the trees leading from camp to camp and the paths leading back to the outhouses and the can of lime for sprinkling, and at the souvenir counters at the store the miniature birch-bark canoes and the postcards that showed things looking a little better than they looked. This was the American family at play, escaping the city heat, wondering whether the newcomers in the camp at the head of the cove were "common" or "nice," wondering whether it was true that the people who drove up for Sunday dinner at the farmhouse were turned away because there wasn't enough chicken.

It seemed to me, as I kept remembering all this, that those times and those summers had been infinitely precious and worth saving. There had been jollity and peace and goodness. The arriving (at the beginning of August) had been so big a business in itself, at the railway station the farm wagon drawn up, the first smell of the pine-laden air, the first glimpse of the smiling farmer, and the great importance of the trunks and your father's enormous authority in such matters, and the feel of the wagon under you for the long ten-mile haul, and at the top of the last long hill catching the first view of the lake after eleven months of not seeing this cherished body of water. The shouts and cries of the other campers when they saw you, and the trunks to be unpacked, to give up their rich burden. (Arriving was less exciting nowadays, when you sneaked up in your car and parked it under a tree near the camp and took out the bags and in five minutes it was all over, no fuss, no loud wonderful fuss about trunks.)

Peace and goodness and jollity. The only thing that was wrong   10
now, really, was the sound of the place, an unfamiliar nervous sound of the outboard motors. This was the note that jarred, the one thing that would sometimes break the illusion and set the years moving. In those other summertimes all motors were inboard; and when they were at a little distance, the noise they made was a sedative, an ingredient of summer sleep. They were one-cylinder and two-cylinder engines, and some were make-and-break and some were jump-spark, but they all made a sleepy sound across the lake. The one-lungers throbbed and fluttered, and the twin-cylinder ones purred and purred, and that was a quiet sound, too. But now the campers all had outboards. In the daytime, in the hot mornings, these motors made a petulant, irritable sound; at night, in the still evening when the afterglow lit the water, they whined about one's ears like mosquitoes. My boy loved our rented outboard, and his great desire was to achieve single-handed mastery over it, and authority, and he soon learned the trick of choking it a little (but not too much), and the adjustment of the needle valve. Watching him I would remember the things you could do with the old one-cylinder engine with the heavy flywheel, how you could have it eating out of your hand if you got really close to it spiritually. Motorboats in those days didn't have clutches, and you would make a landing by shutting off the motor at the proper time and coasting in with a dead rudder. But there was a way of reversing them, if you learned the trick, by cutting the switch and putting it on again exactly on the final dying revolution of the flywheel, so that it would kick back against compression and begin reversing. Approaching a dock in a strong following breeze, it was difficult to slow up sufficiently by the ordinary coasting method, and if a boy felt he had complete mastery over his motor, he was tempted to keep it

running beyond its time and then reverse it a few feet from the dock. It took a cool nerve, because if you threw the switch a twentieth of a second too soon you would catch the flywheel when it still had speed enough to go up past center, and the boat would leap ahead, charging bull-fashion at the dock.

We had a good week at the camp. The bass were biting well and the sun shone endlessly, day after day. We would be tired at night and lie down in the accumulated heat of the little bedrooms after the long hot day and the breeze would stir almost imperceptibly outside and the smell of the swamp drift in through the rusty screens. Sleep would come easily and in the morning the red squirrel would be on the roof, tapping out his gay routine. I kept remembering everything, lying in bed in the mornings—the small steamboat that had a long rounded stern like the lip of a Ubangi, and how quietly she ran on the moonlight sails, when the older boys played their mandolins and the girls sang and we ate doughnuts dipped in sugar, and how sweet the music was on the water in the shining night, and what it had felt like to think about girls then. After breakfast we would go up to the store and the things were in the same place—the minnows in a bottle, the plugs and spinners disarranged and pawed over by the youngsters from the boys' camp, the Fig Newtons and the Beeman's gum. Outside, the road was tarred and cars stood in front of the store. Inside, all was just as it had always been, except there was more Coca-Cola and not so much Moxie and root beer and birch beer and sarsaparilla. We would walk out with the bottle of pop apiece and sometimes the pop would backfire up our noses and hurt. We explored the streams, quietly, where the turtles slid off the sunny logs and dug their way into the soft bottom; and we lay on the town wharf and fed worms to the tame bass. Everywhere we went I had trouble making out which was I, the one walking at my side, the one walking in my pants.

One afternoon while we were there at that lake a thunderstorm came up. It was like the revival of an old melodrama that I had seen long ago with childish awe. The second-act climax of the drama of the electrical disturbance over a lake in America had not changed in any important respect. This was the big scene, still the big scene. The whole thing was so familiar, the first feeling of oppression and heat and a general air around camp of not wanting to go very far away. In mid-afternoon (it was all the same) a curious darkening of the sky, and a lull in everything that had made life tick; and then the way the boats suddenly swung the other way at their moorings with the coming of a breeze out of the new quarter, and the premonitory rumble. Then the kettle drum, then the snare, then the bass drum and cymbals, then crackling light against the dark, and the gods grinning and licking their chops in the hills. Afterward the calm, the rain steadily rustling in the calm lake, the return of light and hope and spirits, and the campers running out in joy and relief to go swimming in the rain, their bright cries perpetuating the deathless joke about how they were getting simply drenched, and the children screaming with delight at the new sensation of bathing in the rain, and the joke about getting drenched linking the generations in a strong indestructible chain. And the comedian who waded in carrying an umbrella.

When the others went swimming, my son said he was going in, too. He pulled his dripping trunks from the line where they had hung all through the shower and wrung them out. Languidly, and with no thought of going in, I watched him, his hard little body, skinny and bare, saw him wince slightly as he pulled up around his vitals the small, soggy, icy garment. As he buckled the swollen belt, suddenly my groin felt the chill of death.

☐ *Outward Exploration: Discussion*

1. Why does White begin his essay with a summary of his boyhood trips to the lake?
2. Explain White's sensation that he was his own son and father.
3. How does White make the thunderstorm so vivid (paragraph 12)?
4. What details have remained the same at the lake?
5. What details throughout the essay reveal that change has occurred at the lake? Which changes does the persona acknowledge, and which does he try to ignore?
6. What details throughout the essay foreshadow White's revelation at the end?

☐ *Outward Exploration: Writing*

1. Write an essay about your return to a place that had once been significant to you. Try to give readers a sense of your perspective *then* as well as of your perspective *now*.
2. Write an essay exploring an event in which its locale played a significant role (as the lake plays a significant role in White's visit).

☐ *Style*

Consider the following sentence from White's essay:

We caught two bass, hauling them in briskly as though they were mackerel, pulling them over the side of the boat in a businesslike manner without any landing net, and stunning them with a blow on the back of the head. (paragraph 6)

A brief (four-word) independent clause ("We caught two bass") tells us the point of the sentence. The rest of the sentence is made up of three free modifiers, each beginning with a present participle (*hauling, pulling,* and *stunning*). Such a structure allows the writer to state the main action in one general verb (in this case, *caught*) and then to elaborate on that action, giving specific details about exactly how that general action was accomplished using present participles called **free modifiers** ("*hauling* them in briskly as though they were mackerel, *pulling* them over the side of the boat in a businesslike manner without any landing net, and *stunning* them with a blow on the back of the head"). The free modifiers "unpack" the idea contained in the general verb. Notice also that each present participle is preceded by a comma.

Using your own information, write a sentence that replicates this structure (a brief independent clause followed by three free modifiers separated by commas).

Beauty: When the Other Dancer Is the Self

ALICE WALKER

□ *Inward Exploration*

Often, one particular event seems to be crucial either in establishing a whole chain of subsequent events or in changing a person's vision of himself or herself. For example, a family's moving from a big city to a small town might be the event that allows a shy child to become confident and outgoing, or failing an exam might be the event that triggers a student's reevaluation of self and new dedication to studying, or joining the debate team in high school might build self-confidence in a person's public speaking ability and change his or her social life, or accepting a summer job might reveal a whole new career path that a person had never considered before. Make a list of such seminal events in your life, and write at least one paragraph about one of them.

It is a bright summer day in 1947. My father, a fat, funny man with beautiful eyes and a subversive wit, is trying to decide which of his eight children he will take with him to the county fair. My mother, of course, will not go. She is knocked out from getting most of us ready: I hold my neck stiff against the pressure of her knuckles as she hastily completes the braiding and the beribboning of my hair.

My father is the driver for the rich old white lady up the road. Her name is Miss Mey. She owns all the land for miles around, as well as the house in which we live. All I remember about her is that she once offered to pay my mother thirty-five cents for cleaning her house, raking up piles of her magnolia leaves, and washing her family's clothes, and that my mother—she of no money, eight children, and a chronic earache—refused it. But I do not think of this in 1947. I am two-and a-half years old. I want to go everywhere my daddy goes. I am excited at the prospect of riding in a car. Someone has told me fairs are fun. That there is room in the car for only three of us doesn't faze me at all. Whirling happily in my starchy frock, showing off my biscuit-polished patent-leather shoes and lavender socks, tossing my head in a way that makes my ribbons bounce, I stand, hands on hips, before my father. "Take me, Daddy," I say with assurance; "I'm the prettiest!"

Later, it does not surprise me to find myself in Miss Mey's shiny black car, sharing the back seat with the other lucky ones. Does not surprise me that I thoroughly enjoy the fair. At home that night I tell the unlucky ones all I can remember about the merry-go-round, the man who eats live chickens, and the teddy bears, until they say: that's enough, baby Alice. Shut up now, and go to sleep.

It is Easter Sunday, 1950. I am dressed in a green, flocked, scalloped-hem dress (handmade by my adoring sister, Ruth) that has its own smooth satin petticoat and tiny hot-pink roses tucked into each scallop. My shoes, new T-strap patent leather, again highly biscuit-polished. I am six years old and have learned one of the longest Easter speeches to be heard that day, totally unlike the speech I said when I was two: "Easter lilies / pure and white / blossom in / the morning light." When I rise to give my speech I do so on a great wave of love and pride and expectation. People in the church stop rustling their new crinolines. They seem to hold their breath. I can tell they admire my dress, but it is my spirit, bordering on sassiness (womanishness), they secretly applaud.

"That girl's a little *mess*," they whisper to each other, pleased.   5

Naturally I say my speech without stammer or pause, unlike those who stutter, stammer, or, worst of all, forget. This is before the word "beautiful" exists in people's vocabulary, but "Oh, isn't she the *cutest* thing!" frequently floats my way. "And got so much sense!" they gratefully add . . . for which thoughtful addition I thank them to this day.

It was great fun being cute. But then, one day, it ended.

I am eight years old and a tomboy. I have a cowboy hat, cowboy boots, checkered shirt and pants, all red. My playmates are my brothers, two and four years older than I. Their colors are black and green, the only difference in the way we are dressed. On Saturday nights we all go to the picture show, even my mother; Westerns are her favorite kind of movie. Back home, "on the ranch," we pretend we are Tom Mix, Hopalong Cassidy, Lash LaRue (we've even named one of our dogs Lash LaRue); we chase each other for hours rustling cattle, being outlaws, delivering damsels from distress. Then my parents decide to buy my brothers guns. These are not "real" guns. They shoot BBs, copper pellets my brothers say will kill birds. Because I am a girl, I do not get a gun. Instantly I am relegated to the position of Indian. Now there appears a great distance between us. They shoot and shoot at everything with their new guns. I try to keep up with my bow and arrows.

One day while I am standing on top of our makeshift "garage"— pieces of tin nailed across some poles—holding my bow and arrow and looking out toward the fields, I feel an incredible blow in my right eye. I look down just in time to see my brother lower his gun.

Both brothers rush to my side. My eye stings, and I cover it with   10 my hand. "If you tell," they say, "we will get a whipping. You don't want that to happen, do you?" I do not. "Here is a piece of wire," says the older brother, picking it up from the roof; "say you stepped on one end of it and the other flew up and hit you." The pain is beginning to start. "Yes," I say. "Yes, I will say that is what happened." If I do not say this is what happened, I know my brothers will find ways to make me wish I had. But now I will say anything that gets me to my mother.

Confronted by our parents we stick to the lie agreed upon. They place me on a bench on the porch and I close my left eye while they examine the right. There is a tree growing from underneath the porch that climbs past the railing to the roof. It is the last thing my right eye sees. I watch as its trunk, its branches, and then its leaves are blotted out by the rising blood.

I am in shock. First there is intense fever, which my father tries to break using lily leaves bound around my head. Then there are chills: my mother tries to get me to eat soup. Eventually, I do not know how, my parents learn what has happened. A week after the "accident" they take me to see a doctor. "Why did you wait so long to come?" he asks, looking into my eye and shaking his head. "Eyes are sympathetic," he says. "If one is blind, the other will likely become blind too."

This comment of the doctor's terrifies me. But it is really how I look that bothers me most. Where the BB pellet struck there is a glob of whitish scar tissue, a hideous cataract, on my eye. Now when I stare at people—a favorite pastime, up to now—they will stare back. Not at the "cute" little girl, but at her scar. For six years I do not stare at anyone, because I do not raise my head.

Years later, in the throes of a mid-life crisis, I ask my mother and sister whether I changed after the "accident." "No," they say, puzzled. "What do you mean?"

What do I mean?   15

I am eight, and, for the first time, doing poorly in school, where I have been something of a whiz since I was four. We have just moved to the place where the "accident" occurred. We do not know any of the people around us because this is a different county. The only time I see the friends I knew is when we go back to our old church. The new school is the former state penitentiary. It is a large stone building, cold and drafty, crammed to overflowing with boisterous, ill-disciplined children. On the third floor there is a huge circular imprint of some partition that has been torn out.

"What used to be here?" I ask a sullen girl next to me on our way past it to lunch.

"The electric chair," says she.

At night I have nightmares about the electric chair, and about all the people reputedly "fried" in it. I am afraid of the school, where all the students seem to be budding criminals.

"What's the matter with your eye?" they ask, critically.   20

When I don't answer (I cannot decide whether it was an "accident" or not), they shove me, insist on a fight.

My brother, the one who created the story about the wire, comes to my rescue. But then brags so much about "protecting" me, I become sick.

After months of torture at the school, my parents decide to send me back to our old community, to my old school. I live with my grandparents and the teacher they board. But there is no room for Phoebe, my cat. By the time my grandparents decide there *is* room, and I ask for my cat, she cannot be found. Miss Yarborough, the boarding teacher, takes me under her wing, and begins to teach me to play the piano. But soon she marries an African—a "prince," she says—and is whisked away to his continent.

At my old school there is at least one teacher who loves me. She is the teacher who "knew me before I was born" and bought my first baby clothes. It is she who makes life bearable. It is her presence that finally helps me turn on the one child at the school who continually calls me "one-eyed bitch." One day I simply grab him by his coat and beat him until I am satisfied. It is my teacher who tells me my mother is ill.

My mother is lying in bed in the middle of the day, something I   25
have never seen. She is in too much pain to speak. She has an abscess in her ear. I stand looking down on her, knowing that if she dies, I cannot live. She is being treated with warm oils and hot bricks held against her cheek. Finally a doctor comes. But I must go back to my grandparents' house. The weeks pass but I am hardly aware of it. All I know is that my mother might die, my father is not so jolly, my brothers still have their guns, and I am the one sent away from home.

"You did not change," they say.

Did I imagine the anguish of never looking up?

I am twelve. When relatives come to visit I hide in my room. My cousin Brenda, just my age, whose father works in the post office and whose mother is a nurse, comes to find me. "Hello," she says. And then she asks, looking at my recent school picture, which I did not want taken, and on which the "glob," as I think of it, is clearly visible, "You still can't see out of that eye?"

"No," I say, and flop back on the bed over my book.

That night, as I do almost every night, I abuse my eye. I rant and   30
rave at it, in front of the mirror. I plead with it to clear up before morning. I tell it I hate and despise it. I do not pray for sight. I pray for beauty.

"You did not change," they say.

I am fourteen and baby-sitting for my brother Bill, who lives in Boston. He is my favorite brother and there is a strong bond between us. Understanding my feelings of shame and ugliness he and his wife take me to a local hospital, where the "glob" is removed by a doctor named O. Henry. There is still a small bluish crater where the scar tissue was, but the ugly white stuff is gone. Almost immediately I become a different person from the girl who does not raise her head. Or so I think. Now that I've raised my head I win the boyfriend of my dreams. Now that I've raised my head I have plenty of friends. Now that I've raised my head classwork comes from my lips as faultlessly as Easter speeches did, and I leave high school as valedictorian, most popular student, and *queen,* hardly believing my luck. Ironically, the girl who was voted most beautiful in our class (and was) was later shot twice through the chest by a male companion, using a "real" gun, while she was pregnant. But that's another story in itself. Or is it?

"You did not change," they say.

It is now thirty years since the "accident." A beautiful journalist comes to visit and to interview me. She is going to write a cover story for her magazine that focuses on my latest book. "Decide how you want to look on the cover," she says. "Glamorous, or whatever."

Never mind "glamorous," it is the "whatever" that I hear. Suddenly   35
all I can think of is whether I will get enough sleep the night before the photography session: If I don't, my eye will be tired and wander, as blind eyes will.

At night in bed with my lover I think up reasons why I should not appear on the cover of a magazine. "My meanest critics will say I've sold out," I say. "My family will now realize I write scandalous books."

"But what's the real reason you don't want to do this?" he asks.

"Because in all probability," I say in a rush, "my eye won't be straight."

"It will be straight enough," he says. Then, "Besides, I thought you'd made your peace with that."

And I suddenly remember that I have.   40

I remember:

I am talking to my brother Jimmy, asking if he remembers anything unusual about the day I was shot. He does not know I consider that day the last time my father, with his sweet home remedy of cool lily leaves, chose me, and that I suffered and raged inside because of this. "Well," he says, "all I remember is standing by the side of the highway with Daddy, trying to flag down a car. A white man stopped, but when Daddy said he needed somebody to take his little girl to the doctor, he drove off."

I remember:

I am in the desert for the first time. I fall totally in love with it. I am so overwhelmed by its beauty, I confront for the first time, consciously, the meaning of the doctor's words years ago: "Eyes are sympathetic. If one is blind, the other will likely become blind too." I realize I have dashed about the world madly, looking at this, looking at that, storing up images against the fading of the light. *But I might have missed seeing the desert!* The shock of that possibility—and gratitude for over twenty-five years of sight—sends me literally to my knees. Poem after poem comes—which is perhaps how poets pray.

ON SIGHT

I am so thankful I have seen
The Desert
And the creatures in the desert
And the desert Itself.

The desert has its own moon
Which I have seen
With my own eye.
There is no flag on it.

Trees of the desert have arms
All of which are always up
That is because the moon is up
The sun is up
Also the sky
The Stars
Clouds
None with flags.

If there *were* flags, I doubt
the trees would point.
Would you?

But mostly, I remember this: 45

I am twenty-seven, and my baby daughter is almost three. Since her birth I have worried about her discovery that her mother's eyes are different from other people's. Will she be embarrassed? I think. What will she say? Every day she watches a television program called *Big Blue Marble*. It begins with a picture of the earth as it appears from the moon. It is bluish, a little battered-looking, but full of light, with whitish clouds swirling around it. Every time I see it I weep with love, as if it is a picture of Grandma's house. One day when I am putting Rebecca down for her nap, she suddenly focuses on my eye. Something inside me cringes, gets ready to try to protect myself. All children are cruel about physical differences, I know from experience, and that they don't always mean to be is another matter. I assume Rebecca will be the same.

But no-o-o-o. She studies my face intently as we stand, her inside and me outside her crib. She even holds my face maternally between her dimpled little hands. Then, looking every bit as serious and lawyerlike as her father, she says, as if it may just possibly have slipped my attention: "Mommy, there's a *world* in your eye." (As in, "Don't be alarmed, or do anything crazy.") And then, gently, but with great interest: "Mommy, where did you *get* that world in your eye?"

For the most part, the pain left then. (So what, if my brothers grew up to buy even more powerful pellet guns for their sons and to carry real guns themselves. So what, if a young "Morehouse man" once nearly fell off the steps of Trevor Arnett Library because he thought my eyes were blue.) Crying and laughing I ran to the bathroom, while Rebecca mumbled and sang herself to sleep. Yes indeed, I realized, looking into the mirror. There *was* a world in my eye. And I saw that it was possible to love it: that in fact, for all it had taught me of shame and anger and inner vision, I *did* love it. Even to see it drifting out of orbit in boredom, or rolling up out of fatigue, not to mention floating back at attention in excitement (bearing witness, a friend has called it), deeply suitable to my personality, and even characteristic of me.

That night I dream I am dancing to Stevie Wonder's song "Always" (the name of the song is really "As," but I hear it as "Always"). As I dance, whirling and joyous, happier than I've ever been in my life, another bright-faced dancer joins me. We dance and kiss each other and hold each other through the night. The other dancer has obviously come through all right, as I have done. She is beautiful, whole, and free. And she is also me.

❏ Outward Exploration: Discussion

1. Why is the essay broken up into sections which are separated by white space?
2. Explain how Walker keeps readers informed in each section about when its events occurred. Are there any variations in her technique for informing readers? What effect is achieved by her use of time markers?
3. Are there any places in the essay where Walker disrupts chronology? If so, why does she do so?
4. Why does Walker tell us about the most beautiful girl in her high school class (paragraph 32)?
5. What is Walker suggesting when she tells us that her brothers now own real guns and that they gave their sons "even more powerful pellet guns" (paragraph 48)?

❏ Outward Exploration: Writing

1. If a single event triggered a series of events or a pattern of behavior in your life, write an essay exploring it. Make the event vivid. Make its implications and significance (both personal and global) explicit.
2. Assumptions about gender roles often play a significant part in what activities we grow up enjoying and what expectations we have about what we can do in life. Examine your own childhood for incidents of

pressure to follow gender stereotyping (for instance, Walker's parents give only their sons pellet guns). Select an event or a series of events that illustrate the stereotyping pressures and their effects on you. Write an essay about the effects of such conditioning on you and society.

❏ *Style*

In this essay, Walker uses sentences such as "'You did not change'" and *"I remember"* as though they were refrains in a poem. Consider the effect of such use—does the meaning change with repetition? In your next essay, try to use a phrase or sentence as a refrain that achieves similar effects.

4

Exploring Other People

One way of discovering something about yourself is to try to understand someone else—his or her personality, sense of self, emotions, beliefs, motives, world view. This could be anyone: a relative, a friend, a writer, a celebrity. In examining and questioning that person's life, you end up exploring your own as well.

Such an endeavor includes many of the techniques discussed in Chapter 3, "Exploring Events"—for example, discovering key incidents which reveal the person's traits, describing the person, perhaps reproducing some of his or her dialogue. In addition, the techniques in Chapter 2, "Exploring Yourself," work equally well as you explore the personality of others—considering the person from different vantage points, considering his or her different identities and roles. In short, you have already worked with several of the techniques that will help you.

WRITER-BASED GOALS

There are four writer-based goals: (1) to choose a person who is significant in some way to you; (2) to discover and explore that person's complexity; (3) to discover and explore his or her significance to you; (4) to discover and explore something about yourself in relation to that person.

READER-BASED GOALS

There are four reader-based goals: (1) to create an interesting and accurate portrait; (2) to reveal the chosen person's complex personality; (3) to reveal his or her significance to you; (4) to reveal something about your inner self.

SELECTING SOMEONE TO WRITE ABOUT

You should select someone whose personality, motives, world view, thoughts, beliefs, and emotions interest you. Thus the person should be important or significant to you in some way. However, there is another important limitation on your selection: He or she must be someone about whom you can find information. To present an interesting and accurate portrait to your readers, you will need access to more information than you probably have available at the moment. For example, you will need background facts about that person's life and interests, and you will need to know his or her views on various matters. If he or she is someone you know personally, perhaps you can elicit the needed information directly, in a conversation or by talking to people whom both of you know. If the person is someone you do not know, as in the case of a public figure, the many sources of information available in the library will provide answers to your questions.

Someone You Know

People you know include relatives, friends, co-workers, fellow students, professors. Even a distant relative may have some very significant connections to you. Let's assume that you want to find out more about your dead great-great-grandmother. In such a case, your major source of information will be other relatives such as your parents, grandparents, aunts and uncles. There will probably be family stories about her. Perhaps photographs of her exist or even whole albums of photographs that she collected of others. Either could be revealing. The attic might hold some records—diaries or journals, her business records. Perhaps some artifacts remain such as drawings, a butter churn, quilt, or carving she made, some letters or poetry she wrote. You might be able to find some objects that were associated with her such as jewelry, clothing, tools, a wallet. Maybe a building in town is still associated with her—or she built a business that still bears her name, or a shed she built is still standing. Perhaps a family recipe that she invented or a technique for doing something, such as how to chop wood, has been passed down. You might even have some memories that you can check and expand by talking with relatives and family friends.

If you decide to write about a living relative, all the sources just discussed are still potentially useful. In addition, a living relative might herself be a major source of information.

Public and Fictitious Figures

We all make people we don't know a significant part of our lives as well. For example, when I was young, Mickey Mantle was my baseball hero, Thomas Jefferson was my idol from history, and the Hardy Boys were my fictional heroes. As I became an adult, *heroes* were demoted to *favorites*: Sports favorites included K. C. Jones, Johnny Unitas, Larry Bird; favorite actors included Raymond Burr, Kirk Douglas, Burt Lancaster, James Earl Jones, Michael Douglas, Meryl Streep; favorite fictitious characters included Perry Mason, Adam Dalgliesh, Humbert Humbert, Miss Marple; favorite writers included Vladimir Nabokov, William Faulkner, P. D. James, Alice Walker, Margaret Atwood. You get the idea.

The point here is simply this: Because I consciously chose to make these public figures a part of my life (on whatever level), I must have sensed some kind of connection with them. Perhaps they fulfilled some fantasy of mine; for example, Kirk Douglas and Burt Lancaster became favorite actors when they portrayed Doc Holliday and Wyatt Earp in the 1957 movie *Gunfight at the OK Corral*. As an only child, I hankered for a friend that true, a friend that loyal. With writers it is even easier to see the connection. I have been writing since I was eight years old; in fact, I began by writing some pretty terrible imitations of the Hardy Boys novels. Later, writers like William Faulkner captured my imagination with the power of language and a complex interweaving of past and present; Alice Walker grabbed me with her honesty and her range; Vladimir Nabokov touched the punster and game-player in me, and I identified with his constant themes of exile and isolation. My choosing to admire these people thus indicated my significant connection with them, a connection that could be explored.

Further, because they are public figures, I can find information about them that might draw me closer to them—or perhaps reveal the flimsiness of my connection to them, a significant discovery in itself. With all such subjects, I would look first at their creative works (if any)—works such as novels, movies, paintings, autobiographies, collections of letters. Then I would turn to biographies, critical studies, reminiscences by others. Do you see how much potential information is at your fingertips? Since I greatly admire Nabokov, for example, I have read all of his novels, his autobiography, and many critical works about those novels. So I have a huge store of information about him already, even before I begin trying to paint a portrait of him for my readers and to explore and reveal his significance to me. And with that depth of information, I have strengthened my **felt connection** to him.

So I have material to write about, information to pass on to my readers, and insights into myself just waiting to be explored as I begin writing.

Do you see how the process works? It can be exciting.

UNDERSTANDING OTHER PEOPLE

Once having selected our subject, we face a seemingly impossible task—how to gain access to someone else's thoughts and emotions and beliefs. After all, exploring our own inner selves is difficult enough.

Since we can never know with complete certainty our own motives, emotions, and thoughts, isn't it absurd to think that we can decipher those of another person, even if that person is a relative or a famous person about whom much has been written?

If we needed to know someone else's inner self with 100% certainty, the answer would be "yes." But that is not the goal: An exploratory essay's main subject is *you*. In other words, you are not writing a biography of that other person; you are writing an exploratory essay that explores *your vision* of that person and *your felt connection* to that person. Although you can't know exactly what someone else feels or thinks, you can speculate, imagine what thoughts are going through his or her mind, what emotions he or she is feeling. Every day we speculate about other people's inner selves and world views; every day we make educated guesses about what some people think and feel—otherwise, we could never form relationships with anyone. In fact, most of us are always analyzing other people's beliefs (for example, we might ask ourselves or a friend, "What do you think he *really* meant by *that?*") or motives ("Why did he say *that* to *me?*") or feelings ("Does she *really* love *me?*"). And we even try to understand other people's world views ("How can she be against a woman's right to have an abortion and yet be in favor of the death penalty?").

Using the same techniques we employ to explore ourselves, we learn about others by observing them and by considering their past experiences, their present situation, their associates, their stated and implied beliefs, their goals and fears, their environment. As usual, the act of trying to clarify something for your readers often can clarify it for you as well. For example, explaining in detail your subject's present situation may help you see elements that you may have missed before. Through conversations and research you can piece together some key influences on other people's personalities. Similarly, describing a person's associates (relatives, friends, enemies, business associates) might be a good way to understand his or her personality. A person's actions can always be examined in light of his or her stated beliefs, goals, or fears, and, conversely, beliefs, goals, and fears can be inferred from actions.

How, then, do we gain access to people's motives, thoughts, feelings? We've already considered several direct methods: questioning the person, examining artifacts and objects, reading letters and diaries, talking to others who know or knew the person, visiting a place that was particularly important to that person. At least one other direct method—observation—deserves mention.

Observing Someone You Know

Since you already know your subject, the chances are that you have informally observed a great deal already, even if you don't know the person very well. Now, however, you will need to observe your subject carefully. Try to see him or her in different types of situations—interacting in small groups and in large groups, dealing with friends and strangers, discussing important issues and just chatting. Ask questions to learn his or her attitudes about issues. In conversation, you might pose hypothetical situations that raise moral issues so that you can see your subject's beliefs in action. Observe gestures, habitual phrases, and characteristic attitudes. Watch for typical patterns of behavior. Notice what kinds of books, movies, and music your subject enjoys. If he or she is someone you have known a long time, you undoubtedly have acquired a significant amount of information already. Let's assume, for instance, that you are writing an essay about your mother. You have witnessed her in action in all kinds of situations: You have probably seen her interact with strangers, with co-workers, with people she loves and likes, with those she respects, with those she dislikes, and perhaps even with people she fears. You've probably heard her talk about her past, about your relatives, about music and movies and books, about your own relationship with her, about situations both real and fictitious, about the present and about the future. Part of your prewriting in such a case is choosing and organizing some of the information you have informally garnered, then making a coherent whole of it, first for yourself and then for your readers. You, perhaps, will find yourself overwhelmed with so much material that it seems impossible even to begin prewriting. How can you explain your mother even to yourself, let alone to your readers?

According to Charles Darwin (no slouch of an observer himself), we need a theory in order to be effective observers. He believed that without a theory to organize our observations, we would miss key details or misunderstand the importance of what we did notice. Even if the theory turns out ultimately to be wrong, it will have performed its function by alerting us to details.

For some people we know, we already have theories in place. For instance, if you know that your friend comes from a "broken home" which was filled with frightening moments such as drunken fights and abusive harangues, you might theorize that her refusal to confront others stems from that childhood experience. Or you might believe that an aggressive acquaintance is a coward at heart and will back down if someone steps forward and tells him to back off. Or you might believe that your "cheap" friend loves money so much that he wouldn't pay a nickel to save himself hours of frustration.

For other people, we might have no theory yet.

In either case, a good starting point is Nancy Mairs's sentence that we discussed in Chapter 2. Here it is again:

> I'm a white, middle-aged, middle-class, heterosexual, crippled
> feminist of a reclusive and rather bookish temperament, turned

from New England Congregationalist to Roman Catholic social activist in the desert Southwest.

I suggested in Chapter 2 that you use this sentence as a model for exploring aspects of your own identity. Here I am suggesting that you use it for exploring someone else's identity. Try to replace all the terms in the sentence with attributes which describe your subject. Once you've done that, try considering your subject from the vantage points listed on page 83. Further, how many different roles does this person play? Each descriptive term, each vantage point, and each role will help you understand and explain your subject's personality more fully.

Another approach comes from Theophrastus (371–287 B.C.), a Greek philosopher and student of Aristotle. He wrote a series of 30 sketches titled *The Characters*. Each sketch presents a deviation from what were considered acceptable standards of behavior. In all the sketches, the technique is the same: The first sentence names the defining trait, and then Theophrastus provides a detailed portrait of the "character's" habits and conversation. It is important to note that Theophrastus's purpose is not ours; he was describing a type, trying to show the trait in its pure form, whereas we are trying to explore an individual person who will, no doubt, deviate a great deal from any type that we try to impose. The point, though, is that each personality trait can lead to a theory which helps the observer choose and organize information. Saying that your subject is shameless, for example, causes you to observe not only the times when he is indeed shameless but also the times when he is not. Again, every person is complex, and every trait exists in all of us along with at least a trace of its opposite. Among the 30 traits Theophrastus considered were the following: being ironic, flattering, boorish, too anxious to please, demoralized, loquacious, shameless, stingy, slow witted, hostile, superstitious, distrustful, mean, boasting, arrogant, cowardly, and avaricious. Here is a sampling from his sketch titled "The Talker":

> The talker is the sort of man who, when you meet him, if you make any remark to him, will tell you that you are quite wrong; that he himself knows all the facts, and if you listen to him you shall learn what they are. When you reply, he interrupts you with "You've already told me, remember, what you're just going to say"; or "What a good thing you reminded me!" or . . . "Oh, I just forgot to mention—." . . . When he is on a jury he prevents his fellow-jurors from reaching a verdict; in a theatre he won't let you follow the play, at a dinner he won't let you eat. . . . He is actually ready to let his own children make fun of him, when they are feeling sleepy and say to him, "Daddy, talk to us and send us to sleep!"

Notice the details that Theophrastus gives, revealing the frustration caused by the talker but at the same time showing his good-naturedness as well. Although Theophrastus is giving his readers not a picture of Theodoros or Theron the talker but rather a picture of the talker in general, as a type, the example nevertheless shows that using a dominant trait to organize observations can be useful, especially in your prewriting. Try thinking about your subject as having a dominant personality trait. List all the ways he or she illustrates that trait. Then list the ways he or she seems to illustrate the opposite or conflicting traits. Then try writing about the same person as having a different dominant trait, and so forth. This technique may be applied for as long as it continues to reveal aspects of your subject's character.

Observing Someone You Don't Know Personally

Most of us have few opportunities to get to know public figures personally. Our observation of such people usually is limited to their public appearances (in person, on television, in the movies, in their books) and to reports of their behavior. For example, my observations of author Vladimir Nabokov are entirely limited to his books and to reports by various critics and writers who had him as a teacher or friend. Such secondhand accounts can be very useful if you are planning to write about someone you do not know personally.

In addition to observation and the other direct methods mentioned earlier, there are some indirect methods of gaining access to other people's personalities and thoughts and feelings, namely, using yourself as a model, using the techniques of literary analysis, and using literary characters as points of reference. Let's examine each of these methods more closely.

Using Yourself as a Model

Presumably you know no one as well as you know yourself. Assume that you are typical—after all, we are all human beings. According to Carl Sagan, "We share 99.6 percent of our active genes with chimpanzees." Think about that for a moment. Since only 0.4% of our genes make us human and separate us from another species, it is not hard to believe that all human beings must be similar in many respects. Indeed, one of the starting premises of exploratory essays is that each of us is, in many ways, a representative human.

So start your thinking by assuming that the person you're examining is very similar to you in terms of "expected human emotions and thoughts." Although we are all different in many ways, there are still some emotions and thoughts that might be considered nearly universal. For example, if a loved one dies, most people react with great sorrow, often expressed with tears and reminiscences. And they tend to react with questioning: "Why did it have to be X who died?" They also tend to rationalize the death with thoughts such as "At least X died quickly" or "X is better off now, he suffered so with that disease." People also tend to justify doing what they want to by saying, "X would have wanted it this way."

Here's a happier example: When people fall in love, they tend to react with great joy, often expressed with smiles and lighthearted behavior. They also tend to react without serious questioning, although they may ask rhetorical questions such as "Why was I chosen to be so happy?" They also tend to feel a cosmic wonder at the whole thing, marveling at the power of coincidence ("Imagine, if I hadn't suddenly decided I wanted an ice cream and turned that corner, I would never have bumped into you and we would never have met") or at the power of fate ("We were meant to be together"). And they tend to talk in generalities ("We talk about everything" and "She is my best friend as well as the love of my life"). Those caught in the throes of a new love feel special, they feel blessed, they feel separated from all others by the depth and magic of their love. Further, they tend to make long-range plans and look forward to each day with anticipation.

Ultimately, it is important to go beyond such expected emotions and thoughts when you explore yourself, and it is important to go beyond them when you write about other people as well. Yet there is no reason that you should not *start* with such expected emotions and thoughts. The important thing is to identify the particular ways your chosen subject embodies these expected emotions and thoughts. Having established that base, you can begin to pay attention to the ways in which the person deviates from the expected. For example, my friend John's reaction to falling in love differs markedly from the sketch I just gave. He is giddy and lighthearted for about a week, tops. Then he starts worrying about everything. Instead of remaining in that romantic haze as long as possible (as most people do), he fights it. He starts looking for reasons why his beloved will desert him. Such an attitude strikes me as perverse and massively self-defeating. He begins looking for the first signs of her waning interest. Such a scrutiny naturally unnerves most women, particularly since John continues to pretend he's still in that romantic haze.

Because his attitude and actions strike me as atypical, that would be one area to explore in his personality. I might begin my essay by describing a typical new lover, then I would describe John's deviation from that norm. I would call on all that I know about him, trying to find the causes and motives for such behavior. I might talk to him about it as well.

Obviously I will not find the absolute truth about John and his unusual response to love. But I will be able to make educated guesses, to speculate about his conscious motives and about the hidden causes of his actions. In that process of speculation, I will reveal quite a bit about myself, perhaps even as much as I do about John. If I dwell on his child-hood relationship to his mother, for example, that will suggest my theoretical orientation is Freudian or psychological. If, instead, I dwell on his past experiences with women, I reveal my belief in the influence of adult experiences on behavior. If I dwell on his explanation of his actions, then I reveal my belief in conscious motives as the mainspring of behavior. If I focus on all three (and perhaps other possibilities), I reveal myself to be eclectic.

In brief, then, begin with the assumption that we are all essentially similar in many key ways. Once you establish that idea and use yourself as a typical person with typical reactions and ideas, examine the person you are writing about. Once that is done, remember that even though a very limited number of genes make us all human and hence similar, our life experiences modify us in many ways and hence make each of us unique.

Using the Techniques of Literary Analysis

How do we come to know characters in a literary text? We consider all the information that we can gather about them, including their physical characteristics; their dialogue, actions, and contradictions; their reactions to situations; the objects associated with them; their misconceptions; and their patterns of behavior. We can use the same techniques for exploring real people.

PHYSICAL CHARACTERISTICS Physical description is often a key to understanding literary characters because some writers use physical characteristics to signal elements of personality. Consider Jake Barnes's impotence in Ernest Hemingway's *The Sun Also Rises* or the Misfit's nearsightedness in Flannery O'Connor's "A Good Man Is Hard to Find." The famous gap in the teeth of Chaucer's Wife of Bath is meant to suggest her lusty nature. In fact, Chaucer uses many of the medieval assumptions about the connection between personality and appearance. Although we modern people might proclaim such assumptions silly, most of us still secretly think they exist—otherwise, we could all get rid of notions such as killers' looking like killers and sneaky people's having shifty eyes. So, giving a physical description of our subject and focusing on key details can help our readers see and understand the person better.

BACKGROUND AND CHILDHOOD EXPERIENCES Often writers fill us in on their characters' backgrounds and childhood experiences. For example, in *House of Mirth* Edith Wharton makes a point of telling us that Lily Bart grew up under the guidance of a mother who talked of nothing except Lily's using her beauty to catch a rich husband. Lily's mother never taught her to economize or to save something in case of disaster. Those same traits show up in Lily throughout her adulthood. The same is true in real life: Early events and lessons from our childhood often exert an influence far into our adult years.

DIALOGUE   Characters often explain their beliefs and ideas and their own version of their motives as well as comment on the actions of others. Their choice of words and patterns of speech can also be revealing: For example, who can forget Uriah Heep's "Umble, sir, very umble" in Charles Dickens's *David Copperfield*? When writing about other people in exploratory essays, try to give your reader some of their spoken words (dialogue), some of their explanations of their own actions or beliefs.

ACTIONS   Everyone knows the adage "Actions speak louder than words." In both fiction and real life, it is often true. We learn about characters' personalities by observing what they do and how they do it. As with phrases, some gestures or habitual actions have come to be associated with particular characters and thus to suggest particular personality traits. For example, Lady Macbeth's washing her hands to get rid of the nonexistent blood tells us about her subconscious guilt, and the same is often said of Pontius Pilate's washing of his hands after sentencing Jesus to be crucified. Catherine's repeated tantrums in Emily Brontë's *Wuthering Heights* reveal her self-centered vision of the world. Does your subject have any characteristic gestures or habitual actions?

CONTRADICTIONS   The discrepancy between what is said and what is done can be quite revealing. If a character tells his wife, "You are the most important thing in my life" and then spends 20 hours a day at the job, we have to account for that discrepancy in some way. Either he is lying to her and perhaps to himself (and then we speculate about why he is lying) or he has a different definition of *important* than most of us do. In real life, people often proclaim one thing as their belief and yet act in the opposite way. Explore such contradictions.

REACTIONS TO SITUATIONS   Either consciously or unconsciously, we consider how we (or people we know) would react to a similar situation. Then we judge the character's reactions in terms of that. Consider, for example, how Gurov, in Anton Chekov's "The Lady with the Pet Dog," carefully slices himself a piece of watermelon and listens silently for half an hour as Anna bemoans the fact that she has become a fallen woman by making love with him. Such nonchalance reveals both that he sees himself as merely "taking a slice out of her life" and that he does not believe she is speaking sincerely. Readers are forced to wonder if they would react with similar disdain.

Sometimes writers provide another character (a foil) to react to a similar situation in a different way. For instance, in *Hamlet,* Hamlet delays avenging his father's death for five acts; in contrast, when Laertes learns that Hamlet has killed his father, Polonius, Laertes springs into action. Thus Shakespeare invites us to compare the reactions of the two sons in similar situations.

Consider how your subject reacts to situations. Do you know someone else (from life or fiction) who reacts differently to similar situations? If so, how do you account for the difference?

OBJECTS ASSOCIATED WITH CHARACTERS   Another good clue about characters' personalities is the objects associated with them. Who can forget Hester's scarlet "A" in Nathaniel Hawthorne's *The Scarlet Letter* or Madame Defarge's "knitted register" of crimes in Dickens's *A Tale of Two Cities* or Arnold Friend's ill-fitting boots and gold car in Joyce Carol Oates's "Where Are You Going, Where Have You Been?" The term *objects* here includes such things as clothing, jewelry, cars, rooms/homes, decorations—in short, any inanimate item. In real life as in literature, many people become associated in our minds with particular objects. For example, some people wear only particular types of clothing or use only one type of pen. One of my friends loves old Studebaker cars (there have been no new Studebakers for over 20 years)—he has photographs of Studebaker Hawks on his walls, true-to-scale versions of several years' models on his bookcase shelves. Despite his obvious fascination with that car, he never even owned a Studebaker. Another friend has a boyhood compass that he still carries with him everywhere, although I've never seen him use it. Such objects individualize people for your readers and are worth exploring. I would ask, Why are they attached to these particular objects? Why not a Jaguar and a pocketknife instead of the Studebaker and the compass? What's the significance of those particular objects to those people?

MISPERCEPTIONS   Often we learn a lot about characters' personalities by observing their misperceptions of other characters or of situations. In Vladimir Nabokov's *Pale Fire,* for example, Charles Kinbote has a dogged belief that the poet John Shade views him as a close friend despite evidence to the contrary. That belief reveals (1) Kinbote's insecurity, (2) his loneliness, (3) his technique for overcoming loneliness (fantasy), and (4) his inability to see reality clearly. Most of us know people who misperceive situations and other people's motives (at least according to our perception of the situations and people). Exploring such misperceptions can reveal a lot about your subject and about you.

PATTERNS OF BEHAVIOR   Many characters repeatedly get themselves into the same or similar situations. For example, in Edith Wharton's *House of Mirth,* the beautiful Lily Bart has a plan (one of the few options open to her as a well-bred nineteenth-century woman) to marry a rich husband whose wealth will keep her in the high social circles to which she has become accustomed but which her dwindling resources cannot support much longer. Yet each time she has captured the affections of a "perfect match," she does something that destroys all possibility of a marriage between them. One such episode could be a mistake or a miscalculation; more than one begins to look like a pattern of behavior. Once we identify a pattern of behavior, we try to understand the motivations that lead the character to follow such a pattern.

Similarly, most of us find ourselves in situations which have become typical for us. Eric, a former student of mine, for example, would always plan out his week's work and fun very carefully. Then, at the last minute, he would grab any opportunity to trash the plan and would inevitably end up pulling all-nighters in a frantic (and not always successful) attempt to finish papers and study for exams. Angela, another former student, would begin each semester with a realistic number of extracurricular activities but would almost immediately begin "heaping her plate" with additional commitments until it was impossible to fulfill her nonacademic commitments (let alone her academic ones). She'd audit courses she didn't need, agree to chair some committee in which she had little interest, and volunteer to hostess meetings with alumnae, with visiting scholars, with visiting potential students. All of these activities were worthwhile, but by consistently taking on too many of them, she managed to turn a four-year academic career into five years.

In literature, we would look for reasons and motivations for the typical situation and typical behavior as in the case of Lily Bart. The same is true with real people. In the examples I have just given, we have two different people who share similar typical situations—good initial planning which they then ignore, thereby endangering their academic performance. Are the students driven by the same reasons, the same motives?

In the first case, Eric came from a military family and had been taught self-discipline since he emerged from the womb. His parents had already made plans for him to attend law school after he received his bachelor's degree, and they had constantly stressed the importance of his succeeding at whatever he did. Consciously Eric believed that schedules and self-discipline were the best path to success and happiness. His self-imposed daily schedules—useful and well thought out though they were—echoed the discipline and stress he had felt throughout his childhood. My speculation, however, is that on a subconscious level he resented having his life all planned out by others. I believe that subconsciously he was rebelling against his own conscious beliefs and against the parents who put them in his mind in the first place. The mediocre papers produced during all-nighters and the exams that he failed after sleepless nights were Eric's unconscious message to his parents that he needed to create his own goals and his own life. They also functioned as an unconsciously applied punishment to himself because he felt guilty about disobeying his parents and about ignoring the system of self-discipline which he consciously believed to be an effective way of life.

Angela's problem had different causes. In part, her overcommitments probably came from her desire to be an important woman on campus. She once told me that she liked the fact that everyone on campus knew who she was. There is nothing wrong with the desire to be an important person on campus, and there's nothing wrong with enjoying high visibility. Yet those desires pushed her into significant academic troubles. Another issue contributed as well. Although she could be pretty successful academically when she devoted her full attention to studies, Angela lacked a strong sense of her own abilities and of her own worth. Coming from a severely dysfunctional home, she had never been made to feel important and capable of accomplishing anything. Her mother had fought the idea of her attending college, her brother was always being kicked out of high school for some infraction, and her father insulted her on the few occasions when he saw her. I believe that Angela's subconscious drive to prove her self-worth and to make herself feel needed and loved led to her overcommitments.

Applying the Techniques of Literary Analysis to Real People

It is a short jump from analyzing a literary character to analyzing real people. Although we are not privy to the unspoken thoughts of real people, we certainly hear what they say and we hear their explanations of their thoughts and motives; we observe their patterns of behavior; we see how they react to situations; we watch their actions in general; we notice their habitual gestures and hear their habitual phrases; we see the objects with which they associate themselves. Using our own perceptions as a touchstone, we can consider what seem to be their misperceptions of certain people or situations.

Using Literary Characters in Another Way

Another effective use of literary texts in your endeavor to explore other people is to compare your real-life subject to a literary or fictional character. For example, let's assume that I'm writing an exploratory essay about my friend John (mentioned earlier) who expects every romance to fail before it has had a chance to start. What if I began by thinking that John is like Alceste in Molière's *The Misanthrope*? Alceste is indeed a misanthrope, someone who dislikes other people, believing that they are superficial and can never be trusted to tell the total truth. In fact, Alceste so little trusts his own instincts and perceptions that he needs people to tell the total truth in order to know where he stands. He can't even recognize the devotion of his best friend. In the play, Alceste falls in love with the beautiful Célimene despite himself. She is the opposite of himself: She adores society, she excels at flirting, she loves to hear pretty compliments no matter how outrageous or untrue. After Alceste discovers her flirtatious letters to others, he demands that she join him in a solitary life, scorning society and other humans, the two of them thus becoming a world unto themselves. Appalled, she rejects that idea because she is, first and foremost, a social creature. Yet she does agree to marry him if they can continue to live in society. He rejects that idea. Saying that she obviously does not love him totally, he feels justified in claiming that he now hates her. In other words, Alceste falls in love with the worst possible woman for him, then objects to everything in her that probably attracted him in the first place (her social skills, her charm, and her flirtatious nature), demands that she totally change, and, when she refuses, feels morally justified in stomping off alone because once more humankind has proven itself unworthy of his affection. Of course, he is left alone.

Such a comparison of John to Alceste opens up several avenues of exploration. For instance, does John tend to choose women who will inevitably disappoint him? Does he impose impossible standards or expectations on them? Is his constant fear of being rejected the mainspring of his fault-finding? Does he dislike humans in general? Does he fear that his own instincts are faulty so that he needs to be constantly reassured about the woman's feelings? Is his demand for exclusivity in the relationship (he wants the woman to be entirely focused on him, to not "waste" time on other people including women friends) closely connected to Alceste's desire to tromp off to a "wild, trackless, solitary place" with the fair Célimene? Answering those questions will move me into a much deeper exploration of John's attitudes than I might have made otherwise. If I discover that John isn't like Alceste, then the final draft of my essay won't even mention Molière's character. However, if he is similar to the misanthrope in some respects, I might well use the comparison to enhance my readers' understanding as well.

Do you see how powerful a device such a comparison can be?

Further, notice the technique I used in the preceding comparison. I gave a summary of the play's plot and explained my interpretation of Alceste's personality in depth before I started writing about John. I wanted to be sure that you understood the play and Alceste, and, of course, I couldn't be positive that you had read or seen the play (or, if you had, that your interpretation of Alceste's personality matched mine). It is a safe bet that your readers—even if they are members of your class—do not share all of your reading or viewing experiences. If you decide to compare a person to a Shakespearean character such as Hamlet or Lady Macbeth, you can't be positive that everyone has read the particular play or has done so recently enough to remember key details. Even if you can be sure that your reader is familiar with a text you are referring to, not everyone will agree with your interpretation of a character's personality. So it is important that you explicitly explain your interpretation of the relevant character and mention any plot details that you might wish to connect to your subject's activities.

Using all of these methods, then, will help you understand and explore other people and, in the process, will help you reveal significant aspects of yourself to your readers.

Exploring Complexities

As with writing about yourself, it is crucial to remember that all of us are complex beings. Nobody feels just one emotion about someone or something. Nobody has just one belief about a course of action. Several emotions and beliefs are in conflict within us about almost every decision we make. What we think our motives are may not be *all* of our motives. In the past 10 years or so, the popular press has highlighted the idea of people having a *hidden agenda*. What that means is this: Either consciously or unconsciously, people often have more reasons for doing what they do than they tell other people about. The term *hidden agenda* has a negative connotation related to the idea of people trying to manipulate us, but there is nothing necessarily sinister about unspoken or unperceived motives: We are simply more complex than we usually wish to believe we are. In writing exploratory essays about other people, one of your goals is to reveal some of that complexity and, in the process, to discover some of your own complexity as well.

Here are two more examples, Brett and Mona. Brett wrote that his parents wanted him to be totally independent. Yet in the same essay he noted that his father was always calling him at college with unsolicited advice about which courses he should take and with subtle pressure to switch into a premed program. In a later draft Brett addressed that inconsistency, deciding that sometimes parents have conflicting impulses: On one level they want their children to grow into adults, but on another level they want to feel needed or in control, so they subconsciously fight against their own efforts to foster independence in their children. In other words, Brett recognized and discussed the complexity of his father's feelings by looking at the discrepancy between what his father always told him—"I want you to be independent"—and what the father did. Building on that insight, Brett discovered that he too had conflicting emotions. On one hand, Brett wanted total freedom to make his own decisions about his major and the courses he took. On the other hand, at times he didn't want to assume all of that responsibility: At those times he wanted to be taken care of, to have his father make the decisions.

Similarly, in an early draft, Mona complained that her mother was too "nosy," always asking questions about what Mona was doing, whom she was dating, what she was thinking. Mona assumed her mother thought that she was not responsible and was "checking up on her." Putting her irritation aside in later drafts, Mona pushed more deeply into her mother's personality by first thinking about other reasons why parents might be "nosy." She concluded that the "nosy" approach of parents often involves control as well as a fear that the child lacks responsibility. Reflecting on their earlier relationship, Mona also realized that in high school she and her mother had had a free exchange of ideas and information about such topics as dating, drugs, smoking, drinking. When Mona got to college, however, her intimate conversations were reserved for her best friends and her mother was left out. Mona concluded that perhaps her mother's nosiness might be an attempt to reestablish that intimacy rather than an implied criticism of Mona's irresponsibility. Also, Mona started to wonder if her mother might, in some way, be trying to live vicariously through her daughter. Again, the complexity of people and of situations is fertile territory to explore.

EXPLORING GROUPS

Throughout this chapter I have suggested ways of exploring individuals. It is also possible to explore groups. Often, too, our exploration of an individual will lead to statements about the larger groups that the individual belongs to (for example, fathers, friends, politicians).

The trick to writing an exploratory essay about a group is to focus on a group that shares some significant trait and then to do enough observation and research to move your analysis beyond the superficial. Usually it helps to select a group that you already know a lot about. Use the techniques in this chapter and others, as well as insights from such classes as sociology and psychology. Look for the threads that bring the people in the group together. What do they gain from their association with the group? What do they lose? Consider the group from the vantage points mentioned in Chapter 2. Think about the composition of the group—who belongs and who is excluded, and why?

EXPLORING SIGNIFICANCE

Usually you will begin your research for this type of essay with a sense of the subject's significance for you. Sometimes the significance will be obvious—you are writing about a parent or a best friend or a mentor. Don't, however, assume that your readers will know exactly in what ways this particular parent or friend is significant to you unless you tell them. For instance, we can assume that a father is a significant person for most of us. Yet reading essays in this book will show you that different fathers have different significance for their children. Thus you should always state explicitly what that significance is for you. For example, what behaviors and attitudes and beliefs did you learn from your father, and which did you reject because they were his? Did he give you a sense of self-confidence or of worthlessness? Did he encourage your dreams and plans, or did he impose his own? And why? What fictitious or historical father is he most like and why? Such questions lead to a better understanding of your subject and of you.

In the process of gathering and organizing information about any subject, you will probably discover other areas of significance that you may not have thought of before. Don't ignore those. Probe them in the early drafts to see where they lead.

Other people are significant to us in many ways. For example, they are significant because we feel strong emotions (either positive or negative) toward them; explore the reasons for your emotions as you explore the person. They are significant because they form some sort of relationship with us—or because they play particular roles in our lives as mentors, role models, friends, teachers, enemies, or rivals. They are significant because we admire them, their personality traits, their accomplishments, their lifestyles. They are significant because they have had a positive or negative impact on our lives or on our sense of ourselves—or because their situations or problems approximate our own and we learn from them how to cope. Finally, they are significant to us simply because they interest us or because we identify with them in some way. Naming their significance helps us in our exploration of both them and ourselves.

Like emotions, significance is complex and often multilayered. Each of the techniques mentioned in this chapter will help you find and explore some of that complexity. Never forget that everything you have learned is part of your personal experience and should be available for use in your exploratory essays. Insights from other courses such as psychology, sociology, anthropology, history, and literature will add depth to your analysis of yourself and others. Remember also Iris Murdoch's belief in deep gazing, described in Chapter 2. By gazing outward at others, we ultimately also gaze inward at ourselves.

SUGGESTIONS FOR WRITING

1. Select someone who is important to you. Write an exploratory essay about him or her.

2. Select a public figure who seems significant to you. Write an exploratory essay about him or her.

3. Select a group that seems significant to you. Write an exploratory essay about that group.

My Uncle Willie

MAYA ANGELOU

📖 *Inward Exploration*

List five memorable people from your life. Select one of those people and write at least one paragraph vividly describing him or her—try to catch that person's physical appearance and personality.

When Bailey was six and I a year younger, we used to rattle off the   *1*
times tables with the speed I was later to see Chinese children in San Francisco employ on their abacuses. Our summer-gray pot-bellied stove bloomed rosy red during winter, and became a severe disciplinarian threat if we were so foolish as to indulge in making mistakes.

Uncle Willie used to sit, like a giant black Z (he had been crippled as a child), and hear us testify to the Lafayette County Training Schools' abilities. His face pulled down on the left side, as if a pulley had been attached to his lower teeth, and his left hand was only a mite bigger than Bailey's, but on the second mistake or on the third hesitation his big overgrown right hand would catch one of us behind the collar, and in the same moment would thrust the culprit toward the dull red heater, which throbbed like a devil's toothache. We were never burned, although once I might have been when I was so terrified I tried to jump onto the stove to remove the possibility of its remaining a threat. Like most children, I thought if I could face the worst danger voluntarily, and *triumph,* I would forever have power over it. But in my case of sacrificial effort I was thwarted. Uncle Willie held tight to my dress and I only got close enough to smell the clean dry scent of hot iron. We learned the times tables without understanding their grand principle, simply because we had the capacity and no alternative.

The tragedy of lameness seems so unfair to children that they are embarrassed in its presence. And they, most recently off nature's mold, sense that they have only narrowly missed being another of her jokes. In relief at the narrow escape, they vent their emotions in impatience and criticism of the unlucky cripple.

Momma related times without end, and without any show of emotion, how Uncle Willie had been dropped when he was three years old by a woman who was minding him. She seemed to hold no rancor against the baby-sitter, nor for her just God who allowed the accident. She felt it necessary to explain over and over again to those who knew the story by heart that he wasn't "born that way."

In our society, where two-legged, two-armed strong Black men   *5*
were able at best to eke out only the necessities of life, Uncle Willie,
with his starched shirts, shined shoes and shelves full of food, was the
whipping boy and butt of jokes of the underemployed and underpaid.
Fate not only disabled him but laid a double-tiered barrier in his path.
He was also proud and sensitive. Therefore he couldn't pretend that he
wasn't crippled, nor could he deceive himself that people were not re-
pelled by his defect.

Only once in all the years of trying not to watch him, I saw him
pretend to himself and others that he wasn't lame.

Coming home from school one day, I saw a dark car in our front
yard. I rushed in to find a strange man and woman (Uncle Willie said
later they were schoolteachers from Little Rock) drinking Dr. Pepper in
the cool of the Store. I sensed a wrongness around me, like an alarm
clock that had gone off without being set.

I knew it couldn't be the strangers. Not frequently, but often
enough, travelers pulled off the main road to buy tobacco or soft drinks
in the only Negro store in Stamps. When I looked at Uncle Willie, I
knew what was pulling my mind's coattails. He was standing erect behind the counter, not leaning forward or resting on the small shelf that
had been built for him. Erect. His eyes seemed to hold me with a mixture of threats and appeal.

I dutifully greeted the strangers and roamed my eyes around for his
walking stick. It was nowhere to be seen. He said, "Uh . . . this this . . .
this . . . uh, my niece. She's . . . uh . . . just come from school." Then
to the couple—"You know . . . how, uh, children are . . . th–th–these
days . . . they play all d–d–day at school and c–c–can't wait to get home
and pl–play some more."

The people smiled, very friendly.   *10*

He added, "Go on out and pl–play, Sister."

The lady laughed in a soft Arkansas voice and said, "Well, you
know, Mr. Johnson, they say, you're only a child once. Have you children of your own?"

Uncle Willie looked at me with an impatience I hadn't seen in his
face even when he took thirty minutes to loop the laces over his high-
topped shoes. "I . . . I thought I told you to go . . . go outside and
play."

Before I left I saw him lean back on the shelves of Garret Snuff,
Prince Albert and Spark Plug chewing tobacco.

"No, ma'am . . . no ch–children and no wife." He tried a laugh. "I   *15*
have an old m–m–mother and my brother's t–two children to l–look
after."

I didn't mind his using us to make himself look good. In fact, I
would have pretended to be his daughter if he wanted me to. Not only
did I not feel any loyalty to my own father, I figured that if I had been
Uncle Willie's child I would have received much better treatment.

The couple left after a few minutes, and from the back of the house I watched the red car scare chickens, raise dust and disappear toward Magnolia.

Uncle Willie was making his way down the long shadowed aisle between the shelves and the counter—hand over hand, like a man climbing out of a dream. I stayed quiet and watched him lurch from one side, bumping to the other, until he reached the coal-oil tank. He put his hand behind that dark recess and took his cane in the strong fist and shifted his weight on the wooden support. He thought he had pulled it off.

I'll never know why it was important to him that the couple (he said later that he'd never seen them before) would take a picture of a whole Mr. Johnson back to Little Rock.

He must have tired of being crippled, as prisoners tire of penitentiary bars and the guilty tire of blame. The high-topped shoes and the cane, his uncontrollable muscles and thick tongue, and the looks he suffered of either contempt or pity had simply worn him out, and for one afternoon, one part of an afternoon, he wanted no part of them.   20

I understood and felt closer to him at that moment than ever before or since.

📓 Outward Exploration: Discussion

1. Specifically, what encouraged Angelou and Bailey to learn their multiplication tables?

2. What do you think of Uncle Willie's method of encouraging the children to learn? What is Angelou's opinion of it?

3. What techniques does Angelou use to convey information about Uncle Willie's appearance and personality?

4. According to Angelou, why do children mock and criticize people with physical handicaps? Do you agree? Explain.

5. How had Willie been hurt originally? What are Momma's feelings about the accident? Why does she tell the story over and over?

6. Why does Angelou recount this particular episode?

7. What is her attitude toward Uncle Willie?

8. What is suggested by her sentence "He thought he had pulled it off"?

9. What is the real reason that Uncle Willie pretended not to be crippled?

10. Why does Angelou understand and feel closer to Uncle Willie "at that moment than ever before or since"?

◻ *Outward Exploration: Writing*

1. Other essays in this book such as Nancy Mairs's "On Being a Cripple" and Sucheng Chan's "You're Short, Besides!" discuss handicaps from the perspective of those with the handicaps. This essay adopts an outsider's perspective. Using at least these three essays (you may consult other sources if you wish), discuss the concept of being crippled or handicapped in some other way.

2. Write a vivid essay about an event that revealed an aspect of someone's personality which you had not realized before. Although you do not have to follow Angelou's structure, you should include the same elements that she does: background information and context for the event, the event itself, your speculations about the person's motives and feelings and thoughts, and the significance to you of the event or revelation about the person.

Afterthoughts

JEAN ERVIN

❑ *Inward Exploration*

Make a list of people who have had an impact on your life. Select one and write at least one paragraph about that person. Try to assign a one- or two-word description that fits each person into some stereotypical category such as the "bachelor uncle" or the "family's black sheep." Then write at least one paragraph defining the concept of "old maid."

I had been hearing about old maids and the dangers of becoming   *1* one all my life. It was said that once a woman reached thirty unmarried she was an old maid, which meant a domineering, fussy spoilsport who gossiped too much. But there were odd contradictions in my elders' composite pictures because I noticed that timid single women were often included with their too assertive sisters. Zona Gale's 1920s best-selling novel *Miss Lulu Bett,* though it seems overdrawn today, reflected many households where an unmarried sister or aunt became a virtual servant. But whatever her personality—domineering gossip or shrinking violet—if she remained unmarried, a woman was almost invariably referred to as a "girl" forever after. I got the impression that to be an old maid was akin to contracting an unmentionable disease. Certainly it was a family disgrace. A friend of mine whose older sister was living at home and working during the 1930s recalls that every morning at the breakfast table her mother would open up the paper and read off the announcements of engagements and weddings in their Boston suburb.

Single women were required to walk a tightrope, and though the very ones who eluded the epithet "spoilsport" might even be considered good sports, there was a catch there, too, for a good sport might be loose or easy, to use two of my parents' favorite terms. Some of the single women we knew came to Springfield and Northampton, Massachusetts, from little towns such as Turner's Falls and Chesterfield and Conway to find jobs and often stayed with relatives while they looked for work. Then they were expected to room in a boardinghouse. Others, who had parents in the area, lived on with their families until the older generation died. Married couples herded them like cattle into a pen marked "leftovers," and they were usually invited to someone's home only as an afterthought. More than once I had heard my mother say, "Oh, and bring Ginny"—or Ellie or Rose—"if you'd like; we haven't had her to the house in a long time." The "oh" told it all: It was a word you used when you added a postscript.

Although old maids were considered not quite up to code as females, I noticed that they had more freedom than married women and that they did not have to ask a husband for money to get a new pair of silk stockings or whether it was all right to skip making dinner in order to go to a meeting. Many of these unmarried women had become the financial mainstays of their families during the Great Depression. Because she had a good job even during the worst years, Mary's generosity to her sister's family meant that they had been able to keep their house when her brother-in-law was out of work and when many other people were losing their homes. She was domineering and often annoyed me with her rules and regulations that I, too, was expected to follow when I played with her niece and nephew. When we shared a cottage at the beach one summer, she got it into her head that we children should brush our teeth before eating a meal. Argue as I might, I wasn't able to shake her idea and for some reason my mother did not bother to interfere, so I found myself lined up with the other children dutifully brushing away before each meal. Momentarily, I could have killed her.

But Mary was as generous with her time as she was with her money, and she introduced us to complicated card games that were a godsend during some of New England's cold and rainy summer days. She was not prissy by any means and enjoyed a party as much as anyone. She was a great raconteur and told stories about growing up in a New England mill town during the early years of the century. Her daily adventures as a businesswoman in the small city of Springfield were as exciting to me as if they had taken place in Paris or New York. I can still see her as she sat in one of her good-looking skirts roaring with laughter after the punch line. Mary was a heavy smoker and one of the things that impressed me most was her ability to continue talking as smoke spilled from her nostrils. In today's sensible clean air world, it is hard to explain how impressive that was to a young girl in the 1930s, when few people worried about the dangers of smoking. Women who smoked then were considered not quite ladylike. What I detected in Mary's ability to wave her cigarette, tell a story, and snort smoke at the same time was a control over the world that too few of the women around me had achieved.

The ideal combination of nurturer and tyrant in the classroom, my   5
favorite elementary school teacher, Miss Powers, was unmarried and probably over thirty, but I never thought of her as an old maid. She was extremely pretty and used a little more makeup than was considered respectable even during the 1930s, when lacquered faces were fashionable. She got me to grapple with fractions; no mean feat. She knew how to have fun, and I can still hear her marvelous laugh ringing through the classroom. I loved it when Mrs. Ryder from across the hall sent in one of her pupils with a picture of a spider or some other crawly

creature because everyone knew it was the one thing that could make Miss Powers shriek. But if I sassed her or tried to put down another child, she had all the verbal equivalents of the ruler on the knuckle. I knew that she lived with her parents in a small town some distance away because they needed her support, financially and otherwise. This sort of arrangement was simply expected of single women at the time, and I don't recall anyone ever considering Hazel Powers a martyr or especially remarkable for her long drives to work and for living on with the old folks.

But there were Miss Lulu Betts hovering at the periphery of my family's social life, single women who laughed too readily at everyone else's jokes and asked polite questions of me as if they felt it was the price of being admitted to the magic circle of family life, if only for an afternoon or evening. My mother was forever trying to fix up Vi with any single male she and my father knew, and for a time she actually hoped that Vi would marry one of my father's colleagues, a man who was inclined to violence when he drank. Maybe Mother believed that by having stepped over the magic line into her thirties unwed, Vi couldn't be too particular.

My father's cousins, the Farrell "girls," in some ways came closest to fitting the classic picture of old maids: they disapproved of alcohol and sometimes had narrow-minded attitudes toward people. For many years Marian and Clara had taught in the Springfield public school system and were financially comfortable. With their eighty-year-old mother, Ellen, they had developed a reverse parent–child relationship, teasing her about her tightfistedness, laughing that her black coat was turning green from age.

When I first knew her, Marian was about fifty and her hair was already snow white. Because she was more talkative than her sister and tended to blush and because her voice always suggested a little girl's, my mother and father decided that she was a lightweight. Clara, the elder of the two daughters, was the one they favored. I could see that she often put a damper on Marian's gushing, as though even at fifty Marian was still the little sister who rushed into things with a dangerous warmth and enthusiasm that might lead to trouble.

Ellen Farrell died in the late 1930s. A few years later, Clara had a stroke and Marian retired early from her teaching job to care for her. I don't suppose anyone ever suggested that she should do otherwise, although people in her school district told us that she was a successful and much-loved fifth-grade teacher; she often spoke affectionately of individual pupils, following their subsequent lives with genuine interest.

After her sister died, Marian was as lost as a widow who has devoted   *10* all her life to her family. Her teaching job and the two people she cared for most in the world were gone. She had friends and few of the financial problems that many women had in old age, particularly in those days, yet she seemed to be totally adrift, leaning on my parents for advice in any practical undertaking. All during the Second World War and in the austerity period afterward, Marian and Clara had sent a family of Scotch relations food packages, a thoughtfulness that must have made life much easier under Britain's grim living conditions. Not long after Clara's death, Marian wrote to them asking if she might visit for a week, but these small-minded people wrote back that it was quite inconvenient to have her stay with them.

Soon Marian decided that she could no longer drive her car—she was in her mid-sixties but seemed much older—and then with a rush came the broken hip, giving up her comfortable home, and moving in as a boarder with a rather chilly woman who took care of her physical needs but not much else.

My parents invited her to spend holidays and some weekends at their house, although she had to be fitted in around their time with friends and children. She was a leftover. One Christmas I had forgotten that she would be there for the family gathering. Hastily, I wrapped up an extra studio photograph of our eighteen-month-old son to give her, but it must have been obvious to her that it was an afterthought. The day was centered on our child, with both sets of grandparents making much of him; it could not have been easy for Marian to sit on the sidelines, but that is where life had placed her. At the end of the day, when my father and I drove her to the house where she boarded and helped her from the car—she was on crutches by then—Marian said to her landlady, "Shall I go upstairs or stay down here, Wanda?" clearly hoping that in the holiday spirit her landlady would invite her to sit downstairs for a while. But Wanda dismissed her. "You can go right up to your room," she said in a voice that told all. I was in my late twenties then, and with an icy shaft shooting down my spine, I envisioned the day when someone might send me upstairs.

Eight years earlier, in the summer of 1945, I was standing somewhere in the Chicago Loop waiting to meet a woman named Madge Clark. I was twenty and had gone from Massachusetts to stay in Winnetka with a classmate from Smith College while attending the summer session at Northwestern University. Madge was a retired governess, my great-uncle Ben's sister-in-law. She was not even a real relation but, because of my family's tendency to cling to any Scotch connection, my father had written to her telling her that I would be in the area.

Madge was wearing a small navy hat, white gloves, and a suitable blue print dress which I recognized as quality. Everything down to her navy purse and shoes spelled a proper lady. White-haired, blue-eyed Scotch men and women proliferated in our family, but I was surprised at how handsome she was, with fine bones and a trim figure. Her coloring made me think of snow and ice. Madge had come to Chicago from Scotland many years earlier to be near her sister Aggie, who was married to my great-uncle Ben, and there she had found a place as a governess. In another sense such women learned their place early in life and, short of marriage, expected nothing more than to keep a respectable job for as long as it lasted. And then, if their references were in order, they could hope to find another place. This usually meant living in. "Living in" is a peculiarly apt term, for it was not just a question of being given board and room for part of your salary. Live-in help lived in other people's lives as well as their homes.

As a governess, Madge was hired to "do" for the little girls and boys   *15*
of men and women who did not want to be bothered with their own children. When I saw her in the summer of 1945 she had been retired for a time, but during the previous year one of her former charges, now grown and married, had called frantically. "Clarkie, you've got to help me out; I can't cope with these kids of mine."

"When I got thurr, I was shocked," she said in a soft Scots burr. "Mary Beth wants to do nothing but sit around her pool and drink cocktails instead of taking care of the gerruls." As the train bore us to our afternoon's destination, there was much clucking over Mary Beth's lapses as a mother, but I sensed that Madge's indignation was rhetorical, for her former charge's failings meant that she was needed once again. It was the eternal "I don't know what's happening to young people these days" response, and like so many grandmothers before and since her time, Madge had gone to the rescue of her surrogate child, now grown but forever a child in her eyes. She told me proudly that she had been teaching the little girls to write with a good hand, finish their homework, mind their manners, and get to bed on time.

"Now you can read their writing, they know to stand and curtsy whenever someone enters the room, and they're in bed at a decent hour, not hanging about where they've got no business downstairs."

When Madge had called to make this date with me, I expected nothing more than a dull but comforting chat about family news. But not at all. We were headed for the Washington Park racetrack. On the train she warned me, "Now watch out for your handbag, the place is overrun with the soldiers, and there're so many coloreds and foreigners and who-knows-what about. This town hasn't been the same since the war." I looked at the other passengers uneasily, yet she spoke so softly I hoped that no one around us could hear her.

I was a snob about racetracks because I associated gambling and racing with the disreputable side of my father's life. Certainly Madge's concerns with bringing up proper young ladies seemed at odds with a day at the races, and as for going to them without a man, it was at once unseemly and downright comical, like sex between people over the age of forty-five.

As we entered the racetrack grounds, I groaned inwardly; the noise   *20*
and the crowds were worse than I had expected, and the place seemed to be populated chiefly with men in those clownlike but menacing outfits called zoot suits and women whose bright hair colors signified only

one thing. The smells—a compound of horse dung, sweat, alcohol, and dimestore Lily of the Valley perfume—did nothing to reassure me. But it was clear that Madge was a habitué of the track, for she knew where the refreshment stand was located and soon was pressing into my hand a paper cup full of whisky. "This will help us pick the winners." Smelling the horrible stuff, I decided that only by faking sips would I ever be able to get through the afternoon without being sick, yet I did not have the nerve to refuse her. It was obvious that this was Madge's idea of a holiday.

Too many of my male relatives had taken to the bottle with a vengeance and some had died violent deaths as a result. My father was already a problem drinker and as a child I had grown to hate the very smell of alcohol, but when I entered college I found that I was made to feel like a kid hanging out with the grownups if I ordered a Coke while the rest of the group had something stronger. During several weekend trips to New York I had discovered the joys of sipping a Pink Lady or a Clover Club in the Biltmore Hotel cocktail lounge after meeting a date under the clock. This, I considered, was sophistication, worlds away from the shots of rye my father and his cronies would down standing at a bar. Young people often have very high standards for their elders, so I was uneasy at the sight of Madge drinking alcohol in the daytime and in public, too. It was all right for me to order a Pink Lady at the Biltmore, but not for a woman of my mother's age, and certainly not for Madge, who was nearly as old as my grandparents.

"Come now, dear, what do you think for the first race? Which horse appeals to you?" The afternoon's entertainment was serious business.

I hesitated since I had saved barely enough from farm work early in the summer to pay for my expenses. Even if I had had some loose cash, my distaste for betting would likely have prevented me. But good hostess that she was, Madge insisted that I take her money, urging this twenty-year-old snob from the East to loosen up, have a drink, place some money on the ponies. At this enormous track it was impossible to locate the horse I had bet on—Iwo Jima or Guadalcanal—and anyway I assumed the money had been thrown away. But Madge was visibly excited, although her voice never rose above the well-modulated tone suitable for the classroom. To my surprise, my horse came in first, and, embarrassed that I was feeling so ambivalent about the afternoon's entertainment, I tried to make her take my winnings. But she would not hear of it. "It's yours, lass, you picked the right one!"

Soon I got into the spirit and followed her lead. We lost on a few, but by the end of the day we were ahead by enough money so that Madge pronounced it "an afternoon well spent!" as though we had soaked up the cultural offerings of the Art Institute and the Museum of Science and Industry. Prig that I was, I doubt that I was fully able to take in the humorous scene: this blue-eyed, white-haired woman, the very picture of respectable grandmotherhood, studying her greensheet and placing her bets with the expertise of a Damon Runyon character while knocking back rotgut rye on a hot summer's day. What it certainly did take many more years for me to understand was that Madge's life may well have been so circumscribed by rules and regulations, those she had to impose on the children she cared for as well as the ones imposed on her, that a day at the races was a much-needed safety valve. She was having fun.

After the races, Madge announced that we were to dine at the Berghoff, a famous restaurant back in the city. As we entered, she pointed out the men's bar where women were not allowed and, like Madge, I accepted this, perfectly content to stand in line for twenty minutes before being shepherded to a table with a less than favorable location for two unescorted women.

Like many other things during the four years that America had been at war, cigarettes were in short supply, so we smoked a variety of peculiar weeds, some of them similar to the cornsilk I had been introduced to at the age of eight. When we were seated, resourceful Madge pulled out a package of little cigars called Puppies. I lit my Puppy expecting something slightly stronger than a Chesterfield or a Camel, but even a dedicated smoker like myself found it a challenge. The smell was somewhere between burning rubber and linseed oil, and I feared that each time I inhaled I'd have to bolt for the ladies' room, but I finally managed to puff away with Madge as we exchanged family news.

She told me that many years before, when her sister Aggie and my great-uncle Ben were to have a baby, she had come to Chicago to help out, but the baby died and there were to be no other children. Madge had stayed on and, over the years, they had formed a tight little island of family far from home. A few years before my visit, Ben and Aggie, both in poor health, had left Chicago for a warmer climate when Ben retired, and now, an old woman, Madge was on her own. I had seen Ben and Aggie a few times when I was younger, but to me they were simply an elderly couple who, for all I knew, had always been that age. During the late 1930s they had stayed with us in Massachusetts before sailing for a vacation in Scotland, and I had memories of Madge's sister Aggie as a rather grand lady with an impenetrable accent. Now for the first time it occurred to me that those staid old folks, with brown spots on their hands and faces, had once been young and in love; they had had a sex life and their own private tragedy.

I was just emerging from that stage in which it seems that the only friends worth having are those your own age, and as we talked I realized that Madge was confiding in me, not as an adult to a child, but as one adult to another. I was flattered that she would talk to me as if my opinion were worth something; it was the first time that I had become acquainted with an older family connection away from my parents and their tendency to pull the rug out from any naive admiration I might develop. So I was glad to sort out Madge for myself, with her odd combination of softspoken Old World gentility and her zest for some of the earthy pleasures in this city filled with New World push.

On another Saturday, we went after lunch to visit two more Scotch women. Staying in upper-class Winnetka, what I had not realized was that on some streets away from the glittering façade of apartment buildings and mansions on the Gold Coast of the Lake Shore Drive, most Chicagoans spent their lives in narrow little houses like the one the Campbells lived in. Unlike trim Madge, with her crown of white hair and her sapphire eyes, the Campbells were pedestrian in looks and manner, black-haired and fat and dull. One of them spent all of the time we were there ironing. Madge produced a pack of Puppies, and in the close quarters of the Campbells' home they smelled worse than ever. The talk dragged, and even peppy Madge seemed humdrum in the presence of the Campbells. I wondered why she had taken me there, but now I realize that, living in, she had no home of her own to take me to.

At the time, few of us could comprehend that those four years of war had created a deep ravine between the old America and the new. On one side stood women like Madge and the Campbells, who had learned to trim their lives to fit those of their employers. On the other side were many younger women, who might also have ended up caring for the children of the privileged or cleaning up after their parents had it not been for the opportunity provided by the world disaster. When the country geared up for war, defense plants met the labor shortage by hiring women and paying wages that far outstripped those of the average maid. These women discovered the pleasures of leading lives that were not in service to someone else, and in those four years America lost its servant class. Few returned to work as maids.

But Madge was not exactly a servant, for the governess has traditionally belonged neither downstairs nor upstairs. Just before I left home for Chicago, my mother had told me that Madge discovered a kickback scheme between the kitchen help and the family grocer at one place, and had brought the scam to the attention of her employer, an act which must have taken more than a little courage. And there was something else. Living in meant living with the quality, and perhaps Madge had learned to live *like* the quality in some ways.

I viewed her as a bit racy, but I was impressed by her independence because I was not accustomed to the women in my family being so self-confident. In getting about Chicago, Madge displayed none of the uncertainty that I so often discerned in my mother when she went to the smaller city of Boston for the day. Even more impressive was Madge's unapologetic enjoyment of Chicago, a far cry from the way Mother and her friends felt—they had to have a good story ready for their husbands when they got home. They were always saying, "He'd kill me if he knew how much I paid for . . ." or "I'd better get home by five or there'll be hell to pay." Madge was really part of my grandparents' generation, but she was a person in her own right.

30

In the 1940s, Madge's refusal to settle back into the prison of old ladydom took far more courage than it would today, when no one takes a second look if a white-haired woman gets on an overseas flight with running shoes and a backpack or decides to run for governor, but in 1945 older women were expected to "act their age," which meant drawing into a cocoon of dullness and conformity. And I see now that Madge was lonely and I was family, however tenuously. For a brief period that summer, perhaps she saw me as the niece she did not have in this country. With her good looks, her poise, and her commonsense intelligence, she would have been a much-valued addition to any family, and she must have commanded a good salary. But in recent years I have wondered if the children she raised repaid her in the most important way, with affection. If not, it did not show, for I never got a whiff of self-pity from her.

To many Easterners, Chicago was considered a joke in those days, a city that had burned to the ground only seventy-some years before, dubbed Hogtown and famous as the setting for lively gang warfare, notably the St. Valentine's Day Massacre of 1929. But to me, Chicago in 1945 was a cornucopia of urbanity, offering far more than I could gather up in the six weeks of the summer session at Northwestern. Through the friends I was staying with in Winnetka, I heard about the city's chic hangouts—or so they seemed to me—such as the Pump Room at the Ambassador East Hotel, where the waiters wore satin knee britches and coffee boys sported turbans and the dishes were flaming. I never made it to the Pump Room, but one evening after an outdoor concert at Ravinia Park, I drove with some friends to an elegant suburban cocktail lounge where the self-appointed sophisticate of our group ordered Ramos Fizzes all around. It was hard to swallow this frothy booze—it seemed like nothing more than a gin milkshake—but I considered that, like the Ravinia Festival concerts, a Ramos Fizz was part of the haut monde I had come West to find, unlike the Washington Park racetrack with its paper cups of rye.

The place I most longed to go was a nightclub of unimaginable 35 glamour, and when Madge asked me what I hoped to see before I went back home, I mentioned the Edgewater Beach Hotel on Lake Michigan where they had dancing under the stars.

"Then we'll go, Saturday night."

Excited at the prospect of finally being at the Edgewater Beach, I wore my one good outfit, a black suit with a bolero jacket and bright yellow blouse. Madge had on one of her well-cut summer print dresses. In our prim little hats and white gloves, we must have looked exactly like mother and daughter at a proper tea party. At Madge's urging, I ordered a Planter's Punch and she insisted that I have the most expensive meal on the menu. As we ate dinner on the terrace, we watched a spotlit dancer execute what seemed to be Balinese–Latin American swirlings.

That night Madge talked more about the war than she had before, the experiences of her family still in Scotland, and the recent election in Great Britain, where Winston Churchill had been voted out of office.

"After all he's done for them, saving the country, such *ingratitude*." Several times she returned to those "incredible ingrates."

I was feeling increasingly uneasy about the evening. It was all too   *40* clear that we made a very odd couple in this Hollywoodish nightclub on the edge of a lake that was a virtual sea. Here I was at the start of my adulthood, with an old woman who was nearing the end of hers, a life of living in other people's lives. I was only half listening as Madge said, "I have a dear friend, Alf, a gardener who worked at one of my places here, but a great opportunity took him East."

Bored and let down by my foray into the elegant fleshpot, I wondered what had led me to an evening of drinking Planter's Punches and smoking the horrible Puppies with an elderly woman. The floor show at the Edgewater Beach alternated with a dance band that played the syrupy slow popular tunes of the day—"A Boy in Khaki, a Girl in Lace," and "When the Lights Go On Again All Over the World"—for couples doing the sedate fox trot. I felt that I should be here with some attractive Air Force pilot, and I could not imagine why Madge was going on about an old Scotch gardener whom she might marry when she finished her present job, for I couldn't imagine someone that age being in love.

Madge was subdued that night, perhaps realizing that this outing, which must have cost her a good deal of money, had fallen flat. She offered me an after-dinner brandy but, aware that we were both feeling out of place, I politely refused. After she had walked me to my train for Winnetka, we shook hands. "Goodbye, dear, my love to your folks." That evening, I was struck once again with the snow and ice of her coloring, but I saw too that there was fire underneath that northern ice; she had done her best to loosen up an old maid of twenty.

🗌 *Outward Exploration: Discussion*

1. Why does Ervin begin her essay with a statement about "old maids"?
2. What connotations did the term "old maid" have for Ervin?
3. What examples of old maids does Ervin mention?
4. What stereotype do you have of the Scottish? Where does it come from?
5. What impression do you get of Madge from Ervin's first description of her (paragraph 14)? Which details gave you that impression?
6. In what details does Ervin's 20-year-old persona reveal her own prejudices and assumptions?
7. How does the *Ervin-now* evaluate the *Ervin-then* (at 20 years of age)?
8. What is the significance of the essay's title?

❑ *Outward Exploration: Writing*

1. Write an essay about a significant person in your life. Try to capture the person the way Ervin captures Madge—for example, through physical description, actions, opinions, and attitudes. Try also to capture your complex feelings about the person—don't settle for simply one response.

2. Starting with a stereotypical category such as old maid or family black sheep, write an essay that shows how someone significant in your life transcends such a classification. Use Ervin's essay as a model.

❑ *Style*

Consider the following sentence from Ervin's essay:

Madge was subdued that night, perhaps realizing that this outing, which must have cost her a good deal of money, had fallen flat. (paragraph 42)

subject ("Madge")

predicate verb ("was subdued")

comma (commas always separate free modifiers from the independent clause)

adverb ("perhaps")

present participle ("realizing")

relative pronoun ("that") [notice—no comma before *that* clauses]

subject of the first dependent clause ("this outing")

comma (commas usually separate *which* clauses from their surroundings)

second relative dependent clause ("which . . . money")

comma (to signal the end of the *which* clause)

verb of the first dependent clause ("had fallen")

adverb ("flat")

period.

In this sentence, a short independent clause (five words—"Madge . . . night") is followed by a long *free modifier* ("perhaps realizing . . . flat") that includes two relative dependent clauses ("that . . . flat" and, within it, "which . . . money").

Using your own information, write a sentence that replicates this structure. Begin with a short independent clause followed by a comma and a free modifier which includes one or more dependent clauses.

My Father's Life

RAYMOND CARVER

☐ *Inward Exploration*

Make a list of relatives who have been important in your life. From that list, select one about whose life you know a great deal of information. Write at least one paragraph about that relative, summarizing the details of his or her life.

My dad's name was Clevie Raymond Carver. His family called him   1
Raymond and friends called him C. R. I was named Raymond Clevie
Carver Jr. I hated the "Junior" part. When I was little my dad called me
Frog, which was okay. But later, like everybody else in the family, he
began calling me Junior. He went on calling me this until I was thirteen
or fourteen and announced that I wouldn't answer to that name any
longer. So he began calling me Doc. From then until his death, on
June 17, 1967, he called me Doc, or else Son.

When he died, my mother telephoned my wife with the news. I was
away from my family at the time, between lives, trying to enroll in the
School of Library Science at the University of Iowa. When my wife
answered the phone, my mother blurted out, "Raymond's dead!" For a
moment, my wife thought my mother was telling her that I was dead.
Then my mother made it clear *which* Raymond she was talking about
and my wife said, "Thank God. I thought you meant *my* Raymond."

My dad walked, hitched rides, and rode in empty boxcars when he
went from Arkansas to Washington State in 1934, looking for work. I
don't know whether he was pursuing a dream when he went out to
Washington. I doubt it. I don't think he dreamed much. I believe he was
simply looking for steady work at decent pay. Steady work was meaningful work. He picked apples for a time and then landed a construction
laborer's job on the Grand Coulee Dam. After he'd put aside a little
money, he bought a car and drove back to Arkansas to help his folks,
my grandparents, pack up for the move west. He said later that they
were about to starve down there, and this wasn't meant as a figure of
speech. It was during that short while in Arkansas, in a town called
Leola, that my mother met my dad on the sidewalk as he came out of
a tavern.

"He was drunk," she said. "I don't know why I let him talk to me.
His eyes were glittery. I wish I'd had a crystal ball." They'd met once,
a year or so before, at a dance. He'd had girlfriends before her, my
mother told me. "Your dad always had a girlfriend, even after we

married. He was my first and last. I never had another man. But I didn't miss anything."

They were married by a justice of the peace on the day they left   5
for Washington, this big, tall country girl and a farmhand–turned–construction worker. My mother spent her wedding night with my dad and his folks, all of them camped beside the road in Arkansas.

In Omak, Washington, my dad and mother lived in a little place not much bigger than a cabin. My grandparents lived next door. My dad was still working on the dam, and later, with the huge turbines producing electricity and the water backed up for a hundred miles into Canada, he stood in the crowd and heard Franklin D. Roosevelt when he spoke at the construction site. "He never mentioned those guys who died building that dam," my dad said. Some of his friends had died there, men from Arkansas, Oklahoma, and Missouri.

He then took a job in a sawmill in Clatskanie, Oregon, a little town alongside the Columbia River. I was born there, and my mother has a picture of my dad standing in front of the gate to the mill, proudly holding me up to face the camera. My bonnet is on crooked and about to come untied. His hat is pushed back on his forehead, and he's wearing a big grin. Was he going in to work or just finishing his shift? It doesn't matter. In either case, he had a job and a family. These were his salad days.

In 1941 we moved to Yakima, Washington, where my dad went to work as a saw filer, a skilled trade he'd learned in Clatskanie. When war broke out, he was given a deferment because his work was considered necessary to the war effort. Finished lumber was in demand by the armed services, and he kept his saws so sharp they could shave the hair off your arm.

After my dad had moved us to Yakima, he moved his folks into the same neighborhood. By the mid-1940s the rest of my dad's family—his brother, his sister, and her husband, as well as uncles, cousins, nephews, and most of their extended family and friends—had come out from Arkansas. All because my dad came out first. The men went to work at Boise Cascade, where my dad worked, and the women packed apples in the canneries. And in just a little while, it seemed—according to my mother—everybody was better off than my dad. "Your dad couldn't keep money," my mother said. "Money burned a hole in his pocket. He was always doing for others."

The first house I clearly remember living in, at 1515 South Fifteenth   10
Street, in Yakima, had an outdoor toilet. On Halloween night, or just any night, for the hell of it, neighbor kids, kids in their early teens, would carry our toilet away and leave it next to the road. My dad would have to get somebody to help him bring it home. Or these kids would take the toilet and stand it in somebody else's backyard. Once they actually set it on fire, but ours wasn't the only house that had an

outdoor toilet. When I was old enough to know what I was doing, I threw rocks at the other toilets when I'd see someone go inside. This was called bombing the toilets. After a while, though, everyone went to indoor plumbing until, suddenly, our toilet was the last outdoor one in the neighborhood. I remember the shame I felt when my third-grade teacher, Mr. Wise, drove me home from school one day. I asked him to stop at the house just before ours, claiming I lived there.

I can recall what happened one night when my dad came home late to find that my mother had locked all the doors on him from the inside. He was drunk, and we could feel the house shudder as he rattled the door. When he'd managed to force open a window, she hit him between the eyes with a colander and knocked him out. We could see him down there on the grass. For years afterward, I used to pick up this colander—it was as heavy as a rolling pin—and imagine what it would feel like to be hit in the head with something like that.

It was during this period that I remember my dad taking me into the bedroom, sitting me down on the bed, and telling me that I might have to go live with my Aunt LaVon for a while. I couldn't understand what I'd done that meant I'd have to go away from home to live. But this, too—whatever prompted it—must have blown over, more or less, anyway, because we stayed together, and I didn't have to go live with her or anyone else.

I remember my mother pouring his whiskey down the sink. Sometimes she'd pour it all out and sometimes, if she was afraid of getting caught, she'd only pour half of it out and then add water to the rest. I tasted some of his whiskey once myself. It was terrible stuff, and I don't see how anybody could drink it.

After a long time without one, we finally got a car, in 1949 or 1950, a 1938 Ford. But it threw a rod the first week we had it, and my dad had to have the motor rebuilt.

"We drove the oldest car in town," my mother said. "We could have   *15* had a Cadillac for all he spent on car repairs." One time she found someone else's tube of lipstick on the floorboard, along with a lacy handkerchief. "See this?" she said to me. "Some floozy left this in the car."

Once I saw her take a pan of warm water into the bedroom where my dad was sleeping. She took his hand from under the covers and held it in the water. I stood in the doorway and watched. I wanted to know what was going on. This would make him talk in his sleep, she told me. There were things she needed to know, things she was sure he was keeping from her.

Every year or so, when I was little, we would take the North Coast Limited across the Cascade Range from Yakima to Seattle and stay in the Vance Hotel and eat, I remember, at a place called the Dinner Bell Cafe. Once we went to Ivar's Acres of Clams and drank glasses of warm clam broth.

In 1956, the year I was to graduate from high school, my dad quit his job at the mill in Yakima and took a job in Chester, a little sawmill town in northern California. The reasons given at the time for his taking the job had to do with a higher hourly wage and the vague promise that he might, in a few years' time, succeed to the job of head filer in this new mill. But I think, in the main, that my dad had grown restless and simply wanted to try his luck elsewhere. Things had gotten a little too predictable for him in Yakima. Also, the year before, there had been the deaths, within six months of each other, of both his parents.

But just a few days after graduation, when my mother and I were packed to move to Chester, my dad penciled a letter to say he'd been sick for a while. He didn't want us to worry, he said, but he'd cut himself on a saw. Maybe he'd got a tiny sliver of steel in his blood. Anyway, something had happened and he'd had to miss work, he said. In the same mail was an unsigned postcard from somebody down there telling my mother that my dad was about to die and that he was drinking "raw whiskey."

When we arrived in Chester, my dad was living in a trailer that   20
belonged to the company. I didn't recognize him immediately. I guess for a moment I didn't want to recognize him. He was skinny and pale and looked bewildered. His pants wouldn't stay up. He didn't look like my dad. My mother began to cry. My dad put his arm around her and patted her shoulder vaguely, like he didn't know what this was all about, either. The three of us took up life together in the trailer, and we looked after him as best we could. But my dad was sick, and he couldn't get any better. I worked with him in the mill that summer and part of the fall. We'd get up in the mornings and eat eggs and toast while we listened to the radio, and then go out the door with our lunch pails. We'd pass through the gate together at eight in the morning, and I wouldn't see him again until quitting time. In November I went back to Yakima to be closer to my girlfriend, the girl I'd made up my mind I was going to marry.

He worked at the mill in Chester until the following February, when he collapsed on the job and was taken to the hospital. My mother asked if I would come down there and help. I caught a bus from Yakima to Chester, intending to drive them back to Yakima. But now, in addition to being physically sick, my dad was in the midst of a nervous breakdown, though none of us knew to call it that at the time. During the entire trip back to Yakima, he didn't speak, not even when asked a direct question. ("How do you feel, Raymond?" "You okay, Dad?") He'd communicate if he communicated at all, by moving his head or by turning his palms up as if to say he didn't know or care. The only time he said anything on the trip, and for nearly a month afterward, was when I was speeding down a gravel road in Oregon and the car muffler came loose. "You were going too fast," he said.

Back in Yakima a doctor saw to it that my dad went to a psychiatrist. My mother and dad had to go on relief, as it was called, and the county paid for the psychiatrist. The psychiatrist asked my dad, "Who is the President?" He'd had a question put to him that he could answer. "Ike," my dad said. Nevertheless, they put him on the fifth floor of Valley Memorial Hospital and began giving him electroshock treatments. I was married by then and about to start my own family. My dad was still locked up when my wife went into this same hospital, just one floor down, to have our first baby. After she had delivered, I went upstairs to give my dad the news. They let me in through a steel door and showed me where I could find him. He was sitting on a couch with a blanket over his lap. *Hey,* I thought. *What in hell is happening to my dad?* I sat down next to him and told him he was a grandfather. He waited a minute and then said, "I feel like a grandfather." That's all he said. He didn't smile or move. He was in a big room with a lot of other people. Then I hugged him, and he began to cry.

Somehow he got out of there. But now came the years when he couldn't work and just sat around the house trying to figure what next and what he'd done wrong in his life that he'd wound up like this. My mother went from job to crummy job. Much later she referred to that time he was in the hospital, and those years just afterward, as "when Raymond was sick." The word *sick* was never the same for me again.

In 1964, through the help of a friend, he was lucky enough to be hired on at a mill in Klamath, California. He moved down there by himself to see if he could hack it. He lived not far from the mill, in a one-room cabin not much different from the place he and my mother had started out living in when they went west. He scrawled letters to my mother, and if I called she'd read them aloud to me over the phone. In the letters, he said it was touch and go. Every day that he went to work, he felt like it was the most important day of his life. But every day, he told her, made the next day that much easier. He said for her to tell me he said hello. If he couldn't sleep at night, he said, he thought about me and the good times we used to have. Finally, after a couple of months, he regained some of his confidence. He could do the work and didn't think he had to worry that he'd let anybody down ever again. When he was sure, he sent for my mother.

He'd been off from work for six years and had lost everything in that time—home, car, furniture, and appliances, including the big freezer that had been my mother's pride and joy. He'd lost his good name too—Raymond Carver was someone who couldn't pay his bills— and his self-respect was gone. He'd even lost his virility. My mother told my wife, "All during that time Raymond was sick we slept together in the same bed, but we didn't have relations. He wanted to a few times, but nothing happened. I didn't miss it, but I think he wanted to, you know."

During those years I was trying to raise my own family and earn a living. But, one thing and another, we found ourselves having to move a lot. I couldn't keep track of what was going down in my dad's life. But I did have a chance one Christmas to tell him I wanted to be a writer. I might as well have told him I wanted to become a plastic surgeon. "What are you going to write about?" he wanted to know. Then, as if to help me out, he said, "Write about stuff you know about. Write about some of those fishing trips we took." I said I would, but I knew I wouldn't. "Send me what you write," he said. I said I'd do that, but then I didn't. I wasn't writing anything about fishing, and I didn't think he'd particularly care about, or even necessarily understand, what I was writing in those days. Besides, he wasn't a reader. Not the sort, anyway, I imagined I was writing for.

Then he died. I was a long way off, in Iowa City, with things still to say to him. I didn't have the chance to tell him goodbye, or that I thought he was doing great at his new job. That I was proud of him for making a comeback.

My mother said he came in from work that night and ate a big supper. Then he sat at the table by himself and finished what was left of a bottle of whiskey, a bottle she found hidden in the bottom of the garbage under some coffee grounds a day or so later. Then he got up and went to bed, where my mother joined him a little later. But in the night she had to get up and make a bed for herself on the couch. "He was snoring so loud I couldn't sleep," she said. The next morning when she looked in on him, he was on his back with his mouth open, his cheeks caved in. *Graylooking,* she said. She knew he was dead—she didn't need a doctor to tell her that. But she called one anyway, and then she called my wife.

Among the pictures my mother kept of my dad and herself during those early days in Washington was a photograph of him standing in front of a car, holding a beer and a stringer of fish. In the photograph he is wearing his hat back on his forehead and has this awkward grin on his face. I asked her for it and she gave it to me, along with some others. I put it up on my wall, and each time we moved, I took the picture along and put it up on another wall. I looked at it carefully from time to time, trying to figure out some things about my dad, and maybe myself in the process. But I couldn't. My dad just kept moving further and further away from me and back into time. Finally, in the course of another move, I lost the photograph. It was then that I tried to recall it, and at the same time make an attempt to say something about my dad, and how I thought that in some important ways we might be alike. I wrote the poem when I was living in an apartment house in an urban area south of San Francisco, at a time when I found myself, like my dad, having trouble with alcohol. The poem was a way of trying to connect up with him.

PHOTOGRAPH OF MY FATHER
IN HIS TWENTY-SECOND YEAR

October. Here in this dank, unfamiliar kitchen
I study my father's embarrassed young man's face.
Sheepish grin, he holds in one hand a string
of spiny yellow perch, in the other
a bottle of Carlsberg beer.

In jeans and flannel shirt, he leans
against the front fender of a 1934 Ford.
He would like to pose brave and hearty for his posterity,
wear his old hat cocked over his ear.
All his life my father wanted to be bold.

But the eyes give him away, and the hands
that limply offer the string of dead perch
and the bottle of beer. Father, I love you,
yet how can I say thank you, I who can't hold my liquor either
and don't even know the places to fish.

The poem is true in its particulars, except that my dad died in June
and not October, as the first word of the poem says. I wanted a word
with more than one syllable to it to make it linger a little. But more than
that, I wanted a month appropriate to what I felt at the time I wrote the
poem—a month of short days and failing light, smoke in the air, things
perishing. June was summer nights and days, graduations, my wedding
anniversary, the birthday of one of my children. June wasn't a month
your father died in.

After the service at the funeral home, after we had moved outside, a
woman I didn't know came over to me and said, "He's happier where he
is now." I stared at this woman until she moved away. I still remember
the little knob of a hat she was wearing. Then one of my dad's cousins—
I didn't know the man's name—reached out and took my hand, "We all
miss him," he said, and I knew he wasn't saying it just to be polite.

I began to weep for the first time since receiving the news. I hadn't
been able to before. I hadn't had the time, for one thing. Now, suddenly,
I couldn't stop. I held my wife and wept while she said and did what she
could do to comfort me there in the middle of that summer afternoon.

I listened to people say consoling things to my mother, and I was
glad that my dad's family had turned up, had come to where he was. I
thought I'd remember everything that was said and done that day and
maybe find a way to tell it sometime. But I didn't. I forgot it all, or
nearly. What I do remember is that I heard our name used a lot that
afternoon, my dad's name and mine. But I knew they were talking about
my dad. *Raymond,* these people kept saying in their beautiful voices out
of my childhood. *Raymond.*

❏ *Outward Exploration: Discussion*

1. What are the major traits of Carver's father?
2. What traits does Carver seem to share with his father? In what ways is he different?
3. Why does Carver include the poem in this essay?
4. How does the last paragraph connect to the essay's beginning?

❏ *Outward Exploration: Writing*

Write an essay about a relative who has had a significant impact on your life. Follow Carver's lead, summarizing the details of that relative's life as well as speculating about his or her motives, feelings, and thoughts. Be explicit about the nature of that person's impact on your inner world.

❏ *Style*

Consider the following sentence from Carver's essay:

Among the pictures my mother kept of my dad and herself during those early days in Washington was a photograph of him standing in front of a car, holding a beer and a stringer of fish. (paragraph 29)

This is the sentence's structure:

prepositional phrase ("among the pictures")
implied relative pronoun beginning a dependent clause ("that")
subject of dependent clause ("my mother")
verb of dependent clause ("kept")
prepositional phrase ("of . . . herself")
prepositional phrase ("during . . . days")
prepositional phrase ("in Washington")
predicate verb of the sentence ("was")
subject of the sentence ("a photograph")
prepositional phrase ("of him")
participial phrase ("standing . . . car")
comma
participial phrase ("holding . . . fish")
period.

The noteworthy elements of this structure are three: (1) The sentence begins with a prepositional phrase and a dependent clause, thus delaying the announcement of the sentence's subject and verb until the 18th and 19th words (yet the sentence is easy to process because the prepositional phrase alerts us that the subject will be one of the *pictures*); (2) the sentence's subject and verb are inverted (which is smoothly done with forms of *to be*); (3) the sentence ends with two participial phrases which modify *him* (the phrases add specific details). Notice the comma before *holding*; it's used because free modifiers are usually separated from the rest of the sentence with commas. Such attention-grabbing structures should be used sparingly since we should usually fulfill readers' expectations (the subject's appearing near the beginning of the sentence, the subject's coming before its verb), but occasional use of such structures adds variety and interest to our style.

Using your own information, create a sentence that replicates these three structural elements.

Raymond Carver, Mentor

JAY MCINERNEY

📖 *Inward Exploration*

In "My Father's Life," Raymond Carver remembers one of the most influential family members in his life. In the following essay, one of Carver's former students explores the impact that Carver had on him. Make a list of nonrelatives who have had an important impact on your life. From that list, select one person and write at least one paragraph describing him or her, and write at least one more paragraph explaining the nature of that person's impact on you.

A year after his death, the recurring image I associate with Raymond Carver is one of people leaning toward him, working very hard at the act of listening. He mumbled. T. S. Eliot once described Ezra Pound, qua mentor, as "a man trying to convey to a very deaf person the fact that the house is on fire." Raymond Carver had precisely the opposite manner. The smoke could be filling the room, flames streaking across the carpet, before Carver would ask, "Is it, uh, getting a little hot in here, maybe?" And you would be sitting in your chair, bent achingly forward at the waist, saying, "Beg pardon, Ray?" Never insisting, rarely asserting, he was an unlikely teacher.

I once sat in and listened while Carver was interviewed for two and a half hours. The writer conducting the interview moved the tape recorder closer and closer and finally asked if Carver would put it in his lap. A few days later the interviewer called up, near despair: Ray's voice on the tapes was nearly inaudible. The word "soft-spoken" hardly begins to do justice to his speech; this condition was aggravated whenever he was pressed into the regions of generality or prescription.

As I say, he mumbled, and if it once seemed merely a physical tic, akin to cracking knuckles or the drumming of a foot, I now think it was a function of a deep humility and a respect for the language bordering on awe, a reflection of his sense that words should be handled very, very gingerly. As if it might be almost impossible to say what you wanted to say. As if it might be dangerous, even. Listening to him talking about writing in the classroom or in the living room of the big Victorian house he shared with Tess Gallagher in Syracuse, you sensed a writer who loved the words of the masters who had handed the language down to him, and who was concerned that he might not be worthy to pick up the instrument. You feel this respect for the language—humility bordering on dread—in every sentence of his work.

1

Encountering Carver's fiction early in the 1970s was a transforming experience for many writers of my generation, an experience perhaps comparable to discovering Hemingway's sentences in the twenties. In fact, Carver's language was unmistakably like Hemingway's—the simplicity and clarity, the repetitions, the nearly conversational rhythms, the precision of physical description. But Carver completely dispensed with the romantic egoism that made the Hemingway idiom such an awkward model for other writers in the late twentieth century. The cafés and *pensions* and battlefields of Europe were replaced by trailer parks and apartment complexes, the glamorous occupations by dead-end jobs. The trout in Carver's streams were apt to be pollution-deformed mutants. The good *vin du pays* was replaced by cheap gin, the romance of drinking by the dull grind of full-time alcoholism. Some commentators found his work depressing for these reasons. For many young writers it was terribly liberating.

One aspect of what Carver seemed to say to us—even to someone who had never been inside a lumber mill or a trailer park—was that literature could be fashioned out of strict observation of real life, wherever and however it was lived, even if it was lived with a bottle of Heinz ketchup on the table and the television set droning. This was news at a time when academic metafiction was the regnant mode. His example reinvigorated realism as well as the short story form.

Though he was a teacher for much of his life, Carver never consciously gathered a band of disciples around himself. But when I was knocking around between graduate schools and the New York publishing world in the late seventies and early eighties, no other writer was as much discussed and mimicked by the writers one met at readings and writers' conferences. Probably not since Donald Barthelme began publishing in the 1960s had a story writer generated such a buzz in the literary world.

Having fallen under Carver's spell on reading his first collection, *Will You Please Be Quiet, Please?*, a book I would have bought on the basis of the title alone, I was lucky enough to meet him a few years later and eventually to become his student at Syracuse University in the early eighties. Despite the existence of several thousand creative writing programs around the country, there is probably no good answer to the question of whether writing can be taught. Saying that Faulkner and Fitzgerald never got M.F.A.s is beside the point. Novelists and short story writers like to eat as much as anyone else, and tend to sniff out subsidies while they pursue their creative work. For writers in the twenties, the exchange rate was favorable in Paris, and in the thirties there was the WPA, and a gold rush of sorts in Hollywood. The universities have become the creative writers' WPA in recent years.

Carver was himself a product of the new system, having studied writing at the University of Iowa Writers' Workshop and at Stanford, and later earned a living teaching. It was something he did out of necessity, a role he was uncomfortable with. He did it to make a living, because it was easier than the other jobs he'd had—working at a sawmill and a hospital, working as a service station attendant, a janitor, a delivery boy, a textbook editor. Though grateful for genteel employment, he didn't really see why people who had a gift for writing should necessarily be able to teach. And he was very shy. The idea of facing a class made him nervous every time. On the days he had to teach he would get agitated, as if he himself were a student on the day of the final exam.

Like many writers in residence at universities, Ray was required to teach English courses in addition to creative writing courses. One was called Form and Theory of the Short Story, a title Ray inherited from the graduate English catalogue. His method in these classes was to assign a book of stories he liked each week, including contemporary and nineteenth-century authors as well as works in translation. We would read the books and discuss them for two hours. Flannery O'Connor, Chekhov, Ann Beattie, Maupassant, Frank O'Connor, John Cheever, Mary Robison, Turgenev, and more Chekhov. (He loved all the nineteenth-century Russians.) Class would begin with Ray saying something like, "Well, guys, how'd you like Eudora Welty?" He preferred listening to lecturing, but he would read his favorite passages, talk about what he loved in the book he had chosen. He dealt in specifics, stayed close to the text, and eventually there would come a moment when the nervousness would lift off of him as he spoke about writing that moved him.

One semester, a very earnest Ph.D. candidate found his way into   10
this class, composed mainly of writers. At that time, the English department, like many around the country, had become a battleground between theorists and humanists, and post-structuralism lay heavy upon the campus. After a few weeks of Carver's free-ranging and impressionistic approach to literature, the young theorist registered a strong protest: "This class is called Form and Theory of the Short Story but all we do is sit around and talk about the books. Where's the form and the theory?"

Ray looked distressed. He nodded and pulled extra hard on his cigarette. "Well, that's a good question," he said. After a long pause, he said, "I guess I'd say that the point here is that we read good books and discuss them. . . . And then you *form* your own *theory*." Then he smiled.

As a teacher of creative writing, too, Carver had a light touch. He did not consider it his job to discourage anyone. He said that there was enough discouragement out there for anyone trying against all odds to be a writer, and he clearly spoke from experience. Criticism, like fiction, was an act of empathy for Ray, putting yourself in the other guy's shoes. He couldn't understand writers who wrote negative reviews and once chided me for doing so. He believed fiction and poetry were fraternal enterprises. Among the very few people that Ray vocally disliked were a poet who had refused to lend him $50 when his car broke down in Salt

Lake City, two critics who had attacked his own work, and writers who had attacked any of his friends.

For a shy man, his gregarious generosity of spirit was remarkable. He kept up a correspondence with dozens of other writers, students, and fans. He wrote letters of recommendation and encouragement, helped people get jobs and grants, editors and agents, accompanied friends in need to their first AA meetings.

One day when I berated him for going easy on a student I thought was turning out poor work, he told me a story: he had recently been a judge in a prestigious fiction contest. The unanimous winner, whose work has since drawn much praise, turned out to be a former student of his, probably the worst, least promising student he'd had in twenty years. "What if I had discouraged her?" he said.

His harshest critical formula was: "I think it's good you got that story behind you." Meaning, I guess, that one has to drive through some ugly country on the way to Parnassus. If Carver had had his way, classes and workshops would have been conducted entirely by students, but his approval was too highly valued for him to remain mute. 15

Once he sat through the reading of a long, strange story in his graduate writing workshop: as I recall, the story fleshed out two disparate characters, brought them together, followed their courtship and eventual marriage. After a series of false starts they decided to open a restaurant together, the preparations for which were described in great detail. On the day it opened a band of submachine-gun–toting terrorists burst in and killed everyone in the restaurant. End of story. After nearly everyone in the smoky seminar room had expressed dissatisfaction with this plot, we all turned to Ray. He was clearly at a loss. Finally, he said softly, "Well, sometimes a story needs a submachine gun." This answer seemed to satisfy the author no less than those who felt the story in question had been efficiently put out of its misery.

My first semester, Ray somehow forgot to enter my grade for workshop. I pointed this out to him, and we went together to the English office to rectify the situation. "You did some real good work," he said, informing me that I would get an A. I was very pleased with myself, but perhaps a little less so when Ray opened the grade book and wrote an A next to my name underneath a solid column of identical grades. Everybody did good work, apparently. In workshop he approached every story with respect—treating each as if it were a living entity, a little sick, possibly, or lame, but something that could be nursed and trained to health.

Though Ray was always encouraging, he could be rigorous if he knew criticism was welcome. Fortunate students had their stories subjected to the same process he employed on his own numerous drafts. Manuscripts came back thoroughly ventilated with Carver deletions, substitutions, question marks, and chicken-scratch queries. I took one story back to him seven times; he must have spent fifteen or twenty hours on it. He was a meticulous, obsessive line editor. One on one, in his office, he almost became a tough guy, his voice gradually swelling with conviction.

Once we spent some ten or fifteen minutes debating my use of the word "earth." Carver felt it had to be "ground," and he felt it was worth the trouble of talking it through. That one exchange was invaluable; I think of it constantly when I'm working. Carver himself used the same example later in an essay he wrote that year, in discussing the influence of his mentor, John Gardner. "Ground is ground, he'd say, it means *ground,* dirt, that kind of stuff. But if you say 'earth,' that's something else, that word has other ramifications."

John Gardner, the novelist, was Ray's first writing teacher. They 20 met at Chico State College in California in the 1960s. Ray said that all of his writing life he had felt Gardner looking over his shoulder when he wrote, approving or disapproving of certain words, phrases, and strategies. Calling fouls. He said a good writing teacher is something like a literary conscience, a friendly critical voice in your ear. I know what he meant. (I have one; it mumbles.)

After almost twenty years Carver had a reunion with his old teacher, who was living and teaching less than a hundred miles from Syracuse, in Binghamton, New York, and Gardner's approval of his work had meant a great deal to him. In the spring of 1982, I happened to stop by Ray's house a few minutes after he heard that Gardner had died in a motorcycle crash. Distraught, he couldn't sit still. We walked around the house and the back yard as he talked about Gardner.

"Back then I didn't even know what a writer looked like," Ray said. "John looked like a writer. He had that hair, and he used to wear this thing that was like a cape. I tried to copy the way he walked. He used to let me work in his office because I didn't have a quiet place to work. I'd go through his files and steal the titles of his stories, use them on my stories."

So he must have understood when we all shamelessly cribbed from him, we students at Syracuse, and Iowa and Stanford and all the other writing workshops in the country where almost everyone seemed to be writing and publishing stories with Raymond Carver titles like "Do You Mind If I Smoke?" or "How About This, Honey?" He certainly didn't want clones. But he knew that imitation was part of finding your own voice.

I encountered Carver near the beginning of what he liked to call his "second life," after he had quit drinking. I heard stories about the bad old Ray, stories he liked to tell on himself. When I met him I thought of writers as luminous madmen who drank too much and drove too fast and scattered brilliant pages along their doomed trajectories. Maybe at one time he did, too. In his essay "Fires," he says, "I understood writers to be people who didn't spend their Saturdays at the laundromat." Would Hemingway be caught dead doing laundry? No, but William Carlos Williams would. Ditto Carver's beloved Chekhov. In the classroom and on the page, Carver somehow delivered the tonic news that there was laundry in the kingdom of letters.

Not that, by this time, Ray was spending much time at the laundromat, life having been good to him toward the end in a way for which he seemed constantly to be grateful. But hearing the typewriter of one of the masters of American prose clacking just up the street, while a neighbor raked leaves and some kids threw a Frisbee as the dogs went on with their doggy life—this was a lesson in itself for me. Whatever dark mysteries lurk at the heart of the writing process, he insisted on a single trade secret: that you had to survive, find some quiet, and work hard every day. And seeing him for coffee, or watching a ball game or a dumb movie with him, put into perspective certain dangerous myths about the writing life that he preferred not to lecture on—although he sometimes would, if he thought it might help. When we first became acquainted, in New York, he felt obliged to advise me, in a series of wonderful letters, and a year later I moved upstate to become his student.

Reading the dialogues of Plato, one eventually realizes that Socrates' self-deprecation is something of a ploy. Ray's humility, however, was profound and unself-conscious and one of the most astonishing things about him. When he asked a student, "What do you think?" he clearly wanted to know. This seemed a rare and inspiring didactic stance. His own opinions were expressed with such caution that you knew how carefully they had been measured.

For someone who claimed he didn't love to teach, he made a great deal of difference to a great many students. He certainly changed my life irrevocably and I have heard others say the same thing.

I'm still leaning forward with my head cocked to one side, straining to hear his voice.

❑ *Outward Exploration: Discussion*

1. Explain McInerney's technique for describing Carver as a teacher in the first paragraph.
2. What was Carver's "trade secret" for writing?
3. Based on this essay, what kind of person was Carver?
4. What message did Carver seem to send about literature?
5. If you read Carver's "My Father's Life," how accurate do you find McInerney's description of Carver's style (paragraph 4)?

Outward Exploration: Writing

Following McInerney's lead, write an essay about someone who has been an important influence in your life. Try to capture the person's personality and demeanor as McInerney has done.

Style

Consider the following sentence from McInerney's essay:

For someone who claimed he didn't love to teach, he made a great deal of difference to a great many students. (paragraph 27)

Notice that the first part of the sentence ("For . . . teach") sums up several ideas from throughout the essay. The rest of the sentence does not contradict that opening section (for example, it doesn't say "he really did love to teach" or even "he devoted most of his time to teaching"), but it does reveal a kind of paradox (he didn't love teaching but he did it well).

Write a sentence of your own that follows this structure and states a paradox about someone. Feel free to use the same "For someone who . . . , that person . . ." structure.

Notes of a Native Son

JAMES BALDWIN

❏ *Inward Exploration*

Make a list of the negative effects of racism.

Make a list of people with whom you have had a complex and perhaps tempestuous relationship. Select one and write at least one paragraph explaining the complexities in that relationship.

I

On the 29th of July, in 1943, my father died. On the same day, a few hours later, his last child was born. Over a month before this, while all our energies were concentrated in waiting for these events, there had been, in Detroit, one of the bloodiest race riots of the century. A few hours after my father's funeral, while he lay in state in the undertaker's chapel, a race riot broke out in Harlem. On the morning of the 3rd of August, we drove my father to the graveyard through a wilderness of smashed plate glass.

The day of my father's funeral had also been my nineteenth birthday. As we drove him to the graveyard, the spoils of injustice, anarchy, discontent, and hatred were all around us. It seemed to me that God himself had devised, to mark my father's end, the most sustained and brutally dissonant of codas. And it seemed to me, too, that the violence which rose all about us as my father left the world had been devised as a corrective for the pride of his eldest son. I had declined to believe in that apocalypse which had been central to my father's vision; very well, life seemed to be saying, here is something that will certainly pass for an apocalypse until the real thing comes along. I had inclined to be contemptuous of my father for the conditions of his life, for the conditions of our lives. When his life had ended I began to wonder about that life and also, in a new way, to be apprehensive about my own.

I had not known my father very well. We had got on badly, partly because we shared, in our different fashions, the vice of stubborn pride. When he was dead I realized that I had hardly ever spoken to him. When he had been dead a long time I began to wish I had. It seems to be typical of life in America, where opportunities, real and fancied, are thicker than anywhere else on the globe, that the second generation has no time to talk to the first. No one, including my father, seems to have known exactly how old he was, but his mother had been born during slavery.

He was of the first generation of free men. He, along with thousands of other Negroes, came North after 1919 and I was part of that generation which had never seen the landscape of what Negroes sometimes call the Old Country.

He had been born in New Orleans and had been a quite young man there during the time that Louis Armstrong, a boy, was running errands for the dives and honky-tonks of what was always presented to me as one of the most wicked of cities—to this day, whenever I think of New Orleans, I also helplessly think of Sodom and Gomorrah. My father never mentioned Louis Armstrong, except to forbid us to play his records; but there was a picture of him on our wall for a long time. One of my father's strong-willed female relatives had placed it there and forbade my father to take it down. He never did, but he eventually maneuvered her out of the house and when, some years later, she was in trouble and near death, he refused to do anything to help her.

He was, I think, very handsome. I gather this from photographs and from my own memories of him, dressed in his Sunday best and on his way to preach a sermon somewhere, when I was little. Handsome, proud, and ingrown, "like a toe-nail," somebody said. But he looked to me, as I grew older, like pictures I had seen of African tribal chieftains: he really should have been naked, with war-paint on and barbaric mementos, standing among spears. He could be chilling in the pulpit and indescribably cruel in his personal life and he was certainly the most bitter man I have ever met; yet it must be said that there was something else in him, buried in him, which lent him his tremendous power and, even, a rather crushing charm. It had something to do with his blackness, I think—he was very black—with his blackness and his beauty, and with the fact that he knew that he was black but did not know that he was beautiful. He claimed to be proud of his blackness but it had also been the cause of much humiliation and it had fixed bleak boundaries to his life. He was not a young man when we were growing up and he had already suffered many kinds of ruin; in his outrageously demanding and protective way he loved his children, who were black like him and menaced, like him; and all these things sometimes showed in his face when he tried, never to my knowledge with any success, to establish contact with any of us. When he took one of his children on his knee to play, the child always became fretful and began to cry; when he tried to help one of us with our homework the absolutely unabating tension which emanated from him caused our minds and our tongues to become paralyzed, so that he, scarcely knowing why, flew into a rage and the child, not knowing why, was punished. If it ever entered his head to bring a surprise home for his children, it was, almost unfailingly, the wrong surprise and even the big watermelons he often brought home on his back in the summertime led to the most appalling scenes. I do not remember, in all those years, that one of his children was ever glad to see him come home. From what I was able to gather of his early life, it

5

seemed that this inability to establish contact with other people had always marked him and had been one of the things which had driven him out of New Orleans. There was something in him, therefore, groping and tentative, which was never expressed and which was buried with him. One saw it most clearly when he was facing new people and hoping to impress them. But he never did, not for long. We went from church to smaller and more improbable church, he found himself in less and less demand as a minister, and by the time he died none of his friends had come to see him for a long time. He had lived and died in an intolerable bitterness of spirit and it frightened me, as we drove him to the graveyard through those unquiet, ruined streets, to see how powerful and overflowing this bitterness could be and to realize that this bitterness now was mine.

When he died I had been away from home for a little over a year. In that year I had had time to become aware of the meaning of all my father's bitter warnings, had discovered the secret of his proudly pursed lips and rigid carriage: I had discovered the weight of white people in the world. I saw that this had been for my ancestors and now would be for me an awful thing to live with and that the bitterness which had helped to kill my father could also kill me.

He had been ill a long time—in the mind, as we now realized, reliving instances of his fantastic intransigence in the new light of his affliction and endeavoring to feel a sorrow for him which never, quite, came true. We had not known that he was being eaten up by paranoia, and the discovery that his cruelty, to our bodies and our minds, had been one of the symptoms of his illness was not, then, enough to enable us to forgive him. The younger children felt, quite simply, relief that he would not be coming home anymore. My mother's observation that it was he, after all, who had kept them alive all these years meant nothing because the problems of keeping children alive are not real for children. The older children felt, with my father gone, that they could invite their friends to the house without fear that their friends would be insulted or, as had sometimes happened with me, being told that their friends were in league with the devil and intended to rob our family of everything we owned. (I didn't fail to wonder, and it made me hate him, what on earth we owned that anybody else would want.)

His illness was beyond all hope of healing before anyone realized that he was ill. He had always been so strange and had lived, like a prophet, in such unimaginably close communion with the Lord that his long silences which were punctuated by moans and hallelujahs and snatches of old songs while he sat at the living-room window never seemed odd to us. It was not until he refused to eat because, he said, his family was trying to poison him that my mother was forced to accept as a fact what had, until then, been only an unwilling suspicion. When he was committed, it was discovered that he had tuberculosis and, as it turned out, the disease of his mind allowed the disease of his body to destroy him. For the doctors could not force him to eat, either, and, though he was fed intravenously, it was clear from the beginning that there was no hope for him.

In my mind's eye I could see him, sitting at the window, locked up in his terrors; hating and fearing every living soul including his children who had betrayed him, too, by reaching towards the world which had despised him. There were nine of us. I began to wonder what it could have felt like for such a man to have had nine children whom he could barely feed. He used to make little jokes about our poverty, which never, of course, seemed very funny to us; they could not have seemed very funny to him, either, or else our all too feeble response to them would never have caused such rages. He spent great energy and achieved, to our chagrin, no small amount of success in keeping us away from the people who surrounded us, people who had all-night rent parties to which we listened when we should have been sleeping, people who cursed and drank and flashed razor blades on Lenox Avenue. He could not understand why, if they had so much energy to spare, they could not use it to make their lives better. He treated almost everybody on our block with a most uncharitable asperity and neither they, nor, of course, their children were slow to reciprocate.

The only white people who came to our house were welfare workers   *10* and bill collectors. It was almost always my mother who dealt with them, for my father's temper, which was at the mercy of his pride, was never to be trusted. It was clear that he felt their very presence in his home to be a violation: this was conveyed by his carriage, almost ludicrously stiff, and by his voice, harsh and vindictively polite. When I was around nine or ten I wrote a play which was directed by a young, white schoolteacher, a woman, who then took an interest in me, and gave me books to read and, in order to corroborate my theatrical bent, decided to take me to see what she somewhat tactlessly referred to as "real" plays. Theatergoing was forbidden in our house, but, with the really cruel intuitiveness of a child, I suspected that the color of this woman's skin would carry the day for me. When, at school, she suggested taking me to the theater, I did not, as I might have done if she had been a Negro, find a way of discouraging her, but agreed that she should pick me up at my house one evening. I then, very cleverly, left all the rest to my mother, who suggested to my father, as I knew she would, that it would not be very nice to let such a kind woman make the trip for nothing. Also, since it was a schoolteacher, I imagine that my mother countered the idea of sin with the idea of "education," which word, even with my father, carried a kind of bitter weight.

Before the teacher came my father took me aside to ask *why* she was coming, what *interest* she could possibly have in our house, in a boy like me. I said I didn't know but I, too, suggested that it had something to do with education. And I understood that my father was waiting for me to say something—I didn't quite know what; perhaps that I wanted his protection against this teacher and her "education." I said none of these things and the teacher came and we went out. It was clear, during the brief interview in our living room, that my father was agreeing very much against his will and that he would have refused permission if he had dared. The fact that he did not dare caused me to despise him: I had no way of knowing that he was facing in that living room a wholly unprecedented and frightening situation.

Later, when my father had been laid off from his job, this woman became very important to us. She was really a very sweet and generous woman and went to a great deal of trouble to be of help to us, particularly during one awful winter. My mother called her by the highest name she knew: She said she was a "christian." My father could scarcely disagree but during the four or five years of our relatively close association he never trusted her and was always trying to surprise in her open, Midwestern face the genuine, cunningly hidden, and hideous motivation. In later years, particularly when it began to be clear that this "education" of mine was going to lead me to perdition, he became more explicit and warned me that my white friends in high school were not really my friends and that I would see, when I was older, how white people would do anything to keep a Negro down. Some of them could be nice, he admitted, but none of them were to be trusted and most of them were not even nice. The best thing was to have as little to do with them as possible. I did not feel this way and I was certain, in my innocence, that I never would.

But the year which preceded my father's death had made a great change in my life. I had been living in New Jersey, working in defense plants, working and living among southerners, white and black. I knew about the south, of course, and about how southerners treated Negroes and how they expected them to behave, but it had never entered my mind that anyone would look at me and expect *me* to behave that way. I learned in New Jersey that to be a Negro meant, precisely, that one was never looked at but was simply at the mercy of the reflexes the color of one's skin caused in other people. I acted in New Jersey as I had always acted, that is as though I thought a great deal of myself—I had to *act* that way—with results that were, simply, unbelievable. I had scarcely arrived before I had earned the enmity, which was extraordinarily ingenious, of all my superiors and nearly all my co-workers. In the beginning, to make matters worse, I simply did not know what was happening. I did not know what I had done, and I shortly began to wonder what *anyone* could possibly do, to bring about such unanimous, active, and unbearably vocal hostility. I knew about jim-crow but I had never experienced it. I went to the same self-service restaurant three times and stood with all the Princeton boys before the counter, waiting for a hamburger and coffee; it was always an extraordinarily long time before anything was set before me; but it was not until the fourth visit that I learned that, in fact, nothing had ever been set before me: I had simply picked something up. Negroes were not served there, I was told, and they had been waiting for me to realize that I was always the only Negro present. Once I was told this, I determined to go there all the time. But now they were ready for me and, though some dreadful scenes were subsequently enacted in that restaurant, I never ate there again.

It was the same story all over New Jersey, in bars, bowling alleys, diners, places to live. I was always being forced to leave, silently, or with mutual imprecations. I very shortly became notorious and children giggled behind me when I passed and their elders whispered or shouted—they really believed that I was mad. And it did begin to work on my mind, of course; I began to be afraid to go anywhere and to compensate for this I went places to which I really should not have gone and where, God knows, I had no desire to be. My reputation in town naturally enhanced my reputation at work and my working day became one long series of acrobatics designed to keep me out of trouble. I cannot say that these acrobatics succeeded. It began to seem that the machinery of the organization I worked for was turning over, day and night, with but one aim: to eject me. I was fired once, and contrived, with the aid of a friend from New York, to get back on the payroll; was fired again, and bounced back again. It took a while to fire me for the third time, but the third time took. There were no loopholes anywhere. There was not even any way of getting back inside the gates.

That year in New Jersey lives in my mind as though it were the year 15 during which, having an unsuspected predilection for it, I first contracted some dread, chronic disease, the unfailing symptom of which is a kind of blind fever, a pounding in the skull and fire in the bowels. Once this disease is contracted, one can never be really carefree again, for the fever, without an instant's warning, can recur at any moment. It can wreck more important things than race relations. There is not a Negro alive who does not have this rage in his blood—one has the choice, merely, of living with it consciously or surrendering to it. As for me, this fever has recurred in me, and does, and will until the day I die.

My last night in New Jersey, a white friend from New York took me to the nearest big town, Trenton, to go to the movies and have a few drinks. As it turned out, he also saved me from, at the very least, a violent whipping. Almost every detail of that night stands out very clearly in my memory. I even remember the name of the movie we saw because its title impressed me as being so patly ironical. It was a movie about the German occupation of France, starring Maureen O'Hara and Charles Laughton and called *This Land Is Mine*. I remember the name of the diner we walked into when the movie ended: it was the "American Diner." When we walked in the counterman asked what we wanted and I remember answering with the casual sharpness which had become my habit: "We want a hamburger and a cup of coffee, what do you think we want?" I do not know why, after a year of such rebuffs, I so completely failed to anticipate his answer, which was, of course, "We don't serve Negroes here." This reply failed to discompose me, at least for the moment. I made some sardonic comment about the name of the diner and we walked out into the streets.

This was the time of what was called the "brown-out," when the lights in all American cities were very dim. When we re-entered the streets something happened to me which had the force of an optical illusion, or a nightmare. The streets were very crowded and I was facing north. People were moving in every direction but it seemed to me, in that instant, that all of the people I could see, and many more than that, were moving toward me, against me, and that everyone was white. I remember how their faces gleamed. And I felt, like a physical sensation, a *click* at the nape of my neck as though some interior string connecting my head to my body had been cut. I began to walk. I heard my friend call after me, but I ignored him. Heaven only knows what was going on in his mind, but he had the good sense not to touch me—I don't know what would have happened if he had—and to keep me in sight. I don't know what was going on in my mind, either; I certainly had no conscious plan. I wanted to do something to crush these white faces, which were crushing me. I walked for perhaps a block or two until I came to an enormous, glittering, and fashionable restaurant in which I knew not even the intercession of the Virgin would cause me to be served. I pushed through the doors and took the first vacant seat I saw, at a table for two, and waited.

I do not know how long I waited and I rather wonder, until today, what I could possibly have looked like. Whatever I looked like, I frightened the waitress who shortly appeared, and the moment she appeared all of my fury flowed towards her. I hated her for her white face, and for her great, astounded, frightened eyes. I felt that if she found a black man so frightening I would make her fright worth-while.

She did not ask me what I wanted, but repeated, as though she had learned it somewhere, "We don't serve Negroes here." She did not say it with the blunt, derisive hostility to which I had grown so accustomed but, rather, with a note of apology in her voice, and fear. This made me colder and more murderous than ever. I felt I had to do something with my hands. I wanted her to come close enough for me to get her neck between my hands.

So I pretended not to have understood her, hoping to draw her   20
closer. And she did step a very short step closer, with her pencil poised incongruously over her pad, and repeated the formula: ". . . don't serve Negroes here."

Somehow, with the repetition of that phrase, which was already ringing in my head like a thousand bells of a nightmare, I realized that she would never come any closer and that I would have to strike from a distance. There was nothing on the table but an ordinary water-mug half full of water, and I picked this up and hurled it with all my strength at her. She ducked and it missed her and shattered against the mirror behind the bar. And, with that sound, my frozen blood abruptly thawed, I returned from wherever I had been, I *saw,* for the first time, the restaurant, the people with their mouths open, already, as it seemed to me, rising as one man, and I realized what I had done, and where I was, and I was frightened. I rose and began running for the door. A round, potbellied man grabbed me by the nape of the neck just as I reached the doors and began to beat me about the face. I kicked him and got loose and ran into the streets. My friend whispered, *"Run!"* and I ran.

My friend stayed outside the restaurant long enough to misdirect my pursuers and the police, who arrived, he told me, at once. I do not know what I said to him when he came to my room that night. I could not have said much. I felt, in the oddest, most awful way, that I had somehow betrayed him. I lived it over and over and over again, the way one relives an automobile accident after it has happened and one finds oneself alone and safe. I could not get over two facts, both equally difficult for the imagination to grasp, and one was that I could have been murdered. But the other was that I had been ready to commit murder. I saw nothing very clearly but I did see this: that my life, my *real* life, was in danger, and not from anything other people might do but from the hatred I carried in my own heart.

II

I had returned home around the second week in June—in great haste because it seemed that my father's death and my mother's confinement were both but a matter of hours. In the case of my mother, it soon became clear that she had simply made a miscalculation. This had always been her tendency and I don't believe that a single one of us arrived in the world, or has since arrived anywhere else, on time. But none of us dawdled so intolerably about the business of being born as did my baby sister. We sometimes amused ourselves, during those endless, stifling weeks, by picturing the baby sitting within the safe, warm dark, bitterly regretting the necessity of becoming a part of our chaos and stubbornly putting it off as long as possible. I understood her perfectly and congratulated her on showing such good sense so soon. Death, however, sat as purposefully at my father's bedside as life stirred within my mother's womb and it was harder to understand why he so lingered in that long shadow. It seemed that he had bent, and for a long time, too, all of his energies towards dying. Now death was ready for him but my father held back.

All of Harlem, indeed, seemed to be infected by waiting. I had never before known it to be so violently still. Racial tensions throughout this country were exacerbated during the early years of the war, partly because the labor market brought together hundreds of thousands of ill-prepared people and partly because Negro soldiers, regardless of where they were born, received their military training in the south. What happened in defense plants and army camps had repercussions, naturally, in every Negro ghetto. The situation in Harlem had grown bad enough for clergymen, policemen, educators, politicians, and social workers to assert in one breath that there was no "crime wave" and to offer, in the very next breath, suggestions as to how to combat it. These suggestions always seemed to involve playgrounds, despite the fact that racial skirmishes were occurring in the playgrounds, too. Playground or not, crime wave or not, the Harlem police force had been augmented in March, and the unrest grew—perhaps, in fact, partly as a result of the ghetto's instinctive hatred of policemen. Perhaps the most revealing news item, out of the steady parade of reports of muggings, stabbings, shootings, assaults, gang wars, and accusations of police brutality is the item concerning six Negro girls who set upon a white girl in the subway because, as they all too accurately put it, she was stepping on their toes. Indeed she was, all over the nation.

I had never before been so aware of policemen, on foot, on horse-   25
back, on corners, everywhere, always two by two. Nor had I ever been so aware of small knots of people. They were on stoops and on corners and in doorways, and what was striking about them, I think, was that they did not seem to be talking. Never, when I passed these groups, did the usual sound of a curse or a laugh ring out and neither did there seem to be any hum of gossip. There was certainly, on the other hand, occurring between them communication extraordinarily intense. Another thing that was striking was the unexpected diversity of the people who made up these groups. Usually, for example, one would see a group of sharpies standing on the street corner, jiving the passing chicks; or a group of older men, usually, for some reason, in the vicinity of a barber shop, discussing baseball scores, or the numbers or making rather chilling observations about women they had known. Women, in a general way, tended to be seen less often together—unless they were church women, or very young girls, or prostitutes met together for an unprofessional instant. But that summer I saw the strangest combinations: large, respectable, churchly matrons standing on the stoops or the corners with their hair tied up, together with a girl in sleazy satin whose face bore the marks of gin and the razor, or heavy-set, abrupt, no-nonsense older men, in company with the most disreputable and fanatical "race" men, or these same "race" men with the sharpies, or these sharpies with the churchly women. Seventh Day Adventists and Methodists and Spiritualists seemed to be hobnobbing with Holyrollers and they were all, alike, entangled with the most flagrant disbelievers; something heavy in their stance seemed to indicate that they had all, incredibly, seen a common vision, and on each face there seemed to be the same strange, bitter shadow.

The churchly women and the matter-of-fact, no–nonsense men had children in the Army. The sleazy girls they talked to had lovers there, the sharpies and the "race" men had friends and brothers there. It would have demanded an unquestioning patriotism, happily as uncommon in this country as it is undesirable, for these people not to have been disturbed by the bitter letters they received, by the newspaper stories they read, not to have been enraged by the posters, then to be found all over New York, which described the Japanese as "yellow-bellied Japs." It was only the "race" men, to be sure, who spoke ceaselessly of being revenged—how this vengeance was to be exacted was not clear—for the indignities and dangers suffered by Negro boys in uniform; but everybody felt a directionless, hopeless bitterness, as well as that panic which can scarcely be suppressed when one knows that a human being one loves is beyond one's reach, and in danger. This helplessness and this gnawing uneasiness does something, at length, to even the toughest mind. Perhaps the best way to sum all this up is to say that the people I knew felt, mainly, a peculiar kind of relief when they knew that their boys were being shipped out of the south, to do battle overseas. It was, perhaps, like feeling that the most dangerous part of a dangerous journey had been passed and that now, even if death should come, it would come with honor and without the complicity of their countrymen. Such a death would be, in short, a fact with which one could hope to live.

It was on the 28th of July, which I believe was a Wednesday, that I visited my father for the first time during his illness and for the last time in his life. The moment I saw him I knew why I had put off this visit so long. I had told my mother that I did not want to see him because I hated him. But this was not true. It was only that I *had* hated him and I wanted to hold on to this hatred. I did not want to look on him as a ruin; it was not a ruin I had hated. I imagine that one of the reasons people cling to their hates so stubbornly is because they sense, once hate is gone, that they will be forced to deal with pain.

We traveled out to him, his older sister and myself, to what seemed to be the very end of a very Long Island. It was hot and dusty and we wrangled, my aunt and I, all the way out, over the fact that I had recently begun to smoke and, as she said, to give myself airs. But I knew that she wrangled with me because she could not bear to face the fact of her brother's dying. Neither could I endure the reality of her despair, her unstated bafflement as to what had happened to her brother's life, and her own. So we wrangled and I smoked and from time to time she fell into a heavy reverie. Covertly, I watched her face, which was the face of an old woman; it had fallen in, the eyes were sunken and lightless; soon she would be dying, too.

In my childhood—it had not been so long ago—I had thought her beautiful. She had been quick-witted and quick-moving and very generous with all the children and each of her visits had been an event. At one time one of my brothers and myself had thought of running away to live with her. Now she could no longer produce out of her handbag some unexpected and yet familiar delight. She made me feel pity and revulsion and fear. It was awful to realize that she no longer caused me to feel affection. The closer we came to the hospital the more querulous she became and at the same time, naturally, grew more dependent on me. Between pity and guilt and fear I began to feel that there was another me trapped in my skull like a jack-in-the-box who might escape my control at any moment and fill the air with screaming.

She began to cry the moment we entered the room and she saw him   *30* lying there, all shriveled and still, like a little black monkey. The great, gleaming apparatus which fed him and would have compelled him to be still even if he had been able to move brought to mind, not beneficence, but torture; the tubes entering his arm made me think of pictures I had seen when a child, of Gulliver, tied down by the pygmies on that island. My aunt wept and wept, there was a whistling sound in my father's throat; nothing was said; he could not speak. I wanted to take his hand, to say something. But I do not know what I could have said, even if he could have heard me. He was not really in that room with us, he had at last really embarked on his journey; and though my aunt told me that he said he was going to meet Jesus, I did not hear anything except that whistling in his throat. The doctor came back and we left, into that unbearable train again, and home. In the morning came the telegram saying that he was dead. Then the house was suddenly full of relatives, friends, hysteria, and confusion and I quickly left my mother and the children to the care of those impressive women, who, in Negro communities at least, automatically appear at times of bereavement armed with lotions, proverbs, and patience, and an ability to cook. I went downtown. By the time I returned, later the same day, my mother had been carried to the hospital and the baby had been born.

III

For my father's funeral I had nothing black to wear and this posed a nagging problem all day long. It was one of those problems, simple, or impossible of solution, to which the mind insanely clings in order to avoid the mind's real trouble. I spent most of that day at the downtown apartment of a girl I knew, celebrating my birthday with whiskey and wondering what to wear that night. When planning a birthday celebration one naturally does not expect that it will be up against competition from a funeral and this girl had anticipated taking me out that night, for a big dinner and a night club afterwards. Sometime during the course of that long day we decided that we would go out anyway, when my father's funeral service was over. I imagine *I* decided it, since, as the funeral hour approached, it became clearer and clearer to me that I would not know what to do with myself when it was over. The girl, stifling her very lively concern as to the possible effects of the whiskey on one of my father's chief mourners, concentrated on being conciliatory and practically helpful. She found a black shirt for me somewhere and ironed it and, dressed in the darkest pants and jacket I owned, and slightly drunk, I made my way to my father's funeral.

The chapel was full, but not packed, and very quiet. There were, mainly, my father's relatives, and his children, and here and there I saw faces I had not seen since childhood, the faces of my father's one-time friends. They were very dark and solemn now, seeming somehow to suggest that they had known all along that something like this would happen. Chief among the mourners was my aunt, who had quarreled with my father all his life; by which I do not mean to suggest that her mourning was insincere or that she had not loved him. I suppose that she was one of the few people in the world who had, and their incessant quarreling proved precisely the strength of the tie that bound them. The only other person in the world, as far as I knew, whose relationship to my father rivaled my aunt's in depth was my mother, who was not there.

It seemed to me, of course, that it was a very long funeral. But it was, if anything, a rather shorter funeral than most, nor, since there were no overwhelming, uncontrollable expressions of grief, could it be called—if I dare to use the word—successful. The minister who preached my father's funeral sermon was one of the few my father had still been seeing as he neared his end. He presented to us in his sermon a man whom none of us had ever seen—a man thoughtful, patient, and forbearing, a Christian inspiration to all who knew him, and a model for his children. And no doubt the children, in their disturbed and guilty state, were almost ready to believe this; he had been remote enough to be anything and, anyway, the shock of the incontrovertible, that it was really our father lying up there in that casket, prepared the mind for anything. His sister moaned and this grief-stricken moaning was taken as corroboration. The other faces held a dark, non-committal thoughtfulness. This was not the man they had known, but they had scarcely expected to be confronted with *him;* this was, in a sense deeper than questions of fact, the man they had not known, and the man they had not known may have been the real one. The real man, whoever he had been, had suffered and now he was dead: this was all that was sure and all that mattered now. Every man in the chapel hoped that when his hour came he, too, would be eulogized, which is to say forgiven, and that all of his lapses, greeds, errors, and strayings from the truth would be invested with coherence and looked upon with charity. This was perhaps the last thing human beings could give each other and it was what they demanded, after all, of the Lord. Only the Lord saw the midnight tears, only He was present when one of His children, moaning and wringing hands, paced up and down the room. When one slapped one's child in anger the recoil in the heart reverberated through heaven and became part of the pain of the universe. And when the children were hungry and sullen and distrustful and one watched them, daily, growing wilder, and further away, and running headlong into danger, it was the Lord who knew what the charged heart endured as the strap was laid to the backside; the Lord alone who knew what one *would* have said if one had had, like the Lord, the gift of the living word. It was the Lord who knew of the impossibility every parent in that room faced: how to prepare the child for the day when the child would be despised and how to *create* in the child—by what means?—a stronger antidote to this poison than one had found for oneself. The avenues, side streets, bars, billiard halls, hospitals, police stations, and even the playgrounds of Harlem— not to mention the houses of correction, the jails, and the morgue— testified to the potency of the poison while remaining silent as to the efficacy of whatever antidote, irresistibly raising the question of whether or not such an antidote existed; raising, which was worse, the question of whether or not an antidote was desirable; perhaps poison should be fought with poison. With these several schisms in the mind and with more terrors in the heart than could be named, it was better not to judge the man who had gone down under an impossible burden. It was better to remember: *Thou knowest this man's fall; but thou knowest not his wrassling.*

While the preacher talked and I watched the children—years of changing their diapers, scrubbing them, slapping them, taking them to school, and scolding them had had the perhaps inevitable result of making me love them, though I am not sure I knew this then—my mind was busily breaking out with a rash of disconnected impressions. Snatches of popular songs, indecent jokes, bits of books I had read, movie sequences, faces, voices, political issues—I thought I was going mad; all these impressions suspended, as it were, in the solution of the faint nausea produced in me by the heat and liquor. For a moment I had the impression that my alcoholic breath, inefficiently disguised with chewing gum, filled the entire chapel. Then someone began singing one of my father's favorite songs and, abruptly, I was with him, sitting on his knee, in the hot, enormous, crowded church which was the first church we attended. It was the Abyssinia Baptist Church on 138th Street. We had not gone there long. With this image, a host of others came. I had forgotten, in the rage of my growing up, how proud my father had been of me when I was little. Apparently, I had had a voice and my father had liked to show me off before the members of the church. I had forgotten what he had looked like when he was pleased but now I remembered that he had always been grinning with pleasure when my solos ended. I even remembered certain expressions on his face when he teased my mother—had he loved her? I would never know. And when had it all begun to change? For now it seemed that he had not always been cruel. I remembered being taken for a haircut and scraping my knee on the footrest of the barber's chair and I remembered my father's face as he soothed my crying and applied the stinging iodine. Then I remembered our fights, fights which had been of the worst possible kind because my technique had been silence.

I remembered the one time in all our life together when we had really spoken to each other. 35

It was on a Sunday and it must have been shortly before I left home. We were walking, just the two of us, in our usual silence, to or from church. I was in high school and had been doing a lot of writing and I was, at about this time, the editor of the high school magazine. But I had also been a Young Minister and had been preaching from the pulpit. Lately, I had been taking fewer engagements and preached as rarely as possible. It was said in the church, quite truthfully, that I was "cooling off."

My father asked me abruptly, "You'd rather write than preach, wouldn't you?"

I was astonished at his question—because it was a real question. I answered, "Yes."

That was all we said. It was awful to remember that that was all we had *ever* said.

The casket now was opened and the mourners were being led up the aisle to look for the last time on the deceased. The assumption was that the family was too overcome with grief to be allowed to make this journey alone and I watched while my aunt was led to the casket and, muffled in black, and shaking, led back to her seat. I disapproved of forcing the children to look on their dead father, considering that the shock of his death, or, more truthfully, the shock of death as a reality, was already a little more than a child could bear, but my judgment in this matter had been overruled and there they were, bewildered and frightened and very small, being led, one by one, to the casket. But there is also something very gallant about children at such moments. It has something to do with their silence and gravity and with the fact that one cannot help them. Their legs, somehow, seem *exposed,* so that it is at once incredible and terribly clear that their legs are all they have to hold them up. 40

I had not wanted to go to the casket myself and I certainly had not wished to be led there, but there was no way of avoiding either of these forms. One of the deacons led me up and I looked on my father's face. I cannot say that it looked like him at all. His blackness had been equivocated by powder and there was no suggestion in that casket of what his power had or could have been. He was simply an old man dead, and it was hard to believe that he had ever given anyone either joy or pain. Yet, his life filled that room. Further up the avenue his wife was holding his newborn child. Life and death so close together, and love and hatred, and right and wrong, said something to me which I did not want to hear concerning man, concerning the life of man.

After the funeral, while I was downtown desperately celebrating my birthday, a Negro soldier, in the lobby of the Hotel Braddock, got into a fight with a white policeman over a Negro girl. Negro girls, white policemen, in or out of uniform, and Negro males—in or out of uniform—were part of the furniture of the lobby of the Hotel Braddock and this was certainly not the first time such an incident had occurred. It was destined, however, to receive an unprecedented publicity, for the fight between the policeman and the soldier ended with the shooting of the soldier. Rumor, flowing immediately to the streets outside, stated that the soldier had been shot in the back, an instantaneous and revealing invention, and that the soldier had died protecting a Negro woman. The facts were somewhat different—for example, the soldier had not been shot in the back, and was not dead, and the girl seems to have been as dubious a symbol of womanhood as her white counterpart in Georgia usually is, but no one was interested in the facts. They preferred the invention because this invention expressed and corroborated their hates and fears so perfectly. It is just as well to remember that people are always doing this. Perhaps many of those legends, including Christianity, to which the world clings began their conquest of the world with just some such concerted surrender to distortion. The effect, in Harlem, of this particular legend was like the effect of a lit match in a tin of gasoline. The mob gathered before the doors of the Hotel Braddock simply began to swell and to spread in every direction, and Harlem exploded.

The mob did not cross the ghetto lines. It would have been easy, for example, to have gone over Morningside Park on the west side or to have crossed the Grand Central railroad tracks at 125th Street on the east side, to wreak havoc in white neighborhoods. The mob seems to have been mainly interested in something more potent and real than the white face, that is, in white power, and the principal damage done during the riot of the summer of 1943 was to white business establishments in Harlem. It might have been a far bloodier story, of course, if, at the hour the riot began, these establishments had still been open. From the Hotel Braddock the mob fanned out, east and west along 125th Street, and for the entire length of Lenox, Seventh, and Eighth avenues. Along each of these avenues, and along each major side street—116th, 125th, 135th, and so on—bars, stores, pawnshops, restaurants, even little luncheonettes had been smashed open and entered and looted—looted, it might be added, with more haste than efficiency. The shelves really looked as though a bomb had struck them. Cans of beans and soup and dog food, along with toilet paper, corn flakes, sardines and milk tumbled every which way, and abandoned cash registers and cases of beer leaned crazily out of the splintered windows and were strewn along the avenues. Sheets, blankets, and clothing of every description formed a kind of path, as though people had dropped them while running. I truly had not realized that Harlem *had* so many stores until I saw them all smashed open; the first time the word *wealth* ever entered my mind in relation to Harlem was when I saw it scattered in the streets. But one's first, incongruous impression of plenty was countered immediately by an impression of waste. None of this was doing anybody any good. It would have been better to have left the plate glass as it had been and the goods lying in the stores.

It would have been better, but it would also have been intolerable, for Harlem had needed something to smash. To smash something is the ghetto's chronic need. Most of the time it is the members of the ghetto who smash each other, and themselves. But as long as the ghetto walls are standing there will always come a moment when these outlets do not work. That summer, for example, it was not enough to get into a fight on Lenox Avenue, or curse out one's cronies in the barber shops. If ever, indeed, the violence which fills Harlem's churches, pool halls, and bars erupts outward in a more direct fashion, Harlem and its citizens are likely to vanish in an apocalyptic flood. That this is not likely to happen is due to a great many reasons, most hidden and powerful among them the Negro's real relation to the white American. This relation prohibits, simply, anything as uncomplicated and satisfactory as pure hatred. In order really to hate white people, one has to blot so much out of the mind—and the heart—that this hatred itself becomes an exhausting and self-destructive pose. But this does not mean, on the other hand, that love comes easily: the white world is too powerful, too complacent, too ready with gratuitous humiliation, and, above all, too ignorant and too innocent for that. One is absolutely forced to make perpetual qualifications and one's own reactions are always canceling each other out. It is this, really, which has driven so many people mad, both white and black. One is always in the position of having to decide between amputation and gangrene. Amputation is swift but time may prove that the amputation was not necessary—or one may delay the amputation too long. Gangrene is slow, but it is impossible to be sure that one is reading one's symptoms right. The idea of going through life as a cripple is more than one can bear, and equally unbearable is the risk of swelling up slowly, in agony, with poison. And the trouble, finally, is that the risks are real even if the choices do not exist.

"But as for me and my house," my father had said, "we will serve the Lord." I wondered, as we drove him to his resting place, what this line had meant for him. I had heard him preach it many times. I had preached it once myself, proudly giving it an interpretation different from my father's. Now the whole thing came back to me, as though my father and I were on our way to Sunday school and I were memorizing the golden text: *And if it seem evil unto you to serve the Lord, choose you this day whom you will serve; whether the gods which your fathers served that were on the other side of the flood, or the gods of the Amorites, in whose land ye dwell: but as for me and my house, we will serve the Lord.* I suspected in these familiar lines a meaning which had never been there for me before. All

45

of my father's texts and songs, which I had decided were meaningless, were arranged before me at his death like empty bottles, waiting to hold the meaning which life would give them for me. This was his legacy: nothing is ever escaped. That bleakly memorable morning I hated the unbelievable streets and the Negroes and whites who had, equally, made them that way. But I knew that it was folly, as my father would have said, this bitterness was folly. It was necessary to hold on to the things that mattered. The dead man mattered, the new life mattered; blackness and whiteness did not matter; to believe that they did was to acquiesce in one's own destruction. Hatred, which could destroy so much, never failed to destroy the man who hated and this was an immutable law.

It began to seem that one would have to hold in the mind forever two ideas which seemed to be in opposition. The first idea was acceptance, the acceptance, totally without rancor, of life as it is, and men as they are: in the light of this idea, it goes without saying that injustice is a commonplace. But this did not mean that one could be complacent, for the second idea was of equal power: that one must never, in one's own life, accept these injustices as commonplace but must fight them with all one's strength. This fight begins, however, in the heart and it now had been laid to my charge to keep my own heart free of hatred and despair. This intimation made my heart heavy and, now that my father was irrecoverable, I wished that he had been beside me so that I could have searched his face for the answers which only the future would give me now.

Outward Exploration: Discussion

1. What trait does Baldwin feel he and his father shared?
2. Describe the personality of Baldwin's father.
3. What traits does Baldwin seem to share with his father?
4. Explain the nature of the "rage" in Baldwin's blood (paragraph 15). Where did it come from? Do you think African Americans and other minorities feel a similar rage now? Why or why not?
5. What's ironic about the movie title and the name of the diner (paragraph 16)?
6. What realization does Baldwin come to after the episode in the restaurant?
7. What does Baldwin mean when he says the white–black relationship "prohibits, simply, anything as uncomplicated and satisfactory as pure hatred" (paragraph 44)?
8. Do you think it is possible to "hold in the mind forever two ideas which seemed to be in opposition," namely acceptance and the desire for equal power (paragraph 46)? Explain.

❑ *Outward Exploration: Writing*

Write an essay about an important person in your life, one with whom your relationship has not always been easy. Search for the sources of that person's attitudes as Baldwin speculates about the sources of his father's.

❑ *Style*

1. Consider the following sentence from Baldwin's essay:

That was his legacy: nothing is ever escaped. (paragraph 45)

This short compound sentence joins two independent clauses with a colon, indicating that the second clause is an elaboration on the first. Using your own information, create a sentence that replicates this structure. The first clause should introduce the second (as the word *legacy* prepares us for the explanation of what that legacy is).

2. Consider the repeating structures and rhythm of Baldwin's opening five sentences:

On the 29th of July, in 1943, my father died. On the same day, a few hours later, his last child was born. Over a month before this, while all our energies were concentrated in waiting for these events, there had been, in Detroit, one of the bloodiest race riots of the century. A few hours after my father's funeral, while he lay in state in the undertaker's chapel, a race riot broke out in Harlem. On the morning of the 3rd of August, we drove my father to the graveyard through a wilderness of smashed plate glass. (paragraph 1)

Notice the similarities:

None of these sentences begin with the subject.

The first, second, third, and fifth sentences all begin with prepositional phrases followed by commas. The fourth sentence begins with a time marker plus a prepositional phrase followed by a comma. In other words, their first elements are not the sentences' subjects.

The **first elements** of the first four sentences are followed by another grammatical unit that is also set off with commas, causing a halting rhythm. In the first sentence, a prepositional phrase follows the first comma; in the second, a time marker plus a prepositional phrase fills that slot; in the third and fourth sentences, a dependent *while* clause is in that slot. Only in the fifth sentence does the subject (*we*) follow the first element, breaking the pattern and rhythm previously established.

In the first, second, and fourth sentences, the subject occurs next (*my father, his last child, a race riot*). In the third sentence, the subject and the verb are inverted (thanks to the expletive *there—there had been*). Notice that in this third sentence—the middle sentence of this grouping of five—an additional interrupter (*in Detroit*) separates the verb (*had been*) from the subject (*one*) and is also set off with commas.

In short, the rhythms of those opening sentences mirror each other. Baldwin's interesting use of commas to create pauses causes us to read more slowly, more meditatively than we might otherwise do. Try reading those five sentences aloud, pausing briefly at each comma, listening to the rhythms. Try putting emphasis on different parts of the sentences.

Using your own information, write a series of four or five sentences whose structure and rhythm mirror each other in the same way. Since there is nothing unusual if the sentences all follow the subject–verb–everything-else structure, there is no noticeable gain in rhythm using that structure. Therefore, make the structure of those sentences a bit distinctive. Feel free to use Baldwin's prepositional-phrase opening or some other opening that has caught your attention.

5

Exploring Relationships

Writing about relationships overlaps significantly with writing about other people. How could it not? Yet there is a subtle difference in focus. As we discovered in the previous chapter, writing about another person requires you to explore his or her personality, motives, emotions. Often you provide a physical description to augment or highlight your analysis. In addition to painting a portrait of that person, you are concerned with that person's impact on you. In fact, you might never have even met the person you write about: Many people we don't know personally have had a profound effect on us (for example, political figures, artists).

Writing about a relationship, on the other hand, requires that you know the person; the very term *relationship* implies a two-way connection. Given that you need to know the other person, exploring a relationship might seem to be a simple mathematical operation: Explore the other person, explore yourself, and write "The End." As in so many areas, however, the sum is greater than the parts. Although there are obviously two (or more) individuals involved in each relationship, the relationship is more than a case of simple addition: The relationship has a life of its own, dynamics of its own, a history of its own. To explore a relationship, then, requires a thorough consideration of the interactions between you and the other person, an examination of how the relationship affected or affects you, and an exploration of the reasons for the dynamics in that particular relationship. In addition, you might find that a pattern emerges from several different relationships.

It is also possible to discuss a relationship between others that has a significant impact on you. The most obvious example is the relationship of your parents—a relationship about which you probably have a great deal of "insider" information and which you may have had many opportunities to observe. Further, it clearly has a significant impact on you. If you do decide to analyze and explore a relationship that influences you without your being a partner in that relationship, the personal significance for you will then grow from your relationship with the relationship rather than with the participants individually. (Naturally, you could explore your relationship with your mother or with your father, but those essays would be different from an essay about your connection to their relationship with each other.)

Exploring relationships is important because, at least in part, we define ourselves in terms of our relationships with others, including romantic partners, friends, enemies, rivals, parents, siblings, teachers, students, employers, and employees. In fact, it is difficult to imagine an explanation of our personalities without reference to how we interact with others. Exploring relationships, then, is a crucial aspect of exploratory writing, for relationships reveal our personality traits in action, help us grow and develop, and offer correctives and qualifications to our self-portrait.

Yet often it is difficult to think very deeply about our relationships. Most of the time we tend simply to accept the majority of relationships in our lives without much thought. The exception occurs, of course, when the relationship changes suddenly or when there is trouble in the relationship (for example, the breakup of a romance or a friendship). Then we probably think of little else.

This chapter discusses how to explore relationships, indicating various areas and issues that you should consider. Not all are likely to be part of any one essay, but your overall understanding of yourself and of yourself as part of that relationship will be much greater if you prewrite about all the areas, pushing yourself to delve deeper than you ever have before. You might be surprised at what you discover.

Fortunately, many of the skills that you have practiced so far, particularly those involving analysis, will help you explore relationships as well. Now, however, you will be analyzing the motives, thoughts, emotions, and reactions of others *and* of yourself. You will be looking for sources of individual *and* mutual reactions and for reasons why all the participants are in the relationship to begin with.

You should also consider the contexts of the relationship you are exploring. Think again, for example, about the vantage points discussed in Chapter 2—how did such vantage points as economic class or gender or family influence the formation of the relationship or its continuation? Consider also the role(s) that the relationship plays in your life as well as the role that each participant plays within the relationship itself. Return to Chapter 1 for a moment and consider the relationship from some of the perspectives listed there. What might the skeptic say about the relationship? The advocate? The observer? The joker? The flea?

In addition to using all the techniques you've learned so far, writing an exploratory essay about relationships can use many organizational strategies. For example, you could include a significant amount of narration. In that case, you could dramatize one or two key events that illustrate crucial elements or moments in the relationship (for instance, the first time the participants met and the big fight that ended the relationship) while merely summarizing or alluding to other events. On the other hand, the exploratory essay might primarily feature analysis. In this case, you could summarize key events while spending most of your time explaining attitudes, assumptions, and the relationship's dynamics. Or the essay might include a mixture of the two strategies. Another way to begin would be to make a general statement that reflects some truth you've learned about this relationship or about relationships in general. Or you might begin by talking about famous relationships (factual or fictional) which are similar to yours, setting your readers up for an extended comparison and contrast in the essay itself. Or you could explain what you think the ideal version of such a relationship should be. Or you might begin with a quotation from some "expert" about this particular type of relationship (texts such as *Bartlett's Familiar Quotations* are good sources). You could even examine several different relationships, analyzing their similarities and differences, looking for a common thread or pattern. In all cases, however, there should be some explicit statements about the relationship's significance to you.

As noted in earlier chapters, people and relationships are complex, and one goal of exploratory essays is to reveal and examine that complexity. For example, we don't just love or hate someone—we have other feelings at the same moment, feelings such as resentment, admiration, envy, pride, fear. In short, we always feel mixed emotions about anyone of significance in our life. It is crucial to keep such complexity in mind in exploratory essays.

WRITER-BASED GOALS

There are at least six writer-based goals. First, try to discover something new about an important relationship in your life. For example: Why is the relationship important (over and beyond the obvious reasons)? What are your expectations, hopes, and fears about this type of relationship?

Second, explore the dynamics of the relationship. Many times we tend to play down one of the roles in a relationship: For instance, we might ignore our own role in causing the ups and downs in a relationship, or, conversely, we might take all the blame on ourselves instead of seeing that each person in a relationship shares some of the blame. As you work on this essay, try to see the whole picture, try to see both people's roles (which may, of course, change over time).

Third, deepen your understanding of how you connect with people. You might discover your strengths as a partner in a relationship as well as your weaknesses. You might find out that you are a better (or worse) friend, child, partner, teacher, parent, mentor, employee, employer or supervisor than you previously thought.

Fourth, look for patterns in your relationships, some of which might be beneficial and others harmful or nonproductive.

Fifth, try to uncover not only the sources of those patterns but also the sources of your expectations and hopes and fears about relationships.

Sixth, try to articulate the global significance of your experiences in a particular kind of relationship or series of relationships.

READER-BASED GOALS

There are three reader-based goals. First, reveal something new about your personality, about your feelings and thoughts.

Second, try to offer insights into relationships in general, insights that might apply to readers' own relationships.

Third, make the essay interesting by using all the elements of writing that seem appropriate. For example, use vivid narration to dramatize key moments in the relationship. Use your analytical skills to explore the dynamics of the relationship. Use figurative language to express your thoughts and emotions.

SELECTING A RELATIONSHIP

Select a relationship that seems meaningful to you, even if you're not sure what that meaning is yet. The following are some obvious possibilities:

parent–child

same-sex friendship

different-sex friendship

dating

romance

love

leader–led

employer–employee

co-worker

peer

mentor

UNDERSTANDING THE RELATIONSHIP

Understanding a relationship includes a great deal of analysis—of yourself, of the other person, of the context of the relationship, of your beliefs and of the sources of your beliefs about what this type of relationship should be, at least in an ideal world. Because we have already considered techniques for such analysis in earlier chapters, this section focuses on the sources of our assumptions about relationships, the patterns of roles in relationships, the obstacles to writing about relationships, and it offers an approach for exploring relationships more deeply.

Sources of Our Assumptions

Chapter 2 discussed some of the sources of our assumptions about ourselves and others: They are also the sources of our assumptions about relationships, and they bear repeating here. Assumptions come from our status as human beings of a particular gender in a particular society in a particular era. Assumptions also come from our belonging to specific groups (for example, regional, religious, ethnic, social) and to particular families. Some assumptions have developed from our own personal experiences through time, such as events that happened to us, texts we've encountered, conversations we've had with others.

Patterns

For our purposes, a **pattern** is any or all of the following: (1) a consistent mode of behavior, (2) a consistent role that you play over and over, (3) a particular personality type that you continue to be attracted to. One of the best ways to understand a relationship is to look for recurring patterns either within the relationship itself or among different relationships.

PATTERNS WITHIN THE RELATIONSHIP   Within any relationship, we tend to assume the same role or set of roles over and over. For example, Mike tends to be the "realist" (or "pessimist") in a friendship: He's the one who reminds Ayal that neither of them has the money to toss a big party next weekend, the one who suggests they study for the exam tomorrow before going out for pizza. Ayal, on the other hand, is the "idealist" (or optimist) who assumes the funds can be found somewhere and keeps on planning or argues for the benefits of studying on a full stomach. Realist, idealist.

Juan always anticipates the worst rather than hopes for the best, believing that if the worst doesn't occur then he will feel good and if the worst does occur he won't feel disappointed. His girlfriend, Mary, on the other hand, always anticipates the best. Nay-sayer, yea-sayer.

PATTERNS AMONG RELATIONSHIPS   In a like manner, we tend to continue playing similar roles in different relationships. If you are the optimist in one friendship, you are probably the optimist in all of your friendships. If you are the leader in one relationship, you probably play that role in most of the relationships you form.

On another level, we tend to replicate patterns in relationships themselves. For instance, if we are attracted to one aggressive problem solver as a romantic partner, we will probably be attracted to other aggressive problem solvers as romantic partners. If we are in one relationship with a submissive, passive friend, then we will tend to form friendships with similar personality types over and over.

Of course, we are not doomed to repeat the same patterns. We can break the patterns and assume different roles. Yet to do so usually requires a conscious effort that begins with our recognition of a pattern. Until we see and understand the pattern, we don't even realize that it requires "breaking."

Obstacles to Exploring Relationships

Writing about a relationship requires that you try to step out of the relationship for a while so that you can see it more objectively. Usually, it is easier to write an interesting essay about a relationship that is either finished or going badly than about a current relationship that is going well.

There are at least five reasons for this phenomenon. First, the negative, unhappy, and disappointing aspects of our lives hang over us, perhaps even haunt us. Given the opportunity and the tools to dig into a negative relationship, we can demystify it, analyze why it has had a lingering effect on us, and thus reduce its power in our lives.

Second, many of us probably spend more time thinking about and regretting negatives than we do thinking about positives.

Third, most of us fear examining the good things too closely. For example, we fear that examining a new romance too closely might ruin it. Too close an examination may reveal flaws in the other person or in the relationship or in us. The old advice "If it ain't broke, don't fix it" could be modified slightly here to "If it feels good, don't examine it." The happiness is new, and we don't want to taint it or jinx it.

Fourth, although few of us ever feel just one emotion about something as complex as a relationship, happiness seems to prevent our looking at or even noticing the other emotions that exist at the same time, emotions such as discomfort, resentment, fear, doubt, relief, or confusion. Perhaps this attitude reflects a superstitious belief that the gods will take away the good stuff if we question it. Another cliché warns us, "Don't look a gift horse in the mouth." Of course, that advice was followed by the ancient Trojans and look what happened to them. But it is difficult to bring ourselves to analyze happiness, in part because analysis, by its very nature, is asking questions . . . and no one wants to question happiness since it might just go away, insulted.

Finally, most of us perceive happiness as much more fragile than unhappiness, perhaps because we value the former and don't value the latter. Happiness often seems like a delicate piece of beautiful glass. Such fragile items do not bear up well under repeated scrutiny: All of that handling and twisting the item this way and that in the light of analysis can lead to an accident—beauty shattered on the floor.

Whatever the reasons, many writers find it more difficult to explore the good things in their lives than the not-so-good things. This difficulty should not, however, prevent your writing about the good things. Happiness examined is much stronger than happiness unexamined. If we don't examine happiness, then that happiness is resting on a shaky foundation, namely, fear.

Nevertheless, if you find yourself blocked by any of these impediments, abandon your current relationship as a topic. You can always explore it another time. Write about a past relationship instead. The point is to explore some relationship.

An Approach to Understanding Relationships

Regardless of which type of relationship you wish to write about, it makes sense to begin by exploring your expectations about that type of relationship. Expectations include your hopes about the relationship, your hopes about the other person(s) in the relationship, your fears about that relationship, the sources of each of your hopes and fears. Once that list is made, make another, this one of the traits you believe an ideal partner in the relationship should possess (for example, what are the traits of an ideal mother, brother, friend?). Once you've explored your expectations fully, list and explain your criteria for a successful relationship.

Having established your expectations, hopes, and assumptions about this type of relationship in general, consider the particular relationship you've selected in terms of this background information. Also ask yourself how this particular relationship has changed you or how it could have changed you if you had allowed it to. In the process of doing this, you might also:

explore the situation leading up to the relationship

explore what brought the participants together

explore the good times

explore the bad times

explore the event that caused a significant change in the relationship

Another element that can help in exploring a relationship is placing it in the context of other relationships. Each of us is familiar with hundreds of relationships. For instance, consider your familiarity with many different relationships involving just your parents: as parents of you and perhaps of other children; perhaps as siblings themselves; as relatives of their own parents; as friends of other people their own age as well as younger and older; as business associates; as members of various groups. Then add the relationships you know which involve your other relatives, friends, and acquaintances.

To that total, add all the relationships that you've experienced secondhand through texts such as novels, poetry, television series, movies, and plays. Classes you may have had in psychology, sociology, anthropology, and literature examine relationships from different perspectives. Finally, to get a better analytical handle on the relationship you've chosen to explore, do some research in the library. Such research will give you even more information as well as help you recognize your essay's wider significance.

That is a lot of relationships and a lot of information.

An especially good way to use those relationships to help yourself better understand the relationship you are exploring is to compare and contrast your relationship to some of them, both factual and fictional. From all the relationships you are familiar with, which is most like yours? Why? Which is most unlike yours? Why?

For the sake of illustration, the rest of this chapter focuses on writing about one particular type of relationship—a romantic relationship. What is said about how to write about romantic relationships, however, is applicable to writing about all types of relationships.

ROMANTIC RELATIONSHIPS

Few topics are as volatile, perhaps, as romantic relationships. Even in this supposedly enlightened age of recognizing alternate lifestyles, our culture is unrelenting in its insistence that, as in poker, a pair is always better than a single. More and more segments of our society have come to accept the idea that a pair might be two males or two females rather than one of each, but the idea that a twosome is the final goal has not changed much over the years. Most of the popular texts we encounter bombard us with images of couples.

So romantic love has a high priority for most of us. To write an exploratory essay about any kind of relationship, however, it is important that we understand the exact nature of our expectations of the relationship: our hopes, our definition of an ideal partner, and our fears.

Our Hopes for the Romantic Relationship

These are some elements most of us expect from love: *fulfillment, sharing, caring, support, nurturing, passion*. Each of those words is a suitcase term and requires unpacking.

One prewriting technique for unpacking a term is to have a dialogue with yourself: One part of you is the questioner, the other part is the answerer. Let's use the term *fulfillment* as an example. Here is my unpacking of that term:

What do I mean by fulfillment?

I mean that the relationship will help me feel fulfilled.

What will make me feel fulfilled?

Reaching my full potential as a human being.

Which potential? Don't I have many—for example, potential for good, for evil, potential as a basketball player, as a writer, as a chess player, as a . . . ?

Okay. Well, I want to reach my potential as a writer, as a teacher, and as a person.

Can one relationship really do all that?

Yes.

How?

Well, to help me fulfill my potential as a writer, the relationship would have to have boundaries.

Why?

Because I need blocks of quiet time to write. I can't write when there's a lot of noise going on or when I'm constantly being interrupted. So my partner will have to be sensitive to that need and give me enough time and space to write.

Why do I say she'll have to give me enough time and space? Can't I claim it as my own—make that a stipulation of the relationship?

Relationships aren't legal contracts, for Pete's sake. They sort of evolve. Yes, I'll need to make that point when we first start dating. If I'm going great guns on a story or something, I might not be able to keep a date or spend all the time I might normally with her. But I'll always make it up to her later.

Let's go back to my earlier statement. How will a relationship help me fulfill myself as a person?

This is very complex. I want to be able to love without fear.

Fear of what?

Of being absorbed emotionally.

Why on earth would that happen . . . how could that happen?

I've always had trouble with emotional boundaries. Something from my childhood, no doubt. I have a tendency to want to merge with my partner. Total oblivion of the self. Maybe I read too much D. H. Lawrence in my formative years. Anyway, since I encourage the partner to emotionally merge with me, few have been able to resist (maybe a lot of people have my problem or maybe I keep selecting women who have this trait).

What do I mean by merging?

I lose all sight of myself, my own needs, my own desires. During most of my previous relationships I haven't written seriously because I've been too busy anticipating and filling all of my partner's needs. So I am stunted as a writer and as a person. I don't have time to explore new interests or even to notice new interests because the woman dominates my horizon.

So what do I need in a partner?

Someone who has a strong sense of her own boundaries, a strong sense of herself as an individual. Someone who will resist the appeal of having me take total care of her (and hence become her caretaker). If my partner is strong that way, then I can learn from her how to maintain boundaries and can address some of my own needs and desires. With me, there's never a danger that I will ignore the needs of others. Instead, the danger is that I'll ignore mine.

Do you see how the technique works? Notice how relentless the questioner is, how the questioner picks up an idea from the previous answer and pushes the answerer to go deeper, to explain more clearly. This dialogue, by the way, usually works best if you do it in writing. Having a record of what issues you are covering is useful. If you go off on a tangent, for instance, you can always look back at what you were talking about before the tangent beckoned. Of course, you may also discover that what seemed like a tangent is really a path you want to explore. In the preceding example, I strayed from the issue of fulfillment into the characteristics of the ideal partner and my problems with boundaries, but that is fine. This is all prewriting; it is all discovery. If you discover something different from what you thought, so what? A discovery is always worthwhile.

☐ *Exercise 1*

With as much specific detail as possible, make a list of hopes you would feel in the beginning of a new relationship. As with all the exercises in this chapter, write about whatever type of relationship you wish to explore. In other words, this list does not have to be about a romantic relationship.

The Ideal Other Person in the Relationship

Although we may not have thought much about it consciously, we all harbor some sort of image of the ideal other person—we all feel a vague sense of what an ideal love partner or sibling or friend or parent or teacher should be like. Usually we don't vocalize such idealizations. Often, in fact, we discover particular elements or traits only by their absence. For example, we might say, "I wish he could take a joke" or "If only my father were more flexible." Such statements reveal criteria that we hold (probably unconsciously). We believe that an ideal friend should "take a joke" (presumably without getting insulted or angry at us) and that an ideal father should be more flexible about whatever we want.

Here are some generalized expectations about a romantic partner:

The partner should be attractive, successful or potentially successful, fun to be with, filled with admiration for all our own good qualities, able to overlook whatever minor flaws we happen to have, able to share a lot of our interests.

☐ *Exercise 2*

With as much specific detail as possible, make a list of the personality traits you'd like an ideal partner (or friend, parent, boss, or whatever) to have. If it helps, use the questioner/answerer technique.

Next, make a list of the attitudes, social skills, abilities, and interests you'd like that person to have.

Then make lists of your own personality traits and your own attitudes, social skills, abilities, hobbies.

Our Fears about Romantic Relationships

If we are very secure people, we may have few fears about new relationships. Or, to put that another way, few people are brave enough to even consider the fears they have. Most of us are into serious denial about fears. Nothing, we tell ourselves, could go wrong with *this* relationship. Intensely we want to believe that is true. Of course, sometimes it is true.

But most of us do have some fears. In those dark lonely evenings when the partner is somewhere else and we have had a day filled with disappointments—on such nights, perhaps some of the fears slip into our conscious mind. Some people even slide into "negative rehearsal"—a routine in which they start imagining all sorts of horrible scenarios for the relationship. I admit that in the past I've been known to drive myself crazy like this at times.

Here are some general fears: We fear that the relationship will end; that the partner will reject and abandon us; that some old pattern of our behavior that a previous partner hated will suddenly become hateful to this new partner; that while we were mistakenly involved with this partner the real Mr. or Ms. Right walked right through our lives and we missed him or her.

☐ *Exercise 3*

With as much specific detail as possible, make a list of the fears you would feel in beginning a new relationship.

Sources of Our Expectations about Relationships

It is important to look for the sources of our expectations. Generalizing about sources is easy: society, the media, our parents, our friends. The difficult part is being specific. For example, exactly from whom did I learn that partners should be each other's best friend? This concept is now a truism, but I believed it long before I knew it was popular. Perhaps I learned it from my parents who, by choice, had few friends (a lot of acquaintances but very few of what I would call friends). They were each other's confidant. Or were they? Am I just superimposing that on them? Perhaps I learned it from movies or books long since forgotten. I could check old newspapers or some published guide to movies to see what flicks I might have seen during my formative years. I might visit my hometown library and scan the juvenile shelves to see what books I might have been influenced by. I might ask my parents. In short, I could do some research if my memory were not sufficient.

☐ *Exercise 4*

With as much specific detail as possible, make a list of the sources of your expectations about relationships in general. Start by looking at the lists you've already made and trying to remember or imagine the source(s) for each. Be very specific.

Criteria for a Good Relationship

You undoubtedly have given some thought to criteria in listing your expectations and their sources, but criteria warrant separate consideration. You have been formulating your *ideal* vision of a relationship, but, as you think more critically about the standards you have been applying, you move toward a more *realistic* vision. What criteria must be met if a relationship is to have a chance of being successful? For example, I have a student friend who refuses to date anyone not in her co-ed dorm. She claims that she can't "get to really know what the guy's like if he lives clear across campus." So one criterion for her is "the partner must live in the same dorm." Once you have identified your criteria, you might want to evaluate them, perhaps in the essay you write. For instance, although my friend has a reason for wanting her boyfriend to live in the same dorm, I wonder if that criterion is too limiting—there are probably many suitable men whose company she would enjoy living in other dorms or off campus. But limiting her options with that criterion, she will probably miss the chance of dating them. So, consider writing about relationships as a chance to assess your criteria as well as to discover and explain them.

☐ *Exercise 5*

With as much specific detail as possible, make a list of the realistic criteria that are necessary if a relationship is to work. Start by looking at the lists of expectations and their sources that you've already made, but don't be limited by them; simply expand them if you make new discoveries.

EXPLORING A FORMER RELATIONSHIP

Let's consider the exploration of a specific relationship from the past. To illustrate how such a relationship might be approached, I here summarize my relationship with Sue (the name and a few minor details have been changed to protect the innocent) during my senior year at college. Remember, this summary is not an exploratory *essay;* it is merely a brief explanation of what I remembered before I began serious prewriting:

> I first met Sue in Bar Harbor, a popular summer tourist town, in early September just before I began my senior year at the University of Maine. I was unhappy and had gone there to "get away" from it all.
>
> I saw an attractive woman coming out of one of the motels. Apparently she was going for a walk. I followed her into a restaurant. Soon we started a conversation. It was amazing how quickly we hit it off. We talked about everything that night. I was amazed to learn she actually lived in Bangor, the city across the river from my hometown (and 10 miles from campus). She was a teller in a bank. Within weeks we were a steady and exclusive couple.
>
> Eleven months later we broke up. Ironically, we broke up in Bar Harbor, the same place where we had met. Sue had suggested we go there for dinner, and the hour-long ride there was not pleasant. She wanted us to get married and live in Maine; I wanted to get a Ph.D. at Brown University in Rhode Island. By the time dinner was over, so were we. In silence we drove back, both of us angry and hurt.

Not surprisingly, the summary lacks details, emotions, thoughts, analysis, and any effort to establish broader significance. Frankly, there are no people either—simply two black squiggles on the page—*Sue* and *I.* Except for a couple of facts such as my wanting to go to Brown University and her wanting to get married, little information is given. What was the nature of this relationship? Was it a wild, passionate love affair? A meeting of two soul mates? Was it filled with trust or with suspicion? With support or with recriminations? With constant conflicts or with frivolous fun? Other than marriage, what did she want from the relationship? What didn't she like in the relationship? And how about me? What did I want from the relationship? What did I dislike about it? Why did I choose Brown University over Sue? Did I ever think of taking Sue to Brown with me? Or of asking her to wait for me? Why or why not?

The unanswered questions here are many. That is what prewriting and drafting are all about—generating information to answer such questions as these.

Let's examine closely what is missing and how I might develop some of that material to increase my understanding of the relationship. Some (and perhaps even all) of the material thus developed may not appear in the final essay, but it will deepen my sense of the relationship, of what I was like then, and of my attitudes toward that relationship now. I would begin by examining all the lists that I had already made in response to this chapter's exercises, selecting whatever point seemed most comfortable as my starting point.

Notice as well that I have a split perspective here. This relationship occurred many years ago. I have been in several committed relationships since then, and I like to believe that I have learned something about myself and my view of relationships from each one. So the Steve-now who is exploring the relationship and the Steve-then who lived through it are two very different people. Where possible, I will try to indicate that split because it can be an important concept in any exploratory essay.

My Criteria Then and Now

When I was a senior in college, my criteria were simple: My ideal partner and I should somehow be "made for each other," we should share similar interests, we should enjoy the same things, dislike the same things, be similar in political and philosophical beliefs. And we shouldn't argue about things. In fact, we should "be as one" in all senses of the word. As the musical group Fifth Dimension put it in the song "Never, My Love," "What makes you think love will end / When you know my whole life depends on you?" That is what I wanted then—for our two whole lives to depend on each other.

Looking back on that period in my life, I find such criteria simplistic and that last criterion downright dangerous. *Now* I ask myself, should someone's whole life depend on another person? And my answer is "NO!" But *then* my answer was, "Yes—it has to."

I still believe that my partner and I should share similar beliefs and an interest in several (not necessarily *all*) of the same things. In addition, however, I believe that partners should respect each other as individuals, a respect that allows room for personal growth and serious discussions about issues of disagreement. I now believe that the merger of two people in the way I used to desire can only do psychological harm. Partners should support each other in all ways, but they should not fear pointing out that the other is making a possible mistake. Partners should help each other open up to new people and new experiences rather than engulfing each other. They should enjoy the emotional high of attraction but should also be savvy enough to think about the implications of the relationship.

Desirable Traits of My Ideal Partner Then and Now

In my college days, the desirable traits of a partner did not form a long list. Although I would never have consciously thought this then, I realize now that the primary criterion for a partner was that she love me and value me and my accomplishments. This meant laughing at my jokes and crying at my poems (rather than crying at the former and laughing at the latter). We had to be compatible, by which I meant she had to enjoy reading, listening to rock music, dancing, "hanging out" with me. She had to be attractive.

The Steve-now has different criteria, and I would use those to evaluate and understand the relationship with Sue in the past. Now I believe that the ideal partner for me must respect herself and me as individuals with great potential. She should be as empathetic as I am. She should be compassionate, concerned about life beyond our limited sphere (in other words, be concerned about human rights), intelligent, witty, funny, capable of backing away from me when she needs space and when I need space. And supportive. And attractive. And intellectually curious about the world. She must be a companion, someone I enjoy spending time with even if we're doing nothing of significance.

Hopes for and Fears about the Relationship

I hoped that the relationship would be fulfilling for both of us, that it would make us feel good about ourselves, that it would allow us to become the persons we wanted to become, that once started it would last forever.

My basic fear was that none of the hopes would come true. I feared that the relationship would end badly, with one or both of us emotionally scarred. And I worried about the future, fearing that she would at first accept me and love me and then ultimately reject me and leave.

Sources of These Expectations

Other than the sources I've already listed in the earlier section, major sources included my own past experiences and those of my friends. My parents had (and still have) a long-lasting marriage, yet my grandmother had gone through a divorce and never remarried (the message I heard there was "If you lose one chance, you might not get another"). The radio airwaves were filled with two types of songs—those about undying love such as "Never, My Love" and those about love that had died such as "One Less Bell to Answer." The movie screen was filled with women falling for James Bond types (of which I am not an example) and with unfaithful wives and girlfriends (I didn't notice the unfaithful boyfriends and husbands). All around me, friends were losing their girlfriends; love that had been proclaimed to be forever ended up lasting a few weeks.

ANALYZING A RELATIONSHIP

Armed with all the preceding prewriting information, I am now ready to think about the specific relationship with Sue.

What Was the Context?

In my brief summary, I said that I was unhappy before Sue and I met. What was I unhappy about? Elaine and I had just broken up after an on-again-off-again year-long relationship. It was summer, and that meant most of the college women were not on campus but were back in their hometowns earning money through summer jobs. Prospects of finding someone else to date seriously were slim until classes started again.

More important, I was feeling very bad about myself. Although I believed at the time that I was filled with self-confidence, in point of fact I suffered from very low self-esteem. Any rejection of any sort knocked me for a loop. Elaine had been vague but determined about why we shouldn't date any longer. The vagueness was perfect—it allowed me to fill in any personality trait I wanted to feel bad about. Was I too possessive? Not possessive enough? Too devoted? Not devoted enough? Too sarcastic about her friends? Too forgiving of my own friends? Too giving? Not giving enough? Whatever was my "fear for the day" about myself fit nicely into that vague slot.

What Attracted Us to Each Other?

What attracted me to Sue? The first thing I noticed was that she was walking the street alone. That suggested she might be available. Second, she was very pretty. Third, she was blonde (Elaine had been brunette). After I actually met her and had talked with her, I was attracted to her independence: While I was still in college and not earning enough to fully support even a thin cat with no appetite, she was working full-time as a bank teller and had her own apartment (with the requisite obnoxious roommate). She picked up and went when she felt like it. Her parents lived in Pennsylvania, so she was truly "on her own." I was attracted to her common sense, her intelligence, and the fact that she laughed at my jokes. Also, she seemed impressed with me, with my plans to attend graduate school, to become a college professor and writer.

Explaining what attracted me to her is significantly easier than saying what attracted her to me. Based on what she said, on her actions, and on what I came to know about her, however, I can make an educated guess. More to the point, my "reading" of her motives is revealing about me even if it is all wrong about her real motives.

First, I pursued her into the restaurant, making a real effort to meet her. That showed the depth of my initial interest, and Sue found that attractive. On a deeper level, I think Sue was beginning to feel the need to get her life going. She had been working full-time for three years in a relatively dead-end job. She had no college education and no desire to get one, so "getting on with her life" meant taking the next socially ordained steps—marriage and then children. All her friends at the bank and from high school were married, and several already had children. Here I was, a college senior, doing well in school with a firm job offer from a newspaper in my pocket for the day after I graduated. I seemed mature, thoughtful, and eligible. Of course, she was probably a bit slowed by my talk about graduate school, but Sue had enough friends to know that such talk was often only that—talk. Plenty of her married friends had talked a lot about dreams before they married and "fell back into reality."

Lest you think I'm cynical, I don't believe for a moment that these thoughts were consciously in Sue's mind. But I think her life circumstances had given her that subconscious agenda.

What Were the Good Times and the Bad Times?

There were a lot of good things and good times. Attending the wedding of some mutual friends, walks along the beach (clichéd though they were), dinners in the Bangor House, campus concerts by famous rock groups and jazz musicians, receiving her daily letters when I was out of state for a couple of weeks. Throughout most of this time we spent together, I was very happy.

There were very few bad times. In part, we were so head-over-heels about each other that we ignored all the little danger signals. For example, we didn't have much to talk about if we weren't talking about us as a couple. I didn't really care about all the office gossip, and she really didn't care about the details of my progress on this or that academic paper. Also, we felt a bit out of place with each other's friends.

What Was the Most Significant Event in the Relationship?

The breakup of a relationship, or whatever other event you single out as the most significant, requires careful thought. In terms of my relationship with Sue, our meeting and our breakup were the two key events. Since I've already discussed our meeting, the focus here will be on the breakup. The procedure is the same for whatever event you decide to explore.

WAS THERE A TRIGGERING EVENT?   In the case of Sue and me, there wasn't a single triggering event. But my sending out graduate school applications was probably a contributing factor—it caused a long and sometimes tearful discussion. My joy at being accepted by Brown was a second element of stress in the relationship.

WERE THERE OTHER CAUSES?   Although I didn't realize it then, my never mentioning the future except in terms of Brown was probably a major cause. Even now I don't understand my actions or reasons. I believed that I loved Sue and that she loved me. I believed that we'd always be together (of course, I believed that about any relationship I was in until it ended—that is one of my patterns of behavior). But I never suggested marriage even though we discussed it as though I had (or perhaps, more accurately, as though we both assumed that marriage was the next logical step we'd take). Why didn't I suggest that Sue wait for me until I got one year of graduate school under my belt? I never did, even when we started fighting about Brown. Barring marriage or simple waiting, another option was rather obvious: I could have suggested that she move to Providence with me. We could live together, or, if that were unacceptable, she could get an apartment there and we could let our relationship continue to develop. But I never suggested it. Why not?

I don't know.

But my guess is that on some deep level I feared that staying connected with Sue would defeat me. I wanted a Ph.D., I wanted to teach on the college level and to have time to write. Staying connected with Sue would prevent that from happening. This is not to say that Sue was evil or was even unsupportive. But I know myself well enough to realize that I couldn't stand the guilt of seeing her trying to work full-time to help me through several years of graduate school. I couldn't stand the guilt of knowing she wanted to start having a family while my pursuit of my Ph.D. prevented it from being economically possible. Sue would not ask me to sacrifice my plans and academic career, but my subconscious would sacrifice them anyway. On another level, going away to Brown was making a break with my childhood and youth: My whole life until then had been spent entirely in Maine.

What Was the Personal Significance of the Relationship?

This relationship had a profound effect on me. First, it was my first serious consideration of marriage. Second, I discovered that I had the power to say no to love and to a woman that I thought I loved. The world didn't end. Third, I had believed that attaining love was my ultimate goal in life, and yet I found that other goals could be equally important. Fourth, I later realized that my subconscious had alerted me to the fact that no matter how attracted Sue and I were to each other, we might not be the perfect couple. Blinded by passion and probably by a fear of facing the unknown future alone, my conscious mind ignored several danger signs such as our lack of common interests and our different life goals. Viewed in terms of my present criteria for an ideal partner, Sue doesn't even approach what I want in a partner. I'm sure that viewed from her present criteria, I don't even approach what she wants in a partner either. Fortunately for both of us, my subconscious got my attention.

What Is the Wider Significance of the Relationship?

Combined with observations of my friends' romantic relationships throughout the years, my relationship with Sue leads me to believe that it is very difficult to select a partner. With vision clouded by hopes and passion and fears, people often choose the wrong person. The reasons for selecting a partner can also be influenced by externals that have nothing to do with the person herself: In my case, my subconscious concern about leaving a "safe" environment to start a new life in a new state no doubt inclined me to marry Sue. Having been bombarded my whole life by society's vision that young people should marry and start families, I felt internal pressure to stay with Sue that had nothing to do with my fears or her appeal—it had only to do with my social conditioning. Presumably we are all conditioned by society to seek particular goals which may or may not conform to our personal goals.

Having done all that prewriting, I would now be ready to write an essay about my relationship with Sue.

Pitfalls of Writing about a Romantic Relationship

What are the pitfalls of writing about a personal relationship? Probably the greatest is that we may be unable to gain sufficient perspective on our emotions in the relationship to avoid embarrassing rather than enlightening the reader. As has been said in the book several times before, if a subject is too painful, choose another. Remember that your purpose in writing an exploratory essay is always to enlarge your own and your reader's understanding, not to "just let it all hang out." Exploratory essays are valuable because they are insightful, not because they are confessional. Beyond this major pitfall are several others that can keep an essay from being interesting and illuminating:

lack of details

lack of context

abundance of suitcase terms whose meaning only the writer totally understands

fear of looking into the motivations of ourselves and of others

fear of seeing a frightening pattern continued in this relationship

In the process of drafting your essays, keep these pitfalls in mind. As you revise, pay particular attention to supplying details and context and motivations. Take care to define key abstract terms (suitcase terms) whose meaning may be obvious to you but may not be to your readers. When in doubt, define.

In conclusion, using the techniques and exercises presented in this chapter will help you explore any type of relationship, not just a romantic one. Any significant relationship is a good topic for an exploratory essay.

☐ *Exercise 6*

Think of a relationship that you'd like to explore. It might be a past relationship or a past phase of an ongoing relationship. Describe that relationship in detail, analyze it in terms of the criteria you've set forth, describe and analyze how that relationship either changed or ended. What have you learned from that relationship?

Photographs of My Parents

MAXINE HONG KINGSTON

☐ *Inward Exploration*

List photographs or other objects that are closely associated with a relative or friend. Select one and write at least one paragraph about it.

Once in a long while, four times so far for me, my mother brings   1
out the metal tube that holds her medical diploma. On the tube are gold circles crossed with seven red lines each—"joy" ideographs in abstract. There are also little flowers that look like gears for a gold machine. According to the scraps of labels with Chinese and American addresses, stamps, and postmarks, the family airmailed the can from Hong Kong in 1950. It got crushed in the middle, and whoever tried to peel the labels off stopped because the red and gold paint came off too, leaving silver scratches that rust. Somebody tried to pry the end off before discovering that the tube pulls apart. When I open it, the smell of China flies out, a thousand-year-old bat flying heavy-headed out of the Chinese caverns where bats are as white as dust, a smell that comes from long ago, far back in the brain. Crates from Canton, Hong Kong, Singapore, and Taiwan have that smell too, only stronger because they are more recently come from the Chinese.

Inside the can are three scrolls, one inside another. The largest says that in the twenty-third year of the National Republic, the To Keung School of Midwifery, where she has had two years of instruction and Hospital Practice, awards its Diploma to my mother, who has shown through oral and written examination her Proficiency in Midwifery, Pediatrics, Gynecology, "Medecine," "Surgary," Therapeutics, Ophthalmology, Bacteriology, Dermatology, Nursing and Bandage. This document has eight stamps on it: one, the school's English and Chinese names embossed together in a circle; one, as the Chinese enumerate, a stork and a big baby in lavender ink; one, the school's Chinese seal; one, an orangish paper stamp pasted in the border design; one, the red seal of Dr. Wu Pak-liang, M.D., Lyon, Berlin, president and "Ex-assistant étranger à la clinique chirugicale et d'accouchement de l'université de Lyon"; one, the red seal of Dean Woo Yin-kam, M.D.; one, my mother's seal, her chop mark larger than the president's and the dean's; and one, the number 1279 on the back. Dean Woo's signature is followed by "(Hackett)." I read in a history book that Hackett Medical College for

Women at Canton was founded in the nineteenth century by European women doctors.

The school seal has been pressed over a photograph of my mother at the age of thirty-seven. The diploma gives her age as twenty-seven. She looks younger than I do, her eyebrows are thicker, her lips fuller. Her naturally curly hair is parted on the left, one wavy wisp tendrilling off to the right. She wears a scholar's white gown, and she is not thinking about her appearance. She stares straight ahead as if she could see me and past me to her grandchildren and grandchildren's grandchildren. She has spacy eyes, as all people recently from Asia have. Her eyes do not focus on the camera. My mother is not smiling; Chinese do not smile for photographs. Their faces command relatives in foreign lands— "Send money"—and posterity forever—"Put food in front of this picture." My mother does not understand Chinese-American snapshots. "What are you laughing at?" she asks.

The second scroll is a long narrow photograph of the graduating class with the school officials seated in front. I picked out my mother immediately. Her face is exactly her own, though forty years younger. She is so familiar, I can only tell whether or not she is pretty or happy or smart by comparing her to the other women. For this formal group picture she straightened her hair with oil to make a chinlength bob like the others'. On the other women, strangers, I can recognize a curled lip, a sidelong glance, pinched shoulders. My mother is not soft; the girl with the small nose and dimpled underlip is soft. My mother is not humorous, not like the girl at the end who lifts her mocking chin to pose like Girl Graduate. My mother does not have smiling eyes; the old woman teacher (Dean Woo?) in front crinkles happily, and the one faculty member in the western suit smiles westernly. Most of the graduates are girls whose faces have not yet formed; my mother's face will not change anymore, except to age. She is intelligent, alert, pretty. I can't tell if she's happy.

The graduates seem to have been looking elsewhere when they pinned the rose, zinnia, or chrysanthemum on their precise black dresses. One thin girl wears hers in the middle of her chest. A few have a flower over a left or a right nipple. My mother put hers, a chrysanthemum, below her left breast. Chinese dresses at that time were dartless, cut as if women did not have breasts; these young doctors, unaccustomed to decorations, may have seen their chests as black expanses with no reference points for flowers. Perhaps they couldn't shorten that far gaze that lasts only a few years after a Chinese emigrates. In this picture too my mother's eyes are big with what they held—reaches of oceans beyond China, land beyond oceans. Most emigrants learn the barbarians' directness—how to gather themselves and stare rudely into talking faces as if trying to catch lies. In America my mother has eyes as strong as boulders, never once skittering off a face, but she has not learned to place decorations and phonograph needles, nor has she stopped seeing land on the other side of the oceans. Now her eyes include the relatives in China, as they once included my father smiling and smiling in his many western outfits, a different one for each photograph that he sent from America.

He and his friends took pictures of one another in bathing suits at Coney Island beach, the salt wind from the Atlantic blowing their hair. He's the one in the middle with his arms about the necks of his buddies. They pose in the cockpit of a biplane, on a motorcycle, and on a lawn beside the "Keep Off the Grass" sign. They are always laughing. My father, white shirt sleeves rolled up, smiles in front of a wall of clean laundry. In the spring he wears a new straw hat, cocked at a Fred Astaire angle. He steps out, dancing down the stairs, one foot forward, one back, a hand in his pocket. He wrote to her about the American custom of stomping on straw hats come fall. "If you want to save your hat for next year," he said, "you have to put it away early, or else when you're riding the subway or walking along Fifth Avenue, any stranger can snatch it off your head and put his foot through it. That's the way they celebrate the change of seasons here." In the winter he wears a gray felt hat with his gray overcoat. He is sitting on a rock in Central Park. In one snapshot he is not smiling; someone took it when he was studying, blurred in the glare of the desk lamp.

There are no snapshots of my mother. In two small portraits, however, there is a black thumbprint on her forehead, as if someone had inked in bangs, as if someone had marked her.

"Mother, did bangs come into fashion after you had the picture taken?" One time she said yes. Another time when I asked, "Why do you have fingerprints on your forehead?" she said, "Your First Uncle did that." I disliked the unsureness in her voice.

The last scroll has columns of Chinese words. The only English is "Department of Health, Canton," imprinted on my mother's face, the same photograph as on the diploma. I keep looking to see whether she was afraid. Year after year my father did not come home or send for her. Their two children had been dead for ten years. If he did not return soon, there would be no more children. ("They were three and two years old, a boy and a girl. They could talk already.") My father did send money regularly, though, and she had nobody to spend it on but herself. She bought good clothes and shoes. Then she decided to use the money for becoming a doctor. She did not leave for Canton immediately after the children died. In China there was time to complete feelings. As my father had done, my mother left the village by ship. There was a sea bird painted on the ship to protect it against shipwreck and winds. She was in luck. The following ship was boarded by river pirates, who kidnapped every passenger, even old ladies. "Sixty dollars for an old lady" was what the bandits used to say. "I sailed alone," she says, "to the capital of the entire province." She took a brown leather suitcase and a seabag stuffed with two quilts.

☐ *Outward Exploration: Discussion*

1. Why does Kingston give us so much detail about the appearances of the scrolls?
2. According to Kingston, why don't Chinese smile for photographs? For what reasons do most Americans smile for pictures?
3. In paragraph 4, what technique does Kingston use to determine (and, by extension, to tell us) how her mother looked in the photograph?
4. Describe the differences between the photographs of her mother and those of her father. What do the differences tell you?
5. What terms would you use to describe her parents' relationship?

☐ *Outward Exploration: Writing*

Find some photographs of two or three people who are closely connected and whom you know well. For instance, these might be photographs of your parents, two best friends, a parent and a child, or two siblings. Like Kingston, use the photographs as a way of exploring the relationship between the people. Use your knowledge of them and your insights into human nature as well as the photographs, but try to tie the insights to the photographs in some way.

☐ *Style*

Consider the following sentence from Kingston's essay:

> In two small portraits, however, there is a black thumbprint on her forehead, as if someone had inked in bangs, as if someone had marked her. (paragraph 7)

What's remarkable about this sentence is its ending, those two *as if* clauses which introduce two different interpretations of the thumbprint on her head.

Write a sentence of your own in which you offer two interpretations of a fact stated in the first part of your sentence. Use two *as if* clauses, and join them only with a comma. Leave out the coordinating conjunction—*or*—which we would usually use between the two clauses in order to achieve the same effect that Kingston does.

Like Mexicans

GARY SOTO

☐ *Inward Exploration*

What is your background? Make a list of terms that describe your religious, philosophical, ethnic, racial, economic, and social class background.

Has anyone ever given you advice about what to look for in a romantic partner or about whom not to date? If so, write a paragraph explaining the advice and why you think you were given that advice.

My grandmother gave me bad advice and good advice when I was   1
in my early teens. For the bad advice, she said that I should become a barber because they made good money and listened to the radio all day. "Honey, they don't work como burros," she would say every time I visited her. She made the sound of donkeys braying. "Like that, honey!" For the good advice, she said that I should marry a Mexican girl. "No Okies, hijo"—she would say—"Look my son. He marry one and they fight every day about I don't know what and I don't know what." For her, everyone who wasn't Mexican, black, or Asian were Okies. The French were Okies, the Italians in suits were Okies. When I asked about Jews, whom I had read about, she asked for a picture. I rode home on my bicycle and returned with a calendar depicting the important races of the world. "Pues si, son Okies tambien!" she said, nodding her head. She saved the calendar away and we went to the living room where she lectured me on the virtues of the Mexican girl: first, she could cook and, second, she acted like a woman, not a man, in her husband's home. She said she would tell me about a third when I got a little older.

I asked my mother about it—becoming a barber and marrying Mexican. She was in the kitchen. Steam curled from a pot of boiling beans, the radio was on, looking as squat as a loaf of bread. "Well, if you want to be a barber—they say they make good money." She slapped a round steak with a knife, her glasses slipping down with each strike. She stopped and looked up. "If you find a good Mexican girl, marry her of course." She returned to slapping the meat and I went to the backyard where my brother and David King were sitting on the lawn feeling the inside of their cheeks.

"This is what girls feel like," my brother said, rubbing the inside of his cheek. David put three fingers inside his mouth and scratched. I ignored them and climbed the back fence to see my best friend, Scott, a second-generation Okie. I called him and his mother pointed to the side of the house where his bedroom was a small aluminum trailer, the kind you gawk at when they're flipped over on the freeway, wheels spinning in the air. I went around to find Scott pitching horseshoes.

I picked up a set of rusty ones and joined him. While we played, we talked about school and friends and record albums. The horseshoes scuffed up dirt, sometimes ringing the iron that threw out a meager shadow like a sundial. After three argued-over games, we pulled two oranges apiece from his tree and started down the alley still talking school and friends and record albums. We pulled more oranges from the alley and talked about who we would marry. "No offense, Scott," I said with an orange slice in my mouth, "but I would never marry an Okie." We walked in step, almost touching, with a sled of shadows dragging behind us. "No offense, Gary," Scott said, "but I would *never* marry a Mexican." I looked at him: a fang of orange slice showed from his munching mouth. I didn't think anything of it. He had his girl and I had mine. But our seventh-grade vision was the same: to marry, get jobs, buy cars and maybe a house if we had money left over.

We talked about our future lives until, to our surprise, we were on   5
the downtown mall, two miles from home. We bought a bag of popcorn at Penneys and sat on a bench near the fountain watching Mexican and Okie girls pass. "That one's mine," I pointed with my chin when a girl with eyebrows arched into black rainbows ambled by. "She's cute," Scott said about a girl with yellow hair and a mouthful of gum. We dreamed aloud, our chins busy pointing out girls. We agreed that we couldn't wait to become men and lift them onto our laps.

But the woman I married was not Mexican but Japanese. It was a surprise to me. For years, I went about wide-eyed in my search for the brown girl in a white dress at a dance. I searched the playground at the baseball diamond. When the girls raced for grounders, their hair bounced like something that couldn't be caught. When they sat together in the lunchroom, heads pressed together, I knew they were talking about us Mexican guys. I saw them and dreamed them. I threw my face into my pillow, making up sentences that were good as in the movies.

But when I was twenty, I fell in love with this other girl who worried my mother, who had my grandmother asking once again to see the calendar of the Important Races of the World. I told her I had thrown it away years before. I took a much-glanced-at snapshot from my wallet. We looked at it together, in silence. Then grandma reclined in her chair, lit a cigarette, and said, "Es pretty." She blew and asked with all her worry pushed up to her forehead: "Chinese?"

I was in love and there was no looking back. She was the one, I told my mother who was slapping hamburger into patties. "Well, sure if you want to marry her," she said. But the more I talked, the more concerned she became. Later I began to worry. Was it all a mistake? "Marry a Mexican girl," I heard my mother say in my mind. I heard it at breakfast. I heard it over math problems, between Western Civilization and cultural geography. But then one afternoon while I was hitchhiking home from school, it struck me like a baseball in the back: my mother wanted me to marry someone of my own social class—a poor girl. I considered my fiancee, Carolyn, and she didn't look poor, though I knew she came from a family of farm workers and pull-yourself-up-by-your-bootstraps ranchers. I asked my brother, who was marrying Mexican poor that fall, if I should marry a poor girl. He screamed "Yeah" above his terrible guitar playing in his bedroom. I considered my sister who had married Mexican. Cousins were dating Mexican. Uncles were remarrying poor women. I asked Scott, who was still my best friend, and he said, "She's too good for you, so you better not."

I worried about it until Carolyn took me home to meet her parents. We drove in her Plymouth until the houses gave way to farms and ranches and finally her house fifty feet from the highway. When we pulled into the drive, I panicked and begged Carolyn to make a U-turn and go back so we could talk about it over a soda. She pinched my cheek, calling me a "silly boy." I felt better, though, when I got out of the car and saw the house: the chipped paint, a cracked window, boards for a walk to the back door. There were rusting cars near the barn. A tractor with a net of spiderwebs under a mulberry. A field. A bale of barbed wire like children's scribbling leaning against an empty chicken coop. Carolyn took my hand and pulled me to my future mother-in-law who was coming out to greet us.

We had lunch: sandwiches, potato chips, and iced tea. Carolyn and her mother talked mostly about neighbors and the congregation at the Japanese Methodist Church in West Fresno. Her father, who was in khaki work clothes, excused himself with a wave that was almost a salute and went outside. I heard a truck start, a dog bark, and then the truck rattle away.

Carolyn's mother offered another sandwich, but I declined with a shake of my head and a smile. I looked around when I could, when I was not saying over and over that I was a college student, hinting that I could take care of her daughter. I shifted my chair. I saw newspapers piled in corners, dusty cereal boxes and vinegar bottles in corners. The wallpaper was bubbled from rain that had come in from a bad roof. Dust. Dust lay on lamp shades and window sills. These people are just like Mexicans, I thought. Poor people.

Carolyn's mother asked me through Carolyn if I would like a *sushi*. A plate of black and white things were held in front of me. I took one, wide-eyed, and turned it over like a foreign coin. I was biting into one when I saw a kitten crawl up the window screen over the sink. I chewed and the kitten opened its mouth of terror as she crawled higher, wanting in to paw the leftovers from our plates. I looked at Carolyn who said that the cat was just showing off. I looked up in time to see it fall. It crawled up, then fell again.

We talked for an hour and had apple pie and coffee, slowly. Finally, we got up with Carolyn taking my hand. Slightly embarrassed, I tried to pull away but her grip held me. I let her have her way as she led me down the hallway with her mother right behind me. When I opened the door, I was startled by a kitten clinging to the screen door, its mouth screaming "cat food, dog biscuits, *sushi.* . . ." I opened the door and the kitten, still holding on, whined in the language of hungry animals. When I got into Carolyn's car, I looked back: the cat was still clinging. I asked Carolyn if it were possibly hungry, but she said the cat was being silly. She started the car, waved to her mother, and bounced us over the rain-poked drive, patting my thigh for being her lover baby. Carolyn waved again. I looked back, waving, then gawking at a window screen where there were now three kittens clawing and screaming to get in. Like Mexicans, I thought. I remembered the Molinas and how the cats clung to their screens—cats they shot down with squirt guns. On the highway, I felt happy, pleased by it all. I patted Carolyn's thigh. Her people were like Mexicans, only different.

❑ *Outward Exploration: Discussion*

1. What was the grandmother's bad advice and her good advice?
2. Why was the bad advice bad? What assumptions underlie her advice about the kind of job her grandson should get? Why does she make those assumptions?
3. Does the grandmother seem prejudiced to you? Explain.
4. Based on only this essay, what careers seemed available for Mexican American women at the time?
5. Ultimately, does Soto follow his grandmother's good advice? Explain.
6. What details does Soto give to "prove" Carolyn's socioeconomic status?
7. How does Soto come to interpret the advice from his mother and grandmother? Why?

❑ *Outward Exploration: Writing*

1. Soto says he spent years searching for a Mexican woman to marry because of his grandmother's advice. Presumably this quest kept him from noticing other possibilities (interestingly, he doesn't explain Carolyn and his meeting and courtship). Have you had a set of criteria in your mind about what the ideal partner should be? What are some of those criteria? Where did they come from? Write an essay exploring your criteria, their sources, and their impact on your dating.

2. How do you feel about people from your socioeconomic class marrying above or below their class? List reasons why doing so is a good idea and reasons why it is a bad idea. Where do your reasons come from—for example, from cases you know personally? from advice given you by family and friends? from fairy tales? from movies? from books? You could do some research into social class (your research librarian will be a great asset). Then write an essay exploring this issue and answering the question "What criteria are valid for selecting a partner?"

3. Consider your own background. Write an essay about the advantages and disadvantages of growing up with the ethnic, racial, religious, and socioeconomic class background that you did. Pay particular attention to the assumptions you make about the world, about yourself, about your own possibilities.

❏ *Style*

Consider the following technique from Soto's essay:

Slightly embarrassed, I tried to pull away but her grip held me. (paragraph 13)

What's particularly nice about this short complex sentence is its use of a two-word descriptive phrase at the beginning (*Slightly embarrassed*) which is then separated by a comma from the word it modifies (*I*, which is also the subject of the first independent clause). Notice as well that the two independent clauses (*I tried to pull away* and *her grip held me*) are so short that Soto felt no comma was needed before the word *but*. Write your own sentence that begins with a two-word descriptive phrase which is then separated by a comma from the noun or pronoun that it modifies (a noun or pronoun which is also the subject of the sentence or of the first independent clause in the sentence).

Students and Teachers

ALAN LIGHTMAN

❏ *Inward Exploration*

Make a list of teachers who have had a significant impact on you in some way. Select one and write a paragraph in which you explain what that impact was.

In the fall of 1934, one year after his Ph.D., John Archibald Wheeler   *1*
traveled to Copenhagen to study with the great atomic physicist Niels
Bohr. At his Institute for Theoretical Physics, a house-sized building
on Blegdamsvej 15, Bohr had created a scientific "school" in which the
daily stimulation from brilliant seminars and disturbing new ideas could
dismast slow thinkers. Among the students who had held up well were
Felix Bloch, Max Delbrück, Linus Pauling, and Harold Urey, all future
Nobel Prize winners like their teacher. As Wheeler arrived at the institute on bicycle one morning, he noticed a workman tearing down the
vines that had grown thickly over the gray stucco front. On closer view,
he saw it was Bohr himself, "following his usual modest but direct approach to a problem." Thus began Wheeler's tutelage.

I am, through Wheeler, a great grandstudent of Bohr. I had forgotten this fact until a recent venture to the Boston studio of painter Paul
Ingbretson, who immediately announced his own pedagogical descent
from R. H. Ives Gammell, a student of William Paxton, a student of the
academic painter Jean-Léon Gérôme. In the art world it is commonly
said that the days of the master and apprentice tradition ended two centuries ago, that the classical method of severe and thorough training has
been lost, except by a handful of painters. Ingbretson, 34 years old, is
one of that handful. He treasures the technique and style and wisdom
garnered from his teachers and tries to give away some of it to his pupils
here in the Fenway Studios, where Paxton worked from 1905 to 1914.
What he learned from Gammell and Paxton cannot be written down.
He is a living painting, full of their brush strokes and visions. In science, such personal inheritance receives less currency, following the idea
that a cut-and-dried objectivity outlives questions of style. You rarely
witness a scientist exhibiting his pedagogical lineage. Yet without a
good teacher, a young student of science could read a row of textbooks
stretching to the moon and not learn how to practice the trade. Exactly
what is it, in this age of massive information storage and retrieval, that
you can't learn from a book?

"Squint your eyes; squint your eyes," Ingbretson was admonishing one of his students. By squinting the eyes as you study your subject, minor details fade, leaving only the highlights, the dominant lights and darks. Ingbretson's charges, with their easels and paper and charcoal, were clustered around a classical marble bust, lit from windows rising to the 16-foot ceiling of the studio. "It's all a question of learning to see," Ingbretson was saying. This phrase "learning to see" was one Gammell often used. It typifies the method of painting from nature practiced by the early twentieth-century Boston school, the blend of the exacting academic style with impressionism.

Wheeler, now 72, had his own method of learning how to see, which he taught to my teacher Kip Thorne: "If you're having trouble thinking clearly, imagine programming a computer to solve your problem. After mentally automating the necessary logic, step by step, you can then dispense with the computer." On occasion, marching through a problem in such a fashion will lead to an unexpected contradiction, and this is where the fun really begins. Wheeler loves to teach physics in terms of paradoxes, a habit he picked up from Bohr. In the 1920s and 1930s—when quantum mechanics was in its infancy and physicists were slowly adjusting to the strange fact that an electron behaves both as a localizable particle and as a wave, spread over many places at once—Bohr realized that several apparently conflicting views can be equally essential for understanding some phenomena. A student doesn't get this kind of thinking from books. Wheeler recalls Bohr's usual method of explanation as a one-man tennis match, in which each hit of the ball would be some telling contradiction to previous results, raised by a new experiment or theory. After each hit Bohr would run around to the other side of the court quickly enough to return his own shot. "No progress without a paradox." The worst thing that could happen in a visitor's seminar was the absence of surprises, after which Bohr had to utter those dreaded words, "That was interesting."

I was slowly circling an odd still-life arrangement in the clutter of   5
Ingbretson's studio—an upright porcelain plate with a diagonal pattern, a bowl, a matchbox, a bit of dried flowers. On an easel nearby was an extremely effective rendering by one of Ingbretson's advanced pupils, clearly taken from the pale still life in front of me, yet more interesting somehow. Then I slipped around to the precise viewing angle of the drawing and suddenly the objects on the table leaped out at me in a wonderful way. "Some artists," said Ingbretson, "will arrange and re-arrange a still life for hours until they find just the right grouping and viewing angle." You look at it from the wrong direction and all you've got is a collection of junk. "Sometimes reality isn't enough. I was once doing a still life in Gammell's class, and we had meticulously chosen and arranged the objects beforehand. After I was finished Gammell stared at my work for a few minutes and then told me to draw in a nonexistent knicknack in the corner. It turned out he was right."

Graduate students in science, unanchored to a knowledgeable thesis adviser, have wasted years circling around for a good project. Every so often an application comes in from a Third World student wanting a research position abroad, and you can tell he's highly competent mathematically and he's been combing the journals equation by equation, but his teachers are isolated from mainstream research, and he has no clue as to what projects are worth working on. The Nobel-Prize–winning Soviet physicist Lev Landau kept a notebook of about thirty important unsolved problems, which he would show to students if and when they successfully passed a barrage of tests known affectionately as the Landau Minimum. Significant research projects in science are often no more difficult than insignificant ones. Projects out of Landau's notebook had guaranteed significance.

As a student, you could always tell which projects Thorne was hot on, because the hallway near his office was lined with framed wagers between himself and other scientific eminences. "Kip Steven Thorne wagers S. Chandrasekhar that rotating black holes will prove to be stable. K. S. T. places forward a year's subscription to *The Listener;* S. C. places forward a year's subscription to *Playboy.*" And so on. Thorne, red-bearded and wiry, would sit quietly in his office filling pages with equations, while passing students contemplated those wagers in the hall and were set on fire.

Beethoven and Czerny and Liszt, Socrates and Plato and Aristotle, Verrocchio and Leonardo, Pushkin and Baryshnikov. As we stood in the studio, Ingbretson walked over to a pupil who had succeeded in putting down three questionable lines in the last hour and told her to start from scratch. Ingbretson's own teacher demanded a lot from his students and didn't mind a little humiliation to get a point across. One day while a younger Ingbretson was smugly reflecting on his painting, Gammell, a bald, wizened man with the head of a bulldog, standing not much over five feet, took Ingbretson by his pinky, led him around the room to some white paint, dipped the little finger in the paint, then led him back to the canvas and applied the finger to a strategic spot. "There," said Gammell, "now you've got the highlight." Hans Krebs, winner of the 1953 Nobel Prize in medicine or physiology, a student of Nobelist Otto Warburg, a student of Nobelist Emil Fischer, wrote that scientists of distinction, above all, "teach a high standard of research. We measure everything, including ourselves, by comparisons; and in the absence of someone with outstanding ability there is a risk that we easily come to believe we are excellent. . . . Mediocre people may appear big to themselves (and to others) if they are surrounded by small circumstances. By the same token big people feel dwarfed in the company of giants, and this is a most useful feeling. . . . If I ask myself how it came about that one day I found myself in Stockholm, I have not the slightest doubt that I owe this good fortune to the circumstance that I had an outstanding teacher at the critical stage of my scientific career."

Rulers and plumb bobs appear regularly in Ingbretson's studio. A plumb bob is a weight attached to a string and, when freely hung in the earth's gravitational pull, gives an unerring reading of the vertical direction. Rulers and plumb bobs serve as invaluable tools for getting proportion and angles exactly right. This old tradition of expert draftsmanship was gleaned from Gammell, who learned it from Paxton. Paxton's portraits are stunning in their precision, with a reality and sensuality far exceeding any photograph. Of Paxton, Gammell once wrote "His unsurpassed visual acuity combined with great technical command enabled him to report his impressions with astounding veracity."

One of Ingbretson's students was struggling with angles in her drawing of the marble bust. Lines were going awry and wandering aimlessly. The sacred plumb bob wasn't working. "Aha," he offered, "your paper's gotten tilted."

Learning good draftsmanship requires constant feedback between teacher and student, Ingbretson explained. But good draftsmanship isn't enough. After mastering technique, you then must decide what to emphasize on the canvas. This tricky combination of formal method and individual impression has the flavor of the balance between mathematical rigor and physical intuition required in science. Thorne believes a feeling for such balance is one of the crucial things he learned from Wheeler. "Many scientists move at a snail's pace because they are too mathematical and don't know how to think physically. And vice versa for people too sloppy in their mathematics." Consider, for example, a quantitative description of marbles rolling around on a floor with holes in it. You try to derive an equation that tells how the number of marbles decreases in time. A most useful check of that equation is to set the hole size to a small number, which should yield the result that you don't lose any of your marbles. Or else the equation is wrong. This check wouldn't naturally occur to you unless you have a physical picture in your head of marbles rolling around and falling, one by one, through the holes. The mathematical equation itself, right or wrong, is quite content to stare back with an unrevealing jumble of its marble-conserving and marble-nonconserving parts.

Niels Bohr was a barrel-chested man, a football hero in his younger days. He was also gentle, and made his penetrating points in a soft voice. Bohr had many ideas he never tried to copyright. Likewise, his student John Wheeler, who quietly introduced numerous seminal ideas in physics, who performed an important but little-known role advising the Du Pont company during the Manhattan Project. Personal style can be inherited. Wheeler's student, Kip Thorne, has always bent over backward to give credit to other scientists. He begins seminars by attributing most of his results to particular students. Modesty, and its opposite, set the tone of a research group.

Ghirlandajo and Michelangelo, Koussevitsky and Bernstein, Lastman and Rembrandt, Fermi and Bethe, Luria and Watson. Of the 286 Nobel laureates named between 1901 and 1972, 41 percent had a master or senior collaborator who was also a Nobelist. Many Nobelists have surrounded themselves with spirited schools of students. A cluster of apprentices seems to generate, en masse, the necessary speed for takeoff. Among the great recent masters in physics were Thomson and Rutherford in England, Landau and Zel'dovich in the Soviet Union, Bohr in Denmark, Fermi and Oppenheimer and Alvarez in the United States— all with large research groups that spawned other eminent scientists. At Caltech, Thorne has always insisted on cloistering his half dozen students within adjacent rooms, with an unwritten rule that office and lab doors remain open. Someone, in a group of creative people working together, is usually quivering at the edge of discovery, and the vibrations spread.

Gazing out from a photograph of the Boston Museum's 1913 life-drawing class is a mustached, steady-eyed Paxton, sitting among his seventeen students. On the front left is Gammell, twenty years old, wearing an overcoat and a full head of hair. His expression is serious. The other pupils stand or sit, some wear elegant suits and others short sleeves and smocks, some look frightened and others bored, but they lean into each other with hands on shoulders, and there is electricity in the air.

The light was fading from the tall windows in Ingbretson's studio *15* and his pupils were packing up their materials. "You know, Gammell wasn't perfect. His gestures were forced. Look at that arm." Ingbretson held up an illustration in a book of Gammell's paintings. "That's unnatural. It took me a while to see it. I was relieved."

Nothing is more bracing for students than to discover the fallibility of their exalted teachers. Students, God knows, are brimming with their own human weaknesses, and if their great mentors can make mistakes, well then, anything might happen. Thorne remembers that, during his second year of graduate school, Wheeler stuck by some erroneous statements about black holes. The realization of Wheeler's errors provided its own kind of inspiration. When Wheeler was in Copenhagen in 1934, he sought Bohr's assessment of some calculations on the so-called dispersion theory, extending it from applications where particles move slowly to applications where they move at nearly the speed of light. Bohr was skeptical of Wheeler's work and discouraged publication. Bohr was wrong. Perhaps, in the end, our own imperfection is the most vital thing we learn from teachers. At the dedication of the giant statue of Einstein in Washington a few years ago, Wheeler said "How can we best symbolize that science reaches after the eternal? . . . Not by a pompous figure on a pedestal. No, a figure over which children can crawl. . . ."

❏ *Outward Exploration: Discussion*

1. According to Ingbretson, what is art a question of doing? Does that advice have application for you as a writer? Explain.

2. What does Bohr think is crucial for progress in science?

3. According to Lightman, what is the advantage of having "a knowledgeable thesis adviser" in science?

4. Lightman is a physicist, yet several of his examples are drawn from the world of painting and music. Why?

❏ *Outward Exploration: Writing*

1. Lightman gives us a great deal of information about a variety of teacher-student relationships. Write an essay exploring a significant relationship that you have had with a teacher or with another student. Feel free to refer to some of the various relationships Lightman explains as a way of setting your particular relationship in context and as a way of achieving global significance.

2. According to Bohr, there is "no progress without a paradox." Devise a paradox of your own or find one in a source, and write an essay exploring the way that paradox sheds light on your personality. For instance, St. Paul says, "For when I am weak, then I am strong"; Pablo Picasso says, "Art is a form of lying in order to tell the truth"; Gertrude Stein says, "But the essence of that ugliness is the thing which will always make it beautiful"; and Edward Young says, "The less we copy the renowned ancients, the more we shall resemble them." In addition, the works of such writers as John Donne and Oscar Wilde offer many provocative examples.

3. Have you ever had the experience of changing your viewing angle and suddenly seeing something "in a wonderful way" as Lightman did in Ingbretson's studio (paragraph 5)? This might have been a change in a physical viewing angle, but it might also have been a metaphysical change in viewing angle as you considered an event or a person in a different light or used a different set of criteria or focused on a different element (for example, instead of thinking about your responses to your friend's complaints, you metaphorically "put yourself in your friend's shoes" and suddenly saw your own actions from his or her point of view). If such an experience has happened to you, explore it in an essay.

My Horse and I

N. Scott Momaday

I sometimes think of what it means that in their heyday—in 1830,   *1* say—the Kiowas owned more horses *per capita* than any other tribe on the Great Plains, that the Plains Indian culture, the last culture to evolve in North America, is also known as "the horse culture" and "the centaur culture," that the Kiowas tell the story of a horse that died of shame after its owner committed an act of cowardice, that I am a Kiowa, that therefore there is in me, as there is in the Tartars, an old, sacred notion of the horse. I believe that at some point in my racial life, this notion must needs be expressed in order that I may be true to my nature.

It happened so: I was thirteen years old, and my parents gave me a horse. It was a small nine-year-old gelding of that rare, soft color that is called strawberry roan. This my horse and I came to be, in the course of our life together, in good understanding, of one mind, a true story and history of that large landscape in which we made the one entity of whole motion, one and the same center of an intricate, pastoral composition, evanescent, ever changing. And to this my horse I gave the name Pecos.

On the back of my horse I had a different view of the world. I could see more of it, how it reached away beyond all the horizons I had ever seen; and yet it was more concentrated in its appearance, too, and more accessible to my mind, my imagination. My mind loomed upon the farthest edges of the earth, where I could feel the full force of the planet whirling into space. There was nothing of the air and light that was not pure exhilaration, and nothing of time and eternity. Oh, Pecos, *un poquito mas!* Oh, my hunting horse! Bear me away, bear me away!

It was appropriate that I should make a long journey. Accordingly I set out one early morning, traveling light. Such a journey must begin in the nick of time, on the spur of the moment, and one must say to himself at the outset: Let there be wonderful things along the way; let me hold to the way and be thoughtful in my going; let this journey be made in beauty and belief.

I sang in the sunshine and heard the birds call out on either side. Bits   *5*
of down from the cottonwoods drifted across the air, and butterflies fluttered in the sage. I could feel my horse under me, rocking at my legs, the bobbing of the reins in my hand; I could feel the sun on my face and the stirring of a little wind at my hair. And through the hard hooves, the slender limbs, the supple shoulders, the fluent back of my horse I felt the earth under me. Everything was under me, buoying me up; I rode across the top of the world. My mind soared; time and again I saw the fleeting shadow of my mind moving about me as it went winding upon the sun.

When the song, which was a song of riding, was finished, I had Pecos pick up the pace. Far down on the road to San Ysidro I overtook my friend Pasqual Fragua. He was riding a rangy, stiff-legged black and white stallion, half wild, which horse he was breaking for the rancher Cass Goodner. The horse skittered and blew as I drew up beside him. Pecos began to prance, as he did always in the company of another horse. "Where are you going?" I asked in the Jemez language. And he replied, "I am going down the road." The stallion was hard to manage, and Pasqual had to keep his mind upon it; I saw that I had taken him by surprise. "You know," he said after a moment, "when you rode up just now I did not know who you were." We rode on for a time in silence, and our horses got used to each other, but still they wanted their heads. The longer I looked at the stallion the more I admired it, and I suppose that Pasqual knew this, for he began to say good things about it: that it was a thing of good blood, that it was very strong and fast, that it felt very good to ride it. The thing was this: that the stallion was half wild, and I came to wonder about the wild half of it; I wanted to know what its wildness was worth in the riding. "Let us trade horses for a while," I said, and, well, all right, he agreed. At first it was exciting to ride the stallion, for every once in a while it pitched and bucked and wanted to run. But it was heavy and raw-boned and full of resistance, and every step was a jolt that I could feel deep down in my bones. I saw soon enough that I had made a bad bargain, and I wanted my horse back, but I was ashamed to admit it. There came a time in the late afternoon, in the vast plain far south of San Ysidro, after thirty miles, perhaps, when I no longer knew whether it was I who was riding the stallion or the stallion who was riding me. "Well, let us go back now," said Pasqual at last. "No, I am going on; and I will have my horse back, please," I said, and he was surprised and sorry to hear it, and we said goodbye. "If you are going south or east," he said, "look out for the sun, and keep your face in the shadow of your hat. *Vaya con Dios.*" And I went on my way alone then, wiser and better mounted, and thereafter I held on to my horse. I saw no one for a long time, but I saw four falling stars and any number of jackrabbits, roadrunners, and coyotes, and once, across a distance, I saw a bear, small and black, lumbering in a ravine. The mountains drew close and withdrew and drew close again, and after several days I swung east.

Now and then I came upon settlements. For the most part they were dry, burnt places with Spanish names: Arroyo Seco, Las Piedras, Tres Casas. In one of these I found myself in a narrow street between high adobe walls. Just ahead, on my left, was a door in the wall. As I approached the door was flung open, and a small boy came running out, rolling a hoop. This happened so suddenly that Pecos shied very sharply, and I fell to the ground, jamming the thumb of my left hand. The little boy looked very worried and said that he was sorry to have caused such an accident. I waved the matter off, as if it were nothing; but as a matter of fact my hand hurt so much that tears welled up in my eyes. And the pain lasted for many days. I have fallen many times from a horse, both before and after that, and a few times I fell from a running horse on dangerous ground, but that was the most painful of them all.

In another settlement there were some boys who were interested in racing. They had good horses, some of them, but their horses were not so good as mine, and I won easily. After that, I began to think of ways in which I might even the odds a little, might give some advantage to my competitors. Once or twice I gave them a head start, a reasonable head start of, say, five or ten yards to the hundred, but that was too simple, and I won anyway. Then it came to me that I might try this: we should all line up in the usual way, side by side, but my competitors should be mounted and I should not. When the signal was given I should then have to get up on my horse while the others were breaking away; I should have to mount my horse during the race. This idea appealed to me greatly, for it was both imaginative and difficult, not to mention dangerous; Pecos and I should have to work very closely together. The first few times we tried this I had little success, and over a course of a hundred yards I lost four races out of five. The principal problem was that Pecos simply could not hold still among the other horses. Even before they broke away he was hard to manage, and when they were set running nothing could hold him back, even for an instant. I could not get my foot in the stirrup, but I had to throw myself up across the saddle on my stomach, hold on as best I could, and twist myself into position, and all this while racing at full speed. I could ride well enough to accomplish this feat, but it was a very awkward and inefficient business. I had to find some way to use the whole energy of my horse, to get it all into the race. Thus far I had managed only to break his motion, to divert him from his purpose and mine. To correct this I took Pecos away and worked with him through the better part of a long afternoon on a broad reach of level ground beside an irrigation ditch. And it was hot, hard work. I began by teaching him to run straight away while I ran beside him a few steps, holding on to the saddle horn, with no pressure on the reins. Then, when we had mastered this trick, we proceeded to the next one, which was this: I placed my weight on my arms, hanging from the saddle horn, threw my feet out in front of me, struck them to the ground, and sprang up against the saddle. This I did again and again, until Pecos came to expect it and did not flinch or lose his stride. I sprang a little higher each time. It was in all a slow process of trial and error, and after two or three hours both Pecos and I were covered with bruises and soaked through with perspiration. But we had much to show for our efforts, and at last the moment came when we must put the whole performance together. I had not yet leaped into the saddle, but I was quite confident that I could now do so; only I must be sure to get high enough. We began this dress rehearsal then from a standing position. At my signal Pecos lurched and was running at once, straight away and smoothly. And at the same time I sprinted forward two steps and gathered myself up, placing my weight precisely at my wrists, throwing my feet out and together, perfectly. I brought my feet down sharply to the ground and sprang up hard, as hard as I could, bringing my legs astraddle of my horse—and everything was just right, except that I sprang too high. I vaulted all the way over my horse, clearing the saddle by a considerable margin, and came down into the irrigation ditch. It was a good trick, but it was not the one I had in mind, and I wonder what Pecos thought of it after all. Anyway, after a while I could mount my horse in this way and so well that there was no challenge in it, and I went on winning race after race.

I went on, farther and farther into the wide world. Many things happened. And in all this I knew one thing: I knew where the journey was begun, that it was itself a learning of the beginning, that the beginning was infinitely worth the learning. The journey was well undertaken, and somewhere in it I sold my horse to an old Spanish man of Vallecitos. I do not know how long Pecos lived. I had used him hard and well, and it may be that in his last days an image of me like thought shimmered in his brain.

Outward Exploration: Discussion

1. What does Momaday mean when he says that on the back of his horse he "had a different view of the world" (paragraph 3)?
2. Explain the tone of the last three sentences in paragraph 3. How does Momaday achieve this tone?
3. What is the significance of Momaday's switching horses with his friend Pasqual?
4. What does this essay reveal about Momaday's personality?

5. Does the meaning of the term *long journey* change in the course of the essay?

6. Why did Momaday sell Pecos? Explain your response to the fact that he sold Pecos and doesn't even know how long the horse lived.

❑ *Outward Exploration: Writing*

In order to reach adulthood, each of us has to "make a long journey" like Momaday's, even if the length of our journey is measured in time or emotional distance rather than in kilometers or miles. If you have taken such a journey, write an essay about it.

❑ *Style*

Consider the following sentence from Momaday's essay:

I could feel my horse under me, rocking at my legs, the bobbing of the reins in my hand; I could feel the sun on my face and the stirring of a little wind at my hair. (paragraph 5)

Notice the parallel structure in this sentence. This parallelism occurs in three ways. First, Momaday repeats "I could feel . . ." at the start of each of the two independent clauses. Second, each verb *feel* has two direct objects (*my horse* and *the bobbing* in the first clause, *the sun* and *the stirring* in the second). Third, the second direct object in each clause is a present participle acting as a gerund (a form of the verb acting as a noun—namely, *bobbing* and *stirring*). In terms of punctuation, notice that Momaday uses only a semicolon to join the two independent clauses, a decision that makes sense given the fact that the first independent clause already contains two commas and he wished to avoid confusion about what functions his commas were performing.

Replicate this subtle parallelism in a sentence of your own. Feel free to use the "I could feel . . ." phrasing. Give each verb two direct objects, and make the second direct object of each clause a gerund.

On Being Raised by a Daughter

NANCY MAIRS

☐ *Inward Exploration*

Just looking at the title of Nancy Mairs's essay should make you wonder, "In what ways did I raise my parents?" Write at least one paragraph answering that question.

Mothering. I didn't know how to do it. Does anyone? If there really *1*
were a maternal instinct, as a good many otherwise quite responsible human beings have claimed, then would we need men like Dr. Alan Guttmacher and Dr. Benjamin Spock to teach us how to mother, and would we be forever scrambling to keep up with the shifts in their child-bearing and child-rearing theories? Would we turn, shaken by our sense of our female incapacity, to the reassuring instructive voices of the fathers, who increasingly come in both sexes, murmuring how much weight to gain or lose, how long to offer the breast, how soon to toilet train, to send to school? Does the salmon ask for a map to the spawning ground? Does the bee send to the Department of Agriculture for a manual on honeymaking?

No, I came with no motherly chromosomes to pattern my gestures comfortably. Not only did I not know how to do it, I'm not even sure now that I wanted to do it. These days people choose whether or not to have children. I am not so very old—my forty-first birthday falls this month—yet I can say with the verity of a wrinkled granny that we did things differently in my day. I no more chose to have children than I had chosen to get married. I simply did what I had been raised to do. Right on schedule (or actually a little ahead of schedule, since I hadn't yet finished college) I wrapped myself in yards of white taffeta and put orange blossoms in my hair and marched myself, in front of the fond, approving gaze of a couple of hundred people, into the arms of a boy in a morning coat who was doing what he had been raised to do. After a year or so, the fond, approving gaze shifted to my belly, which I made swell to magnificent proportions before expelling an unpromising scrap of human flesh on whom the gaze could turn. This was Anne, created in a heedless gesture as close to instinctual as any I would ever perform: satisfaction of the social expectation that I, young, vigorous, equipped with functioning uterus and ovaries and breasts, would sanctify my union with George by bringing forth a son. (I missed, though I had better luck next time.)

The birth of Anne was dreadful, and at the beginning I hated her, briefly, more fiercely than I had ever hated anyone. My doctor, a small round elderly GP who delivered whatever babies came along in Bath, Maine, told me that my protracted pelvis might necessitate a Caesarian section, but he never instructed me what to do during this birth by whatever means. I guess I was supposed not to do but to endure. I remember, hours into a lengthy and complicated labor that ended in Dr. Fichtner's extracting Anne with forceps like a six-pound thirteen-ounce wisdom tooth, twisting my fingers through my hair, yanking, raking my face with my nails, shrieking at the nurse beside me, "Get this thing out of me! I hate it!" Until then I had rather liked Anne, as she humped up bigger and bigger each night under the bedsheet, her wriggles and thumps giving a constant undertone of companionship to my often solitary daily activities. But now I was sure she was killing me. The nurse loosened my fingers and soothed, "You'll feel differently in a little while."

She was right. In a rather long while I did feel differently. I was no longer in pain. But I didn't feel motherly. In fact, Anne on the outside wasn't half so companionable as Anne on the inside, and I think I felt a little lonely. And frightened. I hadn't the faintest idea what I was doing with this mite with the crossed blue eyes and the whoosh of hair sticking straight up. And now, more than eighteen years later, I still have the frequent sense that I don't know what I'm doing, complicated now, of course, by the guilt that I don't know what I've done and the terror that I don't know what I'm going to do. How, I wonder when a young woman comes into my room and speaks to me, her hair blown dry to casual elegance and her eyes uncrossed behind round brown frames, how did you get here? And where, when you turn and walk out of here, out of my house and out of the dailiness of my life, where will you go?

I have been mystified by motherhood largely because motherhood   5 itself has been mystified. Perhaps before Freud I might have raised my children without knowing consciously my power to damage their spirits beyond human repair, but the signs have always been there: the Good Mother and the Terrible Mother, the dead saint and the wicked step-mother waiting to offer disguised poisons, shoes of hellfire. The one is as alien as the other. If you live in a culture where all children are raised by mothers, Nancy Chodorow points out in *The Reproduction of Mothering,* and if half those children are males who must separate with some violence from the mother in order to establish their different gender, and if the males have the power to determine, through the creation of symbolic systems like language and art, what culture itself is, then you will get a cultural view of mothers as others, on whom are projected traits that even they (who speak some form of the language, who look at the pictures even if they don't paint them) come to assume are their own. We live in a culture of object-mothers. The subject-mothers, cul-turally silenced for millennia, are only just beginning to speak.

The voices of authority tell me I may harm, even ruin my daughter (in large measure by spoiling her for the pleasurable uses of men). At first they issue from the eminences of science, in measured tones like those of Carl Jung: "Thus, if the child of an over-anxious mother regularly dreams that she is a terrifying animal or a witch, these experiences point to a split in the child's psyche that predisposes it to a neurosis." I am the stuff of my daughter's nightmares. Gradually the pronouncements trickle down into the market place and are reformulated for popular consumption by voices like Nancy Friday's in that long whine of sexual anxiety *My Mother/My Self,* which was on the bestseller list some years back: "When mother's silent and threatening disapproval adds dark colors to the girl's emergent sexuality, this fear becomes eroticized in such strange forms as masochism, love of the brute, rape fantasies—the thrill of whatever is most forbidden." I make of my daughter's life a waking nightmare as well. A book like *My Mother/My Self,* in dealing with our earliest relationship, out of which our ability to form all other relationships grows, taps a rich subterranean vein of desire and disappointment, but it does so only to portray daughter as victim.

The real danger these voices pose lies not so much in what they say as in what they leave out about motherhood, whether through ignorance or through incapacity. Jung was not a woman at all, at least socially speaking (archetypally, of course, he had an anima, which doesn't seem to have caused him much trouble). And Friday refused to have children on the grounds that if she chanced to have a daughter, she'd ruin her child just as her mother had ruined her (such an assumption suggests that her choice was a wise one). But neither these two nor the vast crowd of fellow motherhood-mystifiers between them takes into adequate account the persistence of human development, which keeps the personality malleable indefinitely, if it is allowed to, or the implacable power of six pounds thirteen ounces of human flesh from the moment it draws a breath and wails its spirit out into the world.

Among all the uncertainties I have experienced about myself as a mother, of one point I feel sure: that I am not today the woman I would have been had Anne not been born one September evening almost nineteen years ago. I cannot prove this hypothesis, there being no control in this experiment, no twenty-two-year-old Nancy Mairs that night who had a son instead, whose baby died, who had had a miscarriage, who had not been able to get pregnant at all, who never married and lives now in a small, well-appointed apartment on the Marina in San Francisco, walking her Burmese cats on leashes in Golden Gate Park. There is only this Nancy Mairs who, for nearly half her life, has in raising been raised by a daughter.

Anne can't have found her job an easy one. Raising a mother is difficult enough under the best of circumstances. But when you get one who's both crippled and neurotic—who doesn't do her fair share of the housework, who lurches around the house and crashes to the floor in front of your friends, whose spirits flag and crumple unpredictably, who gets attacks of anxiety in the middle of stores and has to be cajoled into finishing simple errands—then you have your work cut out for you. Of all the things Anne has taught me, perhaps the most important is that one can live under difficult circumstances with a remarkable amount of equanimity and good humor. It's a lesson I need daily.

My education began, no doubt, from the moment of her birth. Perhaps even before. Perhaps from the moment I perceived her presence in the absence of my period, or from the instant (Christmas Eve, I'm convinced) of her conception, or even from the time I began to dream her. But then she was anonymous. As soon as she appeared, she took me firmly in diminutive hand and trained me much as I've come to see that my cats have trained me, rewarding my good behavior (what difference a smile or a purr?) and punishing my bad (they've both tended to bite). But I don't think of my education as being under way till about nine months later when one day she heaved herself up in her car-bed, raised one arm in a stiff wave, and called, "Hi there!" A baby who could talk with me was beyond my ken. After all, I was raised before the days when dolls had electronic voice-boxes in their tummies and quavered "Hi there!" when you pulled the string. And anyway, Anne didn't have a string. *She* chose to speak to *me*.

I've never been the same.

Birth is, I think, an attenuated process, though we tend to use the word to describe only the physical separation of the baby from the mother. Fortunately, those first hours of birth were the worst, in terms of pain, or I don't think I'd have lasted. Each phase of the process involves separation, which may or may not be physical but always carries heavy psychic freight. For me, Anne's speech was a major step. It set her apart from me, over there, an entity with whom I could, literally, have a dialogue. It made her an other.

Feminist psychologists note that psychical birth, the process of differentiating self from other, is particularly problematic for female children. As Chodorow writes,

> Because they are the same gender as their daughters and have
> been girls, mothers of daughters tend not to experience these
> infant daughters as separate from them in the same way as do
> mothers of infant sons. . . . Primary identification and symbiosis
> with daughters tend to be stronger and cathexis of daughters is
> more likely to retain and emphasize narcissistic elements, that
> is, to be based on experiencing a daughter as an extension or
> double of a mother herself, with cathexis of the daughter as a
> sexual other usually remaining a weaker, less significant theme.

The consequence of this feeling of continuity between mother and daughter is that "separation and individuation remain particularly fe-

10

male developmental issues." But "problematic" doesn't mean "bad," a leap that Friday makes when she lifts "symbiosis" out of the psycho-analytic context in which Chodorow uses it and applies it to noninfan-tile relationships, giving it then not its full range of meaning but that portion of meaning which suits her program: symbiosis as a kind of perverse parasitism: a large but weak organism feeding on a smaller but strong host which, as it grows, weakens until the two are evenly matched in size and incapacity. According to Friday, the mother limits her daughter's autonomy and independence, extinguishes her sexuality, terrifies her witless of men, then packages her in Saran Wrap to keep her fresh and hands her over to some man who, if she's not careful, will get on her a daughter on whom she will perform the same hideous rites.

I'm not saying that no mother does such things. Apparently Nancy Friday's mother did, and I recognize any number of my own experiences in hers. Nor am I saying that, through some virtue or miracle, I have avoided doing them to Anne. Of course I would want to think so; but God and Anne alone know what horrors I've perpetrated. All I can be sure of is that if Anne handed me a list of grievances, most of them would probably surprise me. If they didn't, I'd be a monster, not a mother.

What I am saying is that such things are not intrinsic to the mother–daughter relationship. As Chodorow notes in her study "Family Structure and Female Personality," women in societies as various as those in Atjeh, Java, and East London, where their "kin role, and in particular the mother role, is central and positively valued," have experiences and develop self-images very different from those of Western middle-class women:

> There is another important aspect of the situation in these soci-
> eties. The continuing structural and practical importance of the
> mother–daughter tie not only ensures that a daughter develops
> a positive personal and role identification with her mother, but
> also requires that the close psychological tie between mother
> and daughter become firmly grounded in real role expectations.
> These provide a certain constraint and limitation upon the rela-
> tionship, as well as an avenue for its expression through com-
> mon spheres of interest based in the external social world.

Thus, although the problem of differentiation exists wherever mothers mother daughters, its implications vary from one social setting to an-other. If a woman like Friday's mother teaches her daughter that sex is risky at best and in general downright nasty, she does so not because she is a mother but because she is the product of a patriarchal order that demands that its women be chaste and compliant so that men may be sure of their paternity. In fact, such a concern is extrinsic to the mother–daughter relationship, which exists in essence outside the sphere of men. As soon as one can identify it for what it is, the concern of a particular group of human beings for maintaining a particular kind of power, one is free to choose whether or not to perpetuate it.

Thus, Friday's rationale for refusing to bear children, that she would inevitably visit upon her daughter the same evils her mother visited upon her, is off the mark, rooted in a sense of powerlessness in the face of the existing social order which seems to stem from belief in a biologically predetermined parasitism. Mothers, inexorably, must eat out the hearts of their daughters alive. Neither a mother nor a daughter has the power to avoid the dreadful outcome. They are only helpless women. But if we step outside socially imposed injunctions, then Friday is wrong, and daughters and their mothers wield powers for one another's help as well as harm. They may even make of one another revolutionaries.

Symbiosis is a spacious word. It may encompass parasitism and helotism (though the *Shorter Oxford Dictionary* disallows this meaning by requiring that the entities involved be mutually supportive). But it also—even chiefly—means commensalism, mutualism, "the intimate living together," says *Webster's Third,* "of two dissimilar organisms in any of various mutually beneficial relationships." The crux is the living-withness the word demands: We may live with one another well or badly. To live together reciprocally, each contributing to the other's support, in the figurative sense in which symbiosis represents human relationship, requires delicate balance, difficult to establish and to maintain. Both partners must give to it and take from it. Both must flourish under its influence, or it is no longer symbiotic. For these reasons, a symbiotic relationship between a mother and her growing daughter—or between any other two people, for that matter—may be rather rare. For these reasons, also, emotional symbiosis is not an ascribed characteristic of a relationship; rather, it is the outcome of the dynamics of some relationships between some people some of the time.

Symbiosis as I am now using the word—not like Chodorow to represent the phase of total infantile dependence or like Friday to suggest emotional vampirism but rather as a metaphor for the interdependence characteristic of living together well—does not result in identity. On the contrary, every definition I've found requires the difference of the entities involved. Thus, after the demands of infancy have been made and met, individuation is necessary if a true symbiotic system is to be maintained. Otherwise you get something else, some solid lump of psychic flesh whose name I do not know.

All the analyses I've read of mother–daughter relationships fail to account for my experience of Anne's power in our mutual life. The assumption seems to be that I'm the one in control, not just because I'm older than she is and, until recently, bigger and stronger, but because I have society's acknowledgment and support in the venture and she doesn't. I'm engaged in the honorable occupation of child-rearing, and if I can't figure the procedures out for myself, I can find shelves of manuals in any bookstore or library. No one even notices that Anne is engaged in mother-rearing, much less offers her any hot tips; indeed, books like *My Mother/My Self* only reinforce her powerlessness, making her out a victim of maternal solicitude and submerged rage, whose only recourse is more rage, rebellion, rejection: not an actor but a reactor. Such lopsided accounts arise, I suppose, from the premise—the consequence of a hierarchical view of human development—that adulthood signifies completion. But the fluidity, the pains and delights, the spurts of growth and sluggish spells of childhood never cease, though we may cease to acknowledge them in an effort to establish difference from, and hence authority over, our children. Out of the new arrivals in our lives—the odd word stumbled upon in a difficult text, the handsome black stranger who bursts in one night through the cat door, the telephone call out of a friend's silence of years, the sudden greeting from the girl-child—we constantly make of ourselves our selves.

When Anne waved and called out to me, she made an other not only 20 of herself but of me. Language is the ultimate alienator. When she spoke she created for herself a self so remote from me that it could communicate with me only—imprecisely, imperfectly—through words. Shortly thereafter she named me, and went on naming me, into place, a slowish process. When she was not quite two, I left the world. I went into a state mental hospital and stayed there six months. During that time Anne lived with my mother, another Anne, and the two of them built a life around a space that they both expected me to come back to and fill. One afternoon, sitting in a basket in the checkout line at the IGA, Anne struck up a conversation with the man behind her who, gesturing toward Mother, said something about her mummy. "That's not my Mummy," Anne informed him, drawing herself high and fixing him with one crossed eye. "It's my Grandma. My Mummy is in the hospital." When Mother told me this story, I heard the message as I've heard it ever since: I'm the Mummy, the only Mummy (though I've grown up to be Mom, that hearty jokey apple-pie name, for reasons known only to my children), and that's who I've got to be.

As Mummy I have emphatically never been permitted to be Anne. Whatever fantasies I may have had, at some subliminal level, of my new daughter as a waxen dolly that I could pinch and pat into my likeness, Anne scotched them early, probably when she first spat puréed liver into my face (not to mention when she became the only one in the family who today eats liver in any form), certainly by the time she shouted out "Hi there!" (not "Mama" or "Dada," no private communiqué, but a greeting to all the world). Nor can I ever make her me. She wouldn't let me. Hence the possibility for our symbiosis, a state that demands two creatures for its establishment and maintenance. Anne has schooled me in the art of living well together by letting go.

Like any daughter's, hers hasn't been a simple task, but I don't think that the kind of gritty spirit it's called up in her will stand her in bad stead. She has been hampered by my own terror of separation, brought on perhaps by my early separation from my mother because of illness or my somewhat later permanent separation from my father through death. She has been helped, I think, by my curiosity to see what she would do next and by the fact that I've worked at jobs I enjoy since she was nine months old and that I've remained married, in considerable contentment, to her father, for as Chodorow points out, when "women do meaningful productive work, have ongoing adult companionship while they are parenting, and have satisfying emotional relationships with other adults, they are less likely to overinvest in children." And at least I've always *wanted* to let go. I just haven't always known how or when. Anne, through her peculiar quiet stubborn self-determination, has time after time peeled my white-knuckled fingers loose and shrugged away from my grasp.

Neither of us has had a whole lot of help from the world at large. We live in a society that still expects, even demands, that mothers control and manipulate their children's actions right into adulthood; that judges them according to the acceptability or unacceptability of their children's appearance and behavior; and that ensures their dependence on maternity for a sense, however diffuse, of self by giving them precious little else of interest to do. The mother who does let go, especially of a daughter, is still often considered irresponsible at best, unnatural at worst.

When Anne was sixteen, for instance, she decided to join a volunteer organization called Amigos de las Americas, training in Spanish and public health for several months and then going to Honduras to vaccinate pigs against hog cholera. United States policies in Central America hadn't yet created thoroughgoing chaos, and George and I thought this a wonderful way for her to begin inserting herself into the world. But George's parents, on a visit during her preparations, challenged me about Anne's plans. She ought not to be allowed to go, they said. It would be too much for her. The shock of entering a new culture would make her emotionally ill. "Ugh," Mum Mairs shuddered, "girls shouldn't have to dig latrines." (At that time, Anne hadn't yet received her assignment, but I presume that girls shouldn't have to slog around in pigshit either.) I was so startled by this attack, in terms I had not thought of before, that I doubt I said much to allay their fears, though I did ask Anne to tell them about her training in order to reassure them that she wasn't being thrust into the jungle naked and naive. Meanwhile, I thought about those terms, those feminine terms, forgotten at least momentarily by me, foreign as a source of motivation to Anne: nicety, physical and emotional frailty, passivity: all rolled into that statement that girls shouldn't have to dig latrines. (The logical extension of this attitude, I suppose, is that if a girl is all you've got, then you don't get a latrine. Ugh.)

Later, comparing notes with George, I learned that his parents had   25
never mentioned the matter to him. I was at first hurt, angry, feeling
picked on; later I came to understand that I was the natural target of
their misgivings. George couldn't be counted on to know what girls
should or shouldn't do, or to communicate his knowledge if he did. But
I could. I was Anne's mother. And in letting her go to Latin America
to live, if only briefly, in poverty, perhaps in squalor, and to perform
manual labor, I was derelict in my duty.

Thus challenged, I had to rethink this duty. To Mum and Dad
Mairs, obviously, it entailed the same protection I received growing up:
keeping Anne safe and comfortable, even keeping her pure, at bottom
probably protecting her maidenhead, though this mission is buried so
deep in our cultural unconscious that I think they would be shocked at
the mention of it. I recognized a different duty, a harsher one: to promote Anne's intellectual and spiritual growth even if it meant her leaving
me. I didn't think that safety and comfort tended to lead to growth. As
for protecting her maidenhead, I figured that was her responsibility,
since she was the one who had it, or didn't have it, as the case might
be. My duty, I saw, might in fact *be* dereliction, in the form of releasing
her into the flood of choice and chance that would be her life. I thought
she could swim. More important, she thought she could swim. Nonetheless, while she was gone I ran around distracted and stricken with
guilt, mumbling primitive prayers to Our Lady of Guadalupe to take
up the watch I had left off. Then she came home, bearing rum and
machetes wide-eyed right through customs, with a new taste for man-
goes and a new delight in hot showers but without even the lice and
dysentery and other gruesome manifestations of tropical fauna she had
been promised.

She came back but never, of course, all the way back. Each departure contains an irrevocable element of private growth and self-
sufficiency. For the most part I have thought her departures thrilling:
the month she spent in New England with her grandparents when she
was eight, flying back to Tucson alone; her first period; the first night
she spent (quite chastely) with a boy, and later her first lover; her excellence at calculus; her choice to leave lover and family and lifelong friends
to go to college on the other side of the country. As long as her new
flights give her joy, I rejoice. Where I balk—and balk badly—is at those
junctures where the growing hurts her.

One night a couple of winters ago, I woke from heavy early sleep
to a young man standing in the dark by my bed: David, Anne's boyfriend. "Mrs. Mairs," he whispered, "I think you'd better come. Anne
is drunk and she's really sick and I think you should take care of her."
Clearly David wasn't drunk, hadn't been at the same party, he explained,
but had met up with Anne afterward. He'd taken her to a friend's house,
and though Chris wasn't at home, his mother had kindly taken them in,
given them some tea, let Anne throw up in her toilet. But it was getting

late, and David had a deadline. He had to bring Anne home, but he didn't dare leave her alone.

I hauled myself out of bed and padded to the other end of the cold house, where Anne was in her bathroom washing her face. When she heard my voice, she hissed, "David. I'll kill you," then came out and burst into tears. I sent David along as I held and rocked her, listening to her wretched tale. She certainly was drunk. The fumes rising from my sodden lap were enough to make me tiddly. Gradually I got her quieted and tucked into bed. The next day she felt suitably miserable. To this day she prefers milk to alcohol.

The children were surprised that I wasn't angry about this episode.   *30* In a way I was surprised myself. After all, I had forbidden Anne to drink alcohol outside our house, and she had disobeyed me. Wasn't anger the appropriate response to a disobedient child? But though I specialize in appropriate responses, I did not feel angry. Instead, I felt overwhelmingly sad. For days I was stabbed to the heart by the thought of Anne reeling and stumbling along a darkened street, her emotions black and muddled, abandoned by the group of nasty little boys who had given her beer and vodka and then gone off to have some other fun.

By that one act she stripped me of whatever vestiges of magical thinking I was clinging to about mothers and daughters. Until then, I think, I had still believed that through my wisdom and love I could protect her from the pains I had endured as a child. Suddenly my shield was in tatters. It was a thing of gauze and tissue anyway. She has taught me the bitterest lesson in child-rearing I've yet had to learn: that she will have pain, must have it if she is to get to—and through—this place I am now and the places to which I have yet to go. For, as Juliet Mitchell writes, "pain and lack of satisfaction are the point, the triggers that evoke desire," that essential longing which marks our being in the world, both Anne's and mine, as human.

In teaching me to be her mother, Anne has, among all her other gifts, given me my own mother in ways that have often surprised me. For, as the French theorist Julia Kristeva writes in *Desire in Language,* "By giving birth, the woman enters into contact with her mother; she becomes, she is her own mother, they are the same continuity differentiating itself." Old rebellions have softened, old resentments cooled, now that I see my mother stereoscopically, the lens of motherhood superimposed on that of daughterhood. Every child, I'm sure, takes stern and secret vows along these lines: "When I grow up, I'm never going to make my child clean her room every Saturday, wear orange hair ribbons, babysit her sister, eat pea soup . . ."; and every mother must experience those moments of startlement and sometimes horror when she opens her mouth and hears issue forth not her own voice but the voice of her mother. Surprisingly often, I have found, my mother's voice speaks something that I, as a mother, want to say. I can remember that, when I had accepted a date with Fred—squat, chubby, a little loud, a French kisser, the bane of my high-school love life—and then got a better offer, Mother told me I had only two choices, to go with Fred or to stay home. I vowed then that I would never interfere with my child's social life. But I have had occasion to issue the same injunction, not because I can't tell where my mother ends and I begin, nor because I want Anne to suffer the same horrors I endured in the course of becoming a woman, but because I believe that the habit of courtesy toward one's fellow creatures is more durable than a fabulous night at the prom. Mother may have thought so too.

I gave Mother more trouble throughout my years at home than Anne has given me because, through some psychic and/or biochemical aberration, I was a depressive, though neither she nor I knew so at the time. I recognized that my behavior was erratic and that she got very angry with me for it. What I didn't see, and maybe she didn't either, was that behind her anger lay the anxiety and frustration caused by her helplessness to protect me from my pain. When, finally, I cracked up sufficiently to be sent to a mental hospital, I sensed that she was blaming herself for my troubledness (and no wonder in the disastrous wake of Freud), and I felt impatient with her for believing such silliness. But she was only exhibiting that reflexive maternal guilt which emerges at the infant's first wail: "I'm sorry. I'm sorry. I'm sorry I pushed you from this warm womb into the arms of strangers, me among them. I'm sorry I can't keep you perfectly full, perfectly dry, perfectly free from gas and fear, perfectly, perfectly happy." Any mother knows that if she could do these things, her infant would die more surely than if she covered its face with a rose-printed pillow. Still, part of her desire is to prevent the replication of desire.

Because I knew I had so often infuriated and wearied her, when I left for college I thought only of Mother's relief, never of the possibility that she might miss me. Why should she? The house was still crammed without me, my sister Sally still there, and my stepfather and the babies, and my grandmother too, not to mention an elderly Irish setter and a marmalade cat. As soon as I'd gone, Mother bought a dishwasher, and I figured that took care of any gap I'd left. Not until Anne began the process of selecting a college, finding a summer job in Wisconsin, packing away her mementoes, filling her suitcases did I think that Mother's first-born daughter (and not just a pair of hands in the dishpan) had once left her, and she must have grieved at the separation too. I love to visit her now because I know at last that she is delighted to have me there— not just glad of the company—but warmed and entertained by *me*, one of the daughters who raised her.

I am aware, too, that she once raised a mother, Granna, who lived *35* with us for many years. And Granna raised a mother, Grandma Virchow, with whom she and Mother lived for many years. And Grandma must have raised a mother as well, left behind in Germany in the 1890s, who must herself have raised a mother. "For we think back through our mothers if we are women," writes Virginia Woolf in *A Room of One's Own*. Anne has helped me in that backward dreaming. When she tells me that she doesn't plan to have children, I feel sad, but not because I won't have grandchildren. I mean, I'd welcome them, but I have quite enough characters populating my life to keep me entertained. Rather, I would like her to have this particular adventure, this becoming that a daughter forces.

Overall, I think Anne has done a pretty good job with me. Even without encouragement, in a society that doesn't consider her task authentic, she's done her share of leaning and hauling, shaping me to her needs, forcing me to learn and practice a role I have often found wearying and frightening. Maybe some women are mothers by nature, needing only an infant in their arms to bloom. I'm not. I've needed a lot of nurture. And still I hate it sometimes, especially when she makes me into an authoritarian ogre rumbling disapproval (just as I did to Mother, oh, how many times?). But she's firm and often fair. She doesn't coddle me. Years ago, before I got my brace, I used to have a lot of trouble putting on my left shoe and she would help me with it; the right shoe she'd hand me, saying, "You can do this one yourself." But on my birthday she bakes me lemon bread and, when I ask her what I smell, tells me she's washing dishes in lemon-scented detergent. I believe her and so am surprised by my birthday party. She is tolerant when I stamp my feet (figuratively speaking—if I really stamped my feet I'd fall in a heap and then we'd both get the giggles) and refuse to let her take my peach-colored gauze shirt to Honduras. But she is severe about suicide attempts. She has no use for my short stories, in which she says nothing ever happens, but she likes my essays, especially the ones she appears in, and sometimes my poems. She admires my clothing (especially my peach-colored gauze shirt), my hair, my cooking, but not my taste in music or in men. When my black cat, Bête Noire, the beast of my heart, was killed, she let me weep, hunched over, my tears splashing on the linoleum, and she never said, "Don't cry."

Before long Anne will have to consider the job done. A daughter can't spend a lifetime raising her mother any more than a mother can spend a lifetime raising her daughter; they both have other work to get on with. I can remember the liberating moment when I recognized that it was no longer my task to educate my mother in the ways of the real world; she'd just have to make the best of what she'd learned and muddle along on her own. Mother muddles well. I like to think because I gave her a good start. Anne deserves such a moment.

And I deserve her having it. It's what we've come this way for. Last summer, when George was visiting his parents, his mother sighed, "Life is never so good after the children have gone." George is her only child, and he's been gone for twenty-five years. I can't imagine sustaining a quarter of a century of anticlimax. Anne and I both confront transformation into women with wholly new sets of adventures as we learn to live well apart. I feel pretty well prepared now for muddling along on my own.

☐ *Outward Exploration: Discussion*

1. What is the major concept being explored in this essay? How do you know?
2. What strategies does Mairs use to develop her points?
3. Where did the idea of bad mothering originate?
4. What does she mean by the idea of a child raising a parent?
5. Explain Mairs's concept of birth.
6. Explain Mairs's extended definition of symbiosis.
7. How does Mairs's personal experience differ from what the books tell her about the mother–daughter relationship?
8. What goal did Anne and her mother share? Why was it difficult to achieve?
9. Explain Mairs's use of the Honduras example.
10. What new insights into her own mother does Mairs have after raising Anne (in paragraphs 32–35)?

☐ *Outward Exploration: Writing*

1. Using Mairs's mixture of research and personal experience, write an essay about the experience of raising your father or your mother.
2. Analyze some relationship other than parent/child using Mairs's mixture of research and personal experience.

☐ *Style*

Pick two passages in which Mairs integrates a quotation from a source into her own prose. Find a source (it can be Mairs's essay); then write two sentences, each of which integrates a quotation in the same way that Mairs does.

Unlearning Romance

GLORIA STEINEM

☐ *Inward Exploration*

Write at least one paragraph giving your definition of romance. What are its characteristics? How does it make you feel?

"I *cannot* live without my life! I *cannot* live without my soul!"
—HEATHCLIFF

"Nelly, I *am* Heathcliff!"
—CATHERINE

What do you remember about the story of *Wuthering Heights,* whether from the novel, the classic movie, or the myth that has become a part of our culture?

I remember the yearning of two people to be together—and the intensity, the merging, the loss of boundaries when they were. There was an obsessiveness and a sense of fate about these two lifelong lovers that made even the romantic yearnings of Romeo and Juliet seem pale.

In Emily Brontë's novel, their romance begins when they are children. From the moment Heathcliff, a dark-skinned urchin found wandering the streets of Liverpool, is rescued and brought home as an adopted servant by little Catherine's father, they are soul mates. But divided as they grow up by chasms of class and race, their union as adults seems so impossible that Catherine agrees to marry a kind and wealthy neighbor. Humiliated by her idea that marriage to him would "degrade" her, Heathcliff runs away to sea, and Catherine nearly dies from a fever that is an almost literal lovesickness. By the time a newly prosperous Heathcliff returns three years later, it is too late: Catherine has married Edgar Linton. Heathcliff rages, swears vengeance, and marries Linton's sister to get control of her property and to spite the family—but Catherine knows she is the cause of all this suffering. Torn between her alter ego and her kind husband, and also pregnant, she falls ill but lives long enough to give birth to a daughter.

It's one of the departures of this novel that its heroine dies halfway through it. We then see almost twenty years of Heathcliff raging, mourning, and trying to control everything Catherine ever touched. When he finally succeeds, he seems to will himself to die, as if this obsession had been the only thing keeping him alive. At his request, he is buried next to "my Cathy" at the edge of the moors where they once roamed happily as children, with the facing sides of their coffins cut away so nothing will separate them for eternity.

When this magical novel was first published under the pen name of Ellis Bell in 1847, English critics were shocked by its intimate, romantic focus; a departure from the big canvas, many characters, and broad issues that characterized the Victorian novel. When the author was revealed to be the reclusive daughter of a country clergyman, a woman who had died at thirty from consumption and what we would now call anorexia, and who had little experience of life apart from what she had gleaned from voluminous reading, there began generations of scholarly efforts to understand how such a woman could have produced this masterful novel—the first in English, one critic was to say a century later, "which invites the same kind of attention that we give to *Macbeth*."[1] The most fervent part of the search was for the man who was the model for the passionate, brooding, and very "masculine" Heathcliff.

Some literary investigators theorized that Emily Brontë must have carried on an affair with one of her father's curates, almost the only unrelated men around, though there was no evidence for it. Others thought that, like her contemporary Charles Dickens, she had observed a variety of lives around her, copied down character names from gravestones, and stitched together a novelistic quilt from scraps of reality. Still others assumed that Heathcliff's excesses had been copied from Emily's tormented brother, Branwell, who died young from an excess of gin and opium. Whatever his source in reality, many called her an immoral woman for including such a character as Heathcliff in her novel at all. As one scholarly introduction to *Wuthering Heights* admitted: "Those critics who feel compelled to 'explain' a work of art by tracing it to its origins and who assume that the imagination simply adds up experiences in the external world are ill at ease with this novel."[2]

Only when the most recent wave of feminism brought a less traditional view of women's inner lives into the mainstream of criticism did there begin to be a body of scholars who believed *Wuthering Heights* could have come from one isolated woman's imagination. Long ago, she had given us a major clue when she said, in the guise of Catherine, "I *am* Heathcliff." Emily Brontë was *both* the capricious, suffering girl who could not escape the restrictions of a female life, and the dark, adventurous, rebellious outsider. Like each of our true selves, her nature was *both* "masculine" and "feminine," but unlike most of us, she lived in such isolation that, far from being handicapped, she seems to have preserved more of that wholeness. Growing up outside schools and conventional society, choosing to be reclusive even by the standards of her own isolated family, she was free to commune with nature on the moors, to turn inward, to learn from an inner universe. Though she read a great deal—novels, poetry, and the many political journals her father brought into the house—she missed the social training that convinces women we must not identify with men—and vice versa.

As her older and more gregarious sister, Charlotte Brontë, explained about both Emily and their younger sister, Anne, who also died young: "Nether Emily nor Anne was learned; they had no thought of filling their pitchers at the wellspring of other minds; they always wrote from the impulse of nature, the dictates of intuition."[3]

But it was in Emily that "masculine" and "feminine" seemed most perfectly blended; Emily who was the most creative of a gifted family; and Emily in whom Charlotte, herself to become the author of *Jane Eyre* and other classic novels, found endless fascination. "In Emily's nature," Charlotte wrote, "the extremes of vigour and simplicity seemed to meet. Under an . . . unpretending outside, lay a secret power and fire that might have informed the brain and kindled the veins of a hero." This fascination began the moment Charlotte found Emily's secret stash of poems and persuaded her retiring sister to let them be published under a pseudonym. As Charlotte later explained, "Something more than surprise seized me,—a deep conviction that these were not common effusions, or at all like the poetry women generally write. I thought them condensed and terse, vigorous and genuine. To my ear, they had also had a peculiar music—wild, melancholy, and elevating." Her obsession with Emily's enigmatic strength and independent spirit continued long past her sister's death from consumption. After watching Emily hasten her demise by refusing to eat, a means she had often used to gain control over her otherwise dependent life, Charlotte wrote: "Never in all her life had she lingered over any task that lay before her. . . . She made haste to leave us. Yet, while physically she perished, mentally she grew stronger. . . . I have seen nothing like it; but indeed, I have never seen her parallel in anything. Stronger than a man, simpler than a child, her nature stood alone."[4]

A few years later, when *Wuthering Heights* became popular enough   *10* to be reissued in a new edition, Charlotte wrote a preface in which she tried to disarm its critics by first joining their disapproval of its tortured hero ("Whether it is right or advisable to create beings like Heathcliff, I do not know: I scarcely think it is"), then defending her sister by explaining, "The writer who possesses the creative gift owns something of which he is not always master—something that, at times, strangely wills and works for itself." Heathcliff, she makes clear, is "a man's shape animated by demon life." That demon lived within her quiet sister, who "rarely crossed the threshold of home."

Charlotte also defended Emily for endowing Catherine's husband with such "feminine" traits as "constancy and tenderness."

> Some people will think these qualities do not shine so well incarnate in a man as they would do in a woman, but Ellis Bell [Emily's pseudonym] could never be brought to comprehend

this notion: nothing moved her more than any insinuation that the faithfulness and clemency, the long-suffering and loving-kindness which are esteemed virtues in the daughters of Eve, become foibles in the sons of Adam.

Clearly, Emily believed in the presence of *all* human qualities in both men and women. At the very end of the novel, when Catherine's daughter marries a cousin raised by Heathcliff, thus uniting the two families he had sought to divide and destroy, the union seems to symbolize Emily's hope for future wholeness in both women and men. The romance between Catherine and Heathcliff had been the result of an inner void within each of them, and the story tells of their impossible effort to fill it with the body and soul of the other. Indeed, in Heathcliff, Emily created the perfect vision of a self in which the "masculine" is totally bereft of the "feminine": energetic, focused, strong-willed, controlling, even violent, unable to empathize beyond his own boundaries or to love without possessing. Catherine embodied the fate of the "feminine" without the "masculine": vulnerable, diffused, too connected, more aware of the needs around her than of her own.

In Emily herself, of course, there were both; yet this unity was forbidden. The bond between the lovers who were born of her imagination, as poet and theorist Adrienne Rich has written, "is the archetypal bond between the split fragments of the psyche, the masculine and feminine elements ripped apart and longing for reunion."[5]

No wonder the romance of *Wuthering Heights* endures—as do romantic myths in almost every culture. Indeed, the more patriarchal and gender-polarized a culture is, the more addicted to romance. These myths embody our yearning to be whole.

No wonder romance so often begins at a physical distance or across a psychic chasm of class and race,° and thrives on death and separation.   15

Emily Brontë may have had in mind a racial distance greater than that between the gently bred Catherine and a "dark-skinned gypsy," as Heathcliff was described. Jamaican-American writer Michelle Cliff points out in her unpublished essay, "Caliban's Daughter," that Liverpool was a center of the slave trade, where discarded Africans, perhaps also children fathered by slave traders, lived in the streets. Catherine's father brought home this boy who was "dark as if it came from the devil" and speaking "some gibberish that nobody could understand" only after he had unsuccessfully "enquired for its owner." Later, when Heathcliff runs away to become rich enough to marry Catherine, what trade other than slave ships could have earned him such a fortune in three years? And if that self-betrayal was the source of his wealth, no wonder he was in such pain when he returned to find that even this blood money couldn't give him Catherine. Perhaps Emily Brontë, wandering over moors she must have known were part of a slave trader's estate, was drawing parallels between a Heathcliff who could be bought (and forced to sell others) and a Catherine who could be sold in marriage. Or perhaps as an outsider by sex who had written imaginary stories about Africa as a child, she was simply finding within herself the emotions of an outsider by race—just as Aphra Behn, the first professional woman writer in England, had done almost two hundred years earlier.

Projecting our lost qualities onto someone else can be done more easily from a distance.

No wonder romance grows weaker with closeness, dailiness, and familiarity. *No one can be or give to us the rest of our unique self.*

No wonder many women need romance more than men do. Since most human qualities are labeled "masculine," and only a few are "feminine"—and even those are marginalized—*women have an even greater need to project life-giving parts of themselves onto another human being.*

No wonder that, while it lasts, romance brings such an explosive feeling of melting, merging, and losing boundaries. *We are making love to the rest of ourselves.*

Do you fall in love when you're feeling vulnerable or not so good about yourself? When you fall *out* of love, do you "crash," as if you had been on a drug? Have you noticed that friendship, shared values, working together, almost *anything* is more likely to lead to a lasting love than the usual romance—yet you still find yourself thinking *this* romance will be different? Are you waiting to make basic decisions in your life because those should be determined by a future partner? If you already have a partner, do you spend more time thinking about pleasing and/or improving him or her than pleasing and/or improving yourself? When you're not in a romance, are you prone to too much eating or drinking or other addictions? If the person you are in love with would only change or solve his or her problems, do you feel your problems would be solved, too? Do you feel a "rush" of adrenaline and power when a coveted person agrees to go to bed with you (more usual for men) or professes love for you (more usual for women)? In general, is your sense of well-being determined more by the state of your love life than by your own life?

If you can answer yes to any of those questions—as so many of us   *20* can—then you are still playing a role in some version of the classic script in which romance blooms at a distance, bursts into obsession, and then diminishes into ordinariness—or perhaps unrequited pain. In the true sense of the word's root, *addicere,* "to give oneself up" or "to devote or surrender oneself to something habitually or obsessively," romance can become an addiction, and this cycle can repeat itself again and again. That twelve-step program originated by and for alcoholics, and then expanded to include many other addictions, has now been adapted by those addicted to sex and romance.

But like other addicts, many of us are still in denial: we still believe we can find the rest of ourselves in a foreign substance; that is, in the body and mind of another person. But we didn't invent this dilemma.

Think about it: On the one hand, each of us is born with a full circle of human qualities, and also with a unique version of them. On the other hand, societies ask us to play totalitarian gender roles that divide labor, assign behavior, provide the paradigm for race and class, and are so accepted that they may be seen as part of nature. Societies have been so intent on creating an elaborate difference where none exists that in many languages, even inanimate objects are genderized; thus, one kind of pen may be "feminine" (*la plume*) and another "masculine" (*le stylo*). Yet despite all of these pervasive efforts to categorize and limit everyone and everything, the little boy who is ridiculed for crying "like a girl" doesn't stop feeling sad, he just buries that emotion; and the little girl who is punished for willfulness as a "tomboy" just takes that spirit underground. Later, since both have been told that some parts of themselves are appropriate only to the "opposite sex," they will look for them in other people. In search of inner wholeness, they will try to absorb and possess someone else as Catherine and Heathcliff did—and as you and I probably have done, too.

This polarization of "feminine" and "masculine," this internal mutilation of our whole selves, would be cruel enough if its effects went no further, but the two halves aren't really "halves" at all. Male dominance means that admired qualities are called "masculine" and are more plentiful, while "feminine" ones are not only fewer but also less valued. Thus, boys as a group have higher self-esteem because they are literally allowed more of a self *and* because the qualities they must suppress are less desirable, while girls as a group have lower self-esteem because they are expected to suppress more of themselves *and* because society denigrates what is left. Once adolescence and hormones hit, this lack of a true self in both sexes, this feeling of being incomplete and perhaps also ashamed of parts of oneself that "belong" to the opposite sex, combines with society's intensified gender expectations to make many of us construct a false social persona—in a big way. The boy who has been allowed to retain more than the usual amount of self-esteem by his upbringing may resist this tendency, or only pretend to conform; especially if he has an adult model to follow, support for some "unmasculine" talent, or perhaps a racial, sexual, or other status that strengthens an "outsider" identity. The girl with exceptional self-esteem may get away with such "masculine" qualities as assertiveness and tomboyish behavior—after all, imitation is the sincerest form of flattery, so it's more okay for girls to imitate boys than vice versa—as long as she compensates by becoming a female impersonator in romantic and other social areas. But with low self-esteem, both males and females are likely to seek refuge and approval in exaggerated versions of their gender roles, and thus to become even less complete as they grow up. Inflexibility, dogmatism, competitiveness, aggression, distance from any female quality or person, homophobia, even cruelty and violence, become the classic gender masks of low self-esteem in men. Submissiveness, dependency, need for male approval, fear of conflict, self-blame, and inability to express anger are classic gender masks of low self-esteem in women.

This means that, with low self-esteem, men and women grow more polarized and have more suppressed parts of themselves to project onto others. They then become the objects of an affair, romance, "falling" in love—all the words we instinctively use to describe the addictive "rush" and withdrawal of adrenaline that is so different from the steady well-being of love. In a survey of 400 U.S. psychiatrists by *Medical Aspects of Human Sexuality,* for instance, the majority reported that both women and men with low self-esteem were more likely to be promiscuous, to have difficulty finding fulfillment in sexual relationships, and to be *less* likely to fall *deeply* in love.[6] Even among women and men with healthy self-esteem, a temporary setback or insecurity can increase the appeal of romance, whether it's the scared young man going off to war who falls in love with someone he's only known a few days, or the scared pregnant woman who falls in love with her obstetrician. Indeed, any strong gender trigger may create a romantic chimera for a while, from the woman who gets a crush on a man because he leads masterfully on the dance floor, to the man who falls in love with a secretary who is being paid to support him.

In her novel *The Company She Keeps,* Mary McCarthy described this phenomenon in her heroine: "Now for the first time she saw her own extremity, saw that it was some failure in self-love that obliged her to snatch blindly at the love of others, hoping to love herself through them, borrowing their feelings, as the moon borrowed light. She herself was a dead planet."

Playwright Sherwood Anderson confessed the same thing from a man's point of view: "I've never been able to work without a woman to love. Perhaps I'm cruel . . . I'm like an Irish peasant taking potatoes out of the ground . . . I take from her. I know damned well I don't give enough."[7]

But if romance has its source in an incompleteness of self, it's unlikely to turn into love: the neediness and low self-esteem of the lovers is the worst adversary of anything deeper and more lasting. As Linda Sanford and Mary Ellen Donovan report in *Women and Self-Esteem,* low self-esteem is perhaps the single greatest barrier to intimacy. It makes a woman "terrified of letting someone get too close lest they discover the real her and reject her."[8] And, of course, men experience the same terror, and often an added fear that dependence on a woman or the discovery of "feminine" feelings within themselves will undermine their carefully constructed facade of manliness.

Obviously, jealousy also springs from these feelings of inadequacy and incompleteness. It increases as self-esteem diminishes. The more incomplete we feel, the more obsessed we become with owning someone on whom we've projected all our missing qualities, hence the more jealous we become. Yet gender masks of low self-esteem also make us feel more interchangeable with any other woman or man.

This cycle of gender roles, low self-esteem, romance, jealousy, lack of love and intimacy, even lower self-esteem, *more* exaggerated gender

roles, and so on, can be dangerous in every way. As four family therapists found in a study of abusive relationships, it is precisely when men
and women conform to traditional roles most rigidly that abuse is most
likely to occur. In their words: "*Abusive relationships exemplify, in extremis, the stereotypical gender arrangements that structure intimacy between
men and women generally.*" And, of course, this violence also has the
larger political purpose of turning half the population into a support
system for the other half. It polices and perpetuates gender politics by
keeping the female half fearful of the moods and approval of the male
half. In fact, patriarchy *requires* violence or the subliminal threat of violence in order to maintain itself. Furthermore, the seeming naturalness
of gender roles makes male/female violence seem excusable, even inevitable. As G. H. Hatherill, Police Commander of London, put it, "There
are only about twenty murders a year in London and not all are serious—some are just husbands killing their wives."[10]

Romance itself serves a larger political purpose by offering at least a
temporary reward for gender roles and threatening rebels with loneliness and rejection. It also minimizes the very antipatriarchal and revolutionary possibility that women and men will realize each other's shared
humanity when we are together physically for the sexual and procrea-
tive purposes society needs. Finally, it privatizes our hopes and distracts
us from making societal changes. The Roman "bread and circuses" way
of keeping the masses happy—and the French saying that "marriage is
the only adventure open to the middle class"—might now be updated.
The circus of romance distracts us with what is, from society's point of
view, a safe adventure. When it fails, we blame only ourselves.

Perhaps the greatest testimony to the power of this "feminine/
masculine" romantic paradigm is that even same-sex couples are not
immune to it. Though lesbians and gay men often create more equal
partnerships that opposite-sex couples would do well to learn from—
especially now that both feminism and the gay movement have challenged old gender roles—we are all living in the same culture, and most
of us were born into families where this pattern was assumed to be
the only one. Sometimes, gender roles produce an exaggerated version
known as doubling, in which two men together may become twice
as aggressive, unempathetic, unavailable for intimacy but promiscuous
about sex; or two women together may become twice as passive, dependent on one another, and focused on intimacy, with or without sex. For
all the internal and external sufferings of same-gender couples in a biased
culture, however, at least society doesn't polarize the partners when they
leave home every day, and that in itself allows more freedom to explore
new forms of balance.

In short, the internal wholeness that allows one to love both one's
self and another, freely and joyously, is hard to find anywhere. On the
other hand, the personal wreckage caused by romantic obsession is a

30

feature of our everyday landscape. We have only to open a newspaper in any country of the world to read about someone who has been murdered, beaten, or imprisoned in what is known as a "crime of passion." In more than twenty years of speaking on campuses here and in other countries, for instance, I've yet to find one where, within the memory of current students, there wasn't at least one young woman murdered by a jealous lover. Statistically, the man most likely to physically attack or even murder a woman is not a stranger, but someone to whom she is romantically attached. The most dangerous situation for a woman is not an unknown man in the street, or even the enemy in wartime, but a husband or lover in the isolation of their own home. Though women mainly become violent in self-defense or in defense of their children, the power of romantic obsession is so great—and women are so much more subject to it—that even "feminine" nonviolent conditioning can be overcome. When women *do* commit violent crimes, they are even more likely than a man's to be attributable to romance rather than to economics, whether that means the rare crime in which a woman kills out of jealousy or the more frequent one in which a woman is an accessory to a crime initiated by her husband or lover.

What's wrong with romance is neatly summed up by the Valentine's Day 1991 statistics given to me by a judge in Tennessee. In his county courthouse that services Knoxville and environs, there were on that one day: 30 applications for marriage licenses, 60 applications for divorce, and 90 applications for orders of protection against violent spouses.

Will self-esteem cause the withering away of romance? Yes—but only in its current form. After all, romance is one additional very important thing: the most intense form of curiosity. If we weren't so needy, so full of illusions about a magic rescue, so hooked on trying to *own* someone—in other words, if the conscious goal of romance were stretching our understanding of ourselves and others, and not, as it was for Catherine and Heathcliff, looking for the completion of our souls—romance could be a deep, intimate, sensual, empathetic way of learning: of seeing through someone else's eyes, feeling with their nerve endings, absorbing another culture or way of life from the inside, stretching our boundaries, and bringing into ourselves a wider view of the world. If there were equality of power and high self-esteem among women and men, or between two lovers of the same gender, both could have the pleasure of learning and of teaching in this all-five-senses way—without feeling incomplete, angry, or abandoned when romance has run its course.

In the meantime, romance remains among the experiences most written about but least understood. But it's beginning to be demythologized and taken more seriously. Psychologist Charlotte Davis Kasl compares its symptoms ("mood swings . . . distortions of reality") to those of manic-depressive disorders.[11] In many cultures it is "a sacred form of insanity, as sacred as cows are in India," as family therapist Frank Pitt-man has written.[12] Like every other kind of illness, romance tells us a lot about what is lacking in us—and what to do about it. If, for example, we think about episodes from our own personal romantic histories, we can learn what we're missing, and then consider what we need to do to grow and change. I've contributed a memory of mine in the hope that it will lead you to meditate on one of your own.

Like Heathcliff as a lost child and Catherine as a six-year-old, or like Dante who fell in love with the real Beatrice when both were only eight, children, too, are vulnerable to romance. They're too young for sex and hormones to have much to do with it, but not too young to be restricted by gender and so begin to yearn for wholeness. I remember spending second-grade recesses watching a kind, quiet, dark-haired boy as he ran in the cold with no mittens and a hand-me-down coat. It's the first time I remember feeling "in love," and we exchanged serious valentines. Only now do I understand that I was watching a part of myself race across that playground reserved for boys while girls played quietly by a wall, or that his poverty made him an outsider, and therefore someone I could identify with. Only now do I notice that this first romance came just after a teacher had insisted I could not possibly have written my Thanksgiving poem because its refrain (something like *Not only for the dead but for the living*) was too "adult."

I realize that I kept on falling in love with men who were outsiders, particularly those doing work I longed for myself but assumed I could only do by helping them. I also fell in love with their families, since I was longing for parents, too. Fortunately, I chose kind men with good hearts who loved me back—whether due to good luck or the self-respect my mother had tried to instill in me—and so we remained friends even after the intensity of romance was gone. In this way, I proceeded through college and beyond, trying on the name and life of each man I thought I might marry—thought I would *have* to marry eventually if I was to be a whole person—and acquired one of women's survival skills: getting men to fall in love with us, a form of self-protection that is also a female version of men's sexual conquering. (I'm sure that, as long as shopping and romance are two of women's few paths to a sense of power and well-being in this culture, both will continue to be addictive—and for the same reason.) But since we really believed then that a husband would decide the rest of our lives, marriage became a decision almost impossible to make. If it closed off all other decisions, then it was like a little death. *I'll definitely get married,* I kept thinking, *but not right now. There's this one thing I want to do first . . .* Fortunately, feminism came along to help me and millions of others try to become ourselves, with or without marriage; to understand, in the brilliant phrase of some anonymous feminist, that we could "become the men we wanted to marry." I realized that everyone didn't *have* to live the same way, and this led to a more personal discovery: *I was happy.* If life is what happens while we are making other plans, I had found work I loved and a chosen family of friends while I was waiting for a mythical future.

But sometimes in the middle of life, as Dante said, we come upon "a shadowed forest . . . dense and difficult." That's where I found myself at the end of my forties. Having chosen a particularly insecure, stretched-thin kind of life in a movement trying to change the oldest power difference, but with relatively little power to do it, I had spent most of two decades getting on a treadmill of traveling, organizing, fund-raising, lobbying, working on *Ms.* magazine, and generally doing a triage of emergencies every morning—then falling off the treadmill into bed every night only to get back on it the next day. Though I was privileged to be working in this movement that had given me life and friends I loved, I had less and less time to replenish lost energy—or even to pick up my dry cleaning. Pressure is cumulative. In retrospect, I was redoing the grisly experiment in which a frog, dropped in hot water, jumps out and saves itself; but a frog put in water that is heated *very gradually* stays there and boils to death. After many years in varying kinds of hot water, I was well on my way to becoming the second frog.

Into this time of exhaustion came a man different from others I had known. Instead of working in fields where progress was measured by change in people, he lived in a world where progress was measured in numbers and things. Contrary to my habit of keeping former lovers as chosen family, which seemed odd to many people, his alienation from women who had been his important romances seemed odd to me. Unlike other men in my life, who were as interested in my work as I was in theirs, and who took as much pleasure in finding books, articles, or movies that I might like as I did in doing the same for them, this man answered questions about his own life and childhood, but didn't know how to ask them of someone else.

On the other hand, he had traits I found magnetic. For one thing, he had enormous energy and a kind of Little-Engine-That-Could attitude toward his work that I found very moving. Being work obsessed, too, he didn't mind all my traveling and crazy schedules. For another, he made every social decision (via his staff), so all I had to do was show up, look appropriate, listen, relax at dinners, dance, laugh at his wonderfully told jokes—whatever was on his agenda. I found this very restful. Since I had been helplessly recreating my caretaking pattern left over from childhood, he seemed the perfect answer: someone I *couldn't* take care of. For a third, he was miserable and said he wanted to change his life, to use his considerable power in new and creative ways. Since I was hooked on helping people change as a way of proving that *I* was alive and valuable, a man who said he was miserable was irresistible. Finally, I was just so . . . *tired.* When I arrived at the airport late one night to find that he had sent a car, its sheltering presence loomed out of all proportion. Remember the scene in *Bus Stop* when Marilyn Monroe, a desperate singer in a poor café, wraps herself in the warm, rescuing skeepskin jacket of her cowboy lover? Well, that was the way I felt sinking into that car.

So I reverted to a primordial skill that I hadn't used since feminism had helped me to make my own life: getting a man to fall in love with me. As many women can testify, this is alarmingly easy, providing you're willing to play down who you are and play up who he wants you to be. In this case, I was aided by my travel and his work and social schedule, which left us with little time to find out how very different we were. And also by something I didn't want to admit: a burnout and an erosion of self so deep that outcroppings of a scared sixteen-year-old had begun to show through. Like a friend who lost weight and, with the burning away of her body fat, reexperienced an anesthetic that had been stored in it from an operation years before, I had lost so much energy and hope that I was reexperiencing romantic rescue fantasies that had been forgotten long ago.

The only problem was that, having got this man to fall in love with an inauthentic me, I had to *keep on* not being myself. Thus, I had to ignore the fact that the cost of a casually purchased painting on his wall was equal to what I had come up with for movement groups in years of desperate fund-raising—and was by a famously misogynist artist at that. I had to suppress the thought that his weekend house cost more than several years' worth of funds for the entire women's movement in this country—and maybe a couple of other countries besides. If I was to be his companion, I had to ignore how obliterated most of my chosen family felt in the company and conversation he enjoyed; indeed, how marginalized they made me feel, too. If I was to be properly appreciative for the advice he gave to me and some of the women I worked with— advice I'm sure he thought of as helpful—I had to forget that, like a gourmet recipe for people with no groceries, it had no practical application. Indeed, even the laughter we first so delightfully shared turned out to be generated by very different senses of humor: his centered around jokes he collected in a notebook and recited wonderfully, complete with ethnic accents; mine was improvised and had a you-had-to-be-there perishability.

I'm sure you know what's coming. So did all my friends. But it took me much longer. Having for the first time in my life made a lover out of a man who wasn't a friend first—my mistake, not his, since I was the one being untrue to myself—I had a huge stake in justifying what I had done. When he supported the same policies and hierarchies that I was working to change, I thought: Nobody said we had to have the same views. When I told him about a trip I'd made to raise a few thousand dollars for a battered women's shelter that was about to close down, and he in the next breath celebrated an unexpected six-figure check that, he joked, would buy a good dinner, I said to myself: It's not his fault he can't empathize—and besides, everyone can change. When a small inner voice began to miss the comfort and eroticism that comes with empathy and sensuality, I thought: If I treat him as I want to be treated, this can change, too. In other words, I made all the classic errors of romance, including one I'd never made before: loving someone for what *I needed* instead of for what *he was*. Far from being a light in my Dantesque "shadowed forest," this relationship became a final clue that I was really lost.

I got lonely and depressed—and then more lonely and more depressed. When I finally tried to voice these feelings that I'd been having all along but *not* voicing, he got mystified—and then angry. But there's something to be said for hitting bottom: as with swimming, it may be the only way to propel oneself back up again. To quote Dante, let me "retell the good discovered there."

After two years, when my last bit of energy and faith in my own judgment was fast disappearing, I finally got down past the scared sixteen-year-old, and came to a clear childhood voice that actually said, "Are you going to condemn yourself to this?" It was such a surprise that it made me laugh. Of course, my well-socialized adult self ignored it for quite a while—but it was the beginning.

Slowly, I began to realize there might have been a reason why I was attracted to someone so obviously wrong for me. If I had been drawn to a man totally focused on his own agenda, *maybe I needed to have an agenda of my own.* Finally, I began to make time to write. If I had felt comforted by the elaborate organization of his life, *maybe I needed some comfort and organization in my own.* Therefore, I enlisted the help of friends to take the stacks of cardboard boxes out of my apartment and started the long process of making it into a pleasant place to live. I even began to save money for the first time in my life. If I had been drawn to simple-minded fun and dancing, *maybe I should get off the treadmill and ask myself the revolutionary question: What do I enjoy?* Finally, I interrupted my triage of emergencies and started taking the initiative to do a few things I loved. If I had glossed over the world's most obvious differences in values (for instance, he advocated trade with a government I got arrested for protesting), *maybe I should have a more realistic idea of what distances I could bridge.* I began to focus my energy on what I might be able to do—and to question why I was so often drawn to attempting what I couldn't. Finally, if I had been interested for the first time in my life in a man who really didn't know what other people were thinking or feeling, *perhaps I had to face the fact that I had the usually "feminine" disease of being empathy sick—of knowing other people's feelings better than my own.* It was a crucial signal that I needed to look inward for solutions instead of outward—a change of which this book is a part.

And perhaps most of all, if I had fallen in love with a powerful man, I had to realize that I was in mourning for the power women need and rarely have, myself included.

I don't mean to make this a neat ending. Romances don't have them. I had deceived him by deceiving myself, and I'm still working on what I learned. But I do know that I chose an opposite as a dramatic example of what I missed in myself. Even allowing for my dissembling, perhaps that's what he was doing, too.

Clearly, romance can arrive with all its obsession whenever we're feeling incomplete, at any age or station of life—and as I can testify, even when we know better. We hurt both ourselves and other people when we become who they want us to be instead of who we really are. Nonetheless, the prospect of getting unhooked from this obsession sometimes creates as much anxiety as giving up *any* addiction: Where will that "rush" of excitement come from? Who will we become?

I think the truth is that finding ourselves brings more excitement   *50* and well-being than anything romance has to offer, and somewhere, we know that. Think of the joy of self-discovery: solving a problem, making a bookcase, inventing a dance step, losing oneself in a sport, cooking for friends, writing a poem—all by reaching within for a vision and then making it real. As for who we will be, the answer is: We don't know; we *are* on the edge of history. But we do know that growth comes from saying yes to the unknown.

Donna Jensen, a friend and an expert on how we relate to one another—in couples, families, and organizations—gave me this list of past excesses and the golden mean that is the future:

"Masculine" *Extreme*	*Wholeness*	*"Feminine"* *Extreme*
Domineering	Creative	Victimized
Angry	Relaxed	Depressed
Dictates	Invites	Begs or schemes
Knows everything	Curious	Knows nothing
Arrogant	Attentive	Shut down, numb
Out of touch with one's own feelings	Draws self-wisdom from feelings	Overwhelmed by one's own feelings
Unwilling to show weakness	Flexible	Unwilling to show strength
Ignores own mistakes or blames others	Learns from mistakes	Makes excuses or obsesses about mistakes
Feels superior	Feels equal	Feels inferior

When the choice is so clear, who wouldn't say yes to a whole self in the center?

To figure out more personally what you need to do to get there, try this exercise:

Write down—in whatever order or form they come to you—all the things you want in an ideal lover.

Notes

1. G. D. Klingopulos, "The Novel as Dramatic Poem," quoted in Emily Brontë, *Wuthering Heights,* New York: Random House, Modern Library Edition, 1978, p. xvii.

2. Royal A. Gettmann, "Introduction," *Wuthering Heights,* p. ix.

3. Charlotte Brontë, "Biographical Notice of Ellis and Acton Bell," *Wuthering Heights,* pp. xxv–xxvi.

4. Ibid., pp. xxv, xx, and xxiv–xxv.

5. Adrienne Rich, "Jane Eyre: The Temptations of a Motherless Woman," *On Lies, Secrets, and Silence,* New York: W. W. Norton, 1979, p. 90.

6. "Survey: Sex and Self-Esteem," *Medical Aspects of Human Sexuality,* volume 17, number 5, May 1983, pp. 197–211.

7. Helen Handley, editor, *The Lovers' Quotation Book,* Wainscott, New York: Pushcart Press, 1986, p. 63.

8. Linda Sanford and Mary Ellen Donovan, *Women and Self-Esteem,* New York: Anchor/Doubleday, 1984, p. 123.

9. Virginia Goldner, Peggy Penn, Marcia Sheinberg, Gillian Walker, "Love and Violence: Gender Paradoxes in Volatile Attachments," *Family Process,* December 1990, volume 20, number 4, p. 343.

10. Handley, *Lovers' Quotation Book,* p. 45.

11. Charlotte Davis Kasl, *Women, Sex, and Addiction: A Search for Love and Power,* New York: Ticknor & Fields, 1989, p. 130.

12. Frank Pittman, *Private Lies,* New York: W. W. Norton, 1989, p. 183

☐ *Outward Exploration: Discussion*

1. Why does Steinem give us a brief summary of *Wuthering Heights* at the beginning of her essay?

2. According to Steinem, which traits are considered masculine and which feminine?

3. According to Steinem, what's the problem with society pressuring us to suppress some of our human emotions?

4. Explain what she means by the term *romance*.

5. How effective are Steinem's direct addresses to the reader (for example, in paragraph 19)?
6. Why does Steinem quote various writers?
7. Why is romance unlikely to turn into love?
8. What cycle does this suppression of traits (paragraph 22) cause?
9. How effective is her analysis of her relationships (starting in paragraph 36)? Explain.

Outward Exploration: Writing

1. If you have grown in a relationship by saying "yes to the unknown," write an essay about it.
2. Find a text that at least partially illustrates a particular romantic relationship from your past (this can be any kind of text, including a novel, a poem, a television series, a movie, a song). Using Steinem's approach, begin by summarizing the text and then analyze the relationship, making connections where appropriate with the text.
3. Striving for a depth of analysis similar to Steinem's, write an essay about a romance from your past.

Style

Consider the structure of Steinem's essay—she begins with several paragraphs about a text—*Wuthering Heights*—which vividly illustrates romance, then moves to an analysis of romance and society's role in it, sprinkling references to *Wuthering Heights* throughout the essay as a unifying device. In other words, *Wuthering Heights* becomes the touchstone to which she refers several times. Add this structural device of the touchstone to your writing repertoire and use it when appropriate.

6

Exploring Concepts

On some level you can't help but write about **concepts,** those thoughts and general ideas that we infer from specific instances or events. Every essay you've written so far and every episode you've thought about so far has had, at its core, a concept. In earlier chapters, you've been encouraged to explore your thoughts as well as your feelings by starting with yourself, with events, with other people, and with relationships. When we *start with* a concept as the subject for an exploratory essay, the kinds of issues we encounter can sometimes differ from those we find when writing about other subjects. For example, when exploring a concept we need to be very clear about the definitions of important terms. In fact, sometimes a whole essay is an extended definition of one key term. In exploratory essays about concepts, we often resort to various sources for confirmation or for information about points of contention. As our understanding of a concept grows, that concept becomes one of the tools to help us dig even deeper into our present and past experiences. And the more sophisticated and detailed the sources we explore, the deeper and more sophisticated will be our understanding of the concept. Exploring concepts allows us to expand our knowledge by looking outward at sources as well as inward at ourselves.

WRITER-BASED GOALS

There are two writer-based goals for exploring concepts: (1) to learn more about a concept that interests you; (2) to expand your knowledge about yourself. You achieve these goals by expanding your search beyond your personal experience, moving outward to include other sources such as books, articles, newspapers, computer databases, and interviews with experts. Such research deepens your experience of the concept and becomes part of your knowledge of the world. Along the way, you may discover connections between concepts that you never realized existed before, or you may discover that what you thought you believed isn't supported by your own experiences or by those of others. Exploring concepts can be very exciting.

READER-BASED GOALS

There are four reader-based goals for exploring concepts: (1) to deepen your readers' knowledge of the concept; (2) to place your understanding of it in the wider context of the sources that you consulted; (3) to explore your thoughts and feelings about the particular concept; (4) to explain the sources of your understanding (for example, a personal experience, something you read or saw or heard).

THE PROCESS FOR EXPLORING CONCEPTS

As with all exploratory writing, the process for exploring concepts can be exciting. First, find a concept that interests you. It does not have to be one that you believe in; it may simply be one that you want to learn more about or even one that you oppose and wish to explore in order to expose all of its dangerous implications. Second, by thinking and writing, discover what you already know about the concept. Third, explore other sources for additional information you need and to learn how others understand the concept. Once the prewriting is completed, you are ready to draft and revise your essay.

Select an Idea That Interests You

We all have personal definitions of concepts that affect or interest us, even if we haven't verbalized them yet. In fact, putting them into words is one way we learn about ourselves and find out what we really understand. In addition to the idea-generation techniques mentioned in Chapter 1 (for example, freewriting, listing, brainstorming), two other techniques can help prime the pump—"Dictionary Seek-and-Write" and "Titles."

DICTIONARY SEEK-AND-WRITE   With your eyes closed, randomly open a dictionary and place your finger on a page. Whatever word you find under your finger is your topic for this exercise. Write for 10 minutes about that word. Let your mind play. If you find yourself going off on a tangent, follow it since tangents often lead to interesting insights. Sometimes you'll get an "easy" word like *truth* or *justice;* at times, though, you might get unusual words such as *lute* or *repellent* or *splurge.* Whatever the word, try writing about it. If your finger finds a word about which you have nothing to say, however, feel free to select another word (perhaps take the word above or below the original selection, or start all over).

TITLES   Titles is a particularly effective approach because it not only stimulates thinking but also suggests at least a first source to read. The technique is simple but powerful: Use the titles of existing essays to spark your own exploratory writing.

Your task here is not to duplicate or approximate what the original author wrote about a concept. Instead, your task is to find out what you think about the concept. Later you can read the author's essay as part of your research into what other people have thought about it. If a title doesn't apply literally to you, see if it applies figuratively. Suppose that I were using the title of Nancy Mairs's "On Being a Cripple" to spark my writing. I am not a cripple in the literal sense (although I have been in a cast twice). But in the figurative sense I am a cripple (probably we all are in some way). For instance, I'm a "social cripple": In large gatherings of strangers I can't make small talk; I can't ask provocative questions that get other people rambling on about themselves—instead, I stand around holding a glass and wondering when I can politely bolt for the door. In short, taking a title figuratively can be as productive as taking it literally.

SAMPLE OF DIRECTED FREEWRITING   For the sake of illustration, let's select one concept; how we approach defining it will illustrate the process of exploring any concept. Here is a sample of the directed freewriting that I did for the concept of *mothering:*

> *Mothering* is all about the female parent's job. So it is about tasks and doing. What does a mother do? Or is the concept connected somehow to biological birth as well? No, *mothering* is what happens after the birth—the birth itself is something else—maybe just *birthing.* Of course, the opposite is true of fathers. Why do we never say *fathering* or "he *fathered* his son or daughter"— except to mean *impregnating the mother?* Yet she "mothered" her son never means "gave birth to." Apparently there has been no historical equivalent to *mothering* on the part of men, or at least none that society has acknowledged with an official term.
>
> Anyway, *mothering* is the process that follows conception and birth. Usually it has a positive sense—caring for the child, helping him or her, giving advice and support, nurturing. Does it include the idea of *unconditional love?* Does anything include

the idea of *unconditional love?* It is hard for me to see this yet—maybe I'll return to the idea later.

The concept of *mothering* acquires negative connotations if it continues past the point when society assumes the child no longer needs it. Or, at least, no longer needs such attention from his or her actual mother. People certainly say that a man's wife "mothers" him—sometimes that is said as a positive thing about the wife suggesting that she "takes good care of him" and sometimes as a negative thing about the husband suggesting that he's not "man enough" to prevent her from "babying" him—a very negative term for inappropriate mothering. *Attention* is a key idea too, I think, for that can include psychological as well as physical stuff. Maybe most mothers would like to continue mothering when it is no longer appropriate, but most of us have carved out our own lives. When mothers do overstep the boundaries, it might simply be that we don't have that day-to-day connection with them that we did when we were children, so they can't know anymore what is an appropriate area for their attention and what isn't.

Maybe *mothering* is a comfortable and fulfilling role for mothers to play. Perhaps it gives the illusion of protecting the child and keeping the bad things away. Folksy examples abound in TV ads—the whole idea of "Dr. Mom," of mothers putting bandaids on children's skinned knees and cooking that special dinner when the child gets a good report card.

Discover What You Already Know About the Concept

After selecting a concept and getting some of your initial thoughts about it down on paper (or in the computer's memory), discover what you already know about the concept. Such discovery includes at least four elements:

Define the concept clearly and explicitly.

Explore the origins and sources of your definition of the concept.

Explore any experiences from your life that illustrate the concept.

Explore any experiences from the lives of your family or friends that illustrate the concept.

DEFINING THE CONCEPT   There are several strategies of definition. For example, you can write a one-sentence definition of the concept, give examples to illustrate the concept (for instance, my mother, famous mothers in history or literature), trace the roots and history of the word that names the concept, compare and contrast the concept with other concepts (for example, *mothering* with *fathering*), give negative definitions (for example, *mothering* is not *birthing*). A combination of such techniques will often produce an exploratory essay about the concept.

   One-Sentence Definitions.   Any good one-sentence definition accomplishes at least two things: It sets the object to be defined in a context of similar things (the *class* to which it belongs) and then shows how it differs from each of those other things (its *distinguishing characteristics*). Let's say that we want to define the concept *chair*. First, the class. My first thought was that a chair is "a piece of furniture." Okay. But the concept *furniture* includes many objects—for example, beds, sofas, chairs, tables, bureaus, and desks. A more useful (because smaller) class, then, would be "furniture designed for sitting." That eliminates beds, tables, desks, and bureaus.

   We have located the concept *chair* within a workable class that includes only four other items: stools, sofas, love seats, and benches. However, now we need to find the characteristics that separate the chair from those other four items. Often the best method for achieving this is to proceed one item at a time. For example, what separates a chair from a sofa? The latter is designed to hold more than one person whereas a chair is designed to hold only one person. That is our first distinguishing characteristic, and it eliminates everything in the list except *stool*. What separates a chair from a stool? Well, a chair always has a seat and a back; it sometimes has arms; it sometimes has four legs (beanbag chairs, of course, are legless). A stool, on the other hand, has legs but never a back or arms. So our information gathering is complete. We structure the sentence definition by introducing the item to be defined first, then the class to which it belongs, and then the distinguishing characteristics:

> A *chair* is a piece of furniture designed to be sat in by one person; it always has a back and may or may not have arms and legs.

Of course, there are other ways of setting up the sentence, ways that are less direct but still effective. For example, we might use **subordinate clauses:**

> *Although designed to be sat in by only one person,* a chair can sometimes hold two persons *if one sits on top of the other since the chair's back prevents the two from toppling backwards.*

As you can see from this rather silly example, the first subordinate clause provides basic information and the other subordinating clauses provide additional information.

   Another structural device that is useful for definition is the **appositive phrase.** An appositive is a noun which renames a previous noun, and it is usually located next to that noun. Consider the following example:

He quickly drew a sketch of a chair, *a piece of furniture which is designed to be sat in by one person and which always has a back.*

Another strategy of definition is the **comparative definition.** Here two or more terms are used to define each other. You might use contrasting clauses that start with words such as *although, despite, even though,* or you might use parallel phrases that follow a colon or a verb:

Although both have backs, the love seat is designed *to be sat in by two people* whereas the chair is designed *to be sat in by only one person.*

The chair is designed to be sat in *by one person;* the love seat is designed *for two.*

The Mothering *Example.* Let's return to the more abstract concept of *mothering.* How would we define this concept? It might make sense to begin with the root word, *mother.* The first place to look is a dictionary. *Webster's New World Dictionary* (2nd edition), for example, says *mother* (both noun and verb) has the following meanings:

—**n.** **1.** a woman who has borne a child; esp., a woman as she is related to her child or children **2.** *a)* a stepmother *b)* a mother-in-law **3.** the female parent of a plant or animal **4.** that which gives birth to something, is the origin or source of something, or nurtures in the manner of a mother **5.** *a)* a woman having the responsibility and authority of a mother *b)* a woman who is the head (*mother superior*) of a religious establishment **6.** an elderly woman: used as a title of affectionate respect **7.** the qualities of a mother

—**vt.** **1.** to be the mother or giving birth to: often used figuratively **2.** to look after or care for as a mother does **3.** to acknowledge or admit that one is the mother, author, or originator of

In addition, we could consult the *Oxford English Dictionary (OED),* which features extensive definitions as well as numerous quotations to illustrate the shades of meaning that a term has. We might consult a book of quotations such as *Bartlett's Familiar Quotations* to see what famous people have said about *mothering.* Ultimately, we might come up with the following one-sentence definition, which will require a lot of expansion via examples, word history, negative definition, comparison and contrast, and other sources and might even explore related issues such as the various types of mothers (biological, foster, adoptive, and step):

Mothering is the process in which a female parents a child, a process that includes raising, nurturing, educating, supporting, and loving that child.

EXPLORING THE SOURCES OF YOUR PERSONAL DEFINITION   This is one of the ways that this type of essay is deeply exploratory. Where did your original understanding of this concept come from? No idea pops full-grown into our minds. Each idea comes from someplace, or, rather, from many places. Discovering and exploring those sources are important and sometimes crucial endeavors. Some obvious sources to consider are your own experiences and reading, your parents and other family members, your friends, co-workers, and acquaintances. Especially be aware that our concepts and beliefs are sometimes ruthlessly shaped and manipulated by public figures and by the media, often for their own unstated ends. Every book, movie, television show, and advertisement that we encounter is trying to define concepts for us—everything from *masculinity* and *femininity* to *courage* and *cowardice*. Only when we make ourselves aware of the subtexts and hidden messages can we see how we have been influenced by them.

EXAMINING EXPERIENCES THAT ILLUSTRATE THE CONCEPT   Whatever concept you have chosen to explore, you must have had some experience with it or you wouldn't have chosen it. Again you might start with freewriting to discover that experience and explore its significance. Or perhaps some experience you've already written about in another context involved the concept you're exploring. Examine that experience again. Don't forget about experiences which your family members and friends have told you; they, too, can be useful.

Gather Information from Outside Sources

After formulating your thoughts and ideas, it is time to turn to outside sources. Explore books, movies, or television shows for illustrations and for complementary or competing definitions of the concept.

EXAMINING OUTSIDE SOURCES THAT ILLUSTRATE OR DISCUSS THE CONCEPT   Often sources with which we are familiar will illustrate a concept for us in surprising ways. Stephen King's *Carrie,* for instance, provides examples of *fanaticism* and *isolation* and the *tribe mentality,* as well as an interesting example of *mothering.* Other sources might also help. Take a moment to consider what academic disciplines might be involved with the concept you've selected. For our example of *mothering,* psychology, sociology, anthropology, women's studies, feminist studies, literature, and folklore all spring immediately to mind. No doubt there are others. You should consider at least two types of sources for each discipline you can think of: texts and people.

Texts.   In addition to dictionaries and books of quotations, such as the *OED* and *Bartlett's Familiar Quotations* mentioned earlier, popular and specialized academic journals might be useful. Biographical and autobiographical texts also are wonderful sources. Don't forget about diaries, letters, and private journals (some families have attics loaded with rich material, and some libraries now are gathering such materials). Works which discuss famous (or infamous) examples in history, myth, and literature are helpful as well. All of these texts can help you develop a context for the concept you are exploring, as well as help you understand the global significance of that concept.

People.   In addition to gathering the insights and examples of family members and friends, you may find it useful to conduct surveys and interview experts. For example, you might conduct an informal survey of your fellow students (on your dorm floor, in a particular class, or in the dining hall) for their ideas about a concept like *fairness* or *procrastination*. Your paper would have more credibility, however, if you could also interview an expert; for *fairness,* you might interview a professor in the philosophy, political science, anthropology, or religion department. For *procrastination,* you might interview a member of the psychology department or perhaps one of the on-campus counselors, who no doubt daily helps clients afflicted with the problem.

Interviewing an expert might seem overwhelming at first, but it isn't. Briefly, here's how to arrange and conduct a successful interview. First, contact the person you wish to interview ahead of time to set up an appointment. State exactly what your topic is (for instance, *mothering*) and, as specifically as possible, the kinds of information you'd like (suggestions about sources, facts, opinions).

Go to the interview with your questions written out on the first page of the notebook you will use to take notes. This will prevent your forgetting to ask something. But remember that an interview is really a conversation, not a question-and-answer session. Often the expert will surprise you with an idea or a fact that leads you away from your written questions. Follow such tangents as far as they go. One advantage of having written questions is that they free you to follow conversational tangents without fear of losing your focus since you can always flip back to the first page and ask any questions not already covered.

It is also a good idea to take notes during the interview (memories are not dependable). This may seem impolite, but it isn't. Experts are usually familiar with the interview process, and in any event they prefer to be quoted accurately. To get used to the process, try interviewing a couple of your friends first, taking notes. Then you will feel at ease with the process when you interview the expert. Even better, if you have access to a small tape recorder and if the expert agrees, tape the interview and then you can get the quotations and facts exactly right. Many journalists who use tape recorders, however, still take notes during the interview in order to highlight important insights on the spot.

Conducting surveys might be less useful than interviewing, but it is an option that you should at least consider. For exploratory writing, the point of a survey is to set a context or to establish global significance. With *mothering,* for example, you might survey your dorm floor to find out what students think the term means or to find out how many people on the floor believe they received appropriate mothering.

RESPONDING TO OTHERS' VISIONS OF THE CONCEPT   Once you've gathered information, it is time to assess and respond to it. For example, you might agree with someone else's definition of *mothering* and therefore decide to broaden your own definition to accommodate it. Or you might argue against someone else's definition, thus extending your own. Exploring *why* you reject a particular definition reveals you and your thought processes as well as expanding your readers' understanding of the concept. In short, once you've done the research, use it creatively.

STRUCTURE OF AN ESSAY EXPLORING A CONCEPT

An essay exploring a concept affords you the same freedom of structure as any other exploratory essay. As with other such essays, however, you must consider your readers' needs as you begin to revise. You may need to use a process narration if, for instance, the concept you are explaining is something like "how to become a friend after being an acquaintance" or if you wish to dramatize the process of coming to your present understanding of the concept. You may need to define the concept negatively first in order to clear away the deadwood assumptions you feel your readers might have. At times you will find yourself comparing and contrasting concepts or elements (how is a *friend* different from an *acquaintance?*). Or you might be looking for causes or effects or both. Often you will be classifying or dividing. If you use the ideas or words of other people, be sure to indicate any quotations correctly and to give your sources proper credit, following an accepted form of documentation such as that recommended by the Modern Language Association (MLA) or the American Psychological Association (APA).

Among the elements your essays might include are the following (but the order is determined by your particular approach to the concept you are exploring):

your personal definition of the concept

your analysis of its implications

examples drawn from your personal experience

an explanation of the sources of your definition (sources could range from Aristotle to Aunt Agnes, from an advertisement to a Bible verse)

definitions by other people who have thought deeply about this concept and its implications an exploration of the difference between your definition and theirs

an explanation of how your definition has changed to accommodate or to include the definitions of others

POSSIBLE PLACES TO EXPAND YOUR DRAFT

As with all exploratory essays, the further you probe into the topic and the more you reveal about yourself, the better the essay is likely to be. In the case of essays that explore concepts, the problems that most often require attention once a draft is done are the following: (1) Your definition of the concept is not complete enough; (2) your exploration of the concept's implications (for you, for other people in your life, for relationships, for the world) is not extensive enough; (3) you haven't discussed (or discussed fully enough) other sources of your personal definition; (4) you haven't offered a satisfactory answer to the question of why this particular concept is important to you; (5) you need to do more research to broaden your understanding of the concept and its significance; (6) an assumption that "everyone knows what this concept means" has prevented you from delving far enough into it; (7) your essay could be structured more effectively for your readers.

Such areas for revision, however, are opportunities to increase even more your understanding of the concept. Perceiving the nuances of a concept can be one of the essayist's most exciting and useful accomplishments and is, after all, one of the reasons why we write in the first place—to deepen our knowledge.

SUGGESTIONS FOR WRITING

1. Open a dictionary at random and let your finger land on a word. Write for 10 minutes about that word. Be inventive, considering the word metaphorically, symbolically, or figuratively as well as literally. Play with the concept.

2. Select a concept that interests you. Write briefly explaining why it interests you. Then fully investigate the concept. Write an essay about it, explaining it for your readers, its implications, and why it interested or still interests you.

3. Select one or more of the titles below, and write for 10 minutes on the concept in the title. The end product will not be a full-fledged essay, but it will be the start of exploring a concept. If you get off onto a fruitful tangent, follow it. You can always play with the concept in the original title later. Here are some of Nancy Mairs's titles: "On Having Adventures," "On Being a Cripple," "On Touching by Accident," "On

Being a Scientific Booby," "On Being Raised by a Daughter," "On Not Liking Sex," "On Loving Men," "On Living Behind Bars."

Michel de Montaigne's titles include: "Of Cannibals," "Of Idleness," "Of Liars," "Of Friendship," "Of Moderation," "Of Sleep," "Of Names," "Of the Power of the Imagination."

Here are some of Francis Bacon's titles: "Of Truth," "Of Death," "Of Revenge," "Of Envy," "Of Nobility," "Of Superstition," "Of Cunning," "Of Innovations," "Of Deformity," "Of Studies," "Of Suitors."

Other possibilities include: "On Education," "On Responsibility," "On Justice," "On Fairness," "On Beauty," "On Reading," "On Conversing," "On Laughing," "On Crying," "On Freedom," "On Moving," "On Staying Still," "On the Perfect Day," "On April" (substitute any month), "On *Can,*" "On *Should,*" "On Hot or Cold Weather," "On Farms or Cities or Towns," "On Siblings," "On Fathers," "On Fathers and Sons," "On Mothers," "On Mothers and Daughters," "On Fathers and Daughters," "On Mothers and Sons," "On Dogs," "On Cats," "On Fish," "On Tame or Wild Birds," "On Winnie the Pooh," "On Rock and Roll," "On Beer," "On Drugs," "On Sex," "On Jazz," "On the Seashore," "On Returning or Leaving," "On Control," "On Self-Respect," "On Cheating," "On Honesty," "On Books," "On Nature," "On Truth," "On Organization," "On Procrastination," "On Movies," "On TV," "On Arguing," "On Being Happy or Depressed," "On Horror Movies," "On Love Songs."

"Mommy, What Does 'Nigger' Mean?"

GLORIA NAYLOR

❏ *Inward Exploration*

Write at least one paragraph defining the word nigger. *Make a list of other, similar words. Which one of those words seems the most hateful, the most hurtful, the most powerful. Why?*

Language is the subject. It is the written form with which I've man-   1
aged to keep the wolf away from the door and, in diaries, to keep my sanity. In spite of this, I consider the written word inferior to the spoken, and much of the frustration experienced by novelists is the awareness that whatever we manage to capture in even the most transcendent passages falls far short of the richness of life. Dialogue achieves its power in the dynamics of a fleeting moment of sight, sound, smell and touch.

I'm not going to enter the debate here about whether it is language that shapes reality or vice versa. That battle is doomed to be waged whenever we seek intermittent reprieve from the chicken and egg dispute. I will simply take the position that the spoken word, like the written word, amounts to a nonsensical arrangement of sounds or letters without a consensus that assigns "meaning." And building from the meanings of what we hear, we order reality. Words themselves are innocuous; it is the consensus that gives them true power.

I remember the first time I heard the word "nigger." In my third-grade class, our math tests were being passed down the rows, and as I handed the papers to a little boy in back of me, I remarked that once again he had received a much lower mark than I did. He snatched his test from me and spit out that word. Had he called me a nymphomaniac or a necrophiliac, I couldn't have been more puzzled. I didn't know what a nigger was, but I knew that whatever it meant, it was something he shouldn't have called me. This was verified when I raised my hand, and in a loud voice repeated what he had said and watched the teacher scold him for using a "bad" word. I was later to go home and ask the inevitable question that every black parent must face—"Mommy, what does 'nigger' mean?"

And what exactly did it mean? Thinking back, I realize that this could not have been the first time the word was used in my presence. I was part of a large extended family that had migrated from the rural South after World War II and formed a close-knit network that gravitated around my maternal grandparents. Their ground-floor apartment in one of the buildings they owned in Harlem was a weekend mecca for my immediate family, along with countless aunts, uncles and cousins who brought along assorted friends. It was a bustling and open house with assorted neighbors and tenants popping in and out to exchange bits of gossip, pick up an old quarrel or referee the ongoing checkers game in which my grandmother cheated shamelessly. They were all there to let down their hair and put up their feet after a week of labor in the factories, laundries and shipyards of New York.

Amid the clamor, which could reach deafening proportions— two or three conversations going on simultaneously, punctuated by the sound of a baby's crying somewhere in the back rooms or out on the street—there was still a rigid set of rules about what was said and how. Older children were sent out of the living room when it was time to get into the juicy details about "you-know-who" up on the third floor who had gone and gotten herself "p-r-e-g-n-a-n-t!" But my parents, knowing that I could spell well beyond my years, always demanded that I follow the others out to play. Beyond sexual misconduct and death, everything else was considered harmless for our young ears. And so among the anecdotes of the triumphs and disappointments in the various workings of their lives, the word "nigger" was used in my presence, but it was set within contexts and inflections that caused it to register in my mind as something else.

In the singular, the word was always applied to a man who had distinguished himself in some situation that brought their approval for his strength, intelligence or drive:

"Did Johnny really do that?"

"I'm telling you, that nigger pulled in $6,000 of overtime last year. Said he got enough for a down payment on a house."

When used with a possessive adjective by a woman—"my nigger"—it became a term of endearment for husband or boyfriend. But it could be more than just a term applied to a man. In their mouths it became the pure essence of manhood—a disembodied force that channeled their past history of struggle and present survival against the odds into a victorious statement of being: "Yeah, that old foreman found out quick enough—you don't mess with a nigger."

In the plural, it became a description of some group within the community that had overstepped the bounds of decency as my family defined it: Parents who neglected their children, a drunken couple who fought in public, people who simply refused to look for work, those with excessively dirty mouths or unkempt households were all "trifling niggers." This particular circle could forgive hard times, unemployment, the occasional bout of depression—they had gone through all of that themselves—but the unforgivable sin was lack of self-respect.

A woman could never be a "nigger" in the singular, with its connotation of confirming worth. The noun "girl" was its closest equivalent in that sense, but only when used in direct address and regardless of the gender doing the addressing. "Girl" was a token of respect for a woman. The one-syllable word was drawn out to sound like three in recognition of the extra ounce of wit, nerve or daring that the woman had shown in the situation under discussion.

"G-i-r-l, stop. You mean you said that to his face?"

But if the word was used in a third-person reference or shortened so that it almost snapped out of the mouth, it always involved some element of communal disapproval. And age became an important factor in these exchanges. It was only between individuals of the same generation, or from an older person to a younger (but never the other way around), that "girl" would be considered a compliment.

I don't agree with the argument that use of the word nigger at this social stratum of the black community was an internalization of racism. The dynamics were the exact opposite: the people in my grandmother's living room took a word that whites used to signify worthlessness or degradation and rendered it impotent. Gathering there together, they transformed "nigger" to signify the varied and complex human beings they knew themselves to be. If the word was to disappear totally from the mouths of even the most liberal of white society, no one in that room was naïve enough to believe it would disappear from white minds. Meeting the word head-on, they proved it had absolutely nothing to do with the way they were determined to live their lives.

So there must have been dozens of times that the word "nigger" was   *15* spoken in front of me before I reached the third grade. But I didn't "hear" it until it was said by a small pair of lips that had already learned it could be a way to humiliate me. That was the word I went home and asked my mother about. And since she knew that I had to grow up in America, she took me in her lap and explained.

🗋 *Outward Exploration: Discussion*

1. According to Naylor, what gives words their power?

2. Explain the various meanings of the word *nigger*.

3. Why was the term *nigger* in the singular never used to refer to a woman?

4. What term of approbation was used for women?

5. Why did Naylor's family use the term *nigger* at all? Does this seem like a good strategy? Have you ever used a similar strategy with a term?

6. How does Naylor use personal experience in this essay?

7. Based on her definitions of the terms *nigger* and *girl,* what traits and types of behavior does her extended family (and, presumably, the wider population of Harlem) value and which do they scorn?

❑ *Outward Exploration: Writing*

Select a meaningful term that has multiple meanings (this does not have to be a term like *nigger*—it could be a term like *love, justice, fairness*). Write an essay exploring its various meanings. Do some research to broaden your understanding of the term (the *Oxford English Dictionary* and sources such as *Bartlett's Familiar Quotations* will give you numerous definitions for the same term, and the reference librarian can suggest other sources).

❑ *Style*

Consider the following sentence from Naylor's essay:

Words themselves are innocuous; it is the consensus that gives them true power. (paragraph 2)

Notice this sentence's structure: *"x are y"* semicolon *"it is w that z"* period. Write a sentence of your own that replicates this structure.

Americanization Is Tough on "Macho"

ROSE DEL CASTILLO GUILBAULT

❏ *Inward Exploration*

Make a list of personality traits that you associate with the term macho.

What is *macho?* That depends which side of the border you come 1
from.

Although it's not unusual for words and expressions to lose their subtlety in translation, the negative connotations of *macho* in this country are troublesome to Hispanics.

Take the newspaper descriptions of alleged mass murderer Ramon Salcido. That an insensitive, insanely jealous, hard-drinking, violent Latin male is referred to as *macho* makes Hispanics cringe.

"*Es muy macho,*" the women in my family nod approvingly, describing a man they respect. But in the United States, when women say, "He's so macho," it's with disdain.

The Hispanic *macho* is manly, responsible, hardworking, a man in 5
charge, a patriarch. A man who expresses strength through silence. What the Yiddish language would call a *mensch.*

The American *macho* is a chauvinist, a brute, uncouth, selfish, loud, abrasive, capable of inflicting pain, and sexually promiscuous.

Quintessential *macho* models in this country are Sylvester Stallone, Arnold Schwarzenegger, and Charles Bronson. In their movies, they exude toughness, independence, masculinity. But a closer look reveals their machismo is really violence masquerading as courage, sullenness disguised as silence and irresponsibility camouflaged as independence.

If the Hispanic ideal of *macho* were translated to American screen roles, they might be Jimmy Stewart, Sean Connery, and Laurence Olivier.

In Spanish, *macho* ennobles Latin males. In English it devalues them. This pattern seems consistent with the conflicts ethnic minority males experience in this country. Typically the cultural traits other societies value don't translate as desirable characteristics in America.

I watched my own father struggle with these cultural ambiguities. 10
He worked on a farm for 20 years. He laid down miles of irrigation pipe, carefully plowed long, neat rows in fields, hacked away at recalci-

trant weeds and drove tractors through whirlpools of dust. He stoically worked 20-hour days during harvest season, accepting the long hours as part of agricultural work. When the boss complained or upbraided him for minor mistakes, he kept quiet, even when it was obvious the boss had erred.

He handled the most menial tasks with pride. At home he was a good provider, helped out my mother's family in Mexico without complaint, and was indulgent with me. Arguments between my mother and him generally had to do with money, or with his stubborn reluctance to share his troubles. He tried to work them out in his own silence. He didn't want to trouble my mother—a course that backfired, because the imagined is always worse than the reality.

Americans regarded my father as decidedly un-*macho*. His character was interpreted as non-assertive, his loyalty non-ambition, and his quietness, ignorance. I once overheard the boss's son blame him for plowing crooked rows in a field. My father merely smiled at the lie, knowing the boy had done it, but didn't refute it, confident his good work was well known. But the boss instead ridiculed him for being "stupid" and letting a kid get away with a lie. Seeing my embarrassment, my father dismissed the incident, saying "They're the dumb ones. Imagine, me fighting with a kid."

I tried not to look at him with American eyes because sometimes the reflection hurt.

Listening to my aunts' clucks of approval, my vision focused on the qualities America overlooked. "He's such a hard worker. So serious, so responsible," my aunts would secretly compliment my mother. The unspoken comparison was that he was not like some of their husbands, who drank and womanized. My uncles represented the darker side of *macho*.

In a patriarchal society, few challenge their roles. If men drink, it's because it's the manly thing to do. If they gamble, it's because it's how men relax. And if they fool around, well, it's because a man simply can't hold back so much man! My aunts didn't exactly meekly sit back, but they put up with these transgressions because Mexican society dictated this was their lot in life.

In the United States, I believe it was the feminist movement of the early '70s that changed *macho*'s meaning. Perhaps my generation of Latin women was in part responsible. I recall Chicanas complaining about the chauvinistic nature of Latin men and the notion they wanted their women barefoot, pregnant, and in the kitchen. The generalization that Latin men embodied chauvinistic traits led to this interesting twist of semantics. Suddenly a word that represented something positive in one culture became a negative prototype in another.

The problem with the use of *macho* today is that it's become an accepted stereotype of the Latin male. And like all stereotypes, it distorts truth.

The impact of language in our society is undeniable. And the misuse of *macho* hints at a deeper cultural misunderstanding that extends beyond mere word definitions.

Outward Exploration: Discussion

1. Why do Hispanics cringe when a mass murderer is described as *macho?*

2. In paragraphs 5 and 6, Guilbault succinctly defines the term *macho* as it is used by Hispanics and by Americans. Explain the differences between the two definitions. Are there any areas in either definition that require more explanation? Based on the rest of the essay, what would you add to these definitions? Try to explain how the Hispanic definition was transformed into the American; in other words, are the traits in these definitions really "two sides to the same coin"?

3. How well do her examples of American macho men fit the definition she gives in paragraph 6? Can you think of better examples, either celebrities or people from your own life? Does she add more characteristics to her definition?

4. What are the political implications of the changes Americans have made in the definition of *macho?* Can you think of examples which support her contention?

5. In paragraph 14, Guilbault seems to acknowledge that there is a "darker side of *macho.*" How does this darker side compare to the American definition of *macho?*

6. In paragraph 15, she defines *manly* and explains some of the implications of *being a patriarch.* What is her definition? What is yours?

7. To whom are the "negative" aspects of *macho* negative? If everyone saw such traits and behavior as negative, would being macho still be so popular? Would the actors she identifies as macho be so admired and emulated? Explain.

Outward Exploration: Writing

Select a complex term that includes a number of traits or behaviors (for example, what does it mean to be a *man* or to be a *woman?* to be a *hero* or a *villain?* to be *honest* or *dishonest?* to be *just* or *unjust?* to be a *liberal* or a *conservative?*). Write an essay defining the term and attacking incorrect definitions that have been offered of that term. This essay will probably require some research.

❏ *Style*

Consider the following sentence from this essay:

The Hispanic *macho* is manly, responsible, hardworking, a man in charge, a patriarch. (paragraph 5)

The structure is as follows:

subject ("The Hispanic *macho*")

verb ("is")

three adjectives joined by **commas** ("manly, responsible, hardworking")

comma (a comma usually separates an appositive from the noun it renames)

a noun functioning as an appositive renaming "*macho*" ("man")

prepositional phrase modifying "man" ("in charge")

comma (separating a second appositive)

a noun functioning as a second appositive for "*macho*" ("a patriarch")

period.

Write a sentence that replicates this subtle structure: After a form of *to be,* describe the sentence's subject with three adjectives followed by a comma and two appositives.

On the Decay of the Art of Lying

MARK TWAIN

☐ *Inward Exploration*

Write at least one paragraph about telling lies. For example, you might explain when (if ever) it is all right to tell lies, or you might explain exactly what the term lying *means to you.*

Essay, for discussion, read at a meeting of the Historical and Antiquarian Club of Hartford, and offered for the thirty-dollar prize. Now first published.*

Observe, I do not mean to suggest that the *custom* of lying has suf-   1
fered any decay or interruption—no, for the Lie, as a Virtue, a Principle, is eternal; the Lie, as a recreation, a solace, a refuge in time of need, the fourth Grace, the tenth Muse, man's best and surest friend, is immortal, and cannot perish from the earth while this Club remains. My complaint simply concerns the decay of the *art* of lying. No high-minded man, no man of right feeling, can contemplate the lumbering and slovenly lying of the present day without grieving to see a noble art so prostituted. In this veteran presence I naturally enter upon this theme with diffidence; it is like an old maid trying to teach nursery matters to the mothers in Israel. It would not become me to criticise you, gentlemen, who are nearly all my elders—and my superiors, in this thing—and so, if I should here and there *seem* to do it, I trust it will in most cases be more in a spirit of admiration than of fault-finding; indeed if this finest of the fine arts had everywhere received the attention, encouragement, and conscientious practice and development which this Club has devoted to it, I should not need to utter this lament, or shed a single tear. I do not say this to flatter: I say it in a spirit of just and appreciative recognition. [It had been my intention, at this point, to mention names and give illustrative specimens, but indications observable about me admonished me to beware of particulars and confine myself to generalities.]

No fact is more firmly established than that lying is a necessity of our circumstances—the deduction that it is then a Virtue goes without saying. No virtue can reach its highest usefulness without careful and diligent cultivation—therefore, it goes without saying, that this one

―――――――

*Did not take the prize.

ought to be taught in the public schools—at the fireside—even in the newspapers. What chance has the ignorant, uncultivated liar against the educated expert? What chance have I against Mr. Per—against a lawyer? *Judicious* lying is what the world needs. I sometimes think it were even better and safer not to lie at all than to lie injudiciously. An awkward, unscientific lie is often as ineffectual as the truth.

Now let us see what the philosophers say. Note that venerable proverb: Children and fools *always* speak the truth. The deduction is plain— adults and wise persons *never* speak it. Parkman, the historian, says, "The principle of truth may itself be carried into an absurdity." In another place in the same chapter he says, "The saying is old that truth should not be spoken at all times; and those whom a sick conscience worries into habitual violation of the maxim are imbeciles and nuisances." It is strong language, but true. None of us could *live* with an habitual truth-teller; but thank goodness none of us has to. An habitual truth-teller is simply an impossible creature; he does not exist; he never has existed. Of course there are people who *think* they never lie, but it is not so—and this ignorance is one of the very things that shame our so-called civilization. Everybody lies—every day; every hour; awake; asleep; in his dreams; in his joy; in his mourning; if he keeps his tongue still, his hands, his feet, his eyes, his attitude, will convey deception— and purposely. Even in sermons—but that is a platitude.

In a far country where I once lived the ladies used to go around paying calls, under the humane and kindly pretence of wanting to see each other; and when they returned home, they would cry out with a glad voice, saying, "We made sixteen calls and found fourteen of them out"—not meaning that they found out anything against the fourteen— no, that was only a colloquial phrase to signify that they were not at home—and their manner of saying it expressed their lively satisfaction in that fact. Now their pretence of wanting to see the fourteen—and the other two whom they had been less lucky with—was that commonest and mildest form of lying which is sufficiently described as a deflection from the truth. Is it justifiable? Most certainly. It is beautiful, it is noble; for its object is, *not* to reap profit, but to convey a pleasure to the sixteen. The iron-souled truth-monger would plainly manifest, or even utter the fact that he didn't want to see those people—and he would be an ass, and inflict a totally unnecessary pain. And next, those ladies in that far country—but never mind, they had a thousand pleasant ways of lying, that grew out of gentle impulses, and were a credit to their intelligence and an honor to their hearts. Let the particulars go.

The men in that far country were liars, every one. Their mere   5 howdy-do was a lie, because *they* didn't care how you did, except they were undertakers. To the ordinary inquirer you lied in return; for you made no conscientious diagnosis of your case, but answered at random, and usually missed it considerably: You lied to the undertaker, and said your health was failing—a wholly commendable lie, since it cost you nothing and pleased the other man. If a stranger called and interrupted you, you said with your hearty tongue, "I'm glad to see you," and said with your heartier soul, "I wish you were with the cannibals and it was dinner-time." When he went, you said regretfully, "*Must* you go?" and followed it with a "Call again;" but you did no harm, for you did not deceive anybody nor inflict any hurt, whereas the truth would have made you both unhappy.

I think that all this courteous lying is a sweet and loving art, and should be cultivated. The highest perfection of politeness is only a beautiful edifice, built, from the base to the dome, of graceful and gilded forms of charitable and unselfish lying.

What I bemoan is the growing prevalence of the brutal truth. Let us do what we can to eradicate it. An injurious truth has no merit over an injurious lie. Neither should ever be uttered. The man who speaks an injurious truth lest his soul be not saved if he do otherwise, should reflect that that sort of a soul is not strictly worth saving. The man who tells a lie to help a poor devil out of trouble, is one of whom the angels doubtless say, "Lo, here is an heroic soul who casts his own welfare into jeopardy to succor his neighbor's; let us exalt this magnanimous liar."

An injurious lie is an uncommendable thing; and so, also, and in the same degree, is an injurious truth—a fact which is recognized by the law of libel.

Among other common lies, we have the *silent* lie—the deception which one conveys by simply keeping still and concealing the truth. Many obstinate truth-mongers indulge in this dissipation, imagining that if they *speak* no lie, they lie not at all. In that far country where I once lived, there was a lovely spirit, a lady whose impulses were always high and pure, and whose character answered to them. One day I was there at dinner, and remarked, in a general way, that we are all liars. She was amazed, and said, "Not *all?*" It was before "Pinafore's" time, so I did not make the response which would naturally follow in our day, but frankly said, "Yes, *all*—we are all liars; there are no exceptions." She looked almost offended, and said, "Why, do you include *me?*" "Certainly," I said. "I think you even rank as an expert." She said, "'Sh—'sh! the children!" So the subject was changed in deference to the children's presence, and we went on talking about other things. But as soon as the young people were out of the way, the lady came warmly back to the matter and said, "I have made it the rule of my life to never tell a lie; and I have never departed from it in a single instance." I said, "I don't mean the least harm or disrespect, but really you have been lying like smoke ever since I've been sitting here. It has caused me a good deal of pain, because I am not used to it." She required of me an instance—just a single instance. So I said—

"Well, here is the unfilled duplicate of the blank which the Oakland hospital people sent to you by the hand of the sick-nurse when she came here to nurse your little nephew through his dangerous illness. This

10

blank asks all manner of questions as to the conduct of that sick-nurse: 'Did she ever sleep on her watch? Did she ever forget to give the medicine?' and so forth and so on. You are warned to be very careful and explicit in your answers, for the welfare of the service requires that the nurses be promptly fined or otherwise punished for derelictions. You told me you were perfectly delighted with that nurse—that she had a thousand perfections and only one fault: you found you never could depend on her wrapping Johnny up half sufficiently while he waited in a chilly chair for her to rearrange the warm bed. You filled up the duplicate of this paper, and sent it back to the hospital by the hand of the nurse. How did you answer this question—'Was the nurse at any time guilty of a negligence which was likely to result in the patient's taking cold?' Come—everything is decided by a bet here in California: ten dollars to ten cents you lied when you answered that question." She said, "I didn't; *I left it blank!*" "Just so—you have told a *silent* lie; you have left it to be inferred that you had no fault to find in that matter." She said, "Oh, was that a lie? And how *could* I mention her one single fault, and she so good?—it would have been cruel." I said, "One ought always to lie, when one can do good by it; your impulse was right, but your judgment was crude; this comes of unintelligent practice. Now observe the result of this inexpert deflection of yours. You know Mr. Jones's Willie is lying very low with scarlet-fever; well, your recommendation was so enthusiastic that that girl is there nursing him, and the worn-out family have all been trustingly sound asleep for the last fourteen hours, leaving their darling with full confidence in those fatal hands, because you, like young George Washington, have a reputa—However, if you are not going to have anything to do, I will come around to-morrow and we'll attend the funeral together, for, of course, you'll naturally feel a peculiar interest in Willie's case—as personal a one, in fact, as the undertaker."

But that was all lost. Before I was half-way through she was in a carriage and making thirty miles an hour toward the Jones mansion to save what was left of Willie and tell all she knew about the deadly nurse. All of which was unnecessary, as Willie wasn't sick, I had been lying myself. But that same day, all the same, she sent a line to the hospital which filled up the neglected blank, and stated the *facts,* too, in the squarest possible manner.

Now, you see, this lady's fault was *not* in lying, but only in lying injudiciously. She should have told the truth, *there,* and made it up to the nurse with a fraudulent compliment further along in the paper. She could have said, "In one respect this sick-nurse is perfection—when she is on watch, she never snores." Almost any little pleasant lie would have taken the sting out of that troublesome but necessary expression of the truth.

Lying is universal—we *all* do it; we all *must* do it. Therefore, the wise thing is for us diligently to train ourselves to lie thoughtfully, judiciously; to lie with a good object, and not an evil one; to lie for others' advantage, and not our own; to lie healingly, charitably, humanely, not cruelly, hurtfully, maliciously; to lie gracefully and graciously, not awkwardly and clumsily; to lie firmly, frankly, squarely, with head erect, not haltingly, tortuously, with pusillanimous mien, as being ashamed of our high calling. Then shall we be rid of the rank and pestilent truth that is rotting the land; then shall we be great and good and beautiful, and worthy dwellers in a world where even benign Nature habitually lies, except when she promises execrable weather. Then—But I am but a new and feeble student in this gracious art; I cannot instruct *this* Club.

Joking aside, I think there is much need of wise examination into what sort of lies are best and wholesomest to be indulged, seeing we *must* all lie and *do* all lie, and what sorts it may be best to avoid—and this is a thing which I feel I can confidently put into the hands of this experienced Club—a ripe body, who may be termed, in this regard, and without undue flattery, Old Masters.

☐ Outward Exploration: Discussion

1. Explain exactly what Twain means by *judicious lying*.
2. What is Twain's attitude toward his immediate audience, members of the Historical and Antiquarian Club of Hartford?
3. In paragraph 2, Twain says that the truth is often ineffectual. Is that true? Explain.
4. According to Twain, what is a "*silent* lie"? Have you ever been guilty of such silent lies? Are they as "bad" or "wrong" as actual lies that you speak? Explain.
5. In paragraph 11, Twain ends the story of the woman and the nurse by saying that he himself had lied to the woman about the Jones's son being ill. Why did he lie?
6. Is Twain right about the desirability of lying? Give some examples from your own experience.
7. If Twain is right that everyone lies, how does that make you feel as the receiver of possible lies?

☐ Outward Exploration: Writing

1. Write a humorous essay of your own in which you follow Twain's lead but on a different topic. Try to select a topic which will seem outrageous at first but which has some defendable points in its favor as does lying.
2. Write a serious essay about some moral issue, arguing that it should be taken more seriously or less seriously.
3. Write a rebuttal of Twain's essay.

4. Write an essay that describes a personal experience in which you found lying was preferable to telling the truth. Explore the implications of the situation. If you can, derive a general rule-of-thumb from the experience about lying and truth-telling.

5. List the lies you heard last week. Can they be classified in some way (for example, malicious lies and polite lies)? Write an essay about lying that explores areas that Twain does not develop at length.

On Natural Death

LEWIS THOMAS

❑ *Inward Exploration*

Write at least one paragraph expressing your thoughts about the term natural death.

There are so many new books about dying that there are now special shelves set aside for them in bookshops, along with the health-diet and home-repair paperbacks and the sex manuals. Some of them are so packed with detailed information and step-by-step instructions for performing the function that you'd think this was a new sort of skill which all of us are now required to learn. The strongest impression the casual reader gets, leafing through, is that proper dying has become an extraordinary, even an exotic experience, something only the specially trained get to do.

Also, you could be led to believe that we are the only creatures capable of the awareness of death, that when all the rest of nature is being cycled through dying, one generation after another, it is a different kind of process, done automatically and trivially, more "natural," as we say.

An elm in our backyard caught the blight this summer and dropped stone dead, leafless, almost overnight. One weekend it was a normal-looking elm, maybe a little bare in spots but nothing alarming, and the next weekend it was gone, passed over, departed, taken. Taken is right, for the tree surgeon came by yesterday with his crew of young helpers and their cherry picker, and took it down branch by branch and carted it off in the back of a red truck, everyone singing.

The dying of a field mouse, at the jaws of an amiable household cat, is a spectacle I have beheld many times. It used to make me wince. Early in life I gave up throwing sticks at the cat to make him drop the mouse, because the dropped mouse regularly went ahead and died anyway, but I always shouted unaffections at the cat to let him know the sort of animal he had become. Nature, I thought, was an abomination.

Recently I've done some thinking about that mouse, and I wonder if his dying is necessarily all that different from the passing of our elm. The main difference, if there is one, would be in the matter of pain. I do not believe that an elm tree has pain receptors, and even so, the blight seems to me a relatively painless way to go even if there were nerve endings in a tree, which there are not. But the mouse dangling tail-down from the teeth of a gray cat is something else again, with pain beyond bearing, you'd think, all over his small body.

There are now some plausible reasons for thinking it is not like that at all, and you can make up an entirely different story about the mouse and his dying if you like. At the instant of being trapped and penetrated by teeth, peptide hormones are released by cells in the hypothalamus and the pituitary gland; instantly these substances, called endorphins, are attached to the surface of other cells responsible for pain perception; the hormones have the pharmacologic properties of opium; there is no pain. Thus it is that the mouse seems always to dangle so languidly from the jaws, lies there so quietly when dropped, dies of his injuries without a struggle. If a mouse could shrug, he'd shrug.

I do not know if this is true or not, nor do I know how to prove it if it is true. Maybe if you could get in there quickly enough and administer naloxone, a specific morphine antagonist, you could turn off the endorphins and observe the restoration of pain, but this is not something I would care to do or see. I think I will leave it there, as a good guess about the dying of a cat-chewed mouse, perhaps about dying in general.

Montaigne had a hunch about dying, based on his own close call in a riding accident. He was so badly injured as to be believed dead by his companions, and was carried home with lamentations, "all bloody, stained all over with the blood I had thrown up." He remembers the entire episode, despite having been "dead, for two full hours," with wonderment:

> It seemed to me that my life was hanging only by the tip of my lips. I closed my eyes in order, it seemed to me, to help push it out, and took pleasure in growing languid and letting myself go. It was an idea that was only floating on the surface of my soul, as delicate and feeble as all the rest, but in truth not only free from distress but mingled with that sweet feeling that people have who have let themselves slide into sleep. I believe that this is the same state in which people find themselves whom we see fainting in the agony of death, and I maintain that we pity them without cause. . . . In order to get used to the idea of death, I find there is nothing like coming close to it.

Later, in another essay, Montaigne returns to it:

> If you know not how to die, never trouble yourself; Nature will in a moment fully and sufficiently instruct you; she will exactly do that business for you; take you no care for it.

The worst accident I've ever seen was in Okinawa, in the early days of the invasion, when a jeep ran into a troop carrier and was crushed nearly flat. Inside were two young MPs, trapped in bent steel, both mortally hurt, with only their heads and shoulders visible. We had a conversation while people with the right tools were prying them free. Sorry about the accident, they said. No, they said, they felt fine. Is everyone else okay, one of them said. Well, the other one said, no hurry now. And then they died.

Pain is useful for avoidance, for getting away when there's time to get away, but when it is end game, and no way back, pain is likely to be turned off, and the mechanisms for this are wonderfully precise and quick. If I had to design an ecosystem in which creatures had to live off each other and in which dying was an indispensable part of living, I could not think of a better way to manage.

☐ *Outward Exploration: Discussion*

1. What books is Thomas responding to in this essay? What do they seem to suggest?
2. What creatures are aware of death?
3. Why does Thomas believe that the mouse feels no pain?
4. Why does Thomas tell us about the tree and the mouse?
5. What is the use of pain in Nature?
6. What is Thomas's purpose in writing this essay?
7. How comforting do you find this essay? Why?

☐ *Outward Exploration: Writing*

1. Formulate your own ideas about death. Write them down. Then read what some other writers with a different perspective have to say about death. You might look for articles written by psychologists and philosophers as well as those written in earlier times by such writers as Michel de Montaigne and Francis Bacon. Then write an essay about death, using the information you have gathered and explaining your own view and its sources.
2. Select any complex concept and write an essay exploring it. Do research to deepen and broaden your understanding of that concept.

Selections from *The Devil's Dictionary*

AMBROSE BIERCE

❏ *Inward Exploration*

Write at least one paragraph defining your understanding of the term dic-tionary. Consider, for example, what exactly you expect to find in a dictionary. What is appropriate and inappropriate for inclusion in a dictionary?

abdication, *n.* An act whereby a sovereign attests his sense of the high   1
temperature of the throne.

abscond, *v.i.* To "move in a mysterious way," commonly with the
property of another.

absent, *adj.* Peculiarly exposed to the tooth of detraction; vilified; hope-lessly in the wrong; superseded in the consideration and affection of
another.

accident, *n.* An inevitable occurrence due to the action of immutable
natural laws.

accordion, *n.* An instrument in harmony with the sentiments of an   5
assassin.

achievement, *n.* The death of endeavor and the birth of disgust.

admiration, *n.* Our polite recognition of another's resemblance to
ourselves.

alone, *adj.* In bad company.

applause, *n.* The echo of a platitude.

ardor, *n.* The quality that distinguishes love without knowledge.   10

bore, *n.* A person who talks when you wish him to listen.

cemetery, *n.* An isolated suburban spot where mourners match lies,
poets write at a target and stone-cutters spell for a wager. The inscrip-tion following will serve to illustrate the success attained in these
Olympian games:

> His virtues were so conspicuous that his enemies, unable to
> overlook them, denied them, and his friends, to whose loose
> lives they were a rebuke, represented them as vices. They are
> here commemorated by his family, who shared them.

childhood, *n.* The period of human life intermediate between the idi-ocy of infancy and the folly of youth—two removes from the sin of
manhood and three from the remorse of age.

Christian, *n.* One who believes that the New Testament is a divinely
inspired book admirably suited to the spiritual needs of his neighbor.

One who follows the teachings of Christ in so far as they are not inconsistent with a life of sin.

compulsion, *n.* The eloquence of power.

congratulation, *n.* The civility of envy.

conservative, *n.* A statesman who is enamored of existing evils, as distinguished from the Liberal, who wishes to replace them with others.

consult, *v.t.* To seek another's approval of a course already decided on.

contempt, *n.* The feeling of a prudent man for an enemy who is too formidable safely to be opposed.

coward, *n.* One who in a perilous emergency thinks with his legs.

debauchee, *n.* One who has so earnestly pursued pleasure that he has had the misfortune to overtake it.

destiny, *n.* A tyrant's authority for crime and a fool's excuse for failure.

diplomacy, *n.* The patriotic art of lying for one's country.

distance, *n.* The only thing that the rich are willing for the poor to call theirs and keep.

duty, *n.* That which sternly impels us in the direction of profit, along the line of desire.

education, *n.* That which discloses to the wise and disguises from the foolish their lack of understanding.

erudition, *n.* Dust shaken out of a book into an empty skull.

extinction, *n.* The raw material out of which theology created the future state.

faith, *n.* Belief without evidence in what is told by one who speaks without knowledge, of things without parallel.

genealogy, *n.* An account of one's descent from an ancestor who did not particularly care to trace his own.

ghost, *n.* The outward and visible sign of an inward fear.

habit, *n.* A shackle for the free.

heaven, *n.* A place where the wicked cease from troubling you with talk of their personal affairs, and the good listen with attention while you expound your own.

historian, *n.* A broad-gauge gossip

hope, *n.* Desire and expectation rolled into one.

hypocrite, *n.* One who, professing virtues that he does not respect, secures the advantage of seeming to be what he despises.

impiety, *n.* Your irreverence toward my deity.

impunity, *n.* Wealth.

language, *n.* The music with which we charm the serpents guarding another's treasure.

logic, *n.* The art of thinking and reasoning in strict accordance with the limitations and incapacities of the human misunderstanding. The basis of logic is the syllogism, consisting of a major and a minor premise and a conclusion—thus:

Major Premise: Sixty men can do a piece of work sixty times as quickly as one man.

Minor Premise: One man can dig a post-hole in sixty seconds; therefore—

Conclusion: Sixty men can dig a post-hole in one second.

This may be called the syllogism arithmetical, in which, by combining logic and mathematics, we obtain a double certainty and are twice blessed.

love, *n.* A temporary insanity curable by marriage or by removal of the patient from the influences under which he incurred the disorder. This disease, like *caries* and many other ailments, is prevalent only among civilized races living under artificial conditions; barbarous nations breathing pure air and eating simple food enjoy immunity from its ravages. It is sometimes fatal, but more frequently to the physician than to the patient.

miracle, *n.* An act or event out of the order of nature and unaccountable, as beating a normal hand of four kings and an ace with four aces and a king.

monkey, *n.* An arboreal animal which makes itself at home in genealogical trees.

mouth, *n.* In man, the gateway to the soul; in woman, the outlet of the heart.

non-combatant, *n.* A dead Quaker. 45

platitude, *n.* The fundamental element and special glory of popular literature. A thought that snores in words that smoke. The wisdom of a million fools in the diction of a dullard. A fossil sentiment in artificial rock. A moral without the fable. All that is mortal of a departed truth. A demi-tasse of milk-and-morality. The Pope's-nose of a featherless peacock. A jelly-fish withering on the shore of the sea of thought. The cackle surviving the egg. A desiccated epigram.

pray, *v.* To ask that the laws of the universe be annulled in behalf of a single petitioner confessedly unworthy.

presidency, *n.* The greased pig in the field game of American politics.

prude, *n.* A bawd hiding behind the back of her demeanor.

rapacity, *n.* Providence without industry. The thrift of power. 50

reason, *v.i.* To weigh probabilities in the scales of desire.

religion, *n.* A daughter of Hope and Fear, explaining to Ignorance the nature of the Unknowable.

resolute, *adj.* Obstinate in a course that we approve.

retaliation, *n.* The natural rock upon which is reared the Temple of Law.

saint, *n.* A dead sinner revised and edited. 55

The Duchess of Orleans relates that the irreverent old calumniator, Marshal Villeroi, who in his youth had known St. Francis de Sales, said, on hearing him called saint: "I am delighted to hear that Monsieur de Sales is a saint. He was fond of saying indelicate things, and used to cheat at cards. In other respects he was a perfect gentleman, though a fool."

valor, *n.* A soldierly compound of vanity, duty and the gambler's hope:

> "Why have you halted?" roared the commander of a division at Chickamauga, who had ordered a charge; "move forward, sir, at once."
>
> "General," said the commander of the delinquent brigade, "I am persuaded that any further display of valor by my troops will bring them into collision with the enemy."

☐ *Outward Exploration: Discussion*

1. What topics does Bierce seem to return to several times? Do you find any consistency in his vision of these topics?

2. Assume (for the sake of discussion) that the inscription included in the definition of *cemetery* was meant to refer to Bierce. What does it suggest about his vision of himself and of his relationship to the world?

3. For discussion, pick out two or three definitions that particularly strike you.

☐ *Outward Exploration: Writing*

1. Using this selection from *The Devil's Dictionary,* write an essay exploring Bierce's vision of life. You may use other texts by Bierce if you wish.

2. Select one of Bierce's definitions (or a collection of definitions that share a common topic or attitude) and write an essay exploring them.

3. Select a term of your own, and write an imaginative and revealing definition in the manner of Bierce. Then write an essay explaining the implications of your definition.

The Ignored Lesson of Anne Frank

BRUNO BETTELHEIM

☐ *Inward Exploration*

1. *If you have ever read* The Diary of Anne Frank *or seen the play or one of the movie versions, write at least one paragraph describing what you remember about it. Include whatever emotional response you remember feeling as you experienced the text and your overall emotional evaluation of the text now as you look back on it. For example, by the end of the text, did you feel saddened, uplifted, agitated, calm, or . . . ?*

2. *In your own words, define the term* civilized behavior. *How important is such behavior to you?*

3. *In psychology, the term* anxiety *suggests a more serious emotion than the way most laypeople use the term. Look up the term in a dictionary of psychological terms or in a textbook. As you read the essay, think about how that definition/explanation fits into Bettelheim's usage of the term throughout this essay.*

   Note: In the following essay, Bruno Bettelheim uses his insights as a psychoanalyst and as a survivor of Nazi concentration camps to examine both the experiences of several European Jewish families during World War II (and particularly the Frank family) and the responses of American audiences to the various versions of The Diary of Anne Frank. *Bettelheim makes every effort to keep these two topics clearly separated, but the issues are complex so you need to read very carefully.*

When the world first learned about the Nazi concentration and death camps, most civilized people felt the horrors committed in them to be so uncanny as to be unbelievable. It came as a severe shock that supposedly civilized nations could stoop to such inhuman acts. The implication that modern man has such inadequate control over his cruel and destructive proclivities was felt as a threat to our views of ourselves and our humanity. Three different psychological mechanisms were most frequently used for dealing with the appalling revelation of what had gone on in the camps:

(1) its applicability to man in general was denied by asserting—contrary to evidence—that the acts of torture and mass murder were committed by a small group of insane or perverted persons;

(2) the truth of the reports was denied by declaring them vastly exaggerated and ascribing them to propaganda (this originated with the German government, which called all reports on terror in the camps "horror propaganda"—*Greuelpropaganda*);

(3) the reports were believed, but the knowledge of the horror repressed as soon as possible.

All three mechanisms could be seen at work after liberation of those prisoners remaining. At first, after the discovery of the camps and their death-dealing, a wave of extreme outrage swept the Allied nations. It was soon followed by a general repression of the discovery in people's minds. Possibly this reaction was due to something more than the blow dealt to modern man's narcissism by the realization that cruelty is still rampant among men. Also present may have been the dim but extremely threatening realization that the modern state now has available the means for changing personality, and for destroying millions it deems undesirable. The ideas that in our day a people's personalities might be changed against their will by the state, and that other populations might be wholly or partially exterminated, are so fearful that one tries to free oneself of them and their impact by defensive denial, or by repression.

The extraordinary world-wide success of the book, play, and movie *The Diary of Anne Frank* suggests the power of the desire to counteract the realization of the personality-destroying and murderous nature of the camps by concentrating all attention on what is experienced as a demonstration that private and intimate life can continue to flourish even under the direct persecution by the most ruthless totalitarian system. And this although Anne Frank's fate demonstrates how efforts at disregarding in private life what goes on around one in society can hasten one's own destruction.

What concerns me here is not what actually happened to the Frank family, how they tried—and failed—to survive their terrible ordeal. It would be very wrong to take apart so humane and moving a story, which aroused so much well-merited compassion for gentle Anne Frank and her tragic fate. What is at issue is the universal and uncritical response to her diary and to the play and movie based on it, and what this reaction tells about our attempts to cope with the feelings her fate—used by us to serve as a symbol of a most human reaction to Nazi terror—arouses in us. I believe that the world-wide acclaim given her story cannot be explained unless we recognize in it our wish to forget the gas chambers, and our effort to do so by glorifying the ability to retreat into an extremely private, gentle, sensitive world, and there to cling as much as possible to what have been one's usual daily attitudes and activities, although surrounded by a maelstrom apt to engulf one at any moment.

The Frank family's attitude that life could be carried on as before may well have been what led to their destruction. By eulogizing how they lived in their hiding place while neglecting to examine first whether it was a reasonable or an effective choice, we are able to ignore the crucial lesson of their story—that such an attitude can be fatal in extreme circumstances.

While the Franks were making their preparations for going passively into hiding, thousands of other Jews in Holland (as elsewhere in Europe) were trying to escape to the free world, in order to survive and/or fight. Others who could not escape went underground—into hiding—each family member with, for example, a different gentile family. We gather from the diary, however, that the chief desire of the Frank family was to continue living as nearly as possible in the same fashion to which they had been accustomed in happier times.

Little Anne, too, wanted only to go on with life as usual, and what *10* else could she have done but fall in with the pattern her parents created for her existence? But hers was not a necessary fate, much less a heroic one; it was a terrible but also a senseless fate. Anne had a good chance to survive, as did many Jewish children in Holland. But she would have had to leave her parents and go to live with a gentile Dutch family, posing as their own child, something her parents would have had to arrange for her.

Everyone who recognized the obvious knew that the hardest way to go underground was to do it as a family; to hide out together made detection by the SS most likely; and when detected, everybody was doomed. By hiding singly, even when one got caught, the others had a chance to survive. The Franks, with their excellent connections among gentile Dutch families, might well have been able to hide out singly, each with a different family. But instead, the main principle of their planning was continuing their beloved family life—an understandable desire, but highly unrealistic in those times. Choosing any other course would have meant not merely giving up living together, but also realizing the full measure of the danger to their lives.

The Franks were unable to accept that going on living as a family as they had done before the Nazi invasion of Holland was no longer a desirable way of life, much as they loved each other; in fact, for them and others like them, it was most dangerous behavior. But even given their wish not to separate, they failed to make appropriate preparations for what was likely to happen.

There is little doubt that the Franks, who were able to provide themselves with so much while arranging for going into hiding, and even while hiding, could have provided themselves with some weapons had they wished. Had they had a gun, Mr. Frank could have shot down at least one or two of the "green police" who came for them. There was no surplus of such police, and the loss of an SS with every Jew arrested would have noticeably hindered the functioning of the police state. Even a butcher knife, which they certainly could have taken with them into hiding, could have been used by them in self-defense. The fate of the Franks wouldn't have been very different, because they all died anyway except for Anne's father. But they could have sold their lives for a high price, instead of walking to their death. Still, although one must assume that Mr. Frank would have fought courageously, as we know he did when a soldier in the first World War, it is not everybody who can plan to kill those who are bent on killing him, although many who would not be ready to contemplate doing so would be willing to kill those who are bent on murdering not only them but also their wives and little daughters.

An entirely different matter would have been planning for escape in case of discovery. The Franks' hiding place had only one entrance; it did not have any other exit. Despite this fact, during their many months of hiding, they did not try to devise one. Nor did they make other plans for escape, such as that one of the family members—as likely as not Mr. Frank—would try to detain the police in the narrow entrance way—maybe even fight them, as suggested above—thus giving other members of the family a chance to escape, either by reaching the roofs of adjacent houses, or down a ladder into the alley behind the house in which they were living.

Any of this would have required recognizing and accepting the des-   15
perate straits in which they found themselves, and concentrating on how best to cope with them. This was quite possible to do, even under the terrible conditions in which the Jews found themselves after the Nazi occupation of Holland. It can be seen from many other accounts, for example from the story of Marga Minco, a girl of about Anne Frank's age who lived to tell about it. Her parents had planned that when the police should come for them, the father would try to detain them by arguing and fighting with them, to give the wife and daughter a chance to escape through a rear door. Unfortunately it did not quite work out this way, and both parents got killed. But their short-lived resistance permitted their daughter to make her escape as planned and to reach a Dutch family who saved her.°

This is not mentioned as a criticism that the Frank family did not plan or behave along similar lines. A family has every right to arrange their life as they wish or think best, and to take the risks they want to take. My point is not to criticize what the Franks did, but only the universal admiration of their way of coping, or rather of not coping. The story of little Marga who survived, every bit as touching, remains totally neglected by comparison.

Many Jews—unlike the Franks, who through listening to British radio news were better informed than most—had no detailed knowledge of the extermination camps. Thus it was easier for them to make themselves believe that complete compliance with even the most outrageously debilitating and degrading Nazi orders might offer a chance

---

Marga Minco, *Bitter Herbs* (New York: Oxford University Press, 1960).

for survival. But neither tremendous anxiety that inhibits clear thinking and with it well-planned and determined action, nor ignorance about what happened to those who responded with passive waiting for being rounded up for their extermination, can explain the reaction of audiences to the play and movie retelling Anne's story, which are all about such waiting that results finally in destruction.

I think it is the fictitious ending that explains the enormous success of this play and movie. At the conclusion we hear Anne's voice from the beyond, saying, "In spite of everything, I still believe that people are really good at heart." This improbable sentiment is supposedly from a girl who had been starved to death, had watched her sister meet the same fate before she did, knew that her mother had been murdered, and had watched untold thousands of adults and children being killed. This statement is not justified by anything Anne actually told her diary.

Going on with intimate family living, no matter how dangerous it might be to survival, was fatal to all too many during the Nazi regime. And if all men are good, then indeed we can all go on with living our lives as we have been accustomed to in times of undisturbed safety and can afford to forget about Auschwitz. But Anne, her sister, her mother, may well have died because her parents could not get themselves to believe in Auschwitz.

While play and movie are ostensibly about Nazi persecution and destruction, in actuality what we watch is the way that, despite this terror, lovable people manage to continue living their satisfying intimate lives with each other. The heroine grows from a child into a young adult as normally as any other girl would, despite the most abnormal conditions of all other aspects of her existence, and that of her family. Thus the play reassures us that despite the destructiveness of Nazi racism and tyranny in general, it is possible to disregard it in one's private life much of the time, even if one is Jewish. 20

True, the ending happens just as the Franks and their friends had feared all along; their hiding place is discovered, and they are carried away to their doom. But the fictitious declaration of faith in the goodness of all men which concludes the play falsely reassures us since it impresses on us that in the combat between Nazi terror and continuance of intimate family living the latter wins out, since Anne has the last word. This is simply contrary to fact, because it was she who got killed. Her seeming survival through her moving statement about the goodness of men releases us effectively of the need to cope with the problems Auschwitz presents. That is why we are so relieved by her statement. It explains why millions loved play and movie, because while it confronts us with the fact that Auschwitz existed, it encourages us at the same time to ignore any of its implications. If all men are good at heart, there never really was an Auschwitz; nor is there any possibility that it may recur.

The desire of Anne Frank's parents not to interrupt their intimate family living, and their inability to plan more effectively for their survival, reflect the failure of all too many others faced with the threat of Nazi terror. It is a failure that deserves close examination because of the inherent warnings it contains for us, the living.

Submission to the threatening power of the Nazi state often led both to the disintegration of what had once seemed well-integrated personalities and to a return to an immature disregard for the dangers of reality. Those Jews who submitted passively to Nazi persecution came to depend on primitive and infantile thought processes: wishful thinking and disregard for the possibility of death. Many persuaded themselves that they, out of all the others, would be spared. Many more simply disbelieved in the possibility of their own death. Not believing in it, they did not take what seemed to them desperate precautions, such as giving up everything to hide out singly; or trying to escape even if it meant risking their lives in doing so; or preparing to fight for their lives when no escape was possible and death had become an immediate possibility. It is true that defending their lives in active combat before they were rounded up to be transported into the camps might have hastened their deaths, and so, up to a point, they were protecting themselves by "rolling with the punches" of the enemy.

But the longer one rolls with the punches dealt not by the normal vagaries of life, but by one's eventual executioner, the more likely it becomes that one will no longer have the strength to resist when death becomes imminent. This is particularly true if yielding to the enemy is accompanied not by a commensurate strengthening of the personality, but by an inner disintegration. We can observe such a process among the Franks, who bickered with each other over trifles, instead of supporting each other's ability to resist the demoralizing impact of their living conditions.

Those who faced up to the announced intentions of the Nazis prepared for the worst as a real and imminent possibility. It meant risking one's life for a self-chosen purpose, but in doing so, creating at least a small chance for saving one's own life or those of others, or both. When Jews in Germany were restricted to their homes, those who did not succumb to inertia took the new restrictions as a warning that it was high time to go underground, join the resistance movement, provide themselves with forged papers, and so on, if they had not done so long ago. Many of them survived.

Some distant relatives of mine may furnish an example. Early in the war, a young man living in a small Hungarian town banded together with a number of other Jews to prepare against a German invasion. As soon as the Nazis imposed curfews on the Jews, his group left for Budapest—because the bigger capital city with its greater anonymity offered chances for escaping detection. Similar groups from other towns converged in Budapest and joined forces. From among themselves they selected typically "Aryan"-looking men who equipped themselves with false papers and immediately joined the Hungarian SS. These spies were then able to warn of impending persecution and raids.

Many of these groups survived intact. Furthermore, they had also equipped themselves with small arms, so that if they were detected, they could put up enough of a fight for the majority to escape while a few would die fighting to make the escape possible. A few of the Jews who had joined the SS were discovered and immediately shot, probably a death preferable to one in the gas chambers. But most of even these Jews survived, hiding within the SS until liberation.

Compare these arrangements not just to the Franks' selection of a hiding place that was basically a trap without an outlet but with Mr. Frank's teaching typically academic high-school subjects to his children rather than how to make a getaway: a token of his inability to face the seriousness of the threat of death. Teaching high-school subjects had, of course, its constructive aspects. It relieved the ever-present anxiety about their fate to some degree by concentrating on different matters, and by implication it encouraged hope for a future in which such knowledge would be useful. In this sense such teaching was purposeful, but it was erroneous in that it took the place of much more pertinent teaching and planning: how best to try to escape when detected.

Unfortunately the Franks were by no means the only ones who, out of anxiety, became unable to contemplate their true situation and with it to plan accordingly. Anxiety, and the wish to counteract it by clinging to each other, and to reduce its sting by continuing as much as possible with their usual way of life incapacitated many, particularly when survival plans required changing radically old ways of living that they cherished, and which had become their only source of satisfaction.

My young relative, for example, was unable to persuade other members of his family to go with him when he left the small town where he had lived with them. Three times, at tremendous risk to himself, he returned to plead with his relatives, pointing out first the growing persecution of the Jews, and later the fact that transport to the gas chambers had already begun. He could not convince these Jews to leave their homes and break up their families to go singly into hiding.

As their desperation mounted, they clung more determinedly to their old living arrangements and to each other, became less able to consider giving up the possessions they had accumulated through hard work over a lifetime. The more severely their freedom to act was reduced, and what little they were still permitted to do restricted by insensible and degrading regulations imposed by the Nazis, the more did they become unable to contemplate independent action. Their life energies drained out of them, sapped by their ever-greater anxiety. The less they found strength in themselves, the more they held on to the little that was left of what had given them security in the past—their old surroundings, their customary way of life, their possessions—all these seemed to give their lives some permanency, offer some symbols of security. Only what had once been symbols of security now endangered life, since they were excuses for avoiding change. On each successive visit the young man found his relatives more incapacitated, less willing or able to take his advice, more frozen into inactivity, and with it further along the way to the crematoria where, in fact, they all died.

Levin renders a detailed account of the desperate but fruitless efforts made by small Jewish groups determined to survive to try to save the rest. She tells how messengers were "sent into the provinces to warn Jews that deportation meant death, but their warnings were ignored because most Jews refused to contemplate their own annihilation."° I believe the reason for such refusal has to be found in their inability to take action. If we are certain that we are helpless to protect ourselves against the danger of destruction, we cannot contemplate it. We can consider the danger only as long as we believe there are ways to protect ourselves, to fight back, to escape. If we are convinced none of this is possible for us, then there is no point in thinking about the danger; on the contrary, it is best to refuse to do so.

As a prisoner in Buchenwald, I talked to hundreds of German Jewish prisoners who were brought there as part of the huge pogrom in the wake of the murder of vom Rath in the fall of 1938. I asked them why they had not left Germany, given the utterly degrading conditions they had been subjected to. Their answer was: How could we leave? It would have meant giving up our homes, our work, our sources of income. Having been deprived by Nazi persecution and degradation of much of their self-respect, they had become unable to give up what still gave them a semblance of it: their earthly belongings. But instead of using possessions, they became captivated by them, and this possession by earthly goods became the fatal mask for their possession by anxiety, fear, and denial.

How the investment of personal property with one's life energy could make people die bit by bit was illustrated throughout the Nazi persecution of the Jews. At the time of the first boycott of Jewish stores, the chief external goal of the Nazis was to acquire the possessions of the Jews. They even let Jews take some things out of the country at that time if they would leave the bulk of their property behind. For a long time the intention of the Nazis, and the goal of their first discriminatory laws, was to force undesirable minorities, including Jews, into emigration.

Although the extermination policy was in line with the inner logic *35* of Nazi racial ideology, one may wonder whether the idea that millions of Jews (and other foreign nationals) could be submitted to extermination did not partially result from seeing the degree of degradation Jews

---

Nora Levin, *The Holocaust* (New York: Thomas Y. Crowell, 1968).

accepted without fighting back. When no violent resistance occurred, persecution of the Jews worsened, slow step by slow step.

Many Jews who on the invasion of Poland were able to survey their situation and draw the right conclusions survived the Second World War. As the Germans approached, they left everything behind and fled to Russia, much as they distrusted and disliked the Soviet system. But there, while badly treated, they could at least survive. Those who stayed on in Poland believing they could go on with life-as-before sealed their fate. Thus in the deepest sense the walk to the gas chamber was only the last consequence of these Jews' inability to comprehend what was in store; it was the final step of surrender to the death instinct, which might also be called the principle of inertia. The first step was taken long before arrival at the death camp.

We can find a dramatic demonstration of how far the surrender to inertia can be carried, and the wish not to know because knowing would create unbearable anxiety, in an experience of Olga Lengyel.° She reports that although she and her fellow prisoners lived just a few hundred yards from the crematoria and the gas chambers and knew what they were for, most prisoners denied knowledge of them for months. If they had grasped their true situation, it might have helped them save either the lives they themselves were fated to lose, or the lives of others.

When Mrs. Lengyel's fellow prisoners were selected to be sent to the gas chambers, they did not try to break away from the group, as she successfully did. Worse, the first time she tried to escape the gas chambers, some of the other selected prisoners told the supervisors that she was trying to get away. Mrs. Lengyel desperately asks the question: How was it possible that people denied the existence of the gas chambers when all day long they saw the crematoria burning and smelled the odor of burning flesh? Why did they prefer ignoring the exterminations to fighting for their very own lives? She can offer no explanation, only the observation that they resented anyone who tried to save himself from the common fate, because they lacked enough courage to risk action themselves. I believe they did it because they had given up their will to live and permitted their death tendencies to engulf them. As a result, such prisoners were in the thrall of the murdering SS not only physically but also psychologically, while this was not true for those prisoners who still had a grip on life.

Some prisoners even began to serve their executioners, to help speed the death of their own kind. Then things had progressed beyond simple inertia to the death instinct running rampant. Those who tried to serve their executioners in what were once their civilian capacities were merely continuing life as usual and thereby opening the door to their death.

Olga Lengyel, *Five Chimneys: The Story of Auschwitz* (Chicago: Ziff-Davis, 1947).

For example, Mrs. Lengyel speaks of Dr. Mengele, SS physician at   *40*
Auschwitz, as a typical example of the "business as usual" attitude that
enabled some prisoners, and certainly the SS, to retain whatever balance
they could despite what they were doing. She describes how Dr. Mengele took all correct medical precautions during childbirth, rigorously
observing all aseptic principles, cutting the umbilical cord with greatest
care, etc. But only half an hour later he sent mother and infant to be
burned in the crematorium.

Having made his choice, Dr. Mengele and others like him had to
delude themselves to be able to live with themselves and their experience. Only one personal document on the subject has come to my attention, that of Dr. Nyiszli, a prisoner serving as "research physician" at
Auschwitz.° How Dr. Nyiszli deluded himself can be seen, for example,
in the way he repeatedly refers to himself as working in Auschwitz as a
physician, although he worked as the assistant of a criminal murderer.
He speaks of the Institute for Race, Biological, and Anthropological
Investigation as "one of the most qualified medical centers of the Third
Reich," although it was devoted to proving falsehoods. That Nyiszli
was a doctor didn't alter the fact that he—like any of the prisoner fore-
men who served the SS better than some SS were willing to serve it—
was a participant in the crimes of the SS. How could he do it and live
with himself?

The answer is: by taking pride in his professional skills, irrespective
of the purpose they served. Dr. Nyiszli and Dr. Mengele were only two
among hundreds of other—and far more prominent—physicians who
participated in the Nazis' murderous pseudo-scientific human experiments. It was the peculiar pride of these men in their professional skill
and knowledge, without regard for moral implications, that made them
so dangerous. Although the concentration camps and crematoria are no
longer here, this kind of pride still remains with us; it is characteristic of
a modern society in which fascination with technical competence has
dulled concern for human feelings. Auschwitz is gone, but so long as
this attitude persists, we shall not be safe from cruel indifference to life
at the core.

I have met many Jews as well as gentile anti-Nazis, similar to the
activist group in Hungary described earlier, who survived in Nazi Germany and in the occupied countries. These people realized that when a
world goes to pieces and inhumanity reigns supreme, man cannot go on
living his private life as he was wont to do, and would like to do; he
cannot, as the loving head of a family, keep the family living together
peacefully, undisturbed by the surrounding world; nor can he continue
to take pride in his profession or possessions, when either will deprive

---

Miklos Nyiszli, *Auschwitz: A Doctor's Eyewitness Account* (New York: Frederick Fell,
1960).

him of his humanity, if not also of his life. In such times, one must radically reevaluate all of what one has done, believed in, and stood for in order to know how to act. In short, one has to take a stand on the new reality—a firm stand, not one of retirement into an even more private world.

If today, Negroes in Africa march against the guns of a police that defends *apartheid*—even if hundreds of dissenters are shot down and tens of thousands rounded up in camps—their fight will sooner or later assure them of a chance for liberty and equality. Millions of the Jews of Europe who did not or could not escape in time or go underground as many thousands did, could at least have died fighting as some did in the Warsaw ghetto at the end, instead of passively waiting to be rounded up for their own extermination.

Outward Exploration: Discussion

1. Summarize your reactions, both intellectual and emotional, to this essay.

2. In paragraph 6, Bettelheim suggests the major reason for the success of *The Diary of Anne Frank*. What exactly is it? Does he imply a warning to us today in this paragraph?

3. In paragraph 7, Bettelheim says that "[i]t would be very wrong to take apart so humane and moving a story" as that of Anne Frank. Yet in several parts of the essay, he criticizes the behavior of the Frank family. Is this a contradiction, or is he doing something other than "take it apart"? If it is a contradiction, is there some reason why he feels it necessary to make this misleading statement near the beginning of his essay?

4. In several places throughout the essay, Bettelheim mentions other Jewish families in circumstances similar to the Franks's. Why does he mention them? What comparisons and contrasts is he drawing? How effective are they?

5. In paragraph 10, Bettelheim says that Anne's was "not a necessary fate, much less a heroic one." What does he mean by that?

6. Beginning with paragraph 12, Bettelheim argues that even given the Franks's unrealistic desire to stay together, they made several mistakes. What were they? Ultimately, what caused them to make those mistakes?

7. In paragraph 16, Bettelheim reiterates that he is not criticizing the Frank family. What does he say his purpose is?

8. In paragraph 20, Bettelheim says that the play and movie versions are not really about Nazi persecution and destruction. What are they about?

9. In paragraph 22, Bettelheim moves beyond the Frank family to explore the "failure" of many others to react realistically to the Nazi threat. According to him, what was the effect of the Nazi threats?

10. Paragraph 28 explains the constructive and destructive aspects of Mr. Frank teaching his children traditional high school subjects. Explain them.

11. Throughout the essay, Bettelheim gives us many psychological observations about how people react to anxiety and fear, about the disintegration of personality, about why people cling to behavior that no longer is an adequate response to a changed reality. List those observations.

☐ *Outward Exploration: Writing*

1. Have you ever been in a situation where you reacted ineffectively? For example, have you ever clung to an old style of behavior (the way you write a paper, the way you ask people out on dates, the way you deal with sexual harassment, the way you deal with stress) that no longer worked? If so, write an essay explaining the pattern of behavior, give one detailed event which displayed the behavior, and then try to analyze the reasons why you behaved that way. Feel free to quote from Bettelheim if his concepts seem appropriate.

2. Use one or more of the passages you wrote for "Inward Exploration" as the basis for writing an essay which explores some of the issues raised in Bettelheim's essay or which argues for or against his position.

3. In paragraph 5, Bettelheim says that "the modern state now has available the means for changing personality, and for destroying millions it deems undesirable." This one sentence raises several issues that you might explore in an essay. For example, what countries now seem to you to have such hatred of one of their own groups or of some other nation that they would like to exterminate them? Explore why that hatred exists (this will no doubt require some library research into historical and economic causes). Examine your own feelings toward and thoughts about that group.

4. Using that same passage in #3 above, have you ever personally felt a desire—no matter how briefly—to totally destroy some other group? If so, write an essay exploring the circumstances surrounding that emotion. Speculate about the underlying reasons why you felt that way.

5. Still using the passage in #3 above, explain what means of changing someone's personality exist in our world. For example, you might consider advertising (which is really propaganda aimed at consumers) and "managed news" (reading or rereading Molly Ivins's "The

Perils and Pitfalls of Reporting in the Lone Star State" in "Further Readings" would be helpful here). Have you ever been a member of a group that has actively tried to change your personality? This is not necessarily a sinister operation, of course, since any organization tries to change elements of human personality. For example, most religious organizations try to make humans more forgiving, more moral, less aggressive. Most colleges try to make humans more thoughtful, less prone to impulsive behavior. Most nations try to change people into better citizens (you might define what a "good citizen" is for your country). Further, most therapists try to modify patients' behavior, usually at the patients' request. Explore your reactions to such attempts to change your personality and your attitudes. Speculate carefully about how to differentiate between "good" modifications of your behavior and "sinister" ones.

6. If you have ever been in extraordinary circumstances, write an essay about it. Try to document your feelings and thoughts then as well as your thoughts and feelings now as you look back on them. Try to use some of Bettelheim's insights and observations to analyze your thoughts and feelings then, but don't limit yourself to Bettelheim's ideas.

7. Taking an overview of humankind, would you say that people are really good at heart? Write an essay explaining your response. Do research to broaden your understanding, using quotations to support your view or as points to argue against.

8. Most of us do things "in the heat of the moment" that we later regret doing. Sometimes we even do things which, when we think about them later, amaze or frighten us—"How could I have done such a thing?" we ask ourselves. If you have ever done something that, on later reflection, seemed unlike you or that seemed against your moral code, write an essay exploring it. Analyze the reasons why you did something which, normally, you would not approve of doing. Try to think of as many reasons, both internal (psychological) and external (such as pressure from peers or from economic circumstances) as possible.

9. What exactly is the "surrender to inertia" that Bettelheim refers to in paragraph 37? Have you ever surrendered to inertia in a less dramatic fashion? If so, write an essay about it.

☐ *Style*

Consider the following sentence from Bettelheim's essay:

The more severely their freedom to act was reduced, and what little they were still permitted to do restricted by insensible and degrading regulations imposed by the Nazis, the more did they become unable to contemplate independent action. (paragraph 31)

What is noteworthy in this sentence is "the more x . . . , the more y" structure. This achieves a sense of balance within the sentence while suggesting a cause-and-effect relationship between the elements mentioned (the greater restrictions on freedom caused the withering of their ability to contemplate action on their own). Write a sentence of your own that uses this structure ("the more . . . , the more").

7

Exploring Beliefs

The inward–outward pattern of exploratory writers is perhaps most clearly illustrated when we write about beliefs: You look inward to discover your thoughts and feelings, then outward to see if they coincide with those of people in the real world; then you carry new real-world information back inward to see how it alters or adds to the inner world's attitudes and beliefs, then move outward again to discover the views of others, then back inward to weigh their ideas against yours.

WHAT IS A BELIEF?

A **belief** is an idea or a concept which we accept as true. Ethical or moral beliefs are those that we use to justify or condemn the actions of ourselves and of others. Such beliefs make up our **moral code,** a collection of beliefs that function as guidelines of our behavior as well as tools of analysis. Underlying our moral code is our **philosophy of life,** a system of beliefs about the "big" questions, both secular and religious: What is the meaning of life? Is there a God? Is there human progress throughout history or only the illusion of progress? What is happiness? What is success? What are good and evil? What makes a society good? What makes an individual person good? What is basic human nature (for instance, good, bad, selfish, selfless)? What makes us do the things we do? Is free will a reality or only an illusion? What is reality? Is there such a thing as objective reality, or is reality merely a creation of each individual's subjective perception? That is a sampling of the "big" questions; no doubt others occur to you as well.

When beliefs remain unconscious, we call them **assumptions.**

When we are forced to examine those assumptions, we sometimes discover that they are in conflict with other assumptions or with ideas that we have consciously accepted as beliefs—hence the desirability of writing about beliefs. By exploring their implications and consequences, we learn more about ourselves.

Beliefs are built on beliefs: Consider, for instance, your political beliefs, which are based, at least in part, on your beliefs about the nature of humans and about what makes a person good and a society just. If you assume that humans cannot be trusted to make decisions based on anything other than short-term self-interest (for example, taking advantage of the lack of banking regulations to steal money from savings and loan institutions), then you are likely to believe that laws should regulate as much behavior as possible (imposing more restrictions on banking practices). If, on the other hand, you assume that humans are innately good and are corrupted by bad institutions, you are likely to believe that the solution to human misbehavior is to eliminate bad institutions. For example, if you believe that the structure of political campaigning forces candidates to accept donations from big corporations which then have undue influence over them, you may favor giving all candidates free access to the media, eliminating the need for huge "war chests." Often we work backward, beginning with the conscious belief (create more banking regulations) to discover the underlying assumptions (humans can think only about short-term benefits to themselves). In the process of exploring conscious beliefs, then, we discover some of our unconscious assumptions and thus learn more about ourselves and how we view the world.

With all of this in mind, you can see that much of what was said in the previous chapter about ideas and concepts also applies here. In some ways, much of this text has been, at least implicitly, about beliefs. For example, we have explored beliefs about events (Chapter 3), as well as beliefs about love, friendship, marriage, and parenting (Chapter 5). In a sense, this whole book is ultimately dedicated to your exploring your own beliefs about yourself and about the world outside your skin.

Stating a Belief

Stating a belief in words, although seemingly simple, can be difficult. It is, nevertheless, important to try. Doing so will clarify your thoughts.

Often, beliefs or systems of belief have public names already (for example, *fairness, existentialism, socialism, hedonism, humanism*). Such public names are a good place to start. They are not, however, enough for an exploratory essay because the public name often hides many nuances and variations. Consider existentialism, for example. Practically every existentialist writer and philosopher has his or her own slant, from Christian existentialism to atheistic existentialism and all stops in between. Simply proclaiming oneself an existentialist, then, leaves a great deal unsaid and unexplored.

This is not to say you shouldn't use the public name, for it can accomplish at least two things for you as a writer: First, the name will raise some ideas in the minds of your readers (even if those ideas have to be countered or altered later in your essay) and, second, it is a tool that will allow you to investigate what other writers have said about that belief.

So, using the public name of the belief is a good starting place, but you need to explain what the belief means for you as well.

Considering the Implications of a Belief

What are the implications of a belief in self-reliance? Well, if everyone should be self-reliant, then maybe the government should eliminate welfare payments, price supports to farmers, tariffs on foreign goods, tax breaks to parents with children in college. And what are the implications of animals' having rights? If animals really do have rights, maybe everyone should be a vegetarian. Perhaps medical research involving animals should stop.

Looking at the possible implications of a belief, then, helps you (and ultimately your readers) evaluate it more fully. For example, self-reliance certainly seems to be a wonderful ideal. But most of us would agree that some people cannot be totally self-reliant (for example, the very young, the very old, and the sick). Realizing this, we might decide to modify the statement of our belief. Instead of saying "Everyone must be self-reliant," we might say "Everyone should be as self-reliant *as his or her capabilities allow.*" Adequately considering the implications of a belief may require several pages, including examples to make the implications clear.

Considering the Sources of a Belief

You will also need to consider where your belief came from. Often a belief has more than one source. Take self-reliance as an example. Consider all the television shows, movies, books, plays, and advertisements whose heroes are loners, solitary individuals standing up for themselves (Superman, Clint Eastwood's movie characters, Robinson Crusoe, and James Bond). Ralph Waldo Emerson, hardly a pop culture figure, wrote a major essay on the concept. Henry David Thoreau, living beside Walden Pond, provided a 24-hour-a-day example of self-reliance. More immediately, parents, family members, and friends often tell us to "look out for ourselves." In fact, our whole culture seems to celebrate self-reliance, even if this belief has proven to have some practical limitations. In an essay about self-reliance, then, you might quote Emerson, Thoreau, and your parents and friends, and you could also allude to various films and plays as sources of this particular belief.

But these are not the only kind of sources. Return to the list of identities and vantage points in Chapter 2 ("Exploring Yourself"). Each of those, too, might turn out to be a source of beliefs. For example, all of the following can influence our beliefs: racial, sexual, social, political, religious, and geographic identity; economic class; age; temperament; family; education; and, of course, personal experiences. Consider these as you examine the sources of your beliefs.

A lot of beliefs are floating around out there, all competing for our attention. Why do we heed some and not others? Why do some messages get through and others get blocked? In other words, what makes us receptive to some beliefs and deaf to others?

Our receptiveness is a complex issue. First and probably most important, our receptiveness is affected by our background. Once again, the identities and vantage points mentioned in the previous section come into play. For example, our parents, family members, peers, neighborhood, and society as a whole condition us to accept certain beliefs. Some of this conditioning is conscious: For example, the parents who repeatedly tell their children not to take something that doesn't belong to them are consciously conditioning those children to respect property rights. Often, however, the conditioning is unconscious—for example, the parents who preach honesty but who lie on their income tax returns, or who consciously condition their children to avoid drugs while they down three or four cocktails each evening. The messages here are mixed, of course, yet for some reason the unconscious conditioning (seeing the parents lie or drink) usually seems to overpower the parents' conscious conditioning.

Second, we all have a certain amount of credulity and rebellion in our makeup. Some of us are quick to see hypocrisy (or at least inconsistencies in behavior) and slow to believe goodness; others of us are the opposite—more than willing to believe the good and slow to see the hypocrisy or evil. All of us have a certain amount of "talent" in assessing concepts offered to us for belief. Just as some of us have more talent for playing the piano than others, so some of us have more talent for weighing beliefs than others. If we are very active and impulsive people, then we probably act first and justify later, perhaps developing beliefs to explain our actions as we go along. If we are very meditative and reflective people, perhaps we have the beliefs in place and analyze our choices carefully before making a decision. Each approach has its advantages and its disadvantages. The important thing is to recognize which approach you tend to favor as you discuss your beliefs.

Third, we all make conscious decisions to act in certain ways. For instance, we might have decided to behave honestly during exams, regardless of the pressure to cheat along with some friends. Or we might decide to be the designated driver at tonight's party and hence drink only soda. Decisions about moral actions such as these require underlying beliefs. Even if we haven't consciously decided to be honest in all of our dealings, the decision to behave honestly during the exam suggests a belief in the value of at least the ideal of honesty. The decision to be the designated driver indicates a belief in friends being responsible for friends and a belief in the importance of accepting responsibility.

As you write to explore your beliefs, you will often find that exploring one belief reveals another acting as its foundation. In fact, you may find yourself digging through several layers of beliefs. Therefore, a lot of prewriting and perhaps several drafts may be needed before you are ready to begin polishing your prose for the final draft.

WRITER-BASED GOALS

There are five writer-based goals: (1) to discover and to explore deeply one of your beliefs; (2) to examine the opinions of others; (3) to become more aware of the assumptions that influence your actions; (4) to explore the implications of your belief—for example, what actions it leads to or endorses, what other beliefs it supports; (5) to discover the sources of your belief and the reasons for your receptivity to that belief.

READER-BASED GOALS

There are four reader-based goals: (1) to help your readers understand you better; (2) to inform them of a belief of yours; (3) to show them how you arrived at that belief; (4) to show how the belief manifests itself in your actions or in your support of particular positions or programs.

STRUCTURING THE ESSAY

One effective structure is suggested by the reader-based goals just listed. Begin with your statement of the belief, examine its sources, and then show how the belief manifests itself in your behavior.

Another strategy is to begin with the statement of a belief you have subsequently revised ("All people should be self-reliant") and then *to dramatize your process of discovery* as you think through the belief's implications and sources, perhaps prompted by some experience. Such an approach might work well for exploring the question of how very young, very old, or very sick people could be self-reliant. You might use an example or recount an event to show someone's inability to care for himself or herself. The next section might pose questions: for example, "How can such people be self-reliant? Does the principle of self-reliance fail here?" In the rest of the essay you might refine and qualify your original tentative statement of the belief until the essay ends with the more developed, more complex belief.

BELIEFS IN ACTION

You might begin with an event—for instance, a time when you passed up an offer of much needed help in order to appear self-reliant—and then "meditate" on its meaning and implications, thus ending with a statement of your belief.

A variation of this approach is to create a "what-if" situation to see how you would respond. You might begin by describing the situation, explain its ethical or moral significance, and then tell what you would do in that situation and *why*—that is, lay out the beliefs underlying your hypothetical actions. Or you could select a situation that happened to someone you know, comparing and contrasting your beliefs and resulting actions with those of the person involved.

Of course, many other structures and approaches are possible as the essays included in this book prove. Select one that feels comfortable and which allows you to probe your beliefs. You might even return to the essay you wrote exploring an event (Chapter 3) and dig deeper into the beliefs that underlay your actions and reactions.

LOOKING FOR COMPLEXITY

The more complex the situation you choose, the better test of your belief it is—and the more interesting the essay is likely to be.

What makes a situation complex? Conflict between two or more beliefs or between a belief and a goal is the main source of ethical complexity. In the real world, we face ethical situations almost daily. Those situations can become dilemmas when two or more of our beliefs are placed in conflict or when ethical implications conflict with practical ones.

Let's look at a hypothetical example. Ellen has a good friend named Mike who begs to borrow the "A" paper she wrote last year for her nineteenth-century American history class. He is taking the same course this semester, and he wants to pass in her paper as his own. He offers her several "good" reasons why he didn't manage to write a paper on his own, but she suspects that he simply procrastinated. Also, she knows that he doesn't take school as seriously as she does.

What should Ellen do?

Caught in a moral dilemma, she decides to examine her beliefs in order to gain insight into what she should do. She lists the following beliefs:

Honesty is the best policy.

Friends should help friends, even if giving such help hurts.

People should work for what they get.

Individuals must make up their own minds about their own moral codes.

I am an honest person.

People must pay back debts.

The major conflict is between her belief that "friends should help out friends" and her belief that "honesty is the best policy." To resolve the conflict, Ellen might invoke her belief that "people should work for what they get": Presumably Mike would get a good grade on the copied paper, a grade that he didn't deserve. Further, her belief in herself as "an honest person" would be shaken by helping Mike cheat.

Countering those beliefs, however, might be the sense that "individuals must make up their own moral codes." Ellen might ask herself, "Who am I to impose my code of honesty on my friend?" She might even say to herself, "I am not being dishonest in lending him my paper. By giving him the paper I am merely responding to a friend's request. What he does with it is his business and his responsibility, not mine."

Do you see how the conflict between the beliefs leads to an interesting and revealing situation?

If that's not enough complexity, there might be some practical considerations as well. For instance, Ellen might worry about the ramifications if Mike got caught using her paper. Perhaps the paper was memorable, and, armed with the certainty that he'd read it before, the professor would confront Mike, who might confess. What would happen to Mike? An "F" for the course? Expulsion? What would be the practical consequences for Ellen? Would the professor also confront her? What would Ellen say in her defense? She would probably not face any grade penalty (after all, she's not in the course). Yet there could still be serious ramifications for her. For example, Ellen's reputation among faculty members might be damaged. Other factors might be included in the calculation of her risk. For example, what if she were a history major? Would being caught endanger her academic reputation, and would the professors she must depend on for recommendations in her major be less willing to write those recommendations? Or what if she never planned to take another history course again? Would she be "less vulnerable" if Mike got caught? And should either of those circumstances influence her decision whether to lend him the paper?

To make it more complicated, what if Mike had a different professor from the one Ellen had? Would the very remote chance of his (and her) getting caught make it easier to lend him the paper?

Worse yet, what if Mike had done her a huge favor only a week earlier? That would bring into play her belief that "people must pay back their debts." What if Mike were her only real friend? Would she be afraid that he would drop her as a friend? If she feared that, should she give him the paper? Is fear ever a good reason for making any decision?

Everyday life is filled with such dilemmas or potential dilemmas. Probing a situation that seriously puts one or more of your beliefs to the test is the key to learning more about your beliefs and yourself in general. It is also the key to illuminating something significant for your readers.

AVOIDING COMMON PROBLEMS

The most common problems with essays about beliefs are the following:

1. The writer assumes readers understand everything once they read the belief's public name. This just isn't true. Even some members of the same group can disagree about what the true meaning of the belief is. (Just look at all the various branches of Christianity or Judaism or all the different types of Democrats or Republicans.) It's important to define your terms clearly and to stick to those meanings throughout your essay. Remember that one of your goals is to inform your readers, so give them information that they probably don't already have.

2. The writer does not do enough research, relying instead only on his or her version of the belief. For example, if you consider yourself to be a stoic, you need to explain the range of beliefs and assumptions that position carries.

☐ *Exercise 1*

1. From the following list, choose three beliefs that would be worth exploring in an essay and be prepared to discuss your choices. Feel free to add any beliefs you wish to the list. After all, it is hardly complete; in fact, it barely scratches the surface. Each item in the list should also suggest its opposite (for instance, *liberal* might suggest *conservative*):

    vegetarianism

    pacifist

    stoicism

    humanism

    Judaism

    Hinduism

    Christianity

    atheism

    agnosticism

    conservative

    liberal

    Freudian

    Jungian

self-interest

hedonism

selflessness

selfishness

intellect

emotions

rationalism

existentialism

ecofeminism

feminism

Marxism

socialism

democracy

2. Below are the bare-bones of several hypothetical moral situations. Skip those which would not pose a dilemma for you. Select one (or more) of the remaining ones, and write about what you would do and about the beliefs that would underlie your decision. Feel free to add as many details as you'd like or to alter the situation. The point is to explore.

   a. In a restaurant the waitress forgets to charge you and your companion for dessert. Do you call her attention to the problem or simply leave her a bigger tip? Or do you take some other action?

   b. On an airplane, an annoying old woman asks if you would switch seats with her since she would like to look out the window. Assume that you made a point of making an early reservation in order to get a window seat. Do you switch seats with the woman?

   c. A good friend has just bought an expensive outfit and asks your opinion both of the outfit and about whether it is appropriate to wear to a formal function with faculty and parents. You think the outfit is ugly, that it makes her look "cheap" and fat, and that it is incredibly inappropriate. What do you say to your friend?

   d. Soon after marriage, you discover that your mate is dead-set against having children, even though having children was one of the main reasons you decided to get married in the first place. Do you leave your mate?

   e. A friend confides in you that he is going to commit suicide tonight and asks you to promise not to interfere. Do you promise? If so, do you keep your promise?

f. Returning from the mall, you discover that an acquaintance who accompanied you has stolen over $60 worth of CDs. What do you do? What if it's your best friend who stole the CDs?

g. Although you are in a supposedly "committed" relationship with X, you find yourself strongly attracted to Y. When X goes home for the weekend, Y invites you to go out. What do you do? Why? Do you tell X later?

h. The person with whom you have been in a "committed" relationship has been unfaithful to you. What do you do?

i. Despite all your good advice, a friend continues to behave obnoxiously when you are together with other people. Do you pull away from the friendship?

j. You are a lawyer. In your conversations with your client, he not only admits to committing the crime of which he is accused, but he also brags about committing several other crimes. Do you still defend him? If so, do you do your best to get him acquitted, or do you do a mediocre job knowing that he deserves punishment and that he will be a threat to society if he is acquitted?

k. As a well-respected person in your community, you are asked by a friend to publicly endorse her candidacy for the school committee. You don't agree with many of her ideas about education and you do not plan to vote for her, but she is a friend. What do you do?

l. You accidentally erase all the files on one of your mother's computer disks while using it without permission. She blames your sibling. Do you confess? What if you had been unjustly punished for something that your sibling did last week? Would that fact alter your decision?

m. Faced with a 10-page paper and a major exam in a course which you are failing, you receive a midnight phone call from a friend begging you to come over and comfort her. She has just broken up with her boyfriend and is distraught. What do you do? What if she is threatening to commit suicide?

n. You are applying for a job which requires expertise that you don't have, even though your present job title suggests that you do. You have faith that you can learn what you need to know while on the job. Do you lie in the interview and pretend that you have the expertise?

o. Your roommate is away for the weekend. While looking for a pencil to borrow from the roommate's desk, you find his or her private journal. Do you read it?

p. You suspect that an acquaintance is being physically abused by her boyfriend. When you try to raise the issue indirectly, it's clear that she does not want to acknowledge the fact or discuss the issue. What do you do?

q. Your friend's drinking has started to get more and more out-of-hand. At times your friend gets so drunk that he or she can't even find the way back to the dorm. Your friend brushes off any attempts on your part to offer help or suggestions, maintaining loudly that there is no drinking problem. What do you do?

r. While on a first date, both you and the woman you are with have too much to drink. Knowing her reputation as being pretty strict about having sex, you are surprised when she invites you back to her room. Once there, you realize that she is much drunker than you and that under sober conditions she would never have invited you back there on a first date. Still, she is very attractive and you plan to ask her out again. Do you take advantage of the situation?

s. You are the woman in situation #18. The man has sex with you while you are too drunk to stop him. The next morning you realize what happened. What action, if any, do you take? Why?

t. You are a reporter for a newspaper. Ms. X has been a good source of off-the-record information for you, and three of your best stories have been the result of leads you received from her. Now you discover that Ms. X has herself been guilty of a job-related crime. Breaking the story will be another milestone in your career, and you are pretty sure that the story will lead to a promotion for you. You are also 95% sure that no other reporters will ever get this story; in other words, if you don't report the story, Ms. X's crime will never be known. Practical considerations include (but are not limited to) the following: (1) Her crime is the type which will no doubt get her fired from her job but will probably not result in legal prosecution; (2) she has been friendly to you and helped your career when she gained nothing from helping you except your friendship; (3) her job is such that she will probably continue to give you tips that will lead to revelations of corruption in elected officials, so keeping her on the job will probably lead to the apprehension of more corrupt public officials. What options are open to you? What belief(s) are involved? What would you do—write the story and expose her or kill the story? Why?

Was the World Made for Man?

MARK TWAIN

☐ *Inward Exploration*

Write a paragraph explaining your beliefs or thoughts about the creation of the world, including how it was created and, if applicable, why it was created.

I seem to be the only scientist and theologian still remaining to be   *1*
heard from on this important matter of whether the world was made for
man or not. I feel that it is time for me to speak.

I stand almost with the others. They believe the world was made
for man, I believe it likely that it was made for man; they think there
is proof, astronomical mainly, that it was made for man, I think there is
evidence only, not proof, that it was made for him. It is too early, yet,
to arrange the verdict, the returns are not all in. When they are all in, I
think they will show that the world was made for man; but we must not
hurry, we must patiently wait till they are all in.

Now as far as we have got, astronomy is on our side. Mr. Wallace°
has clearly shown this. He has clearly shown two things: that the world
was made for man, and that the universe was made for the world—
to stiddy it, you know. The astronomy part is settled, and cannot be
challenged.

We come now to the geological part. This is the one where the evidence is not all in, yet. It is coming in, hourly, daily, coming in all the
time, but naturally it comes with geological carefulness and deliberation, and we must not be impatient, we must not get excited, we must
be calm, and wait. To lose our tranquillity will not hurry geology; nothing hurries geology.

It takes a long time to prepare a world for man, such a thing is not   *5*
done in a day. Some of the great scientists, carefully ciphering the evi
dences furnished by geology, have arrived at the conviction that our
world is prodigiously old, and they may be right, but Lord Kelvin° is
not of their opinion. He takes a cautious, conservative view, in order to
be on the safe side, and feels sure it is not so old as they think. As Lord
Kelvin is the highest authority in science now living, I think we must
yield to him and accept his view. He does not concede that the world is

---

Mr. Wallace: Alfred Russell Wallace, English naturalist, 1823–1913.
Lord Kelvin: William Thomson Kelvin, British mathematician and physicist, 1824–1907.

more than a hundred million years old. He believes it is that old, but not older. Lyell° believed that our race was introduced into the world 31,000 years ago, Herbert Spencer° makes it 32,000. Lord Kelvin agrees with Spencer.

Very well. According to these figures it took 99,968,000 years to prepare the world for man, impatient as the Creator doubtless was to see him and admire him. But a large enterprise like this has to be conducted warily, painstakingly, logically. It was foreseen that man would have to have the oyster. Therefore the first preparation was made for the oyster. Very well, you cannot make an oyster out of whole cloth, you must make the oyster's ancestor first. This is not done in a day. You must make a vast variety of invertebrates, to start with—belemnites, trilobites, jebusites, amalekites, and that sort of fry, and put them to soak in a primary sea, and wait and see what will happen. Some will be a disappointment—the belemnites, the ammonites and such; they will be failures, they will die out and become extinct, in the course of the 19,000,000 years covered by the experiment, but all is not lost, for the amalekites will fetch the home-stake; they will develop gradually into encrinites, and stalactites, and blatherskites, and one thing and another as the mighty ages creep on and the Archaean and the Cambrian Periods pile their lofty crags in the primordial seas, and at last the first grand stage in the preparation of the world for man stands completed, the Oyster is done. An oyster has hardly any more reasoning power than a scientist has; and so it is reasonably certain that this one jumped to the conclusion that the nineteen-million years was a preparation for *him;* but that would be just like an oyster, which is the most conceited animal there is, except man. And anyway, this one could not know, at that early date, that he was only an incident in a scheme, and that there was some more to the scheme, yet.

The oyster being achieved, the next thing to be arranged for in the preparation of the world for man, was fish. Fish, and coal—to fry it with. So the Old Silurian seas were opened up to breed the fish in, and at the same time the great work of building Old Red Sandstone mountains 80,000 feet high to cold-storage their fossils in was begun. This latter was quite indispensable, for there would be no end of failures again, no end of extinctions—millions of them—and it would be cheaper and less trouble to can them in the rocks than keep tally of them in a book. One does not build the coal beds and 80,000 feet of perpendicular Old Red Sandstone in a brief time—no, it took twenty million years. In the first place, a coal bed is a slow and troublesome and tiresome thing to construct. You have to grow prodigious forests of tree-ferns and reeds and calamites and such things in a marshy region; then

---

Lyell: Sir Charles Lyell, British geologist, 1797–1875.
Spencer: Herbert Spencer, English philosopher, 1820–1903.

you have to sink them under out of sight and let them rot; then you have to turn the streams on them, so as to bury them under several feet of sediment, and the sediment must have time to harden and turn to rock; next you must grow another forest on top, then sink it and put on another layer of sediment and harden it; then more forest and more rock, layer upon layer, three miles deep—ah, indeed it is a sickening slow job to build a coal-measure and do it right!

So the millions of years drag on; and meantime the fish-culture is lazying along and frazzling out in a way to make a person tired. You have developed ten thousand kinds of fishes from the oyster; and come to look, you have raised nothing but fossils, nothing but extinctions. There is nothing left alive and progressive but a ganoid or two and perhaps half a dozen asteroids. Even the cat wouldn't eat such.

Still, it is no great matter; there is plenty of time, yet, and they will develop into something tasty before man is ready for them. Even a ganoid can be depended on for that, when he is not going to be called on for sixty million years.

The Palaeozoic time-limit having now been reached, it was necessary to begin the next stage in the preparation of the world for man, by opening up the Mesozoic Age and instituting some reptiles. For man would need reptiles. Not to eat, but to develop himself from. This being the most important detail of the scheme, a spacious liberality of time was set apart for it—thirty million years. What wonders followed! From the remaining ganoids and asteroids and alkaloids were developed by slow and steady and pains-taking culture those stupendous saurians that used to prowl about the steamy world in those remote ages, with their snaky heads reared forty feet in the air and sixty feet of body and tail racing and thrashing after. All gone, now, alas—all extinct, except the little handful of Arkansawrians left stranded and lonely with us here upon this far-flung verge and fringe of time.

Yes, it took thirty million years and twenty million reptiles to get one that would stick long enough to develop into something else and let the scheme proceed to the next step.

Then the Pterodactyl burst upon the world in all his impressive solemnity and grandeur, and all Nature recognized that the Cainozoic threshold was crossed and a new Period open for business, a new stage begun in the preparation of the globe for man. It may be that the Pterodactyl thought the thirty million years had been intended as a preparation for himself, for there was nothing too foolish for a Pterodactyl to imagine, but he was in error, the preparation was for man. Without doubt the Pterodactyl attracted great attention, for even the least observant could see that there was the making of a bird in him. And so it turned out. Also the makings of a mammal, in time. One thing we have to say to his credit, that in the matter of picturesqueness he was the triumph of his Period; he wore wings and had teeth, and was a starchy and wonderful mixture altogether, a kind of long-distance premonitory symptom of Kipling's marine:

> 'E isn't one o' the reg'lar Line, nor 'e isn't one of the crew,
> 'E's a kind of a giddy harumfrodite—soldier an' sailor too!

From this time onward for nearly another thirty million years the preparation moved briskly. From the Pterodactyl was developed the bird; from the bird the kangaroo, from the kangaroo the other marsupials; from these the mastodon, the megatherium, the giant sloth, the Irish elk, and all that crowd that you make useful and instructive fossils out of—then came the first great Ice Sheet, and they all retreated before it and crossed over the bridge at Behring's strait and wandered around over Europe and Asia and died. All except a few, to carry on the preparation with. Six Glacial Periods with two million years between Periods chased these poor orphans up and down and about the earth, from weather to weather—from tropic swelter at the poles to Arctic frost at the equator and back again and to and fro, they never knowing what kind of weather was going to turn up next; and if ever they settled down anywhere the whole continent suddenly sank under them without the least notice and they had to trade places with the fishes and scramble off to where the seas had been, and scarcely a dry rag on them; and when there was nothing else doing a volcano would let go and fire them out from wherever they had located. They led this unsettled and irritating life for twenty-five million years, half the time afloat, half the time aground, and always wondering what it was all for, they never suspecting, of course, that it was a preparation for man and had to be done just so or it wouldn't be any proper and harmonious place for him when he arrived.

And at last came the monkey, and anybody could see that man wasn't far off, now. And in truth that was so. The monkey went on developing for close upon 5,000,000 years, and then turned into a man—to all appearances.

Such is the history of it. Man has been here 32,000 years. That it took a hundred million years to prepare the world for him is proof that that is what it was done for. I suppose it is. I dunno. If the Eiffel tower were now representing the world's age, the skin of paint on the pinnacle-knob at its summit would represent man's share of that age; and anybody would perceive that that skin was what the tower was built for. I reckon they would, I dunno.

🔲 *Outward Exploration: Discussion*

1. At the beginning of the essay, what exactly is Twain's position on the question of whether the world was made for humans?

2. According to the figures Twain accepts from Lord Kelvin, how many years were required to prepare the world for humans? Why did it take so long?

3. What theory does Twain assume is valid as he explains about the oyster?

4. Why does Twain select the oyster instead of some other animal?

5. In paragraph 6, what is the point of Twain's saying that "[a]n oyster has hardly any more reasoning power than a scientist has" and that an oyster is more conceited than any other animal "except man"?

6. How does Twain explain the formation of coal?

7. What image of God does this essay imply?

8. Why does Twain repeat "I dunno" in the last paragraph?

9. Explain the point of Twain's comparing the world's history to the Eiffel Tower in the last paragraph. Have you ever encountered such analogies and comparisons elsewhere?

☐ *Outward Exploration: Writing*

Write an essay in which you adopt a persona similar to Twain's and seemingly support exactly the point you are really attacking. As does Twain, make your point humorously clear at the end without overtly saying "I don't believe this."

☐ *Style*

Notice the effect Twain achieves with his Eiffel Tower comparison: The comparison helps us grasp the enormity of the world's history and to see humankind's insignificant amount of time in that history. Create a comparison similar to Twain's. Use your comparison to explain a concept just as Twain does.

The Death of the Moth

Virginia Woolf

☐ *Inward Exploration*

Write at least one paragraph exploring your idea of what death is.

Moths that fly by day are not properly to be called moths; they do   1
not excite that pleasant sense of dark autumn nights and ivy-blossom
which the commonest yellow-underwing asleep in the shadow of the
curtain never fails to rouse in us. They are hybrid creatures, neither
gay like butterflies nor sombre like their own species. Nevertheless the
present specimen, with his narrow hay-coloured wings, fringed with a
tassel of the same colour, seemed to be content with life. It was a pleasant morning, mid-September, mild, benignant, yet with a keener breath
than that of the summer months. The plough was already scoring the
field opposite the window, and where the share had been, the earth was
pressed flat and gleamed with moisture. Such vigour came rolling in
from the fields and the down beyond that it was difficult to keep the
eyes strictly turned upon the book. The rooks too were keeping one of
their annual festivities; soaring round the tree tops until it looked as if a
vast net with thousands of black knots in it had been cast up into the air;
which, after a few moments sank slowly down upon the trees until every
twig seemed to have a knot at the end of it. Then, suddenly, the net
would be thrown into the air again in a wider circle this time, with the
utmost clamour and vociferation, as though to be thrown into the air
and settle slowly down upon the tree tops were a tremendously exciting
experience.

The same energy which inspired the rooks, the ploughmen, the
horses, and even, it seemed, the lean bare-backed downs, sent the moth
fluttering from side to side of his square of the window-pane. One could
not help watching him. One was, indeed, conscious of a queer feeling
of pity for him. The possibilities of pleasure seemed that morning so
enormous and so various that to have only a moth's part in life, and a
day moth's at that, appeared a hard fate, and his zest in enjoying his
meagre opportunities to the full, pathetic. He flew vigorously to one
corner of his compartment, and, after waiting there a second, flew
across to the other. What remained for him but to fly to a third corner
and then to a fourth? That was all he could do, in spite of the size of
the downs, the width of the sky, the far-off smoke of houses, and the

romantic voice, now and then, of a steamer out at sea. What he could do he did. Watching him, it seemed as if a fibre, very thin, but pure, of the enormous energy of the world had been thrust into his frail and diminutive body. As often as he crossed the pane, I could fancy that a thread of vital light became visible. He was little or nothing but life.

Yet, because he was so small, and so simple a form of the energy that was rolling in at the open window and driving its way through so many narrow and intricate corridors in my own brain and in those of other human beings, there was something marvellous as well as pathetic about him. It was as if someone had taken a tiny bead of pure life and decking it as lightly as possible with down and feathers, had set it dancing and zigzagging to show us the true nature of life. Thus displayed one could not get over the strangeness of it. One is apt to forget all about life, seeing it humped and bossed and garnished and cumbered so that it has to move with the greatest circumspection and dignity. Again, the thought of all that life might have been had he been born in any other shape caused one to view his simple activities with a kind of pity.

After a time, tired by his dancing apparently, he settled on the window ledge in the sun, and, the queer spectacle being at an end, I forgot about him. Then, looking up, my eye was caught by him. He was trying to resume his dancing, but seemed either so stiff or so awkward that he could only flutter to the bottom of the window-pane; and when he tried to fly across it he failed. Being intent on other matters I watched these futile attempts for a time without thinking, unconsciously waiting for him to resume his flight, as one waits for a machine, that has stopped momentarily, to start again without considering the reason of its failure. After perhaps a seventh attempt he slipped from the wooden ledge and fell, fluttering his wings, on to his back on the window sill. The helplessness of his attitude roused me. It flashed upon me that he was in difficulties; he could no longer raise himself; his legs struggled vainly. But, as I stretched out a pencil, meaning to help him to right himself, it came over me that the failure and awkwardness were the approach of death. I laid the pencil down again.

The legs agitated themselves once more. I looked as if for the enemy *5*
against which he struggled. I looked out of doors. What had happened there? Presumably it was mid-day, and work in the fields had stopped. Stillness and quiet had replaced the previous animation. The birds had taken themselves off to feed in the brooks. The horses stood still. Yet the power was there all the same, massed outside indifferent, impersonal, not attending to anything in particular. Somehow it was opposed to the little hay-coloured moth. It was useless to try to do anything. One could only watch the extraordinary efforts made by those tiny legs against an oncoming doom which could, had it chosen, have submerged an entire city, not merely a city, but masses of human beings; nothing, I knew, had any chance against death. Nevertheless, after a

pause of exhaustion the legs fluttered again. It was superb this last protest, and so frantic that he succeeded at last in righting himself. One's
sympathies, of course, were all on the side of life. Also, when there
was nobody to care or to know, this gigantic effort on the part of
an insignificant little moth, against a power of such magnitude, to retain what no one else valued or desired to keep, moved one strangely.
Again, somehow, one saw life, a pure bead. I lifted the pencil again,
useless though I knew it to be. But even as I did so, the unmistakable
tokens of death showed themselves. The body relaxed, and instantly
grew stiff. The struggle was over. The insignificant little creature now
knew death. As I looked at the dead moth, this minute wayside triumph
of so great a force over so mean an antagonist filled me with wonder.
Just as life had been strange a few minutes before, so death was now as
strange. The moth having righted himself now lay most decently and
uncomplainingly composed. O yes, he seemed to say, death is stronger
than I am.

☐ Outward Exploration: Discussion

1. Before the episode she describes in the essay, what was Woolf's attitude toward day moths?

2. What is the moth's attitude toward life at the start of the essay? How
   does Woolf know this?

3. What activity is she engaged in? What distracts her from it?

4. What does the moth come to symbolize for Woolf as she watches
   him? How does she suggest this symbolic significance?

5. Why does she see the moth as both "pathetic" and "marvellous"?

6. Throughout most of the essay before paragraph 4, Woolf has primarily used the impersonal pronoun *one* (exceptions occur at the
   end of paragraph 2, she does use *I* once, and in paragraph 3 she
   mentions "*my* own brain"). Beginning in paragraph 4, however,
   Woolf switches pronouns from the impersonal *one* to the personal
   I. Why?

7. Point out the vivid verbs and colorful adjectives that Woolf uses in
   her various descriptions of the moth. Which strike you as the most
   effective?

8. Why does Woolf refrain from using the pencil to help the moth?

9. What does Woolf notice as she looks around for "the enemy against
   which he struggled"?

10. What insight about death does the moth's death give Woolf?

11. Why does she return to the impersonal pronoun *one* when she says,
    "One's sympathies, of course, were all on the side of life"?

❏ *Outward Exploration: Writing*

1. Closely observe an event in Nature (for instance, ducks feeding in a pond, some insect or group of insects gathering food, or a cat stalking a bird). Write a detailed description of what you observed. Then write an essay that uses that event as a way of explaining some belief of yours.

2. Write an essay explaining your beliefs about death. You should read at least Lewis Thomas's "On Natural Death" and Annie Dillard's "Living Like Weasels" to get different perspectives on the issue.

❏ *Style*

Consider the following sentences from Woolf's essay:

> The rooks too were keeping one of their annual festivities; soaring round the tree tops until it looked as if a vast net with thousands of black knots in it had been cast up into the air; which, after a few moments sank slowly down upon the trees until every twig seemed to have a knot at the end of it. Then, suddenly, the net would be thrown into the air again in a wider circle this time, with the utmost clamour and vociferation, as though to be thrown into the air and settle slowly down upon the tree tops were a tremendously exciting experience. (paragraph 1)

In this sentence, Woolf creates a vivid visual image—the black rooks look like the knots in a large net—and continues the image in her following sentence to describe the experience of seeing the net flung high in the air, then settling on the trees and then flung high again.

Create a visual image of your own in one sentence, and continue it in the following sentence.

The Perils and Pitfalls of Reporting in the Lone Star State

MOLLY IVINS

☐ *Inward Exploration*

Write at least one paragraph which explains your vision of reporters and newspapers. You might include such issues as the following: How factual are most newspaper accounts of events? How objective is most newspaper writing? How objective is the best newspaper writing? How much truth is there in newspaper stories, and how do you know? What is distinctive about the newspaper style of writing? How does it differ from academic report writing? How does it differ from the style of the essays in this book?

The *Houston Journalism Review,* may it rest in peace, once got me to set down my beliefs about being a reporter. Reading it now, I conclude that I was quite an idealistic young thing. Even odder, I still believe it all.

I think the reason the editors of this publication asked me to write   *1* an article on the pitfalls of being a reporter is because it's clear to them that I have fallen into every pit possible. I'm not insulted: I see it as an opportunity to practice participatory journalism. And a little advocacy journalism as well: there are a lot of pits out of which you should stay.

I have yet to enter into sexual congress with any of my news sources (which probably reflects as unfavorably on their appeal as it does favorably on my good sense), but apart from that, I believe I've hit all the pits. The first was cynicism. As a fledgling female reporter I had two splendid models to choose from—Brenda Starr and Poteet Canyon. But I hadda go and choose Hildy Johnson to imitate. Bogey in a trench coat figures in there somewhere, too. It is my considered opinion that Hildy has done more harm to American journalism than Frank Munsey, Spiro Agnew, and Everett Collier, combined. Generation after generation of pimply-faced kids have come staggering out of J schools and into city rooms pretending to be characters out of *The Front Page.* At least young reporters just pretend to be cynical. With most older reporters, cynicism is a habit. A stupid, vitiating habit sustained by sloth.

During a discussion of corruption in Texas politics not long ago, one of Houston's finest remarked, "Look, baby, that's the way it always has been and that's the way it always will be." Whereupon he took a particularly worldly toke off his Pall Mall. He should only get lung cancer. Failing that, he should get his ass out of journalism.

Being a cynic is so contemptibly easy. If you let yourself think that nothing you're working on is ever going to make any difference, why bust your tail over it? Why care? If you're a cynic, you don't have to invest anything in your work. No effort, no pride, no compassion, no sense of excellence, nothing. You can sit around on your butt for most of the day, because, as has been proved time and again on Houston newspapers, you don't really have to produce much of anything to pull down $160 a week. The rest of your time you can spend in bars impressing young reporters with your worldly wisdom.

Best get yourself straight early on about why you're in this business.   5
Not for the money, we trust. Some people are in it because it's so seldom boring, which I regard as an acceptable excuse. This next part is extremely sticky because it's a damn sight simpler to criticize other people's ideas than it is to set forth your own. One is never in so much danger of making an ass of one's self as when one is engaged in saying, "This I believe . . ."

Having adequately prefaced my credo, I'm ready to fire. I believe that ignorance is the root of all evil. And that no one knows the truth. I believe that the people is not dumb. Ignorant, bigoted, and meanminded, maybe, but not stupid. I just think it helps, anything and everything, if the people know. Know what the hell is going on. What they do about it once they know is not my problem.

The discerning reader will have noticed several pitfalls in the preceding paragraph. For example, the people pit. I have meditated on the people pit and have come to the conclusion that it has always been there and always will be. Reporters are constrained to think of readers and viewers and listeners abstractly, a great, gray blob, out there. But what amazes me is the ubiquitous reportorial attitude which holds that the masses *out* there are the masses *down* there. Every newspaper I've ever worked on has had a Mythical Average Reader. In Minneapolis, our MAR was the retarded wife of a North Dakota farmer. In Houston, I am told, the MAR is an Aggie sophomore.

Any good teacher will tell you that aiming at the lowest common denominator is poor practice. In communicating anything, you do better if you aim slightly above the heads of your audience. If you make them stretch a little, they respond better. If you keep aiming at the dumb ones, you never challenge them and you bore the hell out of the bright ones. You also commit the grievous and pernicious error of thinking that the people is dumb. One of the most horrific results is that the people start to think so themselves.

If in fact you hold that the people is dumb, if that attitude is not a pose, you're in the wrong business. Go join an ad agency.

The people pit cannot be cured, but it can be ameliorated by knowl-   10
edge. Every reporter in Houston should know and know well Bellaire,

Pasadena, The Fifth Ward, River Oaks/Memorial. You should know those areas and the people in them on a good-or-better basis. You should have friends in those areas and you should know the areas geographically, sociologically, historically, economically, and culturally. S'funny, once you know people you tend to care about them.

Also, in cultivating your regard for the people, the readers, it helps if you don't read the letters-to-the-editor column.

The kind of contempt for readers represented by the MAR concept is what leads reporters into the Great Pit, the most absurd perversion in our business. In-ism has become so acute that a reporter can be generally defined as a person who knows, but doesn't tell. You can find out more about what's going on at the state capitol by spending one night drinking with the capitol press corps than you can in months of reading the papers those reporters write for. The same is true of city hall reporters, court reporters, police reporters, education writers—any of us. In city rooms and in the bars where newspeople drink, you can find out what's going on. You can't find it in the papers.

There is a degree to which the structure and values of the Establishment press are responsible for this phenomenon. Reporters learn early on that there are certain central truths they cannot tell readers—for example, the governor of Texas is definitely a dimwit. Such truths are invariably denounced as subjective or even subversive observation and are edited out forthwith.

But reporters, in general, tend to fall in with the Establishment's limitations on truth with alarming complaisance. It is as though we had internalized the restraints. Despite the fact that most of us object to them intellectually, we obey them unconsciously after a while. There's not a major newspaper I know of in this country that's going to let you tell it like you find it. But that's no excuse for giving up. You have no business sitting around with your friends over beers telling them what *really* happened at today's city council meeting. The very least you owe yourself and your readers is to try to get out what you know. Playing the get-the-facts-straight-and-let-the-truth-go-hang-itself game is management's bag. Your obligation, your responsibility is not to the management of the *Houston Post,* the *Houston Chronicle,* or the *Houston Whatever.* It is to yourself, to your own standards of excellence, and to your readers. If your readers don't know as much as you know about your beat, you're a failure. So damn many of us write about the surface and save the juicy stuff for our friends; we can dine out on what we don't put in our stories.

You know and I know that it's not easy to get the truth into newspapers—so much of it is not family fare. But you can't have been in this business for a year without learning at least the basics of all the gimmicks there are for getting the stuff through. The curve ball, the slideroo, the old put-it-in-the-17th-graf trick. Tell your editor the opposition will have the story in its next edition. Show 'em where *The*

15

New York Times, or better yet, the *Dallas Morning News,* has already done this story. If you haven't got enough points with management to pull off a strong story on your own, give it to one of your colleagues. Find another angle on it. Localize the hell out of it. Disguise it as a feature.

Or, you can use the Janis Joplin–Zarko Franks take-another-little-chunk-of-their-ass-out technique. The inimitable Zarko, the Chronk's city editor, was grousing one day about all these g.d. kids he's got working for him who want to tell the Truth allatime, fer Chrissakes. "I tell 'em," said Zark, "you can't tell the *truth,* honey, this is a *daily newspaper.* Every day these kids wanna write "War and Peace." I tell 'em, look, baby, today you just tell the readers a little bit of the truth. That's all we got room for. Then tomorrow you go back and you pick up another little piece of the truth. And the day after that, another piece. You'll get it all eventually, but you ain't never gonna get none of it if you shoot for the whole wad every day."

If all else fails, pass your story along to the *Texas Observer.*

Whatever you do, don't give up. Because all you can do once you've given up is bitch. I've known some great bitchers in my time. With some it's a passion, with others an art. With all of them, it is a dissipation of the energy they should be putting into reporting. I know, I know, the reason why newspeople bitch so much is because they've got a lot to bitch about. It's still a waste of time. Think Pollyanna. Read George Bernard Shaw or go listen to Ralph Yarborough. Anything but full-time bitching.

One of the most depressing aspects of reporters-as-a-group is that they tend to be fairly ignorant themselves. There is no excuse for it and there is a complete cure for it. Read, read, read. At least one good paper every day. It's kind of fun to switch them around: Monday, the *Christian Science Monitor;* Tuesday, the *Louisville Courier-Journal;* Wednesday, the *Washington Post;* Thursday, *Le Monde;* Friday, the *L.A. Times;* Saturday, *Manchester Guardian;* Sunday, *The New York Times.* Better yet, all of them every day, plus the major papers in Texas. You should be reading every good magazine you've ever heard of and most of the bad ones. Concentrate on opening your mind. If you're 55 and straight, read *Rolling Stone.* If you're 25 and hip, *Reader's Digest.* If you're liberal, read the *National Review;* conservative, read *New Republic.* You should be reading at least one good book a week—history, anthropology, sociology, politics, urban problems. If you were a fine arts major, read about economics. If you were a business major, find out about ballet. I'm not joking about any of this. You have got to stretch your mind, further and further. The alternative is letting it congeal, harden, and contract. You must be able to see more and understand more than most folks or you're never going to be able to explain what you do see to most folks. This isn't elitist; it's just part of the basic job requirement—the same way a pianist has to keep his hands limber or a mechanic will start boning up on the Wankel. It's your job, that's all.

George Orwell wrote a preface to *Animal Farm* concerning freedom 20
of the press, which was published for the first time a few months ago. In it he speaks of the phenomenon of voluntary censorship, of the orthodoxies of fashionable thought and how subtly we censor ourselves. In order to be able to resist intellectual fashions, you have to be well informed. Very well informed. I sometimes think that reporters should be required to go through an experience analogous to that required of psychiatrists, who must themselves be analyzed before they are allowed to practice. We need to be aware of our own biases in order to compensate for them, aware of our own vanities and weaknesses.

Reporters need to be people people. It helps if you're an extrovert, but it's not necessary. I have frequently been amazed, when taking a colleague along to a meeting of radicals or blacks, to find my colleague actually afraid of such people. I find it absurd and wrong when reporters are ill at ease with people, just plain people, who happen not to be like them. There are reporters who simply can't deal with anyone who's not white, college-educated, middle class. I'm not sure whether that's sad or funny, but I know it doesn't make for good journalism. I don't know how you learn to relate to people—listen to them, I suppose. Spend enough time around very different kinds of people so that they don't strike you as odd. Maybe read some of the *I'm O.K., You're O.K.* genre of interpersonal relations. Dale Carnegie, anyone?

As a final thought about job qualifications, I'd like to suggest to you that it's racist for any Texas reporter south of Lubbock not to be able to speak Spanish.

One of the happy side effects of doing a lot of reading is that it will improve your writing, which needs it. Would you like to know why people don't read newspapers anymore? Because newspapers are boring. Dull. Tedious. Unreadable. No fun. I don't need your excuses: I read both Houston papers every day and I'd rather listen to local television news myself.

An editor once told me, "Adjectives and adverbs are dangerous words." There went half the English language. "Facts," Norman Mailer said to Judge Julius Hoffman, "mean nothing, sir, without their nuance." Nuances, I grant you, are very damned hard to get by the copy desk. Every desk has someone on it who is convinced that both *whispered* and *screamed* mean the same thing as *said*. I dare say, we have all seen our fair share of murmurs, croaks, rasps, shouts, and gasps bite the dust, not to mention all the adjectives and adverbs of our lives. Nevertheless, recalling previous pits, you will be neither cynical, discouraged, or bitchy about this. Right? Right. You will try. And try again. And again. And you will smile. Because it's so much healthier than crying or throwing up.

Be comforted, good writing is the wave of the future. *The New York*   25
Times gets more readable every day: it's hard to find a pure-fact pyramid
story in a good paper anymore. They throw in little hints now about
what the facts mean. If you do get discouraged about trying to bring a
little humanity into your writing in the face of constant desk opposition,
think of yourself as part of the anti-anomie brigade. Fight alienation.
Get on John Donne's side. There are too damn many lonely people in
the world who just can't handle it, who are afraid of other people, who
don't understand what's going on, who fear change. It doesn't help them
to get a newspaper plopped on their front stoops every day that reduces
the whole rich, human, comic, tragic, absurd, exasperating, and exciting parade of one day's events into a dehydrated lifeless set of unrelated
facts. We keep writing about events as though they were pictures on a
wall, something we could stand off and look at, when in fact they are
the stuff of our lives. The news gets sanitized, homogenized, pasteur-
ized, dehumanized, and wrapped in cellophane. No wonder people forget they're human. Fight it. Use adjectives.

Which brings us to the serious pitfall. That is, taking one's self seriously. In a way, I'm afraid to broach this one, since there's no shortage
of cynics to remind us that the product only costs 10 cents and most
people use it to wrap their fish.

How easily we come to accept the power, such as it is, that we carry
around with us. I imagine most of you have had the experience, on an
investigation, of walking up to some crook and saying, "I'm Joe Smith
from the *Daily Hallelujah*" and watching the poor beggar start to sweat.
Now there's a power trip. So is watching a pol, as you whip out your
notebook, shift out of his normal style, get glassy-eyed, take on a fake
heartiness, and say, "Well now Joe, let me tell you about my stand on
that issue. . . ." The mayor calls you by your first name. So does the
superintendent of schools and the head of the black power movement in
town. Not to mention the bartender at the Press Club. You're in with
the big people, all right. With any luck at all, Ben Barnes not only remembers your name but stops to josh with you about the time you asked
him a tough one in Amarillo. Preston and Sissy never remember anybody's name, but it's In to know that, too. You got people you can drop
in on. Big people in this town. Developers, bankers, lawyers, judges.
They all know you. Hell no, you never have been asked to join the Cap
Club, but you drink there a lot. Mecom, Mischer, Moody. Been in a
few poker games with the judge. . . . Remember the time the mayor
asked me, he said, Joe . . . Talked to Herman about that the other
day . . . Wortham, Welch, Wyatt, Winchester . . . Ike Arnold says . . .
Hell, ol' Percy hisself told me she was guilty . . . Guy I know knows
Connally real well and . . . Saw George Brown at the Petroleum Club
with . . . Heard the latest 'bout Gertrude . . . Stumpf, Cummings,
L.C. . . . Roy's real sick . . . Palm's craziern a loon . . . Barbara'll take
Curtis with no sweat.

Sure we talk about the biggies among ourselves with our best Hildy Johnson sneers on. And we all have our Genuines for comfort—those Real People we discovered all by ourselves, usually on feature assignments. The lady in Baytown with twelve kids who got her engineering degree when she was forty-seven; the woman in the Heights with kidney disease who won't take charity; the black dentist who thinks he's got the answer on biodegradable cans; and we all have our favorite welfare case, don't we? And we all keep going back to the Cap Club, don't we? Dugger once said of John Connally, "He never messes with the top waters." In the Cap Club, that's a compliment. Look, we know the movers and the shakers because they make news and that's what we write about. But watch your ass, reporter, or you'll wind up like most of your brethren—a power groupie. Power is an insidious commodity. It's fascinating. Once you get into who's doing what to whom for why, it's as addictive as smack. And it works the same way: you need more and more of it and you produce less and less. You start to identify with your sources and then you're gone. You spend so much time with those people that you can't imagine the city being run in any other way. "That's the way it always has been and that's the way it always will be, baby." That's why it's called Establishment journalism. You concentrate on the people at the top, the people with power; you watch, you study how they make their moves, you get fascinated by it, and pretty soon you can't see anything else—just the top, just the power. And the others, the people, the readers, matter so little that you don't even bother to let them know what's going on. You start to think like the people you cover. It can happen on any beat—business, police, politics, education. The stuff you want is from the top—you want to quote the chief, the superintendent, the chairman of the board. There are no reliable sources who earn less than $10,000 a year.

There are ways to kick the habit. Institutional reporting (Haynes Johnson on labor), human reporting (Ernie Pyle on a war), investigative reporting (Sy Hersh isn't talking to General Lavelle about that illegal bombing—he's talking to the pilots who did it).

Cultivate clerks and secretaries. They haven't got as big a stake as their bosses in covering up what's going on. There's no point in asking Herman Short about police brutality. Go look at Johnny Coward's foot and eye and chest. Don't listen to the president of Armco tell you about ship channel pollution: go look at the ship channel.

Do not go to press conferences. An abomination. A manipulative device. Stop letting sources get away with lies because they hold high positions and titles. The *Chronicle* ran a front-page story not long ago about some astronaut blasting the government for cutting back the space program. The astronaut was quoted as saying that 80 percent of the federal budget went for welfare programs. Don't let him get away with that just because he's an astronaut. Right after that quote, the *Chronicle* should have run the actual percentage of the budget that goes for welfare programs. There's no excuse for spreading misinformation just because it comes from someone in a high place.

I am told that a Houston editor is fond of reminding his reporters, "This is not a crusading newspaper." I think that's too bad myself, but I could live with it. Us crusaders screw up with alarming frequency, too. Don Rottenberg, late of the *Chicago Journalism Review,* declared in his farewell article, "There are still places where people think the function of the media is to provide information." I'd settle for that. And I don't think you should settle for anything less.

☐ *Outward Exploration: Discussion*

1. What specific advice does Ivins give for becoming a good reporter?

2. She advises aspiring journalists to read a different newspaper every day and at least "every good magazine you've ever heard of" and "at least one good book a week—history, anthropology, sociology, politics, urban problems." If you don't wish to be a journalist, does her advice apply to you? Explain your response.

3. In paragraph 25, Ivins suggests her desire to portray "the whole rich, human, comic, tragic, absurd, exasperating, and exciting parade of one day's events." Does that goal suggest the goals of other types of writers?

4. According to Ivins, why is it so hard to get the truth into the newspaper?

5. Where do you get most of your "news"—newspapers, TV, magazines, etc.? How would you judge the amount of truth (using Ivins's definition) that you get as opposed to simply facts?

6. Do you agree with Ivins's definition of *truth* and her opposition of *truth* to *facts?* Explain.

7. As usual, the audience that an essay is intended for influences how that essay is written. This essay was written for a very particular audience, namely, the readers of the *Houston Journalism Review.* What do you imagine Ivins's assumptions were about her readers' attitudes, careers or career goals, and beliefs? Consider the possible impact that having such an audience had on Ivins in terms of her approach, her tone, her use of language, her structure, her references.

8. How practical do you find her argument that the obligation and responsibility of all reporters (and, by extension, all writers of any kind) is not to the newspaper (or magazine or publisher) that prints what they write but to themselves, to their own standards of excellence, and to their readers? Explore.

9. In your own words, explain what Ivins means by "Establishment journalism."

10. Here are three opening paragraphs from different newspapers covering the same story. Comment on each. Which story do you believe? Why? Which opening do you think Ivins would most approve of? Why?

    a. On Tuesday evening, the city council discussed rezoning Park Street, replacing sewer pipes in the Norris section of town, and installing five streetlights along the section of Route 8 known as "deadman's mile." Representatives of the Keep Park Street for Homes committee and Rezoning for Progress offered conflicting ideas and information about the potential impact of the proposed zoning changes. The council tabled the motion pending further study.

    b. On Tuesday evening, the city council heard arguments about rezoning Park Street, replacing sewer pipes in the Norris section of town, and installing five streetlights along the section of Route 8 known as "deadman's mile." Amid loud exchanges of information and misinformation about the rezoning proposal, the council finally gave up and tabled the proposal until it could discover some hard facts about the issue.

    c. On Tuesday evening, the city council meeting was flooded with misinformation as various interest groups argued loudly and ineffectively about three issues: rezoning Park Street, replacing sewer pipes in the Norris section of town, and installing five streetlights along the section of Route 8 known as "deadman's mile." For example, representatives of the Keep Park Street for Homes committee persisted in making false claims based on unfounded speculation in their attempt to thwart progress once again in an area of the city that is crying out for development. Cowed by the vocal minority represented by that committee, the council once again failed to take a stand and tabled the proposal with cowardly haste, saying once again it needs more "hard facts," facts it seems incapable of discovering for itself.

☐ Outward Exploration: Writing

1. Write an essay that explores one of the questions listed in "Inward Exploration."

2. Ultimately, how do Molly Ivins's recommendations about how to be a good reporter apply to you even if you don't plan to be a journalist? You might write a whole essay exploring how they apply and what you think you would get from following her advice, both as a writer and as a human being.

3. Equipped with the insights from Ivins's essay, read about the same major event in a number of different sources. For example, you might read about the event in your local newspaper, the *New York Times*, the *Washington Post, Time, U.S. News and World Report, The Nation* and listen to at least one national television newscast and one local radio newscast about the event. Your task here is to look for differences in emphasis (for example, what gets mentioned first, what receives the most time or space devoted to it) and for differences in style and tone. You might begin your essay by explaining your assumptions about news reporting before you did this reading, and then explore the similarities and differences among the various sources you considered, ending with your evaluation of the possibility of objectivity. What are the advantages and disadvantages of the "newspaper style" of writing?

4. In this essay, Ivins explicitly gives us many of her assumptions about people and reporting. Some of these she comments on at some length. Others she simply mentions in passing. Consider her assertion that "it helps, anything and everything, if the people know. Know what the hell is going on. What they do about it once they know is not my problem." This comment raises two very difficult questions. First, does it always help when the general public knows what's going on? There have been many cases in the history of the United States when the general public has been purposely kept in the dark to achieve some end seen as being desirable (for example, the various machinations of the Roosevelt administration to help the Allies with equipment well before the United States joined World War II). You might do some historical research here. Second, is it really desirable for reporters to report information that they believe will harm some cause or program whose purpose they wholeheartedly support? Write an essay taking a position on such issues.

5. Using Ivins's concept and approach, write an essay about the perils and pitfalls of doing some activity that you know how to do well. Try to express your feelings as well as your thoughts about the various details of the activity. Use keen observation of others who perform the activity as well as the way Ivins comments on the "pretend cynicism" of young reporters and the habitual cynicism of older reporters.

6. According to Ivins, "One is never in so much danger of making an ass of one's self as when one is engaged in saying, 'This I believe. . . .'" Ivins runs the risk by telling us what she deeply believes about reporting and about being a good person. Risk making an ass of yourself by writing an essay about something you believe in strongly.

7. In paragraph 27, Ivins drops many names to illustrate the appeal of "In-ism." Make a list of the "power" people you would most like

to be on a first-name basis with, the people you would most like to mention to other people as being your friends. For example, these "power people" might be celebrities from the worlds of music, movies, television, or the arts, or they might be important people from national or local politics. Whichever world(s) they come from, make a list of the top 10 or 15 power people you'd be impressed to know personally. In your mind, imagine what it would be like to be at parties with those people. Think about what it would be like to have those people confide secrets to you, secrets that might hurt them if the public found out about them. Think about how exciting it would be to have such people trust you, about how important you would feel. Then imagine trying to write an "objective" essay about those secrets, one that informed the public. Write an essay exploring the appeal of knowing such people.

Living Like Weasels

ANNIE DILLARD

☐ *Inward Exploration*

Write at least one paragraph about the habits of whatever animal you know best (for example, a pet or some animal you observed at a zoo).

A weasel is wild. Who knows what he thinks? He sleeps in his 1
underground den, his tail draped over his nose. Sometimes he lives in his den for two days without leaving. Outside, he stalks rabbits, mice, muskrats, and birds, killing more bodies than he can eat warm, and often dragging the carcasses home. Obedient to instinct, he bites his prey at the neck, either splitting the jugular vein at the throat or crunching the brain at the base of the skull, and he does not let go. One naturalist refused to kill a weasel who was socketed into his hand deeply as a rattlesnake. The man could in no way pry the tiny weasel off, and he had to walk half a mile to water, the weasel dangling from his palm, and soak him off like a stubborn label.

And once, says Ernest Thompson Seton—once, a man shot an eagle out of the sky. He examined the eagle and found the dry skull of a weasel fixed by the jaws to his throat. The supposition is that the eagle had pounced on the weasel and the weasel swiveled and bit as instinct taught him, tooth to neck, and nearly won. I would like to have seen that eagle from the air a few weeks or months before he was shot: was the whole weasel still attached to his feathered throat, a fur pendant? Or did the eagle eat what he could reach, gutting the living weasel with his talons before his breast, bending his beak, cleaning the beautiful airborne bones?

I have been reading about weasels because I saw one last week. I startled a weasel who startled me, and we exchanged a long glance.

Twenty minutes from my house, through the woods by the quarry and across the highway, is Hollins Pond, a remarkable piece of shallowness, where I like to go at sunset and sit on a tree trunk. Hollins Pond is also called Murray's Pond; it covers two acres of bottomland near Tinker Creek with six inches of water and six thousand lily pads. In winter, brown-and-white steers stand in the middle of it, merely dampening their hooves; from the distant shore they look like miracle itself, complete with miracle's nonchalance. Now, in summer, the steers are gone. The water lilies have blossomed and spread to a green horizontal plane that is terra firma to plodding blackbirds, and tremulous ceiling to black leeches, crayfish, and carp.

This is, mind you, suburbia. It is a five-minute walk in three direc-   *5* tions to rows of houses, though none is visible here. There's a 55 mph highway at one end of the pond, and a nesting pair of wood ducks at the other. Under every bush is a muskrat hole or a beer can. The far end is an alternating series of fields and woods, fields and woods, threaded everywhere with motorcycle tracks—in whose bare clay wild turtles lay eggs.

So. I had crossed the highway, stepped over two low barbed-wire fences, and traced the motorcycle path in all gratitude through the wild rose and poison ivy of the pond's shoreline up into high grassy fields. Then I cut down through the woods to the mossy fallen tree where I sit. This tree is excellent. It makes a dry, upholstered bench at the upper, marshy end of the pond, a plush jetty raised from the thorny shore between a shallow blue body of water and a deep blue body of sky.

The sun had just set. I was relaxed on the tree trunk, ensconced in the lap of lichen, watching the lily pads at my feet tremble and part dreamily over the thrusting path of a carp. A yellow bird appeared to my right and flew behind me. It caught my eye; I swiveled around—and the next instant, inexplicably, I was looking down at a weasel, who was looking up at me.

Weasel! I'd never seen one wild before. He was ten inches long, thin as a curve, a muscled ribbon, brown as fruitwood, soft-furred, alert. His face was fierce, small and pointed as a lizard's; he would have made a good arrowhead. There was just a dot of chin, maybe two brown hairs' worth, and then the pure white fur began that spread down his underside. He had two black eyes I didn't see, any more than you see a window.

The weasel was stunned into stillness as he was emerging from beneath an enormous shaggy wild rose bush four feet away. I was stunned into stillness twisted backward on the tree trunk. Our eyes locked, and someone threw away the key.

Our look was as if two lovers, or deadly enemies, met unexpectedly   *10* on an overgrown path when each had been thinking of something else: a clearing blow to the gut. It was also a bright blow to the brain, or a sudden beating of brains, with all the charge and intimate grate of rubbed balloons. It emptied our lungs. It felled the forest, moved the fields, and drained the pond; the world dismantled and tumbled into that black hole of eyes. If you and I looked at each other that way, our skulls would split and drop to our shoulders. But we don't. We keep our skulls. So.

He disappeared. This was only last week, and already I don't remember what shattered the enchantment. I think I blinked, I think I retrieved my brain from the weasel's brain, and tried to memorize what

I was seeing, and the weasel felt the yank of separation, the careening splashdown into real life and the urgent current of instinct. He vanished under the wild rose. I waited motionless, my mind suddenly full of data and my spirit with pleadings, but he didn't return.

Please do not tell me about "approach-avoidance conflicts." I tell you I've been in that weasel's brain for sixty seconds, and he was in mine. Brains are private places, muttering through unique and secret tapes—but the weasel and I both plugged into another tape simultaneously, for a sweet and shocking time. Can I help it if it was a blank?

What goes on in his brain the rest of the time? What does a weasel think about? He won't say. His journal is tracks in clay, a spray of feathers, mouse blood and bone: uncollected, unconnected, loose-leaf, and blown.

I would like to learn, or remember, how to live. I come to Hollins Pond not so much to learn how to live as, frankly, to forget about it. That is, I don't think I can learn from a wild animal how to live in particular—shall I suck warm blood, hold my tail high, walk with my footprints precisely over the prints of my hands?—but I might learn something of mindlessness, something of the purity of living in the physical senses and the dignity of living without bias or motive. The weasel lives in necessity and we live in choice, hating necessity and dying at the last ignobly in its talons. I would like to live as I should, as the weasel lives as he should. And I suspect that for me the way is like the weasel's: open to time and death painlessly, noticing everything, remembering nothing, choosing the given with a fierce and pointed will.

I missed my chance. I should have gone for the throat. I should have 15 lunged for that streak of white under the weasel's chin and held on, held on through mud and into the wild rose, held on for a dearer life. We could live under the wild rose wild as weasels, mute and uncomprehending. I could very calmly go wild. I could live two days in the den, curled, leaning on mouse fur, sniffing bird bones, blinking, licking, breathing musk, my hair tangled in the roots of grasses. Down is a good place to go, where the mind is single. Down is out, out of your ever-loving mind and back to your careless senses. I remember muteness as a prolonged and giddy fast, where every moment is a feast of utterance received. Time and events are merely poured, unremarked, and ingested directly, like blood pulsed into my gut through a jugular vein. Could two live that way? Could two live under the wild rose, and explore by the pond, so that the smooth mind of each is as everywhere present to the other, and as received and as unchallenged, as falling snow?

We could, you know. We can live any way we want. People take vows of poverty, chastity, and obedience—even of silence—by choice. The thing is to stalk your calling in a certain skilled and supple way, to locate the most tender and live spot and plug into that pulse. This is yielding, not fighting. A weasel doesn't "attack" anything; a weasel lives as he's meant to, yielding at every moment to the perfect freedom of single necessity.

I think it would be well, and proper, and obedient, and pure, to grasp your one necessity and not let it go, to dangle from it limp wherever it takes you. Then even death, where you're going no matter how you live, cannot you part. Seize it and let it seize you up aloft even, till your eyes burn out and drop; let your musky flesh fall off in shreds, and let your very bones unhinge and scatter, loosened over fields, over fields and woods, lightly, thoughtless, from any height at all, from as high as eagles.

❑ *Outward Exploration: Discussion*

1. What are the purposes of the essay's first two paragraphs?
2. Why does Dillard mention the fact that the pond has two names?
3. At the end of paragraph 4, why does Dillard tell us that the water lilies are "terra firma to plodding blackbirds, and tremulous ceiling to black leeches, crayfish, and carp"?
4. What's the significance of the fact that "[u]nder every bush is a muskrat hole or a beer can" (paragraph 5)?
5. Why does Dillard break her essay into sections using extra white space? Do the breaks help the structure work? Why or why not?
6. What details of Dillard's description of the weasel strike you as particularly vivid?
7. In paragraph 10, what device(s) does Dillard use to convey the impact of seeing the weasel?
8. According to Dillard, why does she go to the pond?
9. What does she think she can and cannot learn from animals?
10. What does Dillard mean when she says she should live as she should, "open to time and death painlessly, noticing everything, remembering nothing, choosing the given with a fierce and pointed will" (paragraph 14)? In particular, how can someone choose the given since, by its very definition, the given is not a matter of choosing or not choosing?
11. In what ways does Dillard's approach to a natural event differ from Virginia Woolf's approach in "The Death of a Moth"? Why does Dillard take a different approach?

❏ *Outward Exploration: Writing*

1. Using the habits of whatever animal you know best (for example, a pet or some animal you observed at a zoo or perhaps some animal examined on a television nature show), explore one of your beliefs as Dillard does.

2. What do you see as your life's "calling" or your "one necessity"? Write an essay exploring it. Consider explaining the sources of your conviction that this is indeed your "calling" or your "one necessity."

❏ *Style*

Consider the following sentence from Dillard's essay:

He was ten inches long, thin as a curve, a muscled ribbon, brown as fruitwood, soft-furred, alert. (paragraph 8)

Notice the mixture of precise detail ("ten inches long"), description ("brown as fruitwood," "alert"), unusually phrased adjective ("soft-furred"), simile ("thin as a curve"), and metaphor ("a muscled ribbon"). Notice that the *ribbon* metaphor is an elaboration on the simile's *curve*. Using Dillard's technique, write a one-sentence description of some animal or object or person; namely, give a precise detail first, followed by a simile, then a metaphor (which plays off the idea in the simile just given), and end with three adjectives (if possible, follow Dillard's rhythm here—a three-word adjective followed by a two-word adjective, followed by a one-word adjective).

Where I Lived, and What I Lived For

Henry David Thoreau

☐ *Inward Exploration*

Write a one-paragraph answer to this question: What do you live for?

When first I took up my abode in the woods, that is, began to spend   1
my nights as well as days there, which, by accident, was on Independence Day, or the Fourth of July, 1845, my house was not finished for winter, but was merely a defence against the rain, without plastering or chimney, the walls being of rough, weather-stained boards, with wide chinks, which made it cool at night. The upright white hewn studs and freshly planed door and window casings gave it a clean and airy look, especially in the morning, when its timbers were saturated with dew, so that I fancied that by noon some sweet gum would exude from them. To my imagination it retained throughout the day more or less of this auroral character, reminding me of a certain house on a mountain which I had visited a year before. This was an airy and unplastered cabin, fit to entertain a travelling god, and where a goddess might trail her garments. The winds which passed over my dwelling were such as sweep over the ridges of mountains, bearing the broken strains, or celestial parts only, of terrestrial music. The morning wind forever blows, the poem of creation is uninterrupted; but few are the ears that hear it. Olympus is but the outside of the earth everywhere.

The only house I had been the owner of before, if I except a boat, was a tent, which I used occasionally when making excursions in the summer, and this is still rolled up in my garret; but the boat, after passing from hand to hand, has gone down the stream of time. With this more substantial shelter about me, I had made some progress toward settling in the world. This frame, so slightly clad, was a sort of crystallization around me, and reacted on the builder. It was suggestive somewhat as a picture in outlines. I did not need to go out of doors to take the air, for the atmosphere within had lost none of its freshness. It was not so much within doors as being a door where I sat, even in the rainiest weather. The Harivansa° says, "An abode without birds is like a meat

---

Harivansa: a fifth-century Hindu epic.

without seasoning." Such was not my abode, for I found myself suddenly neighbor to the birds; not by having imprisoned one, but having caged myself near them. I was not only nearer to some of those which commonly frequent the garden and the orchard, but to those wilder and more thrilling songsters of the forest which never, or rarely, serenade a villager,—the wood-thrush, the veery, the scarlet tanager, the field-sparrow, the whippoorwill, and many others.

I was seated by the shore of a small pond, about a mile and half south of the village of Concord and somewhat higher than it, in the midst of an extensive wood between that town and Lincoln, and about two miles south of that our only field known to fame, Concord Battle Ground; but I was so low in the woods that the opposite shore, half a mile off, like the rest, covered with wood, was my most distant horizon. For the first week, whenever I looked out on the pond it impressed me like a tarn high up on the side of a mountain, its bottom far above the surface of other lakes, and, as the sun arose, I saw it throwing off its nightly clothing of mist, and here and there, by degrees, its soft ripples or its smooth reflecting surface was revealed, while the mists, like ghosts, were stealthily withdrawing in every direction into the woods, as at the breaking up of some nocturnal conventicle. The very dew seemed to hang upon the trees later into the day than usual, as on the sides of mountains.

This small lake was of most value as a neighbor in the intervals of a gentle rain-storm in August, when, both air and water being perfectly still, but the sky overcast, mid-afternoon had all the serenity of evening, and the wood thrush sang around, and was heard from shore to shore. A lake like this is never smoother than at such a time; and the clear portion of the air above it being shallow and darkened by clouds, the water, full of light and reflections, becomes a lower heaven itself so much the more important. From a hilltop near by, where the wood had been recently cut off, there was a pleasing vista southward across the pond, through a wide indentation in the hills which form the shore there, where their opposite sides sloping toward each other suggested a stream flowing out in that direction through a wooded valley, but stream there was none. That way I looked between and over the near green hills to some distant and higher ones in the horizon, tinged with blue. Indeed, by standing on tiptoe I could catch a glimpse of some of the peaks of the still bluer and more distant mountain ranges in the northwest, those true-blue coins from heaven's own mint, and also of some portion of the village. But in other directions, even from this point, I could not see over or beyond the woods which surrounded me. It is well to have some water in your neighborhood, to give buoyancy to and float the earth. One value even of the smallest well is, that when you look into it you see that earth is not continent but insular. This is as important as that it keeps butter cool. When I looked across the pond from this peak toward the Sudbury meadows, which in time of flood I distinguished elevated perhaps by a mirage in their seething valley, like a coin in a basin, all the earth beyond the pond appeared like a thin crust insulated and floated even by this small sheet of intervening water, and I was reminded that this on which I dwelt was but *dry land*.

Though the view from my door was still more contracted, I did not   5 feel crowded or confined in the least. There was pasture enough for my imagination. The low shrub oak plateau to which the opposite shore arose stretched away toward the prairies of the West and the steppes of Tartary, affording ample room for all the roving families of men. "There are none happy in the world but beings who enjoy freely a vast horizon,"—said Damodara,° when his herds required new and larger pastures.

Both place and time were changed, and I dwelt nearer to those parts of the universe and to those eras in history which had most attracted me. Where I lived was as far off as many a region viewed nightly by astronomers. We are wont to imagine rare and delectable places in some remote and more celestial corner of the system, behind the constellation of Cassiopeia's Chair, far from noise and disturbance. I discovered that my house actually had its site in such a withdrawn, but forever new and unprofaned, part of the universe. If it were worth the while to settle in those parts near to the Pleiades or the Hyades, to Aldebaran or Altair,° then I was really there, or at an equal remoteness from the life which I had left behind, divided and twinkling with as fine a ray to my nearest neighbor, and to be seen only in moonless nights by him. Such was that part of creation where I had squatted;—

> "There was a shepherd that did live,
>   And held his thoughts as high
> As were the mounts whereon his flocks
>   Did hourly feed him by."

What should we think of the shepherd's life if his flocks always wandered to higher pastures than his thoughts?

Every morning was a cheerful invitation to make my life of equal simplicity, and I may say innocence, with Nature herself. I have been as sincere a worshipper of Aurora° as the Greeks. I got up early and bathed in the pond; that was a religious exercise, and one of the best things which I did. They say that characters were engraven on the bathing tub of King Tchingthang° to this effect—"Renew thyself completely each day; do it again, and again, and forever again." I can understand that. Morning brings back the heroic ages. I was as much affected by the faint

---

Damodara: Krishna; in the Hindu religion, the incarnation of the God Vishnu.
Pleiades, Hyades, Aldebaran, Altair: names of stars and constellations.
Aurora: the classical goddess of dawn.
King Tchingthang: Confucius (551–479 B.C.), China's greatest sage.

hum of a mosquito making its invisible and unimaginable tour through my apartment at earliest dawn, when I was sitting with door and windows open, as I could be by any trumpet that ever sang of fame. It was Homer's requiem; itself an Iliad and Odyssey in the air, singing its own wrath and wanderings. There was something cosmical about it; a standing advertisement, till forbidden, of the everlasting vigor and fertility of the world. The morning, which is the most memorable season of the day, is the awakening hour. Then there is least somnolence in us; and for an hour, at least, some part of us awakes which slumbers all the rest of the day and night. Little is to be expected of that day, if it can be called a day, to which we are not awakened by our Genius, but by the mechanical nudgings of some servitor, are not awakened by our own newly acquired force and aspirations from within, accompanied by the undulations of celestial music, instead of factory bells, and a fragrance filling the air—to a higher life than we fell asleep from; and thus the darkness bear its fruit, and prove itself to be good, no less than the light. The man who does not believe that each day contains an earlier, more sacred, and auroral hour than he has yet profaned, has despaired of life, and is pursuing a descending and darkening way. After a partial cessation of his sensuous life, the soul of man, or its organs rather, are reinvigorated each day, and his Genius tries again what noble life it can make. All memorable events, I should say, transpire in morning time and in a morning atmosphere. The Vedas° say, "All intelligences awake with the morning." Poetry and art, and the fairest and most memorable of the actions of men, date from such an hour. All poets and heroes, like Memmon,° are the children of Aurora, and emit their music at sunrise. To him whose elastic and vigorous thought keeps pace with the sun, the day is a perpetual morning. It matters not what the clocks say or the attitudes and labors of men. Morning is when I am awake and there is a dawn in me. Moral reform is the effort to throw off sleep. Why is it that men give so poor an account of their day if they have not been slumbering? They are not such poor calculators. If they had not been overcome with drowsiness, they would have performed something. The millions are awake enough for physical labor; but only one in a million is awake enough for effective intellectual exertion, only one in a hundred millions to a poetic or divine life. To be awake is to be alive. I have never yet met a man who was quite awake. How could I have looked him in the face?

We must learn to reawaken and keep ourselves awake, not by mechanical aids, but by an infinite expectation of the dawn, which does not forsake us in our soundest sleep. I know of no more encouraging fact than the unquestionable ability of man to elevate his life by a conscious endeavor. It is something to be able to paint a particular picture, or to

---

Vedas: ancient Hindu scriptures.
Memmon: at Thebes the statue of Memmon was said to emit music at dawn.

carve a statue, and so to make a few objects beautiful; but it is far more glorious to carve and paint the very atmosphere and medium through which we look, which morally we can do. To affect the quality of the day, that is the highest of arts. Every man is tasked to make his life, even in its details, worthy of the contemplation of his most elevated and critical hour. If we refused, or rather used up, such paltry information as we get, the oracles would distinctly inform us how this might be done.

I went to the woods because I wished to live deliberately, to front only the essential facts of life, and see if I could not learn what it had to teach, and not, when I came to die, discover that I had not lived. I did not wish to live what was not life, living is so dear, nor did I wish to practice resignation, unless it was quite necessary. I wanted to live deep and suck out all the marrow of life, to live so sturdily and Spartan-like as to put to rout all that was not life, to cut a broad swath and shave close, to drive life into a corner, and reduce it to its lowest terms, and, if it proved to be mean, why then to get the whole and genuine meanness of it, and publish its meanness to the world; or if it were sublime, to know it by experience, and be able to give a true account of it in my next excursion. For most men, it appears to me, are in a strange uncertainty about it, whether it is of the devil or of God and have *somewhat hastily* concluded that it is the chief end of man here to "glorify God and enjoy him forever."

Still we live meanly, like ants; though the fable tells us that we were   *10* long ago changed into men; like pygmies we fight with cranes; it is error upon error, and clout upon clout, and our best virtue has for its occasion a superfluous and evitable wretchedness. Our life is frittered away by detail. An honest man has hardly need to count more than his ten fingers, or in extreme cases he may add his ten toes, and lump the rest. Simplicity, simplicity, simplicity! I say, let your affairs be as two or three, and not a hundred or a thousand; instead of a million count half a dozen, and keep your accounts on your thumb-nail. In the midst of this chopping sea of civilized life, such are the clouds and storms and quicksands and thousand-and-one items to be allowed for, that a man has to live, if he would not founder and go to the bottom and not make his port at all, by dead reckoning, and he must be a great calculator indeed who succeeds. Simplify, simplify. Instead of three meals a day, if it be necessary eat but one; instead of a hundred dishes, five; and reduce other things in proportion. Our life is like a German Confederacy, made up of petty states, with its boundary forever fluctuating, so that even a German cannot tell you how it is bounded at any moment. The nation itself, with all its so-called internal improvements, which, by the way, are all external and superficial, is just such an unwieldly and overgrown establishment, cluttered with furniture and tripped up by its own traps, ruined by luxury and heedless expense, by want of calculation and a worthy aim, as the million households in the land; and the only cure for it, as for them, is in a rigid economy, a stern and more than Spartan simplicity of life and elevation of purpose. It lives too fast. Men think that it is essential that the *Nation* have commerce, and export ice, and talk through a telegraph, and ride thirty miles an hour, without a doubt, whether *they* do or not; but whether we should live like baboons or like men, is a little uncertain. If we do not get out sleepers,° and forge rails, and devote days and nights to the work, but go to tinkering upon our *lives* to improve *them,* who will build railroads? And if railroads are not built, how shall we get to Heaven in season? But if we stay at home and mind our business, who will want railroads? We do not ride on the railroad; it rides upon us. Did you ever think what those sleepers are that underlie the railroad? Each one is a man, an Irishman, or a Yankee man. The rails are laid on them, and they are covered with sand, and the cars run smoothly over them. They are sound sleepers, I assure you. And every few years a new lot is laid down and run over; so that, if some have the pleasure of riding on a rail, others have the misfortune to be ridden upon. And when they run over a man that is walking in his sleep, a supernumerary sleeper in the wrong position, and wake him up, they suddenly stop the cars, and make a hue and cry about it, as if this were an exception. I am glad to know that it takes a gang of men for every five miles to keep the sleepers down and level in their beds as it is, for this is a sign that they may sometime get up again.

Why should we live with such hurry and waste of life? We are determined to be starved before we are hungry. Men say that a stitch in time saves nine, and so they take a thousand stitches to-day to save nine to-morrow. As for *work,* we haven't any of any consequence. We have the Saint Vitus' dance, and cannot possibly keep our heads still. If I should only give a few pulls at the parish bell-rope, as for a fire, that is, without setting the bell, there is hardly a man on his farm in the outskirts of Concord, notwithstanding that press of engagements which was his excuse so many times this morning, nor a boy, nor a woman, I might almost say, but would forsake all and follow that sound, not mainly to save property from the flames, but, if we will confess the truth, much more to see it burn, since burn it must, and we, be it known, did not set it on fire,—or to see it put out, and have a hand in it, if that is done as handsomely; yes, even if it were the parish church itself. Hardly a man takes a half-hour's nap after dinner, but when he wakes he holds up his head and asks, "What's the news?" as if the rest of mankind had stood his sentinels. Some give directions to be waked every half-hour, doubtless for no other purpose; and then, to pay for it, they tell what they have dreamed. After a night's sleep the news is as indispensable as the breakfast. "Pray tell me anything new that has happened to a man anywhere on this globe,"—and he reads it over his coffee and rolls, that a man has had his eyes gouged out this morning on the Wachito River,

---

sleepers: railroad ties.

never dreaming the while that he lives in the dark unfathomed mammoth cave of this world, and has but the rudiment of an eye himself.

For my part, I could easily do without the post-office. I think that there are very few important communications made through it. To speak critically, I never received more than one or two letters in my life—I wrote this some years ago—that were worth the postage. The penny-post is, commonly, an institution through which you seriously offer a man that penny for his thoughts which is so often safely offered in jest. And I am sure that I never read any memorable news in a newspaper. If we read of one man robbed, or murdered, or killed by accident, or one house burned, or one vessel wrecked, or one steamboat blown up, or one cow run over on the Western Railroad, or one mad dog killed, or one lot of grasshoppers in the winter,—we never read of another. One is enough. If you are acquainted with the principle, what do you care for a myriad instances and applications? To a philosopher all *news,* as it is called, is gossip and they who edit and read it are old women over their tea. Yet not a few are greedy after this gossip. There was such a rush, as I hear, the other day at one of the offices to learn the foreign news by the last arrival, that several large squares of plate glass belonging to the establishment were broken by the pressure,—news which I seriously think a ready wit might write a twelvemonth, or twelve years, beforehand with sufficient accuracy. As for Spain, for instance, if you know how to throw in Don Carlos and the Infanta, and Don Pedro and Seville and Granada, from time to time in the right proportions,—they may have changed the names a little since I saw the papers,—and serve up a bull-fight when other entertainments fail, it will be true to the letter, and give us as good an idea of the exact state of ruin of things in Spain as the most succinct and lucid reports under this head in the newspapers: and as for England, almost the last significant scrap of news from that quarter was the revolution of 1649, and if you have learned the history of her crops for an average year, you never need attend to that thing again, unless your speculations are of a merely pecuniary character. If one may judge who rarely looks into the newspapers, nothing new does ever happen in foreign parts, a French revolution not excepted.

What news! how much more important to know what that is which was never old! "Kieou-he-yu (great dignitary of the state of Wei) sent a man to Khoung-tseu to know his news. Khoung-tseu caused the messenger to be seated near him, and questioned him in these terms: What is your master doing? The messenger answered with respect: My master desires to diminish the number of his faults, but he cannot come to the end of them. The messenger being gone, the philosopher remarked: 'What a worthy messenger! What a worthy messenger!'" The preacher, instead of vexing the ears of drowsy farmers on their day of rest at the end of the week,—for Sunday is the fit conclusion of an ill-spent week, and not the fresh and brave beginning of a new one,—with this one other draggle-tail of a sermon, should shout with thundering voice, "Pause! Avast! Why so seeming fast, but deadly slow?"

Shams and delusions are esteemed for soundest truths, while reality is fabulous. If men would steadily observe realities only, and not allow themselves to be deluded, life, to compare it with such things as we know, would be like a fairy tale and the Arabian Nights' Entertainments. If we respected only what is inevitable and has a right to be, music and poetry would resound along the streets. When we are unhurried and wise, we perceive that only great and worthy things have any permanent and absolute existence, that petty fears and petty pleasures are but the shadow of the reality. This is always exhilarating and sublime. By closing the eyes and slumbering, and consenting to be deceived by shows, men establish and confirm their daily life of routine and habit everywhere, which still is built on purely illusory foundations. Children, who play life, discern its true law and relations more clearly than men, who fail to live it worthily, but who think that they are wiser by experience, that is, by failure. I have read in a Hindoo book, that "there was a king's son, who, being expelled in infancy from his native city, was brought up by a forester, and growing up to maturity in that state, imagined himself to belong to the barbarous race with which he lived. One of his father's ministers having discovered him, revealed to him what he was, and the misconception of his character was removed, and he knew himself to be a prince. So soul," continues the Hindoo philosopher, "from the circumstances in which it is placed, mistakes its own character, until the truth is revealed to it by some holy teacher, and then it knows itself to be *Brahma.*" I perceive that we inhabitants of New England live this mean life that we do because our vision does not penetrate the surface of things. We think that that *is* which *appears* to be. If a man should walk through this town and see only the reality, where, think you, would the "Mill-dam" go to? If he should give us an account of the realities he beheld there, we should not recognize the place in his description. Look at a meeting-house, or a court-house, or a jail, or a shop, or a dwelling-house, and say what that thing really is before a true gaze, and they would all go to pieces in your account of them. Men esteem truth remote, in the outskirts of the system, behind the farthest star, before Adam and after the last man. In eternity there is indeed something true and sublime. But all these times and places and occasions are now and here. God himself culminates in the present moment, and will never be more divine in the lapse of all the ages. And we are enabled to apprehend at all what is sublime and noble only by the perpetual instilling and drenching of the reality that surrounds us. The universe constantly and obediently answers to our conceptions; whether we travel fast or slow, the track is laid for us. Let us spend our lives in conceiving then. The poet or the artist never yet had so fair and noble a design but some of his posterity at least could accomplish it.

Let us spend one day as deliberately as Nature, and not be thrown   15 off the track by every nutshell and mosquito's wing that falls on the rails. Let us rise early and fast, or break fast, gently and without perturbation; let company come and let company go, let the bells ring and the children cry,—determined to make a day of it. Why should we knock under and go with the stream? Let us not be upset and overwhelmed in that terrible rapid and whirlpool called a dinner, situated in the meridian shallows. Weather this danger and you are safe, for the rest of the way is down hill. With unrelaxed nerves, with morning vigor, sail by it, looking another way, tied to the mast like Ulysses. If the engine whistles, let it whistle till it is hoarse for its pains. If the bell rings, why should we run? We will consider what kind of music they are like. Let us settle ourselves, and work and wedge our feet downward through the mud and slush of opinion, and prejudice, and tradition, and delusion, and appearance, that alluvion which covers the globe, through Paris and London, through New York and Boston and Concord, through Church and State, through poetry and philosophy and religion, till we come to a hard bottom and rocks in place, which we can call *reality,* and say, This is, and no mistake; and then begin, having a *point d'appui,*° below freshet and frost and fire, a place where you might found a wall or a state, or set a lamp-post safely, or perhaps a gauge, not a Nilometer,° but a Realometer, that future ages might know how deep a freshet of shams and appearances had gathered from time to time. If you stand right fronting and face to face to a fact, you will see the sun glimmer on both its surfaces, as if it were a cimeter,° and feel its sweet edge dividing you through the heart and marrow, and so you will happily conclude your mortal career. Be it life or death, we crave only reality. If we are really dying, let us hear the rattle in our throats and feel cold in the extremities; if we are alive, let us go about our business.

Time is but the stream I go a-fishing in. I drink at it; but while I drink I see the sandy bottom and detect how shallow it is. Its thin current slides away, but eternity remains. I would drink deeper; fish in the sky, whose bottom is pebbly with stars. I cannot count one. I know not the first letter of the alphabet. I have always been regretting that I was not as wise as the day I was born. The intellect is a cleaver; it discerns and rifts its way into the secret of things. I do not wish to be any more busy with my hands than is necessary. My head is hands and feet. I feel all my best faculties concentrated in it. My instinct tells me that my head is an organ for burrowing, as some creatures use their snout and fore paws, and with it I would mine and burrow my way through these hills. I think that the richest vein is somewhere hereabouts; so by the divining-rod and thin rising vapors I judge; and here I will begin to mine.

---

point d'appui: a point of support or foundation.
Nilometer: a device to measure the water level in the Nile River.
cimeter: a curved sword.

❏ *Outward Exploration: Discussion*

1. Explain your reaction to Thoreau's description of his cabin.

2. What is the effect of the quotations and the classic allusions throughout the essay?

3. One of Thoreau's beliefs is that "[t]he millions are awake enough for physical labor; but only one in a million is awake enough for effective intellectual exertion, only one in a hundred millions to a poetic or divine life. To be awake is to be alive." What does Thoreau mean by "being awake"? Do you agree or disagree? Explain.

4. Why did Thoreau go to the woods?

5. Do you agree that "our life is frittered away by detail"? Explain.

6. What is Thoreau's attitude toward the technology of his day (for example, telegraphs and railroads)? What do you think his attitude would be about today's technology? Explain.

7. What is his attitude toward work? Do you agree?

8. Explain his attitude toward the post office and newspapers. Do you agree? Why or why not?

❏ *Outward Exploration: Writing*

1. According to Thoreau, "Little is to be expected of that day, if it can be called a day, to which we are not awakened by our Genius, but by the mechanical nudgings of some servitor, are not awakened by our own newly acquired force and aspirations from within, accompanied by the undulations of celestial music, instead of factory bells, and a fragrance filling the air—to a higher life than we fell asleep from" (paragraph 8). Few people in our society have the luxury of waking when their "Genius" feels it's time; most people awake to the noise of an alarm clock or the pounding of a friend on the door. Write an essay about time and schedules. You might compare and contrast the ways Thoreau and the modern world see time. How do you view time?

2. Thoreau believes that "[e]very man is tasked to make his life, even in its details, worthy of the contemplation of his most elevated and critical hour" (paragraph 8). Write an essay agreeing or disagreeing with this belief. Support the essay with references to outside sources as well as with details from your own life.

3. Thoreau says that he "wanted to live deep and suck out all the marrow of life" (paragraph 9). How did he achieve that goal? What is your life goal? How are you going about achieving it? Write an essay exploring this topic.

4. Select one or more of Thoreau's beliefs and write an essay about it. You might agree with it and support it with examples from your own readings and your own life, or you might attack it and support your attack with examples from your own readings and your own life.

5. Write an essay about what you live for.

❏ *Style*

Look again at the extended image in paragraph 10. Thoreau compares our individual lives to the German Confederacy—made up of petty states with boundaries forever in dispute, the confederacy an overgrown establishment cluttered with unnecessary things and lacking purpose and direction. Think about your life or the lives of those you see around you. Create an image that captures the essence of what you see, then try to extend the image as Thoreau does.

The Four Idols

FRANCIS BACON

☐ *Inward Exploration*

Write at least one paragraph detailing an error in judgment or in perception that you have made. Explain what happened, why you think it happened, and its end result. Or write at least one paragraph explaining how you reach a decision about something. Be as specific and as analytical as possible.

The idols and false notions which are now in possession of the human understanding, and have taken deep root therein, not only so beset men's minds that truth can hardly find entrance, but even after entrance obtained, they will again in the very instauration° of the sciences meet and trouble us, unless men being forewarned of the danger fortify themselves as far as may be against their assaults.

There are four classes of idols which beset men's minds. To these for distinction's sake I have assigned names—calling the first class *Idols of the Tribe;* the second, *Idols of the Cave;* the third, *Idols of the Marketplace;* the fourth, *Idols of the Theater.*

The formation of ideas and axioms by true induction° is no doubt the proper remedy to be applied for the keeping off and clearing away of idols. To point them out, however, is of great use; for the doctrine of idols is to the interpretation of nature what the doctrine of the refutation of sophisms° is to common logic.

The *Idols of the Tribe* have their foundation in human nature itself, and in the tribe or race of men. For it is a false assertion that the sense of man is the measure of things. On the contrary, all perceptions as well of the sense as of the mind are according to the measure of the individual and not according to the measure of the universe. And the human understanding is like a false mirror, which, receiving rays irregularly, dis-

1

---

instauration: renovation, restoration, or the establishment of something.
induction: for Bacon, the method of gathering and categorizing many individual examples of a phenomenon in the hope that the truth about them will emerge through inference. Bacon offered induction as a replacement for Aristotle's method of *deduction,* beginning with a theory and drawing conclusions from that theory.
sophisms: plausible but incorrect arguments. In fifth-century BC Greece, a group of philosophers were known as the Sophists; they came to be seen as specialists in elaborate and devious argumentation.

torts and discolors the nature of things by mingling its own nature with it.

The *Idols of the Cave* are the idols of the individual man. For everyone (besides the errors common to human nature in general) has a cave or den of his own, which refracts and discolors the light of nature; owing either to his own proper and peculiar nature; or to his education and conversation with others; or to the reading of books, and the authority of those whom he esteems and admires; or to the differences of impressions, accordingly as they take place in a mind preoccupied and predisposed or in a mind indifferent and settled; or the like. So that the spirit of man (according as it is meted out to different individuals) is in fact a thing variable and full of perturbation,° and governed as it were by chance. Whence it was well observed by Heraclitus° that men look for sciences in their own lesser worlds, and not in the greater or common world.

There are also idols formed by the intercourse and association of men with each other, which I call *Idols of the Marketplace,* on account of the commerce and consort of men there. For it is by discourse that men associate; and words are imposed according to the apprehension of the vulgar. And therefore the ill and unfit choice of words wonderfully obstructs the understanding. Nor do the definitions or explanations wherewith in some things learned men are wont to guard and defend themselves, by any means set the matter right. But words plainly force and overrule the understanding, and throw all into confusion and lead men away into numberless empty controversies and idle fancies.

Lastly, there are idols which have immigrated into men's minds from the various dogmas of philosophies, and also from wrong laws of demonstration. These I call *Idols of the Theater;* because in my judgment all the received systems are but so many stage-plays, representing worlds of their own creation after an unreal and scenic fashion. Nor is it only of the systems now in vogue, or only of the ancient sects and philosophies, that I speak; for many more plays of the same kind may yet be composed and in like artificial manner set forth; seeing that errors the most widely different have nevertheless causes for the most part alike. Neither again do I mean this only of entire systems, but also of many principles and axioms in science, which by tradition, credulity, and negligence, have come to be received.

But of these several kinds of idols I must speak more largely and exactly, that the understanding may be duly cautioned.

---

perturbation: disturbance or agitation. In physics and astronomy, the term means the variation in a designated orbit (for example, a planet's orbit) which is caused by the influence of one or more external bodies.

Heraclitus: Greek philosopher (around 500 BC) who believed that strife and change are the natural conditions of the universe. He saw fire as the basic building block of the world.

The human understanding is of its own nature prone to suppose the existence of more order and regularity in the world than it finds. And though there be many things in nature which are singular and unmatched, yet it devises for them parallels and conjugates and relatives° which do not exist. Hence the fiction that all celestial bodies move in perfect circles; spirals and dragons being (except in name) utterly rejected. Hence too the element of fire with its orb is brought in, to make up the square with the other three which the sense perceives. Hence also the ratio of density° of the so-called elements is arbitrarily fixed at ten to one. And so on of other dreams. And these fancies affect not dogmas only, but simple notions also.

The human understanding when it has once adopted an opinion   *10* (either as being the received opinion or as being agreeable to itself) draws all things else to support and agree with it. And though there be a greater number and weight of instances to be found on the other side, yet these it either neglects and despises, or else by some distinction sets aside and rejects; in order that by this great and pernicious predetermination the authority of its former conclusions may remain inviolate. And therefore it was a good answer that was made by one who when they showed him hanging in a temple a picture of those who had paid their vows as having escaped shipwreck, and would have him say whether he did not now acknowledge the power of the gods—"Ay," asked he again, "but where are they painted that were drowned after their vows?" And such is the way of all superstition, whether in astrology, dreams, omens, divine judgments, or the like; wherein men having a delight in such vanities, mark the events where they are fulfilled, but where they fail, though this happen much oftener, neglect and pass them by. But with far more subtlety does this mischief insinuate itself into philosophy and the sciences; in which the first conclusion colors and brings into conformity with itself all that come after, though far sounder and better. Besides, independently of that delight and vanity which I have described, it is the peculiar and perpetual error of the human intellect to be more moved and excited by affirmatives than by negatives; whereas it ought properly to hold itself indifferently disposed towards both alike. Indeed, in the establishment of any true axiom, the negative instance is the more forcible of the two.

The human understanding is moved by those things most which strike and enter the mind simultaneously and suddenly, and so fill the

---

parallels and conjugates and relatives: refers to the assumption that there are forms of order.
ratio of density: an inaccurate and fanciful table of weights in which Earth was thought to be ten times heavier than an equal volume of water, and water was ten times heavier than air, and air, in turn, was ten times heavier than fire. This ratio was obtained by deduction rather than observation and turned out to be false. For Bacon, another example of the dangers of deduction.

imagination; and then it feigns and supposes all other things to be some-how, though it cannot see how, similar to those few things by which it is surrounded. But for that going to and fro to remote and heterogene-ous instances, by which axioms are tried as in the fire, the intellect is altogether slow and unfit, unless it be forced thereto by severe laws and overruling authority.

The human understanding is unquiet; it cannot stop or rest, and still presses onward, but in vain. Therefore it is that we cannot conceive of any end or limit to the world, but always as of necessity it occurs to us that there is something beyond. Neither again can it be conceived how eternity has flowed down to the present day; for that distinction which is commonly received of infinity in time past and in time to come can by no means hold; for it would thence follow that one infinity is greater than another, and that infinity is wasting away and tending to become finite. The like subtlety arises touching the infinite divisibility of lines,° from the same inability of thought to stop. But this inability interferes more mischievously in the discovery of causes:° for although the most general principles in nature ought to be held merely positive, as they are discovered, and cannot with truth be referred to a cause; nevertheless, the human understanding being unable to rest still seeks something prior in the order of nature. And then it is that in struggling towards that which is further off, it falls back upon that which is more nigh at hand; namely, on final causes: which have relation clearly to the nature of man rather than to the nature of the universe, and from this source have strangely defiled philosophy. But he is no less an unskilled and shallow philosopher who seeks causes of that which is most general, than he who in things subordinate and subaltern omits to do so.

The human understanding is no dry light, but receives an infusion from the will and affections; whence proceed sciences which may be called "sciences as one would." For what a man had rather were true he

---

the infinite divisibility of lines: This belief underlies the paradox of the Greek philosopher Zeno of Elea. Zeno's paradox "proved" the impossibility of ever reaching a destination. For instance, if a person shot an arrow from point A toward the bulls-eye at point B, Zeno argued that the arrow had to cover half the distance between A and B, and then it had to cover half the distance from that midpoint to B, then half the remaining distance, ad infinitum. Following this line of thought based on commonly accepted truths (you obviously have to go half the distance between points A and B before you can cover all the distance between A and B), it seems logical that the arrow can never reach point B since it is always going only half of the remaining distance. According to Bacon, such "inability of thought to stop" leads to absurdities and confusion.

the discovery of causes: In Bacon's day it was common belief that people learned about the world by pondering its four questions (or *causes*): Who made it? (the efficient cause); What is it composed of? (the material cause); What shape does it have? (the formal cause); and For what purpose was it made? (the final cause). Bacon believed science should focus only on the material and formal causes, yet scholastics focused on efficient and final purposes, hence confusing religion and superstition with science.

more readily believes. Therefore he rejects difficult things from impatience of research; sober things, because they narrow hope; the deeper things of nature, from superstition; the light of experience, from arrogance and pride, lest his mind should seem to be occupied with things mean and transitory; things not commonly believed, out of deference to the opinion of the vulgar. Numberless in short are the ways, and sometimes imperceptible, in which the affections color and infect the understanding.

But by far the greatest hindrance and aberration of the human understanding proceeds from the dullness, incompetency, and deceptions of the senses; in that things which strike the sense outweigh things which do not immediately strike it, though they be more important. Hence it is that speculation commonly ceases where sight ceases; insomuch that of things invisible there is little or no observation. Hence all the working of the spirits enclosed in tangible bodies lies hid and unobserved of men. So also all the more subtle changes of form in the parts of coarser substances (which they commonly call alteration, though it is in truth local motion through exceedingly small spaces) is in like manner unobserved. And yet unless these two things just mentioned be searched out and brought to light, nothing great can be achieved in nature, as far as the production of works is concerned. So again the essential nature of our common air, and of all bodies less dense than air (which are very many) is almost unknown. For the sense by itself is a thing infirm and erring; neither can instruments for enlarging or sharpening the senses do much; but all the truer kind of interpretation of nature is effected by instances and experiments fit and apposite; wherein the sense decides touching the experiment only, and the experiment touching the point in nature and the thing itself.

The human understanding is of its own nature prone to abstractions   15
and gives a substance and reality to things which are fleeting. But to resolve nature into abstractions is less to our purpose than to dissect her into parts; as did the school of Democritus,° which went further into nature than the rest. Matter rather than forms should be the object of our attention, its configurations and changes of configuration, and simple action, and law of action or motion; for forms are figments of the human mind, unless you will call those laws of action forms.

Such then are the idols which I call *Idols of the Tribe;* and which take their rise either from the homogeneity of the substance of the human spirit, or from its preoccupation, or from its narrowness, or from its restless motion, or from an infusion of the affections, or from the incompetency of the senses, or from the mode of impression.

The *Idols of the Cave* take their rise in the peculiar constitution, mental or bodily, of each individual; and also in education, habit, and

---

Democritus: a Greek philosopher who theorized that the world is made up of atoms.

accident. Of this kind there is a great number and variety; but I will instance those the pointing out of which contains the most important caution, and which have most effect in disturbing the clearness of the understanding.

Men become attached to certain particular sciences and speculations, either because they fancy themselves the authors and inventors thereof, or because they have bestowed the greatest pains upon them and become most habituated to them. But men of this kind, if they betake themselves to philosophy and contemplations of a general character, distort and color them in obedience to their former fancies; a thing especially to be noticed in Aristotle, who made his natural philosophy° a mere bondservant to his logic, thereby rendering it contentious and well nigh useless. The race of chemists° again out of a few experiments of the furnace have built up a fantastic philosophy, framed with reference to a few things; and Gilbert° also, after he had employed himself most laboriously in the study and observation of the loadstone, proceeded at once to construct an entire system in accordance with his favorite subject.

There is one principal and, as it were, radical distinction between different minds, in respect of philosophy and the sciences, which is this: that some minds are stronger and apter to mark the differences of things, others to mark their resemblances. The steady and acute mind can fix its contemplations and dwell and fasten on the subtlest distinctions: the lofty and discursive mind recognizes and puts together the finest and most general resemblances. Both kinds however easily err in excess, by catching the one at gradations, the other at shadows.

There are found some minds given to an extreme admiration of antiquity, others to an extreme love and appetite for novelty; but few so duly tempered that they can hold the mean, neither carping at what has been well laid down by the ancients, nor despising what is well introduced by the moderns. This however turns to the great injury of the sciences and philosophy; since these affectations of antiquity and novelty are the humors of partisans rather than judgments; and truth is to be sought for not in the felicity of any age, which is an unstable thing, but in the light of nature and experience, which is eternal. These factions therefore must be abjured, and care must be taken that the intellect be not hurried by them into assent.

Contemplations of nature and of bodies in their simple form break

20

---

natural philosophy: in Bacon's era, the name given to the scientific study of the natural world.

chemists: alchemists, practitioners of a medieval chemical philosophy who devoted themselves to creating the elixir of longevity, the discovery of the panacea, and the transmutation of lead into gold.

William Gilbert: Bacon's English contemporary and author of *De Magnete* (1600). Bacon felt that Gilbert did not have enough evidence to justify his dogmatic and broad conclusions.

up and distract the understanding, while contemplations of nature and bodies in their composition and configuration overpower and dissolve the understanding: a distinction well seen in the school of Leucippus° and Democritus as compared with the other philosophies. For that school is so busied with the particles that it hardly attends to the structure; while the others are so lost in admiration of the structure that they do not penetrate to the simplicity of nature. These kinds of contemplation should therefore be alternated and taken by turns; that so the understanding may be rendered at once penetrating and comprehensive, and the inconveniences above mentioned, with the idols which proceed from them, may be avoided.

Let such then be our provision and contemplative prudence for keeping off and dislodging the *Idols of the Cave,* which grow for the most part either out of the predominance of a favorite subject, or out of an excessive tendency to compare or to distinguish, or out of partiality for particular ages, or out of the largeness or minuteness of the objects contemplated. And generally let every student of nature take this as a rule—that whatever his mind seizes and dwells upon with peculiar satisfaction is to be held in suspicion, and that so much the more care is to be taken in dealing with such questions to keep the understanding even and clear.

But the *Idols of the Marketplace* are the most troublesome of all: idols which have crept into the understanding through the alliances of words and names. For men believe that their reason governs words; but it is also true that words react on the understanding; and this it is that has rendered philosophy and the sciences sophistical and inactive. Now words, being commonly framed and applied according to the capacity of the vulgar, follow those lines of division which are most obvious to the vulgar understanding. And whenever an understanding of greater acuteness or a more diligent observation would alter those lines to suit the true divisions of nature, words stand in the way and resist the change. Whence it comes to pass that the high and formal discussions of learned men end oftentimes in disputes about words and names; with which (according to the use and wisdom of the mathematicians) it would be more prudent to begin, and so by means of definitions reduce them to order. Yet even definitions cannot cure this evil in dealing with natural and material things; since the definitions themselves consist of words, and those words beget others: so that it is necessary to recur to individual instances, and those in due series and order; as I shall say presently when I come to the method and scheme for the formation of notions and axioms.

Leucippus: a fifth-century BC Greek philosopher who is thought to have been the teacher of Democritus.

The idols imposed by words on the understanding are of two kinds. They are either names of things which do not exist (for as there are things left unnamed through lack of observation, so likewise are there names which result from fantastic suppositions and to which nothing in reality responds), or they are names of things which exist, but yet confused and ill-defined, and hastily and irregularly derived from realities. Of the former kind are Fortune, the Prime Mover, Planetary Orbits, Element of Fire, and like fictions which owe their origin to false and idle theories. And this class of idols is more easily expelled, because to get rid of them it is only necessary that all theories should be steadily rejected and dismissed as obsolete.

But the other class, which springs out of a faulty and unskillful abstraction, is intricate and deeply rooted. Let us take for example such a word as *humid;* and see how far the several things which the word is used to signify agree with each other; and we shall find the word *humid* to be nothing else than a mark loosely and confusedly applied to denote a variety of actions which will not bear to be reduced to any constant meaning. For it both signifies that which easily spreads itself round any other body; and that which in itself is indeterminate and cannot solidize; and that which readily yields in every direction; and that which easily divides and scatters itself; and that which easily unites and collects itself; and that which readily flows and is put in motion; and that which readily clings to another body and wets it; and that which is easily reduced to a liquid, or being solid easily melts. Accordingly when you come to apply the word—if you take it in one sense, flame is humid; if in another, air is not humid; if in another, fine dust is humid; if in another, glass is humid. So that it is easy to see that the notion is taken by abstraction only from water and common and ordinary liquids, without any due verification.

There are however in words certain degrees of distortion and error. One of the least faulty kinds is that of names of substances, especially of lowest species and well-deduced (for the notion of *chalk* and of *mud* is good, of *earth* bad);° a more faulty kind is that of actions, as *to generate, to corrupt, to alter;* the most faulty is of qualities (except such as are the immediate objects of the sense), as *heavy, light, rare, dense,* and the like. Yet in all these cases some notions are of necessity a little better than others, in proportion to the greater variety of subjects that fall within the range of the human sense.

But the *Idols of the Theater* are not innate, nor do they steal into the understanding secretly, but are plainly impressed and received into the mind from the play-books of philosophical systems and the perverted rules of demonstration. To attempt refutations in this case would be

25

---

chalk and *mud:* Because these substances were seen as useful, they are termed good.

merely inconsistent with what I have already said: for since we agree neither upon principles nor upon demonstrations, there is no place for argument. And this is so far well, inasmuch as it leaves the honor of the ancients untouched. For they are no wise disparaged—the question between them and me being only as to the way. For as the saying is, the lame man who keeps the right road outstrips the runner who takes a wrong one. Nay, it is obvious that when a man runs the wrong way, the more active and swift he is the further he will go astray.

But the course I propose for the discovery of sciences is such as leaves but little to the acuteness and strength of wits, but places all wits and understandings nearly on a level. For as in the drawing of a straight line or perfect circle, much depends on the steadiness and practice of the hand, if it be done by aim of hand only, but if with the aid of rule or compass, little or nothing; so is it exactly with my plan. But though particular confutations would be of no avail, yet touching the sects and general divisions of such systems I must say something; something also touching the external signs which show that they are unsound; and finally something touching the causes of such great infelicity and of such lasting and general agreement in error; that so the access to truth may be made less difficult, and the human understanding may the more willingly submit to its purgation and dismiss its idols.

Idols of the Theater, or of systems, are many, and there can be and perhaps will be yet many more. For were it not that now for many ages men's minds have been busied with religion and theology; and were it not that civil governments, especially monarchies, have been averse to such novelties, even in matters speculative; so that men labor therein to the peril and harming of their fortunes—not only unrewarded, but exposed also to contempt and envy; doubtless there would have arisen many other philosophical sects like to those which in great variety flourished once among the Greeks. For as on the phenomena of the heavens many hypotheses may be constructed, so likewise (and more also) many various dogmas may be set up and established on the phenomena of philosophy. And in the plays of this philosophical theater you may observe the same thing which is found in the theater of the poets, that stories invented for the stage are more compact and elegant, and more as one would wish them to be, than true stories out of history.

In general, however, there is taken for the material of philosophy   *30*
either a great deal out of a few things, or a very little out of many things; so that on both sides philosophy is based on too narrow a foundation of experiment and natural history, and decides on the authority of too few cases. For the rational school of philosophers° snatches from experience a variety of common instances, neither duly ascertained nor diligently

---

the rational school of philosophers: followers of Plato who put all of their faith in human reason and ignored the value of experimentation.

examined and weighed, and leaves all the rest to meditation and agitation of wit.

There is also another class of philosophers,° who having bestowed much diligent and careful labor on a few experiments, have thence made bold to educe and construct systems; wresting all other facts in a strange fashion to conformity therewith.

And there is yet a third class,° consisting of those who out of faith and veneration mix their philosophy with theology and traditions; among whom the vanity of some has gone so far aside as to seek the origin of sciences among spirits and genii. So that this parent stock of errors—this false philosophy—is of three kinds; the sophistical, the empirical, and the superstitious. . . .

But the corruption of philosophy by superstition and an admixture of theology is far more widely spread, and does the greatest harm, whether to entire systems or to their parts. For the human understanding is obnoxious to the influence of the imagination no less than to the influence of common notions. For the contentious and sophistical kind of philosophy ensnares the understanding; but this kind, being fanciful and tumid and half poetical, misleads it more by flattery. For there is in man an ambition of the understanding, no less than of the will, especially in high and lofty spirits.

Of this kind we have among the Greeks a striking example in Pythagoras, though he united with it a coarser and more cumbrous superstition; another in Plato and his school,° more dangerous and subtle. It shows itself likewise in parts of other philosophies, in the introduction of abstract forms and final causes and first causes, with the omission in most cases of causes intermediate, and the like. Upon this point the greatest caution should be used. For nothing is so mischievous as the apotheosis of error; and it is a very plague of the understanding for vanity to become the object of veneration. Yet in this vanity some of the moderns have with extreme levity indulged so far as to attempt to found a system of natural philosophy on the first chapter of Genesis, on the book of Job, and other parts of the sacred writings; seeking for the dead among the living: which also makes the inhibition and repression of it the more important, because from this unwholesome mixture of things human and divine there arises not only a fantastic philosophy but also an heretical religion. Very meet it is therefore that we be sober-minded, and give to faith that only which is faith's. . . .

So much concerning the several classes of Idols, and their equipage: 35

---

another class of philosophers: a reference to William Gilbert again.
a third class: a group of philosophers including Pythagoras, a Greek philosopher who worked on mathematics, music, and a theory of reincarnation.
Plato and his school: a probable reference to Plotinus, a third-century philosopher who further developed Plato's religious ideas.

all of which must be renounced and put away with a fixed and solemn determination, and the understanding thoroughly freed and cleansed; the entrance into the kingdom of man, founded on the sciences, being not much other than the entrance into the kingdom of heaven, whereunto none may enter except as a little child.

☐ *Outward Exploration: Discussion*

1. What is Bacon's purpose in writing this essay?
2. Carefully and clearly explain each of Bacon's four idols.
3. Inherent in the name of each idol is an image. Discuss the implications of each image. How effective are the names? Can you think of more effective or clearer names?
4. Which of these idols is a problem for our world now? Discuss and give examples.
5. Throughout the essay are several memorable statements and ideas. Select two or three that particularly strike you and bring them up in class for discussion.

☐ *Outward Exploration: Writing*

1. Which of Bacon's idols most applies to you? Write an essay exploring that idol's role in your life.
2. Examine some text (a story, another essay, a novel, a movie) in terms of the four idols. For instance, the protagonists in Nathaniel Hawthorne's "Young Goodman Brown" and in Jack London's "To Build a Fire" certainly seem to have some problems perceiving reality, so you might analyze one or both of them in terms of the four idols. Essays such as Annie Dillard's "Seeing" and Virginia Woolf's "The Death of the Moth" deal with close observation of nature and drawing conclusions from those observations, and hence they too might be worth exploring in terms of the four idols.
3. Write an essay exploring the reason(s) why the four idols have been so persistent throughout the ages. How do people learn them? How did you learn them? Are there new ways to learn them in our modern world?
4. Throughout the essay are several memorable statements and ideas. Select one that particularly strikes you and write an essay exploring its implications both for you personally and more generally.

8

Exploring Controversies

Not surprising, exploring one area can often lead to another: For example, exploring an event can lead to exploring other people, which, in turn, can lead to exploring relationships. Similarly, exploring beliefs can lead to exploring controversies. In fact, we might say that your stand on controversial issues is the public expression of your private beliefs. To explore controversies, you should use all the techniques that you've encountered throughout this book. A major difference in exploring controversies is that you will need to turn to a significant number of outside sources and incorporate your findings in your essay.

In exploring controversies, not only will you explore your beliefs and their sources and implications, but you also will make an argument. That is, you will try to convince your readers that your position on the issue is more reasonable than other positions. All the understanding you've gained by exploring yourself will stand you in good stead here, for it will have provided insights into how belief builds on belief; that knowledge can alert you to weaknesses in your positions so that you can revise them or buttress them with evidence. Seeing weaknesses in your own position will also help you anticipate opposing arguments and counter them.

WRITING ABOUT CONTROVERSIES

A **controversy** is any issue about which intelligent, educated, fair-minded people can disagree and argue logically. Notice the description of your potential readers in that sentence: *intelligent, educated,* and <u>*fair-minded*</u> people who can *argue logically*. If some people lack the intelligence to understand the concepts and assumptions necessary for the argument, then you should not bother to write to them about that issue. If they lack the educational sophistication to understand the concepts, then either give them the necessary background or do not bother to address them in your argument. For instance, if you are arguing for an esoteric new formulation in physics and your readers have never even taken an introductory course in physics, you should select another topic because they do not have the necessary education to make a reasoned judgment about what you say. Finally, even though people may be intelligent and educated, they may not be fair-minded. In other words, some people may not be interested in exploring an issue to discover the truth, either because one of their cherished beliefs is involved or because they have a vested interest in maintaining their position. These diehards simply will not listen with anything approaching an open mind. Such diehards are not to be confused with those who firmly believe in a position. Most people are willing to listen, to hear more evidence, and perhaps even to consider changing their minds if enough evidence is placed before them. These are fair-minded people. In addition, the term **argue** suggests the give-and-take of debate, a willingness to share ideas and assumptions, not the "I don't want to talk about it" attitude of the diehards. Finally, the term **logically** implies the use of reason. Something other than emotion has to be appealed to when exploring controversies.

Here are a few controversial issues: abortion, academic morality, AIDS, biomedical ethics, business ethics, church–state relations, a citizen's role and duties in modern society, civil liberties, condom distribution in schools, crime and law enforcement, date rape, the death penalty, the drinking age, divorce in America, education's mission and role in society, euthanasia, free speech, gays in the military, the government's role in our everyday lives, gun control, health care reform, immigration laws, the rights of the individual versus those of society, the legalization of drugs, limited terms for members of Congress, a one-term, six-year presidency, male and female roles, the media's role in our society, the military's role in a changing world, pass/fail for college courses, "politically correct" language and attitudes, religion in schools, course requirements at your college, sex education in the schools, sexual values, smoking bans, social justice, suicide, welfare. This list is but a sampling. Obviously any belief can become the subject of a controversy—all you need is someone with logical arguments against it.

Selecting a controversy about which you feel deeply should lead to an interesting and revealing exploratory essay. In such an essay, you delve into your reasons for taking the stand that you do on a particular issue, and you try to discover the sources of those reasons. The process is the same as in writing about beliefs. After searching inward, you move outward, looking both for arguments against your position and for evidence that will support it.

CHOOSING A CONTROVERSY

For most of us, there are three kinds of issues. First, there are those issues which make us angry because they seem so clearly to have only one right side; we can't see the other side's position at all. Second, there are issues about which we can't make up our minds—issues that raise conflicting goals or beliefs in us; they leave us frustrated because we see both sides and realize that both have strong points and weak points. Third, there are issues about which we don't care one way or the other. These issues don't seem to have any impact on our lives, or they don't seem to involve any of our cherished beliefs.

If a controversy doesn't spring immediately to mind, try freewriting or any of the other idea-generation devices mentioned in Chapter 1. Any essay in this book, as well as any article or book that you read for other classes or on your own, might suggest a controversy. So might a news story or a documentary on television or an editorial in the newspaper.

Once you find a topic, follow the same procedure as you did for exploring beliefs. The only difference is that this time you'll have to argue against those who disagree with you, marshaling evidence you have gained from outside sources as well as using your own logic.

WRITER-BASED GOALS

There are five writer-based goals: (1) to discover your position on a controversial issue; (2) to explore your reasons (emotional and intellectual) for taking the position that you do on that particular issue; (3) to discover and explore the sources of those reasons; (4) to find evidence to support your position; (5) to understand the views and reasoning of people who disagree with your position.

In the case of an issue that seems to have only one defensible side, the challenge for you is to find and consider the arguments on the other side. This is difficult because you have to move beyond what you deeply believe in order to see what the opponents think and what reasons they have for believing as they do. Only then can you begin to formulate effective counterarguments to your opponents' points. Only then can you begin to see the weaknesses in your own position and to shore them up.

If you write about an issue that seems too complex to take a stand on, a major challenge will be to uncover the sources of your conflicting views: For example, two of your primary beliefs might be in conflict over the issue, or a belief passed down from family or friends might conflict with a belief you've developed on your own. Using that insight, explore the issue more fully. Knowing the sources of the conflict might help you decide about the issue itself. Even if it doesn't, you will have deepened your self-knowledge.

READER-BASED GOALS

The five reader-based goals are (1) to identify the issue, its background, and the reasons why it is controversial; (2) to reveal to readers the arguments for and against your particular position; (3) to reveal your values and beliefs; (4) to reveal your thought processes and the way you use logic; and (5) to have an impact on your readers' beliefs about the issue or at least to win respect for your own position.

TYPES OF READERS

What kind of effect on your readers it is possible for you to have depends on the type of readers you are addressing. Basically, there are four types of audiences you might write to: friendly, hostile, undecided, and mixed.

Friendly readers already agree with your position. Your goals in writing to them are to reinforce their beliefs, to give them additional information which they might use to convince others, and, most likely, to spur them to some kind of action. For example, you might inspire them to write letters of protest, boycott some company, or attend a rally. In essays to such readers, emotional appeals and emotionally loaded language can be effective (as long as you don't become so extreme that you frighten or repel your audience). Appealing to logic as well as to emotions, however, will pay bigger dividends because your readers will then be able to apply your logic and evidence in convincing others.

Hostile readers, on the other hand, disagree strongly with your position. Rarely will one essay convince such readers to reverse their own position. Your primary goal with such readers, then, is to establish yourself in their eyes as an educated, intelligent, and fair-minded person and to show them that such a person can disagree with them. That might seem like a minor goal, but it can be very important. Simply knowing that people who oppose them are essentially just like them can have a powerful effect. Such knowledge might slow down their opposition, and it will certainly make them think about your arguments rather than dismissing them out-of-hand.

Between these two extremes reside the *undecided readers*. They may know the arguments on both sides of the issue, but they have not been able to make up their minds. Your goal here is to prove that you share similar basic assumptions with them and that, although you understand your opponents' views, you have been led by the evidence and by logic to conclude that those views are less valid than yours. As with hostile readers, you need to establish your persona as someone who is educated, intelligent, and fair-minded.

Mixed audiences may include readers of all three types. Any time you must write for a large group, the chances are that some will disagree with your position, some will agree with it, and some will be undecided.

In such a case, write as though you are addressing an undecided audience. Doing so will not alienate those who already support your position (in fact, they can feel superior because they know exactly "where you're coming from"), and it will not alienate your opponents since you will be treating their points with polite seriousness.

DEVELOPING STRATEGIES TO EXPLORE CONTROVERSIES

As the reader-based goals suggest, exploring controversies means thinking deeply and analytically not only about your own beliefs but also about your readers and about their beliefs and attitudes. You must anticipate their objections to your position and answer them. In exploring controversies, the single best strategy for dealing with all types of readers is called accommodation. Quite simply, **accommodation** means making your readers feel noticed and understood by you, the writer. No one likes to be ignored or to have cherished notions dismissed out-of-hand. In many ways, accommodation is what makes arguments civilized discussions rather than undisciplined brawls.

Accommodation occurs in at least five ways. The most basic is defining key terms and explaining allusions that your readers might not know. Any writer who doesn't do this for any type of writing risks a breakdown in communication. Second, *early in your essay* you should try to find some common ground that you and even hostile readers can agree on. This common ground is usually an assumption that goes beyond the issue at hand. For example, you and your opponent might disagree about a woman's right to have an abortion, but you agree that individual life is important. Having established that agreement, you might point out the real issue is not abortion but rather which individual's life has precedence—the fetus's or the woman's. Third, you should acknowledge that the issue is complex and difficult. If it weren't, why would intelligent people need to debate it? Although this complexity might seem too obvious to need mentioning, saying explicitly that the issue is complex already reveals that you understand your readers might have good reasons for disagreeing with you. Fourth, whether your readers are hostile or not, you should show them that you know and understand your opponents' views. By stating your opponents' points and answering each of them, you build your readers' confidence in you as an honest and thoughtful person. Fifth, you should anticipate your readers' objections to each of your points. Readers will think of such objections on their own anyway; your anticipating and overtly stating those objections in your essay makes it much easier for readers to believe that you have thought deeply and constructively about the issue.

Two basic strategies exist for dealing with opponents' points. **Refutation** is the act of overcoming opponents' points by using logical reasoning and evidence. **Concession** is the act of admitting that an opposing point has some merit; at the same time, however, you try to show that the merit is less than it might at first appear to be or that it is offset by some other consideration.

The following example is an essay arguing that colleges and universities should pay student athletes. It is addressed to hostile readers. My comments are in the boldface type.

SHOULD COLLEGE ATHLETES BE PAID?

In America, we all expect to get paid for the work we do. For example, if we spend 35 hours a week cooking hamburgers in a fast-food restaurant, we expect that the company will pay us. If we fill in for someone else and do the company a favor by working overtime, we expect to be paid for that effort, too. That is the American way. And if we become employers someday, we will expect to pay workers a fair and honest wage for the work they do. **[This whole first paragraph establishes common ground—nothing is stated here that most Americans would object to in principle.]**

Yet college athletes have been left out of the American system for some reason. **[This opening sentence uses the common ground to lead into the essay's main point.]** They certainly do significant work for their "companies"—the universities—bringing in millions of dollars each year. Further, they risk serious and often permanent physical damage each time they put on their university's uniform to play a game. Yet they receive no wages for their efforts. Is this fair? Is it American? **[The elaboration of details shows how playing a sport is comparable to work. The closing rhetorical questions remind readers of the common ground established in the introduction.]**

Of course, some will argue that athletes do get paid, at least in a manner of speaking. **[Accommodation as author states one of the opponent's points. Notice that the opponent's points are never stated as fact: The sentence does not say, "Of course, athletes do get paid" but rather, "Some will argue that . . . ."]** They argue that athletes receive athletic scholarships to big-name schools, so their education is actually their salary. On one level that makes a great deal of sense. **[Concession.]** But on a deeper level, it doesn't. **[This sentence begins the second part of concession, namely, showing that the conceded point is not as important as it might at first seem.]** When we examine the life of college athletes closely, we discover that those scholarships usually don't deliver the education they promise. My brother, for example, received a scholarship to play football. The coaching staff steered him to all the easy courses, courses for which he didn't even have to take exams in order to get an "A." He missed more classes than he attended, even for "university-required" courses, because practices were time-consuming, studying the playbook took hours each night, and, frankly, he got into the lifestyle of the big man on campus and partied when he wasn't practicing. Once his years of eligibility were up, his scholarship disappeared. In spite of having been in college for four years, my brother had no degree, a group of courses that didn't even add up to the start of a coherent major, and no place to go. Much to his surprise, the NFL passed him by. His best friend on the team—a wide receiver with almost a guaranteed future in the pros—was tackled in the next-to-the-last game of his college career and broke his neck. He'll never walk again. He, too, has no degree and no future. **[This paragraph uses personal experiences.]**

Their experiences are typical. **[The move from personal to expert testimony.]** According to *Big Time College Sports*, college sports require up to 40 hours a week of training, practicing, viewing films, learning plays, traveling, and playing actual games. **[This sentence offers evidence.]** Thus few athletes have the time to study the course material as thoroughly as typical students do. In fact, more than 50% of college athletes don't graduate on time, and many never graduate. **[Evidence.]** Further, many of those who do graduate have almost meaningless majors created especially for them, majors made up of "gut" courses that required little work and taught them even less.

That's not much of a salary, is it? **[Logical conclusion.]**   5

The preceding sample is hardly a complete exploratory argument; in fact, it could use significantly more background information and more discussion of the problems inherent in paying college athletes. Nevertheless, it is a good example of some of the techniques we've been considering.

CLAIMS, EVIDENCE, WARRANTS

Three major elements in most exploratory arguments are claims, evidence, and warrants.

Claims

A **claim** (also called a conclusion, a proposition, or a thesis) is an assertion about the nature of things. It is the proposition that you are trying to prove with evidence. There are *claims of fact*. A fact is a statement that can be verified. "My cat prefers dry cat food to canned cat food" is a claim of fact. Assuming that most people agree about what would constitute verification, such claims seldom lead to controversy or to interesting essays. But facts can be more elusive than we might think. In arguments, a fact is any statement that can be verified *sometime* (that is, in the future as well as in the present). Claims of fact which cannot be easily verified might lead to controversy: "Humans will never travel in space in the ways depicted by science fiction writers." Presumably in the future this statement can be verified, but not now.

There are also *claims of value,* such as "Cats make better pets than dogs." Such claims express a judgment, an evaluation. They often lead to controversy. For example, what exactly is a "better pet"? Is a "better pet" more or less affectionate? Is it more or less independent of humans? Is it easily trainable? Is it less destructive? Does it provide protection? The criteria you select as important support the claim—in other words, if you value "independence" and "less destructive," you would probably agree that cats are better. If you value "protection" and "trainability," you will probably believe that dogs are better. Of course even these "facts" I've just smuggled in are open to question—looking at the destroyed carpeting on the stairs and two ruined chairs, my mother would never agree that cats are less destructive. I would need better evidence than just my opinion to prove that cats were less destructive and more independent.

Finally, there are *claims of policy,* which argue that particular public policies should be enacted or that particular actions should be undertaken (by individuals, by groups, by the nation). For example, "Grades should be abolished and all courses should become pass/fail" is a claim of policy.

Exploratory essays often combine two or even all three kinds of claims. Usually one of them is the primary point, but all three can easily be included.

Evidence

Three major types of **evidence** are particularly useful for exploratory essays: factual evidence, the testimony of experts, and appeals to our personal experiences.

Factual evidence includes examples and hypothetical examples (imaginary situations that illustrate your point), as well as statistics. Factual evidence can be convincing if it meets the following requirements: the information is current; there is a sufficient amount of information; the sources of the information are reliable; the information is relevant to the claim; any examples are typical of the possible examples. Hypothetical examples are effective if the suggested situation clearly involves the issues in question, if it is believable, and if your explanation of the motives and actions and consequences in the example is believable and logical. In most cases, it is the *interpretation* of factual evidence which counts. For example, a nationwide poll revealed that more than 50% of managers felt pressured to compromise their personal ethics for the sake of the organizations for which they worked. That's a statistical fact, but what does it mean? Most likely, we would use the statistic to prove how corrupt the business world now is. Yet the statistic could be interpreted differently. Given the public's perception of businesses as willing to do anything to ensure profits, for example, that statistic might be encouraging—almost 50% of managers perceive their companies as moral.

The *testimony of experts* is, in actuality, their informed opinion and interpretation of facts. This type of evidence, therefore, gains credibility if we establish the credentials of those experts. One of the greatest dangers here is quoting someone who is an expert in one field about an issue in a different field. Advertisements do this all the time, having movie stars say that a particular kind of shoes are best for your feet; although their expertise is acting, they express an opinion about podiatry, not their field of expertise. For the advertisers, of course, the point is having a famous person identified with their product. Unfortunately, consumers, too, seem to give unjustified weight to these illogical associations. For you as a writer, the fame of the expert is not important; what is important is the person's level of expertise in the area you are writing about. You should also consider whether the expert is biased about the issue. Are there underlying motives, either conscious or unconscious, that influence the expert about this subject? If the answer is yes, then that expert is not very useful. Conversely, if you can find such bias in your opponents' experts, you have a solid attack against them. Finally, has the expert provided sufficient evidence to back up his or her interpretation of the facts? Needless to say, if the expert backs up the interpretation with evidence, readers are much more likely to believe that interpretation.

The *writer's personal experiences* are particularly appropriate for exploratory essays, for recounting them is one way that the writer is revealed in the essay. What was just said about the testimony of experts applies to you as well. If you use events from your own life to illustrate a point (for instance, the value of pass/fail grading), be sure to probe far enough into your thoughts and feelings to convince your readers that you are being truthful and complete. If you have a bias (for example, you freeze on exams because you are overly concerned about grades), reveal that bias and discuss it. Doing so will make your essay more convincing than if you try to hide your bias. Also, make sure that your experience is not atypical; talk to your friends and do research in the library about the issue.

Warrants

A **warrant** is an assumption or a general principle that underlies an argument and establishes the relevance of the evidence to the claim. When exploring a controversial issue, you should expose and examine

your assumptions about the issue—that's part of the point of exploratory writing. Perhaps few of those assumptions will be included in your
essay's final draft; the decision to include or exclude them depends on
your purpose, the nature of your readers, and the types of evidence you
are using. Stating your assumptions explicitly so that you can support
them is a strong strategy for anticipating and defeating attacks by opponents. However, even if most of your assumptions are not stated in
the final draft, the exploration itself will give you a firmer sense of what
you believe and what you are arguing for.

Further, unconsidered assumptions are often the weakest points in
arguments; discovering yours might prompt you to eliminate some assertions or to find evidence to support an idea that you were treating as
self-evident. Conversely, exposing the defective warrants of your opponents is a good way to undermine their positions.

Claims, Evidence, and Warrants in Action

Below are claims supported by various types of evidence and warrants. The first one is relatively straightforward:

Claim: I deserve an "A" for this course.

Evidence: The average of all my grades for papers and exams is a 95.

Warrant: The average of all the work done in the course determines
the grade.

That seems like a fairly self-evident warrant, one that would not likely
require being made explicit or supported. Further, the average of all the
work is an easily verifiable fact.

Let's consider a less obvious claim, one whose warrants need to be
made explicit and defended. For convenience's sake, let's say that Hedda
makes the following claim:

Claim: Although my average is 87, I deserve an "A" for this course.

Evidence: I participated often in class.

Warrants: Participation has not already been included in the average.
Participation is an important part of the course's work.
My participation was meaningful and contributed to
learning.

Although the first warrant here is easily verifiable, the second and third
are not. If the professor intended the course to be primarily lectures,
then frequent comments from a student might be seen as interruptions
and disruptions. Or, if the student spoke often but rarely said anything
germane to the issues at hand, then her speaking would again seem to
be an interruption rather than meaningful participation. So the second
and third warrants would have to be supported by evidence.

Here is the same claim with different evidence:

Claim: Although my average is 87, I deserve an "A" for this course.
Evidence: I devoted a lot of time doing homework for this class.
Warrant: Spending a lot of time on homework indicates great dedication and guarantees that learning is occurring.

First, of course, Hedda must define the key term "a lot of time." For some students, three hours a week is "a lot of time." For others, 25 hours a week is "a lot of time." So that phrase requires definition and clarification. Here's the clarified argument:

Claim: Although my average is 87, I deserve an "A" for this course.
Evidence: I spent 15 hours per week doing homework for this class.
Warrant: Spending 15 hours per week on homework reveals great dedication and guarantees that learning is occurring.

This evidence is more clearly stated. Yet still more evidence is needed. For example, what occurred during those 15 hours? Perhaps Hedda simply sat staring at a blank computer screen for hours at a time. Or perhaps she got distracted by friends dropping by or by suddenly deciding to organize her books. Or perhaps she simply needed more time to understand concepts that most of the other students grasped quickly. Perhaps, in fact, she really needed to spend 20 hours per week in order to fully grasp the course's concepts. In short, the evidence and the warrant require a great deal more exploration, and more explanation, for this to be a convincing argument. Here's the same claim supported by different evidence:

Claim: Although my average is 87, I deserve an "A" for this course.
Evidence: I often came back for extra help.
Warrants: Returning for extra help guarantees that learning occurred. Returning for extra help shows dedication and interest in the course's material, and such traits should be rewarded.

Again, the warrants need support. Perhaps the extra help did not work. Perhaps Hedda left the extra help session as confused as when she went in. Also, the professor could easily argue that the extra help has already been rewarded since Hedda would not have earned an 87 average without it. The professor could further argue that although dedication and interest in the course's material are certainly desirable traits, they are not factors in measuring students' performance in the course. Hedda would have to counter such arguments. For example:

Claim: Although my average is 87, I deserve an "A" for this course.
Evidence: I learned more than the tests showed.
Warrant: Tests are not necessarily the best measure of learning.

Again, the warrant needs support, but in this case the evidence is readily available to provide that support. Hedda could find articles in educational journals filled with statistics and expert testimony that some very knowledgeable students simply do not test well. She could use these to support her warrant. If her papers for the course always received "A's" and her tests always received "C's," she could use those facts as further evidence of her claim that the exams did not adequately reveal her understanding of the course's material.

This somewhat fanciful argument illustrates the interplay among claims, evidence, and warrants.

As the essays at the end of this chapter and in the further readings indicate, such neat breakdowns of arguments are an analytical tool, not a model to follow slavishly as you write your own exploratory essays. Writers explore controversial issues using a variety of approaches. To be able to understand your own thought processes, to discover your beliefs and recognize the warrants underlying them, to be able to find evidence in the outside world to support your beliefs, and to be able to marshal beliefs, evidence, and warrants effectively—those are the goals of writing exploratory essays about controversial issues.

SUGGESTION FOR WRITING

Select a controversial issue that interests you and write an exploratory argument about it. This will probably require some research, both to learn the arguments of your opponents and to find evidence to support your own claims. Find the warrants (the assumptions and beliefs) that underlie both your own arguments and those of your opponents. Pay particular attention to the nature of the readers to whom you are writing, and craft your essay to convince them. Remember to accommodate them and to create an impression of yourself as an intelligent, educated, fair-minded person who can argue logically.

Am I Blue?

"Ain't these tears in these eyes tellin' you?"

ALICE WALKER

❑ *Inward Exploration*

Write a paragraph either about the issue of animal rights or about some animal that you have observed.

For about three years my companion and I rented a small house in the country that stood on the edge of a large meadow that appeared to run from the end of our deck straight into the mountains. The mountains, however, were quite far away, and between us and them there was, in fact, a town. It was one of the many pleasant aspects of the house that you never really were aware of this.

It was a house of many windows, low, wide, nearly floor to ceiling in the living room, which faced the meadow, and it was from one of these that I first saw our closest neighbor, a large white horse, cropping grass, flipping its mane, and ambling about—not over the entire meadow, which stretched well out of sight of the house, but over the five or so fenced-in acres that were next to the twenty-odd that we had rented. I soon learned that the horse, whose name was Blue, belonged to a man who lived in another town, but was boarded by our neighbors next door. Occasionally, one of the children, usually a stocky teen-ager, but sometimes a much younger girl or boy, could be seen riding Blue. They would appear in the meadow, climb up on his back, ride furiously for ten or fifteen minutes, then get off, slap Blue on the flanks, and not be seen again for a month or more.

There were many apple trees in our yard, and one by the fence that Blue could almost reach. We were soon in the habit of feeding him apples, which he relished, especially because by the middle of summer the meadow grasses—so green and succulent since January—had dried out from lack of rain, and Blue stumbled about munching the dried stalks half-heartedly. Sometimes he would stand very still just by the apple tree, and when one of us came out he would whinny, snort loudly, or stamp the ground. This meant, of course: I want an apple.

It was quite wonderful to pick a few apples, or collect those that had fallen to the ground overnight, and patiently hold them, one by one, up to his large, toothy mouth. I remained as thrilled as a child by his flexible dark lips, huge, cubelike teeth that crunched the apples, core and all, with such finality, and his high, broad-breasted *enormity;* beside which, I felt small indeed. When I was a child, I used to ride horses, and was especially friendly with one named Nan until the day I was riding and my brother deliberately spooked her and I was thrown, head first, against the trunk of a tree. When I came to, I was in bed and my mother was bending worriedly over me; we silently agreed that perhaps horse-back riding was not the safest sport for me. Since then I have walked, and prefer walking to horseback riding—but I had forgotten the depth of feeling one could see in horses' eyes.

I was therefore unprepared for the expression in Blue's. Blue was   5
lonely. Blue was horribly lonely and bored. I was not shocked that this should be the case; five acres to tramp by yourself, endlessly, even in the most beautiful of meadows—and his was—cannot provide many inter-esting events, and once rainy season turned to dry that was about it. No, I was shocked that I had forgotten that human animals and nonhuman animals can communicate quite well; if we are brought up around ani-mals as children we take this for granted. By the time we are adults we no longer remember. However, the animals have not changed. They are in fact *completed* creations (at least they seem to be, so much more than we) who are not likely *to* change; it is their nature to express themselves. What else are they going to express? And they do. And, generally speak-ing, they are ignored.

After giving Blue the apples, I would wander back to the house, aware that he was observing me. Were more apples not forthcoming then? Was that to be his sole entertainment for the day? My partner's small son had decided he wanted to learn how to piece a quilt; we worked in silence on our respective squares as I thought . . .

Well, about slavery: about white children, who were raised by black people, who knew their first all-accepting love from black women, and then, when they were twelve or so, were told they must "forget" the deep levels of communication between themselves and "mammy" that they knew. Later they would be able to relate quite calmly, "My old mammy was sold to another good family." "My old mammy was ————." Fill in the blank. Many more years later a white woman would say: "I can't understand these Negroes, these blacks. What do they want? They're so different from us."

And about the Indians, considered to be "like animals" by the "settlers" (a very benign euphemism for what they actually were), who did not understand their description as a compliment.

And about the thousands of American men who marry Japanese, Korean, Filipina, and other non–English-speaking women and of how happy they report they are, "*blissfully,*" until their brides learn to speak English, at which point the marriages tend to fall apart. What then did the men see, when they looked into the eyes of the women they married, before they could speak English? Apparently only their own reflections.

I thought of society's impatience with the young. "Why are they   10 playing the music so loud?" Perhaps the children have listened to much of the music of oppressed people their parents danced to before they were born, with its passionate but soft cries for acceptance and love, and they have wondered why their parents failed to hear.

I do not know how long Blue had inhabited his five beautiful, boring acres before we moved into our house; a year after we had arrived— and had also traveled to other valleys, other cities, other worlds—he was still there.

But then, in our second year at the house, something happened in Blue's life. One morning, looking out the window at the fog that lay like a ribbon over the meadow, I saw another horse, a brown one, at the other end of Blue's field. Blue appeared to be afraid of it, and for several days made no attempt to go near. We went away for a week. When we returned, Blue had decided to make friends and the two horses ambled or galloped along together, and Blue did not come nearly as often to the fence underneath the apple tree.

When he did, bringing his new friend with him, there was a different look in his eyes. A look of independence, of self-possession, of inalienable *horse*ness. His friend eventually became pregnant. For months and months there was, it seemed to me, a mutual feeling between me and the horses of justice, of peace. I fed apples to them both. The look in Blue's eyes was one of unabashed "this is *it*ness."

It did not, however, last forever. One day, after a visit to the city, I went out to give Blue some apples. He stood waiting, or so I thought, though not beneath the tree. When I shook the tree and jumped back from the shower of apples, he made no move. I carried some over to him. He managed to half-crunch one. The rest he let fall to the ground. I dreaded looking into his eyes—because I had of course noticed that Brown, his partner, had gone—but I did look. If I had been born into slavery, and my partner had been sold or killed, my eyes would have looked like that. The children next door explained that Blue's partner had been "put with him" (the same expression that old people used, I had noticed, when speaking of an ancestor during slavery who had been impregnated by her owner) so that they could mate and she conceive. Since that was accomplished, she had been taken back by her owner, who lived somewhere else.

Will she be back? I asked.   15

They didn't know.

Blue was like a crazed person. Blue *was,* to me, a crazed person. He galloped furiously, as if he were being ridden, around and around his five beautiful acres. He whinnied until he couldn't. He tore at the ground with his hooves. He butted himself against his single shade tree. He looked always and always toward the road down which his partner had gone. And then, occasionally, when he came up for apples, or I took apples to him, he looked at me. It was a look so piercing, so full of grief, a look so *human,* I almost laughed (I felt too sad to cry) to think there are people who do not know that animals suffer. People like me who have forgotten, and daily forget, all that animals try to tell us. "Everything you do to us will happen to you; we are your teachers, as you are ours. We are one lesson" is essentially it, I think. There are those who never once have even considered animals' rights: those who have been taught that animals actually want to be used and abused by us, as small children "love" to be frightened, or women "love" to be mutilated and raped. . . . They are the great-grandchildren of those who honestly thought, because someone taught them this: "Women can't think," and "niggers can't faint." But most disturbing of all, in Blue's large brown eyes was a new look, more painful than the look of despair: the look of disgust with human beings, with life; the look of hatred. And it was odd what the look of hatred did. It gave him, for the first time, the look of a beast. And what that meant was that he had put up a barrier within to protect himself from further violence; all the apples in the world wouldn't change that fact.

And so Blue remained, a beautiful part of our landscape, very peaceful to look at from the window, white against the grass. Once a friend came to visit and said, looking out on the soothing view: "And it *would* have to be a *white* horse; the very image of freedom." And I thought, yes, the animals are forced to become for us merely "images" of what they once so beautifully expressed. And we are used to drinking milk from containers showing "contented" cows, whose real lives we want to hear nothing about, eating eggs and drumsticks from "happy" hens, and munching hamburgers advertised by bulls of integrity who seem to command their fate.

As we talked of freedom and justice one day for all, we sat down to steaks. I am eating misery, I thought, as I took the first bite. And spit it out.

Outward Exploration: Discussion

1. Why did Walker give up horseback riding as a child?
2. What shocked her about discovering that Blue was lonely?
3. What technique does Walker use to broaden the discussion beyond Blue's restricted and boring life?
4. According to Walker, what creates "beasts"?
5. What is Walker's main point in this essay?

Outward Exploration: Writing

1. Write an essay that reveals the sources of your belief about a controversial subject.

2. In this essay, Walker uses a technique similar to that used by George Orwell in "A Hanging." Select a controversy about which you have strong feelings and write an essay using a similar technique.

❏ *Style*

Consider the following sentence from Walker's essay:

When he did, bringing his new friend with him, there was a different look in his eyes. (paragraph 13)

What's interesting about this sentence is the way Walker separates the introductory dependent clause ("When he did") from the independent clause ("there was a . . . eyes") with a free modifier ("bringing his new friend with him"). Notice that the free modifier is the present participle of the verb (ending in -*ing*) and that the free modifier is set off from the rest of the sentence by commas both before and after. Write a sentence of your own which replicates this structure.

Death and Justice: How Capital Punishment Affirms Life

EDWARD I. KOCH

☐ *Inward Exploration*

Write at least one paragraph that summarizes your attitude toward the death penalty.

Last December a man named Robert Lee Willie, who had been con- 1
victed of raping and murdering an 18-year-old woman, was executed in
the Louisiana state prison. In a statement issued several minutes before
his death, Mr. Willie said: "Killing people is wrong. . . . It makes no
difference whether it's citizens, countries, or governments. Killing is
wrong." Two weeks later in South Carolina, an admitted killer named
Joseph Carl Shaw was put to death for murdering two teenagers. In
an appeal to the governor for clemency, Mr. Shaw wrote: "Killing is
wrong when I did it. Killing is wrong when you do it. I hope you have
the courage and moral strength to stop the killing."

It is a curiosity of modern life that we find ourselves being lectured
on morality by cold-blooded killers. Mr. Willie previously had been
convicted of aggravated rape, aggravated kidnapping, and the murders
of a Louisiana deputy and a man from Missouri. Mr. Shaw committed
another murder a week before the two for which he was executed, and
admitted mutilating the body of the 14-year-old girl he killed. I can't
help wondering what prompted these murderers to speak out against
killing as they entered the deathhouse door. Did their newfound reverence for life stem from the realization that they were about to lose
their own?

Life is indeed precious, and I believe the death penalty helps to affirm this fact. Had the death penalty been a real possibility in the minds
of these murderers, they might well have stayed their hand. They might
have shown moral awareness before their victims died, and not after.
Consider the tragic death of Rosa Velez, who happened to be home
when a man named Luis Vera burglarized her apartment in Brooklyn.
"Yeah, I shot her," Vera admitted. "She knew me, and I knew I
wouldn't go to the chair."

During my twenty-two years in public service, I have heard the pros
and cons of capital punishment expressed with special intensity. As a
district leader, councilman, congressman, and mayor, I have repre-

sented constituencies generally thought of as liberal. Because I support the death penalty for heinous crimes of murder, I have sometimes been the subject of emotional and outraged attacks by voters who find my position reprehensible or worse. I have listened to their ideas. I have weighed their objections carefully. I still support the death penalty. The reasons I maintain my position can be best understood by examining the arguments most frequently heard in opposition.

1. *The death penalty is "barbaric."* Sometimes opponents of capital 5 punishment horrify with tales of lingering death on the gallows, of faulty electric chairs, or of agony in the gas chamber. Partly in response to such protests, several states such as North Carolina and Texas switched to execution by lethal injection. The condemned person is put to death painlessly, without ropes, voltage, bullets, or gas. Did this answer the objections of death penalty opponents? Of course not. On June 22, 1984, the *New York Times* published an editorial that sarcastically attacked the new "hygienic" method of death by injection, and stated that "execution can never be made humane through science." So it's not the method that really troubles opponents. It's the death itself they consider barbaric.

Admittedly, capital punishment is not a pleasant topic. However, one does not have to like the death penalty in order to support it any more than one must like radical surgery, radiation, or chemotherapy in order to find necessary these attempts at curing cancer. Ultimately we may learn how to cure cancer with a simple pill. Unfortunately, that day has not yet arrived. Today we are faced with the choice of letting the cancer spread or trying to cure it with the methods available, methods that one day will almost certainly be considered barbaric. But to give up and do nothing would be far more barbaric and would certainly delay the discovery of an eventual cure. The analogy between cancer and murder is imperfect, because murder is not the "disease" we are trying to cure. The disease is injustice. We may not like the death penalty, but it must be available to punish crimes of cold-blooded murder, cases in which any other form of punishment would be inadequate and, therefore, unjust. If we create a society in which injustice is not tolerated, incidents of murder—the most flagrant form of injustice—will diminish.

2. *No other major democracy uses the death penalty.* No other major democracy—in fact, few other countries of any description—are plagued by a murder rate such as that in the United States. Fewer and fewer Americans can remember the days when unlocked doors were the norm and murder was a rare and terrible offense. In America the murder rate climbed 122 percent between 1963 and 1980. During that same period, the murder rate in New York City increased by almost 400 percent, and the statistics are even worse in many other cities. A study at M.I.T. showed that based on 1970 homicide rates a person who lived in a large

American city ran a greater risk of being murdered than an American soldier in World War II ran of being killed in combat. It is not surprising that the laws of each country differ according to differing conditions and traditions. If other countries had our murder problem, the cry for capital punishment would be just as loud as it is here. And I daresay that any other major democracy where 75 percent of the people supported the death penalty would soon enact it into law.

3. *An innocent person might be executed by mistake.* Consider the work of Hugo Adam Bedau, one of the most implacable foes of capital punishment in this country. According to Mr. Bedau, it is "false sentimentality to argue that the death penalty should be abolished because of the abstract possibility that an innocent person might be executed." He cites a study of the 7,000 executions in this country from 1893 to 1971, and concludes that the record fails to show that such cases occur. The main point, however, is this. If government functioned only when the possibility of error didn't exist, government wouldn't function at all. Human life deserves special protection, and one of the best ways to guarantee that protection is to assure that convicted murderers do not kill again. Only the death penalty can accomplish this end. In a recent case in New Jersey, a man named Richard Biegenwald was freed from prison after serving 18 years for murder; since his release he has been convicted of committing four murders. A prisoner named Lemuel Smith, who, while serving four life sentences for murder (plus two life sentences for kidnapping and robbery) in New York's Green Haven Prison, lured a woman corrections officer into the chaplain's office and strangled her. He then mutilated and dismembered her body. An additional life sentence for Smith is meaningless. Because New York has no death penalty statute, Smith has effectively been given a license to kill.

But the problem of multiple murder is not confined to the nation's penitentiaries. In 1981, 91 police officers were killed in the line of duty in this country. Seven percent of those arrested in the cases that have been solved had a previous arrest for murder. In New York City in 1976 and 1977, 85 persons arrested for homicide had a previous arrest for murder. Six of these individuals had two previous arrests for murder, and one had four previous murder arrests. During those two years the New York police were arresting for murder persons with a previous arrest for murder on the average of one every 8.5 days. This is not surprising when we learn that in 1975, for example, the median time served in Massachusetts for homicide was less than two and a half years. In 1976 a study sponsored by the Twentieth Century Fund found that the average time served in the United States for first-degree murder is ten years. The median time served may be considerably lower.

4. *Capital punishment cheapens the value of human life.* On the contrary, it can be easily demonstrated that the death penalty strengthens the value of human life. If the penalty for rape were lowered, clearly it

10

would signal a lessened regard for the victims' suffering, humiliation, and personal integrity. It would cheapen their horrible experience, and expose them to an increased danger of recurrence. When we lower the penalty for murder, it signals a lessened regard for the value of the victim's life. Some critics of capital punishment, such as columnist Jimmy Breslin, have suggested that a life sentence is actually a harsher penalty for murder than death. This is sophistic nonsense. A few killers may decide not to appeal a death sentence, but the overwhelming majority make every effort to stay alive. It is by exacting the highest penalty for the taking of human life that we affirm the highest value of human life.

5. *The death penalty is applied in a discriminatory manner.* This factor no longer seems to be the problem it once was. The appeals process for a condemned prisoner is lengthy and painstaking. Every effort is made to see that the verdict and sentence were fairly arrived at. However, assertions of discrimination are not an argument for ending the death penalty but for extending it. It is not justice to exclude everyone from the penalty of the law if a few are found to be so favored. Justice requires that the law be applied equally to all.

6. *Thou Shalt Not Kill.* The Bible is our greatest source of moral inspiration. Opponents of the death penalty frequently cite the sixth of the Ten Commandments in an attempt to prove that capital punishment is divinely proscribed. In the original Hebrew, however, the Sixth Commandment reads "Thou Shalt Not Commit Murder," and the Torah specifies capital punishment for a variety of offenses. The biblical viewpoint has been upheld by philosophers throughout history. The greatest thinkers of the 19th century—Kant, Locke, Hobbes, Rousseau, Montesquieu, and Mill—agreed that natural law properly authorizes the sovereign to take life in order to vindicate justice. Only Jeremy Bentham was ambivalent. Washington, Jefferson, and Franklin endorsed it. Abraham Lincoln authorized executions for deserters in wartime. Alexis de Tocqueville, who expressed profound respect for American institutions, believed that the death penalty was indispensable to the support of social order. The United States Constitution, widely admired as one of the seminal achievements in the history of humanity, condemns cruel and inhuman punishment, but does not condemn capital punishment.

7. *The death penalty is state-sanctioned murder.* This is the defense with which Messrs. Willie and Shaw hoped to soften the resolve of those who sentenced them to death. By saying in effect, "You're no better than I am," the murderer seeks to bring his accusers down to his own level. It is also a popular argument among opponents of capital punishment, but a transparently false one. Simply put, the state has rights that the private individual does not. In a democracy, those rights are given to the state by the electorate. The execution of a lawfully condemned killer is no more an act of murder than is legal imprisonment an act of kidnapping. If an individual forces a neighbor to pay him money under threat of

punishment, it's called extortion. If the state does it, it's called taxation. Rights and responsibilities surrendered by the individual are what give the state its power to govern. This contract is the foundation of civilization itself.

Everyone wants his or her rights, and will defend them jealously. Not everyone, however, wants responsibilities, especially the painful responsibilities that come with law enforcement. Twenty-one years ago a woman named Kitty Genovese was assaulted and murdered on a street in New York. Dozens of neighbors heard her cries for help but did nothing to assist her. They didn't even call the police. In such a climate the criminal understandably grows bolder. In the presence of moral cowardice, he lectures us on our supposed failings and tries to equate his crimes with our quest for justice.

The death of anyone—even a convicted killer—diminishes us all. 15 But we are diminished even more by a justice system that fails to function. It is an illusion to let ourselves believe that doing away with capital punishment removes the murderer's deed from our conscience. The rights of society are paramount. When we protect guilty lives, we give up innocent lives in exchange. When opponents of capital punishment say to the state, "I will not let you kill in my name," they are also saying to murderers: "You can kill in your *own* name as long as I have an excuse for not getting involved."

It is hard to imagine anything worse than being murdered while neighbors do nothing. But something worse exists. When those same neighbors shrink back from justly punishing the murderer, the victim dies twice.

🔲 *Outward Exploration: Discussion*

1. Why does Koch begin his essay by telling us about Robert Lee Willie and Joseph Carl Shaw?

2. When does Koch first state his point?

3. What purpose is served by paragraph 4?

4. What structuring technique does Koch use in this essay? Is it effective?

5. Explain Koch's use of analogy in paragraph 6. Is it effective?

6. Although the statistics he quotes are now out of date (the essay was published in 1985), how effective is his strategy of using such statistics?

7. Discuss Koch's strategies in paragraph 8. Are they effective?

8. What is Koch's response to the argument that the death penalty has been applied in an unfair manner?

9. How does Koch respond to the biblical injunction "Thou shalt not kill"?

10. Do you find his argument about state-sanctioned murder convincing? Explain.

11. In what ways does Koch accommodate his readers?

□ *Outward Exploration: Writing*

1. Write an essay in which you argue for or against Koch's position. Your first step should be to research the most recent statistics on murder to update the studies he quotes. Then read other essays and articles on both sides of the argument.

2. Select another controversial topic, research it, and write an essay that asserts a position and develops your thesis by naming and arguing each of the opponent's major points.

□ *Style*

Consider the following sentence from Koch's essay:

If government functioned only when the possibility of error didn't exist, government wouldn't function at all. (paragraph 8)

Notice that the opening dependent clause establishes a condition (if government functioned only when there was no chance that it would commit an error) and that the independent clause draws a logical conclusion from that condition (government wouldn't be able to do anything since humans are always liable to make mistakes). Write a sentence of your own in which your opening dependent clause (probably an *if* clause) establishes a condition and the independent clause draws a logical conclusion from it.

Random Reflections
of a Second-Rate Mind

WOODY ALLEN

❑ *Inward Exploration*

Assume for a moment that you have been asked to write an essay with the same title as this essay by Allen. List at least five ideas that come to mind which you might explore in such an essay. Select one and write at least a paragraph about it.

Dining at a fashionable restaurant on New York's chic Upper East   *1*
Side, I noticed a Holocaust survivor at the next table. A man of sixty or
so was showing his companions a number tattooed on his arm while I
overheard him say he had gotten it at Auschwitz. He was graying and
distinguished-looking with a sad, handsome face, and behind his eyes
there was the predictable haunted look. Clearly he had suffered and
gleaned deep lessons from his anguish. I heard him describe how he
had been beaten and had watched his fellow inmates being hanged and
gassed, and how he had scrounged around in the camp garbage for anything—a discarded potato peel—to keep his corpse-thin body from
giving in to disease. As I eavesdropped I wondered: If an angel had
come to him then, when he was scheming desperately not to be among
those chosen for annihilation, and told him that one day he'd be sitting
on Second Avenue in Manhattan in a trendy Italian restaurant amongst
lovely young women in designer jeans, and that he'd be wearing a
fine suit and ordering lobster salad and baked salmon, would he have
grabbed the angel around the throat and throttled him in a sudden fit of
insanity?

Talk about cognitive dissonance! All I could see as I hunched over
my pasta were truncheons raining blows on his head as second after
second dragged on in unrelieved agony and terror. I saw him weak and
freezing—sick, bewildered, thirsty, and in tears, an emaciated zombie in
stripes. Yet now here he was, portly and jocular, sending back the wine
and telling the waiter it seemed to him slightly too tannic. I knew without a doubt then and there that no philosopher ever to come along, no
matter how profound, could even begin to understand the world.

Later that night I recalled that at the end of Elie Wiesel's fine book,
Night, he said that when his concentration camp was liberated he and
others thought first and foremost of food. Then of their families and
next of sleeping with women, but not of revenge. He made the point

several times that the inmates didn't think of revenge. I find it odd that I, who was a small boy during World War II and who lived in America, unmindful of any of the horror Nazi victims were undergoing, and who never missed a good meal with meat and potatoes and sweet desserts, and who had a soft, safe, warm bed to sleep in at night, and whose memories of those years are only blissful and full of good times and good music—that I think of nothing but revenge.

Confessions of a hustler. At ten I hustled dreidel. I practiced endlessly spinning the little lead top and could make the letters come up in my favor more often than not. After that I mercilessly contrived to play dreidel with kids and took their money.

"Let's play for two cents," I'd say, my eyes waxing wide and inno- 5 cent like a big-time pool shark's. Then I'd lose the first game deliberately. After, I'd move the stakes up. Four cents, maybe six, maybe a dime. Soon the other kid would find himself en route home, gutted and muttering. Dreidel hustling got me through the fifth grade. I often had visions of myself turning pro. I wondered if when I got older I could play my generation's equivalent of Legs Diamond or Dutch Schultz for a hundred thousand a game. I saw myself bathed in won money, sitting around a green felt table or getting off great trains, my best dreidel in a smart carrying case as I went from city to city looking for action, always cleaning up, always drinking bourbon, always taking care of my precious manicured spinning hand.

On the cover of this magazine, under the title, is printed the line: A Bimonthly Jewish Critique of Politics, Culture & Society. But why a Jewish critique? Or a gentile critique? Or any limiting perspective? Why not simply a magazine with articles written by human beings for other humans to read? Aren't there enough real demarcations without creating artificial ones? After all, there's no biological difference between a Jew and a gentile despite what my Uncle Max says. We're talking here about exclusive clubs that serve no good purpose; they exist only to form barriers, trade commercially on human misery, and provide additional differences amongst people so they can further rationalize their natural distrust and aggression.

After all, you know by ten years old there's nothing bloodier or more phony than the world's religious history. What could be more awful than, say, Protestant versus Catholic in Northern Ireland? Or the late Ayatollah? Or the expensive cost of tickets to my local synagogue so my parents can pray on the high holidays? (In the end they could only afford to be seated downstairs, not in the main room, and the service was piped in to them. The smart money sat ringside, of course.) Is there anything uglier than families that don't want their children to marry loved ones because they're of the wrong religion? Or professional clergy whose pitch is as follows: "There is a God. Take my word for it. And I pretty much know what He wants and how to get on with Him and I'll try to help you to get and remain in His good graces, because that way your life won't be so fraught with terror. Of course, it's going to cost you a little for my time and stationery. . . ."

Incidentally, I'm well aware that one day I may have to fight because I'm a Jew, or even die because of it, and no amount of professed apathy to religion will save me. On the other hand, those who say they want to kill me because I'm Jewish would find other reasons if I were not Jewish. I mean, think if there were no Jews or Catholics, or if everyone were white or German or American, if the earth was one country, one color; then endless new, creative rationalizations would emerge to kill "other people"—the left-handed, those who prefer vanilla to strawberry, all baritones, any person who wears saddle shoes.

So what was my point before I digressed? Oh—do I really want to contribute to a magazine that subtly helps promulgate phony and harmful differences? (Here I must say that *Tikkun*° appears to me as a generally wonderful journal—politically astute, insightful, and courageously correct on the Israeli-Palestinian issue.)

I experienced this type of ambivalence before when a group wanted   10
me to front and raise money for the establishment of a strong pro-Israel political action committee. I don't approve of PACs, but I've always been a big rooter for Israel. I agonized over the decision and in the end I did front the PAC and helped them raise money and get going. Then, after they were off and running, I quietly slipped out. This was the compromise I made which I've never regretted. Still, I'd be happier contributing to *Tikkun* if it had a different line, or no line, under the title. After all, what if other magazines felt the need to employ their own religious perspectives? You might have: *Field and Stream: A Catholic Critique of Fishing and Hunting.* This month: "Angling for Salmon as You Baptize."

I was amazed at how many intellectuals took issue with me over a piece I wrote a while back for the *New York Times* saying I was against the practice of Israeli soldiers going door-to-door and randomly breaking the hands of Palestinians as a method of combating the intifada. I said also I was against the too quick use of real bullets before other riot control methods were tried. I was for a more flexible attitude on negotiating land for peace. All things I felt to be not only more in keeping with Israel's high moral stature but also in its own best interest. I never doubted the correctness of my feelings and I expected all who read it to agree. Visions of a Nobel danced in my head and, in truth, I had even formulated the first part of my acceptance speech. Now, I have frequently been accused of being a self-hating Jew, and while it's true I am Jewish and I don't like myself very much, it's not because of my persua-

---

Tikkun: The journal in which this essay first appeared.

sion. The reasons lie in totally other areas—like the way I look when I get up in the morning, or that I can never read a road map. In retrospect, the fact that I did not win a peace prize but became an object of some derision was what I should have expected.

"How can you criticize a place you've never been to?" a cabbie asked me. I pointed out I'd never been many places whose politics I took issue with, like Cuba for instance. But this line of reasoning cut no ice.

"Who are you to speak up?" was a frequent question in my hate mail. I replied I was an American citizen and a human being, but neither of these affiliations carried enough weight with the outraged.

The most outlandish cut of all was from the Jewish Defense League, which voted me Pig of the Month. How they misunderstood me! If only they knew how close some of my inner rages have been to theirs. (In my movie *Manhattan,* for example, I suggested breaking up a Nazi rally not with anything the ACLU would approve, but with baseball bats.)

But it was the intellectuals, some of them close friends, who hated   *15* most of all that I had made my opinions public on such a touchy subject. And yet, despite all their evasions and circumlocutions, the central point seemed to me inescapable: Israel was not responding correctly to this new problem.

"The Arabs are guilty for the Middle East mess, the bloodshed, the terrorism, with no leader to even try to negotiate with," reasoned the typical thinker.

"True," I agreed, with Socratic simplicity.

"Victims of the Holocaust deserve a homeland, a place to be free and safe."

"Absolutely." I was totally in accord.

"We can't afford disunity. Israel is in a precarious situation." Here I   *20* began to feel uneasy, because we can afford disunity.

"Do you want the soldiers going door-to-door and breaking hands?" I asked, cutting to the kernel of my complaint.

"Of course not."

"So?"

"I'd still rather you hadn't written ·hat piece." Now I'd be fidgeting in my chair, waiting for a cogent rebuttal to the breaking-of-hands issue. "Besides," my opponent argued, "the *Times* prints only one side."

"But even the Israeli press—"   *25*

"You shouldn't have spoken out," he interrupted.

"Many Israelis agree," I said, "and moral issues apart, why hand the Arabs a needless propaganda victory?"

"Yes, yes, but still you shouldn't have said anything. I was disappointed in you." Much talk followed by both of us about the origins of Israel, the culpability of Arab terrorists, the fact there's no one in charge of the enemy to negotiate with, but in the end it always came down to them saying, "You shouldn't have spoken up," and me saying, "But do you think they should randomly break hands?" and them adding,

"Certainly not—but I'd still feel better if you had just not written that piece."

My mother was the final straw. She cut me out of her will and then tried to kill herself just to hasten my realization that I was getting no inheritance.

At fifteen I received as a gift a pair of cuff links with a William Steig   *30*
cartoon on them. A man with a spear through his body was pictured and the accompanying caption read, "People are no damn good." A generalization, an oversimplification, and yet it was the only way I ever could get my mind around the Holocaust. Even at fifteen I used to read Anne Frank's line about people being basically good and place it on a par with Will Rogers's pandering nonsense, "I never met a man I didn't like."

The questions for me were not: How could a civilized people, and especially the people of Goethe and Mozart, do what they did to another people? And how could the world remain silent? Remain silent and indeed close their doors to millions who could have, with relative simplicity, been plucked from the jaws of agonizing death? At fifteen I felt I knew the answers. If you went with the Anne Frank idea or the Will Rogers line, I reasoned as an adolescent, of course the Nazi horrors became unfathomable. But if you paid more attention to the line on the cuff links, no matter how unpleasant that caption was to swallow, things were not so mysterious.

After all, I had read about all those supposedly wonderful neighbors throughout Europe who lived beside Jews lovingly and amiably. They shared laughter and fun and the same experiences I shared with my community and friends. And I read, also, how they turned their backs on the Jews instantly when it became the fashion and even looted their homes when they were left empty by sudden departure to the camps. This mystery that had confounded all my relatives since World War II was not such a puzzle if I understood that inside every heart lived the worm of self-preservation, of fear, greed, and an animal will to power. And the way I saw it, it was nondiscriminating. It abided in gentile or Jew, black, white, Arab, European, or American. It was part of who we all were, and that the Holocaust could occur was not at all so strange. History had been filled with unending examples of equal bestiality, differing only cosmetically.

The real mystery that got me through my teen years was that every once in a while one found an act of astonishing decency and sacrifice. One heard of people who risked their lives and their family's lives to save lives of people they didn't even know. But these were the rare exceptions and in the end there were not enough humane acts to keep six million from being murdered.

I still own those cuff links. They're in a shoe box along with a lot of memorabilia from my teens. Recently I took them out and looked at them and all these thoughts returned to me. Perhaps I'm not quite as sure of all I was sure of at fifteen, but the waffling may come from just being middle-aged and not as virile. Certainly little has occurred since then to show me much different.

(Reprinted from TIKKUN MAGAZINE, A BI-MONTHLY JEWISH CRITIQUE OF POLITICS, CULTURE, AND SOCIETY. Subscriptions are $31.00 per year from TIKKUN, 251 West 100th Street, 5th floor, New York, NY 10025.)

❏ *Outward Exploration: Discussion*

1. List the main topic of each of the essay's sections.
2. What connects these sections?
3. Why does Allen feel that no philosopher could ever "begin to understand the world"?
4. What point does Allen make about revenge?
5. Comment on Allen's argument in the third section. What exactly is he against? Do you agree? Why or why not?
6. Do you think Allen really envisioned receiving a Nobel Prize for his piece against the breaking of Palestinians' hands? If not, why does he say it?
7. Why does Allen dramatize the conversation about his article? What is the major objection to his article?
8. What does Allen think of Anne Frank's line about people being basically good?
9. According to Allen, what philosophical idea explains the world?

❏ *Outward Exploration: Writing*

1. Using the list of ideas you created or generating another one, write an essay called "My Random Reflections." The trick, though, is to make the essay seem random but, in actuality, to have it as organized as Allen's essay.
2. Like Bruno Bettelheim in "The Ignored Lesson of Anne Frank," Woody Allen wrestles with the question of how humans can do evil things to other humans. After recording your own ideas on paper, consider the sources of those ideas. Write about them. As the final part of your prewriting, you might read what some other thinkers have to say about evil (you might consider articles by such people as a theologian, a philosopher, or a historian). Using Bettelheim and Allen and whatever other sources you've consulted, write an essay exploring the concept of evil.

Against Nature

JOYCE CAROL OATES

❑ *Inward Exploration*

Write a paragraph describing your feelings and ideas about Nature.

We soon get through with Nature. She excites an expectation which she cannot satisfy.

—THOREAU, *Journal,* 1854

Sir, if a man has experienced the inexpressible, he is under no obligation to attempt to express it.

—SAMUEL JOHNSON

The writer's resistance to Nature.

It has no sense of humor: in its beauty, as in its ugliness, or its neutrality, there is no laughter.

It lacks a moral purpose.

It lacks a satiric dimension, registers no irony.

Its pleasures lack resonance, being accidental; its horrors, even when premeditated, are equally perfunctory, "red in tooth and claw," et cetera.

It lacks a symbolic subtext—excepting that provided by man.

It has no (verbal) language.

It has no interest in ours.

It inspires a painfully limited set of responses in "nature writers"—REVERENCE, AWE, PIETY, MYSTICAL ONENESS.

It eludes us even as it prepares to swallow us up, books and all.

I was lying on my back in the dirt gravel of the towpath beside the   *1*
Delaware and Raritan Canal, Titusville, New Jersey, staring up at the
sky and trying, with no success, to overcome a sudden attack of tachycardia that had come upon me out of nowhere—such attacks are always "out of nowhere," that's their charm—and all around me Nature
thrummed with life, the air smelling of moisture and sunlight, the canal
reflecting the sky, red-winged blackbirds testing their spring calls; the
usual. I'd become the jar in Tennessee, a fictitious center, or parenthesis,
aware beyond my erratic heartbeat of the numberless heartbeats of the
earth, its pulsing, pumping life, sheer life, incalculable. Struck down in

the midst of motion—I'd been jogging a minute before—I was "out of time" like a fallen, stunned boxer, privileged (in an abstract manner of speaking) to be an involuntary witness to the random, wayward, nameless motion on all sides of me.

Paroxysmal tachycardia can be fatal, but rarely; if the heartbeat accelerates to 250–270 beats a minute you're in trouble, but the average attack is about 100–150 beats and mine seemed about average; the trick now was to prevent it from getting worse. Brainy people try brainy strategies, such as thinking calming thoughts, pseudo-mystic thoughts, *If I die now it's a good death,* that sort of thing, *if I die this is a good place and good time;* the idea is to deceive the frenzied heartbeat that, really, you don't care: you hadn't any other plans for the afternoon. The important thing with tachycardia is to prevent panic! you must prevent panic! otherwise you'll have to be taken by ambulance to the closest emergency room, which is not so very nice a way to spend the afternoon, really. So I contemplated the blue sky overhead. The earth beneath my head. Nature surrounding me on all sides; I couldn't quite see it but I could hear it, smell it, sense it, there is something *there,* no mistake about it. Completely oblivious to the predicament of the individual but that's only "natural," after all, one hardly expects otherwise.

When you discover yourself lying on the ground, limp and unresisting, head in the dirt, and, let's face it, helpless, the earth seems to shift forward as a presence; hard, emphatic, not mere surface but a genuine force—there is no other word for it but *presence.* To keep in motion is to keep in time, and to be stopped, stilled, is to be abruptly out of time, in another time dimension perhaps, an alien one, where human language has no resonance. Nothing to be said about it expresses it, nothing touches it, it's an absolute against which nothing human can be measured. . . . Moving through space and time by way of your own volition you inhabit an interior consciousness, a hallucinatory consciousness, it might be said, so long as breath, heartbeat, the body's autonomy hold; when motion is stopped you are jarred out of it. The interior is invaded by the exterior. The outside wants to come in, and only the self's fragile membrane prevents it.

The fly buzzing at Emily's death.

Still, the earth *is* your place. A tidy grave site measured to your size.   5
Or, from another angle of vision, one vast democratic grave.

Let's contemplate the sky. Forget the crazy hammering heartbeat, don't listen to it, don't start counting, remember that there is a clever way of breathing that conserves oxygen as if you're lying below the surface of a body of water breathing through a very thin straw but you *can* breathe through it if you're careful, if you don't panic; one breath and then another and then another, isn't that the story of all lives? careers? Just a matter of breathing. Of course it is. But contemplate the sky, it's there to be contemplated. A mild shock to see it so blank, blue, a thin airy ghostly blue, no clouds to disguise its emptiness. You are beginning to feel not only weightless but near-bodiless, lying on the

earth like a scrap of paper about to be blown off. Two dimensions and
you'd imagined you were three! And there's the sky rolling away forever, into infinity—if "infinity" can be "rolled into"—and the forlorn
truth is, that's where you're going too. And the lovely blue isn't even
blue, is it? isn't even there, is it? a mere optical illusion, isn't it? no matter
what art has urged you to believe.

Early Nature memories. Which it's best not to suppress.
. . . Wading, as a small child, in Tonawanda Creek near our house,
and afterward trying to tear off, in a frenzy of terror and revulsion, the
sticky fat black bloodsuckers that had attached themselves to my feet,
particularly between my toes.
. . . Coming upon a friend's dog in a drainage ditch, dead for several
days, evidently the poor creature had been shot by a hunter and left to
die, bleeding to death, and we're stupefied with grief and horror but
can't resist sliding down to where he's lying on his belly, and we can't
resist squatting over him, turning the body over.
. . . The raccoon, mad with rabies, frothing at the mouth and tearing   *10*
at his own belly with his teeth, so that his intestines spill out onto the
ground . . . a sight I seem to remember though in fact I did not see. I've
been told I did not see.

Consequently, my chronic uneasiness with Nature mysticism; Nature adoration; Nature-as-(moral)-instruction-for-mankind. My doubt
that one can, with philosophical validity, address "Nature" as a single
coherent noun, anything other than a Platonic, hence discredited,
is-ness. My resistance to "Nature writing" as a genre, except when it is
brilliantly fictionalized in the service of a writer's individual vision—
Thoreau's books and *Journal,* of course, but also, less known in this
country, the miniaturist prose poems of Colette (*Flowers and Fruit*) and
Ponge (*Taking the Side of Things*)—in which case it becomes yet another,
and ingenious, form of storytelling. The subject is *there* only by the
grace of the author's language.
Nature has no instructions for mankind except that our poor belea-
guered humanist-democratic way of life, our fantasies of the individual's
high worth, our sense that the weak, no less than the strong, have a
right to survive, are absurd. When Edmund of *King Lear* said excitedly,
"Nature, be thou my goddess!" he knew whereof he spoke.
In any case, where *is* Nature, one might (skeptically) inquire. Who
has looked upon her/its face and survived?

But isn't this all exaggeration, in the spirit of rhetorical contentious-
ness? Surely Nature is, for you, as for most reasonably intelligent
people, a "perennial" source of beauty, comfort, peace, escape from the
delirium of civilized life; a respite from the ego's ever-frantic strategies
of self-promotion, as a way of ensuring (at least in fantasy) some small

measure of immortality? Surely Nature, as it is understood in the usual slapdash way, as human, if not dilettante, *experience* (hiking in a national park, jogging on the beach at dawn, even tending, with the usual comical frustrations, a suburban garden), is wonderfully consoling; a place where, when you go there, it has to take you in?—a palimpsest of sorts you choose to read, layer by layer, always with care, always cautiously, in proportion to your psychological strength?

Nature: as in Thoreau's upbeat Transcendentalist mode ("The indescribable innocence and beneficence of Nature,—such health, such cheer, they afford forever! and such sympathy have they ever with our race, that all Nature would be affected . . . if any man should ever for a just cause grieve"), and not in Thoreau's grim mode ("Nature is hard to be overcome but she must be overcome"). 15

Another way of saying, not *Nature-in-itself* but *Nature-as-experience.*

The former, Nature-in-itself, is, to allude slantwise to Melville, a blankness ten times blank; the latter is what we commonly, or perhaps always, mean, when we speak of Nature as a noun, a single entity— something of *ours.* Most of the time it's just an activity, a sort of hobby, a weekend, a few days, perhaps a few hours, staring out the window at the mind-dazzling autumn foliage of, say, northern Michigan, being rendered speechless—temporarily—at the sight of Mt. Shasta, the Grand Canyon, Ansel Adams's West. Or Nature writ small, contained in the back yard. Nature filtered through our optical nerves, our "senses," our fiercely romantic expectations. Nature that pleases us because it mirrors our souls, or gives the comforting illusion of doing so.

Nature as the self's (flattering) mirror, but not ever, no, never, Nature-in-itself.

Nature is mouths, or maybe a single mouth. Why glamorize it, romanticize it?—well, yes, but we must, we're writers, poets, mystics (of a sort) aren't we, precisely what else are we to do but glamorize and romanticize and generally exaggerate the significance of anything we focus the white heat of our "creativity" upon? And why not Nature, since it's there, common property, mute, can't talk back, allows us the possibility of transcending the human condition for a while, writing prettily of mountain ranges, white-tailed deer, the purple crocuses outside this very window, the thrumming dazzling "life force" we imagine we all support. Why not?

Nature *is* more than a mouth—it's a dazzling variety of mouths. 20 And it pleases the senses, in any case, as the physicists' chill universe of numbers certainly does not.

Oscar Wilde, on our subject:

Nature is no great mother who has borne us. She is our creation. It is in our brain that she quickens to life. Things are because

we see them, and what we see, and how we see it, depends on
the Arts that have influenced us. To look at a thing is very different from seeing a thing. . . . At present, people see fogs,
not because there are fogs, but because poets and painters have
taught them the mysterious loveliness of such effects. There
may have been fogs for centuries in London. I dare say there
were. But no one saw them. They did not exist until Art had
invented them. . . . Yesterday evening Mrs. Arundel insisted
on my going to the window and looking at the glorious sky,
as she called it. And so I had to look at it. . . . And what was
it? It was simply a very second-rate Turner, a Turner of a bad
period, with all the painter's worst faults exaggerated and
over-emphasized.

"The Decay of Lying," 1889

(If we were to put it to Oscar Wilde that he exaggerates, his reply might
well be, "Exaggeration? I don't know the meaning of the word.")

Walden, that most artfully composed of prose fictions, concludes, in
the rhapsodic chapter "Spring," with Henry David Thoreau's contemplation of death, decay, and regeneration as it is suggested to him, or to
his protagonist, by the spectacle of vultures feeding off carrion. There
is a dead horse close by his cabin, and the stench of its decomposition,
in certain winds, is daunting. Yet "the assurance it gave me of the strong
appetite and inviolable health of Nature was my compensation for this.
I love to see that Nature is so rife with life that myriads can be afforded
to be sacrificed and suffered to prey upon one another; that tender organizations can be so serenely squashed out of existence like pulp,—
tadpoles which herons gobble up, and tortoises and toads run over in
the road; and that sometimes it has rained flesh and blood! . . . The
impression made on a wise man is that of universal innocence."

Come off it, Henry David. You've grieved these many years for
your elder brother, John, who died a ghastly death of lockjaw; you've
never wholly recovered from the experience of watching him die.
And you know, or must know, that you're fated too to die young of
consumption. . . . But this doctrinaire Transcendentalist passage ends
Walden on just the right note. It's as impersonal, as coolly detached,
as the Oversoul itself: a "wise man" filters his emotions through his
brain.

Or through his prose.

Nietzsche: "We all pretend to ourselves that we are more simple-   25
minded than we are: that is how we get a rest from our fellow men."

Once out of nature I shall never take
My bodily form from any natural thing,

But such a form as Grecian goldsmiths make
Of hammered gold and gold enamelling
To keep a drowsy Emperor awake;
Or set upon a golden bough to sing
To lords and ladies of Byzantium
Of what is past, or passing, or to come.

WILLIAM BUTLER YEATS, "Sailing to Byzantium"

Yet even the golden bird is a "bodily form [taken from a] natural thing."
No, it's impossible to escape!

The writer's resistance to Nature.
Wallace Stevens: "In the presence of extraordinary actuality, consciousness takes the place of imagination."

Once, years ago, in 1972 to be precise, when I seemed to have been another person, related to the person I am now as one is related, tangentially, sometimes embarrassingly, to cousins not seen for decades—once, when we were living in London, and I was very sick, I had a mystical vision. That is, I "had" a "mystical vision"—the heart sinks: such pretension—or something resembling one. A fever dream, let's call it. It impressed me enormously and impresses me still, though I've long since lost the capacity to see it with my mind's eye, or even, I suppose, to believe in it. There is a statute of limitations on "mystical visions," as on romantic love.

I was very sick, and I imagined my life as a thread, a thread of breath, or heartbeat, or pulse, or light—yes, it was light, radiant light; I was burning with fever and I ascended to that plane of serenity that might be mistaken for (or *is,* in fact) Nirvana, where I had a waking dream of uncanny lucidity:

My body is a tall column of light and heat.
My body is not "I" but "it."
My body is not one but many.

My body, which "I" inhabit, is inhabited as well by other creatures, *30* unknown to me, imperceptible—the smallest of them mere sparks of light.

My body, which I perceive as substance, is in fact an organization of infinitely complex, overlapping, imbricated structures, radiant light their manifestation, the "body" a tall column of light and blood heat, a temporary agreement among atoms, like a high-rise building with numberless rooms, corridors, corners, elevator shafts, windows. . . . In this fantastical structure the "I" is deluded as to its sovereignty, let alone its autonomy in the (outside) world; the most astonishing secret is that the "I" doesn't exist!—but it behaves as if it does, as if it were one and not many.

In any case, without the "I" the tall column of light and heat would die, and the microscopic life particles would die with it . . . will die with it. The "I," which doesn't exist, is everything.

But Dr. Johnson is right, the inexpressible need not be expressed. And what resistance, finally? There is none.

This morning, an invasion of tiny black ants. One by one they   *35*
appear, out of nowhere—that's their charm too!—moving single file across the white Parsons table where I am sitting, trying without much success to write a poem. A poem of only three or four lines is what I want, something short, tight, mean; I want it to hurt like a white-hot wire up the nostrils, small and compact and turned in upon itself with the density of a hunk of rock from the planet Jupiter. . . .
But here come the black ants: harbingers, you might say, of spring. One by one by one they appear on the dazzling white table and one by one I kill them with a forefinger, my deft right forefinger, mashing each against the surface of the table and then dropping it into a wastebasket at my side. Idle labor, mesmerizing, effortless, and I'm curious as to how long I can do it—sit here in the brilliant March sunshine .
killing ants with my right forefinger—how long I, and the ants, can keep it up.
After a while I realize that I can do it a long time. And that I've written my poem.

☐ Outward Exploration: Discussion

1. What are Oates's complaints about Nature?
2. In addition to making her argument, Oates also informs her readers. What new information did the essay give you?
3. What elements of Nature does she notice as she lies on the ground, stricken by tachycardia?
4. What are her childhood memories of Nature?
5. Does she state the opposition's vision of Nature? Where?
6. Explain her distinction between *Nature-in-itself* and *Nature-as-experience* (paragraph 16).
7. What argument strategies does Oates use?
8. Are any of her strategies ineffective for traditional arguments?
9. Explain the content of Oates's mystical vision. What are its implications for her argument?
10. What is the point of the last section?
11. What is the function of each section?

❏ *Outward Exploration: Writing*

1. Write an essay arguing against Oates's points. To do so effectively, you will have to explain each of her major points clearly and then either refute or concede each. To be convincing, you will also need evidence—your personal experiences and expert testimony from outside sources.

2. Read an essay or a poem by one of the writers Oates mentions in her essay. Write an essay supporting or disagreeing with that writer's vision of Nature. To be convincing, you will also need evidence—your personal experiences and expert testimony from outside sources.

3. In this book are several essays by such writers as Annie Dillard, Virginia Woolf, Lewis Thomas, E. B. White, and Henry David Thoreau—essays that discuss various elements of Nature. Compare and contrast Oates's essay with one or more of those essays, focusing on their vision of Nature, arguing that one vision of Nature is more effective (or believable or realistic or comforting or whatever) than the other.

❏ *Style*

Consider the following sentence from Oates's essay:

That is, I "had" a "mystical vision"—the heart sinks: such pretension—or something resembling one. (paragraph 28)

This sentence features an interrupter in the middle of the sentence (set off by dashes). What is most interesting about the sentence, though, is the kind of interrupter it is—an independent clause ("the heart sinks") followed by a colon and a noun ("such pretension") that *ironically comments upon the idea stated in the main sentence*. In other words, Oates is calling herself pretentious for thinking that she has had a "mystical vision" rather than a fever-induced delusion or hallucination. Write a sentence of your own that is interrupted by an ironic comment. Be sure to insert a dash on each side of the interrupter to separate it from the rest of the sentence.

Save the Whales, Screw the Shrimp

JOY WILLIAMS

◻ *Inward Exploration*

Write at least a paragraph expressing your thoughts and feelings about ecology and the preservation of endangered species.

I don't want to talk about *me,* of course, but it seems as though far   *1* too much attention has been lavished on *you* lately—that your greed and vanities and quest for self-fulfillment have been catered to far too much. You just want and want and want. You haven't had a mandala dream since the eighties began. To have a mandala dream you'd have to instinctively know that it was an attempt at self-healing on the part of Nature, and you don't believe in Nature anymore. It's too isolated from you. You've abstracted it. It's so messy and damaged and sad. Your eyes glaze as you travel life's highway past all the crushed animals and the Big Gulp cups. You don't even take pleasure in looking at nature photographs these days. Oh, they can be just as pretty, as always, but don't they make you feel increasingly . . . anxious? Filled with more trepidation than peace? So what's the point? You see the picture of the baby condor or the panda munching on a bamboo shoot, and your heart just sinks, doesn't it? A picture of a poor old sea turtle with barnacles on her back, all ancient and exhausted, depositing her five gallons of doomed eggs in the sand hardly fills you with joy, because you realize, quite rightly, that just outside the frame falls the shadow of the condo. What's cropped from the shot of ocean waves crashing on a pristine shore is the plastics plant, and just beyond the dunes lies a parking lot. Hidden from immediate view in the butterfly-bright meadow, in the dusky thicket, in the oak and holly wood, are the surveyors' stakes, for someone wants to build a mall exactly there—some gas stations and supermarkets, some pizza and video shops, a health club, maybe a bulimia treatment center. Those lovely pictures of leopards and herons and wild rivers, well, you just know they're going to be accompanied by a text that will serve only to bring you down. You don't want to think about it! It's all so uncool. And you don't want to feel guilty either. Guilt is uncool. Regret maybe you'll consider. *Maybe.* Regret is a possibility, but don't push me, you say. Nature photographs have become something of a problem, along with almost everything else. Even though they leave the bad stuff out—maybe because you *know* they're leaving all the bad stuff out—such pictures are making you increasingly aware that you're a little too late for Nature. Do you feel that? Twenty years too late, maybe only ten? Not *way* too late, just a little too late? Well, it appears that you are. And since you are, you've decided you're just not going to attend this particular party.

Pascal said that it is easier to endure death without thinking about it than to endure the thought of death without dying. This is how you manage to dance the strange dance with that grim partner, nuclear annihilation. When the U.S. Army notified Winston Churchill that the first atom bomb had been detonated in New Mexico, it chose the code phrase BABIES SATISFACTORILY BORN. So you entered the age of irony, and the strange double life you've been leading with the world ever since. Joyce Carol Oates suggests that the reason writers—*real* writers, one assumes—don't write about Nature is that it lacks a sense of humor and registers no irony. It just doesn't seem to be of the times—these slick, sleek, knowing, objective, indulgent times. And the word *Environment.* Such a bloodless word. A flat-footed word with a shrunken heart. A word increasingly disengaged from its association with the natural world. Urban planners, industrialists, economists, and developers use it. It's a lost word, really. A cold word, mechanistic, suited strangely to the coldness generally felt toward Nature. It's their word now. You don't mind giving it up. As for *Environmentalist,* that's one that can really bring on the yawns, for you've tamed and tidied it, neutered it quite nicely. An environmentalist must be calm, rational, reasonable, and willing to compromise, otherwise you won't listen to him. Still, his beliefs are *opinions* only, for this is the age of radical subjectivism. Not long ago, Barry Commoner spoke to the Environmental Protection Agency. He scolded them. They loved it. The way they protect the environment these days is apparently to find an "acceptable level of harm from a pollutant and then issue rules allowing industry to pollute to that level." Commoner suggested that this was inappropriate. An EPA employee suggested that any other approach would place limits on economic growth and implied that Commoner was advocating this. Limits on economic growth! Commoner vigorously denied this. Oh, it was a healthy exchange of ideas, healthier certainly than our air and water. We needed that little spanking, the EPA felt. It was refreshing. The agency has recently lumbered into action in its campaign to ban dinoseb. You seem to have liked your dinoseb. It's been a popular weed killer, even though it has been directly linked with birth defects. You must hate weeds a lot. Although the EPA appears successful in banning the poison, it will still have to pay the disposal costs and compensate the manufacturers for the market value of the chemicals they still have in stock.

That's ironic, you say, but farmers will suffer losses, too, oh dreadful financial losses, if herbicide and pesticide use is restricted.

Farmers grow way too much stuff anyway. They grow surplus crops with subsidized water created by turning rivers great and small into a plumbing system of dams and canals. Rivers have become *systems*. Wetlands are increasingly being referred to as *filtering systems*—things deigned *useful* because of their ability to absorb urban run-off, oil from roads, et cetera.

We know that. We've known that for years about farmers. We know   5
a lot these days. We're very well informed. If farmers aren't allowed to make a profit by growing surplus crops, they'll have to sell their land to developers, who'll turn all that *arable land* into office parks. Arable land isn't Nature anyway, and besides, we like those office parks and shopping plazas, with their monster supermarkets open twenty-four hours a day with aisle after aisle after aisle of *products*. It's fun. Products are fun.

Farmers like their poisons, but ranchers like them even more. There are well-funded predominantly federal and cooperative programs like the Agriculture Department's Animal Damage Control Unit that poison, shoot, and trap several thousand animals each year. This unit loves to kill things. It was created to kill things—bobcats, foxes, black bears, mountain lions, rabbits, badgers, countless birds—all to make this great land safe for the string bean and the corn, the sheep and the cow, even though you're not consuming as much cow these days. A burger now and then, but burgers are hardly cows at all, you feel. They're not all *our* cows in any case, for some burger matter is imported. There's a bit of Central American burger matter in your bun. Which is contributing to the conversion of tropical rain forest into cow pasture. Even so, you're getting away from meat these days. You're eschewing cow. It's seafood you love, shrimp most of all. And when you love something, it had better watch out, because you have a tendency to love it to death. Shrimp, shrimp, shrimp. It's more common on menus than chicken. In the wilds of Ohio, far, far from watery shores, four out of the six entrées on a menu will be shrimp, for some modest sum. Everywhere, it's all the shrimp you can eat or all you *care* to eat, for sometimes you just don't feel like eating all you *can*. You are intensively *harvesting* shrimp. Soon there won't be any left and then you can stop. It takes that, often, to make you stop. Shrimpers shrimp, of course. That's their *business*. They put out these big nets and in these nets, for each pound of shrimp, they catch more than ten times that amount of fish, turtles, and dolphins. These, quite the worse for wear, they dump back in. There is an object called TED (Turtle Excluder Device), which would save thousands of turtles and some dolphins from dying in the nets, but the shrimpers are loath to use TEDs, as they say it would cut the size of their shrimp catch.

We've heard about TED, you say.

They want you, all of you, to have all the shrimp you can eat and more. At Kiawah Island, off the coast of South Carolina, visitors go out on Jeep "safaris" through the part of the island that hasn't been developed yet. ("Wherever you see trees," the guide says, "really, that's a lot.") The safari comprises six Jeeps, and these days they go out at least four times a day, with more trips promised soon. The tourists drive their own Jeeps and the guide talks to them by radio. Kiawah has nice beaches, and the guide talks about turtles. When he mentions the shrimpers' role in the decline of the turtle, the shrimpers, who share the same frequency, scream at him. Shrimpers and most commercial fishermen (many of them working with drift and gill nets anywhere from six to thirty miles long) think of themselves as an *endangered species.* A recent newspaper headline said, "Shrimpers Spared Anti-Turtle Devices." Even so, with the continuing wanton depletion of shrimp beds, they will undoubtedly have to find some other means of employment soon. They might, for instance, become part of that vast throng laboring in the *tourist industry.*

Tourism has become an industry as destructive as any other. You are no longer benign in your traveling somewhere to look at the scenery. You never thought there was much gain in just looking anyway, you've always preferred to *use* the scenery in some manner. In your desire to get away from what you've got, you've caused there to be no place to get away *to.* You're just all bumpered up out there. Sewage and dumps have become prime indicators of America's lifestyle. In resort towns in New England and the Adirondacks, measuring the flow into the sewage plant serves as a business barometer. Tourism is a growth industry. You believe in growth. *Controlled* growth, of course. Controlled exponential growth is what you'd really like to see. You certainly don't want to put a moratorium or a cap on anything. That's illegal, isn't it? Retro you're not. You don't want to go back or anything. Forward. Maybe ask directions later. Growth is *desirable* as well as being *inevitable.* Growth is the one thing you seem to be powerless before, so you try to be realistic about it. Growth is—it's weird—it's like cancer or something.

Recently you, as tourist, have discovered your national parks and are quickly *overburdening* them. Spare land and it belongs to you! It's exotic land too, not looking like all the stuff around it that looks like everything else. You want to take advantage of this land, of course, and use it in every way you can. Thus the managers—or *stewards,* as they like to be called—have developed *wise* and *multiple-use* plans, keeping in mind exploiters' interests (for they have their needs, too) as well as the desires of the backpackers. Thus mining, timbering, and ranching activities take place in the national forests, where the Forest Service maintains a system of logging roads eight times larger than the interstate highway system. The national parks are more of a public playground and are becoming increasingly Europeanized in their look and management. Lots of concessions and motels. You deserve a clean bed and a hot meal when you go into the wilderness. At least your stewards think that

10

you do. You keep your stewards busy. Not only must they cater to your multiple and conflicting desires, they have to manage your wildlife *resources*. They have managed wildfowl to such an extent that the reasoning has become, If it weren't for hunters, ducks would disappear. Duck stamps and licensing fees support the whole rickety duck-management system. Yes! If it weren't for the people who killed them, wild ducks wouldn't exist! Managers are managing all wild creatures, not just those that fly. They track and tape and tag and band. They relocate, restock, and reintroduce. They cull and control. It's hard to keep it all straight. Protect or poison? Extirpate or just mostly eliminate? Sometimes even the stewards get mixed up.

This is the time of machines and models, hands-on management and master plans. Don't you ever wonder as you pass that billboard advertising another MASTER-PLANNED COMMUNITY just what master they are actually talking about? Not the Big Master, certainly. Something brought to you by one of the tiny masters, of which there are many. But you like these tiny masters and have even come to expect and require them. In Florida they've just started a ten-thousand-acre city in the Everglades. It's a *megaproject,* one of the largest ever in the state. Yes, they must have thought you wanted it. No, what you thought of as the Everglades, the Park, is only a little bitty part of the Everglades. Developers have been gnawing at this irreplaceable, strange land for years. It's like they just *hate* this ancient sea of grass. Maybe you could ask them about this sometime. Roy Rogers is the senior vice president of strategic planning, and the old cowboy says that every tree and bush and inch of sidewalk in the project has been planned. Nevertheless, because the whole thing will take twenty-five years to complete, the plan is going to be constantly changed. You can understand this. The important thing is that there be a blueprint. You trust a blueprint. The tiny masters know what you like. You like *a secure landscape* and *access to services*. You like grass— that is, lawns. The ultimate lawn is the golf course, which you've been told has "some ecological value." You believe this! Not that it really matters, you just like to play golf. These golf courses require a lot of watering. So much that the more inspired of the masters have taken to watering them with effluent, *treated* effluent, but yours, from all the condos and villas built around the stocked artificial lakes you fancy.

I really don't want to think about sewage, you say, but it sounds like progress.

It is true that the masters are struggling with the problems of your incessant flushing. Cuisine is also one of their concerns. Advances in sorbets—sorbet intermezzos—in their clubs and fine restaurants. They know what you want. You want A HAVEN FROM THE ORDINARY WORLD, If you're A NATURE LOVER in the West you want to live in a $200,000 home in A WILD ANIMAL HABITAT. If you're eastern and consider yourself more hip, you want to live in new towns—brand-new reconstructed-from-scratch towns—in a house of NINETEENTH-CENTURY DESIGN. But in these new towns the masters are building, getting around can be confusing. There is an abundance of curves and an infrequency of through streets. It's the new wilderness without any trees. You can get lost, even with all the "mental bread crumbs" the masters scatter about as visual landmarks—the windmill, the water views, the various groupings of landscape "material." You *are* lost, you know. But you trust a Realtor will show you the way. There are many more Realtors than tiny masters, and many of them have to make do with less than a loaf—that is, trying to sell stuff that's already been built in an environment already "enhanced" rather than something being planned—but they're everywhere, willing to show you the path. If Dante returned to Hell today, he'd probably be escorted down by a Realtor, talking all the while about how it was just another level of Paradise.

> When have you last watched a sunset? Do you remember where
> you were? With whom? At Loews Ventana Canyon Resort, the
> Grand Foyer will provide you with that opportunity through
> lighting which is computerized to diminish with the approach-
> ing sunset!

The tiny masters are willing to arrange Nature for you. They will compose it into a picture that you can look at at your leisure, when you're not doing work or something like that. Nature becomes scenery, a prop. At some golf courses in the Southwest, the saguaro cacti are reported to be repaired with green paste when balls blast into their skin. The saguaro can attempt to heal themselves by growing over the balls, but this takes time, and the effect can be somewhat . . . baroque. It's better to get out the pastepot. Nature has become simply a visual form of entertainment, and it had better look snappy.

Listen, you say, we've been at Ventana Canyon. It's in the desert, right? It's very, very nice, a world-class resort. A totally self-contained environment with everything that a person could possibly want, on more than a thousand acres in the middle of zip. It sprawls but nestles, like. And they've maintained the integrity of as much of the desert ecosystem as possible. Give them credit for that. *Great* restaurant, too. We had baby bay scallops there. Coming into the lobby there are these two big hand-carved coyotes, mutely howling. And that's the way we like them, *mute*. God, why do those things howl like that?

> Wildlife is a personal matter, you think. The attitude is up to you.   15
> You can prefer to see it dead or not dead. You might want to let it mosey
> about its business or blow it away. Wild things exist only if you have the
> graciousness to allow them to. Just outside Tucson, Arizona, there is a
> brand-new structure modeled after a French foreign legion outpost. It's
> the *International Wildlife Museum,* and it's full of dead animals. Three
> hundred species are there, at least a third of them—the rarest ones—

killed and collected by one C. J. McElroy, who enjoyed doing it and now shares what's left with you. The museum claims to be educational because you can watch a taxidermist at work or touch a lion's tooth. You can get real close to these dead animals, closer than you can in a zoo. Some of you prefer zoos, however, which are becoming bigger, better, and bioclimatic. New-age zoo designers want the animals to *flow right out into your space*. In Dallas there will soon be a Wilds of Africa exhibit; in San Diego there's a simulated rain forest, where you can thread your way "down the side of a lush canyon, the air filled with a fine mist from 300 high-pressure nozzles"; in New Orleans you've constructed a swamp, the real swamp not far away on the verge of disappearing. Animals in these places are abstractions—wandering relics of their true selves, but that doesn't matter. Animal behavior in a zoo is nothing like natural behavior, but that doesn't really matter, either. Zoos are pretty, contained, and accessible. These new habitats can contain one hundred different species—not more than one or two of each thing, of course—on seven acres, three, one. You don't want to see *too much* of anything, certainly. An *example* will suffice. Sort of like a biological Crabtree & Evelyn basket selected with *you* in mind. You like things reduced, simplified. It's easier to take it all in, park it in your mind. You like things inside better than outside anyway. You are increasingly looking at and living in proxy environments created by substitution and simulation. *Resource economists* are a wee branch in the tree of tiny masters, and one, Martin Krieger, wrote, "Artificial prairies and wildernesses have been created, and there is no reason to believe that these artificial environments need be unsatisfactory for those who experience them. . . . We will have to realize that the way in which we experience nature is conditioned by our society—which more and more is seen to be receptive to responsible intervention."

Nature has become a world of appearances, a mere source of materials. You've been editing it for quite some time; now you're in the process of deleting it. Earth is beginning to look like not much more than a launching pad. Back near Tucson, on the opposite side of the mountain from the dead-animal habitat, you're building Biosphere II (as compared with or opposed to Biosphere I, more commonly known as Earth)—a 2½-acre terrarium, an artificial ecosystem that will include a rain forest, a desert, a thirty-five-foot ocean, and several thousand species of life (lots of microbes), including eight human beings, who will cultivate a bit of farmland. You think it would be nice to colonize other worlds after you've made it necessary to leave this one.

Hey, that's pretty good, you say, all that stuff packed into just 2½ acres. That's only about three times bigger than my entire *house*.

It's small all right, but still not small enough to be, apparently, useful. For the purposes of NASA, say, it would have to be smaller, oh much smaller, and energy-efficient too. Fiddle, fiddle, fiddle. You support fiddling, as well as meddling. This is how you learn. Though it's quite apparent the environment has been grossly polluted and the natural world abused and defiled, you seem to prefer to continue pondering effects rather than preventing causes. You want proof, you insist on proof. A Dr. Lave from Carnegie-Mellon—and he's an expert, an economist, and an environmental *expert*—says that scientists will have to prove to you that you will suffer if you don't become less of a "throwaway society." *If you really want me to give up my car or my air conditioner, you'd better prove to me first that the earth would otherwise be uninhabitable,* Dr. Lave says. *Me* is *you,* I presume, whereas *you* refers to them. You as in me—that is, *me, me, me*—certainly strike a hard bargain. Uninhabitable the world has to get before you rein in your requirements. You're a consumer after all, *the* consumer upon whom so much attention is lavished, the ultimate user of a commodity that has become, these days, everything. To try to appease your appetite for proof, for example, scientists have been leasing for experimentation forty-six pristine lakes in Canada.

They don't want to *keep* them, they just want to *borrow* them.

They've been intentionally contaminating many of the lakes with a variety of pollutants dribbled into the propeller wash of research boats. It's *one of the boldest experiments in lake ecology ever conducted.* They've turned these remote lakes into huge *real-world test tubes.* They've been doing this since 1976! And what they've found so far in these *preliminary* studies is that pollutants are really destructive. The lakes get gross. Life in them ceases. It took about eight years to make this happen in one of them, everything carefully measured and controlled all the while. Now the scientists are slowly reversing the process. But it will take hundreds of years for the lakes to recover. They think.

20

Remember when you used to like rain, the sound of it, the feel of it, the way it made the plants and trees all glisten. We needed that rain, you would say. It looked pretty too, you thought, particularly in the movies. Now it rains and you go, Oh-oh. A nice walloping rain these days means *overtaxing our sewage treatment plants.* It means *untreated waste discharged directly into our waterways.* It means . . .

Okay. Okay.

Acid rain! And we all know what this is. Or most of us do. People of power in government and industry still don't seem to know what it is. Whatever it is, they say, they don't want to curb it, but they're willing to study it some more. Economists call air and water pollution "externalities" anyway. Oh, acid rain. You do get so sick of hearing about it. The words have already become a white-noise kind of thing. But you think in terms of *mitigating* it maybe. As for *the greenhouse effect,* you think in terms of *countering* that. One way that's been discussed recently is the planting of new forests, not for the sake of the forests alone, oh my heavens, no. Not for the sake of majesty and mystery or of Thumper and Bambi, are you kidding me, but because, as every schoolchild knows, trees absorb carbon dioxide. They just soak it up and store it. They just love it. So this is the plan: you plant millions of acres of trees, and you can go on doing pretty much whatever you're doing—driving around, using staggering amounts of energy, keeping those power plants fired to the max. Isn't Nature remarkable? So willing to serve? You wouldn't think it had anything more to offer, but it seems it does. Of course these "forests" wouldn't exactly be forests. They would be more like trees. *Managed* trees. The Forest Service, which now manages our forests by cutting them down, might be called upon to evolve in their thinking and allow these trees to grow. They would probably be patented trees after a time. Fast-growing, uniform, genetically-created-to-be-toxin-eating *machines*. They would be *new-age* trees, because the problem with planting the old-fashioned variety to *combat* the greenhouse effect, which is caused by pollution, is that they're already dying from it. All along the crest of the Appalachians from Maine to Georgia, forests struggle to survive in a toxic soup of poisons. They can't *help* us if we've killed them, now can they?

All right, you say, wow, lighten up will you? Relax. Tell about yourself.

Well, I say, I live in Florida . . .   *25*

Oh my God, you say. Florida! Florida is a joke! How do you expect us to take you seriously if you still live there! Florida is crazy, it's pink concrete. It's paved, it's over. And a little girl just got eaten by an alligator down there. It came out of some swamp next to a subdivision and just carried her off. That set your Endangered Species Act back fifty years, you can bet.

I . . .

Listen, we don't want to hear any more about Florida. We don't want to hear about Phoenix or Hilton Head or California's Central Valley. If our wetlands—our *vanishing* wetlands—are mentioned one more time, we'll scream. And the talk about condors and grizzlies and wolves is becoming too de trop. We had just managed to get whales out of our minds when those three showed up under the ice in Alaska. They even had *names*. Bone is the dead one, right? It's almost the twenty-first century! Those last condors are *pathetic*. Can't we just get this over with?

Aristotle said that all living beings are ensouled and striving to participate in eternity.

Oh, I just bet he said that, you say. That doesn't sound like Aristotle.   *30* He was a humanist. We're all humanists here. This is the age of humanism. And it has been for a long time.

You are driving with a stranger in the car, and it is the stranger behind the wheel. In the back seat are your pals for many years now—DO WHAT YOU LIKE and his swilling sidekick, WHY NOT. A deer, or some emblematic animal, something from that myriad natural world you've come from that you now treat with such indifference and scorn—steps from the dimming woods and tentatively upon the highway. The stranger does not decelerate or brake, not yet, maybe not at all. The feeling is that whatever it is *will get out of the way.* Oh, it's a fine car you've got, a fine machine, and oddly you don't mind the stranger driving it, because in a way, everything has gotten too complicated, way, way out of your control. You've given the wheel to the masters, the managers, the comptrollers. Something is wrong, *maybe,* you feel a little sick, *actually,* but the car is luxurious and fast and you're *moving,* which is the most important thing by far.

Why make a fuss when you're so comfortable? Don't make a fuss, make a baby. Go out and get something to eat, build something. Make *another* baby. Babies are cute. Babies show you have faith in the future. Although faith is perhaps too strong a word. They're everywhere these days, in all the crowds and traffic jams, there are the babies too. You don't seem to associate them with the problems of population increase. They're just babies! And you've come to believe in them again. They're a lot more tangible than the afterlife, which, of course, you haven't believed in in ages. At least not for yourself. The afterlife now belongs to plastics and poisons. Yes, plastics and poisons will have a far more extensive afterlife than you, that's known. A disposable diaper, for example, which is all plastic and wood pulp—you like them for all those babies, so easy to use and toss—will take around four centuries to degrade. Almost all plastics do, centuries and centuries. In the sea, many marine animals die from ingesting or being entangled in discarded plastic. In the dumps, plastic squats on more than 25 percent of dump space. But your heart is disposed toward plastic. Someone, no doubt the plastics industry, told you it was convenient. This same industry is now looking into recycling in an attempt to get the critics of their nefarious, multifarious products off their backs. That should make you feel better, because *recycling* has become an honorable word, no longer merely the hobby of Volvo owners. The fact is that people in plastics are born obscurants. Recycling (practically impossible) won't solve the plastic glut, only reduction of production will, and the plastics industry isn't looking into that, you can be sure. Waste is not just the stuff you throw away, of course, it's the stuff you use to excess. With the exception of *hazardous waste,* which you do worry about from time to time, it's even thought you have a declining sense of emergency about the problem. Builders are building bigger houses because you want bigger. You're trading up. Utility companies are beginning to worry about your constantly rising consumption. Utility companies! You haven't entered a new age at all but one of upscale nihilism, deluxe nihilism.

In the summer, particularly in *the industrial Northeast,* you did get a little excited. The filth cut into your fun time. Dead stuff floating around. Sludge and bloody vials. Hygienic devices—appearing not quite so hygienic out of context—all coming in on the tide. The air smelled funny, too. You tolerate a great deal, but the summer of '88 was truly creepy. It was even thought for a moment that the environment would become a political issue. But it didn't. You didn't want it to be, preferring instead to continue in your politics of subsidizing and advancing avarice. The issues were the same as always—jobs, defense, the economy, maintaining and improving the standard of living in this greedy, selfish, expansionistic, industrialized society.

You're getting a little shrill here, you say.

You're pretty well off. You expect to be better off soon. You do. What does this mean? More software, more scampi, more square footage? You have created an ecological crisis. The earth is infinitely variable and alive, and you are killing it. It seems safer this way. But you are not safe. You want to find wholeness and happiness in a land increasingly damaged and betrayed, and you never will. More than material matters. You must change your ways.   35

What is this? *Sinners in the Hands of an Angry God?*

The ecological crisis cannot be resolved by politics. It cannot be solved by science or technology. It is a crisis caused by culture and character, and a deep change in personal consciousness is needed. Your fundamental attitudes toward the earth have become twisted. You have made only brutal contact with Nature, you cannot comprehend its grace. You must change. Have few desires and simple pleasures. Honor nonhuman life. Control yourself, become more authentic. Live lightly upon the earth and treat it with respect. Redefine the word *progress* and dismiss the managers and masters. Grow inwardly and with knowledge become truly wiser. Make connections. Think differently, behave differently. For this is essentially a moral issue we face and moral decisions must be made.

A moral issue! Okay, this discussion is now toast. A *moral* issue . . . And who's this *we* now? Who are *you* is what I'd like to know. You're not me, anyway. I admit, someone's to blame and something should be done. But I've got to go. It's getting late. That's dusk out there. That is dusk, isn't it? It certainly doesn't look like any dawn I've ever seen. Well, take care.

📖 *Outward Exploration: Discussion*

1. In two or three words, how would you describe the tone of this essay?

2. What is the effect of Williams's first paragraph?

3. Does her opening suggest her goal is something other than persuasion? What other evidence from the essay supports your claim?

4. If her goal is persuasion, why would an accomplished writer who knows all about accommodation write such an essay?

5. Specifically, what problems does Williams address in this essay?

6. Why does she think the word *environment* is not useful anymore?

7. Point out some examples where Williams uses humor.

8. One of Williams's most effective strategies is pointing out her readers' assumptions and warrants. Point out some of those assumptions.

9. What solution to environmental problems does she offer?

10. Does her approach offend you? If so, what passages in particular do so?

☐ *Outward Exploration: Writing*

1. Write an exploratory argument essay responding to Williams's essay.

2. Select an issue about which you feel very frustrated. Using Williams's approach, write an exploratory essay.

☐ *Style*

Consider the following sentence from Williams's essay:

In your desire to get away from what you've got, you've caused there to be no place to get away *to*. (paragraph 9)

Notice Williams's use of irony here. Write a sentence that states a point ironically.

9

Exploring Texts

In a previous chapter you considered exploring relationships with people. Another kind of relationship is the kind we form with texts. As used in this chapter, the term **text** includes anything created to communicate with others—for example, novels and short stories, poems, letters, advertisements, plays (both written and staged versions), and films. The readings to be explored in this book, however, will be short stories, poems, and a short play. With such texts, we discover how the characters think and feel about the situations in which they find themselves. We evaluate their reactions, comparing them to our own. Often, of course, such texts present situations almost totally alien to our own, and in such cases, we often imagine ourselves in those situations. Or we might find out what it is like to see the world through the eyes of someone very different from ourselves. For example, reading Hemingway's *The Sun Also Rises* allows us to view the world through the jaded eyes of Jake Barnes, a World War I veteran who tries to make the best of a bad situation (being impotent and in love), a man who sacrifices important things for a woman who can't be faithful to him. Alice Walker's *The Color Purple* lets us see the world through the eyes of an abused and religious young woman who somehow perseveres against heavy odds. John Gardner's *Grendel* allows us to see a barbaric world of early England through the eyes of an outcast, a monster who can't understand the random violence and cruelty of humans.

In other types of texts, such as those created for advertising purposes, we see ourselves as advertisers think we want to see ourselves—young, physically fit, energetic, relatively rich. We see what various types of experts feel will appeal to us; we see what advertisers want us to be attracted to.

In every type of text imaginable, we find some vision of humans and, hence, some potential vision of ourselves. How we perceive and respond to those visions and to those texts is a good way of exploring our thoughts and emotions.

WRITER-BASED GOALS

There are five writer-based goals for exploring texts: (1) to analyze and interpret the text; (2) to explore the sources of your felt connection to that text; (3) to explore the background and context of that text; (4) to discover some personal connection to the text; (5) to use that connection to gain a better understanding of that text. Hence a reciprocal relationship is established: By closely analyzing the text you discover something about yourself which, in turn, may give you a greater insight into the text, and so forth. You might also discover insights into our society.

READER-BASED GOALS

There are three reader-based goals: (1) to give readers a deeper insight into the text; (2) to give readers a deeper insight into you; and (3) perhaps to give readers a deeper insight into the society and forces which helped to create the text. Such insights should lead readers to see the possibilities of connecting in new ways with the text.

RESPONDING TO LITERARY TEXTS

Perhaps the most common way of responding to texts in a college environment is through **analysis,** an examination of the parts that leads to an **interpretation** (an explicit statement of the text's meaning, of its themes, of its governing idea or world vision). In other words, we often "dismantle" the whole, consider its parts, and then comment on how the parts have combined to make meaning. At other times we analyze and comment on the functioning of a particular part (for instance, the use of point of view in a novel or the use of music in a movie).

We need to pause a moment to consider the act of interpreting a text. At times we analyze the work itself first, looking at such elements as the language, images, symbols, and dramatic situation. Then we use that analysis as evidence to support our vision of the work's meaning. At other times we might begin by considering the "externals": the historical context of the work, the literary period of the work (for instance, William Wordsworth's "I Wandered Lonely As a Cloud" as an illustration of the Romantic Period), the biography of the author, or the conventions and assumptions of the genre (sonnets, say, or the psychological novel); or we might consider the work in the light of the insights offered by a particular perspective such as feminism or psychology. A combination of two or more of these approaches can often lead to an even deeper understanding of the work.

EXPLORATORY ESSAYS ABOUT LITERARY TEXTS

During your academic career you have probably learned several ways to respond to texts. What follows is intended not to supplant the techniques and approaches you have learned but rather to supplement them.

Our first reactions to a text can be a good indicator of the focus of an essay about the text. Ideally, these reactions should be more specific than "I like it" or "It's boring," but even these superficial reactions provide a starting point. Begin by recording your reactions to the text, to its various elements (such as characterization or cinematography), and to the issues it raises. Then, by analyzing *your reactions to the work,* you can often discover much about the work itself—for example, how its structure or language or tone cause you to feel a particular way.

Any information you have from previous classes or from reading you've done can help you respond more fully. For example, knowing about American Transcendentalism or English Romanticism from either literature or history classes would help provide a *literary setting* for Herman Melville's *Moby Dick* and would help you see the novel as a comment on those intellectual movements as well as an implementation of their techniques and assumptions. Knowing what was happening in America during the early nineteenth century could help you understand the novel in the context of Melville's *historical era.* Having read Melville's earlier sea novels or having read about Melville's life would deepen your understanding of and reactions to *Moby Dick.* Having read other accounts of sea voyages, such as Richard Henry Dana's *Two Years Before the Mast,* would provide still more *literary context.* And that's only the beginning of the list. Often, of course, we combine several elements in one exploration.

Another element that comes into play is the thing that attracted you to this particular work. You might think you selected the work because you saw how easy it would be to analyze the protagonist's personality, or because you had read other works by the same author that seemed to illuminate this work. Often, however, something more fundamental and more personal influences the selection. Paying attention to that "something" is one of the ways that the exploration can become more meaningful to both you and your readers.

The First Step: Observe Your Own Responses

The first step in any exploratory writing about a text is observation of your own responses to it. Don't worry about the "why" yet; just focus on the response itself. One student told me that Richard Wright's novel *Black Boy* is painful to read, but he added that it is a great book anyway. Exploring such a dual judgment ("painful" and "great") could lead to a very revealing and illuminating personal essay. Why is the novel painful? The events recounted might be too harsh, too brutal, perhaps setting up echoes that this particular reader doesn't want to feel. It's a triumph for his critical sense that he can get beyond the "gut reaction" of feeling pain to see the novel's literary merits as well. Even more impressive, however, is the fact that he *actively possesses* both reactions: He didn't ignore the personal reaction to talk only about the critical or aesthetic reaction.

We may be all too ready to simply cast aside a book that hits too many of our raw nerves, telling ourselves that "the text is boring" or "it's not interesting" or "it's too difficult to understand." By resisting such an impulse and using our reactions as a way into the text rather than as an excuse to avoid it, we often discover interesting insights into both ourselves and the text.

After observing your own reaction, consider its sources. Sometimes at least part of the reason for your reaction is clear. If an image strikes you as particularly appropriate, why? If a character seems especially believable, why? What issues underlie the plot? Consider Shakespeare's *King Lear,* for example. Have you had any personal experience with an arbitrary parent? Or with a lying sibling? Or have you ever experienced an inability to speak what's "in your heart"? Analyzing your own situation in light of the characters' situations (or vice versa) will give you a more profound insight into both the text and your life. Explaining which character you are most like may also prove illuminating.

The Second Step: Write about Your Responses

Once you're focused on your responses, start writing about them. This writing might become prewriting for a paper or it might simply "clear the air," but in either case it is important. Write quickly; perhaps even freewrite. Get your reactions—both emotional and intellectual—down on paper so that you can look objectively at them later.

The Third Step: Check the Responses of Others

After observing and exploring your own reaction, you may find it valuable to consider the reactions of other readers, such as members of your class or in published reviews or critical articles. Book reviews tend to feature more "gut" reactions (refined though they may be) than critical articles, but both are well worth considering. Perhaps your reaction was unique, or perhaps it mirrors that of other readers. Other readers' reasons for their responses might influence you, or they might not. It is important to find out which is the case with your response.

The Fourth Step: Return to the Text

With your own reactions and those of others duly noted, it's time for a more systematic examination of the cause of those reactions. Look at the text again. This time you should focus on elements which struck you or which other readers have commented on. Record your thoughts about these elements. Such recording is still part of prewriting, so do not waste time worrying about spelling and punctuation. Focus on articulating your thoughts. The very act of putting an idea into words might lead to a more rewarding perception.

The Fifth Step: Write a Draft

In the beginning of exploration, most of us want to write "My Collected Thoughts on This Work." For early drafts, at least, such an approach can be useful. Allow yourself to follow tangents, to state provocative ideas and observations, to discuss your reactions to various elements in the work, to make connections to events in your own life or to other texts, to argue with the reactions or interpretations of others. Remember that some of this information will probably not be included in the final draft of your essay, but it is part of the exploratory process in the early drafts.

The Sixth Step: Revise

There are many different elements to focus on when revising, including organization and style. First, however, it's important to revise the ideas themselves.

For example, it's easy to lose sight of *your* importance in the essay. Avoid the temptation to eliminate your personal reactions. If you include your feelings, sensations, and doubts while analyzing or interpreting, the essay becomes even more interesting because readers start to see the analyst as well as the subject analyzed.

The following discussion suggests some ways of bringing yourself into an essay about a text.

PERSONALIZE THE EXPLORATION   Let me give you a brief example from a film course I taught several years ago. One student, Charles, became less and less comfortable in the class. Our careful analysis of the film texts disconcerted him. I suggested that he include his feelings about the analysis process itself in his essay. A week later I received his response to a 1950s Randolph Scott western. Along with an effective analysis of the movie as part of the "western tradition," he provided a running commentary concerning his doubts and emotions about such analysis. Here's a sample:

> I'm getting tired of seeing sexual stereotypes everywhere. Of course the heroine doesn't do much in this movie: it's a western!

In the old west, women had enough to do just trying to survive. It was also the nineteenth century: women were supposed to be ladylike. Finally, this heroine is a school teacher who came from "back East." Why are we surprised if she doesn't shoot outlaws or bop them over the head when Scott is fighting them? Critics would scream that the film was unrealistic if the heroine acted like a modern-day feminist. I know, of course, that no frontier woman ever looked like the actresses in westerns. And I know that they're all wearing hairdos that were popular the year the movie was made, not styles that were used in the old west.

But all this emphasis on sex roles defeats the purpose of westerns. They are escape, not lessons in how we should all be living now. Constant analysis in other courses has already ruined fiction and plays for me. Movies are my last escape. My best escape. Why does being "smart" mean having to pick everything to pieces?

—CHARLES WOOD, "WESTERNS"

Charles's comments reveal his struggle to respond intellectually to the movie while protesting emotionally to such a response. This personal element strengthens the essay: In the essay, he managed to analyze the film and tried to understand his own reactions to the analysis process. And he raises an interesting issue about what it means to be an intellectual in our society.

RECREATE YOUR PROCESS   With exploratory writing, the point of the essay is not only to reveal something about the text analyzed (for instance, the poem), but also to reveal your process of discovery. This doesn't mean that you are going to give readers your freewriting about the poem; it means you are going to watch yourself explore the poem. You will then structure your essay *to dramatize your process of exploration.*

Let's try an example. Because not everyone approaches a poem (or any other text) in exactly the same way, this example illustrates one particular student's approach, an approach that is not necessarily any better or worse than someone else's. Here is a poem by Stephen Crane:

#35

A man saw a ball of gold in the sky: 1
    He climbed for it,
    And eventually he achieved it—
    It was clay.

Now this is the strange part: 5
When the man went to the earth
And looked up again,
Lo, there was the ball of gold.
Now this is the strange part:

It was a ball of gold.   10
Aye, by the heavens, it was a ball of gold.

I asked the student, Gene, to write a description of his process of thinking about and analyzing this poem. What follows below is not an essay; rather, it is simply the description that I requested. I offer it here to give you insight into how at least one mind gained insight into the poem:

> I read the poem all the way through first, just to see what it was about in general. The first thing I noticed was the lack of a title (just its number in the collected poems), so Crane was giving me no help with a clue to the theme or point of the poem. I decided that the poem is about mankind's greed. But then the second stanza didn't really fit that. If the point was greed, we'd see him climbing back up for the ball, right? So the point must have been something else. Or at least, something in addition to greed. The "gold" makes me think greed is part of the point. In fact, the word *gold* shows up four times in 11 lines. Counting the lines to make that previous statement made me aware of the fact that the poem has two uneven stanzas—the first is 4 lines, the second is 7. Why? There is no rhyme scheme, although some words such as *it* and *gold* recur at the end of lines. And I can't see any real meter like iambic pentameter or anything.
>
> But there is a refrain of sorts—"Now this is the strange part." And that's my big clue, I think. That line, or rather its repetition, makes the theme not greed but the fact that the ball turned from gold to clay to gold. And that's why the second stanza is longer—that's where the real point of the poem is: not the greedy man climbing but the way the ball changes.

Gene pursued this type of inquiry for two more pages; again, he was not writing his essay or even a draft. He was simply recreating his thought processes. Notice the way that looking for "typical" poetic elements (rhyme, meter, refrain) led to his insight into the poem's meaning. Playing with the refrain led him to a second major insight: that the poem focuses not on the man depicted but on the speaker—it's his amazement that we see most. In fact, we do not even know how the man reacted.

Following this directed freewriting, the student reconsidered his notes from class. Discovering that Crane is famous for his irony gave him a further clue to the poem's meaning. Gene then wrote an analytical essay:

IRONY IN STEPHEN CRANE'S POEM #35

In his poem #35, Stephen Crane demonstrates once again   1
the irony for which he is famous. On the surface, the situation
in the poem is quite straightforward. In the first stanza, a man

sees a ball of gold suspended above him, desires it, and finds a way to climb up to get it. When he reaches it, however, he discovers that the ball has turned to clay. In the second stanza, he climbs back to the ground, looks up, and sees that the ball is gold again. A careful reading of the poem reveals that Crane has used this straightforward situation to comment ironically on three topics: man's greed, the nature of reality, and the effect of man's perspective on reality.

Clearly the man's behavior shows greed. He wishes to acquire the ball of gold and indeed goes to a great deal of trouble to get it; the word *eventually* in the third line suggests that it was a task not quickly or easily accomplished. Ironically, however, he fails to satisfy his greed, even though he achieves his goal by climbing high enough to reach the golden ball. Instead of grasping it and bringing it back to earth, he leaves it "in the sky" because he perceives that it is only clay. His desire to own the ball has been frustrated by his perception that it is not after all what he thought it was. There is a further irony in the fact that once back on earth he again sees the ball as made of gold, perhaps setting off another round of greed and frustration.

Crane uses this example of greed as the basis for further irony. On close inspection, the ball is made of clay, yet from a distance it appears to be made of gold. Why? Since the man looks at the world with greedy eyes, trying to see what he can acquire, he sees everything as having potential financial value. Thus he misperceives the ball of clay as a ball of gold. If he were not so greedy, he would be able to see the ball for what it is. Crane is thus suggesting that mankind's vision of reality is so clouded that we see only what we want to see. The man in the poem wants gold, so the ball he sees in the sky appears to be made of gold. Only when he is so close to it that even fantasy cannot fool him does he see that it is only clay. The irony is reasserted when the man returns to earth and once again succumbs to his greedy image of the ball.

And this is Crane's third ironic comment on mankind's ability (or inability) to perceive reality. Even with his firsthand knowledge that the ball is made of clay, the man in the poem still sees it as gold once he returns to earth. In short, he learns nothing from his experience. Not only is he unlikely to be able to transfer what he has learned about balls of clay that look like balls of gold, he can't even separate the fantasy from the reality in connection with the ball he has "achieved." If Crane is right about this, then mankind is doomed to repeat the same misperceptions and follies again and again.

There is one final irony in the way the poem's speaker reacts to the man's once again thinking that the ball is made of gold. He 5 seems amazed. Twice he says, "Now this is the strange part," and twice he asserts, "it was a ball of gold." This repetition suggests that the speaker, presumably a witness to the man's frustrated attempt to acquire the ball of gold, is himself convinced that it was gold instead of clay. Thus Crane's irony takes one final turn, entangling the speaker as well as the greedy climber in the folly of misperception.

This is a well-constructed traditional academic essay. After the initial explanation of the situation depicted in the poem, the writer clearly spells out the thesis (Crane uses the situation in poem #35 to comment ironically on man's greed, the nature of reality, and the effect of man's perception of reality). In the process, he also informs us of the order his paper will follow. He then supports that thesis throughout the rest of the paper. His interpretation of the poem (it's about greed, reality, and man's perception of reality) grows out of the analysis which he had earlier performed. He also does a good job of taking into account the genuinely held opinion of literary scholars that Crane is an ironic poet, arguing that there are at least three ironic elements in the poem, the third the most devastating of all.

The analysis is also well substantiated. The writer begins in paragraph 2 by discussing greed. He comments on particular words (*eventually,* for example) which help explain his insights. He uses the words *ironically* and *irony* in this paragraph to keep that element of his thesis in our minds. He follows the same strategies throughout: In every paragraph he reminds us that irony is at work; in every paragraph he comments on particular words or events described in the poem as evidence to support his thesis. Indeed, as in most traditional academic essays, everything in the essay supports the thesis. The style is straightforward, and the tone is serious and impersonal.

Yet that is not the only way to analyze this poem. Although the essay certainly gives readers a sense of the writer's interpretation, and it does a good job of convincing readers that his interpretation is plausible, still readers learn little about the essay's author or his process of exploration. Did he see all of this immediately? (Remember, other readers of this essay do not have our privileged information about the writer's thought processes.) What kind of connections eluded him at first? Was he unduly influenced by lectures that suggested Crane's ironic view of life?

An exploratory analysis gives an interpretation and evidence, but its writer is also free to reveal his or her own connection to the text. Here's Gene's exploratory analysis of that same poem:

A READING OF CRANE'S #35

When I first read Stephen Crane's poem #35, it seemed simple and straightforward. The situation was clear: a greedy

1

man saw a ball of gold in the sky, climbed up in order to retrieve it, but found once he was beside it that it was made out of clay instead of gold. So he left it up there. Reaching the ground again, he looked up and the ball had turned back into gold. That's a pretty good trick for an inanimate ball, but further readings of the poem showed me that something more sophisticated than simple irony was going on.

First, for example, the emphasis turns out not to be on the greedy man but on the fact that the ball turned back into gold. That's why we get this refrain twice in seven lines: "Now this is the strange part." That was my first real clue that greed wasn't the most important issue here. Crane is after something else.

And then it occurred to me that the speaker of the poem is not necessarily the poet Crane. It could be a created character, like one of the speakers in Browning's monologues. Of course, Browning has very defined characters talking; there's no question about who the speaker is or what his particular biases are. Often he uses the title to give us that information ("Fra Lippo Lippi," for example).

But other poets, such as Edgar Allan Poe, also use speakers, speakers who are less defined and hence can be partially confused with the poet himself. I keep thinking of the speaker in "Annabel Lee." We're not supposed to believe that Poe himself is lying there in the sepulchre with his beloved Annabel. Yet the speaker has no name and the point of the poem does not seem to be a revelation about his prejudices and attitudes. It's simply a dark love poem in the way *Catch 22* is a black comedy.

Anyway, the example of Poe reaffirmed my sense that Crane's poem has a created character as a speaker. Like the climber, that character believes the ball really did turn from gold to clay and then back to gold. We are at first trapped in his perspective, seeing the wonder of the fact that the ball turned back to gold.

Yet Crane wants us to go further, I think, to see that the ball really didn't change at all. How do I know this? In part I have an intuition about it, but by themselves such feelings carry little weight in literary analysis. I think the words the speaker uses show that he too is struck by the change. Notice the progression: "strange part," "Lo" (suggesting some kind of religious expression, this word sounds like it is right out of the Bible), "strange part," "Aye, by the heavens."

That last one in particular helped convince me. The "Aye" is a reaffirmation of the fact, of course, but it suggests to me also a sailor (did sailors in Crane's day say "Aye Aye, sir"?). I always think of sailors as being somehow dreamers, probably because I heard so many stories when I was growing up of adventurous

5

men setting out to sea. More important, though, is the "by the heavens." It's as though he thinks he won't be believed, so he's taking a kind of vow that he's telling the truth.

But there is another question raised that is not so easily dealt with. How does the speaker know that the ball turned to clay when the man got to it? Did the climber tell him? Did he yell in anger, "The damned thing is clay!"? Did the speaker also climb up to the ball? Or had he climbed there sometime earlier? Or does he have a god-like omniscience? Or was he himself the climber and is now commenting in the third person on his earlier adventure? I frankly don't see any way of choosing among all these options. Crane doesn't give us enough information to make a definitive selection. And because Crane doesn't give enough information, I imagine that the answer is ultimately not that important.

What is important, I think, is the ball. If the ball didn't change, what does that fact suggest? Was it gold all the time, or was it clay all the time? In either case, the point is that people's perception is what changed—both that of the climber and that of the speaker who observed the action. So, the point of the poem is that man doesn't see reality clearly, that he lets his desires (in this case greed) obscure his vision.

But that ball still bothers me, and my interpretation above doesn't help. I can't help thinking of that ball as being the sun. That was the first thing I thought of as I read the poem's opening. The ball of gold is obviously the sun, I said to myself. What else could it be—a Christmas tree ornament? A meteor? A comet?

Yet if it is the sun, how would the man climb to it? Obviously it's a symbolic climb, like the Tower of Babel's symbolically touching the floor of heaven. The laws of gravity and physics guarantee that no building without a base as big as the earth could get anywhere near as high as humans have flown in airplanes, let alone in rockets. So, unless heaven was a lot closer to earth in the old days, the biblical writers were speaking figuratively and so is Crane—*if* the ball is the sun.

Yet even that might not be the point. One other word keeps coming back to bother me. In the third line, most of us would say "And eventually he reached it," not "achieved it." In fact, I wrote that myself in an earlier draft of this paper. Why "achieved it"? And that, I think, is the final clue, at least the final clue I can understand at this moment in my life as a college sophomore. This poem isn't really about greed at all; it's about goals. The ball can be the sun, it can be a job, it can be Ms. Right as a wife, it can be a college education—anything that we want or value.

10

If this is true, the poem is no longer amusing. It's scary. Crane is saying that any goal we strive for will not satisfy us. Ultimately, it will seem to be made of clay. (Whether or not it is really made of gold or clay is finally beside the point, for our perceptions are the key.) So a degree in economics (my immediate goal) and a career in banking (my long-range goal) seem really great to me now. Yet, if I'm lucky enough to ever get them, Crane suggests that they will no longer satisfy me. Worse, I'll probably give one or the other up (say, the career in banking) and then turn right around and pursue another career (in insurance, perhaps) that is essentially the same thing—the same pressures, the same dissatisfactions. That is a depressing vision of life.

But most depressing of all is the fact that I think Crane is right. My aunt, for example, has been married three times. Each time she selects a man who is essentially just like the previous husband. She has this knack for getting gamblers. Obviously the man doesn't gamble heavily when they are dating, but once they are married it all starts again. My family says she just has terrible luck with men, but Crane's poem says aloud what I've believed secretly for years: My aunt senses something in each of the men that will turn him into a gambler—some trait, some despair, some recklessness perhaps. But from afar (before marriage) that trait seems golden, it attracts her, just like the ball attracts the climber. Maybe the man is a big spender, or maybe he's exciting because he likes to take risks. Once she gets up close (marriage), however, the trait is revealed for what it is: a tragic character flaw that leads to her suffering. She divorces the man (that is, climbs back to earth) and the next man she meets with that same trait seems golden to her again.

Or even worse is the other possibility. I just recently broke up with Beth. She seemed to be everything I am looking for in a girl—loving, very smart, funny, attractive, and ambitious. Yet when she asked me to go steady with her (did I mention she's also liberated?), I got frightened. I started seeing her good traits as handicaps. Her good looks would always attract other men, her humor got on my nerves when I was trying to be serious, she seemed too smart (smarter than I), her ambition made her think about graduate school instead of getting a job and getting married, and her love for me seemed suddenly possessive. But now I find myself thinking fondly of her, especially since she started dating my best friend seriously. I hate myself for breaking up with her. As I thought about Crane's poem for this paper, I realized that I had done the same thing once before, during my junior year in high school. I was dating a really neat

15

girl—Anne—but when she got too serious I saw all her flaws and broke up with her. Even now she looks very good to me. I wonder what college she ended up attending?

That's twice I've climbed up to the golden ball and thought it was clay. And now I'm on the ground looking back up and thinking it's golden again. I'm not sure which is worse: seeing a clay ball and thinking it's golden (the way my aunt does), or seeing a gold ball up close and thinking it's clay (the way I do). Maybe in the end it doesn't make any difference, since the result is the same. A sense of frustration, a sense of loss, a sense that we've done something stupid. Again.

—GENE KATH

This essay is significantly longer than the traditional analysis because the exploratory essay has not one subject, but two—the text and the explorer of the text.

A comparison of the opening sentences of the two essays is revealing:

In his poem #35, Stephen Crane demonstrates once again the irony for which he is famous. On the surface, the situation in the poem is quite straightforward.

When I first read Stephen Crane's poem #35, it seemed simple and straightforward. The situation was clear: . . .

In the former, the writer is essentially invisible. He has made a general assertion (the poem reveals irony) which he will further limit at the end of his introduction. He indicates that the situation is not straightforward ("On the surface"): In other words, he begins with a limited topic, a thesis, and an impersonal tone.

In the latter, both the poem and the writer ("I") are introduced as the subjects to be explored (and the rest of the essay never loses that sense of dual purpose). Although it too suggests that the poem is not as straightforward as the reader might at first suppose, the perception belongs expressly to the writer ("I"), whereas in the other essay the perception is stated as a general truth with no perceiver indicated. Instead of a thesis at the end of the introduction, the exploratory essay has launched us on a journey of discovery along with the writer ("further readings of the poem showed me"). We see the process of analysis as well as the analysis itself.

This sense of the journey is one crucial characteristic of the exploratory literary analysis. But it is important to remember that we have the fourth, not the first, draft of this essay. As they reshape their material for their audience, exploratory writers are under no obligation to detail every wrong turn they took, every moment of frustration they felt. In other words, *we readers are not actually witnessing their discovery*. Before creating the final draft above, there had been a lot of fumbling in earlier versions, and new concepts were added with each draft. For instance, the personal applications of the poem (Gene's aunt and himself) do not appear until the third draft. Even then, the aunt originally showed up in the middle of the essay while the writer himself was at the beginning.

In other words, Gene *hasn't* given us a blow-by-blow description of how he analyzed the poem. He doesn't tell us about going to the library, for instance, or about looking up *lo* and *achieved* in the dictionary. He has *selected* interesting elements *to dramatize his discovery rather than to document it*. He gives us an experience *comparable* to his but not the *same* as his. His essay is controlled.

Other elements contribute to the essay's effect. The style and language are slightly less formal than in the more traditional academic essay. Although the excessive use of slang and profanity is not encouraged in exploratory writing (you still have to worry about distracting or distressing your readers), an occasional, cautious deviation from "polite discourse" might be permitted (*damned* in paragraph 8, for example). This decision depends entirely on your perception of your readers (for instance, your instructor, your classmates, the editor of the magazine you're submitting the essay to).

Beginning in paragraph 3, Gene recreates part of his thought process. For example, he tells us that the refrain was "my first real clue." His acquaintance with poems read for other courses leads to his perception that the poem's speaker may not be Crane (paragraphs 3 and 4).

He freely admits that "an intuition" helped bring about his insight that Crane wants us to go beyond the realization that the speaker might be unreliable (paragraph 6). This honesty doesn't let him "off the hook," for he still has to support that intuition. If that insight comes from having eaten too much pizza before he read the poem, then it has little validity (although he might write an essay exploring the relationship between a critic's digestion and his literary interpretations). So he turns to the language of the poem to discover the source of his intuition (paragraphs 6 and 7). In paragraphs 8 and 9, he raises questions which he admits he can't answer, questions which are nonetheless worth raising.

Paragraph 10 is a very careful transition to the rest of the paper. Gene has consciously led us through the early parts of the essay and of his interpretation because he knows they have a great deal of value, in what they reveal both about the poem and about him. Yet the paragraph also tells us that the writer's interpretation up to this point only partly satisfies him (and presumably us) because it leaves the ball unexplained. Paragraphs 11 and 12 recreate for us the reasoning process that led him to the conclusion in paragraph 13 that the ball symbolizes goals.

So far, the essay has been obviously exploratory: The writer has offered interpretations and qualifications to those interpretations. He has explained the feelings and ideas that led to his interpretations as well as supplying "hard evidence" from the poem to support them; he has asked questions that he feels the poem raises, even when he cannot provide the answers; he has speculated about the poem's connection to works by other poets; and through all of this he has dramatized and recreated for us his process of discovery. In fact, we feel as though we have made the discoveries and stumbled upon the questions just as he has.

In truth, however, the writer made the exploration much earlier. By the time he wrote this draft, he already knew the wrong turns and the blind alleys. Thus he lets us experience the sense of discovery he felt without the frustration. He has selected meaningful aspects of reality (in this case, his process of analysis) to give the *illusion* of the whole process.

Beginning in paragraph 14, he brings to bear his personal experience of life (his aunt and himself), testing the "truth" of the poem against the facts of his life. It is, of course, *his* truth of the poem and *his* interpretation that are being tested, not *the* truth of the poem. But he convinces us at least that his interpretation is plausible.

Gene implicitly asks three questions that all exploratory essayists should ask about texts:

What does this text say to me?

How does it illuminate my experiences?

How do my experiences illuminate the text?

Finally, it's important to emphasize the care that was taken with this essay. The style is carefully crafted, and the essay builds to a climax. The writer's statement that he has gotten all he can "at this moment" from this poem is also revealing: He believes he may be able to find new insights later, when he is a more experienced person, a wiser and more skillful reader. This idea suggests strongly that we are not to be limited to his interpretation and exploration but that we should do some exploring on our own. That is a useful implicit message since no single reader, perhaps not even the total sum of readers, can ever interpret a literary text totally and completely.

As you can see, the exploratory essay helps us to learn from a text and then to apply what we have learned to our world and to ourselves. We are all interested in what will make our lives better, more interesting, more fulfilling. By relating ourselves directly to the material we're examining, we make the learning personal. And by revealing elements of ourselves as well as the object analyzed, we make the essay more rewarding for the readers as well.

Gene's essay illustrates one of the two most common ways to structure an exploratory essay about a text. He uses Crane's poem as a *touchstone* throughout his essay, returning to the text several times to compare his experiences and feelings to those suggested by the text. A second method is to use your analysis of the text as a *point of departure* for your own meditation. In her essay "Unlearning Romance," Gloria Steinem employs this second approach. There are many variations of these two approaches, and there are many other ways to use texts in exploratory essays. The touchstone and point-of-departure approaches, however, are very useful.

CONDITIONED VERSUS REAL RESPONSES

A more fundamental issue underlies exploratory writing in general and exploratory writing about texts in particular: namely, the issue of who controls our feelings and our thoughts.

During a physical examination, doctors often tap a knee with a little hammer to test our reflex reactions. Such reactions are involuntary and hence are "true" (beyond our conscious control). Other reactions are conscious—for example, we consciously decide to yell at the driver who cuts in front of us. There is a third kind of response as well, namely, the conditioned response. A conditioned response is one which has been taught to us by someone else. All of us are loaded with such conditioned responses. Everything from toilet training to crying at weddings is learned behavior, conditioned responses.

Obviously many conditioned responses are useful. For example, when I was first learning how to drive a car, my father took me to an empty parking lot to train me what to do when the car skids on the ice. No amount of verbal instruction would be sufficient. He took me to a safe place and had me create skids and then react to them. The first time, despite all my father's instructions, I turned the wheel away from the skid and we did a 360-degree turn. When I had managed to turn *into* the skid for the 20th consecutive time, we went home. I had been conditioned to turn into a skid and hence retain control of the car. Such conditioned responses are good.

But many are not good, as can be shown vividly when we interact with texts. We are conditioned to respond to texts in certain ways, just as Pavlov's dogs were conditioned to respond to bells. The conditioning is often caused or reinforced by the texts themselves or by society.

Consider, for a moment, sitcoms on television. All have laugh tracks, the sound of an audience laughing. For the viewers at home, the laugh track is supposed to duplicate the experience of sitting in a theater and sharing the laughter with the audience. The underlying principle is simple: Most of us tend to laugh when others laugh. In the pretelevision days, some comedians would hire professional laughers to sit in the audience and start laughing at appropriate places. These ringers in the audience "primed the pump" and got the laughter started. Television producers took this concept one step further by incorporating the professional laughers into the shows' sound tracks.

Would we really laugh at all the one-liners and silly situations we see in those sitcoms if we weren't conditioned to laugh when we hear laughter? Most such sitcoms are highly derivative: The same plots and characters recur in series after series. Yet we laugh at them because we have been conditioned to do so and are cued to do so by the laugh tracks.

Horror movies are another example. Try listening to a horror movie with your eyes closed. The music will tell you when the tension is mounting, when the psycho killer or monster is moving toward the potential victim. Such clues and heightening are used because most horror movies lack original ideas and new scary situations. (How many movies have some character—usually a beautiful woman—walking into a dark house or dark cellar when we, the audience, suspect or know that the killer or monster lurks in that very place?) The producers fall back on conditioned responses to make us think we're being scared.

All types of movies use such devices, of course. When a truly creative movie maker comes along and introduces new clues to the emotions we're supposed to be feeling, the older conditioning clues sometimes seem suddenly clichéd or old-fashioned. For instance, in the 1950s, solo saxophones or trumpets often signaled sexy or "steamy" moments while violin music suggested romance. Just listening to the opening theme music of any 1950s movie tells you immediately whether the movie is a comedy, a western, or a drama. In other words, even before the action starts on the screen, our conditioning is being invoked. The same is true today, but the conventions used are not so obvious since they are *our* conventions rather than those of an earlier generation.

In short, the concept of using conditioning hasn't changed, only the type of bell to evoke our Pavlovian responses has changed. The trick is to get beyond such conditioned reactions to find your true responses, feelings, and beliefs. Only then can you exercise judgment and make sound decisions. If you're reading or watching a movie or television show only for pleasure, it may not be crucial that you always separate the real response from the conditioned reaction. Even then, though, recognizing the difference will help you not waste time with texts that offer only the latter.

With texts such as advertisements and political propaganda, however, any conditioned reactions are not merely wasteful but also potentially dangerous. With advertisements, you may end up spending your money for something that will do you harm. With political propaganda, you might end up not only believing lies but even supporting someone whose policies are at odds with your beliefs. In these arenas, conditioned reactions are terrifying. Surely, few of us want to be controlled or to be mere pawns for someone else's purposes. In chess, players never hesitate to sacrifice a pawn for even a minor advantage. The same is true for many business or political leaders: Their goal is to make us react in a certain predictable way. If we allow them to push us into reacting that way because we haven't committed ourselves to exploring our responses, then we are nothing more than those expendable pieces on a chessboard.

To help us avoid being manipulated is a practical value of all exploratory writing. Understanding yourself better and examining your conditioned reactions and your real reactions will give you a power over yourself and over your world that every adult needs.

SUGGESTIONS FOR WRITING

Any text (anything written or photographed or filmed or drawn or painted or performed on stage) can be explored in writing. Select something you're interested in understanding better and analyze it. Here are a few possibilities:

1. Explore your favorite poem, movie, novel, or play.

2. Explore a poem, movie, novel, or play that does not appeal to you. Here you wish to determine exactly what turns you off about a text that others have found significant. Obviously, "It's boring" or "It's not interesting" or "It's too difficult to understand" will not be helpful. *Why* is it boring? *What* makes it difficult to understand (which is another way of saying it's not worth the work required to understand it)? Is there some assumption or theme or character or situation that you are reacting against for some reason? If so, explore those reasons.

3. Explore an advertisement or a political speech, including your reaction(s) to it. Try to discover where conditioned responses are being appealed to and how.

4. Another way to respond to texts is to act as an editor. Select from four to ten of your favorite texts in one genre (such as short stories, poems, paintings, buildings, or essays). Assume that you have collected these favorite texts into one volume and write an introduction to that volume that explains your reasons for selecting these works, that explains the connections you see among them, and that explains why all of the texts appeal to you.

Désirée's Baby

KATE CHOPIN

☐ *Inward Exploration*

Write at least one paragraph explaining possible reasons why you might break up with someone you deeply love.

As the day was pleasant, Madame Valmondé drove over to L'Abri   1
to see Désirée and the baby.

It made her laugh to think of Désirée with a baby. Why, it seemed but yesterday that Désirée was little more than a baby herself; when Monsieur in riding through the gateway of Valmondé had found her lying asleep in the shadow of the big stone pillar.

The little one awoke in his arms and began to cry for "Dada." That was as much as she could do or say. Some people thought she might have strayed there of her own accord, for she was of the toddling age. The prevailing belief was that she had been purposely left by a party of Texans, whose canvas-covered wagon, late in the day, had crossed the ferry that Coton Maïs kept, just below the plantation. In time Madame Valmondé abandoned every speculation but the one that Désirée had been sent to her by a beneficent Providence to be the child of her affection, seeing that she was without child of the flesh. For the girl grew to be beautiful and gentle, affectionate and sincere,—the idol of Valmondé.

It was no wonder, when she stood one day against the stone pillar in whose shadow she had lain asleep, eighteen years before, that Armand Aubigny riding by and seeing her there, had fallen in love with her. That was the way all the Aubignys fell in love, as if struck by a pistol shot. The wonder was that he had not loved her before; for he had known her since his father brought him home from Paris, a boy of eight, after his mother died there. The passion that awoke in him that day, when he saw her at the gate, swept along like an avalanche, or like a prairie fire, or like anything that drives headlong over all obstacles.

Monsieur Valmondé grew practical and wanted things well consid-   5
ered: that is, the girl's obscure origin. Armand looked into her eyes and did not care. He was reminded that she was nameless. What did it matter about a name when he could give her one of the oldest and proudest in Louisiana? He ordered the *corbeille*° from Paris, and contained himself with what patience he could until it arrived; then they were married.

---

corbeille: Wedding presents.

Madame Valmondé had not seen Désirée and the baby for four weeks. When she reached L'Abri she shuddered at the first sight of it, as she always did. It was a sad looking place, which for many years had not known the gentle presence of a mistress, old Monsieur Aubigny having married and buried his wife in France, and she having loved her own land too well ever to leave it. The roof came down steep and black like a cowl, reaching out beyond the wide galleries that encircled the yellow stuccoed house. Big, solemn oaks grew close to it, and their thick-leaved, far-reaching branches shadowed it like a pall. Young Aubigny's rule was a strict one, too, and under it his negroes had forgotten how to be gay, as they had been during the old master's easy-going and indulgent lifetime.

The young mother was recovering slowly, and lay full length, in her soft white muslins and laces, upon a couch. The baby was beside her, upon her arm, where he had fallen asleep, at her breast. The yellow nurse woman sat beside a window fanning herself.

Madame Valmondé bent her portly figure over Désirée and kissed her, holding her an instant tenderly in her arms. Then she turned to the child.

"This is not the baby!" she exclaimed, in startled tones. French was the language spoken at Valmondé in those days.

"I knew you would be astonished," laughed Désirée, "at the way he   *10* has grown. The little *cochon de lait!*° Look at his legs, mamma, and his hands and fingernails,—real fingernails. Zandrine had to cut them this morning. Isn't it true, Zandrine?"

The woman bowed her turbaned head majestically, "Mais si,° Madame."

"And the way he cries," went on Désirée, "is deafening. Armand heard him the other day as far away as La Blanche's cabin."

Madame Valmondé had never removed her eyes from the child. She lifted it and walked with it over to the window that was lightest. She scanned the baby narrowly, then looked as searchingly at Zandrine, whose face was turned to gaze across the fields.

"Yes, the child has grown, has changed," said Madame Valmondé, slowly, as she replaced it beside its mother. "What does Armand say?"

Désirée's face became suffused with a glow that was happiness itself.

"Oh, Armand is the proudest father in the parish, I believe, chiefly   *15* because it is a boy, to bear his name; though he says not,—that he would have loved a girl as well. But I know it isn't true. I know he says that to please me. And mamma," she added, drawing Madame Valmondé's head down to her, and speaking in a whisper, "he hasn't punished one

---

cochon de lait: Suckling pig.
Mais si: Yes, indeed!

of them—not one of them—since baby is born. Even Négrillon, who pretended to have burnt his leg that he might rest from work—he only laughed, and said Négrillon was a great scamp. Oh, mamma, I'm so happy; it frightens me."

What Désirée said was true. Marriage, and later the birth of his son had softened Armand Aubigny's imperious and exacting nature greatly. This was what made the gentle Désirée so happy, for she loved him desperately. When he frowned she trembled, but loved him. When he smiled, she asked no greater blessing of God. But Armand's dark, handsome face had not often been disfigured by frowns since the day he fell in love with her.

When the baby was about three months old, Désirée awoke one day to the conviction that there was something in the air menacing her peace. It was at first too subtle to grasp. It had only been a disquieting suggestion; an air of mystery among the blacks; unexpected visits from far-off neighbors who could hardly account for their coming. Then a strange, an awful change in her husband's manner, which she dared not ask him to explain. When he spoke to her, it was with averted eyes, from which the old love-light seemed to have gone out. He absented himself from home; and when there, avoided her presence and that of her child, without excuse. And the very spirit of Satan seemed suddenly to take hold of him in his dealings with the slaves. Désirée was miserable enough to die.

She sat in her room, one hot afternoon, in her *peignoir,* listlessly drawing through her fingers the strands of her long, silky brown hair that hung about her shoulders. The baby, half naked, lay asleep upon her own great mahogany bed, that was like a sumptuous throne, with its satin-lined half-canopy. One of La Blanche's little quadroon boys— half naked too—stood fanning the child slowly with a fan of peacock feathers. Désirée's eyes had been fixed absently and sadly upon the baby, while she was striving to penetrate the threatening mist that she felt closing about her. She looked from her child to the boy who stood beside him, and back again; over and over. "Ah!" It was a cry that she could not help; which she was not conscious of having uttered. The blood turned like ice in her veins, and a clammy moisture gathered upon her face.

She tried to speak to the little quadroon boy; but no sound would come, at first. When he heard his name uttered, he looked up, and his mistress was pointing to the door. He laid aside the great, soft fan, and obediently stole away, over the polished floor, on his bare tiptoes.

She stayed motionless, with gaze riveted upon her child, and her face the picture of fright.

Presently her husband entered the room, and without noticing her, went to a table and began to search among some papers which covered it.

"Armand," she called to him, in a voice which must have stabbed him, if he was human. But he did not notice. "Armand," she said again. Then she rose and tottered towards him. "Armand," she panted once more, clutching his arm, "look at our child. What does it mean? tell me."

He coldly but gently loosened her fingers from about his arm and thrust the hand away from him. "Tell me what it means!" she cried despairingly.

"It means," he answered lightly, "that the child is not white; it   *25* means that you are not white."

A quick conception of all that this accusation meant for her nerved her with unwonted courage to deny it. "It is a lie; it is not true, I am white! Look at my hair, it is brown; and my eyes are gray, Armand, you know they are gray. And my skin is fair," seizing his wrist. "Look at my hand; whiter than yours, Armand," she laughed hysterically.

"As white as La Blanche's," he returned cruelly; and went away leaving her alone with their child.

When she could hold a pen in her hand, she sent a despairing letter to Madame Valmondé.

"My mother, they tell me I am not white. Armand has told me I am not white. For God's sake tell them it is not true. You must know it is not true. I shall die. I must die. I cannot be so unhappy, and live."

The answer that came was as brief: *30*

"My own Désirée: Come home to Valmondé; back to your mother who loves you. Come with your child."

When the letter reached Désirée she went with it to her husband's study, and laid it open upon the desk before which he sat. She was like a stone image; silent, white, motionless after she placed it there.

In silence he ran his cold eyes over the written words. He said nothing. "Shall I go, Armand?" she asked in tones sharp with agonized suspense.

"Yes, go."

"Do you want me to go?"   *35*

"Yes, I want you to go."

He thought Almighty God had dealt cruelly and unjustly with him; and felt, somehow, that he was paying Him back in kind when he stabbed thus into his wife's soul. Moreover he no longer loved her, because of the unconscious injury she had brought upon his home and his name.

She turned away like one stunned by a blow, and walked slowly towards the door, hoping he would call her back.

"Good-by, Armand," she moaned.

He did not answer her. That was his last blow at fate.   *40*

Désirée went in search of her child. Zandrine was pacing the sombre gallery with it. She took the little one from the nurse's arms with no word of explanation, and descending the steps, walked away, under the live-oak branches.

It was an October afternoon; the sun was just sinking. Out in the still fields the negroes were picking cotton.

Désirée had not changed the thin white garment nor the slippers which she wore. Her hair was uncovered and the sun's rays brought a golden gleam from its brown meshes. She did not take the broad, beaten road which led to the far-off plantation of Valmondé. She walked across a deserted field, where the stubble bruised her tender feet, so delicately shod, and tore her thin gown to shreds.

She disappeared among the reeds and willows that grew thick along the banks of the deep, sluggish bayou; and she did not come back again.

Some weeks later there was a curious scene enacted at L'Abri. In the centre of the smoothly swept back yard was a great bonfire. Armand Aubigny sat in the wide hallway that commanded a view of the spectacle; and it was he who dealt out to a half dozen negroes the material which kept this fire ablaze.   *45*

A graceful cradle of willow, with all its dainty furbishings, was laid upon the pyre, which had already been fed with the richness of a priceless *layette.*° Then there were silk gowns, and velvet and satin ones added to these; laces, too, and embroideries; bonnets and gloves; for the *corbeille* had been of rare quality.

The last thing to go was a tiny bundle of letters; innocent little scribblings that Désirée had sent to him during the days of their espousal. There was the remnant of one back in the drawer from which he took them. But it was not Désirée's; it was part of an old letter from his mother to his father. He read it. She was thanking God for the blessing of her husband's love:—

"But, above all," she wrote, "night and day, I thank the good God for having so arranged our lives that our dear Armand will never know that his mother, who adores him, belongs to the race that is cursed with the brand of slavery."

☐ *Outward Exploration: Discussion*

1. Explain Désirée's background.

2. Describe Désirée.

3. Describe Armand's personality. Why didn't he check into Désirée's past more thoroughly?

4. Explain the structure of the story.

———

layette: A complete outfit for a baby.

5. Why is Désirée so distraught when Armand suggests that she is not "white"? What are the implications of this judgment?

6. Why does Armand tell Désirée to go?

7. Is the story's ending a total surprise? Did Chopin play fair with us readers? Explain.

8. Do you think Armand knew the contents of his mother's letter before he cleaned out the desk for the bonfire? Explain.

9. Is the point of this story the surprise ending? If not, what is the story's point?

☐ *Outward Exploration: Writing*

1. Write a paper exploring Chopin's "Désirée's Baby" in some way.

2. Check with your reference librarian for sources that deal with the issue of *passing*. After gaining some background, write an essay about the concept using "Désirée's Baby" as an example (but do not feel you should limit yourself to that one story).

3. If you have ever been surprised by a revelation about your family or your own background, write an essay exploring your thoughts and feelings as well as the impact of the revelation on your day-to-day life.

4. Write an essay on a topic that suggested itself to you when you read this story.

Young Goodman Brown

Nathaniel Hawthorne

◻ *Inward Exploration*

Write at least one paragraph describing a time when you were tempted to do something that you knew you shouldn't do.

Young Goodman Brown came forth at sunset into the street at Salem village; but put his head back, after crossing the threshold, to exchange a parting kiss with his young wife. And Faith, as the wife was aptly named, thrust her own pretty head into the street, letting the wind play with the pink ribbons of her cap while she called to Goodman Brown.

"Dearest heart," whispered she, softly and rather sadly, when her lips were close to his ear, "prithee put off your journey until sunrise and sleep in your own bed to-night. A lone woman is troubled with such dreams and such thoughts that she's afeared of herself sometimes. Pray tarry with me this night, dear husband, of all nights in the year."

"My love and my Faith," replied young Goodman Brown, "of all nights in the year, this one night must I tarry away from thee. My journey, as thou callest it, forth and back again, must needs be done 'twixt now and sunrise. What, my sweet, pretty wife, dost thou doubt me already, and we but three months married?"

"Then God bless you!" said Faith, with the pink ribbons; "and may you find all well when you come back."

"Amen!" cried Goodman Brown. "Say thy prayers, dear Faith, and go to bed at dusk, and no harm will come to thee."

So they parted; and the young man pursued his way until, being about to turn the corner by the meeting-house, he looked back and saw the head of Faith still peeping after him with a melancholy air, in spite of her pink ribbons.

"Poor little Faith!" thought he, for his heart smote him. "What a wretch am I to leave her on such an errand! She talks of dreams, too. Methought as she spoke there was trouble in her face, as if a dream had warned her what work is to be done to-night. But no, no; 't would kill her to think it. Well, she's a blessed angel on earth, and after this one night I'll cling to her skirts and follow her to heaven."

With this excellent resolve for the future, Goodman Brown felt himself justified in making more haste on his present evil purpose. He had taken a dreary road, darkened by all the gloomiest trees of the forest, which barely stood aside to let the narrow path creep through, and closed immediately behind. It was all as lonely as could be; and there is this peculiarity in such a solitude, that the traveller knows not who may be concealed by the innumerable trunks and the thick boughs overhead; so that with lonely footsteps he may yet be passing through an unseen multitude.

"There may be a devilish Indian behind every tree," said Goodman Brown to himself; and he glanced fearfully behind him as he added, "What if the devil himself should be at my very elbow!"

His head being turned back, he passed a crook of the road, and, looking forward again, beheld the figure of a man, in grave and decent attire, seated at the foot of an old tree. He arose at Goodman Brown's approach and walked onward side by side with him.   10

"You are late, Goodman Brown," said he. "The clock of the Old South was striking as I came through Boston, and that is full fifteen minutes agone."

"Faith kept me back a while," replied the young man, with a tremor in his voice, caused by the sudden appearance of his companion, though not wholly unexpected.

It was now deep dusk in the forest, and deepest in that part of it where these two were journeying. As nearly as could be discerned, the second traveller was about fifty years old, apparently in the same rank of life as Goodman Brown, and bearing a considerable resemblance to him, though perhaps more in expression than features. Still they might have been taken for father and son. And yet, though the elder person was as simply clad as the younger, and as simple in manner too, he had an indescribable air of one who knew the world, and who would not have felt abashed at the governor's dinner table or in King William's court, were it possible that his affairs should call him thither. But the only thing about him that could be fixed upon as remarkable was his staff, which bore the likeness of a great black snake, so curiously wrought that it might almost be seen to twist and wriggle itself like a living serpent. This, of course, must have been an ocular deception, assisted by the uncertain light.

"Come, Goodman Brown," cried his fellow traveller, "this is a dull pace for the beginning of a journey. Take my staff, if you are so soon weary."

"Friend," said the other, exchanging his slow pace for a full stop,   15 "having kept covenant by meeting thee here, it is my purpose now to return whence I came. I have scruples touching the matter thou wot'st of."

"Sayest thou so?" replied he of the serpent, smiling apart. "Let us walk on, nevertheless, reasoning as we go; and if I convince thee not thou shalt turn back. We are but a little way in the forest yet."

"Too far! too far!" exclaimed the goodman, unconsciously resuming his walk. "My father never went into the woods on such an errand, nor his father before him. We have been a race of honest men and good Christians since the days of the martyrs; and shall I be the first of the name of Brown that ever took this path and kept"—

"Such company, thou wouldst say," observed the elder person, interpreting his pause. "Well said, Goodman Brown! I have been as well acquainted with your family as with ever a one among the Puritans; and that's no trifle to say. I helped your grandfather, the constable, when he lashed the Quaker woman so smartly through the streets of Salem; and it was I that brought your father a pitch-pine knot, kindled at my own hearth, to set fire to an Indian village, in King Philip's war. They were my good friends, both; and many a pleasant walk have we had along this path, and returned merrily after midnight. I would fain be friends with you for their sake."

"If it be as thou sayest," replied Goodman Brown, "I marvel they never spoke of these matters; or, verily, I marvel not, seeing that the least rumor of the sort would have driven them from New England. We are a people of prayer, and good works to boot, and abide no such wickedness."

"Wickedness or not," said the traveller with the twisted staff, "I *20* have a very general acquaintance here in New England. The deacons of many a church have drunk the communion wine with me; the selectmen of divers towns make me their chairman; and a majority of the Great and General Court are firm supporters of my interest. The governor and I, too—But these are state secrets."

"Can this be so?" cried Goodman Brown, with a stare of amazement at his undisturbed companion. "Howbeit, I have nothing to do with the governor and council; they have their own ways, and are no rule for a simple husbandman like me. But, were I to go on with thee, how should I meet the eye of that good old man, our minister, at Salem village? Oh, his voice would make me tremble both Sabbath day and lecture day."

Thus far the elder traveller had listened with due gravity; but now burst into a fit of irrepressible mirth, shaking himself so violently that his snake-like staff actually seemed to wriggle in sympathy.

"Ha! ha! ha!" shouted he again and again; then composing himself, "Well, go on, Goodman Brown, go on; but, prithee, don't kill me with laughing."

"Well, then, to end the matter at once," said Goodman Brown, considerably nettled, "there is my wife, Faith. It would break her dear little heart; and I'd rather break my own."

"Nay, if that be the case," answered the other, "e'en go thy ways, *25* Goodman Brown. I would not for twenty old women like the one hobbling before us that Faith should come to any harm."

As he spoke he pointed his staff at a female figure on the path, in whom Goodman Brown recognized a very pious and exemplary dame, who had taught him his catechism in youth, and was still his moral and spiritual adviser, jointly with the minister and Deacon Gookin.

"A marvel, truly that Goody Cloyse should be so far in the wilderness at nightfall," said he. "But with your leave, friend, I shall take a cut through the woods until we have left this Christian woman behind. Being a stranger to you, she might ask whom I was consorting with and whither I was going."

"Be it so," said his fellow-traveller. "Betake you to the woods, and let me keep the path."

Accordingly the young man turned aside, but took care to watch his companion, who advanced softly along the road until he had come within a staff's length of the old dame. She, meanwhile, was making the best of her way, with singular speed for so aged a woman, and mumbling some indistinct words—a prayer, doubtless—as she went. The traveller put forth his staff and touched her withered neck with what seemed the serpent's tail.

"The devil!" screamed the pious old lady.   30

"Then Goody Cloyse knows her old friend?" observed the traveller, confronting her and leaning on his writhing stick.

"Ah, forsooth, and is it your worship indeed?" cried the good dame. "Yea, truly is it, and in the very image of my old gossip, Goodman Brown, the grandfather of the silly fellow that now is. But—would your worship believe it?—my broomstick hath strangely disappeared, stolen, as I suspect, by that unhanged witch, Goody Cory, and that, too, when I was all anointed with the juice of smallage, and cinquefoil, and wolf's bane"—

"Mingled with fine wheat and the fat of a new-born babe," said the shape of old Goodman Brown.

"Ah, your worship knows the recipe," cried the old lady, cackling aloud. "So, as I was saying, being all ready for the meeting, and no horse to ride on, I made up my mind to foot it; for they tell me there is a nice young man to be taken into communion to-night. But now your good worship will lend me your arm, and we shall be there in a twinkling."

"That can hardly be," answered her friend. "I may not spare you   35 my arm, Goody Cloyse; but here is my staff, if you will."

So saying, he threw it down at her feet, where, perhaps, it assumed life, being one of the rods which its owner had formerly lent to the Egyptian magi. Of this fact, however, Goodman Brown could not take cognizance. He had cast up his eyes in astonishment, and, looking down again, beheld neither Goody Cloyse nor the serpentine staff, but his fellow-traveller alone, who waited for him as calmly as if nothing had happened.

"That old woman taught me my catechism," said the young man; and there was a world of meaning in this simple comment.

They continued to walk onward, while the elder traveller exhorted his companion to make good speed and persevere in the path, discoursing so aptly that his arguments seemed rather to spring up in the bosom of his auditor than to be suggested by himself. As they went, he plucked a branch of maple to serve for a walking stick, and began to strip it of the twigs and little boughs, which were wet with evening dew. The moment his fingers touched them they became strangely withered and dried up as with a week's sunshine. Thus the pair proceeded, at a good free pace, until suddenly, in a gloomy hollow of the road, Goodman Brown sat himself down on the stump of a tree and refused to go any farther.

"Friend," he said, stubbornly, "my mind is made up. Not another step will I budge on this errand. What if a wretched old woman do choose to go to the devil when I thought she was going to heaven: is that any reason why I should quit my dear Faith and go after her?"

"You will think better of this by and by," said his acquaintance, *40* composedly. "Sit here and rest yourself a while; and when you feel like moving again, there is my staff to help you along."

Without more words, he threw his companion the maple stick, and was as speedily out of sight as if he had vanished into the deepening gloom. The young man sat a few moments by the roadside, applauding himself greatly, and thinking with how clear a conscience he should meet the minister in his morning walk, nor shrink from the eye of good old Deacon Gookin. And what calm sleep would be his that very night, which was to have been spent so wickedly, but so purely and sweetly now, in the arms of Faith! Amidst these pleasant and praiseworthy meditations, Goodman Brown heard the tramp of horses along the road, and deemed it advisable to conceal himself within the verge of the forest, conscious of the guilty purpose that had brought him thither, though now so happily turned from it.

On came the hoof tramps and the voices of the riders, two grave old voices, conversing soberly as they drew near. These mingled sounds appeared to pass along the road, within a few yards of the young man's hiding-place; but, owing doubtless to the depth of the gloom at that particular spot, neither the travellers nor their steeds were visible. Though their figures brushed the small boughs by the wayside, it could not be seen that they intercepted, even for a moment, the faint gleam from the strip of bright sky athwart which they must have passed. Goodman Brown alternately crouched and stood on tiptoe, pulling aside the branches and thrusting forth his head as far as he durst without discerning so much as a shadow. It vexed him the more, because he could have sworn, were such a thing possible, that he recognized the voices of the minister and Deacon Gookin, jogging along quietly, as they were wont to do, when bound to some ordination or ecclesiastical council. While yet within hearing, one of the riders stopped to pluck a switch.

"Of the two, reverend sir," said the voice like the deacon's, "I had rather miss an ordination dinner than to-night's meeting. They tell me that some of our community are to be here from Falmouth and beyond, and others from Connecticut and Rhode Island, besides several of the

Indian powwows, who, after their fashion, know almost as much deviltry as the best of us. Moreover, there is a goodly young woman to be
taken into communion."

"Mighty well, Deacon Gookin!" replied the solemn old tones of the
minister. "Spur up, or we shall be late. Nothing can be done, you know,
until I get on the ground."

The hoofs clattered again; and the voices, talking so strangely in the   45
empty air, passed on through the forest, where no church had ever been
gathered or solitary Christian prayed. Whither, then, could these holy
men be journeying so deep into the heathen wilderness? Young Goodman Brown caught hold of a tree for support, being ready to sink down
on the ground, faint and overburdened with the heavy sickness of his
heart. He looked up to the sky, doubting whether there really was a
heaven above him. Yet there was the blue arch, and the stars brightening
in it.

"With heaven above and Faith below, I will yet stand firm against
the devil!" cried Goodman Brown.

While he still gazed upward into the deep arch of the firmament and
had lifted his hands to pray, a cloud, though no wind was stirring, hurried across the zenith and hid the brightening stars. The blue sky was
still visible, except directly overhead, where this black mass of cloud
was sweeping swiftly northward. Aloft in the air, as if from the depths
of the cloud, came a confused and doubtful sound of voices. Once the
listener fancied that he could distinguish the accents of towns-people of
his own, men and women, both pious and ungodly, many of whom he
had met at the communion table, and had seen others rioting at the
tavern. The next moment, so indistinct were the sounds, he doubted
whether he had heard aught but the murmur of the old forest, whispering without a wind. Then came a stronger swell of those familiar tones,
heard daily in the sunshine at Salem village, but never until now from a
cloud of night. There was one voice, of a young woman, uttering lamentations, yet with an uncertain sorrow, and entreating for some favor,
which, perhaps, it would grieve her to obtain; and all the unseen multitude, both saints and sinners, seemed to encourage her onward.

"Faith!" shouted Goodman Brown, in a voice of agony and desperation; and the echoes of the forest mocked him, crying, "Faith!
Faith!" as if bewildered wretches were seeking her all through the
wilderness.

The cry of grief, rage, and terror was yet piercing the night, when
the unhappy husband held his breath for a response. There was a
scream, drowned immediately in a louder murmur of voices, fading
into far-off laughter, as the dark cloud swept away, leaving the clear
and silent sky above Goodman Brown. But something fluttered lightly
down through the air and caught on the branch of a tree. The young
man seized it, and beheld a pink ribbon.

"My Faith is gone!" cried he after one stupefied moment. "There is *50*
no good on earth; and sin is but a name. Come, devil; for to thee is this
world given."

And, maddened with despair, so that he laughed loud and long, did
Goodman Brown grasp his staff and set forth again, at such a rate that
he seemed to fly along the forest path rather than to walk or run. The
road grew wilder and drearier and more faintly traced, and vanished at
length, leaving him in the heart of the dark wilderness, still rushing
onward with the instinct that guides mortal men to evil. The whole
forest was peopled with frightful sounds—the creaking of the trees, the
howling of wild beasts, and the yell of Indians; while sometimes the
wind tolled like a distant church bell, and sometimes gave a broad roar
around the traveller, as if all Nature were laughing him to scorn. But he
was himself the chief horror of the scene, and shrank not from its other
horrors.

"Ha! Ha! ha!" roared Goodman Brown when the wind laughed at
him. "Let us hear which will laugh loudest. Think not to frighten me
with your deviltry. Come witch, come wizard, come Indian powwow,
come devil himself, and here comes Goodman Brown. You may as well
fear him as he fear you."

In truth, all through the haunted forest there could be nothing more
frightful than the figure of Goodman Brown. On he flew among the
black pines, brandishing his staff with frenzied gestures, now giving
vent to an inspiration of horrid blasphemy, and now shouting forth such
laughter as set all the echoes of the forest laughing like demons around
him. The fiend in his own shape is less hideous than when he rages in
the breast of man. Thus sped the demoniac on his course, until, quivering among the trees, he saw a red light before him, as when the felled
trunks and branches of a clearing have been set on fire, and throw up
their lurid blaze against the sky, at the hour of midnight. He paused, in
a lull of the tempest that had driven him onward, and heard the swell of
what seemed a hymn, rolling solemnly from a distance with the weight
of many voices. He knew the tune; it was a familiar one in the choir of
the village meeting-house. The verse died heavily away, and was length-
ened by a chorus, not of human voices, but of all the sounds of the
benighted wilderness pealing in awful harmony together. Goodman
Brown cried out, and his cry was lost to his own ear by its unison with
the cry of the desert.

In the interval of silence he stole forward until the light glared full
upon his eyes. At one extremity of an open space, hemmed in by the
dark wall of the forest, arose a rock, bearing some rude, natural resemblance either to an altar or a pulpit, and surrounded by four blazing
pines, their tops aflame, their stems untouched, like candles at an evening meeting. The mass of foliage that had overgrown the summit of
the rock was all on fire, blazing high into the night and fitfully illumi-

nating the whole field. Each pendent twig and leafy festoon was in a blaze. As the red light arose and fell, a numerous congregation alternately shone forth, then disappeared in shadow, and again grew, as it were, out of the darkness, peopling the heart of the solitary woods at once.

"A grave and dark–clad company," quoth Goodman Brown.   55

In truth they were such. Among them, quivering to and fro between gloom and splendor, appeared faces that would be seen next day at the council board of the province, and others which, Sabbath after Sabbath, looked devoutly heavenward, and benignantly over the crowded pews, from the holiest pulpits in the land. Some affirm that the lady of the governor was there. At least there were high dames well known to her, and wives of honored husbands, and widows, a great multitude, and ancient maidens, all of excellent repute, and fair young girls, who trembled lest their mothers should espy them. Either the sudden gleams of light flashing over the obscure field bedazzled Goodman Brown, or he recognized a score of the church members of Salem village famous for their especial sanctity. Good old Deacon Gookin had arrived, and waited at the skirts of that venerable saint, his revered pastor. But, irreverently consorting with these grave, reputable, and pious people, these elders of the church, these chaste dames and dewy virgins, there were men of dissolute lives and women of spotted fame, wretches given over to all mean and filthy vice, and suspected even of horrid crimes. It was strange to see that the good shrank not from the wicked, nor were the sinners abashed by the saints. Scattered also among their pale-faced enemies were the Indian priests, or powwows, who had often scared their native forest with more hideous incantations than any known to English witchcraft.

"But where is Faith?" thought Goodman Brown; and, as hope came into his heart, he trembled.

Another verse of the hymn arose, a slow and mournful strain, such as the pious love, but joined to words which expressed all that our nature can conceive of sin, and darkly hinted at far more. Unfathomable to mere mortals is the lore of fiends. Verse after verse was sung; and still the chorus of the desert swelled between like the deepest tone of a mighty organ; and with the final peal of that dreadful anthem there came a sound, as if the roaring wind, the rushing streams, the howling beasts, and every other voice of the unconcerted wilderness were mingling and according with the voice of guilty man in homage to the prince of all. The four blazing pines threw up a loftier flame, and obscurely discovered shapes and visages of horror on the smoke wreaths above the impious assembly. At the same moment the fire on the rock shot redly forth and formed a flowing arch above its base, where now appeared a figure. With reverence be it spoken, the figure bore no slight similitude, both in garb and manner, to some grave divine of the New England churches.

"Bring forth the converts!" cried a voice that echoed through the field and rolled into the forest.

At the word, Goodman Brown stepped forth from the shadow of   60
the trees and approached the congregation, with whom he felt a loathful brotherhood by the sympathy of all that was wicked in his heart. He could have well-nigh sworn that the shape of his own dead father beckoned him to advance, looking downward from a smoke wreath, while a woman, with dim features of despair, threw out her hand to warn him back. Was it his mother? But he had no power to retreat one step, nor to resist, even in thought, when the minister and good old Deacon Gookin seized his arms and led him to the blazing rock. Thither came also the slender form of a veiled female, led between Goody Cloyse, that pious teacher of the catechism, and Martha Carrier, who had received the devil's promise to be queen of hell. A rampant hag was she. And there stood the proselytes beneath the canopy of fire.

"Welcome, my children," said the dark figure, "to the communion of your race. Ye have found thus young your nature and your destiny. My children, look behind you!"

They turned; and flashing forth, as it were, in a sheet of flame, the fiend worshippers were seen; the smile of welcome gleamed darkly on every visage.

"There," resumed the sable form, "are all whom ye have reverenced from youth. Ye deemed them holier than yourselves and shrank from your own sin, contrasting it with their lives of righteousness and prayerful aspirations heavenward. Yet here are they all in my worshipping assembly. This night it shall be granted you to know their secret deeds: how hoary-bearded elders of the church have whispered wanton words to the young maids of their households; how many a woman, eager for widows' weeds, has given her husband a drink at bedtime and let him sleep his last sleep in her bosom; how beardless youths have made haste to inherit their fathers' wealth; and how fair damsels—blush not, sweet ones—have dug little graves in the garden, and bidden me, the sole guest, to an infant's funeral. By the sympathy of your human hearts for sin ye shall scent out all the places—whether in church, bedchamber, street, field, or forest—where crime has been committed, and shall exult to behold the whole earth one stain of guilt, one mighty blood spot. Far more than this. It shall be yours to penetrate, in every bosom, the deep mystery of sin, the fountain of all wicked arts, and which inexhaustibly supplies more evil impulses than human power—than my power at its utmost—can make manifest in deeds. And now, my children, look upon each other."

They did so; and, by the blaze of the hell-kindled torches, the wretched man beheld his Faith, and the wife her husband, trembling before that unhallowed altar.

"Lo, there ye stand, my children," said the figure, in a deep and   65
solemn tone, almost sad with its despairing awfulness, as if his once

angelic nature could yet mourn for our miserable race. "Depending upon one another's hearts, ye had still hoped that virtue were not all a dream. Now are ye undeceived. Evil is the nature of mankind. Evil must be your only happiness. Welcome again, my children, to the communion of your race."

"Welcome," repeated the fiend worshippers, in one cry of despair and triumph.

And there they stood, the only pair, as it seemed, who were yet hesitating on the verge of wickedness in this dark world. A basin was hallowed, naturally, in the rock. Did it contain water, reddened by the lurid light? or was it blood? or, perchance, a liquid flame? Herein did the shape of evil dip his hand and prepare to lay the mark of baptism upon their foreheads, that they might be partakers of the mystery of sin, more conscious of the secret guilt of others, both in deed and thought, than they could now be of their own. The husband cast one look at his pale wife, and Faith at him. What polluted wretches would the next glance show them to each other, shuddering alike at what they disclosed and what they saw!

"Faith! Faith!" cried the husband, "look up to heaven, and resist the wicked one."

Whether Faith obeyed he knew not. Hardly had he spoken when he found himself amid calm night and solitude, listening to a roar of the wind which died heavily away through the forest. He staggered against the rock, and felt it chill and damp; while a hanging twig, that had been all on fire, besprinkled his cheek with the coldest dew.

The next morning young Goodman Brown came slowly into the street of Salem village, staring around him like a bewildered man. The good old minister was taking a walk along the graveyard to get an appetite for breakfast and meditate his sermon, and bestowed a blessing, as he passed, on Goodman Brown. He shrank from the venerable saint as if to avoid an anathema. Old Deacon Gookin was at domestic worship, and the holy words of his prayer were heard through the open window. "What God doth the wizard pray to?" quoth Goodman Brown. Goody Cloyse, that excellent old Christian, stood in the early sunshine at her own lattice, catechizing a little girl who had brought her a pint of morning's milk. Goodman Brown snatched away the child as from the grasp of the fiend himself. Turning the corner by the meeting-house, he spied the head of Faith, with the pink ribbons, gazing anxiously forth, and bursting into such joy at sight of him that she skipped along the street and almost kissed her husband before the whole village. But Goodman Brown looked sternly and sadly into her face, and passed on without a greeting.

Had Goodman Brown fallen asleep in the forest and only dreamed a wild dream of a witch-meeting?

Be it so if you will; but, alas! it was a dream of evil omen for young Goodman Brown. A stern, a sad, a darkly meditative, a distrustful, if

70

not a desperate man did he become from the night of that fearful dream. On the Sabbath day, when the congregation were singing a holy psalm, he could not listen because an anthem of sin rushed loudly upon his ear and drowned all the blessed strain. When the minister spoke from the pulpit with power and fervid eloquence, and, with his hand on the open Bible, of the sacred truths of our religion, and of saint-like lives and triumphant deaths, and of future bliss or misery unutterable, then did Goodman Brown turn pale, dreading lest the roof should thunder down upon the gray blasphemer and his hearers. Often, awaking suddenly at midnight, he shrank from the bosom of Faith; and at morning or eventide, when the family knelt down at prayer, he scowled and muttered to himself, and gazed sternly at his wife, and turned away. And when he had lived long, and was borne to his grave a hoary corpse, followed by Faith, an aged woman, and children and grandchildren, a goodly procession, besides neighbors not a few, they carved no hopeful verse upon his tombstone, for his dying hour was gloom.

☐ *Outward Exploration: Discussion*

1. Why does Goodman Brown go into the forest?
2. Describe the process by which Brown's resistance to the man with the staff slowly erodes.
3. Describe Brown's personality and beliefs.
4. According to the devil, what exactly will Brown and Faith receive once they are baptized into evil?
5. What exactly is Brown's reason for refusing the baptism and lifting his eyes to heaven?
6. Was Brown's "escape" fortunate? In other words, how does Hawthorne want us to feel about Brown—are we supposed to admire his piety?
7. Comment on the symbolism in the story.

☐ *Outward Exploration: Writing*

1. We all take symbolic walks into the forest of temptation. Select one time when you were tempted to do something that you believed you really shouldn't do. Detail the event, exploring the dynamics of the situation, your reasoning then and your insights now as you look back on the event. Using "Young Goodman Brown" either as a point of departure or as a touchstone throughout, compare the psychology

of his decision making to yours. In what ways is Brown's encounter similar to and different from yours?

2. Analyze the story. In the process, comment on the accuracy or inaccuracy of Hawthorne's depiction of how people make moral decisions, using yourself as an example.

3. Ambiguity makes stories more interesting and life more complicated. After analyzing Hawthorne's use of ambiguity, consider the ways life is ambiguous for you. Compare your reactions to ambiguity in your life to your reactions to Hawthorne's ambiguity in the story. Then compare your reactions to ambiguity to those of Brown.

The Dark Wood

JANETTE TURNER HOSPITAL

☐ *Inward Exploration*

Write a paragraph explaining your thoughts and feelings about the phrase "The Dark Wood."

Angela turned off the car radio, not wanting to hear about Princess   *1*
Margaret and boyfriend. Not at high speed on the turnpike with one
death behind her and another one waiting ahead.

She wondered: why do I always pick the wrong men? She was
surely second only to Her Highness in that respect, although she had
been sufficiently adroit never to marry her mistakes and had been spared
the embarrassment of having her terminal romances splashed across the
international press.

And of course her work helped. She could become so absorbed in
cases that she would not remember if there was anyone waiting for her
at home or not. When she thought "home" she meant whichever one-
and-a-half-room studio her Bokharas, pillows, and plants were gracing
at that moment. She travelled light. Decorating style: expensive stark.
Portable elegance. Nothing that could not be relocated in three trips of
her MG with car rack. She moved in and out of her life.

On the turnpike she played with her blinkers like a magician, changing lanes, moving, weaving, dodging. Disengaging. Brendan, however,
kept circling her consciousness like the foggy rings around Saturn.
Brendan and his children, Brendan and his crisis, Brendan and his im-
portunate pleading eyes—as persistent as that green Chrysler dogging
her, arrogantly suffusing her rear-view mirror. With deft timing she
slithered into a momentary space in the next lane then back into the
fast lane two cars ahead. The Chrysler, she saw with pleasure, was a
dwindling green dot in her mirror.

She thought with contempt: all my men have been tail-gaters.   *5*
Clinging. Hampering.

Well, there it was. Death of another relationship. She could not be
encumbered with the debris of Brendan's life when her work was so
important, people depending on her, matters of life and death. There
had been, of course, grey spaces of betrayal in his eyes. That was the
way it was with her men. Impossible demands and messy endings.

But this was misting away at the periphery of her mind. She
changed lanes, jockeying for the exit. She always stayed in the fast lane

until the last possible minute, defying entanglements, winning the off ramp. She parked in her reserved space at the hospital.

Odours come coded. The brackish tang of seaweed can sting the nostrils and suddenly one is feeling for a pitted anklet of scars and hearing an old scream hurtle off the rocks, childhood blood spurting from oyster shells.

Angela smelled the familiar wave of disinfectant, bed pans, assorted medicinal fumes, and felt invigorated. Other people might turn faint at that smell but Angela inhaled power. Within its ambience she had a certain licence to bind and loose. She made mortal arrangements.

Her case-load was heavy but it was the latest admission which most   10
immediately concerned her. The bed of Beatrice Grossetti floated in its own haze of mustiness. The smell of the last century, thought Angela; of oiled furniture and old photographs; the smell of a person long unused.

Only a small fetal arc disturbed the bedding but the face on the pillow was gnome-like and ancient. Angela glanced at her clipboard. This was the clinical data: Beatrice Grossetti was seventy years old. No living relatives. Weight: eighty pounds.

The ancient eyes of the child-body opened.

Angela said briskly, "Good morning, Miss Grossetti."

"*Mrs.* Grossetti. Are you the doctor?"

"Not a medical doctor. I'm here to help you sort out anything that   15
might be worrying you."

The eyes closed again. "I thought the clergy did that."

"They do, if that's what you prefer. Would you like to see a priest?"

"No." Mrs. Grossetti's eyes, startled and skittish as dragonflies, darted out from cover. "I don't know . . . perhaps later. . . . Is it so urgent?"

She was wounded now, a cornered animal.

Angela, releaser of traps, liberator of caged spirits, sat beside   20
the bed.

"No rush," she said.

She was confident that the timing depended on her patient and herself. None of her cases had ever gone before they were ready. She had a certain knack, and the dying have instincts of their own.

"You will know when. And I will be with you."

Mrs. Grossetti's face contorted itself into what would have been a scream if any sound had come out. She clutched at Angela who took both gnarled hands between her own, leaning forward to press them against her cheek.

"It's all right, it's all right," she murmured. "You're not alone. I am   25
with you."

"How can *knowing* . . . how can just the *knowing* . . . ?" The voice of Mrs. Grossetti struggled to assert itself over some rushing undertow.

"Two days ago everything was . . . *usual.* Slow and weak . . . just the usual slow and weak . . . just age. I watered my geraniums and my tomatoes. They're ripening so I have to watch out for the pigeons. . . . I grow them in my window box you know, they'll be ready in about ten days. . . . And then my . . . Mr. Bernstein, the man in my little supermarket . . . he said—such a nice gentleman—he said: 'I'm worried about you, Beatrice. You're looking a little thinner every time I see you. I wish you'd see a doctor.' And just to please him, you know. . . ."

There was a long pause while Mrs. Grossetti's forces deployed themselves. They tapped some wild energy of insight and she sat up abruptly.

"But nothing has changed! Just *knowing* cannot make any difference. Nothing has changed. I want my tomatoes."

She slumped back wearily.

"Couldn't I go home to my tomatoes?" she pleaded. "Don't you   30
think I could just stay home until. . . ." She turned to the wall. "If anything is going to happen, I'd rather be home. I *would* like to see my tomatoes ripen. I'm frightened here. Couldn't I go home? Nothing has happened, except the knowing. Couldn't I go home, please? Just *knowing* can't make any difference."

"It always does make a difference. For everyone."

"I want to *un*-know! I only came as a favour to Mr. Bernstein. Now I want to go away again. Couldn't I, please? Please . . . ?"

After a while Angela gently freed herself from the fingers closed tightly on sleep and hope.

It was well known to the friends of Dr. Angela Carson that she did not like to be paged for personal calls while she was at the hospital. Although she did not explain it in so many words, it seemed to her as obscene as surreptitiously reading a paperback (neatly hidden inside the prayer book) at a funeral service. Consequently when she was summoned to the phone she knew it would be Brendan. No one else, at the moment anyway, would be so rash and desperate. Jacob would have done the same thing once. And then Charles. But there it was again. Birds of a feather.

"Angela, we have to talk. I can't believe you meant what you said   35
yesterday. I'll pick you up at the hospital this evening and we'll go out for dinner. You've been over-reacting because you're overworked."

"Brendan, you know I hate to be called here. Anything you might have to say is irrelevant to me while I am working."

He said wearily: "Angela, I fail to see how some sort of semihuman robot can help the dying."

"Goodbye, Brendan."

"Angela! For god's sake! I don't even understand what happened. What are you afraid of?"

"I'm not afraid of anything. I have responsibilities."   40

"But a visit, for heaven's sake! Do you want me to surrender the right ever to see my children?"

"Of course not. But you can't expect me to get involved in that sort of draining familial situation."

"What's draining about a visit that's already *over?* You're being so irrational. . . ."

She replaced the receiver delicately on its hook.

In all honesty, she thought, I cannot blame myself for this fiasco.   *45*
She had not, after all, been anticipating overnight visits from his children. Infrequent or otherwise.

Angela's profession placed her under a heavy moral obligation. The dying cannot postpone the gathering up of loose ends and the settling of accounts. She owed it to her cases to lead an uncluttered life, to be capable of undivided attention, compassion, total commitment.

When Angela reached the door of Beatrice Grossetti's room, a young intern was moving a stethoscope about her body, pausing and listening, his face creased with solemn inner deliberation. As though he were sounding an old hull for seaworthiness, Angela thought.

"Doctor?" asked Mrs. Grossetti in a small apologetic voice. "What can you tell me?"

As she spoke she reached out tentatively, supplicatingly, and touched his arm. The young intern flinched, moving aside to put his equipment back in its case.

"You're in good hands, Mrs. Grossetti." He smiled paternally.   *50*
"We'll take expert care of you here."

He nodded at Angela as he left the room, flushing slightly before the direct baleful impact of her eyes. It was curious, she thought with anger, the way so many people cringed from contact with death. As though it were catching. As though the patient were already a leper, an outcast, no longer one of us. She had seen it in doctors, relatives, visitors.

The familiar look of shame suffused Mrs. Grossetti's face, the embarrassment of imposing on the living. Angela saw the tears and instinctively leaned over and kissed her gently on the forehead.

"Tell me about yourself, Mrs. Grossetti. Tell me how you came to have your beautiful name. Beatrice has always been one of my favourites, especially if you pronounce it the Italian way."

"I can't blame them, I suppose. It's natural, isn't it?" replied Mrs. Grossetti who walked down her own paths. "You are different though. I suppose you see so many . . . so much of this . . . it seems ordinary to you."

"I do see a lot. Perhaps the difference is the doctors are fighting   *55*
against death. But you see I share it, I stay with my patients. No one is left alone."

"Are you afraid of being alone?"

Angela was disconcerted. "No! Oh no. Not me. I don't want *you* to feel alone."

"I would feel less alone with my geraniums and tomatoes than here. It is very cruel to keep me here. I've lived, you know. I've seen a lot. Buried my only son (he was just a child) and my husband. And a good many friends. I've seen a lot of . . . not as many as you perhaps, but I'm no stranger to . . . at least, I didn't think I was."

Mrs. Grossetti drifted in and out of sleep. Angela had other cases to attend to and she came and went. But she checked with Beatrice every hour. She had an instinct about these things.

Sometimes the frail body stirred and whimpered, and Angela would   60
sit and hold her hand.

"Mrs. Grossetti? I'm here. Is there anything you want?"

"Beatrice. My name is Beatrice."

"It's such a beautiful name."

"My father loved Dante. He taught in a college. My father, that is. You know Dante's Beatrice?"

"Yes indeed. I took one whole course on him in college myself. The   65
professor used to make us recite the Italian aloud because it sounded so beautiful. *I' son Beatrice che ti faccio andare. . . .*"

"Is that the part where she meets him in paradise?"

"No. It's at the beginning, in the dark wood. When he was lost and afraid."

"Such a luxury. To believe there was somebody waiting for him. . . . And then finally all that light and peace. Do you believe it?"

Angela said soothingly, as to a child: "Perhaps, perhaps. I don't know."

"I used to. I wish I still could."   70

"That's not so important. I do know that death itself is a moment of joy and peacefulness. I can *promise* you. I have *seen* it over and over again."

"But after that you can't know, can you, doctor? I wish I'd never been a Catholic. It keeps you scared up to your very last breath."

"Do you want to see a priest?"

"Not yet, not yet. I want to see my tomatoes ripen."

Beatrice slept again and Angela went about her rounds.   75

The surfacing into speech was less frequent, the exchanges with Beatrice more fragmented as the afternoon wore on.

"It is so strange," she said once, quite suddenly, "to think of the tomatoes ripening next week without me. Ripening and rotting all by themselves."

Acceptance, Angela thought. The final stage. "Shall I bring a priest now?"

Beatrice opened her eyes and turned to face Angela.

"You're in such a hurry, doctor. Determined to see me off properly,   80
aren't you?"

"You are a Catholic, Beatrice. It is customary. . . ."

"Yes, yes. For the final promises. And will you believe him? Will
you find the promises reassuring?"

Angela, caught off guard, almost said: I'm not the one who is dying.

Instead she said: "It is what *you* believe that matters, Beatrice."

"It doesn't matter to you yet, doctor. Things *are,* things *are*—   85
whatever we believe. I believed I was healthy two days ago."

She sighed and seemed to lapse back into sleep. Angela was about
to go but Beatrice seized her hand.

"Don't go, doctor. I'm afraid. I'm so frightened."

Angela slipped her arm under the trembling shoulders. On impulse
she raised Beatrice and cuddled her as though she were a small child.
The figure felt light as an infant. Angela rocked back and forth on the
bed, crooning softly.

As Beatrice slithered back across the hazy border into unconscious-
ness, her fingers curled themselves around Angela's wrist. The head,
under its wispy halo of silver grey, sank a little more heavily against
Angela's shoulder. Angela made no attempt to extricate herself. She
continued to rock back and forth, singing a lullaby.

The eyes of the night-shift nurse widened. She stood indecisively in   90
the doorway with her tray of medications. Dr. Angela Carson seemed
oblivious to her presence so she left again. It was something, she
thought with wonder, to recount at coffee break.

An orderly arrived with a note. Angela surfaced as from a great
depth, swaying slightly, to read it.

"Tell Brendan . . . tell the gentleman I can't come down," she said.
"I have to work all night."

She went on stroking Beatrice's hair, rocking, singing.

Shortly after midnight, Beatrice began to struggle.

"No!" she cried out. "No! No! No!"   95

"Shall I bring a priest?"

"No! No!"

Angela held her. "It's all right, Beatrice. I'm here. It's all right."

Beatrice was gasping, scooping in air with a greedy bronchial rattling. Her body tightened and bucked. Angela buzzed for the nurse and
for emergency help, whispering caressingly: "Let go, Beatrice. Just relax and let go now. It's easy, it's peaceful, it's not worth hanging on.
You're *there* now."

Convulsion.   100

With wholly unexpected energy, Beatrice slapped Angela across
the face.

"You are making me sick." Her words flew like grapeshot, low and deadly. "If it's so easy, why don't you try it?" And then, like a baleful Cassandra: "Look! I see the bones behind your face. Go away, you fool, go away, go away, go away!"

Angela drew back from the crescendo of hysteria. She felt disoriented, drunken as a ship snagged suddenly on an uncharted rock. She had a sensation of internal puncture, of ominous seepage. She made way for nurses and the doctor, she moved like a sleep-walker down the corridor.

The cry of Beatrice, a rattling network of panic and malevolent laughter, billowed after her like a vast cobweb, endlessly sticky, grotesquely caressing, wisping away gradually before the blessings of sedation.

Angela sat trembling behind the wheel of her car, poised at the mouth of the entry ramp, unable to propel herself into the slipstream of the turnpike. Already she was reproaching herself for a moment of professional inadequacy. Never before had she allowed one of her cases to die alone. This, she saw clearly, was the cause of her distress.

So late at night the traffic was thin but it hurtled by at a menacing speed, headlamps glaring in the dark like burning eye sockets. There seemed to be a fog of hazard, randomness, in the night air. Suddenly she was astonished that she had miraculously survived so many circuits of that urban racetrack.

Another car purred up the entry ramp behind her and its lights bathed her in gold. She was swamped by a panic compelling as nausea. From out of the heart of the radiance came a rhythm of horns, stern as the trumpets of angels. Beatrice stood on her dark side, mocking.

Angela felt herself to be ten years old again, teetering at the tip of the highest diving board, not knowing how to dive, distant figures far below calling encouragement, the line of people on the ladder rungs growing impatient, the board swaying precariously, no return possible.

She put her car suddenly into reverse, swerved crazily around the vehicle behind her, backed off the ramp, and returned to the parking lot at the hospital where she collapsed over her steering wheel, shaking violently.

The chill air of the parking lot sobered her. But even before she located the night nurse she knew she would be too late.

"It was very peaceful," the nurse said. "She never regained consciousness."

Of course, Angela thought, it could be explained by malevolence. Revenge against youth, against the living. Statistically it was not significant. All the others, every single one, had gone gently, slipping quietly into beatitude, grateful for her presence.

There was, she knew from years of experience, a certain amount of choice at the end. As regards timing, Beatrice had chosen to deny her the last peaceful coda. Just this once she had missed out on the epiphany. Yes.

As she grew calmer she went back to her car, but when she tried to start it the violent trembling returned. She hugged herself, shivering, and waited for the malaise to pass.

❑ *Outward Exploration: Discussion*

1. What is the significance of the story's title?
2. What is her problem with Brendan—why does she see their relationship as dead?
3. Why does Beatrice want to be at home and see her tomatoes rather than stay in the hospital?
4. In the first paragraph, Angela thinks of "one death behind her and another one waiting ahead." What does that mean?
5. Describe Angela's personality.
6. Why does Beatrice verbally attack Angela as she nears death?
7. Why is Angela so shaken by Beatrice's attack?

❑ *Outward Exploration: Writing*

1. Janette Turner Hospital suggests in the story that the qualities which make a person good at a job may be the disadvantages in his or her personal life. What qualities and personality traits would make a person good at whatever career or profession you are contemplating? What impact would those same qualities have on your personal life? Consider these questions carefully; don't settle for the first responses that occur to you. You may even need to talk to people in the profession to get their ideas of the key personality traits. Analyze Hospital's story and use it as a point of departure or as a touchstone in your essay.
2. Analyze the story, making connections to your own thoughts, feelings, and experiences where appropriate.

To Build a Fire

JACK LONDON

◻ *Inward Exploration*

Write at least one paragraph about the biggest mistake or miscalculation you ever made. What caused it? What were its results? Had anyone warned you about it before you did it? If so, why did you ignore the warning?

Day had broken cold and grey, exceedingly cold and grey, when   1
the man turned aside from the main Yukon° trail and climbed the high
earth-bank, where a dim and little-travelled trail led eastward through
the fat spruce timberland. It was a steep bank, and he paused for breath
at the top, excusing the act to himself by looking at his watch. It was
nine o'clock. There was no sun nor hint of sun, though there was not a
cloud in the sky. It was a clear day, and yet there seemed an intangible
pall over the face of things, a subtle gloom that made the day dark, and
that was due to the absence of sun. This fact did not worry the man.
He was used to the lack of sun. It had been days since he had seen the
sun, and he knew that a few more days must pass before that cheerful
orb, due south, would just peep above the skyline and dip immediately
from view.

The man flung a look back along the way he had come. The Yukon°
lay a mile wide and hidden under three feet of ice. On top of this ice
were as many feet of snow. It was all pure white, rolling in gentle undulations where the ice jams of the freeze-up had formed. North and
south, as far as his eye could see, it was unbroken white, save for a dark
hairline that curved and twisted from around the spruce-covered island
to the south, and that curved and twisted away into the north, where it
disappeared behind another spruce-covered island. This dark hairline
was the trail—the main trail—that led south five hundred miles to the
Chilcoot Pass, Dyea, and salt water; and that led north seventy miles
to Dawson, and still on to the north a thousand miles to Nulato,° and

---

Yukon: a large subarctic region in Canada that borders Alaska. It was the site of an 1897
gold rush.
Yukon: The Yukon River flows across Alaska, from the Yukon Territory to the Bering
Sea.
Chilcoot Pass, Dyea, and *Nulato:* Chilcoot Pass is a mountain pass between the Yukon
Territory and Alaska. It was used by those seeking gold to reach Dawson, the town at
the head of the Klondike River. Dyea was a village near the Chilcoot Pass. Nulato was
an Indian village in Alaska.

finally to St. Michael, on the Bering Sea, a thousand miles and half a thousand more.

But all this—the mysterious, far-reaching hairline trail, the absence of sun from the sky, the tremendous cold, and the strangeness and weirdness of it all—made no impression on the man. It was not because he was long used to it. He was a newcomer in the land, a *chechaquo,*° and this was his first winter. The trouble with him was that he was without imagination. He was quick and alert in the things of life, but only in the things, and not in the significances. Fifty degrees below zero meant eighty-odd degrees of frost. Such fact impressed him as being cold and uncomfortable, and that was all. It did not lead him to meditate upon his frailty as a creature of temperature, and upon man's frailty in general, able only to live within certain narrow limits of heat and cold; and from there on it did not lead him to the conjectural field of immortality and man's place in the universe. Fifty degrees below zero stood for a bite of frost that hurt and that must be guarded against by the use of mittens, ear flaps, warm moccasins, and thick socks. Fifty degrees below zero. That there should be anything more to it than that was a thought that never entered his head.

As he turned to go on, he spat speculatively. There was a sharp explosive crackle that startled him. He spat again. And again, in the air, before it could fall to the snow, the spittle crackled. He knew that at fifty below spittle crackled on the snow, but this spittle had crackled in the air. Undoubtedly it was colder than fifty below—how much colder he did not know. But the temperature did not matter. He was bound for the old claim on the left fork of Henderson Creek, where the boys were already. They had come over across the divide from the Indian Creek country, while he had come the roundabout way to take a look at the possibilities of getting out logs in the spring from the islands in the Yukon. He would be in to camp by six o'clock; a bit after dark, it was true, but the boys would be there, a fire would be going, and a hot supper would be ready. As for lunch, he pressed his hand against the protruding bundle under his jacket. It was also under his shirt, wrapped up in a handkerchief and lying against the naked skin. It was the only way to keep the biscuits from freezing. He smiled agreeably to himself as he thought of those biscuits, each cut open and sopped in bacon grease, and each enclosing a generous slice of fried bacon.

He plunged in among the big spruce trees. The trail was faint. A foot of snow had fallen since the last sled had passed over, and he was glad he was without a sled, travelling light. In fact, he carried nothing but the lunch wrapped in the handkerchief. He was surprised, however, at the cold. It certainly was cold, he concluded, as he rubbed his numb nose and cheekbones with his mittened hand. He was a warm-

5

---

chechaquo: a tenderfoot or greenhorn.

whiskered man, but the hair on his face did not protect the high cheek-bones and the eager nose that thrust itself aggressively into the frosty air.

At the man's heels trotted a dog, a big native husky, the proper wolf-dog, grey-coated and without any visible or temperamental difference from its brother, the wild wolf. The animal was depressed by the tremendous cold. It knew that it was no time for travelling. Its instinct told it a truer tale than was told to the man by the man's judgment. In reality, it was not merely colder than fifty below zero; it was colder than sixty below, than seventy below. It was seventy-five below zero. Since the freezing point is thirty-two above zero, it meant that one hundred and seven degrees of frost obtained. The dog did not know anything about thermometers. Possibly in its brain there was no sharp consciousness of a condition of very cold such as was in the man's brain. But the brute had its instinct. It experienced a vague but menacing apprehension that subdued it and made it slink along at the man's heels, and that made it question eagerly every unwonted movement of the man as if expecting him to go into camp or to seek shelter somewhere and build a fire. The dog had learned fire, and it wanted fire, or else to burrow under the snow and cuddle its warmth away from the air.

The frozen moisture of its breathing had settled on its fur in a fine powder of frost, and especially were its jowls, muzzle, and eyelashes whitened by its crystal breath. The man's red beard and moustache were likewise frosted, but more solidly, the deposit taking the form of ice and increasing with every warm, moist breath he exhaled. Also, the man was chewing tobacco, and the muzzle of ice held his lips so rigidly that he was unable to clear his chin when he expelled the juice. The result was a crystal beard of the colour and solidity of amber was increasing its length on his chin. If he fell down it would shatter itself, like glass, into brittle fragments. But he did not mind the appendage. It was the penalty all tobacco chewers paid in that country, and he had been out before in two cold snaps. They had not been so cold as this, he knew, but by the spirit thermometer° at Sixty Mile° he knew they had been registered at fifty below and at fifty-five.

He held on through the level stretch of woods for several miles, crossed a wide flat of nigger heads,° and dropped down a bank to the frozen bed of a small stream. This was Henderson Creek, and he knew he was ten miles from the forks. He looked at his watch. It was ten o'clock. He was making four miles an hour, and he calculated that he would arrive at the forks at half-past twelve. He decided to celebrate that event by eating his lunch there.

---

spirit thermometer: The word *spirit* refers to alcohol.
Sixty Mile: a village located forty miles west of Dawson near the Alaskan border.
nigger heads: a slang term referring to rocks and boulders which were exposed above the snow and ice.

The dog dropped in again at his heels, with a tail drooping discouragement, as the man swung along the creek bed. The furrow of the old sled trail was plainly visible, but a dozen inches of snow covered up the marks of the last runners. In a month no man had come up or down that silent creek. The man held steadily on. He was not much given to thinking, and just then particularly he had nothing to think about save that he would eat lunch at the forks and that at six o'clock he would be in camp with the boys. There was nobody to talk to; and, had there been, speech would have been impossible because of the ice muzzle on his mouth. So he continued monotonously to chew tobacco and to increase the length of his amber beard.

Once in a while the thought reiterated itself that it was very cold *10* and that he had never experienced such cold. As he walked along he rubbed his cheekbones and nose with the back of his mittened hand. He did this automatically, now and again changing hands. But, rub as he would, the instant he stopped his cheekbones went numb, and the following instant the end of his nose went numb. He was sure to frost his cheeks; he knew that, and experienced a pang of regret that he had not devised a nose strap of the sort Bud wore in cold snaps. Such a strap passed across the cheeks, as well, and saved them. But it didn't matter much, after all. What were frosted cheeks? A bit painful, that was all; they were never serious.

Empty as the man's mind was of thoughts, he was keenly observant, and he noticed the changes in the creeks, the curves and bends and timber jams, and always he sharply noted where he placed his feet. Once, coming round a bend, he shied abruptly, like a startled horse, curved away from the place where he had been walking, and retreated several paces back along the trail. The creek he knew was frozen clear to the bottom—no creek could contain water in that arctic winter—but he knew also that there were springs that bubbled out from the hillsides and ran along under the snow and on top of the ice of the creek. He knew that the coldest snaps never froze these springs, and he knew likewise their danger. They were traps. They hid pools of water under the snow that might be three inches deep, or three feet. Sometimes a skin of ice half an inch thick covered them, and in turn was covered by the snow. Sometimes there were alternate layers of water and ice skin, so that when one broke through he kept on breaking through for a while, sometimes wetting himself to the waist.

That was why he had shied in such a panic. He had felt the give under his feet and heard the crackle of a snow-hidden ice skin. And to get his feet wet in such a temperature meant trouble and danger. At the very least it meant delay, for he would be forced to stop and build a fire, and under its protection to bare his feet while he dried his socks and moccasins. He stood and studied the creek bed and its banks, and decided that the flow of water came from the right. He reflected awhile, rubbing his nose and cheeks, then skirted to the left, stepping gingerly and testing the footing for each step. Once clear of the danger, he took a fresh chew of tobacco and swung along at his four-mile gait.

In the course of the next two hours he came upon several similar traps. Usually the snow above the hidden pools had a sunken, candied appearance that advertised the danger. Once again, however, he compelled the dog to go on in front. The dog did not want to go. It hung back until the man shoved it forward, and then it went quickly across the white, unbroken surface. Suddenly it broke through, floundered to one side, and got away to firmer footing. It had wet its forefeet and legs, and almost immediately the water that clung to it turned to ice. It made quick efforts to lick the ice off its legs, then dropped down in the snow and began to bite out the ice that had formed between the toes. This was a matter of instinct. To permit the ice to remain would mean sore feet. It did not know this. It merely obeyed the mysterious prompting that arose from the deep crypts of its being. But the man knew, having achieved a judgment on the subject, and he removed the mitten from his right hand and helped to tear out the ice particles. He did not expose his fingers more than a minute, and was astonished at the swift numbness that smote them. It certainly was cold. He pulled on the mitten hastily, and beat the hand savagely across the chest.

At twelve o'clock the day was at its brightest. Yet the sun was too far south on its winter journey to clear the horizon. The bulge of the earth intervened between it and Henderson Creek, where the man walked under a clear sky at noon and cast no shadow. At half-past twelve, to the minute, he arrived at the forks of the creek. He was pleased at the speed he had made. If he kept it up, he would certainly be with the boys by six. He unbuttoned his jacket and shirt and drew forth his lunch. The action consumed no more than a quarter of a minute, yet in that brief moment the numbness laid hold of the exposed fingers. He did not put the mitten on, but, instead, struck the fingers a dozen sharp smashes against his leg. Then he sat down on a snow-covered log to eat. The sting that followed upon the striking of his fingers against his leg ceased so quickly that he was startled. He had had no chance to take a bite of biscuit. He struck the fingers repeatedly and returned them to the mitten, baring the other hand for the purpose of eating. He tried to take a mouthful, but the ice muzzle prevented. He had forgotten to build a fire and thaw out. He chuckled at his foolishness, and as he chuckled he noted the numbness creeping into the exposed fingers. Also, he noted that the stinging which had first come to his toes when he sat down was already passing away. He wondered whether the toes were warm or numb. He moved them inside the moccasins and decided that they were numb.

He pulled the mitten on hurriedly and stood up. He was a bit frightened. He stamped up and down until the stinging returned into the feet. It certainly was cold, was his thought. That man from Sulphur Creek had spoken the truth when telling how cold it sometimes got in the country. And he had laughed at him at the time! That showed one must not be too sure of things. There was no mistake about it, it *was* cold. He strode up and down, stamping his feet and threshing his arms, until reassured by the returning warmth. Then he got out matches and proceeded to make a fire. From the undergrowth, where high water of the previous spring had lodged a supply of seasoned twigs, he got his firewood. Working carefully from a small beginning, he soon had a roaring fire, over which he thawed the ice from his face and in the protection of which he ate his biscuits. For the moment the cold of space was outwitted. The dog took satisfaction in the fire, stretching out close enough for warmth and far enough away to escape being singed.

When the man had finished, he filled his pipe and took his comfortable time over a smoke. Then he pulled on his mittens, settled the earflaps of his cap firmly about his ears, and took the creek trail up the left fork. The dog was disappointed and yearned back towards the fire. This man did not know cold. Possibly all the generations of his ancestry had been ignorant of cold, of real cold, of cold one hundred and seven degrees below freezing point. But the dog knew; all its ancestry knew, and it had inherited the knowledge. And it knew that it was not good to walk abroad in such fearful cold. It was the time to lie snug in a hole in the snow and wait for a curtain of cloud to be drawn across the face of outer space whence this cold came. On the other hand, there was no keen intimacy between the dog and the man. The one was the toil slave of the other, and the only caresses it had ever received were the caresses of the whip lash and of harsh and menacing throat sounds that threatened the whip lash. So the dog made no effort to communicate its apprehension to the man. It was not concerned in the welfare of the man; it was for its own sake that it yearned back towards the fire. But the man whistled, and spoke to it with the sound of whip lashes, and the dog swung in at the man's heels and followed after.

The man took a chew of tobacco and proceeded to start a new amber beard. Also, his moist breath quickly powdered with white his moustache, eyebrows, and lashes. There did not seem to be so many springs on the left fork of the Henderson, and for half an hour the man saw no signs of any. And then it happened. At a place where there were no signs, where the soft, unbroken snow seemed to advertise solidity beneath, the man broke through. It was not deep. He wet himself halfway to the knees before he floundered out to the firm crust.

He was angry, and cursed his luck aloud. He had hoped to get into camp with the boys at six o'clock, and this would delay him an hour, for he would have to build a fire and dry out his footgear. This was imperative at that low temperature—he knew that much; and he turned aside to the bank, which he climbed. On top, tangled in the underbrush about the trunks of several small spruce trees, was a highwater deposit of dry firewood—sticks and twigs, principally, but also larger portions of seasoned branches and fine, dry, last year's grasses. He threw down several large pieces on top of the snow. This served for a foundation and prevented the young flame from drowning itself in the snow it otherwise would melt. The flame he got by touching a match to a small shred of birch bark that he took from his pocket. This burned even more readily than paper. Placing it on the foundation, he fed the young flame with wisps of dry grass and with the tiniest dry twigs.

He worked slowly and carefully, keenly aware of his danger. Gradually, as the flame grew stronger, he increased the size of the twigs with which he fed it. He squatted in the snow pulling the twigs out from their entanglement in the brush and feeding directly to the flame. He knew there must be no failure. When it is seventy-five below zero, a man must not fail in his first attempt to build a fire—that is, if his feet are wet. If his feet are dry, and he fails, he can run along the trail for half a mile and restore his circulation. But the circulation of wet and freezing feet cannot be restored by running when it is seventy-five below. No matter how fast he runs, the wet feet will freeze the harder.

All this the man knew. The old-timer on Sulphur Creek had told him about it the previous fall, and now he was appreciating the advice. Already all sensation had gone out of his feet. To build the fire he had been forced to remove his mittens, and the fingers had quickly gone numb. His pace of four miles an hour had kept his heart pumping blood to the surface of his body and to all the extremities. But the instant he stopped, the action of the pump eased down. The cold of space smote the unprotected tip of the planet, and he, being on that unprotected tip, received the full force of the blow. The blood of his body recoiled before it. The blood was alive, like the dog, and like the dog it wanted to hide away and cover itself up from the fearful cold. So long as he walked four miles an hour, he pumped that blood, willy-nilly, to the surface; but now it ebbed away and sank down into the recesses of his body. The extremities were the first to feel its absence. His wet feet froze the faster, and his exposed fingers numbed the faster, though they had not yet begun to freeze. Nose and cheeks were already freezing, while the skin of all his body chilled as it lost its blood.

But he was safe. Toes and nose and cheeks would be only touched by the frost, for the fire was beginning to burn with strength. He was feeding it with twigs the size of his finger. In another minute he would be able to feed it with branches the size of his wrist, and then he could remove his wet footgear, and, while it dried, he could keep his naked feet warm by the fire, rubbing them at first, of course, with snow. The fire was a success. He was safe. He remembered the advice of the old-timer on Sulphur Creek, and smiled. The old-timer had been very serious in laying down the law that no man must travel alone in the Klondike after fifty below. Well, here he was; he had had the accident; he was alone; and he had saved himself. Those old-timers were rather womanish, some of them, he thought. All a man had to do was to keep his head, and he was all right. Any who was a man could travel alone. But it was surprising, the rapidity with which his cheeks and nose were freezing. And he had not thought his fingers could go lifeless in so short a time. Lifeless they were, for he could scarcely make them move together to grip a twig, and they seemed remote from his body and from him. When he touched a twig, he had to look and see whether or not he had hold of it. The wires were pretty well down between him and his finger ends.

All of which counted for little. There was the fire, snapping and crackling and promising life with every dancing flame. He started to untie his moccasins. They were coated with ice; the thick German socks were like sheaths of iron halfway to the knees; and the moccasin strings were like rods of steel all twisted and knotted as by some conflagration. For a moment he tugged with his numb fingers, then, realizing the folly of it, he drew his sheath knife.

But before he could cut the strings, it happened. It was his own fault or, rather, his mistake. He should not have built the fire under the spruce tree. He should have built it in the open. But it had been easier to pull the twigs from the brush and drop them directly on the fire. Now the tree under which he had done this carried a weight of snow on its boughs. No wind had blown for weeks, and each bough was fully freighted. Each time he had pulled a twig he had communicated a slight agitation to the tree—an imperceptible agitation, so far as he was concerned, but an agitation sufficient to bring about the disaster. High up in the tree one bough capsized its load of snow. This fell on the boughs beneath, capsizing them. This process continued, spreading out and involving the whole tree. It grew like an avalanche, and it descended without warning upon the man and the fire, and the fire was blotted out! Where it had burned was a mantle of fresh and disordered snow.

The man was shocked. It was as though he had just heard his own sentence of death. For a moment he sat and stared at the spot where the fire had been. Then he grew very calm. Perhaps the old-timer on Sulphur Creek was right. If he had only had a trail mate he would have been in no danger now. The trail mate could have built the fire. Well, it was up to him to build the fire over again, and this second time there must be no failure. Even if he succeeded, he would most likely lose some toes. His feet must be badly frozen by now, and there would be some time before the second fire was ready.

Such were his thoughts, but he did not sit and think them. He was 25 busy all the time they were passing through his mind. He made a new foundation for a fire, this time in the open, where no treacherous tree could blot it out. Next he gathered dry grasses and tiny twigs from the high-water flotsam. He could not bring his fingers together to pull them out, but he was able to gather them by the handful. In this way he got many rotten twigs and bits of green moss that were undesirable, but it was the best he could do. He worked methodically, even collecting an armful of the larger branches to be used later when the fire gathered strength. And all the while the dog sat and watched him, a certain yearning wistfulness in its eyes, for it looked upon him as the fire provider, and the fire was slow in coming.

When all was ready, the man reached in his pocket for a second piece of birch bark. He knew the bark was there, and, though he could not feel it with his fingers, he could hear its crisp rustling as he fumbled for it. Try as he would, he could not clutch hold of it. And all the time, in his consciousness, was the knowledge that each instant his feet were freezing. This thought tended to put him in a panic, but he fought against it and kept calm. He pulled on his mittens with his teeth, and threshed his arms back and forth, beating his hands with all his might against his sides. He did this sitting down, and he stood up to do it; and all the while the dog sat in the snow, its wolf brush of a tail curled around warmly over its forefront, its sharp wolf ears pricked forward intently as it watched the man. And the man, as he beat and threshed with his arms and hands, felt a great surge of envy as he regarded the creature that was warm and secure in its natural covering.

After a time he was aware of the first faraway signals of sensation in his beaten fingers. The faint tingling grew stronger till it evolved into a stinging ache that was excruciating, but which the man hailed with satisfaction. He stripped the mitten from his right hand and fetched forth the birch bark. The exposed fingers were quickly going numb again. Next he brought out his bunch of sulphur matches. But the tremendous cold had already driven the life out of his fingers. In his effort to separate one match from the others, the whole bunch fell in the snow. He tried to pick it out of the snow, but failed. The dead fingers could neither touch nor clutch. He was very careful. He drove the thought of his freezing feet, and nose, and cheeks, out of his mind, devoting his whole soul to the matches. He watched, using the sense of vision in place of that touch, and when he saw his fingers on each side of the bunch, he closed them—that is, he willed to close them, for the wires were down, and the fingers did not obey. He pulled the mitten on the right hand, and beat it fiercely against his knee. Then with both mittened hands, he scooped the bunch of matches, along with much snow, into his lap. Yet he was no better off.

After some manipulation he managed to get the bunch between the heels of his mittened hands. In this fashion he carried it to his mouth. The ice crackled and snapped when by a violent effort he opened his mouth. He drew the lower jaw in, curled the upper lip out of the way, and scraped the bunch with his upper teeth in order to separate a match. He succeeded in getting one, which he dropped on his lap. He was no better off. He could not pick it up. Then he devised a way. He picked it up in his teeth and scratched it on his leg. Twenty times he scratched before he succeeded in lighting it. As it flamed he held it with his teeth to the birch bark. But the burning brimstone went up his nostrils and into his lungs, causing him to cough spasmodically. The match fell into the snow and went out.

The old-timer on Sulphur Creek was right, he thought in the moment of controlled despair that ensued: after fifty below, a man should travel with a partner. He beat his hands, but failed in exciting any sensation. Suddenly he bared both hands, removing the mittens with his teeth. He caught the whole bunch between the heels of his hands. His arm muscles not being frozen enabled him to press the hand heels tightly against the matches. Then he scratched the bunch along his leg. It flared into flame, seventy sulphur matches at once! There was no wind to blow them out. He kept his head to one side to escape the strangling fumes, and held the blazing bunch to the birch bark. As he so held it, he became aware of sensation in his hand. His flesh was burning. He could smell it. Deep down below the surface he could feel it. The sensation developed into pain that grew acute. And still he endured it, holding the flame of the matches clumsily to the bark that would not light readily because his own burning hands were in the way, absorbing most of the flame.

At last, when he could endure no more, he jerked his hands apart.   *30*
The blazing matches fell sizzling into the snow, but the birch bark was alight. He began laying dry grasses and the tiniest twigs on the flame. He could not pick and choose, for he had to lift the fuel between the heels of his hands. Small pieces of rotten wood and green moss clung to the twigs, and he bit them off as well as he could with his teeth. He cherished the flame carefully and awkwardly. It meant life, and it must not perish. The withdrawal of blood from the surface of his body now made him begin to shiver, and he grew more awkward. A large piece of green moss fell squarely on the little fire. He tried to poke it out with his fingers, but his shivering frame made him poke too far, and he disrupted the nucleus of the little fire, the burning grasses and tiny twigs separating and scattering. He tried to poke them together again, but in spite of the tenseness of the effort, his shivering got away with him, and the twigs were hopelessly scattered. Each twig gushed a puff of smoke and went out. The fire provider had failed. As he looked apathetically about him, his eyes chanced on the dog, sitting across the ruins of the fire from him, in the snow, making restless, hunching movements, slightly lifting one forefoot and then the other, shifting its weight back and forth on them with wistful eagerness.

The sight of the dog put a wild idea into his head. He remembered the tale of the man, caught in a blizzard, who killed a steer and crawled inside the carcass, and so was saved. He would kill the dog and bury his hands in the warm body until the numbness went out of them. Then he could build another fire. He spoke to the dog, calling it to him; but in his voice was a strange note of fear that frightened the animal, who had never known the man to speak in such a way before. Something was the matter, and its suspicious nature sensed danger—it knew not what danger, but somewhere, somehow, in its brain arose an apprehension of the man. It flattened its ears down at the sound of the man's voice, and its restless, hunching movements and the liftings and shiftings of its fore-feet became more pronounced; but it would not come to the man. He got on his hands and knees and crawled towards the dog. This unusual posture again excited suspicion, and the animal sidled mincingly away.

The man sat up in the snow for a moment and struggled for calmness. Then he pulled on his mittens, by means of his teeth, and got upon his feet. He glanced down at first in order to assure himself that he was really standing up, for the absence of sensation in his feet left him unrelated to the earth. His erect position in itself started to drive the webs of suspicion from the dog's mind; and when he spoke peremptorily, with the sound of whip lashes in his voice, the dog rendered its customary allegiance and came to him. As it came within reaching distance, the man lost his control. His arms flashed out to the dog, and he experienced genuine surprise when he discovered that his hands could not clutch, that there was neither bend nor feeling in the fingers. He had forgotten for the moment that they were frozen and that they were freezing more and more. All this happened quickly, and before the animal could get away, he encircled its body with his arms. He sat down in the snow, and in this fashion held the dog, while it snarled and whined and struggled.

But it was all he could do, hold its body encircled in his arms and sit there. He realized he could not kill the dog. There was no way to do it. With his helpless hands he could neither draw nor hold his sheath knife nor throttle the animal. He released it, and it plunged wildly away, with tail between its legs, and still snarling. It halted forty feet away and surveyed him curiously, with ears sharply pricked forward.

The man looked down at his hands in order to locate them, and found them hanging on the ends of his arms. It struck him as curious that one should have to use his eyes in order to find out where his hands were. He began threshing his arms back and forth, beating the mittened hands against his sides. He did this for five minutes, violently, and his heart pumped enough blood up to the surface to put a stop to his shivering. But no sensation was aroused in the hands. He had an impression that they hung like weights on the ends of his arms, but when he tried to run the impression down, he could not find it.

A certain fear of death, dull and oppressive, came to him. This fear quickly became poignant as he realized that it was no longer a mere matter of freezing his fingers and toes, or of losing his hands and feet, but that it was a matter of life and death with the chances against him. This threw him into a panic, and he turned and ran up the creek bed along the old, dim trail. The dog joined in behind him and kept up with him. He ran blindly, without intention, in fear such as he had never known in his life. Slowly, as he ploughed and floundered through the snow, he began to see things again—the banks of the creek, the old timber jams, the leafless aspens, and the sky. The running made him feel better. He did not shiver. Maybe, if he ran on, his feet would thaw out; and, anyway, if he ran far enough, he would reach camp and the boys. Without doubt he would lose some fingers and toes and some of his face; but the boys would take care of him, and save the rest of him when he got there. And at the same time there was another thought in his mind that said he would never get to the camp and the boys; that it was too many miles away, that the freezing had too great a start on him, and that he would soon be stiff and dead. This thought he kept in the background and refused to consider. Sometimes it pushed itself forward and demanded to be heard, but he thrust it back and strove to think of other things.

It struck him as curious that he could run at all on feet so frozen that he could not feel them when they struck the earth and took the weight of his body. He seemed to himself to skim along above the surface, and to have no connection with the earth. Somewhere he had once seen a winged Mercury, and he wondered if Mercury felt as he felt when skimming over the earth.

His theory of running until he reached camp and the boys had one flaw in it: he lacked the endurance. Several times he stumbled, and finally he tottered, crumpled up, and fell. When he tried to rise, he failed. He must sit and rest, he decided, and next time he would merely walk and keep on going. As he sat and regained his breath, he noted that he was feeling quite warm and comfortable. He was not shivering, and it even seemed that a warm glow had come to his chest and trunk. And yet, when he touched his nose or cheeks, there was no sensation. Running would not thaw them out. Nor would it thaw out his hands and feet. Then the thought came to him that the frozen portions of his body must be extending. He tried to keep this thought down, to forget it, to think of something else; he was aware of the panicky feeling that it caused, and he was afraid of the panic. But the thought asserted itself, and persisted, until it produced a vision of his body totally frozen. This was too much, and he made another wild run along the trail. Once he slowed down to a walk, but the thought of the freezing extending itself made him run again.

And all the time the dog ran with him, at his heels. When he fell down a second time, it curled its tail over its forefeet and sat in front of him, facing him, curiously eager and intent. The warmth and security of the animal angered him, and he cursed it till it flattened down its ears appeasingly. This time the shivering came more quickly upon the man. He was losing in his battle with the frost. It was creeping into his body from all sides. The thought of it drove him on, but he ran no more than a hundred feet, when he staggered and pitched headlong. It was his last panic. When he had recovered his breath and control, he sat up and entertained in his mind the conception of meeting death with dignity. However, the conception did not come to him in such terms. His idea of it was that he had been making a fool of himself, running around like a chicken with its head cut off—such was the simile that occurred to him. Well, he was bound to freeze anyway, and he might as well take it decently. With this new-found peace of mind came the first glimmerings of drowsiness. A good idea, he thought, to sleep off to death. It was like taking an anaesthetic. Freezing was not so bad as people thought. There were lots worse ways to die.

He pictured the boys finding his body next day. Suddenly he found himself with them, coming along the trail looking for himself. And, still with them, he came around a turn in the trail and found himself lying in the snow. He did not belong with himself any more, for even then he was out of himself, standing with the boys and looking at himself in the snow. It certainly was cold, was his thought. When he got back to the States he could tell the folks what real cold was. He drifted on from this to a vision of the old-timer on Sulphur Creek. He could see him quite clearly, warm and comfortable, and smoking a pipe.

'You were right, old hoss; you were right,' the man mumbled to the old-timer of Sulphur Creek.   40

Then the man drowsed off into what seemed to him the most comfortable and satisfying sleep he had ever known. The dog sat facing him and waiting. The brief day drew to a close in a long, slow twilight. There were no signs of a fire to be made, and, besides, never in the dog's experience had it known a man to sit like that in the snow and make no fire. As the twilight drew on, its eager yearning for the fire mastered it, and with a great lifting and shifting of forefeet, it whined softly, then flattened its ears down in anticipation of being chidden by the man. But the man remained silent. Later the dog whined loudly. And still later it crept close to the man and caught the scent of death. This made the animal bristle and back away. A little longer it delayed, howling under the stars that leaped and danced and shone brightly in the cold sky. Then it turned and trotted up the trail in the direction of the camp it knew, where were the other food providers and fire providers.

Outward Exploration: Discussion

1. Speaking of the protagonist, London says, "The trouble with him was that he was without imagination" (paragraph 3). What does London mean? How is that lack of imagination seen throughout the story?

2. What factors contribute to the man's death?

3. Explore the relationship between the protagonist and the dog.

4. Discuss London's use of irony in the story.

5. Discuss symbolism in the story.

6. Discuss the story's possible themes.

◻️ *Outward Exploration: Writing*

1. Write an essay that interprets "To Build a Fire."

2. One of the failings of the protagonist in "To Build a Fire" is his assumption that he knows more than he actually does. Write an essay exploring a time when you too assumed you knew more—for example, about the situation or about other people—than you really did.

3. One of the failings of the man in London's story is his inability to see the significance of the things he observes. Have you ever been in a situation where you observed the details but failed to see their significance until it was too late? If so, write an essay exploring that event. Feel free to refer to London's story to show similarities and differences between the protagonist's way of perceiving and responding and yours. Also feel free to make connections with other essays in this book (for example, Annie Dillard's "Seeing") or with other texts that you have encountered elsewhere.

4. Write an essay about the topic in either #2 (assumptions) or #3 (seeing the significance of things observed) not about yourself but about someone you either know or admire (for instance, an older sibling, a parent, a celebrity). In any case, you will also be exploring the impact of that person's mistake on your relationship with him or her and the impact on your inner self. For instance, you might discuss an instance in which an older sibling's supposed knowledge got you both into trouble. If you write about someone you do not know personally, you will probably need to do some research.

5. Write an essay exploring the relationship between the protagonist and the dog. You might consider what London is saying symbolically about instinct and intellect. If you like, you might go beyond the story to consider the morality or necessity of such exploitative relationships. If you do so, you might invoke the ideas of other essays in this book (for example, Alice Walker's "Am I Blue?" or Annie Dillard's "Living Like Weasels").

6. Write an essay comparing and contrasting "To Build a Fire" with Nathaniel Hawthorne's "Young Goodman Brown." Among the elements you might consider are the dramatic situation itself, the personalities of the protagonists, the stances of the narrators, and the use of symbolism.

The Censors

Luisa Valenzuela

☐ *Inward Exploration*

Write at least one paragraph explaining what the phrase the censors *suggests to you.*

Poor Juan! One day they caught him with his guard down before he   1
could even realize that what he had taken as a stroke of luck was really
one of fate's dirty tricks. These things happen the minute you're careless,
as one often is. Juancito let happiness—a feeling you can't trust—get the
better of him when he received from a confidential source Mariana's
new address in Paris and knew that she hadn't forgotten him. Without
thinking twice, he sat down at his table and wrote her a letter. *The* letter
that now keeps his mind off his job during the day and won't let him
sleep at night (what had he scrawled, what had he put on that sheet of
paper he sent to Mariana?).

Juan knows there won't be a problem with the letter's contents, that
it's irreproachable, harmless. But what about the rest? He knows that
they examine, sniff, feel, and read between the lines of each and every
letter, and check its tiniest comma and most accidental stain. He knows
that all letters pass from hand to hand and go through all sorts of tests
in the huge censorship offices and that, in the end, very few continue
on their way. Usually it takes months, even years, if there aren't any
snags; all this time the freedom, maybe even the life, of both sender
and receiver is in jeopardy. And that's why Juan's so troubled: thinking
that something might happen to Mariana because of his letters. Of all
people, Mariana, who must finally feel safe there where she always
dreamt she'd live. But he knows that the *Censor's Secret Command* oper-
ates all over the world and cashes in on the discount in air fares; there's
nothing to stop them from going as far as that hidden Paris neighborhood, kidnapping Mariana, and returning to their cozy homes, certain
of having fulfilled their noble mission.

Well, you've got to beat them to the punch, do what everyone tries
to do: sabotage the machinery, throw sand in its gears, get to the bottom
of the problem so as to stop it.

This was Juan's sound plan when he, like many others, applied for a
censor's job—not because he had a calling or needed a job: no, he applied simply to intercept his own letter, a consoling albeit unoriginal

idea. He was hired immediately, for each day more and more censors are needed and no one would bother to check on his references.

Ulterior motives couldn't be overlooked by the *Censorship Division,*   5
but they needn't be too strict with those who applied. They knew how hard it would be for the poor guys to find the letter they wanted and even if they did, what's a letter or two when the new censor would snap up so many others? That's how Juan managed to join the *Post Office's Censorship Division,* with a certain goal in mind.

The building had a festive air on the outside that contrasted with its inner staidness. Little by little, Juan was absorbed by his job, and he felt at peace since he was doing everything he could to get his letter for Mariana. He didn't even worry when, in his first month, he was sent to *Section K* where envelopes are very carefully screened for explosives.

It's true that on the third day, a fellow worker had his right hand blown off by a letter, but the division chief claimed it was sheer negligence on the victim's part. Juan and the other employees were allowed to go back to their work, though feeling less secure. After work, one of them tried to organize a strike to demand higher wages for unhealthy work, but Juan didn't join in; after thinking it over, he reported the man to his superiors and thus got promoted.

You don't form a habit by doing something once, he told himself as he left his boss's office. And when he was transferred to *Section F,* where letters are carefully checked for poison dust, he felt he had climbed a rung in the ladder.

By working hard, he quickly reached *Section E* where the job became more interesting, for he could now read and analyze the letters' contents. Here he could even hope to get hold of his letter, which, judging by the time that had elapsed, had gone through the other sections and was probably floating around in this one.

Soon his work became so absorbing that his noble mission blurred   10
in his mind. Day after day he crossed out whole paragraphs in red ink, pitilessly chucking many letters into the censored basket. These were horrible days when he was shocked by the subtle and conniving ways employed by people to pass on subversive messages; his instincts were so sharp that he found behind a simple "the weather's unsettled" or "prices continue to soar" the wavering hand of someone secretly scheming to overthrow the Government.

His zeal brought him swift promotion. We don't know if this made him happy. Very few letters reached him in *Section B*—only a handful passed the other hurdles—so he read them over and over again, passed them under a magnifying glass, searched for microprint with an electronic microscope, and tuned his sense of smell so that he was beat by the time he made it home. He'd barely manage to warm up his soup, eat some fruit, and fall into bed, satisfied with having done his duty. Only his darling mother worried, but she couldn't get him back on the right track. She'd say, though it wasn't always true: Lola called, she's at the bar with the girls, they miss you, they're waiting for you. Or else she'd leave a bottle of red wine on the table. But Juan wouldn't overdo it: any distraction could make him lose his edge and the perfect censor had to be alert, keen, attentive, and sharp to nab cheats. He had a truly patriotic task, both self-denying and uplifting.

His basket for censored letters became the best fed as well as the most cunning basket in the whole *Censorship Division*. He was about to congratulate himself for having finally discovered his true mission, when his letter to Mariana reached his hands. Naturally, he censored it without regret. And just as naturally, he couldn't stop them from executing him the following morning, another victim of his devotion to his work.

☐ *Outward Exploration: Discussion*

1. At the beginning of the story, what is Juan's problem?
2. How does Juan try to solve this problem?
3. Does anything strike you as unusual about the Censorship Division?
4. Is the need for censorship in the country totally unfounded?
5. Why does Valenzuela never name the country where Juan lives?
6. Document Juan's change from concerned citizen trying to protect himself and Mariana to ultimate bureaucratic censor.
7. Were the passages that he crossed out and the letters he discarded really subversive? Give your reasons for thinking so.
8. Given the fact that Juan no doubt knew what happened to citizens who wrote subversive letters, and given the fact that he knew his original intentions in writing the letter were totally innocent, why does he censor his own letter and thus condemn himself to death? What is Valenzuela suggesting?

☐ *Outward Exploration: Writing*

1. This rich story is highly suggestive, and its lessons can be applied to many areas of life in addition to government censorship. Write an essay that analyzes this story and which also applies its lessons in some way to your own experiences. Let each illuminate the other.
2. Valenzuela and Hawthorne use allegory to make statements about life and about the nature of the world. Write an essay in which you compare and contrast these stories, focusing on such elements as theme, use of allegory, and techniques the authors use for involving their readers in the stories.

Trifles

SUSAN GLASPELL

☐ *Inward Exploration*

What is a trifle? After defining the term, make a list of things you would deem to be trifles.

SCENE

The kitchen in the now abandoned farmhouse of JOHN WRIGHT, *a gloomy kitchen, and left without having been put in order—unwashed pans under the sink, a loaf of bread outside the bread-box, a dish-towel on the table—other signs of incompleted work. At the rear the outer door opens and the* SHERIFF *comes in followed by the* COUNTY ATTORNEY *and* HALE. *The* SHERIFF *and* HALE *are men in middle life, the* COUNTY ATTORNEY *is a young man; all are much bundled up and go at once to the stove. They are followed by the two women—the* SHERIFF'S *wife first; she is a slight wiry woman, a thin nervous face.* MRS. HALE *is larger and would ordinarily be called more comfortable looking, but she is disturbed now and looks fearfully about as she enters. The women have come in slowly, and stand close together near the door.*

COUNTY ATTORNEY (*Rubbing his hands.*) This feels good. Come up to the fire, ladies.

MRS. PETERS (*After taking a step forward.*) I'm not—cold.

SHERIFF (*Unbuttoning his overcoat and stepping away from the stove as if to mark the beginning of official business.*) Now, Mr. Hale, before we move things about, you explain to Mr. Henderson just what you saw when you came here yesterday morning.

COUNTY ATTORNEY By the way, has anything been moved? Are things just as you left them yesterday?

SHERIFF (*Looking about.*) It's just the same. When it dropped below zero last night I thought I'd better send Frank out this morning to make a fire for us—no use getting pneumonia with a big case on, but I told him not to touch anything except the stove—and you know Frank.

COUNTY ATTORNEY Somebody should have been left here yesterday.

SHERIFF Oh—yesterday. When I had to send Frank to Morris Center for that man who went crazy—I want you to know I had my hands full yesterday. I knew you could get back from Omaha by today and as long as I went over everything here myself—

COUNTY ATTORNEY Well, Mr. Hale, tell just what happened when you came here yesterday morning.

HALE Harry and I had started to town with a load of potatoes. We came along the road from my place and as I got here I said, "I'm going to see if I can't get John Wright to go in with me on a party telephone." I spoke to Wright about it once before and he put me off, saying folks talked too much anyway, and all he asked was peace and quiet—I guess you know about how much he talked himself; but I thought maybe if I went to the house and talked about it before his wife, though I said to Harry that I didn't know as what his wife wanted made much difference to John—

COUNTY ATTORNEY Let's talk about that later, Mr. Hale. I do want to talk about that, but tell now just what happened when you got to the house.

HALE I didn't hear or see anything; I knocked at the door, and still it was all quiet inside. I knew they must be up, it was past eight o'clock. So I knocked again, and I thought I heard somebody say, "Come in." I wasn't sure, I'm not sure yet, but I opened the door—this door (*indicating the door by which the two women are still standing*) and there in that rocker—(*pointing to it*) sat Mrs. Wright.

(*They all look at the rocker.*)

COUNTY ATTORNEY What—was she doing?

HALE She was rockin' back and forth. She had her apron in her hand and was kind of—pleating it.

COUNTY ATTORNEY And how did she—look?

HALE Well, she looked queer.

COUNTY ATTORNEY How do you mean—queer?

HALE Well, as if she didn't know what she was going to do next. And kind of done up.

COUNTY ATTORNEY How did she seem to feel about your coming?

HALE Why, I don't think she minded—one way or other. She didn't pay much attention. I said, "How do, Mrs. Wright, it's cold, ain't it?" And she said, "Is it?"—and went on kind of pleating at her apron. Well, I was surprised; she didn't ask me to come up to the stove, or to set down, but just sat there, not even looking at me, so I said, "I want to see John." And then she—laughed. I guess you would call it a laugh. I thought of Harry and the team outside, so I said a little sharp: "Can't I see John?" "No," she says, kind o' dull like. "Ain't he home?" says I. "Yes," says she, "he's home." "Then why can't I see him?" I asked her, out of patience. "'Cause he's dead," says she. "*Dead?*" says I. She just nodded her head, not getting a bit excited, but rockin' back and forth. "Why—where is he?" says I, not knowing what to say. She just pointed upstairs—like that (*himself pointing to the room above*). I got up, with the idea of going up there. I walked from there to here—then I says, "Why, what did he die of?" "He died of a rope round his neck," says she, and just went on pleatin' at her apron. Well, I went out and called Harry. I thought I might—need help. We went upstairs and there he was lyin'—

COUNTY ATTORNEY I think I'd rather have you go into that upstairs, where you can point it all out. Just go on now with the rest of the story.

HALE Well, my first thought was to get that rope off. It looked . . . (*Stops, his face twitches*) . . . but Harry, he went up to him, and he said, "No, he's dead all right, and we'd better not touch anything." So we went back downstairs. She was still sitting that same way. "Has anybody been notified?" I asked. "No," says she, unconcerned. "Who did this, Mrs. Wright?" said Harry. He said it business-like—and she stopped pleatin' of her apron. "I don't know," she says. "You don't *know?*" says Harry. "No," says she. "Weren't you sleepin' in the bed with him?" says Harry. "Yes," says she, "but I was on the inside." "Somebody slipped a rope round his neck and strangled him and you didn't wake up?" says Harry. "I didn't wake up," she said after him. We must 'a looked as if we didn't see how that could be, for after a minute she said, "I sleep sound." Harry was going to ask her more questions but I said maybe we ought to let her tell her story first to the coroner, or the sheriff, so Harry went fast as he could to Rivers' place, where there's a telephone.

COUNTY ATTORNEY And what did Mrs. Wright do when she knew that you had gone for the coroner?

HALE She moved from that chair to this one over here (*Pointing to a small chair in the corner*) and just sat there with her hands held together and looking down. I got a feeling that I ought to make some conversation, so I said I had come in to see if John wanted to put in a telephone, and at that she started to laugh, and then she stopped and looked at me—scared. (*The* County Attorney, *who has had his notebook out, makes a note.*) I dunno, maybe it wasn't scared. I wouldn't like to say it was. Soon Harry got back, and then Dr. Lloyd came, and you, Mr. Peters, and so I guess that's all I know that you don't.

COUNTY ATTORNEY (*Looking around.*) I guess we'll go upstairs first—and then out to the barn and around there. (*To the* Sheriff.) You're convinced that there was nothing important here—nothing that would point to any motive.

SHERIFF Nothing here but kitchen things.

(*The* COUNTY ATTORNEY, *after again looking around the kitchen, opens the door of a cupboard closet. He gets up on a chair and looks on a shelf. Pulls his hand away, sticky.*)

COUNTY ATTORNEY Here's a nice mess.

(*The women draw nearer.*)

MRS. PETERS (*To the other woman.*) Oh, her fruit; it did freeze. (*To the* Lawyer.) She worried about that when it turned so cold. She said the fire'd go out and her jars would break.

SHERIFF Well, can you beat the women! Held for murder and worryin' about her preserves.

COUNTY ATTORNEY I guess before we're through she may have something more serious than preserves to worry about.

HALE Well, women are used to worrying over trifles.

(*The two women move a little closer together.*)

COUNTY ATTORNEY (*With the gallantry of a young politician.*) And yet, for all their worries, what would we do without the ladies? (*The women do not unbend. He goes to the sink, takes a dipperful of water from the pail and pouring it into a basin, washes his hands. Starts to wipe them on the roller-towel, turns it for a cleaner place.*) Dirty towels! (*Kicks his foot against the pans under the sink.*) Not much of a housekeeper, would you say, ladies?

MRS. HALE (*Stiffly.*) There's a great deal of work to be done on a farm.

COUNTY ATTORNEY To be sure. And yet (*With a little bow to her*) I know there are some Dickson county farmhouses which do not have such roller towels.

(*He gives it a pull to expose its full length again.*)

MRS. HALE Those towels get dirty awful quick. Men's hands aren't always as clean as they might be.

COUNTY ATTORNEY Ah, loyal to your sex, I see. But you and Mrs. Wright were neighbors. I suppose you were friends, too.

MRS. HALE (*Shaking her head.*) I've not seen much of her of late years. I've not been in this house—it's more than a year.

COUNTY ATTORNEY And why was that? You didn't like her?

MRS. HALE I liked her all well enough. Farmers' wives have their hands full, Mr. Henderson. And then—

COUNTY ATTORNEY Yes—?

MRS. HALE (*Looking about.*) It never seemed a very cheerful place.

COUNTY ATTORNEY No—it's not cheerful. I shouldn't say she had the homemaking instinct.

MRS. HALE Well, I don't know as Wright had, either.

COUNTY ATTORNEY You mean that they didn't get on very well?

MRS. HALE No, I don't mean anything. But I don't think a place'd be any cheerfuller for John Wright's being in it.

COUNTY ATTORNEY I'd like to talk more of that a little later. I want to get the lay of things upstairs now.

(*He goes to the left, where three steps lead to a stair door.*)

SHERIFF I suppose anything Mrs. Peters does'll be all right. She was to take in some clothes for her, you know, and a few little things. We left in such a hurry yesterday.

COUNTY ATTORNEY Yes, but I would like to see what you take, Mrs. Peters, and keep an eye out for anything that might be of use to us.

MRS. PETERS Yes, Mr. Henderson.

(The women listen to the men's steps on the stairs, then look about the kitchen.)

MRS. HALE I'd hate to have men coming into my kitchen, snooping around and criticizing.

(She arranges the pans under sink which the Lawyer had shoved out of place.)

MRS. PETERS Of course it's no more than their duty.

MRS. HALE Duty's all right, but I guess that deputy sheriff that came out to make the fire might have got a little of this on. *(Gives the roller towel a pull.)* Wish I'd thought of that sooner. Seems mean to talk about her for not having things slicked up when she had to come away in such a hurry.

MRS. PETERS *(Who has gone to a small table in the left rear corner of the room, and lifted one end of a towel that covers a pan.)* She had bread set.

(Stands still.)

MRS. HALE *(Eyes fixed on a loaf of bread beside the breadbox, which is on a low shelf at the other side of the room. Moves slowly toward it.)* She was going to put this in there. *(Picks up loaf, then abruptly drops it. In a manner of returning to familiar things.)* It's a shame about her fruit. I wonder if it's all gone. *(Gets up on the chair and looks.)* I think there's some here that's all right, Mrs. Peters. Yes—here; *(Holding it toward the window)* this is cherries, too. *(Looking again.)* I declare I believe that's the only one. *(Gets down, bottle in her hand. Goes to the sink and wipes it off on the outside.)* She'll feel awful bad after all her hard work in the hot weather. I remember the afternoon I put up my cherries last summer.

(She puts the bottle on the big kitchen table, center of the room. With a sigh, is about to sit down in the rocking-chair. Before she is seated realizes what chair it is; with a slow look at it, steps back. The chair which she has touched rocks back and forth.)

MRS. PETERS Well, I must get those things from the front room closet. *(She goes to the door at the right, but after looking into the other room, steps back.)* You coming with me, Mrs. Hale? You could help me carry them.

(They go in the other room; reappear, MRS. PETERS carrying a dress and skirt, MRS. HALE following with a pair of shoes.)

MRS. PETERS My, it's cold in there.

(*She puts the clothes on the big table, and hurries to the stove.*)

MRS. HALE (*Examining the skirt.*) Wright was close. I think maybe that's why she kept so much to herself. She didn't even belong to the Ladies Aid. I suppose she felt she couldn't do her part, and then you don't enjoy things when you feel shabby. She used to wear pretty clothes and be lively, when she was Minnie Foster, one of the town girls singing in the choir. But that—oh, that was thirty years ago. This all you was to take in?

MRS. PETERS She said she wanted an apron. Funny thing to want, for there isn't much to get you dirty in jail, goodness knows. But I suppose just to make her feel more natural. She said they was in the top drawer in this cupboard. Yes, here. And then her little shawl that always hung behind the door. (*Opens stair door and looks.*) Yes, here it is.

(*Quickly shuts door leading upstairs.*)

MRS. HALE (*Abruptly moving toward her.*) Mrs. Peters?

MRS. PETERS Yes, Mrs. Hale?

MRS. HALE Do you think she did it?

MRS. PETERS (*In a frightened voice.*) Oh, I don't know.

MRS. HALE Well, I don't think she did. Asking for an apron and her little shawl. Worrying about her fruit.

MRS. PETERS (*Starts to speak, glances up, where footsteps are heard in the room above. In a low voice.*) Mr. Peters says it looks bad for her. Mr. Henderson is awful sarcastic in a speech and he'll make fun of her sayin' she didn't wake up.

MRS. HALE Well, I guess John Wright didn't wake when they was slipping that rope under his neck.

MRS. PETERS No, it's strange. It must have been done awful crafty and still. They say it was such a—funny way to kill a man, rigging it all up like that.

MRS. HALE That's just what Mr. Hale said. There was a gun in the house. He says that's what he can't understand.

MRS. PETERS Mr. Henderson said coming out that what was needed for the case was a motive; something to show anger, or—sudden feeling.

MRS. HALE (*Who is standing by the table.*) Well, I don't see any signs of anger around here. (*She puts her hand on the dish towel which lies on the table, stands looking down at table, one half of which is clean, the other half messy.*) It's wiped to here. (*Makes a move as if to finish work, then turns and looks at loaf of bread outside the breadbox. Drops towel. In that voice of coming back to familiar things.*) Wonder how they are finding things upstairs. I hope she had it a little more red-up up there. You know, it seems kind of *sneaking*. Locking her up in town and then coming out here and trying to get her own house to turn against her!

MRS. PETERS But Mrs. Hale, the law is the law.

MRS. HALE I s'pose 'tis. (*Unbuttoning her coat.*) Better loosen up your things, Mrs. Peters. You won't feel them when you go out.

(MRS. PETERS *takes off her fur tippet, goes to hang it on hook at back of room, stands looking at the under part of the small corner table.*)

MRS. PETERS She was piecing a quilt.

(*She brings the large sewing basket and they look at the bright pieces.*)

MRS. HALE It's log cabin pattern. Pretty, isn't it? I wonder if she was goin' to quilt it or just knot it?

(*Footsteps have been heard coming down the stairs. The* SHERIFF *enters followed by* HALE *and the* COUNTY ATTORNEY.)

SHERIFF They wonder if she was going to quilt it or just knot it!

(*The men laugh, the women look abashed.*)

COUNTY ATTORNEY (*Rubbing his hands over the stove.*) Frank's fire didn't do much up there, did it? Well, let's go out to the barn and get that cleared up.

(*The men go outside.*)

MRS. HALE (*Resentfully.*) I don't know as there's anything so strange, our takin' up our time with little things while we're waiting for them to get the evidence. (*She sits down at the big table smoothing out a block with decision.*) I don't see as it's anything to laugh about.

MRS. PETERS (*Apologetically.*) Of course they've got awful important things on their minds.

(*Pulls up a chair and joins* MRS. HALE *at the table.*)

MRS. HALE (*Examining another block.*) Mrs. Peters, look at this one. Here, this is the one she was working on, and look at the sewing! All the rest of it has been so nice and even. And look at this! It's all over the place! Why, it looks as if she didn't know what she was about!

(*After she had said this they look at each other, then start to glance back at the door. After an instant* MRS. HALE *has pulled at a knot and ripped the sewing.*)

MRS. PETERS Oh, what are you doing, Mrs. Hale?

MRS. HALE (*Mildly.*) Just pulling out a stitch or two that's not sewed very good. (*Threading a needle.*) Bad sewing always made me fidgety.

MRS. PETERS (*Nervously.*) I don't think we ought to touch things.

MRS. HALE I'll just finish up this end. (*Suddenly stopping and leaning forward.*) Mrs. Peters?

MRS. PETERS Yes, Mrs. Hale?

MRS. HALE What do you suppose she was so nervous about?

MRS. PETERS Oh—I don't know. I don't know as she was nervous. I sometimes sew awful queer when I'm just tired. (Mrs. Hale *starts to say something, looks at* Mrs. Peters, *then goes on sewing.*) Well I must get these things wrapped up. They may be through sooner than we think. (*Putting apron and other things together.*) I wonder where I can find a piece of paper, and string.

Mrs. Hale In that cupboard, maybe.

Mrs. Peters (*Looking in cupboard.*) Why, here's a bird-cage. (*Holds it up.*) Did she have a bird, Mrs. Hale?

Mrs. Hale Why, I don't know whether she did or not—I've not been here for so long. There was a man around last year selling canaries cheap, but I don't know as she took one; maybe she did. She used to sing real pretty herself.

Mrs. Peters (*Glancing around.*) Seems funny to think of a bird here. But she must have had one, or why would she have a cage? I wonder what happened to it.

Mrs. Hale I s'pose maybe the cat got it.

Mrs. Peters No, she didn't have a cat. She's got that feeling some people have about cats—being afraid of them. My cat got in her room and she was real upset and asked me to take it out.

Mrs. Hale My sister Bessie was like that. Queer, ain't it?

Mrs. Peters (*Examining the cage.*) Why, look at this door. It's broke. One hinge is pulled apart.

Mrs. Hale (*Looking too.*) Looks as if someone must have been rough with it.

Mrs. Peters Why, yes.

(*She brings the cage forward and puts it on the table.*)

Mrs. Hale I wish if they're going to find any evidence they'd be about it. I don't like this place.

Mrs. Peters But I'm awful glad you came with me, Mrs. Hale. It would be lonesome for me sitting here alone.

Mrs. Hale It would, wouldn't it? (*Dropping her sewing.*) But I tell you what I do wish, Mrs. Peters. I wish I had come over sometimes when *she* was here. I—(*Looking around the room*)—wish I had.

Mrs. Peters But of course you were awful busy, Mrs. Hale—your house and your children.

Mrs. Hale I could've come. I stayed away because it weren't cheerful—and that's why I ought to have come. I—I've never liked this place. Maybe because it's down in a hollow and you don't see the road. I dunno what it is, but it's a lonesome place and always was. I wish I had come over to see Minnie Foster sometimes. I can see now—

(*Shakes her head.*)

Mrs. Peters Well, you mustn't reproach yourself, Mrs. Hale. Somehow we just don't see how it is with other folks until—something comes up.

MRS. HALE Not having children makes less work—but it makes a quiet house, and Wright out to work all day, and no company when he did come in. Did you know John Wright, Mrs. Peters?

MRS. PETERS Not to know him; I've seen him in town. They say he was a good man.

MRS. HALE Yes—good; he didn't drink, and kept his word as well as most, I guess, and paid his debts. But he was a hard man, Mrs. Peters. Just to pass the time of day with him—(*Shivers.*) Like a raw wind that gets to the bone. (*Pauses, her eye falling on the cage.*) I should think she would'a wanted a bird. But what do you suppose went with it?

MRS. PETERS I don't know, unless it got sick and died.

(*She reaches over and swings the broken door, swings it again, both women watch it.*)

MRS. HALE You weren't raised round here, were you? (Mrs. Peters *shakes her head.*) You didn't know—her?

MRS. PETERS Not till they brought her yesterday.

MRS. HALE She—come to think of it, she was kind of like a bird herself—real sweet and pretty, but kind of timid and—fluttery. How—she—did—change. (*Silence; then as if struck by a happy thought and relieved to get back to every day things.*) Tell you what, Mrs. Peters, why don't you take the quilt in with you? It might take up her mind.

MRS. PETERS Why, I think that's a real nice idea, Mrs. Hale. There couldn't possibly be any objection to it, could there? Now, just what would I take? I wonder if her patches are in here—and her things.

(*They look in the sewing basket.*)

MRS. HALE Here's some red. I expect this has got sewing things in it. (*Brings out a fancy box.*) What a pretty box. Looks like something somebody would give you. Maybe her scissors are in here. (*Opens box. Suddenly puts her hand to her nose.*) Why—(Mrs. Peters *bends nearer, then turns her face away.*) There's something wrapped up in this piece of silk.

MRS. PETERS Why, this isn't her scissors.

MRS. HALE (*Lifting the silk.*) Oh, Mrs. Peters—its—

(MRS. PETERS *bends closer.*)

MRS. PETERS It's the bird.

MRS. HALE (*Jumping up.*) But, Mrs. Peters—look at it! It's (*sic*) neck! Look at its neck! It's all—other side *to*.

MRS. PETERS Somebody—wrung—its—neck.

(*Their eyes meet. A look of growing comprehension, of horror. Steps are heard outside.* MRS. HALE *slips box under quilt pieces, and sinks into her chair. Enter* SHERIFF *and* COUNTY ATTORNEY. MRS. PETERS *rises.*)

COUNTY ATTORNEY (*As one turning from serious things to little pleasantries.*) Well, ladies, have you decided whether she was going to quilt it or knot it?

MRS. PETERS We think she was going to—knot it.

COUNTY ATTORNEY Well, that's interesting, I'm sure. (*Seeing the birdcage.*) Has the bird flown?

MRS. HALE (*Putting more quilt pieces over the box.*) We think the—cat got it.

COUNTY ATTORNEY (*Preoccupied.*) Is there a cat?

(MRS. HALE *glances in a quick covert way at* MRS. PETERS.)

MRS. PETERS Well, not *now*. They're superstitious, you know. They leave.

COUNTY ATTORNEY (*To* Sheriff Peters, *continuing an interrupted conversation.*) No sign at all of anyone having come from the outside. Their own rope. Now let's go up again and go over it piece by piece. (*They start upstairs.*) It would have to have been someone who knew just the—

(MRS. PETERS *sits down. The two women sit there not looking at one another, but as if peering into something and at the same time holding back. When they talk now it is in the manner of feeling their way over strange ground, as if afraid of what they are saying, but as if they can not help saying it.*)

MRS. HALE She liked the bird. She was going to bury it in that pretty box.

MRS. PETERS (*In a whisper.*) When I was a girl—my kitten—there was a boy took a hatchet, and before my eyes—and before I could get there—(*Covers her face an instant.*) If they hadn't held me back I would have—(*Catches herself, looks upstairs where steps are heard, falters weakly*)—hurt him.

MRS. HALE (*With a slow look around her.*) I wonder how it would seem never to have had any children around. (*Pause.*) No, Wright wouldn't like the bird—a thing that sang. She used to sing. He killed that, too.

MRS. PETERS (*Moving uneasily.*) We don't know who killed the bird.

MRS. HALE I knew John Wright.

MRS. PETERS It was an awful thing was done in this house that night, Mrs. Hale. Killing a man while he slept, slipping a rope around his neck that choked the life out of him.

MRS. HALE His neck. Choked the life out of him.

(*Her hand goes out and rests on the bird-cage.*)

MRS. PETERS (*With rising voice.*) We don't know who killed him. We don't *know*.

MRS. HALE (*Her own feeling not interrupted.*) If there'd been years and years of nothing, then a bird to sing to you, it would be awful—still, after the bird was still.

MRS. PETERS (*Something within her speaking.*) I know what stillness is. When we homesteaded in Dakota, and my first baby died—after he was two years old, and me with no other then—

MRS. HALE (*Moving.*) How soon do you suppose they'll be through, looking for the evidence?

MRS. PETERS I know what stillness is. (*Pulling herself back.*) The law has got to punish crime, Mrs. Hale.

MRS. HALE (*Not as if answering that.*) I wish you'd seen Minnie Foster when she wore a white dress with blue ribbons and stood up there in the choir and sang. (*A look around the room.*) Oh, I *wish* I'd come over here once in a while! That was a crime! That was a crime! Who's going to punish that?

MRS. PETERS (*Looking upstairs.*) We mustn't—take on.

MRS. HALE I might have known she needed help! I know how things can be—for women. I tell you, it's queer, Mrs. Peters. We live close together and we live far apart. We all go through the same things—it's all just a different kind of the same thing. (*Brushes her eyes, noticing the bottle of fruit, reaches out for it.*) If I was you I wouldn't tell her her fruit was gone. Tell her it *ain't*. Tell her it's all right. Take this in to prove it to her. She—she may never know whether it was broke or not.

MRS. PETERS (*Takes the bottle, looks about for something to wrap it in; takes petticoat from the clothes brought from the other room, very nervously begins winding this around the bottle. In a false voice.*) My, it's a good thing the men couldn't hear us. Wouldn't they just laugh! Getting all stirred up over a little thing like a—dead canary. As if that could have anything to do with—with—wouldn't they *laugh!*

(*The men are heard coming down stairs.*)

MRS. HALE (*Under her breath.*) Maybe they would—maybe they wouldn't.

COUNTY ATTORNEY No, Peters, it's all perfectly clear except a reason for doing it. But you know juries when it comes to women. If there was some definite thing. Something to show—something to make a story about—a thing that would connect up with this strange way of doing it—

(*The women's eyes meet for an instant. Enter* HALE *from outer door.*)

HALE Well, I've got the team around. Pretty cold out there.

COUNTY ATTORNEY I'm going to stay here a while by myself. (*To the Sheriff.*) You can send Frank out for me, can't you? I want to go over everything. I'm not satisfied that we can't do better.

SHERIFF Do you want to see what Mrs. Peters is going to take in?

(*The* LAWYER *goes to the table, picks up the apron, laughs.*)

COUNTY ATTORNEY Oh, I guess they're not very dangerous things the ladies have picked out. (*Moves a few things about, disturbing the quilt pieces which cover the box. Steps back.*) No, Mrs. Peters doesn't need supervising. For that matter, a sheriff's wife is married to the law. Ever think of it that way, Mrs. Peters?

MRS. PETERS Not—just that way.

SHERIFF (*Chuckling.*) Married to the law. (*Moves toward the other room.*) I just want you to come in here a minute, George. We ought to take a look at these windows.

COUNTY ATTORNEY (*Scoffingly.*) Oh, windows!

SHERIFF We'll be right out, Mr. Hale.

(HALE *goes outside. The* SHERIFF *follows the* COUNTY ATTORNEY *into the other room. Then* MRS. HALE *rises, hands tight together, looking intensely at* MRS. PETERS, *whose eyes make a slow turn, finally meeting* MRS. HALE'S. *A moment* MRS. HALE *holds her, then her own eyes point the way to where the box is concealed. Suddenly* MRS. PETERS *throws back quilt pieces and tries to put the box in the bag she is wearing. It is too big. She opens box, starts to take bird out, cannot touch it, goes to pieces, stands there helpless. Sound of a knob turning in the other room.* MRS. HALE *snatches the box and puts it in the pocket of her big coat. Enter* COUNTY ATTORNEY *and* SHERIFF.)

COUNTY ATTORNEY (*Facetiously.*) Well, Henry, at least we found out that she was not going to quilt it. She was going to—what is it you call it, ladies?

MRS. HALE (*Her hand against her pocket.*) We call it—knot it, Mr. Henderson.

(CURTAIN)

☐ *Outward Exploration: Discussion*

1. Describe the kitchen when the play opens. Does anything strike you about the description?
2. What is the situation?
3. Although the characters have names—the Sheriff is Mr. Peters and the County Attorney is Mr. Henderson—Glaspell identifies their dialogue throughout the play by their official titles. Why?
4. What picture of John Wright's personality is revealed by everyone's dialogue?
5. What changes occurred in Minnie Foster after she became Mrs. Wright?
6. What is the importance of the weather?
7. Why don't the men believe Mrs. Wright's story?
8. Is there any irony in the play?
9. Why does Mrs. Hale feel guilty?

10. Describe the women's attitudes. Do they change throughout the play?

11. What is Glaspell suggesting about male/female roles? Give evidence to support your claim.

❏ *Outward Exploration: Writing*

1. Analyze the play. You might consider exploring feminist themes in the play, or you might analyze characters' personalities, or you might explore the play's symbolism. Using your analysis either as a point of departure or as a touchstone, explore whatever aspects of yourself that seem appropriate.

2. Several of the works in this book touch on similar themes. Select one or two of them and discuss "Trifles" in terms of them. Make references to your own experiences and ideas where appropriate.

Poem for the Young White Man Who Asked Me How I, An Intelligent, Well-Read Person, Could Believe in the War Between Races

LORNA DEE CERVANTES

❑ *Inward Exploration*

Write at least one paragraph answering the question "Is a war between the races going on in the United States now?"

In my land there are no distinctions.   *1*
The barbed wire politics of oppression
have been torn down long ago. The only reminder
of past battles, lost or won, is a slight
rutting in the fertile fields.   *5*

In my land
people write poems about love,
full of nothing but contented childlike syllables.
Everyone reads Russian short stories and weeps.
There are no boundaries.   *10*
There is no hunger, no
complicated famine or greed.

I am not a revolutionary.
I don't even like political poems.
Do you think I can believe in a war between races?   *15*
I can deny it. I can forget about it
when I'm safe,
living on my own continent of harmony
and home, but I am not
there.   *20*

I believe in revolution
because everywhere the crosses are burning,
sharp-shooting goose-steppers round every corner,
there are snipers in the schools . . .
(I know you don't believe this.   *25*
You think this is nothing

but faddish exaggeration. But they
are not shooting at you.)

I'm marked by the color of my skin.
The bullets are discrete and designed to kill slowly.   *30*
They are aiming at my children.
These are facts.
Let me show you my wounds: my stumbling mind, my
"excuse me" tongue, and this
nagging preoccupation   *35*
with the feeling of not being good enough.

These bullets bury deeper than logic.
Racism is not intellectual.
I can not reason these scars away.

Outside my door   *40*
there is a real enemy
who hates me.

I am a poet
who yearns to dance on rooftops,
to whisper delicate lines about joy   *45*
and the blessings of human understanding.
I try. I go to my land, my tower of words and
bolt the door, but the typewriter doesn't fade out
the sounds of blasting and muffled outrage.
My own days bring me slaps on the face.   *50*
Every day I am deluged with reminders
that this is not
my land

and this is my land.

I do not believe in the war between races   *55*
but in this country
there is war.

☐ *Outward Exploration: Discussion*

1. To whom is the poem addressed?
2. What are the *bullets* referred to in line 30?
3. What are the *wounds* referred to in line 33?
4. What is the speaker's *land* (line 47)?
5. Cervantes is a native Californian of Hispanic origins. Explain the paradox in lines 50–54.
6. What do the last three lines mean?

Outward Exploration: Writing

Think about conversations you have had in which someone did not or could not see your point because he or she found it too unbelievable to even entertain. Use that experience to help you analyze Cervantes' poem.

Five Short Poems

STEPHEN CRANE

❏ *Inward Exploration*

> *Write at least one paragraph defining your sense of the term* irony.
> *What follows is a mini-collection of poetry by Stephen Crane. In his books of poetry, Crane never titled his poems, choosing instead simply to number them, and I've followed his custom here. Consider the following five poems as a sampling. Each poem is a separate entity, yet you may discover thematic or stylistic connections.*

19

A god in wrath   *1*
Was beating a man;
He cuffed him loudly
With thunderous blows
That rang and rolled over the earth.   *5*
All people came running.
The man screamed and struggled,
And bit madly at the feet of the god.
The people cried:
"Ah, what a wicked man!"   *10*
And—
"Ah, what a redoubtable god!"

31

Many workmen   *1*
Built a huge ball of masonry
Upon a mountain-top.
Then they went to the valley below,
And turned to behold their work.   *5*
"It is grand," they said;
They loved the thing.

Of a sudden, it moved:
It came upon them swiftly;
It crushed them all to blood.   *10*
But some had opportunity to squeal.

44

I was in the darkness;   1
I could not see my words
Nor the wishes of my heart.
Then suddenly there was a great light—

"Let me into the darkness again."   5

56

A man feared that he might find an assassin;   1
Another that he might find a victim.
One was more wise than the other.

88

The wayfarer   1
Perceiving the pathway to truth
Was struck with astonishment.
It was thickly grown with weeds.
"Ha," he said,   5
"I see that none has passed here
In a long time."
Later he saw that each weed
Was a singular knife.
"Well," he mumbled at last,   10
"Doubtless there are other roads."

❏ *Outward Exploration: Discussion*

1. In poem #19, what assumptions do the people make about the god
   and about the man?
2. Why do they make those assumptions?
3. Are these assumptions correct?
4. What is the point of poem #19?
5. In poem #31, what does the ball symbolize?
6. What is the point of poem #31?
7. What is the point of poem #44?
8. Poem #56 leaves us with a question: Which man was more wise?
   Discuss the possible answers.
9. In poem #88, what is Crane suggesting about our quest for truth? Is
   he right?

❏ *Outward Exploration: Writing*

1. Write an analysis of any single Crane poem.
2. Write an analysis of Crane's vision of something (for example,

humans, truth, or religion) using more than one of his poems for support.

3. Select one of Crane's poems that speaks particularly to you. Begin by analyzing the poem, then use its insights to illuminate your own experience (and vice versa) as the example essay in Chapter 9 uses Crane's poem #35.

The Woman Hanging from the Thirteenth Floor Window

JOY HARJO

❏ *Inward Exploration*

Write at least one paragraph about what it must be like to feel desperate.

She is the woman hanging from the 13th floor   *1*
window. Her hands are pressed white against the
concrete moulding of the tenement building. She
hangs from the 13th floor window in east Chicago,
with a swirl of birds over her head. They could   *5*
be a halo, or a storm of glass waiting to crush her.

She thinks she will be set free.

The woman hanging from the 13th floor window
on the east side of Chicago is not alone.
She is a woman of children, of the baby, Carlos,   *10*
and of Margaret, and of Jimmy who is the oldest.
She is her mother's daughter and her father's son.
She is several pieces between the two husbands
she has had. She is all the women of the apartment
building who stand watching her, watching themselves.   *15*

When she was young she ate wild rice on scraped down
plates in warm wood rooms. It was in the farther
north and she was the baby then. They rocked her.

She sees Lake Michigan lapping at the shores of
herself. It is a dizzy hole of water and the rich   *20*
live in tall glass houses at the edge of it. In some
places Lake Michigan speaks softly, here, it just sputters
and butts itself against the asphalt. She sees
other buildings just like hers. She sees other
women hanging from many-floored windows   *25*
counting their lives in the palms of their hands
and in the palms of their children's hands.

She is the woman hanging from the 13th floor window
on the Indian side of town. Her belly is soft from
her children's births, her worn levis swing down below   *30*

her waist, and then her feet, and then her heart.
She is dangling.

The woman hanging from the 13th floor hears voices.
They come to her in the night when the lights have gone
dim. Sometimes they are little cats mewing and scratching   35
at the door, sometimes they are her grandmother's voice,
and sometimes they are gigantic men of light whispering
to her to get up, to get up, to get up. That's when she wants
to have another child to hold onto in the night, to be able
to fall back into dreams.   40

And the woman hanging from the 13th floor window
hears other voices. Some of them scream out from below
for her to jump, they would push her over. Others cry softly
from the sidewalks, pull their children up like flowers and gather
them into their arms. They would help her, like themselves.   45

But she is the woman hanging from the 13th floor window,
and she knows she is hanging by her own fingers, her
own skin, her own thread of indecision.

She thinks of Carlos, of Margaret, of Jimmy.
She thinks of her father, and of her mother.   50
She thinks of all the women she has been, of all
the men. She thinks of the color of her skin, and
of Chicago streets, and of waterfalls and pines.
She thinks of moonlight nights, and of cool spring storms.
Her mind chatters like neon and northside bars.   55
She thinks of the 4 a.m. lonelinesses that have folded
her up like death, discordant, without logical and
beautiful conclusion. Her teeth break off at the edges.
She would speak.

The woman hangs from the 13th floor window crying for   60
the lost beauty of her own life. She sees the
sun falling west over the grey plane of Chicago.
She thinks she remembers listening to her own life
break loose, as she falls from the 13th floor
window on the east side of Chicago, or as she   65
climbs back up to claim herself again.

❑ Outward Exploration: Discussion

1. What roles has the woman played in her life?
2. What, if anything, does the woman represent in the poem?

3. What does she mourn?
4. What does the ending mean?

☐ *Outward Exploration: Writing*

Analyze this poem in an exploratory essay. Try to discover connections between the poem's emotions and ideas and some of your own.

Off from Swing Shift

GARRETT HONGO

❑ *Inward Exploration*

Select a room with which you are very familiar. List the objects within that room which suggest the nature of the people who use it, including their socioeconomic class and their interests.

Late, just past midnight,   *1*
freeway noise from the Harbor
and San Diego leaking in
from the vent over the stove,
and he's off from swing shift at Lear's.   *5*
Eight hours of twisting circuitry,
charting ohms and maximum gains
while transformers hum
and helicopters swirl
on the roofs above the small factory.   *10*
He hails me with a head-fake,
then the bob and weave
of a weekend middleweight
learned at the Y on Kapiolani
ten years before I was born.   *15*

The shoes and gold London Fogger
come off first, then the easy grin
saying he's lucky as they come.
He gets into the slippers
my brother gives him every Christmas,   *20*
carries his Thermos over to the sink,
and slides into the one chair at the table
that's made of wood and not yellow plastic.
He pushes aside stacks
of *Sporting News* and *Outdoor Life,*   *25*
big round tins of Holland butter cookies,
and clears a space for his elbows, his pens,
and the *Racing Form*'s Late Evening Final.

His left hand reaches out,
flicks on the Sony transistor   *30*
we bought for his birthday

when I was fifteen.
The right ferries in the earphone,
a small, flesh-colored star,
like a tiny miracle of hearing,   *35*
and fits it into place.
I see him plot black constellations
of figures and calculations
on the magazine's margins,
alternately squint and frown   *40*
as he fingers the knob of the tuner
searching for the one band
that will call out today's results.

There are whole cosmologies
in a single handicap,   *45*
a lifetime of two-dollar losing
in one pick of the Daily Double.

Maybe tonight is his night
for winning, his night
for beating the odds   *50*
of going deaf from a shell
at Anzio still echoing
in the cave of his inner ear,
his night for cashing in
the blue chips of shrapnel still grinding   *55*
at the thickening joints of his legs.

But no one calls
the horse's name, no one
says Shackles, Rebate, or Pouring Rain.
No one speaks a word.   *60*

☐ *Outward Exploration: Discussion*

1. Who is the poem's speaker?
2. What is the man's socioeconomic class? How do you know?
3. What are the man's interests?
4. What is the speaker's attitude toward the man? How do you know?

☐ *Outward Exploration: Writing*

1. Write an exploratory analysis of this poem.
2. Is there someone for whom you have feelings similar to those the
   speaker feels for the man? If so, examine your relationship by analyzing this poem.

Latero Story

TATO LAVIERA

☐ *Inward Exploration*

Write at least one paragraph explaining what the American dream means to you. Be as explicit as possible. Then read the following poem about a latero—a man who collects cans from streets and out of garbage containers. The word latero *comes from the Spanish word* lata, *which means can.*

i am a twentieth-century welfare recipient   *1*
moonlighting in the sun as a latero
a job invented by national state laws
designed to re-cycle aluminum cans
returned to consumer's acid laden   *5*
gastric inflammation pituitary glands
coca diet rites low cal godsons
of artificially flavored malignant
indigestions somewhere down the line
of a cancerous cell   *10*

i collect garbage cans in outdoor facilities
congested with putrid residues
my hands shelving themselves
opening plastic bags never knowing
what they'll encounter   *15*

several times a day i touch evil rituals
cut throats of chickens
tongues of poisoned rats
salivating my index finger
smells of month old rotten foods   *20*
next to pamper's diarrhea
     dry blood infectious diseases
hypodermic needles tissued with
heroin water drops pilfered in
slimy greases hazardous waste materials   *25*
but i cannot use rubber gloves
they undermine my daily profits

i am twentieth-century welfare recipient
moonlighting in the day as a latero
that is the only opportunity i have   *30*

to make it big in america
some day i might become experienced enough
to offer technical assistance
to other lateros
i am thinking of publishing   35
my own guide to latero's collection
and a latero's union offering
medical dental benefits

i am a twentieth-century welfare recipient
moonlighting in the night as a latero   40
i am considered some kind of expert
at collecting cans during fifth avenue parades
i can now hire workers at twenty
five cents an hour guaranteed salary
and fifty per cent two and one half cents   45
profit on each can collected

i am a twentieth-century welfare recipient
moonlighting in midnight as a latero
i am becoming an entrepreneur
an american success story   50
i have hired bag ladies to keep peddlers
from my territories
i have read in some guide to success
that in order to get rich
to make it big   55
i have to sacrifice myself
moonlighting until dawn by digging
deeper into the extra can
margin of profit
i am on my way up the opportunistic   60
ladder of success
in ten years i will quit welfare
to become a legitimate businessman
i'll soon become a latero executive
with corporate conglomerate intents   65
god bless america

☐ Outward Exploration: Discussion

1. Why does the latero give us so much detail about what he encounters in his job?
2. Find elements of irony in the poem.
3. What is the latero's attitude toward what he says? Does his attitude differ from Laviera's? Explain.

❏ *Outward Exploration: Writing*

Write an exploratory analysis of this poem. Include elements of your own plans for the future and understanding of the American dream where appropriate. Try to illuminate your plans by examining his, and illuminate his plans by exploring yours.

The Weak Monk

STEVIE SMITH

❑ *Inward Exploration*

Write a paragraph about religion.

The monk sat in his den,   1
He took the mighty pen
And wrote "Of God and Men."

One day the thought struck him
It was not according to Catholic doctrine;   5
His blood ran dim.

He wrote till he was ninety years old,
Then he shut the book with a clasp of gold
And buried it under the sheep fold.

He'd enjoyed it so much, he loved to plod,   10
And he thought he'd a right to expect that God
Would rescue his book alive from the sod.

Of course it rotted in the snow and rain;
No one will ever know now what he wrote of God and men.
For this the monk is to blame.   15

❑ *Outward Exploration: Discussion*

1. Why is the monk upset that his ideas are not in accordance with Catholic Church doctrine?
2. Why does he believe that he has a right to expect that God will rescue his manuscript?

❑ *Outward Exploration: Writing*

Write an exploratory essay which analyzes this poem. Connect the poem's main point to yourself in some interesting way.

The Youngest Daughter

CATHY SONG

☐ *Inward Exploration*

*Write at least one paragraph that explains what comes to mind when you
hear the term* the youngest daughter.

The sky has been dark   1
for many years.
My skin has become as damp
and pale as rice paper
and feels the way   5
mother's used to before the drying sun
parched it out there in the fields.

    Lately, when I touch my eyelids,
my hands react as if
I had just touched something   10
hot enough to burn.
My skin, aspirin colored,
tingles with migraine. Mother
has been massaging the left side of my face
especially in the evenings   15
when the pain flares up.

This morning
her breathing was graveled,
her voice gruff with affection
when I wheeled her into the bath.   20
She was in a good humor,
making jokes about her great breasts,
floating in the milky water
like two walruses,
flaccid and whiskered around the nipples.   25
I scrubbed them with a sour taste
in my mouth, thinking:
six children and an old man
have sucked from these brown nipples.

I was almost tender   30
when I came to the blue bruises

that freckle her body,
places where she has been injecting insulin
for thirty years. I soaped her slowly,
she sighed deeply, her eyes closed.   *35*
It seems it has always
been like this: the two of us
in this sunless room,
the splashing of the bathwater.

In the afternoons   *40*
when she has rested,
she prepares our ritual of tea and rice,
garnished with a shred of gingered fish,
a slice of pickled turnip,
a token for my white body.   *45*
We eat in the familiar silence.
She knows I am not to be trusted,
even now planning my escape.
As I toast to her health
with the tea she has poured,   *50*
a thousand cranes curtain the window,
fly up in a sudden breeze.

❏ *Outward Exploration: Discussion*

1. What is the situation in the poem?
2. Describe the relationship between the mother and the daughter.
3. What is the significance of the cranes flying past the window at the
   end of the poem?

❏ *Outward Exploration: Writing*

In the process of analyzing this poem, consider a complex relationship of your own which seems somehow connected to (similar to, parallel to, totally different from) the mother–daughter relationship in the
poem. Write an essay in which you use each relationship to help explain
the other.

Hopper's Women

SUE STANDING

❏ *Inward Exploration*

If you don't know the works of the painter Edward Hopper, look up some of his paintings in the library. Select one of his paintings or a painting by any other artist, and write a paragraph responding to it in some way. You might describe the painting, record your reactions to it, or try to imagine the story of which this painting is but a moment.

1. House by the Railroad

She minds the lilacs.   1
What can be saved, she saves:
dried flowers, tarnished costume jewelry,
half-used boxes of face powder.
She imagines a man will call to her from the train: 5
"The fruits of summer are here!"
Sun pierces the house like the whistle
of the train. Inside she waits,
knitting the heavy light of afternoon.
A few pieces of Sandwich glass   10
glow in the windows.
The aspidistra, which never grows,
throws spiky shadows at her feet.

2. East Side Interior

She minds the cool
moonshine in the room.   15
In the frame of the window,
her soft profile, dark mass of hair,
she bends low, sewing.
Her African violets bloom all winter.
She thinks bones, she thinks rivers,   20
she thinks bread and yeast,
the way the white curtain
billows over the bed.
She will stay at the window through dusk
like a ghost at the sewing machine,   25
opaque and beautiful and lost.

3. Nighthawks

She minds her cheap gardenia perfume,
her tight red dress.
The way this reflection goes,
she sees only her angular arms   *30*
and the drugstore counter;
neon blots out the rest, except for fragments
of her dress mirrored on the coffee urn.
The men can't figure why she comes here,
night after night.   *35*
They haven't seen her room and won't.
She wonders why she can't leave
the harsh light of this town, wonders
if every town contains only two stories.

❏ *Outward Exploration: Discussion*

1. What is the mood of the first section, "House by the Railroad"?
2. Why is the woman in "East Side Interior" described as "lost"?
3. What is the woman's situation in "Nighthawks"?

❏ *Outward Exploration: Writing*

1. Write an exploratory essay which analyzes this poem. What is Standing suggesting about the women depicted in the paintings? About women in general?
2. If your professor agrees, select a visual text of your own (for example, a painting, photograph, advertisement, a film, a piece of sculpture or architecture). Write an exploratory essay about it, analyzing the text but also explaining your reactions to it.

Scene from the Movie *GIANT*

TINO VILLANUEVA

☐ *Inward Exploration*

Write a paragraph about a scene in a movie or a play that particularly struck you as important or significant or which simply spoke to you in some way.

What I have from 1956 is one instant at the Holiday   *1*
Theater, where a small dimension of a film, as in
A dream, became the feature of the whole. It
Comes toward the end . . . the café scene, which
Reels off a slow spread of light, a stark desire   *5*

To see itself once more, though there is, at times,
No joy in old time movies. It begins with the
Jingling of bells and the plainer truth of it:
That the front door to a roadside café opens and
Shuts as the Benedicts (Rock Hudson and Elizabeth   *10*

Taylor), their daughter Luz, and daughter-in-law
Juana and grandson Jordy, pass through it not
Unobserved. Nothing sweeps up into an actual act
Of kindness into the eyes of Sarge, who owns this
Joint and has it out for dark-eyed Juana, weary   *15*

Of too much longing that comes with rejection.
Juana, from barely inside the door, and Sarge,
Stout and unpleased from behind his counter, clash
Eye-to-eye, as time stands like heat. Silence is
Everywhere, acquiring the name of hatred and Juana   *20*

Cannot bear the dread—the dark-jowl gaze of Sarge
Against her skin. Suddenly: bells go off again.
By the quiet effort of walking, three Mexican-
Types step in, whom Sarge refuses to serve . . .
Those gestures of his, those looks that could kill   *25*

A heart you carry in memory for years. A scene from
The past has caught me in the act of living: even
To myself I cannot say except with worried phrases
Upon a paper, how I withstood arrogance in a gruff
Voice coming with the deep-dyed colors of the screen;   *30*

How in the beginning I experienced almost nothing to
Say and now wonder if I can ever live enough to tell
The after-tale. I remember this and I remember myself
Locked into a back-row seat—I am a thin, flickering,
Helpless light, local-looking, unthought of at fourteen.   *35*

❑ *Outward Exploration: Discussion*

1. What are the key elements in the scene described?
2. Why does this scene affect Villanueva so much?

❑ *Outward Exploration: Writing*

If your professor agrees, select a movie or play that has had an impact on your life. Write an essay that describes the scene or text and which elaborates upon its effect(s) on you and the reasons why you think it affected you that way.

10

Revising Content

Many of us fear revising. If we don't fear the additional work and effort that revision entails, we fear the loss of spontaneity in our prose. We fear destroying the "unity" of the essay, even though we might find it hard to say exactly what that unity is. If an essay popped out of us in one sitting, we erroneously believe that it must be all of one piece. It is as though these particular ideas, this particular structure, and this particular phrasing have been sanctioned by the gods. It can be a heady feeling.

Yet such an assumption involves a surprising amount of trust: trust that our first idea is our best, that our first phrasing is the best, that the act of self-expression will also be an act of communication with our readers, that every idea and word coming from us at this moment is good whereas ideas and words coming from us later will be worse.

Too much trust, if you ask me.

Would you want a brain surgeon to be spontaneous? The surgeon might say, "Oh what the heck, I feel like entering the brain through the ear this time." Would you want your lawyer to simply drop by the courtroom and argue your case spontaneously? Would you want your professor to stroll into the classroom and start teaching spontaneously? Would you want the author of a long book that you have to read for class over the weekend to have written it spontaneously with no revision. I certainly wouldn't.

WHY REVISE?

Almost anything that is important requires thought and revision, whether it is the surgeon's evaluation of the best surgical technique or the lawyer's careful trial preparation or a professor's lecture—and certainly the book you had to read. Spontaneity is an overrated commodity, and faith in it reflects a sense that we have no real control over our writing. That idea, of course, is false. What we write can always be altered and usually improved. Spontaneity precludes careful reflection and rethinking. As I've suggested throughout this book, revising is the best means of digging deeper into our topics and into ourselves.

Further, most first drafts have several recurring problems. For instance, they almost certainly contain too many words to express the ideas they contain. Moreover, several different ideas often compete for attention, leaving readers wondering exactly what the point of the essay is. Almost always a first draft lacks a sense of proportion, the unimportant receiving too much attention and the very important not receiving enough. In a first draft, the introduction rarely indicates the essay's content adequately, and since it came in that first burst of discovery, the introduction doesn't grab readers' attention as well as it should because it wasn't crafted to do so. Similarly, the rest of the draft's potential effects tend to be scattered and unfocused. Such a draft would frustrate and confuse readers.

As we have noted, self-expression does not equal communication. First drafts (often the creation of spontaneity) are self-expression. Those drafts may tell you what you know and think and feel about the subject. But that information is not organized or crafted for readers. Only through revision can you change your focus from writing for yourself to writing for readers. And that is what communication is all about.

So adios, spontaneity.

Creating the *illusion* of spontaneity, however, is a different matter. Giving your readers the sense that your essay simply flowed from your mind onto the page can be a charming and effective strategy. But note that the word *strategy* implies careful planning. To create the **illusion of spontaneity** requires much revision, much craft, and much attention to word choice, tone, and structure. Consider, for example, how effortlessly a juggler performs her feats. If you have ever tried to duplicate those tricks, however, you probably discovered that a great deal of practice was needed. In other words, the juggler's ease was an illusion. The juggler's practicing is comparable to your revising what you write—few people get the balls flying in synchronization or the language and ideas flashing in harmony on the first try.

When you encounter an essay that seems spontaneous, then, the chances are that you are experiencing the illusion of spontaneity. In fact, the vast majority of the writers whose prose we value are dedicated revisers. Not simply literary writers, but also those economists, social scientists, scientists, and commentators whose writing is praised—all of those writers revise and revise some more. Some go through 10 or 12 drafts before submitting an essay or article for publication. In *Life Work,* poet and essayist Donald Hall says that one of his poems—"Another

Elegy"—has gone through over 500 drafts in 10 years. That is an extreme example, of course, but the point remains true: Good writers revise many times to achieve just the right effects.

What do they revise? Ultimately, just about everything. We tend to think of style when we talk about revision, and certainly style is a major component (see Chapter 11, "Revising Style"). By *style* I mean more than correctness; I mean getting exactly the right word, the right rhythm of sentences. I mean making the prose reader-friendly, providing definitions and transitions.

But revision also means probing the topic more extensively. Once we finish the first draft, many of us feel that we've said everything we can say about the topic. Filled with a sense of accomplishment and, perhaps more important, a belief that the essay is finished, we try to ignore the fact that the discovery process has only just begun when the first draft is finished. This chapter examines some content areas that usually require revision.

For the most part, revising content involves either deleting or adding material. The material you might delete includes ideas or scenes which, though interesting in the early drafts, turn out to be tangential to the finished exploratory essay. Never throw away the material you delete in exploratory writing, however. The scene or idea that doesn't fit in one essay might be the cornerstone of a later one. The material you might add includes more information about the context and background, more details, more speculation about motives, more reflection about significance, and perhaps dialogue.

Deleting Material

For me, this is the most difficult part of revising. Once I've embodied an idea in words, it seems to have a life of its own. Yet every chapter in this book is about half as long as it was in the early drafts. I made a lot of painful decisions to eliminate sentences, paragraphs, examples, even ideas. Often the material I deleted was the stuff that I most enjoyed writing or that I liked the best. But the rule-of-thumb I followed was very clear: "If it doesn't clearly belong here, it must go." Let me hasten to add that none of that "deathless prose" is lost forever to the world—all of it is saved in a computer file called "Graveyard." I can always resurrect it for use in some other piece of writing. Besides, saving deleted material is a good psychological strategy: Moving it to another file seems much less final than simply trashing it.

Adding Material

Any material you add to an essay might spark new exploration or new ideas, so the process of creation is never-ending (until your deadline starts looming, anyway). Among the material that may be added are context and background information, details, dialogue, speculations about motives and meaning, personal and global significance. Let's consider each of these in turn.

ADDING CONTEXT AND BACKGROUND INFORMATION   Often the thing most seriously missing from early drafts is information that provides context and background. Caught up in presenting an event or idea as we are now thinking of it, we often forget that our readers cannot have all the same background information that we have. For example, this information may be about a relationship that has merely been alluded to in the early drafts. Because early drafts are mainly self-expression, we can easily lose sight of the fact that the final draft must succeed as communication, as writing to readers who cannot possibly know as much about our relationships and our thought processes as we do. During revision, we fill in such gaps for those readers.

Don't forget that your earlier self is a potential source during revision. If you are writing about the past, for example, a quotation from your journal or a letter you wrote during that period might convey the feelings and thoughts of you-then with a great deal of accuracy and immediacy.

Here is a brief example which you saw in Chapter 5, "Exploring Relationships." In brackets are the questions I asked myself as I prepared to revise the content:

> I first met Sue in Bar Harbor, a popular summer tourist town, in early September, just before I started my senior year of college at the University of Maine. I was unhappy [Unhappy about what?] and had gone there to "get away" from it all. [What is "it all"?] I saw an attractive woman coming out of one of the motels. [What did she look like?] Apparently she was going for a walk. [How did I know?] I followed her into a restaurant. [Why follow her?] Soon we started a conversation. [Who started it? What was the conversation about?] It was amazing [Why amazing?] how quickly we hit it off. We talked about everything that night. [Such as?] I was amazed to learn she actually lived in Bangor [Why amazed—didn't a lot of people live in Bangor?], the city across the river from my hometown (and 10 miles from campus). [Why was she in Bar Harbor then?] She was a teller in a bank. [Significance of her job? Was that good or bad for our potential relationship? Why?] Within weeks we were a steady and exclusive couple. [How did *that* happen?]
>
>   Eleven months later we broke up. [Why?] Ironically, we broke up in Bar Harbor, the same place where we had met. Sue had suggested we go there for dinner [Any other reason?], and the hour-long ride there was not pleasant. [Why not? What are

some examples of what happened?] She wanted us to get married; I wanted to get a Ph.D. at Brown University in Rhode Island. [Why get married or get a Ph.D.? And why not do both?] By the time dinner was over, so were we. In silence we drove back, both angry and hurt.

All of those annoying questions are actually requests for more background information (for instance, the reasons we were in Bar Harbor) and for additional details. Answering each of those questions with one or more sentences would make the essay more revealing, more interesting, and significantly longer.

ADDING DETAILS   Ideas often reside in the specific details. For an insightful exploration of this need for details, see Abby Frucht's "The Obects of My Invention," reprinted in "Further Readings" in this book. Although Frucht discusses her use of details and objects in fiction, everything that she says applies equally well to exploratory essays because, like fiction writers, exploratory essayists are after the *emotional truth* rather than the mere *factual truth*. Even though we are writing about an event which actually happened, human memory does not record every tiny detail. Rather, it retains the gist of the event and then fills in the gaps with guesses and assumptions. Like Frucht, then, we need to find "details with life, with personality, with influence." In other words, we need suggestive details, details that resound with significance. Often such details come to us in the process of writing. In passing, we may mention an object in one of our drafts and later, when revising, wonder why the object is there. Instead of simply tossing out such a detail, try writing about it. As Frucht says, details on a page have "a kind of presence, however slight; agency, however slight; effect, however slight." Try to enhance that presence, explore the agency, highlight the effect. Begin by describing the object, trying to see its symbolic possibilities. Often our subconscious mind gives us such gifts while we're busy focusing on something else in the draft. So explore the gift before deciding to delete the object.

Consider this example. In an essay about falling in love and entering into a relationship that ended badly, one football player mentioned his old high school football trophy that sat in the corner of his room. The small statue that topped the trophy (a runner with his left arm outstretched) had been beheaded during unpacking in September. Originally the writer had mentioned the trophy in his first draft because he listed everything his room contained. Somehow, though, it survived the cuts in the next two drafts. As he prepared the final draft, he couldn't bring himself to eliminate mention of the trophy. So, instead of cutting the trophy, he described it in some new prewriting. Only then did it strike him: The player on the trophy had "lost his head" just as he, the writer, had "lost his head" over his girlfriend. In his prewriting he pushed the comparison further: He no longer prized the trophy because of the missing head in the same way that the girlfriend no longer prized him because he was acting foolish about her. He planned to discard the trophy, and she had already discarded him.

In the final draft, he didn't make all of this explicit. Instead, he simply devoted a short paragraph to describing the trophy. Later in the essay, as he and the girlfriend sit in his room discussing their relationship, he notes that his eyes rest on the trophy as he tries to avoid her glare. Near the end of the essay, he says, "If I learned any lesson at all from that romance, it was this: You can't lose both your heart and your head if you want to keep your self-respect and your girlfriend. Once I lost my head and started acting as though she was absolutely everything to me, Jenny tired of me and left." That first full description of the trophy, the second reference to the trophy itself, and then this explicit statement about "losing" your head all combine to create an effective symbol. The writer never had to make explicit the connection between the trophy and himself since the combination implied it. Hence the object (in this case the trophy) took on symbolic significance and deepened the essay without the writer's being blatant about the connection. Notice how many objects have a symbolic resonance in the essays in this book.

In addition to objects, emotions can be enhanced with more details. For instance, don't simply tell us, "I was angry." Show us: "My palms suddenly moistened, and my knuckles whitened as I clutched the steering wheel harder than I intended. How dare that ignorant bumpkin tell me that I couldn't drive!" Here *the details* (the sweaty palms, the white knuckles, the clutching of the steering wheel) and *the direct thought* ("How dare . . . drive!") *show* us that the writer was angry without ever using the word *angry*. By adding the details, you involve your readers on an emotional as well as an intellectual level. Always ask yourself, "Would this passage be more effective if I gave details to illustrate rather than simply told what I meant?" If you want your readers to "experience" what you experienced, *showing* is crucial. If you want to appeal to your readers' intellect more than to their emotions, *telling* might be appropriate. Usually, however, a combination of both showing and telling is most effective, for exploratory essays usually appeal both to your readers' reason and to their emotions.

As noted in Chapter 3, "Exploring Events," adding details that describe people and places has a further advantage: Such details help your readers *experience* the events rather than simply hear about them. If your essay doesn't appeal to at least some of the five senses, making it do so will help the revision significantly. If necessary, try remembering exactly what the person or place looks like and jot down the details quickly. Then you can add the important ones to your essay.

Occasionally we mistakenly add details we can't know; for example, we say something like "I opened the door with a frightened look on my face." Think about the logic of saying "with a frightened look on my face." How can you know what your face looked like unless you were gazing in a mirror at the time? What you probably mean is that "anyone opening the door in such circumstances would have a frightened look on his or her face," but such a generalization lacks punch. It's more effective to tell us how your body was feeling. In other words, monitor your physical sensations. For example, when I get frightened my chest feels like a closed fist. That is a physical sensation I can describe and which (I hope) sets up an echo of recognition in my readers. In short, describing your sensations makes more sense (and draws your readers closer to you) than the somewhat clichéd and illogical notion that you know what your face looks like to others. Try describing how your face felt rather than how it looked (for instance, it felt hot, flushed, frozen in a grimace). That is effective too.

As difficult as it may be to believe this, how we experience ourselves in a situation is not necessarily how the rest of the world experiences us. Here's one vivid example. When Ayni and I got married, we made up our own wedding vows. It was as close to a perfect day as is possible, but when it came time for the exchanging of vows, I suddenly became profoundly nervous. The 3-minute vow I had written got reduced to 20 seconds (I just left out a chunk of it). Worse, I could hear my own voice shake as I spoke. When that part of the ceremony was over, I felt like a fool, certain that everyone had heard my voice shaking as though I were standing on a fault during an earthquake. Good friends' reassurances that I had sounded fine rang hollow to my ears. Weeks later, however, my uncle sent us his videotape of the wedding. On the tape, I sounded perfectly normal and under control as I spoke the vows although to my own ears at the time my voice had seemed to shake badly.

In other words, my perception of how I projected myself to the world was wrong. So it is more accurate (as well as more vivid and logical) to describe *what you are feeling* rather than to state that you sounded or looked a certain way to others. If it's important that readers know you had a frightened look on your face, have someone in the essay say, "You look frightened." Or have them react as though they saw a frightened look on your face, perhaps glancing around nervously as though trying to find the person or thing that was frightening you.

ADDING DIALOGUE   Although dialogue does not figure as prominently in exploratory essays as it does in fiction, it still has a place and serves an important function when used. Dialogue is simply another form of detail, of course, but it is a very potent kind of detail. By giving your reader some dialogue instead of a brief summary, you also give yourself a chance to reveal the speakers' tones of voice, gestures, and reactions to particular phrases or ideas. You can show what a speaker noticed while talking. In the football player's essay mentioned earlier, for example, his eyes rest for a moment on the statue in the middle of a dialogue between him and his girlfriend. Further, gestures can reveal a speaker's feelings. A characteristic gesture such as chewing a moustache, tugging on an ear, or playing with some handy object can subtly signal to your readers what a speaker's emotions are (confusion, confidence, fear, happiness, and so forth). Moreover, characteristic phrases can be clues to underlying attitudes. For instance, I have a friend who tends to proclaim his opinions as facts. When he is confronted with the real fact, he inevitably says, "I'm just saying. . . ." That phrase has come to be a signal to his friends that at least subconsciously he knows he's overstepped the facts and this is the bugle call signaling retreat.

There are three tricks to writing effective dialogue. First, create dialogue that both captures the essence of what was said and which does so in language and phrasing that are typical of the speaker (once again, going for the emotional truth rather than the merely factual truth). Second, quote only the key lines of dialogue. No one wants to read dialogue like the following:

> "Hi. How are you?"
> "I'm fine. How about yourself?"
> "Can't complain. What's new with you?"
> "Not much. How about you?"
> "Well, Marge and I just broke up."

This example gives us four lines of boring and nonessential dialogue. Now consider the revision:

> After almost two minutes of small talk, Mike finally blurted out, "Marge and I just broke up."
> I had never thought Marge was right for him anyway, but I felt surprisingly disturbed by his news. "How'd it happen?" I asked, twisting my napkin and watching his downcast eyes.

Here the boring exchanges are justifiably collapsed into the phrase "small talk" and the speakers come alive with the descriptive verbs (*blurted out, twisting*), the descriptions (*downcast eyes*), and with the inclusion of the writer's immediate thoughts and feelings as he heard Mike's news. Notice too the writer's absent-minded gesture—twisting the napkin—as a symbol of his emotions.

Third, save dialogue for key moments that you want to dramatize, mixing in your thoughts and reactions to what is being said.

ADDING SPECULATION ABOUT MOTIVES AND MEANING As noted throughout this book, we can't *know* with certainty the thoughts or inner selves of other people. That fact, however, should not limit our ability to make good guesses, to speculate about people's motives (including our own). When speculating, of course, you should indicate the reasons for your particular speculations. Doing so will give your readers (and you) more confidence in what you say and will also illustrate the way you think.

Here's an example. After dating for several months, your friends Miguel and Crystal suddenly broke up with no explanation to anyone. You write an essay exploring romantic relationships, setting them in the context of such relationships you have observed. Because neither Miguel nor Crystal will talk about the situation, you begin to speculate. At a party the previous weekend, you noticed Miguel's flirting with several other girls. To your mind, such activity would certainly be cause for breaking up. Yet might there be other possible reasons? For example, you know that the stress of midterms was making them irritable. Further, Crystal had complained to you in the past when Miguel seemed to put his studies before her. He was having a particularly difficult time with chemistry, so perhaps he devoted more time to studying than she could tolerate. On the other hand, perhaps Miguel was the one who terminated the relationship. You know from experience that he is very insecure. Perhaps Crystal's smoldering anger about his studying made him feel that she was on the verge of leaving him. Given his need to always save face, you find it believable that he would break up with her in order to avoid her breaking up with him. Finally, you know that relationships in general are hard to maintain because people so easily feel unappreciated by others. If Crystal and Miguel had taken the time to compliment each other, you think, they might still be together.

Are any of these possibilities *the* answer? No. But each speculation reveals something about *your* vision of romantic relationships and your analysis of Crystal's and Miguel's personalities. Notice, for example, that the idea that the breakup was a mutual decision is not entertained. That in itself is revealing. When the evidence is supplied to support your speculations (examples of his flirting, of their irritability and concern about midterms, of his insecurity and need to maintain his pride), readers will have a good sense of you.

The same advice applies to writing about yourself. When you don't know the motive or reason, speculate. Always avoid cop-outs like "I can't remember why I did X" or "It all happened too quickly" or "I have no idea what this all means." Replace them with your speculations: It's perfectly valid to say, for example, "I'm not sure why I did X. Perhaps I feared being revealed as a fool. Perhaps I felt sorry for my friend. Perhaps I was simply a coward. Whatever the reason, I . . . ." Simply spelling out the possibilities helps your readers understand you more fully.

ADDING PERSONAL SIGNIFICANCE   Sometimes the **personal significance** (of a relationship, an event, a concept, a text, or whatever) seems so obvious to us that we fail to state it so that the reader, too, can understand it. When revising, make sure that you have stated the significance clearly and fully. Especially in early drafts, we may become so engaged in exploring one aspect of significance that we forget there may be others. As you go through your drafts, keep these two questions in mind:

> *What other <u>direct significance</u> did this have for you?* In other words, how did what you are writing about affect your vision of the world, your sense of your self, your sense of your own moral code, your understanding of the particular people involved and/ or of people in general?

> *Did it have any <u>indirect significance</u>?* Did exploring the topic lead you to insights about people or relationships that were not directly involved?

Many issues recur in essays—for example, relationships with parents, siblings, friends, lovers), vision of the world (as a good place, a bad place, a complex place), assumptions about how people or institutions work ("The only thing men want is sex," "All politics and politicians are crooked"), attitudes toward the self ("I'm the greatest," "I'm a failure," "I rarely make the right decision"). *Each such issue is a key to personal significance.* Which of those issues seem major in your essay? What is your explicit attitude toward those issues? Should those issues really be the main focus of the essay? Often an issue mentioned merely in passing might be worth further exploration, either in this essay or in an essay of its own. Look for issues that are merely alluded to or mentioned once, then write about their personal significance as well.

ADDING GLOBAL SIGNIFICANCE   Once you have deepened the personal significance, turn your attention to **global significance,** the possible importance that your exploration of a topic might have for your readers and the connections between your own experience and the experience of others (perhaps as revealed in texts). Global significance not only increases your readers' understanding of you but also provides them with a wider context for understanding themselves. Any insight into yourself—into your feelings, ideas, beliefs, and their sources—may have automatic global significance since each of us is, in a sense, humanity in miniature. That is why we can often generalize from our own experiences. For instance, if you are exploring your relationship with a sibling, what insights might you offer about the way siblings interact? How does your experience connect to the experiences of others with siblings that you know? How does it connect to texts you've encountered?

To be made convincing, however, global significance usually requires that as a writer you move outward into the realm of research, reading books and articles on the topic, reviewing your lecture notes from other classes, interviewing experts, viewing documentaries, considering the popular vision of your topic in television shows and movies, and so on.

QUESTIONING

One technique that is particularly useful for deepening and revising content is called **questioning.** After each sentence (assertion) in your draft, ask yourself the following questions. Then write at least a one-sentence answer to the question that seems most penetrating and put your answer to it immediately after the original sentence.

1. What as-yet unstated reasons caused me to act (or think or feel) that particular way?

2. What as-yet unstated emotions was I feeling then (and am I feeling now)?

3. What as-yet unstated assumptions and ideas influenced me then and influence me now (for example, assumptions about the nature of people, the world, and myself)?

4. How does this event (reaction, feeling, or idea) connect to other experiences (either mine or those I have heard or read about)? In what specific ways does it connect?

5. Assuming that my reactions (thoughts or feelings) are not typical, in what ways do they reveal my inner self?

6. In addition to the expected reactions, emotions, and ideas (*expected* in the sense that just about everyone would have them under similar circumstances), what *surprising* reactions, emotions, and ideas did this experience give me?

7. What are the other sources of these reactions, emotions, and ideas?

8. What texts have I encountered that relate to my experience (reactions, emotions, and thoughts)? (Quotations might enhance your essay.)

9. What as-yet unstated beliefs justify or explain my reactions, feelings, and thoughts?

WRITING INTRODUCTIONS

An introduction should let the readers know what the essay will be about. It should also give them at least a hint about your attitude toward the subject. And it should capture the readers' attention. This is a very important element in any exploratory essay. You need to make your readers want to continue to read. Of course, some readers will persevere no matter how boring the introduction is. But do you want reading your essay to be a chore?

Consider a college dance. You have gone there stag. Across the room are two people. One is dressed in an incredibly boring outfit; the other is wearing an eye-catching outfit, subtle but provocative. Which one will you probably ask to dance first?

This is not to imply that, in reality, the one with the dull clothes is dull. That person might turn out to be fascinating company—if you ever get around to requesting a dance. Essay introductions work the same way. You want to entice your readers to continue to read; you want them to willingly get to know you and your ideas better.

Consider the seemingly minor difference between these two opening sentences:

> It was a typical summer day—the sky was balmy and the ocean was full of boats.

> It started off as a typical day—the sky was balmy and the ocean was full of boats.

Frankly, the first is boring. It promises an essay which describes a typical day. Although I don't know how interesting a life its writer leads, I do know that no one would give up an hour of even TV reruns to learn about *my* typical day. Admittedly, the second opening sentence hardly fires our imagination. But notice the difference: The verb—*started off*—suggests that the day did not end up in a typical fashion. Suddenly our interest is aroused.

That's your goal in writing an introduction—spark your readers' interest in some way. You may open with a narrative statement as in the preceding example. Or you may choose some other opening gambit. Many strategies exist to catch your readers' attention. For examples, look at the variety of openings the essayists employ in this book.

A final piece of advice about introductions: Make writing an introduction your last act before you revise for style and prepare your final draft. It is difficult to introduce something until you know exactly what it is that you are introducing; waiting until the rest of the essay is in final form will make writing the introduction easier.

A REVISION CHECKLIST FOR CONTENT

Following the suggestions below as you reexamine your drafts *before* you submit them should significantly improve your essays. Always assume that *all of the following apply to your paper* (don't say to yourself, "Oh, I've already done *that*" because even if you have, you can probably do it with more detail or with more stylistic flair). Prove to yourself that you have indeed done all that can be done.

1. What is the main point of your essay? If you can't find it, create one. If you can't create one, that means you need to do more exploring.

2. About each assertion, ask "Why is this fact or opinion important?" Then answer each "why" in one or more sentences that directly follow the assertion.

3. About each assertion, ask "How do I know this idea is true?" Then write one or more sentences that state (or quote) the evidence which answers that question.

4. Ask yourself, "What is the direct significance of this sentence/paragraph/idea to my essay's point?" Then explain the significance in one or more sentences. If you don't see a connection, do some idea generation exercises to discover the significance of the sentence/paragraph/idea or eliminate it.

5. Keep asking about your own motives and those of others. For example, "What else did I feel and think when X happened?" Then ask, "Why did I feel that way or think that thought?"

6. Ask yourself about the motives of other people involved. In what ways are they more complex than you originally thought?

7. Similarly, keep asking yourself questions about meaning and significance: For example, "What does this text mean to me?" "Why is this event important to me?"

8. What is your essay trying to accomplish? Analyze feelings? Present a world view or life philosophy? Define a belief or concept? Recreate a process of discovery? Analyze a text and relate it to you? If you can't tell, neither can your readers. Make the goal or approach clearer to them.

9. Do you provide your readers with new information? If not, can you do so?

10. Are there places where more information, more analysis, more details, or more examples would help readers believe or understand your points?

11. Have you explored your split perspective, explaining the differences (if any) between your thoughts and feelings then and your thoughts and feelings now?

12. Does your introduction capture your readers' attention and make them want to read on?

13. Does your introduction state directly (or perhaps subtly or indirectly) the major issues or themes you examine in your essay?

14. Would your essay be more effective if it started with your second paragraph instead of the first paragraph?

15. Does the conclusion of this essay really satisfy your readers? That is, has what was started in the introduction been either resolved or, in some significant way, ended to provide a sense of closure?

16. Does the conclusion connect in some significant manner with the introduction? For example, do you allude to your opening strategy or device?

17. Would the progression of your essay be improved by a re-ordering of the sequence of its major sections?

18. Are the events or ideas related in ways that you have not yet shown or explored fully—for example, by means of comparison and contrast or cause and effect or as an illustration of each other?

19. Have you made the descriptions of people vivid, giving memorable details of their appearance, focusing on the "telling details" or features which suggest something about their personalities?

20. Have you shown other people's tones of voice, their characteristic phrasings, their characteristic gestures and movements?

21. Have you indicated the objects or clothing or settings most closely associated with those other people?

22. Have you made the descriptions of place vivid by appealing to all five senses and by recreating its atmosphere?

23. Have you indicated what makes this place different from every other similar place you've ever seen—for example, how is this beach different from all other beaches?

24. Have you made the descriptions of objects vivid by focusing on the key details that make this object different from all others?

25. Have you indicated why you noticed this particular object?

26. Have you made clear who or what is associated with this object and why?

27. Have you suggested how this object signifies or symbolizes something or someone in the scene?

28. Is the essay coherent and unified? Is the connection between ideas clearly implied or stated?

29. Have you provided all the background information that your readers need (such as your age at the time of the event)? Have you provided enough context and global significance?

THE TENSION BETWEEN BEING EXPLICIT AND BEING IMPLICIT

In this chapter, you may have noticed a tension between the advice to make things more explicit (adding context, background, speculation, personal and global significance) and the advice to make them more subtle (adding details and dialogue). Such tension is also visible when you compare a number of essays reprinted in this book—some are very explicit and others are not. Which should be your goal—explicit or implicit?

Unfortunately (from the point of view of those wanting to receive advice and those wanting to give it), there is no easy answer to this question. But that fact is also fortunate for writers and readers since it opens up a wide variety of possibilities. Without question, the ideal deliverer of information is a piece of writing that is totally explicit. In it, everything is spelled out. Perhaps this is why legal documents such as contracts and laws themselves tend to be so long—the information has to be perfectly clear with no ambiguity and no suggestiveness (either of which could lead to litigation). You will notice, however, that no legal documents are reprinted in this book because they are not exploratory essays.

With every essay that you revise, you face the challenge of deciding how much should be made explicit. For each essay you write, the ratio between explicit and implicit will probably change. The reason is twofold: First, your purpose might change with each essay you write. For instance, if it is important to you that readers come away from your essay knowing exactly what you learned from the experience (or what you felt, and so forth), then you will probably make the essay more explicit. If, on the other hand, you want readers to ponder the experience's implications, you might make the essay less explicit. The following is a huge oversimplification, but it might offer some guidance here: Less explicit essays tend to be more artistic; more explicit essays tend to be more intellectual.

Second, different types of exploratory essays lend themselves to different degrees of explicitness. For example, essays exploring events and relationships often tend to be more implicit, using such elements as the details, descriptions, and dialogue to suggest meaning. These essays encourage your readers to interpret, evaluate, and judge. Essays exploring texts and beliefs, on the other hand, tend to be more explicit, in part because their very nature is analytical and interpretative. They encourage readers to understand and consider implications. This, too, is an oversimplification, but it does contain some truth.

Most of the time, you should explicitly state as much of the essay's meaning as possible *for yourself,* and that is the major thrust of the advice throughout this book. After all, one of the major reasons for writing exploratory essays is to discover more about yourself. If you do not make those discoveries explicit, the chances are you will not appreciably increase your self-knowledge. The very act of stating your discoveries clearly gives them substance and staying power. Once you have done that for yourself, however, you face a decision about what to include in your final draft. In addition to considering how comfortable you are about revealing your insights, you should ask what will make your essay more interesting for readers and what will fulfill your purpose more effectively—stating your insights explicitly or leaving them implicit for readers to interpret (and, it must be added, to possibly misinterpret). Finally, it is your decision to make.

11

Revising Style

Able to draw on a wide range of styles and techniques, exploratory essays are, nevertheless, still essays—in other words, they are acts of communication which must convey ideas clearly. In this chapter we consider some of the stylistic options and techniques that you might use to improve the readability of your essays and to make your style as interesting as your content.

WHAT IS STYLE?

Style is your fingerprint in writing. Just as the whorls, swirls, and breaks in the ridges of your fingerprint identify you, so too does that quality of language which is intimately involved with the precise communication of your ideas, feelings, and characteristic habits of thought (in other words, your typical ways of approaching a topic or a problem or an idea and of developing and exploring a concept). **Style** includes the language you use and the ways in which you use it, the ideas you choose to explore and the attitudes you take toward them, the emotions you decide to reveal and the techniques you use to convey them.

As you can see, this definition of *style* includes content as well as prose itself. Hence revision requires further exploration of your ideas (Chapter 10) as well as refinement of your prose. To develop a truly personal style, then, you need to deepen your insights, make ideas your own, explore your emotions, examine your habits of thought, and fine-tune your prose.

For most of us, though, the word *style* suggests such elements as words, figurative language, and sentences. Keeping in mind the fact that style is a reflection of you, we will focus on such elements in this chapter.

Part of developing that style is to understand and appreciate others' styles, to learn from them and perhaps to steal techniques that seem appropriate to you. It has often been said that the immature writer imitates while the mature writer steals. Theft, of course, implies total possession (the thief has made the stolen VCR his own). Such "stealing" of techniques, of course, is a happy tradition in all art forms—borrowing techniques from masters and then making them your own, adapting them to *your* vision and *your* needs. One technique for sharpening your sense of the differences between styles and to learn from them is to read aloud at least one paragraph from each of the published essays you read. Hearing the language is the best way to imprint its patterns in your subconscious and to help them become a part of your stylistic repertoire.

WORDS

With the understanding that the development of a "personal style" involves our thoughts themselves, our attitude toward them, our method of developing those thoughts, our sense of ourselves as writers in addition to precise and accurate prose, let's turn our attention to the particulars of prose. Our basic principle about modern writing style throughout will be the following: The best style is concise, precise, accurate, imaginative, and interesting.

Choosing the Right Word

According to Mark Twain, "The difference between the *almost*-right word and the *right* word is really a large matter—it's the difference between the lightning bug and the lightning" (letter to George Bainton, Oct. 15, 1888). Whenever possible, you want your essay filled with lightning—words which say exactly what you mean and which carry the exact connotations you desire, words that illuminate and excite your readers. Most often the potential for selecting the lightning bug over the lightning occurs with adjectives and verbs, perhaps because the names of things (nouns) are usually easier to be precise about.

Let's take a moment to review three key concepts, namely, denotation, connotation, and synonym. **Denotation** is the dictionary definition of a word, its literal sense. For example, the *American Heritage College Dictionary* (3rd edition) offers the following as its first definition for the adjective *fat*: "Having much or too much fat or flesh; plump or obese." On the other hand, **connotations** are the meanings suggested by or associated with a word or thing. Hence, to our modern sensibility, the word *fat* connotes such things as *overindulgence, pig, lack of exercise.*

Finally, a **synonym** is a word that has the same or nearly the same meaning as another word. Yet language seems to find exact synonyms redundant and thus connotations quickly change exact duplicates into something else. In its own definition of *fat* (quoted above), for example, the dictionary lists *obese* as a synonym for *fat*. But its own definition of *obese* is "extremely fat, grossly overweight." In other words, *obese* is not an exact synonym of *fat*. If we had substituted *obese* for *fat* in our description of a person, we would have changed the meaning of the description: *Obese* carries a more negative connotation than *fat* and also means more than just fat—it means *extremely* fat. The trick, then, is to find the word whose denotation and connotations exactly match your meaning. Presto—lightning.

The quest for just the right word can certainly be aided by a thesaurus. As the previous paragraph implies, however, the danger of a thesaurus is that it seems to suggest that many of the words it lists are exact synonyms, and they aren't. Useful as it is, a thesaurus should always be used in conjunction with a very good dictionary to decrease the chances of selecting a word with the wrong connotations.

❏ *Exercise 1*

Below are lists of synonyms. Try to express the differences in the connotations and shades of meaning among each group.

1. to imitate, to copy, to emulate, to mimic, to impersonate
2. fat, corpulent, fleshy, obese, stout
3. thin, slender, slight, wispy, lean, willowy, svelte
4. to walk, to amble, to traverse, to saunter, to stroll, to strut, to tread

Avoiding Suitcase Words

Suitcases are containers into which we place numerous articles of clothing. We then close the lid so that the articles don't fall out. A secondary result of that lid closing is that others cannot see what we are carrying. Similarly, **suitcase words** are vague or general words which may hold a great deal of meaning for you the writer, but whose meaning cannot be seen from the outside by your readers. We all use suitcase words in early drafts. A particular term has a definite meaning in our minds and perhaps carries a lot of emotion as well. Yet to our readers, the word has little depth or meaning. Perhaps they sense that the word bulges with potential, but they can't discover the potential because they lack X-ray vision. Thus we must unpack those suitcase words, spilling out their emotional and intellectual content so that readers can understand.

For example, Brent wrote that there are a "couple of personal subjects" he doesn't discuss with his parents. A "couple of personal subjects" is a suitcase phrase. What specifically does it mean? It actually tells his readers very little. When I was in college, for instance, I didn't tell my parents about the subject matter of my stories nor did I mention the fact that I was in love in my freshman year—those would be my "couple of personal subjects"—but they weren't Brent's and they probably wouldn't be yours either. To Brent, the phrase had a very specific meaning. But it has *different* specific meanings for everyone else, so the act of communication broke down when he used the phrase in an essay. However, after Brent unpacked that suitcase phrase in a revision, he could explore *why* he didn't talk to his parents about those particular issues. His essay became both more searching and more revealing.

One more example: Laura wrote that in high school she was "rebellious and wanted independence," but what do those suitcase words mean exactly? For some, *independence* might mean being allowed to join a gang and beat up drunks, whereas for others it might mean being able to wear spiked hair, and for still others it might mean being allowed to have lovers in their rooms. Unless such suitcase terms are unpacked, readers don't know much about the writer. The insights into Laura come from seeing in what particular ways she rebelled and what particular issues were involved for *her*.

Eliminating Distancing Words

Some words hinder readers' experiencing the essay's emotions; those words force readers away from the action, the thoughts, the emotions. I call them **distancing words**—the verbs of remembering, thinking, feeling. That we tend to use too many of these words is not surprising: We are merely duplicating our own present experience. For example, as we sit before the computer searching our memory for an event to write about, it's only natural that we begin by writing "I remember the day . . ." because that's exactly what we are doing—remembering as we sit at the computer. But by telling readers that we are remembering, we push them away from the more direct experience of the event itself. Consider the following example:

> I remember the day that Sue and I broke up. I remember that it was raining, and I thought to myself that the rain was appropriate. I wondered why we were breaking up at all. I didn't want to break up with her. I felt myself getting sadder and sadder, and then angrier and angrier. After all, I couldn't help wondering what I had done to deserve such treatment by her.

Here's a revision:

> Appropriately enough, it rained the day Sue and I broke up. Why were we breaking up at all? I certainly didn't want to break

up with her. Sadness filled me, then anger washed it away. What had I done to deserve such treatment?

The *felt experience* of these two passages is different. In the first, readers are removed from the action, hearing about it in summary fashion, the way we hear a news report on the radio. In the second, readers experience the writer's confusion and anger and frustration instead of simply hearing about it. The elimination of all the distancing words—*remember, thought to myself, wondered, felt, wondering*—and the dramatization of the thoughts make the second passage alive in ways that the first isn't.

The first example is written the way many of us write our first drafts. When revising, though, one of the things we should focus on is eliminating distancing words and making the experience of the essay more immediate and dramatic for our readers. In the example, this is accomplished by turning indirect thought ("I wondered why . . . ") into direct thought ("Why were we . . . ?") and by making the emotions ("Sadness filled . . . , anger washed . . . ") the subjects of their clauses accompanied by strong verbs instead of adjectives with state-of-being verbs ("felt myself getting sadder and sadder, and then angrier and angrier"). Notice too that the direct thought maintains the past tense of the whole paragraph; it is a common misperception that if you give direct thought you have to do so in the present tense. Not so.

One final note: Have you ever considered the logic of the phrase *thought to myself?* Assuming that we don't have telepathic powers, to whom else would we think? Although the phrase has achieved idiomatic status, it is redundant.

Avoiding Sexist Language

Sexist language is language which assumes one gender is dominant. We tend to fall into sexist language in exploratory essays when we generalize from our own experiences. Consider the following examples:

> A *child* faces many traumas, and *he* needs to know that there are others who will help *him* to overcome them.

> When a *child* is told or taught to keep things to *himself* and is not permitted to imagine, daydream, or fantasize, *their* unconscious self is repressed.

Some out-of-date grammar books insist that the masculine singular pronoun (*he/him*) is correct when people of either gender are meant; such a "rule" is blatantly sexist and based on old-fashioned notions about male superiority in society. It also leads to pronoun reference problems as in the second example above (*himself . . . their*). Many readers still object to the *he or she* option, and I agree that it becomes tiresome after several consecutive usages. It can lead to horrible wordiness in a sentence such as "He or she must decide for himself or herself."

There are several ways to avoid sexist language without creating new stylistic problems. One way is to begin such sentences or paragraphs using plural nouns (we usually mean the plural anyway). For both of the preceding examples, a simple change of *child* to *children* eliminates the sexism and makes the prose clearer:

> *Children* face many traumas, and *they* need to know that there are others who will help *them* to overcome such traumas.

> When *children* are told or taught to keep things to *themselves* and are not permitted to imagine, daydream, or fantasize, *their* unconscious selves are repressed.

Using the plural can also often help you avoid sexual stereotypes that set you up to use sexist language later on in the sentence:

not: A *lawyer* and *his* advice are rarely parted without a fee.
but: *Lawyers* and *their* advice are rarely parted without a fee.

If using the plural is not an option, rephrase the sentence to eliminate the gender-specific pronoun entirely:

> *not:*   *Anyone* who is illegally parked will have *his* car towed.
> *but:*   Any illegally parked car will be towed.
> *not:*   Each writer must have *his* essay photocopied today.
> *but:*   Each essay must be photocopied today.

or (if appropriate):   *You* must have your essay photocopied today.

A third method is to use inclusive words instead of gender-specific words:

not: *Workmen* and their *wives* were invited to the opening ceremonies.
but: *Workers* and their *spouses* were invited to the opening ceremonies.
not: *Mankind's* time on earth is insignificant when compared to the age of the earth itself.
but: *Humankind's* time on earth is insignificant when compared to the age of the earth itself.
not: *Chairmen* of corporations face great stress every day.
but: *Leaders* of corporations face great stress every day.

There are many gender-specific terms that are now considered sexist. Here are a few examples of words to use to refer to both males and females (a good handbook will provide a much more extensive list): *actor* (replaces *actress*), *poet* (replaces *poetess*), *graduates* (replaces *alumnae, alumni*), *hero* (replaces *heroine*), *nurse* (replaces *male nurse*), *worker-hours* or *staff-hours* (replaces *man-hours*), *go-between* or *intermediary* (replaces *middleman*), and *superstition* (replaces *old wives' tale*).

FIGURATIVE LANGUAGE

Exploratory essays can use all the resources of language. One great resource is **figurative language,** language that is metaphorical or rhetorical and which goes beyond denotation. Perhaps the best known figures of speech are those we call metaphorical, and they are commonly associated with poetry because they can compress ideas or feelings into few words. They can be very useful when your feelings about a topic seem to defy simple explanation. In exploratory essays, the metaphorical figures of speech you are most likely to use are *similes, metaphors, symbols,* and *analogies.*

Simile

A **simile** is an explicitly stated comparison. Because the connection between the two items (say, a man and a horse) is clearly spelled out, readers do not have to puzzle over the simile. Moreover, the image is clearly signaled to the readers by the presence of *like, as,* and *as if.* Consider the following examples:

The man eats like a horse.

The man eats as a horse eats.

The man eats as if he were a horse.

Similes can be highly effective in conveying your ideas, and your personality and inventiveness can be amply displayed by your choice of items to compare. In the above example, for instance, if you had replaced the clichéd *horse* with *fish,* you would have slowed your readers down a bit ("Just how does a fish eat, anyway?"), but their delay would have been well rewarded once they had envisioned a fish eating with its pursed and pulsing lips. In addition, if you put too much food in a fish tank, fish will eat until they kill themselves—a much more appropriate image for a real glutton than the clichéd *horse,* which simply eats a lot of food because it has a big body to feed.

Metaphor

Whereas a simile indicates the point of comparison with a signaling word such as *like,* a **metaphor** *assumes* the connection between the two items and hence offers an implied rather than an explicit comparison. The metaphor, that is, boldly equates the two items and leaves it up to the readers to decide which points of comparison are being considered:

"He eats like a fish." [simile]

"He is a fish." [a metaphor]

Obviously you are leaving a great deal up to the readers here—they have to consider all the characteristics of a fish (e.g., has scales, lives under water, breathes through gills, gets caught by hooks and nets) and then decide which one(s) you want them to consider as they contemplate the man. If they received only that sentence, your readers would of course be hard pressed to determine what you mean. Normally, however, a sentence is read in context. For instance, if the sentence were a part of a paragraph that described a group of people, including the "fish man," at the dinner table or that talked about the high costs of having this man as a live-in guest, the metaphor's meaning would be clear. Because it requires more activity from readers, the metaphor is a more difficult image for readers to decode than the simile, but it may also be more rewarding.

A metaphor can be a very suggestive tool for you as a writer as well as for your readers. For instance, if you write "He is a fish" thinking of the man's gluttony, the metaphor might cause you to ask, "In what other ways is he like a fish?" Think about the parenthetical list of characteristics in the preceding paragraph. Perhaps the man doesn't have a skin condition (scales), but maybe his palm is always clammy when you shake hands (notice the second sea-world metaphor, *clammy*). Maybe this man is so uninformed about what's going on that he might as well live under water. And maybe he will fall for anything (he bought the Brooklyn Bridge, twice!). He can get caught by any wiggling idea that captures his attention. Maybe his wife "netted" him by using her witty repartee as bait.

See how a metaphor can spark your thoughts? Even if everything in the preceding paragraph were unusable in your particular essay, the act of playing with the metaphor could give you new insights and new ways of approaching the topic. Further, the sheer joy of playing with an idea is its own reward—indulging in such playing occasionally will encourage your subconscious to continue to be creative. For instance, I enjoyed pushing the fish metaphor in the previous paragraph.

Another level of metaphor is the **implied metaphor.** Here, instead of naming "fish," you might use words associated with a fish to suggest the connection. Again, this challenges readers more and hence gives them a greater sense of accomplishment when they work it out (which often happens, by the way, on the subconscious level). Thus you might say:

> With his eyes bulging, the man pursed his lips and inhaled the food.

Finally, here's an example of how writers often challenge readers with a metaphor and then extend the metaphor, making some of the points of comparison explicit. The paragraph is from Annie Dillard's essay "Heaven and Earth in Jest":

> I am an explorer, then, and I am also a stalker, or the instrument of the hunt itself. Certain Indians used to carve long grooves

along the wooden shafts of their arrows. They called the grooves "lightning marks," because they resembled the curved fissure lightning slices down the trunks of trees. The function of lightning marks is this: if the arrow fails to kill the game, blood from a deep wound will channel along the lightning mark, streak down the arrow shaft, and spatter to the ground, laying a trail dripped on broadleaves, on stones, that the barefoot and trembling archer can follow into whatever deep or rare wilderness it leads. I am the arrow shaft, carved along my length by unexpected lights and gashes from the very sky, and this book is the straying trail of blood.

This is a complex paragraph with undeniable power. For the point I'm making here, however, consider the "I am the arrow shaft" sentence near the end. Because Dillard assumes that the Indians' lightning marks and arrow shafts are probably unknown to most of us, she spends most of the paragraph explaining them before she offers the metaphor. Then she introduces the other half of the metaphor—herself as writer and as observer. Only when we understand the details of the arrow do we see the implications of her being a shaft. In other words, when you are using a specialized item in your image, be sure to give your readers enough information so that they can understand all the nuances.

Notice too that there are other metaphors in this paragraph which depend on that first one. For instance, Dillard's book is the trail of blood, implying that something else—truth?—is the wounded beast. And what does it mean to be "carved and gashed" by the sky? Can we doubt that she sees herself also as "the barefoot and trembling archer," an identification which she established in the paragraph's first sentence ("I am also a stalker")?

Yes, a complex and compelling paragraph, one that shows the signs of careful and thoughtful crafting. Its lesson to us? Start with a metaphor and let it grow. You never know what you'll end up with.

Here is a very extended metaphor from essayist Thomas Simmons's "Mourning":

> The past is a battlefield strewn with mines whose detonators finally fail: in the end, the oldest miseries no longer explode. Like mines, ominous and encrusted with dirt, they look threatening, but when shaken or dropped after excavation they do not detonate. They lie there, frozen in their treachery, incapable of harm.
>
> My unrelieved earaches, which were such a torment to me in my childhood, no longer wound me in the gut. I hold them in my mind as I would hold a mine, delicately and cautiously, and then I let them fall. Nothing happens. At most they displace a little dust. I am outraged at what I endured, but it rarely frightens me. I am only frightened when I see such torments inflicted in the present on children who unlike me do not live through

the battle. My old memories of earaches, bronchitis, and un-named and unhealed illnesses return with a keen edge, a sharp fear of human beings who impose suffering for the sake of a prin-ciple. But the fear is short-lived. I have learned to move beyond it into a healthy rage.

Other mines, still relatively fresh, have live detonators. Bur-ied in my personal battlefield of high school and college, they remind me how much there is to mourn.

In the first paragraph's first sentence, Simmons establishes two met-aphors: (1) the past is a battlefield and (2) painful events from the past are land mines. The rest of the first paragraph develops the second im-age. The second paragraph makes explicit some of the past events he has in mind and continues the image, showing how their "detonators finally fail." The third paragraph continues the image, suggesting some mines still have "live detonators." Once again, allowing images to develop this way and allowing yourself to play with their implications can lead to powerful passages in your essays.

Symbol

The word *symbol* is used in many different ways. For our purposes in this book, let's define a **symbol** as an object, an event, a gesture, or a person that represents something in addition to itself. Unlike the simile and the metaphor, it does not require a comparison. Often the process of association gives the symbol its additional meaning(s). Note the word *additional* in the previous sentence: *a symbol is, first and foremost, itself.*

There are two kinds of symbols: public (or traditional) and private. Public symbols are easily recognizable: For instance, "Mom" and "apple pie" have come to symbolize a vision of America, and a Christmas tree symbolizes the whole Christmas experience (religious elements, carols, gift-giving, family gatherings, and so forth). Often, however, writers invent their own symbols (private symbols) by investing a particular action, gesture, object, person, or event with special significance. Al-most any literary symbol you can think of—for example, Gogol's over-coat and Hawthorne's scarlet letter—are everyday objects which have gained symbolic value in those particular works through repetition and through the authors' adding significance to them.

In an early draft of an essay about stifling family life, for example, one of my students, Allie, provocatively stated that the "sticky plastic covering on the couch is a pain," then moved on to something else. In that original version, the "pain" she referred to was literal: the discom-fort of sitting on the plastic. That was all. But as she revised, she came to see that the plastic could be turned into a symbol and explored. Not-ing that she felt stifled by her lifestyle, she added these details to her revision:

That plastic sealed the couch. Nothing could get in to harm the couch, and that was good. But the couch couldn't be touched by the outside world. Also, there was a spot on one of the cushions—maybe the cushion came from the factory that way. In any case, the plastic prevented anyone from fixing it. The couch was stuck with that stain. If a couch could breathe, it would suffocate in that plastic. If couches were animate and wanted human contact, that couch would be very lonely. That was my parents' approach to everything they valued: seal it up, keep the outside world outside.

Do you see how Allie has turned the plastic cover into a symbol of her "parents' approach to everything they valued?" Of course, she could have used the plastic cover in other ways. If she had wanted to suggest death with the image instead of isolation, she might have said "the couch was *shrouded* in plastic." The point here is that the plastic cover is not inherently an image of stifling or of death—but it has characteristics that might be used symbolically. The key is to pay attention to the details and then use your description to suggest your own attitudes and feelings.

Here's another example. In E. B. White's essay "Once More to the Lake," the sophisticated symbol of doubling grows with each example—the dragonfly that lands on the pole of White's son and which seems to be the one that landed on White's pole years earlier, the reflected minnows, the repeated jokes about rain and swimming. And in Dillard's "Seeing," the act of seeing takes on symbolic value.

In fact, it is probably impossible to avoid writing symbolically since language itself is, after all, merely a mass of symbols that stand for something else. The trick in exploratory writing is to discover the symbolic potential of what you write. Exploring a symbol and exploring *by means of* symbols are valuable and insight-granting methods of writing. When you notice a symbol or potential symbol as you read over a draft, take time to play with it on a separate sheet of paper (or on the screen if you're using a word processor). You'll be amazed at what you discover.

Analogy

One of the most effective devices is analogy. An **analogy** points out the similarities between two items that are essentially different. The less obvious the connection between the two is, the more powerful and effective the analogy is likely to be. One of the most famous analogies occurs in John Donne's poem "A Valediction: Forbidding Mourning":

If they [our souls] be two, they are two so
  As stiff twin compasses are two;
Thy soul, the fixed foot, makes no show
  To move, but doth, if the other do.

1

And though it in the center sit,   *5*
  Yet when the other far doth roam,
It leans and hearkens after it,
  And grows erect, as that comes home.

Such wilt thou be to me, who must
  Like the other foot, obliquely run: *10*
Thy firmness makes my circle just,
  And makes me end where I begun.

The power of this analogy is that the two items being compared are so dissimilar that we get a shock when Donne brings them together (in this case, lovers are being compared to a connected pair of compasses—the kind used to draw a circle). The analogy becomes a revelation, showing us something about love that we might never have considered before. Even if we did say to ourselves, "Lovers are joined in some way and are never really separate," having the image of the twin compasses makes our knowledge visual; we can *see* the concept in a new way.

There are three dangers with analogies. First, you might select two items that have absolutely nothing of significance in common. In that case, your analogy will fall flat. It will convey nothing except a negative impression of your discernment. Second, you might overuse analogies and thus weaken your essay. Using too many may encourage you not to explore any of them in enough depth. Save the analogy for an important or difficult-to-understand point. Third, you may be tempted to let an analogy serve as proof of something. Don't. Analogies *illustrate* and *make abstract concepts and feelings concrete.* But analogies can't prove anything because the differences between the two items always undercut the logical demonstration of proof.

SENTENCES

According to an old adage, "Variety is the spice of life." That is particularly true of sentences. Having most of your sentences follow one pattern of construction or making them all about the same length can put your readers to sleep. Despite the flash of your ideas, your essay will seem monotonous and dull. Sentence variety is a matter for revision because our focus in early drafts must be on the ideas themselves. Such variety can occur in the length of sentences, in their construction, or in their first elements. The following section will strongly advise that you examine your own prose in ways that you may never have done before. The reason is simple: Scientists observe a phenomenon before doing anything else. Similarly, you should observe the phenomenon of your style before trying to alter it. See what you have now so that you'll know what to change and how to change it.

Sentence Length

A variety of sentence lengths is more effective than any one length. Short sentences are useful for driving home a point and may have a dramatic impact; longer sentences are especially useful for summing up a series of points at the end of a paragraph or section or for qualifying an idea stated in a previous sentence. If most of your sentences are medium or longer, try breaking a few into short sentences. Of course, only you can decide which points you wish to emphasize or qualify. On the other hand, if most of your sentences are short, try combining some of them into longer sentences (doing so usually helps clarify the relationships between the ideas contained in the short sentences).

You may find it worthwhile to count the number of words in each sentence in at least one whole page of your manuscript. List each number on a piece of paper and draw a line under the number for the last sentence in each paragraph. For example, for the previous paragraph and this one the list would look like this:

12
45
16
14
<u>34</u>
23
22
<u>15</u>

Looking at the list tells not only how long each sentence is but also how the sentences are grouped in a paragraph. Assuming that one line of type contains roughly 14 words, we'll say that sentences with 1–14 words are short; those with 15–29 are medium; those with 30–44 are medium long; those with 45–52 are long; and those with 53+ words are extra long. These designations are somewhat arbitrary, but they'll serve as a rough-and-tumble guide. Further, simple addition tells us that the two paragraphs together total 181 words, or 22.6 words per sentence (181 words divided by 8 sentences). In other words, the feel of those two paragraphs together is of medium-length sentences. Also, the first paragraph averages 24.2 words per sentence while the second averages 20 words per sentence. The first paragraph shows good variety; the second, less so (but not disastrously so since it is only three sentences long).

❏ *Exercise 2*

Look at your list for your essay and answer the following questions.

1. How many words are in the *longest* sentence? _____
2. How many words are in the *shortest* sentence? _____

3. Are the long sentences clumped together or spread out? _____

4. Are the short sentences clumped together or spread out? _____

5. Do some paragraphs contain mostly (or only) long sentences? _____

6. Do some paragraphs contain mostly (or only) short sentences? _____

7. What's the average length of your sentences? _____

If numerous sentences of any one length are clumped together, you probably need to revise for length. I've consciously left the term *numerous* vague since the purpose of a particular paragraph may dictate the length of the sentences. A good rule of thumb is the following: If three or more consecutive sentences fall into the same length category, at least one sentence needs to be changed.

Sentence Structure

Not only the length but also the structure of your sentences should be varied. The main ways to create such variety are three: through clauses, through first elements, and through modifiers.

CLAUSES Usually sentence structure is discussed first in terms of independent and dependent clauses. A clause is any group of words that has both a subject and a predicate. An **independent clause** is one that can stand on its own as a complete thought or sentence ("The horse ate the hay"); a **dependent clause** is one that begins with a subordinating conjunction (for instance, *After, Because, While, When*) and sounds incomplete by itself ("Because the horse ate the hay"). Various types of sentences can be constructed using these two types of clauses. A **simple sentence** has one independent clause and no dependent ones:

simple sentence: I told the truth.

simple sentence: In the middle of the night with no stars and no moon shining and with no one around except Marta and Elly and Paula and Nicole and with no help from any of them, I told the truth once and for all in simple and plain words out behind the barn.

Although the second example contains 51 words (and is thus "long"), it is still a simple sentence because it contains no dependent clauses. It is, however, an ungraceful sentence because it strings four prepositional phrases together (stringing together more than two usually sparks concern). But it does prove the point that a simple sentence is not necessarily short.

A **compound sentence** contains two or more independent clauses and no dependent clauses.

compound sentence: I told the truth, and she cried.

compound sentence: At high noon while standing in the middle of the street in front of all our mutual friends, I told the truth, and she cried with nerve-shattering sobs.

compound sentence: I felt terrible, but I told the truth, and she cried.

The second example again gains length by stringing together several prepositional phrases while the third simply adds another independent clause to gain length. All three, however, are compound sentences.

A **complex sentence** contains one independent clause and at least one dependent clause.

complex sentence: She cried when I told the truth.

complex sentence: When I told the truth, she cried.

Notice here that both examples contain exactly the same wording, yet the second example feels as though it has a different structure because the dependent clause has been moved to the front of the sentence.

Finally, a **compound–complex sentence** has at least two independent clauses and at least one dependent clause.

compound–complex: After I told the truth, she cried and I felt guilty.

compound–complex: She cried for two hours after I told her the truth about my beliefs, and I felt guilty both for having lied to her in the first place and for having hurt her now with the truth.

As the first example shows, despite its three-clause requirement, a compound–complex sentence can be short as well as long. The second example gains length and depth by adding prepositional phrases and modifiers.

It is important to note that complex sentences and compound–complex sentences often allow the careful balance, judgment, and qualification necessary to mature critical and analytical thinking. Because they subordinate some ideas to others, they can express the complicated relationship between ideas, between feelings, and between ideas and feelings. An essay containing only such sentences, however, would be as tedious as an essay filled only with simple and compound sentences. Variety is the rule.

☐ *Exercise 3*

Make a list of the structures of the sentences in at least one whole page of your manuscript, using S (simple), C (compound), CX (complex), and CCX (compound–complex) to designate each. As with sentence length, put a line after the designation for the last sentence in each paragraph. As with sentence length, three or more consecutive sentences with the same structure is probably one too many.

FIRST ELEMENTS   Although altering the types of clauses in your sentences sometimes gives the desired sense of variety, sometimes it doesn't. For example, the structure of a complex sentence doesn't really *feel* much different from that of a compound–complex sentence. For this reason, we also use first elements to provide that *felt variety*. A **first element** is the first grammatically detachable unit of a sentence. For example, in this sentence the transitional phrase, *For example,* is the first detachable unit. The first element in this sentence, however, is the subject, *The first element.* If the first element is not the subject, it is often (but not always) followed by a comma.

Consider the following examples:

1. I ran down the street screaming because my shoes were on fire.

2. Screaming, I ran down the street because my shoes were on fire.

3. Down the street I ran screaming because my shoes were on fire.

4. Because my shoes were on fire, I ran down the street screaming.

5. Further, I ran down the street screaming because my shoes were on fire.

6. I ran down the street with fiery shoes on my feet.

In #1, the first element is *I* (the subject); in #2, *Screaming* (the present participle); in #3, *Down the street* (prepositional phrase); in #4, *Because my shoes were on fire* (a dependent clause); in #5, *Further* (a transition); in #6, *I* (the subject).

Notice that sentences #1 and #6 *feel* the same when you read them. In other words, two such structures back to back would not *feel* different to us as we read; hence we would have no sense of variety. Yet their structures are actually different—#1 is a complex sentence while #6 is a simple sentence. In other words, variety in sentence structure alone cannot guarantee that readers will feel a sense of the variety. You also need to vary sentence length and first elements.

As you can see from even that small sample of six sentences given earlier, there are many potential first elements, including the following:

the subject of the sentence

a transitional word or phrase

a prepositional phrase

an expletive (*there, it*)

a modifier (for example, an adverb such as *perhaps* or a participle such as *running*)

a dependent clause

an imperative verb (*Play* outdoors.)

an interrogative (*Why, How*)

a direct object (*The book* he gave to me.)

an indirect object (*To me* he gave the book.)

a predicate adjective (*Happy* she was to see him.)

a predicate nominative (*A doctor* she was.)

Each of these first elements gives variety to your sentence structure. Probably, however, most of your sentences will begin with one of the first six in the list. Too many indirect objects as first elements, for example, would make the prose seem strained.

There is no hard-and-fast rule about when to vary first elements, but here is a good rule of thumb: If more than three consecutive sentences start with the same first element, you probably should change one of them.

☐ *Exercise 4*

Look through one of your manuscripts and find as many different types of first elements as you can. Then try revising several sentences using different first elements.

MODIFIERS   Another way of adding variety to your sentences is to use various types of modifiers. These modifiers also add a touch of elegance to your style and are an effective method of unpacking suitcase words. As with any other device, they should not be overused. There are three types, namely, resumptive, summative, and free modifiers.

A **resumptive modifier** normally comes at the end of a sentence. It begins by repeating a key noun or verb from the sentence and then adds extra information:

In Edith Wharton's *House of Mirth,* Lily Bart enjoys the <u>lifestyle</u> of the rich, <u>a lifestyle</u> filled with parties, leisure, and luxury.

Charles <u>ran</u> into the forest, <u>ran</u> with breath-snatching, gut-twisting speed.

In the first example, the key noun *lifestyle* is repeated and the suitcase phrase *lifestyle of the rich* is unpacked, providing readers with more information and an unusual sentence structure as well. In the second, the predicate verb *ran* is unpacked, providing vivid details about the way Charles ran.

A **summative modifier** also usually comes at the end of the sentence. It begins by summarizing that clause in a word or phrase and then provides additional information:

> In Edith Wharton's *House of Mirth,* Lily Bart often feels anxiety about her growing debts, an <u>experience</u> that deepens her desire to marry a wealthy man.

Here one noun—*experience*—sums up or renames the concept in the first part of the sentence and new information about it is added.

Finally, a **free modifier** can begin or end a sentence. Usually it is a participial phrase (beginning with either the present or past participle of a verb):

> Lily is a woman of powerful emotions, <u>driven</u> by a fear of dinginess and <u>shaken</u> by the love she feels for a poor man.

> <u>Failing</u> to go to church with Peter, <u>gambling</u> at cards until dawn, and <u>choosing</u> Selden's company over his, Lily loses her chance to "secure" Peter's marriage proposal.

In the first example, two past participles—*driven, shaken*—are added to the end of the sentence to elaborate on the final noun before the comma—*emotions*. In the second example, three present participles—*failing, gambling, choosing*—are placed at the beginning to elaborate on the sentence's predicate verb—*loses*.

SENTENCE FRAGMENTS   Yet another form of structural variety is the **sentence fragment.** In exploratory essays, sentence fragments can be dramatically abrupt. A general rule of thumb might help you determine whether a fragment will be effective: The more a fragment looks like a sentence, the less effective it is likely to be. Because readers have certain expectations when they start to read a line of type on a page. Most readers would find my previous "sentence" (actually a long fragment) annoying and confusing. In fact, it also brings up a second rule of thumb: Many readers object to or are confused by fragments that begin with the word *because,* so it's probably a good idea to avoid them. Finally, the longer a sentence fragment is, the greater the chance that your readers will set up false expectations that they are about to receive a complete sentence.

In any event, too many fragments will damage any essay because you then lose the value of surprise—which is what a well-chosen deliberate sentence fragment offers.

COHERENCE

Coherence refers to the presence of a clear relationship between sentences within a paragraph, between paragraphs within a section, and between sections within an essay. For example, coherence occurs when the sentences in a paragraph or an essay all refer to the same "official subject" and its related cluster of ideas. It may also be gained by the maintenance of a single tone or attitude toward your material. The latter works well for short essays but can be difficult to maintain in longer pieces.

Beyond singularity of subject matter or attitude, coherence can also be achieved and signaled by several devices, most notably, by transitional words and phrases, by repeated key terms, by clear time markers, by white space, and by various structural strategies.

Perhaps the most obvious "glue" that holds sentences, paragraphs, sections, and essays together is **transitional words,** the explicit words and phrases which signal the exact connection between their ideas. The relationships that they make explicit for readers include

sequence (*next, first, second, in the second place, last, finally*)

temporal (*then, now, before, after, previously, meanwhile, at the same time*)

spatial (*above, beneath, beside, in front of, behind*)

addition (*in addition, and, also, further, furthermore, moreover*)

logical (*hence, thus, therefore, consequently, as a result*)

examples (*for example, for instance, such as*)

rephrase (*in other words, that is*)

comparison (*similarly, likewise*)

contrast (*on the contrary, but, on the other hand, nevertheless, however, in contrast, conversely*)

Repeating key words or synonyms is another effective technique for establishing coherence. Such repetition reminds readers what they should stay focused on.

Clear **time markers** are yet another device—and one that is particularly important for exploratory essays. Given the extra freedom that exploratory essays have in terms of development strategies, making sure your readers know what happened when is crucial. Flashbacks and flashforwards require clear indications of time. One method of marking time, of course, is verb tenses. If you are writing about an event in the past and then you move to an event that occurred even further back in time, you must signal that move clearly. Consider the following example.

The second time I hurt my knee I felt foolish. Some friends had finally convinced me to play softball with them against another team one Sunday morning. We got to the field early and started practicing. Since no one wanted to play third base, I got the assignment. Although I was a fair to good hitter, I never considered myself much of a fielder. The only reason I didn't

insist on playing deep in the outfield was my throwing arm—
I knew I'd never reach the infield on less than two bounces. So I
figured to take my chances at third. To avoid embarrassing myself during the game, though, I asked Bob to hit a couple of
high fly balls in my direction so I could practice what I consider
the most difficult catch to make. The first one drew me into
the infield, so far into the infield, in fact, that I stepped on the
pitcher's mound. Unfortunately for me, previous pitchers had
scooped a small trench in front of the rubber with their toes
over the years, and into that trench I stepped. And staggered.
And fell. When a couple friends helped me up and asked if I
were okay, I said "No" and asked to be helped to my car. I
recognized the tingling in my knee, all right. I knew I was in
trouble.

But the <u>first time</u> I hurt my knee I wasn't so wise. I <u>had</u> been
playing a pick-up game of basketball with a bunch of strangers.
The game <u>had</u> been going well until I started dribbling the ball
up the court. I was so busy trying to set up a play that I didn't
notice the opponent sneaking up behind me and stealing the
ball. Suddenly I was dribbling thin air and the other player was
heading in the opposite direction, unopposed. With hurt pride
stinging and humiliation flushing my whole body, I gave chase.
I had no hope of catching him, but I couldn't just be a spectator
as he scored. So I ran after him at full speed. Instead of doing
what 99% of ball thiefs would do—namely, running all the way
to the basket for an easy layup—this fool stopped short and fired
up a jump shot. Of course, I tried to jump out of his way to
avoid a surprise collision. I failed. As I landed, my left foot
planted, my knee twisted, and down I went. A moment later I
got up, oblivious to the damage I had done. After we finished
the game, I went to the locker room to change. Since my knee
felt stiff, I did a few knee bends to loosen it up. Two hours later
the knee was so swollen I couldn't climb the stairs. The doctor
who later operated on the knee said the knee bends had not been
a good idea. He was a master of understatement.

This essay then returns to the second time the writer hurt his knee
and the events that occurred afterward. Notice the underlined time
markers at the beginning of the second paragraph. The explicit phrase
the first time is aided by the past perfect verb tense (*had been playing, had
been going*) that starts the paragraph. Notice also, however, that once the
past perfect tense has signaled the change in time, the writer slips back
into simple past tense for the rest of the paragraph (until the final past
perfect verb in the next-to-last sentence which signals that the doctor is
referring to an event previous to his examination of the writer's knee).

In other words, use the past perfect to alert readers that a change has occurred, but then use the simple past thereafter.

Leaving *white space* to separate sections is also a useful device. Such white space alerts readers that the scene and time frame have changed. No one uses white space more effectively than Alice Walker in "Beauty: When the Other Dancer Is the Self" (page 190). Notice, however, that each section after the white space begins with an explicit time marker. Notice as well that Walker saves the white space to suggest significant lapses in time. If you find yourself leaving white space after every paragraph, you're overdoing it. White space is useful occasionally in exploratory essays, and most often when those essays are recounting numerous events that stretch over a long period of time. More reflective and analytical exploratory essays rarely use it.

WORDINESS

Wordiness means using more words than are necessary to convey your meaning. Don't confuse density and texture of language with wordiness. Some ideas require careful discrimination (for example, those in the essays of Gerald Early and Nancy Mairs). Take away that density and texture and the ideas suffer.

Take away wordiness, however, and the ideas improve. Wordiness doesn't add flavor or subtlety to an essay; it simply adds words. Wordiness doesn't clarify ideas; it buries them under a load of useless words. Wordiness cannot be defended by claims such as "That's just the way I write" or "That's the way I speak." If you can't defend the number of words you use on specific stylistic grounds, the odds are that you've used too many words to express your meaning. A part of revision for most good writers is deletion not only of tangential ideas but also of unnecessary words. Most good stylists agree that there are some clear practices which create wordiness, and it is those practices that we will examine next.

Overuse of *I*

Exploratory writing demands that you use the first-person pronoun *I*. Yet even a good thing can be overdone. Consider the following example from Sharon's essay about her mother's discovering a lump in her own breast:

> I was shocked to find out that she had known about the lump on her breast for several months and yet had done nothing about it. I was angry with her for not going to a doctor right away, but at the same time I could sympathize with her fear. I think if the situation were reversed and I had been the one that had discovered a lump in my breast I would have sought professional help

immediately; at least I think I would have. The fear of not knowing the truth would have driven me crazy.

At least half of these usages of *I* can be eliminated and the prose made tighter and cleaner. Consider the following revision:

> How could she have known about this lump for several months and not done anything about it? Although angry with her for not going to a doctor right away, I could also sympathize with her fear. If the situation had been reversed, I would have sought professional help immediately; at least I think I would have. The fear of not knowing the truth would have driven me crazy.

In this revision, notice the techniques used to eliminate the superfluous first-person pronouns. In the first sentence, the "I was shocked" idea is more dramatically conveyed by the indignant question. In the second sentence, the "I was angry" has been turned into a long introductory phrase which not only eliminates an unnecessary *I* but also adds variety to the sentence structure. In the third sentence, the almost always superfluous "I think" is gone, as is the unnecessary repetition of the situation ("If the situation had been reversed" clearly conveys the idea while "and I had been the one that had discovered a lump in my breast" is unnecessarily repetitious). So, the revision has four *I*'s instead of eight, 68 words instead of 97. The prose is tighter and more dramatic.

Let's consider another example.

Original

Having my mother cry in my arms scared me a lot. I began to view myself and my mother in a different light. At that moment I realized that I was an adult, and the reason I think I came to that realization was because my mother had. I was an adult and an adult has to deal with the problems that arise in life. Adults do not run away. In the past, whenever I had a problem I always turned to my parents for advice and help. Now my mother was turning to me for the same things that I used to turn to her for. I began thinking about the power of fear and the role that it played in everyone's life.

Revision

Having my mother cry in my arms was scary. Our relationship had changed—no longer mother and child, but two adults. My mother was seeing me as an adult, and that made me suddenly realize that she was right. I was an adult, and an adult has to deal with the problems that arise in life. Adults do not run away. In the past, I had always turned to my parents for advice and help. Now my mother was turning to me for those same things. I began thinking about the power of fear and the role that it played in everyone's life.

In the revision, the first sentence remains essentially the same, but the second is radically changed, giving additional information (specifying what the previous relationship had been) and eliminating the "I began." The third sentence has eliminated another *I* by changing the focus of the sentence to the mother's perception. The fourth and fifth sentences remain the same. The sixth sentence, however, eliminates information that seems too obvious to need mentioning (the concept of "whenever I had a problem" is clearly included in the "turned to my parents for advice and help" concept). In the seventh sentence, repetition is eliminated ("things that I used to turn to her for") while the sentence's meaning stays the same. The first version has ten *I*'s; the second has three. Further, a total of 124 words in the first version has been reduced to 103. Once again the revised prose is more effective.

In both examples, then, we see how focusing on the number of *I*'s can help us make prose more dramatic, more dynamic, and more concise.

To Be or Not *to Be*

Zeroing in on the number of forms of *to be* (*to be, am, is, are, was, were, being, been*) is probably the single most effective strategy for eliminating unnecessary words. Naturally, forms of *to be* are useful and often indispensable. In early drafts, though, most writers go wild with *to be;* this verb seems to be an essential element in how we record our ideas. Yet it is inevitably overused and thus weakens the writing in which it appears. By searching for forms of *to be* when you revise, you discover various types of wordiness. For example, forms of *to be* often signal the presence of the wordy *progressive* ("he *is* eating" rather than the more concise "he eats"). The progressive has a definite use (to show an action that is in progress while some other action occurs—"He *was eating* when the fire alarm sounded"), but we often use it without thought, hence adding extra useless verbiage to our prose. More important, *to be* forms often signal the presence of the **passive voice** (which in itself emphasizes the receiver of the action rather than the agent or doer of the action, or, in other terms, which often deemphasizes the real topic of the sentence). In addition, *to be* forms function like an = sign; what's on the left equals what's on the right (Linda is a doctor, Linda = doctor), a boring structure at best. In other words, we all love *to be* and find it a very useful verb in some places, but, frankly, it is a dull verb, so it should not be invited to any sentence unless it is absolutely needed.

There are at least five methods of cutting back on the use of *to be* (and hence improving prose).

1. *Eliminate unnecessary progressive verb forms.* Use the progressive only when actually needed. Unless there is reason not to do so, change sentences like "He was eating lunch" to "He ate lunch."

2. *Eliminate the passive voice unless you have a real reason for keeping it.* The passive voice does have important functions. Use it when the receiver of the action is a more important element than the doer. For instance, "The chemicals were mixed" is probably more appropriate than "The lab assistants mixed the chemicals" unless you want to emphasize who did the mixing. Also use the passive to keep the paragraph's main topic in the spotlight (in the subject slot). Consider this brief example:

> Our cat *Gizmo* has diabetes. Before *he* got sick, *he* was always climbing the fence, chasing birds, and having a grand old time outdoors. Once *he* got ill, however, *he* had to stay indoors and lead a much duller life. Worse, my *father* has to give him a shot of insulin every night. *Gizmo* takes the shot like a hero, though, never flinching or even meowing.

All the subjects are italicized. Notice the next-to-last sentence switches our focus away from the cat and onto the father, yet the paragraph is not about the father. In such a case, it would make sense to use a passive to keep the focus squarely on Gizmo: "Worse, he *has to be given* a shot of insulin every night by my father."

But often we use the passive voice even when the **active voice** will serve better or as well. The passive has two faults. First, it usually adds unnecessary words (a form of *to be* and often the preposition *by*). Second, it hides or deemphasizes the doer of the action in a prepositional phrase rather than highlighting the doer in the sentence's subject slot. Consider the following example:

> The rider <u>was thrown</u> by the mule. (passive)
>
> The mule threw the rider. (active)

3. *Substitute more vivid verbs for the forms of* to be. More vivid verbs do not include such words as *exist, become,* or *feel,* which also express states of being rather than actions. Revise to find the most vivid verb that captures exactly the action you envision. In the following example, notice that each change makes the sentence more exact. Although the sentence does become longer, the additional length gives details and information, not simply empty words.

> He <u>was</u> a fool.
>
> He acted like a fool.
>
> Like a fool, he jumped onto his chair and proclaimed his undying devotion to romance at the top of his voice while Jerry tried valiantly to propose to Anne.

In these examples we see a movement from the dull *was* to the vivid action verbs *jumped* and *proclaimed.* In the process of substituting the more vivid verbs, the writer also added details and context.

4. *Combine sentences.* This option is particularly attractive because it allows us to tighten our prose. Often the presence of expletives (*there, it*) or the repetition of key words signals an opportunity to combine sentences. Consider these examples:

> There are several reasons for wanting to eliminate forms of *to be.* These reasons are the following: length of sentences, emphasis, lack of vividness. (24 words)

> We should eliminate forms of *to be* for three reasons: length of sentences, emphasis, lack of vividness. (17 words, 2 forms of *to be* gone)

5. *Eliminate nonproductive relative clauses* (who, which, *and* that *clauses).* Relative clauses often add a touch of elegance and balance to our sentences. However, sometimes they can profitably be eliminated. Consider:

> We loved that car, *which was 15 years old* and *which was actually seen by my family as our heirloom.* (2 relative clauses, 20 words)

> We loved that *15-year-old* car, *a family heirloom.* (no relative clauses, 10 words)

In the revision, the first relative clause became a hyphenated adjective and the second one became an appositive.

Notice, however, that the meaning of the two sentences does differ slightly. The latter suggests that the car really was an heirloom, while the former suggests that the family might have been misguided in its perception of the car as an heirloom. Removing any words will probably slightly change the meaning (it will certainly change the emphasis since fewer or more vivid words highlight what remains). For example, "My foot *went to sleep*" differs from "My foot *went numb*" in its suggestion of the severity of the problem. On a practical level, however, revisions in sentences (particularly when we eliminate unnecessary words) often change the meaning in very insignificant ways while adding to effective communication in very important ways.

Ultimately, revision is a question of options, and you have many options for the phrasing and structuring of each sentence. Select the best option for your purpose. In the preceding car example, a compromise option might be chosen if the author wanted to emphasize his family's misperception about the car's being an heirloom:

> We loved that 15-year-old car, which my family actually saw as an heirloom.

> We loved that 15-year-old car, a car my family actually saw as an heirloom.

Both of these revisions retain the hyphenated adjective, but the first one reinstates the relative (*which*) clause while the second uses a resumptive modifier that acts as an appositive. Both maintain the implication that the family was wrong in its perception of the car as an heirloom.

EDITING

The last function we perform after revising ideas and style is editing for grammar and spelling. Why should we even bother with those things? One good answer is that, practically speaking, although grammar and spelling don't have much to do with the worth of our ideas and insights, readers (including professors, supervisors, personnel directors) often are impressed by correct grammar and spelling and distracted and even prejudiced against the writer by errors. Many personnel directors, for example, reject job application letters and résumés if they find a grammatical or spelling error, on the theory that if the writer is that sloppy in one of the most important documents he or she will ever write, that writer cannot be depended on to pay attention to details on the job. Without question, almost every reader has particular "pet errors" whose absence proves a person is a "good writer" and whose presence proves the person is a "bad writer." Some teachers, especially but not only writing teachers, literally see red when they find a comma splice or a misspelling—they bloody the papers that contain them. In short, justifiably or not, most readers can't get past sloppy editing. At the very least, you and your ideas lose credibility with readers and you have to be twice as brilliant or convincing in order to accomplish your goal.

In any event, don't you want your ideas to be clothed in the best possible language? Effective writers work at their craft, honing their ideas and polishing their style. Imagine trying to be an oil painter if you don't understand how to mix colors, or how to apply paint to the canvas, or which brushes create which effects, or even how to create the illusion of perspective and distance. Being a writer of sophisticated prose is similar to painting in oils. Style isn't something we are born with. We develop it. As with most things in this world, we end up with a style that reflects the amount of work we have put into it. Don't be fooled by the myth of the creative genius who just sits down and writes a masterpiece—no revision, no thought to style. Although there may be a "natural" or two in each generation, the vast majority of good writers—published and student—are made, not born. The harder you work to grasp the basics of your medium and the subtler elements of style, the better writer you will be. Another myth is that great creative leaps in style occur without the writer's knowledge of other writers' styles. Wrong. Picasso, for example, knew everything about his medium and everything about Realism before he pioneered the new style of Cubism. The new style grew out of his deep understanding of all that had been done before. So it is with writing. All great stylists build on the styles of others. Studying the styles of the essayists in this text will be a good start.

FINAL ADVICE ABOUT REVISING STYLE

In this chapter we've looked at several stylistic issues. Concern yourself with such revision issues only after your first draft is written. Go over your prose with *your eyes fixed on only one problem at a time*. Always assume that your essay needs revision. Starting with the question "Does anything need revising here?" too easily leads to the answer "No." Starting with the assertion "The content and style need revising" leads to constructive revision.

Begin by cutting out useless verbiage. A good target might be to eliminate at least 15% of the words you used in the draft (if it contains 1,000 words, cut it down to 850 words using the techniques discussed in this chapter). Then go through the essay looking only at sentence length; make a second pass through the paper looking at sentence variety. You may want to break this process down further—for example, making a separate pass looking only at the first elements of sentences. Only after doing these things should you go through the essay looking at whatever grammatical issues bother you.

Once the essay seems finished, proofread it carefully for errors in spelling, punctuation, and other mechanical matters. If you are using a word processor that includes a spell checker, use it just before you print your paper. But don't forget that spell checkers have limitations. If you write *to* for *too,* for instance, the spell checker can't spot the mistake.

Going through the essay looking at only one problem at a time may at first seem a daunting and onerous task. But after the second or third essay you will discover that you need to do less revising because this process has improved your style.

☐ *Exercise 5*

1. Eliminate wordiness in the following sentences. Try to cut out as many forms of *to be* as possible.
   a. The figures have been checked by an auditor.
   b. My homework was eaten by my dog.
   c. Advocates of abortion are claiming that sanctity of life is an argument against abortion, but they are ignoring one basic fact. That fact is the following: Although there may be a debate about whether or not the fetus is alive from the moment that it is conceived, it is a one-hundred percent fact that the mother is alive. Thus we are asking ourselves one

basic question: Should we be sacrificing the rights of the person that we are sure is alive for the rights of a fetus that may or may not be alive?

d. It makes reasonable sense that if guns are outlawed then only outlaws will be the ones who have guns.

e. In this paper I am going to contend that life is more precious than is a woman's right to control her own body.

f. The modern-day problems concerning abortion are issues of the dangers of the operation, the right to life, and lack of respect for life in general. Of the three, the danger of the operation is, by far, the least important so it is the one with which we will begin our discussion.

g. Although the movie is being filmed by Be Nice studios, it is a rather adult movie which is said to contain a great deal of profanity and there are rumors that there will also be at least three explicit sex scenes, although it is not known if this rumor is true or not.

h. The figures in fairy tales are either good or bad and nothing in between. By showing life to be this way, it *is allowing* the child to see what is good and what is bad without all the complexities of everyday people.

i. Plays and stories are both seen as examples of fictionalization by critics.

j. To me, the article seemed to be both vague and too specific, although I know that this claim by me at first glance may seem to be paradoxical or it might seem to be impossible.

2. In a paper of your own, find two sentences which include forms of *to be*. Revise them to eliminate at least half of the occurrences of forms of *to be*. Use one of the five techniques listed above, or invent your own. Don't be surprised if you end up combining one sentence with another that precedes or follows it. Don't be surprised if such eliminations leave you with half a sentence at times—that's your opportunity to add more information or details, to create a sentence that really says something.

CHECKLIST FOR STYLE

As you read your papers and those written by others, ask yourself, "Specifically, what is good here?" Then ask yourself, "What *must be* changed in this paper?" Fully following the suggestions below as you re-examine your drafts should significantly improve your essays. Always assume that *all of the following apply to your paper* (don't say to yourself, "Oh, I've already done *that*" because even if you have, you can probably do it with more detail or with more stylistic flair).

Unpack each suitcase word (general, vague, abstract nouns) by writing one or more sentences (after that word's *first* use) fully explaining it.

The beginning of each new paragraph should have either a transitional word or phrase and/or a *key* term from the previous paragraph repeated. If this is not true for your paragraphs, make it so.

Say, "I can eliminate 15% of the words I used." Then make it so.

Try to reduce your use of forms of *to be* at least by 25% (includes *to be, am, is, are, was, were, being, been*).

Make verbs more vivid; make them express the action that occurs.

Use occasional fragments for dramatic effect.

Usually the simple verbs of speaking (*say, said, spoke, stated*) are invisible and should be used. Save the vivid speaking verbs for appropriate moments (*whispered, mumbled, screamed, yelled, asserted*).

Eliminate ineffective uses of the first-person *I*.

Further Readings

My Speech to the Graduates

WOODY ALLEN

❑ *Inward Exploration*

Write at least one paragraph documenting your memories of the last graduation-day speech you heard.

More than any other time in history, mankind faces a crossroads. One path leads to despair and utter hopelessness. The other, to total extinction. Let us pray we have the wisdom to choose correctly. I speak, by the way, not with any sense of futility, but with a panicky conviction of the absolute meaninglessness of existence which could easily be misinterpreted as pessimism. It is not. It is merely a healthy concern for the predicament of modern man. (Modern man is here defined as any person born after Nietzsche's edict that "God is dead," but before the hit recording "I Wanna Hold Your Hand.") This "predicament" can be stated one of two ways, though certain linguistic philosophers prefer to reduce it to a mathematical equation where it can be easily solved and even carried around in the wallet.

Put in its simplest form, the problem is: How is it possible to find meaning in a finite world given my waist and shirt size? This is a very difficult question when we realize that science has failed us. True, it has conquered many diseases, broken the genetic code, and even placed human beings on the moon, and yet when a man of eighty is left in a room with two eighteen-year-old cocktail waitresses nothing happens. Because the real problems never change. After all, can the human soul be glimpsed through a microscope? Maybe—but you'd definitely need one of those very good ones with two eyepieces. We know that the most advanced computer in the world does not have a brain as sophisticated as that of an ant. True, we could say that of many of our relatives but we only have to put up with them at weddings or special occasions. Science is something we depend on all the time. If I develop a pain in the chest I must take an X-ray. But what if the radiation from the X-ray causes me deeper problems? Before I know it, I'm going in for surgery. Naturally, while they're giving me oxygen an intern decides to light up a cigarette. The next thing you know I'm rocketing over the World Trade Center in bed clothes. Is this science? True, science has taught us how to pasteurize cheese. And true, this can be fun in mixed company—but what of the H-bomb? Have you ever seen what happens when one of those things falls off a desk accidentally? And where is science when one ponders the eternal riddles? How did the cosmos originate? How long has it been around? Did matter begin with an explosion or by the word of God? And if by the latter, could He not have begun it just two weeks earlier to take advantage of some of the warmer weather? Exactly what do we mean when we say, man is mortal? Obviously it's not a compliment.

Religion too has unfortunately let us down. Miguel de Unamuno writes blithely of the "eternal persistence of consciousness," but this is no easy feat. Particularly when reading Thackeray. I often think how comforting life must have been for early man because he believed in a powerful, benevolent Creator who looked after all things. Imagine his disappointment when he saw his wife putting on weight. Contemporary man, of course, has no such peace of mind. He finds himself in the midst of a crisis of faith. He is what we fashionably call "alienated." He has seen the ravages of war, he has known natural catastrophes, he has been to singles bars. My good friend Jacques Monod spoke often of the randomness of the cosmos. He believed everything in existence occurred by pure chance with the possible exception of his breakfast, which he felt certain was made by his housekeeper. Naturally belief in a divine intelligence inspires tranquillity. But this does not free us from our human responsibilities. Am I my brother's keeper? Yes. Interestingly, in my case I share that honor with the Prospect Park Zoo. Feeling godless then, what we have done is made technology God. And yet can technology really be the answer when a brand new Buick, driven by my close associate, Nat Zipsky, winds up in the window of Chicken Delight causing hundreds of customers to scatter? My toaster has never once worked properly in four years. I follow the instructions and push two slices of bread down in the slots and seconds later they rifle upward. Once they broke the nose of a woman I loved very dearly. Are we counting on nuts and bolts and electricity to solve our problems? Yes, the telephone is a good thing—and the refrigerator—and the air conditioner. But not every air conditioner. Not my sister Henny's, for instance. Hers makes a loud noise and still doesn't cool. When the man comes over to fix it, it gets worse. Either that or he tells her she needs a new one. When she complains, he says not to bother him. This man is truly alienated. Not only is he alienated but he can't stop smiling.

The trouble is, our leaders have not adequately prepared us for a mechanized society. Unfortunately our politicians are either incompetent or corrupt. Sometimes both on the same day. The Government is unresponsive to the needs of the little man. Under five-seven, it is impossible to get your Congressman on the phone. I am not denying that democracy is still the finest form of government. In a democracy at least, civil liberties are upheld. No citizen can be wantonly tortured, imprisoned, or made to sit through certain Broadway shows. And yet this is a far cry from what goes on in the Soviet Union. Under their form of totalitarianism, a person merely caught whistling is sentenced to thirty years in a labor camp. If, after fifteen years, he still will not stop whistling, they shoot him. Along with this brutal fascism we find its handmaiden, terrorism. At no other time in history has man been so afraid to cut into his veal chop for fear that it will explode. Violence breeds more violence and it is predicted that by 1990 kidnapping will be the dominant mode of social interaction. Overpopulation will exacerbate problems to the breaking point. Figures tell us there are already more people on earth than we need to move even the heaviest piano. If we do not call a halt to breeding, by the year 2000 there will be no room to serve dinner unless one is willing to set the table on the heads of strangers. Then they must not move for an hour while we eat. Of course energy will be in short supply and each car owner will be allowed only enough gasoline to back up a few inches.

Instead of facing these challenges we turn instead to distractions like *5* drugs and sex. We live in far too permissive a society. Never before has pornography been this rampant. And those films are lit so badly! We are a people who lack leaders and coherent programs. We have no spiritual center. We are adrift alone in the cosmos wreaking monstrous violence on one another out of frustration and pain. Fortunately, we have not lost our sense of proportion. Summing up, it is clear the future holds great opportunities. It also holds pitfalls. The trick will be to avoid the pitfalls, seize the opportunities, and get back home by six o'clock.

Outward Exploration: Discussion

1. Discuss Allen's use of humorous techniques in the essay.
2. Underlying several of Allen's humorous statements is a serious issue

or concern. Select some of his statements and discuss what issues exist.

3. When Allen says that "the real problems never change," what problems do you think he means?

4. According to Allen, what are the accomplishments and the failures of science?

5. According to Allen, how has religion failed?

6. How has technology failed?

7. How has government failed?

8. What other social issues does Allen mention?

☐ *Outward Exploration: Writing*

1. Write an essay which explores your view of modern American society. Reading some outside sources will deepen your ideas and broaden your essay.

2. Using some of Allen's techniques, write a humorous or satiric essay about a serious subject. This essay should reveal your real opinions and attitudes even though its goal is to be satiric or humorous.

Daze of Wine and Roses

DAVE BARRY

☐ *Inward Exploration*

List words and phrases that come to mind when you see the word wine. *Make a second list of words and phrases that come to mind when you see the word* drunk.

I have never gotten into wine. I'm a beer man. What I like about   1
beer is you basically just drink it, then you order another one. You don't
sniff at it, or hold it up to the light and slosh it around, and above all
you don't drone on and on about it, the way people do with wine. Your
beer drinker tends to be a straightforward, decent, friendly, down-to-
earth person who enjoys talking about the importance of relief pitching,
whereas your serious wine fancier tends to be an insufferable snot.

I realize I am generalizing here, but, as is often the case when I
generalize, I don't care.

Nevertheless, I decided recently to try to learn more about the wine
community. Specifically, I engaged the services of a rental tuxedo and
attended the Grand Finale of the First Annual French Wine Sommelier
Contest in America, which was held at the famous Waldorf-Astoria hotel in New York. For the benefit of those of you with plastic slipcovers,
I should explain that a "sommelier" is a wine steward, the dignified
person who comes up to you at expensive restaurants, hands you the
wine list, and says "Excellent choice, sir," when you point to French
writing that, translated, says "Sales Tax Included."

Several hundred wine-oriented people were on hand for the sommelier competition. First we mingled and drank champagne, then we
sat down to eat dinner and watch the competition. I found it immensely
entertaining, especially after the champagne, because for one thing
many of the speakers were actual French persons who spoke with comical accents, which I suspect they practiced in their hotel rooms ("Zees
epeetomizes zee hrole av zee sommelier sroo-out eestory . . . ," etc.).
Also we in the audience got to drink just gallons of wine. At least I did.
My policy with wine is very similar to my policy with beer, which is
just pretty much drink it and look around for more. The people at my
table, on the other hand, leaned more toward the slosh-and-sniff approach, where you don't so much *drink* the wine as you frown and then
make a thoughtful remark about it such as you might make about a job
applicant ("I find it ambitious, but somewhat strident." Or: "It's lucid,

yes, but almost Episcopalian in its predictability.") As it happened, I was sitting next to a French person named Mary, and I asked her if people in France carry on this way about wine. "No," she said, "they just drink it. They're more used to it."

There were 12 sommeliers from around the country in the contest;   5 they got there by winning regional competitions, and earlier in the day they had taken a written exam with questions like: "Which of the following appellations belong to the Savoie region? (a) Crepy; (b) Seyssel; (c) Arbois; (d) Etoile; (e) Ripple." (I'm just kidding about the Ripple, of course. The Savoie region would not use Ripple as an insecticide.)

The first event of the evening competition was a blind tasting, where the sommeliers had to identify a mystery wine. We in the audience got to try it, too. It was a wine that I would describe as yellow in color, and everybody at my table agreed it was awful. "Much too woody," said one person. "Heavy oxidized," said another. "Bat urine," I offered. The others felt this was a tad harsh. I was the only one who finished my glass.

Next we got a nonmystery wine, red in color, with a French name, and I thought it was swell, gulped it right down, but one of the wine writers at my table got upset because it was a 1979, and the program said we were supposed to get a 1978. If you can imagine. So we got some 1978, and it was swell, too. "They're both credible," said the wine writer, "but there's a great difference in character." I was the only one who laughed, although I think Mary sort of wanted to.

The highlight of the evening was the Harmony of Wine and Food event, where the sommelier contestants were given a menu where the actual nature of the food was disguised via French words ("Crochets sur le Pont en Voiture," etc.), and they had to select a wine for each of the five courses. This is where a sommelier has to be really good, because if he is going to talk an actual paying customer into spending as much money on wine for one meal as it would cost to purchase a half-dozen state legislators for a year, he has to say something more than, "A lotta people like this here chardonnay."

Well, these sommeliers were good. They were *into* the Harmony of Wine and Food, and they expressed firm views. They would say things like: "I felt the (name of French wine) would have the richness to deal with the foie gras," or "My feeling about Roquefort is that. . . ." I thought it was fabulous entertainment, and at least two people at my table asked how I came to be invited.

Anyway, as the Harmony event dragged on, a major issue devel-   10 oped concerning the salad. The salad was Lamb's-Lettuce with—you are going to be shocked when I tell you this—Walnut Vinaigrette. A lot of people in the audience felt that this was a major screw-up, or "gaffe," on the part of the contest organizers, because of course vinaigrette is just going to fight any wine you try to marry it with. "I strongly disagree with the salad dressing," is how one wine writer at my table put it, and I could tell she meant it.

So the contestants were all really battling the vinaigrette problem, and you could just feel a current of unrest in the room. Things finally came to a head, or "tete," when contestant Mark Hightower came right out and said that if the rules hadn't prevented him, he wouldn't have chosen any wine at all with the salad. "Ideally," he said, "I would have liked to have recommended an Evian mineral water." Well, the room just erupted in spontaneous applause, very similar to what you hear at Democratic Party dinners when somebody mentions the Poor.

Anyway, the winning sommelier, who gets a trip to Paris, was Joshua Wesson, who works at a restaurant named Huberts in New York. I knew he'd win, because he began his Harmony of Wine and Food presentation by saying: "Whenever I see oysters on a menu, I am reminded of a quote. . . ." Nobody's ever going to try buying a moderately priced wine from a man who is reminded of a quote by oysters.

It turns out however, that Wesson is actually an OK guy who just happens to have a God-given ability to lay it on with a trowel and get along with the French. I talked to him briefly afterwards, and he didn't seem to take himself too seriously at all. I realize many people think I make things up, so let me assure you ahead of time that this is the actual, complete transcript of the interview:

ME: So. What do you think?

WESSON: I feel good. My arm felt good, my curve ball was popping.   15
I felt I could help the ball team.

ME: What about the vinaigrette?

WESSON: It was definitely the turning point. One can look at vinaigrette from many angles. It's like electricity.

I swear that's what he said, and furthermore at the time it made a lot of sense.

❑ Outward Exploration: Discussion

1. What event does Barry attend in this essay? Why does he go there?

2. What exactly does Barry mock in this essay?

3. Barry's title is a pun off the title of a play and movie, *The Days of Wine and Roses*. That work was a serious and painful examination of the horrors of alcoholism. Is there some reason other than the pun that Barry selected this title?

❑ Outward Exploration: Writing

1. Write an essay about a gathering that you attended but at which you felt out of place. The essay may be humorous or serious.

2. Write an essay satirizing something you feel is worthy of such treatment. Like Barry, reveal yourself as you attack your subject.

3. Drinking alcohol has long been a subject of essays, both serious and humorous. Based on your own experiences of using or seeing others use alcohol or some other drug, write an essay (either serious or humorous) which explores the use of alcohol (or some other drug). Like Barry, try to find the conventions that go along with such use.

Proverbs of Hell

WILLIAM BLAKE

❏ *Inward Exploration*

Write at least one paragraph giving your definition of the word proverb.
Does it have any connotations that similar terms such as adage *or* maxim *lack?*

In seed time learn, in harvest teach, in winter enjoy.   *1*
Drive your cart and your plough over the bones of the dead.
The road of excess leads to the palace of wisdom.
Prudence is a rich, ugly old maid courted by Incapacity.
He who desires but acts not, breeds pestilence.   *5*
The cut worm forgives the plough.
Dip him in the river who loves water.
A fool sees not the same tree that a wise man sees.
He whose face gives no light, shall never become a star.
Eternity is in love with the productions of time.   *10*
The busy bee has no time for sorrow.
The hours of folly are measur'd by the clock; but of wisdom, no
    clock can measure.
All wholesome food is caught without a net or a trap.
Bring out number, weight, and measure in a year of dearth.   *15*
No bird soars too high, if he soars with his own wings.
A dead body revenges not injuries.
The most sublime act is to set another before you.
If the fool would persist in his folly he would become wise.
Folly is the cloak of knavery.   *20*
Shame is Pride's cloak.
Prisons are built with stones of Law, brothels with bricks of
    Religion.
The pride of the peacock is the glory of God.
The lust of the goat is the bounty of God.
The wrath of the lion is the wisdom of God.   *25*
The nakedness of woman is the work of God.
Excess of sorrow laughs. Excess of joy weeps.
The roaring of lions, the howling of wolves, the raging of the
    stormy sea, and the destructive sword are portions of eternity
    too great for the eye of man.   *30*
The fox condemns the trap, not himself.
Joys impregnate. Sorrows bring forth.
Let man wear the fell of the lion, woman the fleece of the sheep.

The bird a nest, the spider a web, man friendship.

The selfish, smiling fool, and the sullen, frowning fool shall be   35
    both thought wise, that they may be a rod.

What is now proved was once only imagin'd.

The rat, the mouse, the fox, the rabbit watch the roots; the lion,
    the tiger, the horse, the elephant watch the fruits.

The cistern contains: the fountain overflows.   40

One thought fills immensity.

Always be ready to speak your mind, and a base man will avoid
    you.

Everything possible to be believ'd is an image of truth.

The eagle never lost so much time as when he submitted to learn
    of the crow.   45

The fox provides for himself; but God provides for the lion.

Think in the morning. Act in the noon. Eat in the evening.
    Sleep in the night.

He who has suffer'd you to impose on him, knows you.

As the plough follows words, so God rewards prayers.   50

The tigers of wrath are wiser than the horses of instruction.

Expect poison from the standing water.

You never know what is enough unless you know what is more
    than enough.

Listen to the fool's reproach! it is a kingly title!   55

The eyes of fire, the nostrils of air, the mouth of water, the
    beard of earth.

The weak in courage is strong in cunning.

The apple tree never asks the beech how he shall grow; nor the
    lion, the horse, how he shall take his prey.   60

The thankful receiver bears a plentiful harvest.

If others had not been foolish, we should be so.

The soul of sweet delight can never be defil'd.

When thou seest an eagle, thou seest a portion of Genius; lift up
    thy head!   65

As the caterpillar chooses the fairest leaves to lay her eggs on, so
    the priest lays his curse on the fairest joys.

To create a little flower is the labor of ages.

Damn braces. Bless relaxes.

The best wine is the oldest, the best water the newest.   70

Prayers plough not! Praises reap not!

Joys laugh not! Sorrows weep not!

The head Sublime, the heart Pathos, the genitals Beauty, the
    hands and feet Proportion.

As the air to a bird or the sea to a fish, so is contempt to the   75
    contemptible.

The crow wish'd everything was black, the owl that everything
    was white.

Exuberance is Beauty.

If the lion was advised by the fox, he would be cunning.   *80*

Improvement makes straight roads; but the crooked roads
 without improvement are roads of Genius.

Sooner murder an infant in its cradle than nurse unacted desires.

Where man is not, nature is barren.

Truth can never be told so as to be understood, and not be
 believ'd.   *85*

Enough! or Too much.

❑ *Outward Exploration: Discussion*

1. Comment on Blake's ideas. Which make sense to you? Which sound outrageous?

2. Discuss the similarities and differences between the philosophy revealed in Blake's "Proverbs of Hell" and the selections from Benjamin Franklin's *Poor Richard's Almanack*.

3. Discuss the significance of Blake's title.

4. Select two or three proverbs that strike you as particularly interesting and bring them up in class discussion.

❑ *Outward Exploration: Writing*

1. Using these "Proverbs of Hell," write an essay exploring Blake's vision of humankind and of the world. If you wish, you might look at Blake's poems, particularly those contained in "Songs of Innocence" and "Songs of Experience" for additional support.

2. The pithy saying is a popular form of literature. Compare and contrast Blake's sayings with those of some other writer (for instance, Ambrose Bierce or Benjamin Franklin). You might consider such things as their structure, style, subject matter, or tone.

3. The Old Testament of the Bible has a whole book called "Proverbs." Read some of the biblical proverbs, then compare and contrast them with Blake's.

4. Select one of Blake's proverbs that seems to speak particularly to you. After explaining its implications, show how it relates to your personal experience.

5. Select several of Blake's related proverbs that seem to speak particularly to you. After explaining their implications, show how they relate to your personal experience.

To My Dear Children

ANNE BRADSTREET

☐ *Inward Exploration*

Anne Bradstreet was an English woman who came to Boston, Massachusetts, in 1630 when Puritans held sway. She wrote poetry while raising her family, and she wrote this spiritual autobiography when she was sick and afraid that she might die. Write at least one paragraph explaining your vision of Puritans and their religious beliefs. Or write at least one paragraph describing a period of suffering or tribulation in your life.

> This book by any yet unread,
> I leave for you when I am dead,
> That, being gone, here you may find
> What was your living mother's mind.
> Make use of what I leave in love
> And God shall bless you from above.

My dear children,

I, knowing by experience that the exhortations of parents take most   *1*
effect when the speakers leave to speak, and those especially sink deepest which are spoke latest—and being ignorant whether on my death bed I shall have opportunity to speak to any of you, much less to all—thought it the best, whilst I was able to compose some short matters (for what else to call them I know not) and bequeath to you, that when I am no more with you, yet I may be daily in your remembrance (although that is the least in my aim in what I now do), but that you may gain some spiritual advantage by my experience. I have not studied in this you read to show my skill, but to declare the truth—not to set forth myself, but the glory of God. If I had minded the former, it had been perhaps better pleasing to you—but seeing the last is the best, let it be best pleasing to you.

The method I will observe shall be this—I will begin with God's dealing with me from my childhood to this day.

In my young years, about 6 or 7 as I take it, I began to make conscience of my ways, and what I knew was sinful, as lying, disobedience to parents, etc. I avoided it. If at any time I was overtaken with the like evils, it was as a great trouble. I could not be at rest till by prayer I had confessed it unto God. I was also troubled at the neglect of private duties, though too often tardy that way. I also found much comfort in reading the Scriptures, especially those places I thought most concerned my condition, and as I grew to have more understanding, so the more solace I took in them.

In a long fit of sickness which I had on my bed I often communed with my heart, and made my supplication to the most High who set me free from that affliction.

But as I grew up to be about 14 or 15 I found my heart more car-   5
nal, and sitting loose from God, vanity and the follies of youth take hold of me.

About 16, the Lord laid His hand sore upon me and smote me with the smallpox. When I was in my affliction, I besought the Lord, and confessed my pride and vanity and He was entreated of me, and again restored me. But I rendered not to Him according to the benefit received.

After a short time I changed my condition and was married, and came into this country, where I found a new world and new manners, at which my heart rose. But after I was convinced it was the way of God, I submitted to it and joined to the church at Boston.

After some time I fell into a lingering sickness like a consumption, together, with a lameness, which correction I saw the Lord sent to humble and try me and do me good: and it was not altogether ineffectual.

It pleased God to keep me a long time without a child, which was a great grief to me, and cost me many prayers and tears before I obtained one, and after him gave me many more, of whom I now take the care, that as I have brought you into the world, and with great pains, weakness, cares, and fears brought you to this, I now travail in birth again of you till Christ be formed in you.

Among all my experiences of God's gracious dealings with me I   10
have constantly observed this, that He hath never suffered me long to sit loose from Him, but by one affliction or other hath made me look home, and search what was amiss—so usually thus it hath been with me that I have no sooner felt my heart out of order, but I have expected correction for it, which most commonly hath been upon my own person, in sickness, weakness, pains, sometimes on my soul, in doubts and fears of God's displeasure, and my sincerity towards Him, sometimes He hath smote a child with a sickness, sometimes chastened by losses in estate—and these times (through His great mercy) have been the times of my greatest getting and advantage, yea I have found them the times when the Lord hath manifested the most love to me. Then have I gone to searching, and have said with David, Lord search me and try me, see what ways of wickedness are in me, and lead me in the way everlasting, and seldom or never but I have found either some sin I lay under which God would have reformed, or some duty neglected which He would have performed. And by His help I have laid vows and bonds upon my soul to perform His righteous commands.

If at any time you are chastened of God, take it as thankfully and joyfully as in greatest mercies, for if ye be His ye shall reap the greatest benefit by it. It hath been no small support to me in times of darkness when the Almighty hath hid His face from me, that yet I have had abundance of sweetness and refreshment after affliction, and more circumspection in my walking after I have been afflicted. I have been with God like an untoward child, that no longer than the rod has been on my back (or at least in sight) but I have been apt to forget Him and myself too. Before I was afflicted I went astray, but now I keep Thy statues.

I have had great experience of God's hearing my prayers, and returning comfortable answers to me, either in granting the thing I prayed for, or else in satisfying my mind without it; and I have been confident it hath been from Him, because I have found my heart through His goodness enlarged in thankfulness to Him.

I have often been perplexed that I have not found that constant joy in my pilgrimage and refreshing which I supposed most of the servants of God have; although He hath not left me altogether without the witness of His holy spirit, who hath oft given me His word and set to His seal that it shall be well with me. I have sometimes tasted of that hidden manna° that the world knows not, and have set up my Ebenezer° and have resolved with myself that against such a promise, such tastes of sweetness, the gates of hell shall never prevail. Yet have I many times sinkings and droopings, and not enjoyed that felicity that sometimes I have done. But when I have been in darkness and seen no light, yet have I desired to stay myself upon the Lord.

And, when I have been in sickness and pain, I have thought if the Lord would but lift up the light of His countenance upon me, although He ground me to powder, it would be but light to me; yea, oft have I thought were I in hell itself, and could there find the love of God toward me, it would be a heaven. And, could I have been in heaven without the love of God, it would have been a hell to me; for, in truth, it is the absence and presence of God that makes heaven or hell.

Many times hath Satan troubled me concerning the verity of the Scriptures, many times by atheism how I could know whether there was a God; I never saw any miracles to confirm me, and those which I read of how did I know but they were feigned. That there is a God my reason would soon tell me by the wondrous works that I see, the vast frame of the heaven and the earth, the order of all things, night and day, summer and winter, spring and autumn, the daily providing for this great house-

15

---

manna: the food which was miraculously provided for the Israelites in the wilderness after their flight from Egypt under the leadership of Moses. The term is often used to symbolize spiritual nourishment that has a divine origin.

Ebenezer: In the Old Testament, the prophet Samuel set up a stone named Ebenezer in order to commemorate a victory by the Hebrews over the Philistines.

hold upon the earth, the preserving and directing of all to its proper end. The consideration of these things would with amazement certainly resolve me that there is an Eternal Being. But how should I know He is such a God as I worship in Trinity, and such a Saviour as I rely upon? Though this hath thousands of times been suggested to me, yet God hath helped me over. I have argued thus with myself. That there is a God I see. If ever this God hath revealed himself, it must be in His Word, and this must be it or none. Have I not found that operation by it that no human invention can work upon the soul? Hath not judgments befallen divers who have scorned and contemned it? Hath it not been preserved through all ages maugre° all the heathen tyrants and all of the enemies who have opposed it? Is there any story but that which shows the beginnings of times, and how the world came to be as we see? Do we not know the prophecies in it fulfilled which could not have been so long foretold by any but God Himself.

When I have got over this block, then have I another put in my way, that admit this be the true God whom we worship, and that be His Word, yet why may not the Popish religion be the right? They have the same God, the same Christ, the same word: they only interpret it one way, we another.

This hath sometimes stuck with me, and more it would, but the vain fooleries that are in their religion, together with their lying miracles and cruel persecutions of the saints, which admit were they as they term them, yet not so to be dealt withal.

The consideration of these things and many the like would soon turn me to my own religion again.

But some new troubles I have had since the world has been filled with blasphemy, and sectaries, and some who have been accounted sincere Christians have been carried away with them, that sometimes I have said, Is there faith upon the earth? and I have not known what to think. But then I have remembered the works of Christ that so it must be, and if it were possible, the very elect should be deceived. Behold, saith our Saviour, I have told you before. That hath stayed my heart, and I can now say, Return, O my Soul, to thy rest, upon this rock Christ Jesus will I build my faith; and, if I perish, I perish. But I know all the Powers of Hell shall never prevail against it. I know whom I have trusted, and whom I have believed, and that He is able to keep that I have committed to His charge.

Now to the King, immortal, eternal and invisible, the only wise God, be honor and glory for ever and ever. Amen.   20

This was written in much sickness and weakness, and is very weakly and imperfectly done; but, if you can pick any benefit out of it, it is the mark which I aimed at.

---

maugre: despite

❏ *Outward Exploration: Discussion*

1. What is Bradstreet's primary reason for writing this letter to her children? Are there other reasons as well?

2. Describe Bradstreet's childhood and her adolescence.

3. According to her, what caused her smallpox when she was 16?

4. In what other ways did God "humble" Bradstreet, test her, and encourage her to be good?

5. In paragraph 9, what did Bradstreet have to do in order to be allowed to have children?

6. What kinds of afflictions and punishments did God use to make Bradstreet mend her ways and be good?

7. How does she characterize her relationship to God?

8. In paragraph 13, what seems missing from her life as a good Christian?

9. How has Bradstreet dealt with this disappointment?

10. Discuss in detail the temptations that Satan has placed in front of her. Analyze her responses. How convincing are her arguments to each of Satan's three temptations?

11. If your mother had written this letter to you, would you be convinced? Explain.

12. Throughout this book, you have been told that specific details are one of the most effective techniques for drawing your readers into your essays and for revealing yourself. In what places does Bradstreet offer specific details? In what places does she remain vague and general? What is the effect of each of those strategies on you? Explain.

❏ *Outward Exploration: Writing*

1. Anne Bradstreet lived the life that Nathaniel Hawthorne alludes to in his short story "Young Goodman Brown." Write an essay in which you explore the connections between the two pieces. For instance, what light does the Puritan faith that Bradstreet explains shed on Young Goodman Brown's decision to go into the forest in the first place? Are her doubts mirrored in Brown's implied doubts (Brown's doubts might be suggested by the temptations the stranger puts in his path)? Is Brown's ultimate response to temptation similar to or different from Bradstreet's?

2. In many ways, Bradstreet's letter is an argument: It is written to convince specific readers of a particular point. Write an essay evaluating Bradstreet's letter as an argument. Consider her use of evidence, her warrants, her vision of her audience. What assumptions

do you think she believed she shared with her readers (her children)? What doubts do you think she has about her children's faith? How does she try to correct those doubts? How effective is this letter as an argument?

3. In many ways, Bradstreet's letter is also a spiritual autobiography. All autobiographies have a guiding principle, an organizing idea which helps the author select and explain events. In Bradstreet's case, the organizing idea is her relationship with God. Write an autobiographical essay of your own. Select an organizing idea that explains much of your life. Here are a few examples: "I have often been lucky" or "My belief in X has guided my decisions" or "My fear of failure has caused me to avoid taking big risks." Use your experiences to explore the organizing idea's effect on your life. Consider its implications. Like Bradstreet, include events that qualify or contradict that organizing idea.

4. If you have read Francis Bacon's "The Four Idols," write an essay evaluating Anne Bradstreet's beliefs and arguments in terms of the four idols. Be specific.

"You're Short, Besides!"

SUCHENG CHAN

☐ *Inward Exploration*

Select one of your physical characteristics or personality traits. Write at least one paragraph about it. Include a description of its effect on your life.

When asked to write about being a physically handicapped Asian American woman, I considered it an insult. After all, my accomplishments are many, yet I was not asked to write about any of them. Is being handicapped the most salient feature about me? The fact that it might be in the eyes of others made me decide to write the essay as requested. I realized that the way I think about myself may differ considerably from the way others perceive me. And maybe that's what being physically handicapped is all about.

I was stricken simultaneously with pneumonia and polio at the age of four. Uncertain whether I had polio of the lungs, seven of the eight doctors who attended me—all practitioners of Western medicine—told my parents they should not feel optimistic about my survival. A Chinese fortune-teller my mother consulted also gave a grim prognosis, but for an entirely different reason: I had been stricken because my name was offensive to the gods. My grandmother had named me "grandchild of wisdom," a name that the fortune-teller said was too presumptuous for a girl. So he advised my parents to change my name to "chaste virgin." All these pessimistic predictions notwithstanding, I hung on to life, if only by a thread. For three years, my body was periodically pierced with electric shocks as the muscles of my legs atrophied. Before my illness, I had been an active, rambunctious, precocious, and very curious child. Being confined to bed was thus a mental agony as great as my physical pain. Living in war-torn China, I received little medical attention; physical therapy was unheard of. But I was determined to walk. So one day, when I was six or seven, I instructed my mother to set up two rows of chairs to face each other so that I could use them as I would parallel bars. I attempted to walk by holding my body up and moving it forward with my arms while dragging my legs along behind. Each time I fell, my mother gasped, but I badgered her until she let me try again. After four nonambulatory years, I finally walked once more by pressing my hands against my thighs so my knees wouldn't buckle.

My father had been away from home during most of those years because of the war. When he returned, I had to confront the guilt he felt about my condition. In many East Asian cultures, there is a strong folk belief that a person's physical state in this life is a reflection of how morally or sinfully he or she lived in previous lives. Furthermore, because of the tendency to view the family as a single unit, it is believed that the fate of one member can be caused by the behavior of another. Some of my father's relatives told him that my illness had doubtless been caused by the wild carousing he did in his youth. A well-meaning but somewhat simple man, my father believed them.

Throughout my childhood, he sometimes apologized to me for having to suffer retribution for his former bad behavior. This upset me; it was bad enough that I had to deal with the anguish of not being able to walk, but to have to assuage his guilt as well was a real burden! In other ways, my father was very good to me. He took me out often, carrying me on his shoulders or back, to give me fresh air and sunshine. He did this until I was too large and heavy for him to carry. And ever since I can remember, he has told me that I am pretty.

After getting over her anxieties about my constant falls, my mother   5
decided to send me to school. I had already learned to read some words of Chinese at the age of three by asking my parents to teach me the sounds and meaning of various characters in the daily newspaper. But between the ages of four and eight, I received no education since just staying alive was a full-time job. Much to her chagrin, my mother found no school in Shanghai, where we lived at the time, which would accept me as a student. Finally, as a last resort, she approached the American School which agreed to enroll me only if my family kept an *amah* (a servant who takes care of children) by my side at all times. The tuition at the school was twenty U.S. dollars per month—a huge sum of money during those years of runaway inflation in China—and payable only in U.S. dollars. My family afforded the high cost of tuition and the expense of employing a full-time *amah* for less than a year.

We left China as the Communist forces swept across the country in victory. We found an apartment in Hong Kong across the street from a school run by Seventh-Day Adventists. By that time I could walk a little, so the principal was persuaded to accept me. An *amah* now had to take care of me only during recess when my classmates might easily knock me over as they ran about the playground.

After a year and a half in Hong Kong, we moved to Malaysia, where my father's family had lived for four generations. There I learned to swim in the lovely warm waters of the tropics and fell in love with the sea. On land I was a cripple; in the ocean I could move with the grace of a fish. I liked the freedom of being in the water so much that many years later, when I was a graduate student in Hawaii, I became greatly enamored with a man just because he called me a "Polynesian water nymph."

As my overall health improved, my mother became less anxious about all aspects of my life. She did everything possible to enable me to lead as normal a life as possible. I remember how once some of her colleagues in the high school where she taught criticized her for letting me wear short skirts. They felt my legs should not be exposed to public view. My mother's response was, "All girls her age wear short skirts, so why shouldn't she?"

The years in Malaysia were the happiest of my childhood, even though I was constantly fending off children who ran after me calling, "*Baikah! Baikah!*" ("Cripple! Cripple!" in the Hokkien dialect commonly spoken in Malaysia). The taunts of children mattered little because I was a star pupil. I won one award after another for general scholarship as well as for art and public speaking. Whenever the school had important visitors my teacher always called on me to recite in front of the class.

A significant event that marked me indelibly occurred when I was   10
twelve. That year my school held a music recital and I was one of the students chosen to play the piano. I managed to get up the steps to the stage without any problem, but as I walked across the stage, I fell. Out of the audience, a voice said loudly and clearly, "Ayah! A *baikah* shouldn't be allowed to perform in public." I got up before anyone could get on stage to help me and, with tears streaming uncontrollably down my face, I rushed to the piano and began to play. Beethoven's "Für Elise" had never been played so fiendishly fast before or since, but I managed to finish the whole piece. That I managed to do so made me feel really strong. I never again feared ridicule.

In later years I was reminded of this experience from time to time. During my fourth year as an assistant professor at the University of California at Berkeley, I won a distinguished teaching award. Some weeks later I ran into a former professor who congratulated me enthusiastically. But I said to him, "You know what? I became a distinguished teacher by *limping* across the stage of Dwinelle 155!" (Dwinelle 155 is a large, cold classroom that most colleagues of mine hate to teach in.) I was rude not because I lacked graciousness but because this man, who had told me that my dissertation was the finest piece of work he had read in fifteen years, had nevertheless advised me to eschew a teaching career.

"Why?" I asked.

"Your leg . . ." he responded.

"What about my leg?" I said, puzzled.

"Well, how would you feel standing in front of a large lecture class?"   15

"If it makes any difference, I want you to know I've won a number of speech contests in my life, and I am not the least bit self-conscious about speaking in front of large audiences. . . . Look, why don't you write me a letter of recommendation to tell people how brilliant I am, and let *me* worry about my leg!"

This incident is worth recounting only because it illustrates a dilemma that handicapped persons face frequently: Those who care about us sometimes get so protective that they unwittingly limit our growth.

This former professor of mine had been one of my greatest supporters for two decades. Time after time, he had written glowing letters of recommendation on my behalf. He had spoken as he did because he thought he had my best interests at heart; he thought that if I got a desk job rather than one that required me to be a visible, public person, I would be spared the misery of being stared at.

Americans, for the most part, do not believe as Asians do that physically handicapped persons are morally flawed. But they are equally inept at interacting with those of us who are not able-bodied. Cultural differences in the perception and treatment of handicapped people are most clearly expressed by adults. Children, regardless of where they are, tend to be openly curious about people who do not look "normal." Adults in Asia have no hesitation in asking visibly handicapped people what is wrong with them, often expressing their sympathy with looks of pity, whereas adults in the United States try desperately to be polite by pretending not to notice.

One interesting response I often elicited from people in Asia but have never encountered in America is the attempt to link my physical condition to the state of my soul. Many a time while living and traveling in Asia people would ask me what religion I belonged to. I would tell them that my mother is a devout Buddhist, that my father was baptized a Catholic but has never practiced Catholicism, and that I am an agnostic. Upon hearing this, people would try strenuously to convert me to their religion so that whichever God they believed in could bless me. If I would only attend this church or that temple regularly, they urged, I would surely get cured. Catholics and Buddhists alike have pressed religious medallions into my palm, telling me if I would wear these, the relevant deity or saint would make me well. Once while visiting the tomb of Muhammad Ali Jinnah in Karachi, Pakistan, an old Muslim, after finishing his evening prayers, spotted me, gestured toward my legs, raised his arms heavenward, and began a new round of prayers, apparently on my behalf.

In the United States adults who try to act "civilized" toward handicapped people by pretending they don't notice anything unusual sometimes end up ignoring handicapped people completely. In the first few months I lived in this country, I was struck by the fact that whenever children asked me what was the matter with my leg, their adult companions would hurriedly shush them up, furtively look at me, mumble apologies, and rush their children away. After a few months of such encounters, I decided it was my responsibility to educate these people. So I would say to the flustered adults, "It's okay, let the kid ask." Turning to the child, I would say, "When I was a little girl, no bigger than you are, I became sick with something called polio. The muscles of my leg shrank up and I couldn't walk very well. You're much luckier than I am because now you can get a vaccine to make sure you never get my disease. So don't cry when your mommy takes you to get a polio vac-

20

cine, okay?" Some adults and their little companions I talked to this
way were glad to be rescued from embarrassment; others thought I was
strange.

Americans have another way of covering up their uneasiness: They
become jovially patronizing. Sometimes when people spot my crutch,
they ask if I've had a skiing accident. When I answer that unfortunately
it is something less glamorous than that, they say, "I bet you *could* ski if
you put your mind to it!" Alternately, at parties where people dance,
men who ask me to dance with them get almost belligerent when I
decline their invitation. They say, "Of course you can dance if you *want*
to!" Some have given me pep talks about how if I would only develop
the right mental attitude, I would have more fun in life.

Different cultural attitudes toward handicapped persons came out
clearly during my wedding. My father-in-law, as solid a representative
of middle America as could be found, had no qualms about objecting to
the marriage on racial grounds, but he could bring himself to comment
on my handicap only indirectly. He wondered why his son, who had
dated numerous high school and college beauty queens, couldn't marry
one of them instead of me. My mother-in-law, a devout Christian, did
not share her husband's prejudices, but she worried aloud about whether
I could have children. Some Chinese friends of my parents, on the other
hand, said that I was lucky to have found such a noble man, one who
would marry me despite my handicap. I, for my part, appeared in
church in a white lace wedding dress I had designed and made myself—a
miniskirt!

How Asian Americans treat me with respect to my handicap tells
me a great deal about their degree of acculturation. Recent immigrants
behave just like Asians in Asia; those who have been here longer or who
grew up in the United States behave more like their white counterparts.
I have not encountered any distinctly Asian American pattern of response. What makes the experience of Asian American handicapped
people unique is the duality of responses we elicit.

Regardless of racial or cultural background, most handicapped
people have to learn to find a balance between the desire to attain physical independence and the need to take care of ourselves by not overtaxing our bodies. In my case, I've had to learn to accept the fact that
leading an active life has its price. Between the ages of eight and eighteen, I walked without using crutches or braces but the effort caused my
right leg to become badly misaligned. Soon after I came to the United
States, I had a series of operations to straighten out the bones of my
right leg; afterwards though my leg looked straighter and presumably
better, I could no longer walk on my own. Initially my doctors fitted
me with a brace, but I found wearing one cumbersome and soon gave it
up. I could move around much more easily—and more important,
faster—by using one crutch. One orthopedist after another warned me

that using a single crutch was a bad practice. They were right. Over the years my spine developed a double-S curve and for the last twenty years I have suffered from severe, chronic back pains, which neither conventional physical therapy nor a lighter work load can eliminate.

The only thing that helps my backaches is a good massage, but the soothing effect lasts no more than a day or two. Massages are expensive, especially when one needs them three times a week. So I found a job that pays better, but at which I have to work longer hours, consequently increasing the physical strain on my body—a sort of vicious circle. When I was in my thirties, my doctors told me that if I kept leading the strenuous life I did, I would be in a wheelchair by the time I was forty. They were right on target: I bought myself a wheelchair when I was forty-one. But being the incorrigible character that I am, I use it only when I am *not* in a hurry!

It is a good thing, however, that I am too busy to think much about my handicap or my backaches because pain can physically debilitate as well as cause depression. And there are days when my spirits get rather low. What has helped me is realizing that being handicapped is akin to growing old at an accelerated rate. The contradiction I experience is that often my mind races along as though I'm only twenty while my body feels about sixty. But fifteen or twenty years hence, unlike my peers who will have to cope with aging for the first time, I shall be full of cheer because I will have already fought, and I hope won, that battle long ago.

Beyond learning how to be physically independent and, for some of us, living with chronic pain or other kinds of discomfort, the most difficult thing a handicapped person has to deal with, especially during puberty and early adulthood, is relating to potential sexual partners. Because American culture places so much emphasis on physical attractiveness, a person with a shriveled limb, or a tilt to the head, or the inability to speak clearly, experiences great uncertainty—indeed trauma—when interacting with someone to whom he or she is attracted. My problem was that I was not only physically handicapped, small, and short, but worse, I also wore glasses and was smarter than all the boys I knew! Alas, an insurmountable combination. Yet somehow I have managed to have intimate relationships, all of them with extraordinary men. Not surprisingly, there have also been countless men who broke my heart—men who enjoyed my company "as a friend," but who never found the courage to date or make love with me, although I am sure my experience in this regard is no different from that of many able-bodied persons.

The day came when my backaches got in the way of having an active sex life. Surprisingly that development was liberating because I stopped worrying about being attractive to men. No matter how headstrong I had been, I, like most women of my generation, had had the desire to

25

be alluring to men ingrained into me. And that longing had always worked like a brake on my behavior. When what men think of me ceased to be compelling, I gained greater freedom to be myself.

I've often wondered if I would have been a different person had I not been physically handicapped. I really don't know, though there is no question that being handicapped has marked me. But at the same time I usually do not *feel* handicapped—and consequently, I do not *act* handicapped. People are therefore less likely to treat me as a handicapped person. There is no doubt, however, that the lives of my parents, sister, husband, other family members, and some close friends have been affected by my physical condition. They have had to learn not to hide me away at home, not to feel embarrassed by how I look or react to people who say silly things to me, and not to resent me for the extra demands my condition makes on them. Perhaps the hardest thing for those who live with handicapped people is to know when and how to offer help. There are no guidelines applicable to all situations. My advice is, when in doubt, ask, but ask in a way that does not smack of pity or embarrassment. Most important, please don't talk to us as though we are children.

So, has being physically handicapped been a handicap? It all depends *30* on one's attitude. Some years ago, I told a friend that I had once said to an affirmative action compliance officer (somewhat sardonically since I do not believe in the head count approach to affirmative action) that the institution which employs me is triply lucky because it can count me as nonwhite, female, and handicapped. He responded, "Why don't you tell them to count you four times? . . . Remember, you're short, besides!"

◻ *Outward Exploration: Discussion*

1. What attitudes does Chan have toward the eight doctors who misdiagnosed her?

2. Explain the East Asian folk belief about people's physical states.

3. How did her father's guilt affect Chan?

4. What was her mother's attitude?

5. What significant event occurred when she was 12 years old?

6. Beginning in paragraph 17, how does the focus of the essay change?

7. Describe the difference between American and Asian attitudes toward the physically handicapped.

8. What balance do handicapped people need to learn?

9. What idea helps Chan deal with her handicap?

❏ *Outward Exploration: Writing*

1. Chan says, "The way I think about myself may differ considerably from the way others perceive me." Write an essay illustrating that idea with yourself as the topic.

2. Compare and contrast this essay with Nancy Mairs's "On Being a Cripple." Which person do you think you would like better if you met her in person? Why?

3. In paragraph 29, Chan ponders what her life would have been like if she hadn't been crippled. Write a *what . . . if* essay, speculating about *what* you would be like now *if* some major event in your life or some key aspect of your physical, emotional, or mental self had been changed. Here are a few examples: If I had been physically gifted in sports, how would my sense of myself be different now? If I had been able to express my needs instead of hiding them even from myself, how would my relationship with X have been different? If I really had the capacity to do advanced physics, how would my world view differ from what it is now?

from *Narrative of the Life of Frederick Douglass, Written by Himself*

FREDERICK DOUGLASS

☐ *Inward Exploration*

Write at least one paragraph on the value of education to you.

Chapter VI

My new mistress proved to be all she appeared when I first met her   *1*
at the door,—a woman of the kindest heart and finest feelings. She had
never had a slave under her control previously to myself, and prior to
her marriage she had been dependent upon her own industry for a living. She was by trade a weaver; and by constant application to her business, she had been in a good degree preserved from the blighting and
dehumanizing effects of slavery. I was utterly astonished at her goodness. I scarcely knew how to behave towards her. She was entirely unlike any other white woman I had ever seen. I could not approach her as
I was accustomed to approach other white ladies. My early instruction
was all out of place. The crouching servility, usually so acceptable a
quality in a slave, did not answer when manifested toward her. Her
favor was not gained by it; she seemed to be disturbed by it. She did not
deem it impudent or unmannerly for a slave to look her in the face. The
meanest slave was put fully at ease in her presence, and none left without
feeling better for having seen her. Her face was made of heavenly smiles,
and her voice of tranquil music.

But, alas! this kind heart had but a short time to remain such. The
fatal poison of irresponsible power was already in her hands, and soon
commenced its infernal work. That cheerful eye, under the influence of
slavery, soon became red with rage; that voice, made all of sweet accord,
changed to one of harsh and horrid discord; and that angelic face gave
place to that of a demon.

Very soon after I went to live with Mr. and Mrs. Auld, she kindly
commenced to teach me the A, B, C. After I had learned this, she assisted me in learning to spell words of three or four letters. Just at this
point of my progress, Mr. Auld found out what was going on, and at
once forbade Mrs. Auld to instruct me further, telling her, among other
things, that it was unlawful, as well as unsafe, to teach a slave to read.
To use his own words further, he said, "If you give a nigger an inch, he
will take an ell. A nigger should know nothing but to obey his mas-

ter—to do as he is told to do. Learning would *spoil* the best nigger in the world. Now," said he, "if you teach that nigger (speaking of myself) how to read, there would be no keeping him. It would forever unfit him to be a slave. He would at once become unmanageable, and of no value to his master. As to himself, it could do him no good, but a great deal of harm. It would make him discontented and unhappy." These words sank deep into my heart, stirred up sentiments within that lay slumbering, and called into existence an entirely new train of thought. It was a new and special revelation, explaining dark and mysterious things, with which my youthful understanding had struggled, but struggled in vain. I now understood what had been to me a most perplexing difficulty—to wit, the white man's power to enslave the black man. It was a grand achievement, and I prized it highly. From that moment, I understood the pathway from slavery to freedom. It was just what I wanted, and I got it at a time when I the least expected it. Whilst I was saddened by the thought of losing the aid of my kind mistress, I was gladdened by the invaluable instruction which, by the merest accident, I had gained from my master. Though conscious of the difficulty of learning without a teacher, I set out with high hope, and a fixed purpose, at whatever cost of trouble, to learn how to read. The very decided manner with which he spoke, and strove to impress his wife with the evil consequences of giving me instruction, served to convince me that he was deeply sensible of the truths he was uttering. It gave me the best assurance that I might rely with the utmost confidence on the results which, he said, would flow from teaching me to read. What he most dreaded, that I most desired. What he most loved, that I most hated. That which to him was a great evil, to be carefully shunned, was to me a great good, to be diligently sought; and the argument which he so warmly urged, against my learning to read, only served to inspire me with a desire and determination to learn. In learning to read, I owe almost as much to the bitter opposition of my master, as to the kindly aid of my mistress. I acknowledge the benefit of both.

I had resided but a short time in Baltimore before I observed a marked difference, in the treatment of slaves, from that which I had witnessed in the country. A city slave is almost a freeman, compared with a slave on the plantation. He is much better fed and clothed, and enjoys privileges altogether unknown to the slave on the plantation. There is a vestige of decency, a sense of shame, that does much to curb and check those outbreaks of atrocious cruelty so commonly enacted upon the plantation. He is a desperate slaveholder, who will shock the humanity of his non-slave-holding neighbors with the cries of his lacerated slave. Few are willing to incur the odium attaching to the reputation of being a cruel master; and above all things, they would not be known as not giving a slave enough to eat. Every city slaveholder is anxious to have it known of him, that he feeds his slaves well; and it is due to them to say that most of them do give their slaves enough to eat. There are, however, some painful exceptions to this rule. Directly opposite to us, on Philpot Street, lived Mr. Thomas Hamilton. He owned two slaves. Their names were Henrietta and Mary. Henrietta was about twenty-two years of age, Mary was about fourteen; and of all the mangled and emaciated creatures I ever looked upon, these two were the most so. His heart must be harder than stone, that could look upon these unmoved. The head, neck, and shoulders of Mary were literally cut to pieces. I have frequently felt her head, and found it nearly covered with festering sores, caused by the lash of her cruel mistress. I do not know that her master ever whipped her, but I have been an eyewitness to the cruelty of Mrs. Hamilton. I used to be in Mr. Hamilton's house nearly every day. Mrs. Hamilton used to sit in a large chair in the middle of the room, with a heavy cowskin always by her side, and scarce an hour passed during the day but was marked by the blood of one of these slaves. The girls seldom passed her without her saying, "Move faster, you *black gip!*" at the same time giving them a blow with the cowskin over the head or shoulders, often drawing the blood. She would then say, "Take that, you *black gip!*"—continuing, "If you don't move faster, I'll move you!" Added to the cruel lashings to which these slaves were subjected, they were kept nearly half-starved. They seldom knew what it was to eat a full meal. I have seen Mary contending with the pigs for the offal thrown into the street. So much was Mary kicked and cut to pieces, that she was oftener called "*pecked*" than by her name.

Chapter VII

I lived in Master Hugh's family about seven years. During this time, I succeeded in learning to read and write. In accomplishing this, I was compelled to resort to various strategems. I had no regular teacher. My mistress, who had kindly commenced to instruct me, had, in compliance with the advice and direction of her husband, not only ceased to instruct, but had set her face against my being instructed by any one else. It is due, however, to my mistress to say of her, that she did not adopt this course of treatment immediately. She at first lacked the depravity indispensable to shutting me up in mental darkness. It was at least necessary for her to have some training in the exercise of irresponsible power, to make her equal to the task of treating me as though I were a brute.

My mistress was, as I have said, a kind and tender-hearted woman; and in the simplicity of her soul she commenced, when I first went to live with her, to treat me as she supposed one human being ought to treat another. In entering upon the duties of a slaveholder, she did not seem to perceive that I sustained to her the relation of a mere chattel, and that for her to treat me as a human being was not only wrong, but dangerously so. Slavery proved as injurious to her as it did to me. When

5

I went there, she was a pious, warm, and tender-hearted woman. There was no sorrow or suffering for which she had not a tear. She had bread for the hungry, clothes for the naked, and comfort for every mourner that came within her reach. Slavery soon proved its ability to divest her of these heavenly qualities. Under its influence, the tender heart became stone, and the lamblike disposition gave way to one of tigerlike fierceness. The first step in her downward course was in her ceasing to instruct me. She now commenced to practise her husband's precepts. She finally became even more violent in her opposition than her husband himself. She was not satisfied with simply doing as well as he had commanded; she seemed anxious to do better. Nothing seemed to make her more angry than to see me with a newspaper. She seemed to think that here lay the danger. I have had her rush at me with a face made all up of fury, and snatch from me a newspaper, in a manner that fully revealed her apprehension. She was an apt woman; and a little experience soon demonstrated, to her satisfaction, that education and slavery were incompatible with each other.

From this time I was most narrowly watched. If I was in a separate room any considerable length of time, I was sure to be suspected of having a book, and was at once called to give an account of myself. All this, however, was too late. The first step had been taken. Mistress, in teaching me the alphabet, had given me the *inch,* and no precaution could prevent me from taking the *ell.*

The plan which I adopted, and the one by which I was most successful, was that of making friends of all the little white boys whom I met in the street. As many of these as I could, I converted into teachers. With their kindly aid, obtained at different times and in different places, I finally succeeded in learning to read. When I was sent of errands, I always took my book with me, and by going one part of my errand quickly, I found time to get a lesson before my return. I used also to carry bread with me, enough of which was always in the house, and to which I was always welcome; for I was much better off in this regard than many of the poor white children in our neighborhood. This bread I used to bestow upon the hungry little urchins, who, in return, would give me that more valuable bread of knowledge. I am strongly tempted to give the names of two or three of those little boys, as a testimonial of the gratitude and affection I bear them; but prudence forbids;—not that it would injure me, but it might embarrass them; for it is almost an unpardonable offence to teach slaves to read in this Christian country. It is enough to say of the dear little fellows, that they lived on Philpot Street, very near Durgin and Bailey's ship-yard. I used to talk this matter of slavery over with them. I would sometimes say to them, I wished I could be as free as they would be when they got to be men. "You will be free as soon as you are twenty-one, *but I am a slave for life!* Have not I as good a right to be free as you have?" These words used to trouble them; they would express for me the liveliest sympathy, and console me with the hope that something would occur by which I might be free.

I was now about twelve years old, and the thought of being *a slave for life* began to bear heavily upon my heart. Just about this time, I got hold of a book entitled "The Columbian Orator." Every opportunity I got, I used to read this book. Among much of other interesting matter, I found in it a dialogue between a master and his slave. The slave was represented as having run away from his master three times. The dialogue represented the conversation which took place between them, when the slave was retaken the third time. In this dialogue, the whole argument in behalf of slavery was brought forward by the master, all of which was disposed of by the slave. The slave was made to say some very smart as well as impressive things in reply to his master—things which had the desired though unexpected effect; for the conversation resulted in the voluntary emancipation of the slave on the part of the master.

In the same book, I met with one of Sheridan's mighty speeches on   10 and in behalf of Catholic emancipation. These were choice documents to me. I read them over and over again with unabated interest. They gave tongue to interesting thoughts of my own soul, which had frequently flashed through my mind, and died away for want of utterance. The moral which I gained from the dialogue was the power of truth over the conscience of even a slaveholder. What I got from Sheridan was a bold denunciation of slavery, and a powerful vindication of human rights. The reading of these documents enabled me to utter my thoughts, and to meet the arguments brought forward to sustain slavery; but while they relieved me of one difficulty, they brought on another even more painful than the one of which I was relieved. The more I read, the more I was led to abhor and detest my enslavers. I could regard them in no other light than a band of successful robbers, who had left their homes, and gone to Africa, and stolen us from our homes, and in a strange land reduced us to slavery. I loathed them as being the meanest as well as the most wicked of men. As I read and contemplated the subject, behold! that very discontentment which Master Hugh had predicted would follow my learning to read had already come, to torment and sting my soul to unutterable anguish. As I writhed under it, I would at times feel that learning to read had been a curse rather than a blessing. It had given me a view of my wretched condition, without the remedy. It opened my eyes to the horrible pit, but to no ladder upon which to get out. In moments of agony, I envied my fellow-slaves for their stupidity. I have often wished myself a beast. I preferred the condition of the meanest reptile to my own. Any thing, no matter what, to get rid of thinking! It was this everlasting thinking of my condition that tormented me. There was no getting rid of it. It was pressed upon me by every object within sight or hearing, animate or inanimate. The silver trump of freedom had roused my soul to eternal wakefulness. Freedom now appeared, to disappear no more forever. It was heard in every sound, and seen in every thing. It was ever present to torment me with a sense of my wretched condition. I saw nothing without seeing it, I heard nothing without hearing it, and felt nothing without feeling. It looked from every star, it smiled in every calm, breathed in every wind, and moved in every storm.

I often found myself regretting my own existence, and wishing myself dead; and but for the hope of being free, I have no doubt but that I should have killed myself, or done something for which I should have been killed. While in this state of mind, I was eager to hear any one speak of slavery. I was a ready listener. Every little while, I could hear something about the abolitionists. It was some time before I found what the word meant. It was always used in such connections as to make it an interesting word to me. If a slave ran away and succeeded in getting clear, or if a slave killed his master, set fire to a barn, or did any thing very wrong in the mind of a slaveholder, it was spoken of as the fruit of *abolition.* Hearing the word in this connection very often, I set about learning what it meant. The dictionary afforded me little or no help. I found it was "the act of abolishing"; but then I did not know what was to be abolished. Here I was perplexed. I did not dare to ask any one about its meaning, for I was satisfied that it was something they wanted me to know very little about. After a patient waiting, I got one of our city papers, containing an account of the number of petitions from the north, praying for the abolition of slavery in the District of Columbia, and of the slave trade between the States. From this time I understood the words *abolition* and *abolitionist,* and always drew near when that word was spoken, expecting to hear something of importance to myself and fellow-slaves. The light broke in upon me by degrees. I went one day down on the wharf of Mr. Waters; and seeing two Irishmen unloading a scow of stone, I went, unasked, and helped them. When we had finished, one of them came to me and asked me if I were a slave. I told him I was. He asked, "Are ye a slave for life?" I told him that I was. The good Irishman seemed to be deeply affected by the statement. He said to the other that it was a pity so fine a little fellow as myself should be a slave for life. He said it was a shame to hold me. They both advised me to run away to the north; that I should find friends there, and that I should be free. I pretended not to be interested in what they said, and treated them as if I did not understand them; for I feared they might be treacherous. White men have been known to encourage slaves to escape, and then, to get the reward, catch them and return them to their masters. I was afraid that these seemingly good men might use me so; but I nevertheless remembered their advice, and from that time I resolved to run away. I looked forward to a time at which it would be safe for me to escape. I was too young to think of doing so immediately; besides, I wished to learn how to write, as I might have occasion to write my own pass. I consoled myself with the hope that I should one day find a good chance. Meanwhile, I would learn to write.

The idea as to how I might learn to write was suggested to me by being in Durgin and Bailey's ship-yard, and frequently seeing the ship carpenters, after hewing, and getting a piece of timber ready for use, write on the timber the name of that part of the ship for which it was intended. When a piece of timber was intended for the larboard side, it would be marked—"L." When a piece was for the starboard side, it would be marked thus—"S." A piece for the larboard side forward, would be marked thus—"L.F." When a piece was for starboard side forward, it would be marked thus—"S.F." For larboard aft, it would be marked thus—"L.A." For starboard aft, it would be marked thus— "S.A." I soon learned the names of these letters, and for what they were intended when placed upon a piece of timber in the ship-yard. I immediately commenced copying them, and in a short time was able to make the four letters named. After that, when I met with any boy who I knew could write, I would tell him I could write as well as he. The next word would be, "I don't believe you. Let me see you try it." I would then make the letters which I had been so fortunate as to learn, and ask him to beat that. In this way I got a good many lessons in writing, which it is quite possible I should never have gotten in any other way. During this time, my copy-book was the board fence, brick way, and pavement; my pen and ink was a lump of chalk. With these, I learned mainly how to write. I then commenced and continued copying the Italics in Webster's Spelling Book, until I could make them all without looking on the book. By this time, my little Master Thomas had gone to school, and learned how to write, and had written over a number of copy-books. These had been brought home, and shown to some of our near neighbors, and then laid aside. My mistress used to go to class meeting at the Wilk Street meetinghouse every Monday afternoon, and leave me to take care of the house. When left thus, I used to spend the time in writing in the spaces left in Master Thomas's copy-book, copying what he had written. I continued to do this until I could write a hand very similar to that of Master Thomas. Thus, after a long, tedious effort for years, I finally succeeded in learning how to write.

📖 *Outward Exploration: Discussion*

1. According to Douglass, why was Mrs. Auld a kind mistress at first?

2. What were Mr. Auld's arguments against his wife's teaching Douglass to read and write?

3. According to Douglass, what transformed Mrs. Auld into a mean-spirited person?

4. What differences does Douglass notice between the treatment of slaves in the city and on the plantation? Why are there such differences?

5. What stratagems did Douglass employ to teach himself to read and write?

6. What does Douglass mean when he says that "[s]lavery proved as injurious to her [Mrs. Auld] as it did to me"?

7. What does Douglass mean when he refrains from naming the boys who helped teach him, saying "it is almost an unpardonable offence to teach slaves to read in this Christian country"?

8. What did Douglass learn from "The Columbian Orator," an anthology of poems, speeches, plays, and dialogues?

☐ *Outward Exploration: Writing*

1. Douglass goes to great effort in order to learn to read and write, skills that many of us take for granted. Using Douglass as a source (you might wish to use others as well), analyze the power of reading and writing in society. One question you might ask yourself is this: If Douglass had not persevered and learned how to read and write, would we have heard of him? Would slavery still be an American institution if Douglass and other slaves had not learned how to read and write?

2. Make an argument that slavery would have ended much earlier (or much later) if all slaves had been taught to read and write as a matter of course.

3. For Douglass, reading and writing were the path to freedom and the tools for helping his people who were still in slavery after he escaped. Write an essay exploring the value of reading and writing for you. You might broaden the topic to include the value of education for you.

4. Write a comparison and contrast essay exploring the similarities and differences between the selections from Frederick Douglass and those from Harriet Jacobs.

The Ghost Dance War

CHARLES ALEXANDER EASTMAN

❏ *Inward Exploration*

Write at least one paragraph explaining your conception of the relationships between white Americans and Native Americans in the late nineteenth century.

A religious craze such as that of 1890–91 was a thing foreign to the   *1*
Indian philosophy.° I recalled that a hundred years before, on the overthrow of the Algonquin nations, a somewhat similar faith was evolved by the astute Delaware prophet, brother to Tecumseh. It meant that the last hope of race entity had departed, and my people were groping blindly after spiritual relief in their bewilderment and misery. I believe that the first prophets of the "Red Christ" were innocent enough and that the people generally were sincere, but there were doubtless some who went into it for self-advertisement, and who introduced new and fantastic features to attract the crowd.

The ghost dancers had gradually concentrated on the Medicine Root creek and the edge of the "Bad Lands," and they were still further isolated by a new order from the agent, calling in all those who had not adhered to the new religion.° Several thousand of these "friendlies" were soon encamped on the White Clay creek, close by the agency.° It was near the middle of December, with weather unusually mild for that season. The dancers held that there would be no snow so long as their rites continued.

A religious craze . . . philosophy: As Anglo-American expansion gained momentum in the last quarter of the nineteenth century and Native Americans found themselves uprooted and exploited, many Native Americans believed in an apocalyptic vision of a future in which the white enemies would be vanquished by the ghosts of the dead Native Americans, and the buffalo would return. Begun by a Piute prophet named Wovoka, this vision gained religious power from a trance-inducing round dance and music. The Ghost Dance was particularly powerful among the Sioux, who were among the hardest hit by the expansion and broken treaties. When Sitting Bull, a believer, was killed while being arrested, Big Foot and his followers escaped the reservation and hoped to find refuge at the Pine Ridge reservation where Eastman worked. They got only as far as Wounded Knee, where they were surrounded by soldiers and massacred with machine guns. At least 150 men, women, and children were killed that day.
The ghost dancers . . . new religion: White officials viewed the Ghost Dance as a dangerous threat.
close by the agency: The agency was situated southwest of Wounded Knee.

An Indian called Little had been guilty of some minor offense on the reservation and had hitherto evaded arrest. Suddenly he appeared at the agency on an issue day, for the express purpose, as it seemed, of defying the authorities. The assembly room of the Indian police, used also as a council room, opened out of my dispensary,° and on this particular morning a council was in progress. I heard some loud talking, but was too busy to pay particular attention, though my assistant had gone in to listen to the speeches. Suddenly the place was in an uproar, and George burst into the inner office, crying excitedly "Look out for yourself, friend! They are going to fight!"

I went around to see what was going on. A crowd had gathered just outside the council room, and the police were surrounded by wild Indians with guns and drawn knives in their hands. "Hurry up with them!" one shouted, while another held his stone war-club over a policeman's head. The attempt to arrest Little had met with a stubborn resistance.

At this critical moment, a fine-looking Indian in citizen's clothes   5
faced the excited throng, and spoke in a clear, steady, almost sarcastic voice.

"Stop! Think! What are you going to do? Kill these men of our own race? Then what? Kill all these helpless white men, women and children? And what then? What will these brave words, brave deeds lead to in the end? How long can you hold out? Your country is surrounded with a network of railroads; thousands of white soldiers will be here within three days. What ammunition have you? what provisions? What will become of your families? Think, think, my brothers! this is a child's madness."

It was the "friendly" chief, American Horse, and it seems to me as I recall the incident that this man's voice had almost magic power. It is likely that he saved us all from massacre, for the murder of the police, who represented the authority of the Government, would surely have been followed by a general massacre. It is a fact that those Indians who upheld the agent were in quite as much danger from their wilder brethren as were the whites, indeed it was said that the feeling against them was even stronger. Jack Red Cloud, son of the chief, thrust the muzzle of a cocked revolver almost into the face of American Horse. "It is you and your kind," he shouted, "who have brought us to this pass!" That brave man never flinched. Ignoring his rash accuser, he quietly reentered the office; the door closed behind him; the mob dispersed, and for the moment the danger seemed over.

---

my dispensary: After graduating from Boston University Medical School, Eastman soon discovered that the only work available to him was as a government doctor on reservations. A few weeks before these events, he had begun working as the reservation doctor at Pine Ridge.

I scarcely knew at the time, but gradually learned afterward, that the Sioux had many grievances and causes for profound discontent, which lay back of and were more or less closely related to the ghost dance craze and the prevailing restlessness and excitement. Rations had been cut from time to time; the people were insufficiently fed, and their protests and appeals were disregarded. Never was more ruthless fraud and graft practiced upon a defenseless people than upon these poor natives by the politicians! Never were there more worthless "scraps of paper" anywhere in the world than many of the Indian treaties and Government documents! Sickness was prevalent and the death rate alarming, especially among the children. Trouble from all these causes had for some time been developing, but might have been checked by humane and conciliatory measures. The "Messiah craze" in itself was scarcely a source of danger, and one might almost as well call upon the army to suppress Billy Sunday° and his hysterical followers. Other tribes than the Sioux who adopted the new religion were let alone, and the craze died a natural death in the course of a few months.

Among the leaders of the malcontents at this time were Jack Red Cloud, No Water, He Dog, Four Bears, Yellow Bear, and Kicking Bear. Friendly leaders included American Horse, Young Man Afraid of His Horses, Bad Wound, Three Stars. There was still another set whose attitude was not clearly defined, and among these men was Red Cloud, the greatest of them all. He who had led his people so brilliantly and with such remarkable results, both in battle and diplomacy, was now an old man of over seventy years, living in a frame house which had been built for him within a half mile of the agency. He would come to council, but said little or nothing. No one knew exactly where he stood, but it seemed that he was broken in spirit as in body and convinced of the hopelessness of his people's cause.

It was Red Cloud who asked the historic question, at a great council   *10* held in the Black Hills region with a Government commission, and after good Bishop Whipple had finished the invocation, "Which God is our brother praying to now? Is it the same God whom they have twice deceived, when they made treaties with us which they afterward broke?"

Early in the morning after the attempted arrest of Little, George rushed into my quarters and awakened me. "Come quick!" he shouted, "the soldiers are here!" I looked along the White Clay creek toward the little railroad town of Rushville, Nebraska, twenty-five miles away, and just as the sun rose above the knife-edged ridges black with stunted pine, I perceived a moving cloud of dust that marked the trail of the Ninth Cavalry. There was instant commotion among the camps of friendly Indians. Many women and children were coming in to the agency for

---

Billy Sunday: A fire-and-brimstone Christian evangelist.

refuge, evidently fearing that the dreaded soldiers might attack their villages by mistake. Some who had not heard of their impending arrival hurried to the offices to ask what it meant. I assured those who appealed to me that the troops were here only to preserve order, but their suspicions were not easily allayed.

As the cavalry came nearer, we saw that they were colored troopers, wearing buffalo overcoats and muskrat caps; the Indians with their quick wit called them "buffalo soldiers." They halted, and established their temporary camp in the open space before the agency enclosure. The news had already gone out through the length and breadth of the reservation, and the wildest rumors were in circulation. Indian scouts might be seen upon every hill top, closely watching the military encampment.

At this juncture came the startling news from Fort Yates, some two hundred and fifty miles to the north of us, that Sitting Bull had been killed by Indian police while resisting arrest, and a number of his men with him, as well as several of the police. We next heard that the remnant of his band had fled in our direction, and soon afterward, that they had been joined by Big Foot's band from the western part of Cheyenne River agency, which lay directly in their road. United States troops continued to gather at strategic points, and of course the press seized upon the opportunity to enlarge upon the strained situation and predict an "Indian uprising." The reporters were among us, and managed to secure much "news" that no one else ever heard of. Border towns were fortified and cowboys and militia gathered in readiness to protect them against the "red devils." Certain classes of the frontier population industriously fomented the excitement for what there was in it for them, since much money is apt to be spent at such times. As for the poor Indians, they were quite as badly scared as the whites and perhaps with more reason.

General Brooke undertook negotiations with the ghost dancers, and finally induced them to come within reach. They camped on a flat about a mile north of us and in full view, while the more tractable bands were still gathered on the south and west. The large boarding school had locked its doors and succeeded in holding its hundreds of Indian children, partly for their own sakes, and partly as hostages for the good behavior of their fathers. At the agency were now gathered all the government employees and their families, except such as had taken flight, together with traders, missionaries, and ranchmen, army officers, and newspaper men. It was a conglomerate population.

During this time of grave anxiety and nervous tension, the cooler heads among us went about our business, and still refused to believe in the tragic possibility of an Indian war. It may be imagined that I was more than busy, though I had not such long distances to cover, for since many Indians accustomed to comfortable log houses were compelled to pass the winter in tents, there was even more sickness than usual. I had access and welcome to the camps of all the various groups and factions, a privilege shared by my good friend Father Jutz, the Catholic missionary, who was completely trusted by his people.

Three days later, we learned that Big Foot's band of ghost dancers from the Cheyenne river reservation north of us was approaching the agency, and that Major Whiteside was in command of troops with orders to intercept them.

Late that afternoon, the Seventh Cavalry under Colonel Forsythe was called to the saddle and rode off toward Wounded Knee creek, eighteen miles away. Father Craft, a Catholic priest with some Indian blood, who knew Sitting Bull and his people, followed an hour or so later, and I was much inclined to go too, but my fiancée pointed out that my duty lay rather at home with our Indians, and I stayed.

The morning of December 29th was sunny and pleasant. We were all straining our ears toward Wounded Knee, and about the middle of the forenoon we distinctly heard the reports of the Hotchkiss guns. Two hours later, a rider was seen approaching at full speed, and in a few minutes he had dismounted from his exhausted horse and handed his message to General Brooke's orderly. The Indians were watching their own messenger, who ran on foot along the northern ridges and carried the news to the so-called "hostile" camp. It was said that he delivered his message at almost the same time as the mounted officer.

The resulting confusion and excitement was unmistakable. The white teepees disappeared as if by magic and soon the caravans were in motion, going toward the natural fortress of the "Bad Lands." In the "friendly" camp there was almost as much turmoil, and crowds of frightened women and children poured into the agency. Big Foot's band had been wiped out by the troops, and reprisals were naturally looked for. The enclosure was not barricaded in any way and we had but a small detachment of troops for our protection. Sentinels were placed, and machine guns trained on the various approaches.

A few hot-headed young braves fired on the sentinels and wounded two of them. The Indian police began to answer by shooting at several braves who were apparently about to set fire to some of the outlying buildings. Every married employee was seeking a place of safety for his family, the interpreter among them. Just then General Brooke ran out into the open, shouting at the top of his voice to the police: "Stop, stop! Doctor, tell them they must not fire until ordered!" I did so, as the bullets whistled by us, and the General's coolness perhaps saved all our lives, for we were in no position to repel a large attacking force. Since we did not reply, the scattered shots soon ceased, but the situation remained critical for several days and nights.

My office was full of refugees. I called one of my good friends aside and asked him to saddle my two horses and stay by them. "When general fighting begins, take them to Miss Goodale and see her to the railroad if you can," I told him. Then I went over to the rectory. Mrs. Cook refused to go without her husband, and Miss Goodale would not leave while there was a chance of being of service. The house was crowded with terrified people, most of them Christian Indians, whom our friends were doing their best to pacify.

At dusk, the Seventh Cavalry returned with their twenty-five dead and I believe thirty-four wounded, most of them by their own comrades, who had encircled the Indians, while few of the latter had guns. A majority of the thirty or more Indian wounded were women and children, including babies in arms. As there were not tents enough for all, Mr. Cook offered us the mission chapel, in which the Christmas tree still stood, for a temporary hospital. We tore out the pews and covered the floor with hay and quilts. There we laid the poor creatures side by side in rows, and the night was devoted to caring for them as best we could. Many were frightfully torn by pieces of shells, and the suffering was terrible. General Brooke placed me in charge and I had to do nearly all the work, for although the army surgeons were more than ready to help as soon as their own men had been cared for, the tortured Indians would scarcely allow a man in uniform to touch them. Mrs. Cook, Miss Goodale, and several of Mr. Cook's Indian helpers acted as volunteer nurses. In spite of all our efforts, we lost the greater part of them, but a few recovered, including several children who had lost all their relatives and who were adopted into kind Christian families.

On the day following the Wounded Knee massacre there was a blizzard, in the midst of which I was ordered out with several Indian police, to look for a policeman who was reported to have been wounded and left some two miles from the agency. We did not find him. This was the only time during the whole affair that I carried a weapon; a friend lent me a revolver which I put in my overcoat pocket, and it was lost on the ride. On the third day it cleared, and the ground was covered with an inch or two of fresh snow. We had feared that some of the Indian wounded might have been left on the field, and a number of us volunteered to go and see. I was placed in charge of the expedition of about a hundred civilians, ten or fifteen of whom were white men. We were supplied with wagons in which to convey any of whom we might find still alive. Of course a photographer and several reporters were of the party.

Fully three miles from the scene of the massacre we found the body of a woman completely covered with a blanket of snow, and from this point on we found them scattered along as they had been relentlessly hunted down and slaughtered while fleeing for their lives. Some of our people discovered relatives or friends among the dead, and there was much wailing and mourning. When we reached the spot where the Indian camp had stood, among the fragments of burned tents and other belongings we saw the frozen bodies lying close together or piled one upon another. I counted eighty bodies of men who had been in the council and who were almost as helpless as the women and babes when the deadly fire began, for nearly all their guns had been taken from them. A reckless and desperate young Indian fired the first shot when the search for weapons was well under way, and immediately the troops opened fire from all sides, killing not only unarmed men, women, and children, but their own comrades who stood opposite them, for the camp was entirely surrounded.

It took all of my nerve to keep my composure in the face of this 25 spectacle, and of the excitement and grief of my Indian companions, nearly every one of whom was crying aloud or singing his death song. The white men became very nervous, but I set them to examining and uncovering every body to see if one were living. Although they had been lying untended in the snow and cold for two days and nights, a number had survived. Among them I found a baby of about a year old warmly wrapped and entirely unhurt. I brought her in, and she was afterward adopted and educated by an army officer. One man who was severely wounded begged me to fill his pipe. When we brought him into the chapel he was welcomed by his wife and daughters with cries of joy, but he died a day or two later.

Under a wagon I discovered an old woman, totally blind and entirely helpless. A few had managed to crawl away to some place of shelter, and we found in a log store near by several who were badly hurt and others who had died after reaching there. After we had dispatched several wagon loads to the agency, we observed groups of warriors watching us from adjacent buttes; probably friends of the victims who had come there for the same purpose as ourselves. A majority of our party, fearing an attack, insisted that some one ride back to the agency for an escort of soldiers, and as mine was the best horse, it fell to me to go. I covered the eighteen miles in quick time and was not interfered with in any way, although if the Indians had meant mischief they could easily have picked me off from any of the ravines and gulches.

All this was a severe ordeal for one who had so lately put all his faith in the Christian love and lofty ideals of the white man. Yet I passed no hasty judgment, and was thankful that I might be of some service and relieve even a small part of the suffering. An appeal published in a Boston paper brought us liberal supplies of much needed clothing, and linen for dressings. We worked on. Bishop Hare of South Dakota visited us, and was overcome by faintness when he entered his mission chapel, thus transformed into a rude hospital.

After some days of extreme tension, and weeks of anxiety, the "hostiles," so called, were at last induced to come in and submit to a general disarmament. Father Jutz, the Catholic missionary, had gone bravely among them and used all his influence toward a peaceful settlement. The troops were all recalled and took part in a grand review before General Milcs, no doubt intended to impress the Indians with their superior force.

❏ *Outward Exploration: Discussion*

1. According to Eastman, what events had led up to the religious craze known as the Ghost Dances?
2. What role did the media play in the events that Eastman recounts?
3. Why did Eastman have access to all the various camps (the "hostiles" as well as the "friendlies")?
4. Explain Eastman's position, both politically and emotionally.
5. Explain Eastman's "severe ordeal."
6. Describe Eastman's narrative approach. How satisfactory is it?

❏ *Outward Exploration: Writing*

1. Do some research about the massacre at Wounded Knee. Write an essay exploring its causes, its impact, and your reactions to it. Feel free to use Eastman as one of your sources.
2. Write an essay defending Eastman's position throughout this selection.
3. If you have ever been in a situation in which panic or misperceptions ruled the day, write an essay making that event come to life for your readers.
4. Write an essay about a time you faced a conflict between two of your beliefs, or between your belief and something else (for example, an event or your heritage).

Leaves from the Mental Portfolio
of an Eurasian

EDITH MAUD EATON (SUI SIN FAR)

❑ *Inward Exploration*

> *Each of us is different in some way from the majority of people who surround us. Write at least one paragraph explaining one way in which you are different from those around you and describing the first time you realized it.*

When I look back over the years I see myself, a little child of scarcely 1 four years of age, walking in front of my nurse, in a green English lane, and listening to her tell another of her kind that my mother is Chinese. "Oh, Lord!" exclaims the informed. She turns me around and scans me curiously from head to foot. Then the two women whisper together. Tho the word "Chinese" conveys very little meaning to my mind, I feel that they are talking about my father and mother and my heart swells with indignation. When we reach home I rush to my mother and try to tell her what I have heard. I am a young child. I fail to make myself intelligible. My mother does not understand, and when the nurse declares to her, "Little Miss Sui is a story-teller," my mother slaps me.

Many a long year has past over my head since that day—the day on which I first learned that I was something different and apart from other children, but tho my mother has forgotten it, I have not.

I see myself again, a few years older. I am playing with another child in a garden. A girl passes by outside the gate. "Mamie," she cries to my companion. "I wouldn't speak to Sui if I were you. Her mamma is Chinese."

"I don't care," answers the little one beside me. And then to me, "Even if your mamma is Chinese, I like you better than I like Annie."

"But I don't like you," I answer, turning my back on her. It is my 5 first conscious lie.

I am at a children's party, given by the wife of an Indian officer whose children were schoolfellows of mine. I am only six years of age, but have attended a private school for over a year, and have already learned that China is a heathen country, being civilized by England. However, for the time being, I am a merry romping child. There are quite a number of grown people present. One, a white haired old man, has his attention called to me by the hostess. He adjusts his eyeglasses and surveys me critically. "Ah, indeed!" he exclaims, "Who would have thought it at first glance. Yet now I see the difference between her and other children. What a peculiar coloring! Her mother's eyes and hair and her father's features, I presume. Very interesting little creature!"

I had been called from my play for the purpose of inspection. I do not return to it. For the rest of the evening I hide myself behind a hall door and refuse to show myself until it is time to go home.

My parents have come to America. We are in Hudson City, N. Y., and we are very poor. I am out with my brother, who is ten months older than myself. We pass a Chinese store, the door of which is open. "Look!" says Charlie, "Those men in there are Chinese!" Eagerly I gaze into the long low room. With the exception of my mother, who is English bred with English ways and manner of dress, I have never seen a Chinese person. The two men within the store are uncouth specimens of their race, drest in working blouses and pantaloons with queues hanging down their backs. I recoil with a sense of shock.

"Oh, Charlie," I cry, "Are we like that?"

"Well, we're Chinese, and they're Chinese, too, so we must be!" returns my seven-year-old brother.   *10*

"Of course you are," puts in a boy who has followed us down the street, and who lives near us and has seen my mother: "Chinky, Chinky, Chinaman, yellow-face, pigtail, rat-eater." A number of other boys and several little girls join in with him.

"Better than you," shouts my brother, facing the crowd. He is younger and smaller than any there, and I am even more insignificant than he; but my spirit revives.

"I'd rather be Chinese than anything else in the world," I scream.

They pull my hair, they tear my clothes, they scratch my face, and all but lame my brother; but the white blood in our veins fights valiantly for the Chinese half of us. When it is all over, exhausted and bedraggled, we crawl home, and report to our mother that we have "won the battle."

"Are you sure?" asks my mother doubtfully.   *15*

"Of course. They ran from us. They were frightened," returns my brother.

My mother smiles with satisfaction.

"Do you hear?" she asks my father.

"Umm," he observes, raising his eyes from his paper for an instant. My childish instinct, however, tells me that he is more interested than he appears to be.

It is tea time, but I cannot eat. Unobserved I crawl away. I do not   *20* sleep that night. I am too excited and I ache all over. Our opponents had been so very much stronger and bigger than we. Toward morning, however, I fall into a doze from which I awake myself, shouting:

"Sound the battle cry;
See the foe is nigh."

My mother believes in sending us to Sunday school. She has been brought up in a Presbyterian college.

The scene of my life shifts to Eastern Canada. The sleigh which has carried us from the station stops in front of a little French Canadian hotel. Immediately we are surrounded by a number of villagers, who stare curiously at my mother as my father assists her to alight from the sleigh. Their curiosity, however, is tempered with kindness, as they watch, one after another, the little black heads of my brothers and sisters and myself emerge out of the buffalo robe, which is part of the sleigh's outfit. There are six of us, four girls and two boys; the eldest, my brother, being only seven years of age. My father and mother are still in their twenties. "Les pauvres enfants," the inhabitants murmur, as they help to carry us into the hotel. Then in lower tones: "Chinoise, Chinoise."

For some time after our arrival, whenever we children are sent for a walk, our footsteps are dogged by a number of young French and English Canadians, who amuse themselves with speculations as to whether, we being Chinese, are susceptible to pinches and hair pulling, while older persons pause and gaze upon us, very much in the same way that I have seen people gaze upon strange animals in a menagerie. Now and then we are stopt and plied with questions as to what we eat and drink, how we go to sleep, if my mother understands what my father says to her, if we sit on chairs or squat on floors, etc., etc., etc.

There are many pitched battles, of course, and we seldom leave the house without being armed for conflict. My mother takes a great interest in our battles, and usually cheers us on, tho I doubt whether she understands the depth of the troubled waters thru which her little children wade. As to my father, peace is his motto, and he deems it wisest to be blind and deaf to many things.

School days are short, but memorable. I am in the same class with   25
my brother, my sister next to me in the class below. The little girl whose desk my sister shares shrinks close against the wall as my sister takes her place. In a little while she raises her hand.

"Please, teacher!"

"Yes, Annie."

"May I change my seat?"

"No, you may not!"

The little girl sobs. "Why should she have to sit beside a ———"   30

Happily my sister does not seem to hear, and before long the two little girls become great friends. I have many such experiences.

My brother is remarkably bright; my sister next to me has a wonderful head for figures, and when only eight years of age helps my father with his night work accounts. My parents compare her with me. She is of sturdier build than I, and, as my father says, "Always has her wits about her." He thinks her more like my mother, who is very bright and interested in every little detail of practical life. My father tells me that I will never make half the woman that my mother is or that my sister will be. I am not as strong as my sisters, which makes me feel somewhat ashamed, for I am the eldest little girl, and more is expected of me. I have no organic disease, but the strength of my feelings seems to take from me the strength of my body. I am prostrated at times with attacks of nervous sickness. The doctor says that my heart is unusually large; but in the light of the present I know that the cross of the Eurasian bore too heavily upon my childish shoulders. I usually hide my weakness from the family until I cannot stand. I do not understand myself, and I have an idea that the others will despise me for not being as strong as they. Therefore, I like to wander away alone, either by the river or in the bush. The green fields and flowing water have a charm for me. At the age of seven, as it is today, a bird on the wing is my emblem of happiness.

I have come from a race on my mother's side which is said to be the most stolid and insensible to feeling of all races, yet I look back over the years and see myself so keenly alive to every shade of sorrow and suffering that it is almost a pain to live.

If there is any trouble in the house in the way of a difference between my father and mother, or if any child is punished, how I suffer! And when harmony is restored, heaven seems to be around me. I can be sad, but I can also be glad. My mother's screams of agony when a baby is born almost drive me wild, and long after her pangs have subsided I feel them in my own body. Sometimes it is a week before I can get to sleep after such an experience.

A debt owing by my father fills me with shame. I feel like a criminal *35* when I pass the creditor's door. I am only ten years old. And all the while the question of nationality perplexes my little brain. Why are we what we are? I and my brothers and sisters. Why did God make us to be hooted and stared at? Papa is English, mamma is Chinese. Why couldn't we have been either one thing or the other? Why is my mother's race despised? I look into the faces of my father and mother. Is she not every bit as dear and good as he? Why? Why? She sings us the songs she learned at her English school. She tells us tales of China. Tho a child when she left her native land she remembers it well, and I am never tired of listening to the story of how she was stolen from her home. She tells us over and over again of her meeting with my father in Shanghai and the romance of their marriage. Why? Why?

I do not confide in my father and mother. They would not understand. How could they? He is English, she is Chinese. I am different to both of them—a stranger, tho their own child. "What are we?" I ask my brother. "It doesn't matter, sissy," he responds. But it does. I love poetry, particularly heroic pieces. I also love fairy tales. Stories of everyday life do not appeal to me. I dream dreams of being great and noble; my sisters and brothers also. I glory in the idea of dying at the stake and a great genie arising from the flames and declaring to those who have scorned us: "Behold, how great and glorious and noble are the Chinese people!"

My sisters are apprenticed to a dressmaker; my brother is entered in an office. I tramp around and sell my father's pictures, also some lace which I make myself. My nationality, if I had only known it at that time, helps to make sales. The ladies who are my customers call me "The Little Chinese Lace Girl." But it is a dangerous life for a very young girl. I come near to "mysteriously disappearing" many a time. The greatest temptation was in the thought of getting far away from where I was known, to where no mocking cries of "Chinese!" "Chinese!" could reach.

Whenever I have the opportunity I steal away to the library and read every book I can find on China and the Chinese. I learn that China is the oldest civilized nation on the face of the earth and a few other things. At eighteen years of age what troubles me is not that I am what I am, but that others are ignorant of my superiority. I am small, but my feelings are big—and great is my vanity.

My sisters attend dancing classes, for which they pay their own fees. In spite of covert smiles and sneers, they are glad to meet and mingle with other young folk. They are not sensitive in the sense that I am. And yet they understand. One of them tells me that she overheard a young man say to another that he would rather marry a pig than a girl with Chinese blood in her veins.

In course of time I too learn shorthand and take a position in an   40 office. Like my sister, I teach myself, but, unlike my sister, I have neither the perseverance nor the ability to perfect myself. Besides, to a temperament like mine, it is torture to spend the hours in transcribing other people's thoughts. Therefore, altho I can always earn a moderately good salary, I do not distinguish myself in the business world as does she.

When I have been working for some years I open an office of my own. The local papers patronize me and give me a number of assignments, including most of the local Chinese reporting. I meet many Chinese persons, and when they get into trouble am often called upon to fight their battles in the papers. This I enjoy. My heart leaps for joy when I read one day an article signed by a New York Chinese in which he declares "The Chinese in America owe an everlasting debt of gratitude to Sui Sin Far for the bold stand she has taken in their defense."

The Chinaman who wrote the article seeks me out and calls upon me. He is a clever and witty man, a graduate of one of the American colleges and as well a Chinese scholar. I learn that he has an American wife and several children. I am very much interested in these children, and when I meet them my heart throbs in sympathetic tune with the tales they relate of their experiences as Eurasians. "Why did papa and mamma born us?" asks one. Why?

I also meet other Chinese men who compare favorably with the white men of my acquaintance in mind and heart qualities. Some of them are quite handsome. They have not as finely cut noses and as well developed chins as the white men, but they have smoother skins and their expression is more serene; their hands are better shaped and their voices softer.

Some little Chinese women whom I interview are very anxious to know whether I would marry a Chinaman. I do not answer No. They clap their hands delightedly, and assure me that the Chinese are much the finest and best of all men. They are, however, a little doubtful as to whether one could be persuaded to care for me, full-blooded Chinese people having a prejudice against the half white.

Fundamentally, I muse, all people are the same. My mother's race is   *45* as prejudiced as my father's. Only when the whole world becomes as one family will human beings be able to see clearly and hear distinctly. I believe that some day a great part of the world will be Eurasian. I cheer myself with the thought that I am but a pioneer. A pioneer should glory in suffering.

"You were walking with a Chinaman yesterday," accuses an acquaintance.

"Yes, what of it?"

"You ought not to. It isn't right."

"Not right to walk with one of my mother's people? Oh, indeed!"

I cannot reconcile his notion of righteousness with my own.   *50*

I am living in a little town away off on the north shore of a big lake. Next to me at the dinner table is the man for whom I work as a stenographer. There are also a couple of business men, a young girl and her mother.

Some one makes a remark about the cars full of Chinamen that past [sic] that morning. A transcontinental railway runs thru the town.

My employer shakes his rugged head. "Somehow or other," says he, "I cannot reconcile myself to the thought that the Chinese are humans like ourselves. They may have immortal souls, but their faces seem to be so utterly devoid of expression that I cannot help but doubt."

"Souls," echoes the town clerk. "Their bodies are enough for me. A Chinaman is, in my eyes, more repulsive than a nigger."

"They always give me such a creepy feeling," puts in the young girl   *55* with a laugh.

"I wouldn't have one in my house," declares my landlady.

"Now, the Japanese are different altogether. There is something bright and likeable about those men," continues Mr. K.

A miserable, cowardly feeling keeps me silent. I am in a Middle West town. If I declare what I am, every person in the place will hear about it the next day. The population is in the main made up of working folks with strong prejudices against my mother's countrymen. The prospect before me is not an enviable one—if I speak. I have no longer an ambition to die at the stake for the sake of demonstrating the greatness and nobleness of the Chinese people.

Mr. K. turns to me with a kindly smile.

"What makes Miss Far so quiet?" he asks.   *60*

"I don't suppose she finds the 'washee washee men' particularly interesting subjects of conversation," volunteers the young manager of the local bank.

With a great effort I raise my eyes from my plate. "Mr. K.," I say, addressing my employer, "the Chinese people may have no souls, no expression on their faces, be altogether beyond the pale of civilization, but whatever they are, I want you to understand that I am—I am a Chinese."

There is silence in the room for a few minutes. Then Mr. K. pushes back his plate and standing up beside me, says:

"I should not have spoken as I did. I know nothing whatever about the Chinese. It was pure prejudice. Forgive me!"

I admire Mr. K.'s moral courage in apologizing to me; he is a   *65* conscientious Christian man, but I do not remain much longer in the little town.

I am under a tropic sky, meeting frequently and conversing with persons who are almost as high up in the world as birth, education and money can set them. The environment is peculiar, for I am also surrounded by a race of people, the reputed descendants of Ham, the son of Noah, whose offspring, it was prophesied, should be the servants of the sons of Shem and Japheth. As I am a descendant, according to the Bible, of both Shem and Japheth, I have a perfect right to set my heel upon the Ham people; but tho I see others around me following out the Bible suggestion, it is not in my nature to be arrogant to any but those who seek to impress me with their superiority, which the poor black maid who has been assigned to me by the hotel certainly does not. My employer's wife takes me to task for this. "It is unnecessary," she says, "to thank a black person for a service."

The novelty of life in the West Indian island is not without its charm. The surroundings, people, manner of living, are so entirely different from what I have been accustomed to up North that I feel as if I were "born again." Mixing with people of fashion, and yet not of them, I am not of sufficient importance to create comment or curiosity. I am busy nearly all day and often well into the night. It is not monotonous work, but it is certainly strenuous. The planters and business men of the island take me as a matter of course and treat me with kindly courtesy. Occasionally an Englishman will warn me against the "brown boys" of the island, little dreaming that I too am of the "brown people" of the earth.

When it begins to be whispered about the place that I am not all white, some of the "sporty" people seek my acquaintance. I am small and look much younger than my years. When, however, they discover that I am a very serious and sober-minded spinster indeed, they retire quite gracefully, leaving me a few amusing reflections.

One evening a card is brought to my room. It bears the name of some naval officer. I go down to my visitor, thinking he is probably some one who, having been told that I am a reporter for the local paper, has brought me an item of news. I find him lounging in an easy chair on the veranda of the hotel—a big, blond, handsome fellow, several years younger than I.

"You are Lieutenant ———?" I inquire. 70

He bows and laughs a little. The laugh doesn't suit him somehow—and it doesn't suit me, either.

"If you have anything to tell me, please tell it quickly, because I'm very busy."

"Oh, you don't really mean that," he answers, with another silly and offensive laugh. "There's always plenty of time for good times. That's what I am here for. I saw you at the races the other day and twice at King's House. My ship will be here for —— weeks."

"Do you wish that noted?" I ask.

"Oh, no! Why—I came just because I had an idea that you might 75 like to know me. I would like to know you. You look such a nice little body. Say, wouldn't you like to go out for a sail this lovely night? I will tell you all about the sweet little Chinese girls I met when we were at Hong Kong. They're not so shy!"

I leave Eastern Canada for the Far West, so reduced by another attack of rheumatic fever that I only weigh eighty-four pounds. I travel on an advertising contract. It is presumed by the railway company that in some way or other I will give them full value for their transportation across the continent. I have been ordered beyond the Rockies by the doctor, who declares that I will never regain my strength in the East. Nevertheless, I am but two days in San Francisco when I start out in search of work. It is the first time that I have sought work as a stranger in a strange town. Both of the other positions away from home were secured for me by home influence. I am quite surprised to find that there is no demand for my services in San Francisco and that no one is particularly interested in me. The best I can do is to accept an offer from a railway agency to typewrite their correspondence for $5 a month. I stipulate, however, that I shall have the privilege of taking in outside work and that my hours shall be light. I am hopeful that the sale of a story or newspaper article may add to my income, and I console myself with the reflection that, considering that I still limp and bear traces of sickness, I am fortunate to secure any work at all.

The proprietor of one of the San Francisco papers, to whom I have a letter of introduction, suggests that I obtain some subscriptions from the people of Chinatown, that district of the city having never been canvassed. This suggestion I carry out with enthusiasm, tho I find that the Chinese merchants and people generally are inclined to regard me with suspicion. They have been imposed upon so many times by unscrupulous white people. Another drawback—save for a few phrases, I am unacquainted with my mother tongue. How, then, can I expect these people to accept me as their own countrywoman? The Americanized Chinamen actually laugh in my face when I tell them that I am of their race. However, they are not all "doubting Thomases." Some little women discover that I have Chinese hair, color of eyes and complexion, also that I love rice and tea. This settles the matter for them—and for their husbands.

My Chinese instincts develop. I am no longer the little girl who shrunk against my brother at the first sight of a Chinaman. Many and many a time, when alone in a strange place, has the appearance of even an humble laundryman given me a sense of protection and made me feel quite at home. This fact of itself proves to me that prejudice can be eradicated by association.

I meet a half Chinese, half white girl. Her face is plastered with a thick white coat of paint and her eyelids and eyebrows are blackened so that the shape of her eyes and the whole expression of her face is changed. She was born in the East, and at the age of eighteen came West in answer to an advertisement. Living for many years among the working class, she had heard little but abuse of the Chinese. It is not difficult, in a land like California, for a half Chinese, half white girl to pass as one of Spanish or Mexican origin. This the poor child does, tho she lives in nervous dread of being "discovered." She becomes engaged to a young man, but fears to tell him what she is, and only does so when compelled by a fearless American girl friend. This girl, who knows her origin, realizing that the truth sooner or later must be told, and better soon than late, advises the Eurasian to confide in the young man, assuring her that he loves her well enough not to allow her nationality to stand, a bar sinister, between them. But the Eurasian prefers to keep her secret, and only reveals it to the man who is to be her husband when driven to bay by the American girl, who declares that if the halfbreed will not tell the truth she will. When the young man hears that the girl he is engaged to has Chinese blood in her veins, he exclaims: "Oh, what will my folks say?" But that is all. Love is stronger than prejudice with him, and neither he nor she deems it necessary to inform his "folks."

The Americans, having for many years manifested a much higher regard for the Japanese than for the Chinese, several half Chinese young men and women, thinking to advance themselves, both in a social and business sense, pass as Japanese. They continue to be known as Eur-

80

asians; but a Japanese Eurasian does not appear in the same light as a Chinese Eurasian. The unfortunate Chinese Eurasians! Are not those who compel them to thus cringe more to be blamed than they?

People, however, are not all alike. I meet white men, and women, too, who are proud to mate with those who have Chinese blood in their veins, and think it a great honor to be distinguished by the friendship of such. There are also Eurasians and Eurasians. I know of one who allowed herself to become engaged to a white man after refusing him nine times. She had discouraged him in every way possible, had warned him that she was half Chinese; that her people were poor, that every week or month she sent home a certain amount of her earnings, and that the man she married would have to do as much, if not more; also, most uncompromising truth of all, that she did not love him and never would. But the resolute and undaunted lover swore that it was a matter of indifference to him whether she was a Chinese or a Hottentot, that it would be his pleasure and privilege to allow her relations double what it was in her power to bestow, and as to not loving him—that did not matter at all. He loved her. So, because the young woman had a married mother and married sisters, who were always picking at her and gossiping over her independent manner of living, she finally consented to marry him, recording the agreement in her diary thus:

"I have promised to become the wife of ———— on ————, 189–, because the world is so cruel and sneering to a single woman—and for no other reason."

Everything went smoothly until one day. The young man was driving a pair of beautiful horses and she was seated by his side, trying very hard to imagine herself in love with him, when a Chinese vegetable gardener's cart came rumbling along. The Chinaman was a jolly-looking individual in blue cotton blouse and pantaloons, his rakish looking hat being kept in place by a long queue which was pulled upward from his neck and wound around it. The young woman was suddenly possest with the spirit of mischief. "Look!" she cried, indicating the Chinaman, "there's my brother. Why don't you salute him?"

The man's face fell a little. He sank into a pensive mood. The wicked one by his side read him like an open book.

"When we are married," said she. "I intend to give a Chinese party every month."

No answer.

"As there are very few aristocratic Chinese in this city, I shall fill up with the laundrymen and vegetable farmers. I don't believe in being exclusive in democratic America, do you?"

He hadn't a grain of humor in his composition, but a sickly smile contorted his features as he replied:

"You shall do just as you please, my darling. But—but—consider a moment. Wouldn't it be just a little pleasanter for us if, after we are married, we allowed it to be presumed that you were—er—Japanese? So many of my friends have inquired of me if that is not your nationality. They would be so charmed to meet a little Japanese lady."

"Hadn't you better oblige them by finding one?"   *90*

"Why—er—what do you mean?"

"Nothing much in particular. Only—I am getting a little tired of this," taking off his ring.

"You don't mean what you say! Oh, put it back, dearest! You know I would not hurt your feelings for the world!"

"You haven't. I'm more than pleased. But I do mean what I say."

That evening the "ungrateful" Chinese Eurasian diaried, among   *95*
other things, the following:

"Joy, oh, joy! I'm free once more. Never again shall I be untrue to my own heart. Never again will I allow any one to 'hound' or 'sneer' me into matrimony."

I secure transportation to many California points. I meet some literary people, chief among whom is the editor of the magazine who took my first Chinese stories. He and his wife give me a warm welcome to their ranch. They are broad-minded people, whose interest in me is sincere and intelligent, not affected and vulgar. I also meet some funny people who advise me to "trade" upon my nationality. They tell me that if I wish to succeed in literature in America I should dress in Chinese costume, carry a fan in my hand, wear a pair of scarlet beaded slippers, live in New York, and come of high birth. Instead of making myself familiar with the Chinese-Americans around me, I should discourse on my spirit acquaintance with Chinese ancestors and quote in between the "Good mornings" and "How d'ye dos" of editors:

> *"Confucius, Confucius, how great is Confucius, Before Confucius,
> there never was Confucius. After Confucius, there never came Confucius," etc., etc., etc.,*

or something like that, both illuminating and obscuring, don't you know. They forget, or perhaps they are not aware that the old Chinese sage taught "The way of sincerity is the way of heaven."

My experiences as an Eurasian never cease; but people are not now as prejudiced as they have been. In the West, too, my friends are more advanced in all lines of thought than those whom I know in Eastern Canada—more genuine, more sincere, with less of the form of religion, but more of its spirit.

So I roam backward and forward across the continent. When I am East, my heart is West. When I am West, my heart is East. Before long I hope to be in China. As my life began in my father's country it may end in my mother's.

After all I have no nationality and am not anxious to claim any.   *100*
Individuality is more than nationality. "You are you and I am I," says

Confucius. I give my right hand to the Occidentals and my left to the Orientals, hoping that between them they will not utterly destroy the insignificant "connecting link." And that's all.

☐ *Outward Exploration: Discussion*

1. Why do you think Eaton's mother has forgotten the conversation with the nurse that alerted Eaton to the fact that she was somehow different from many of the other children (paragraph 2)?
2. In paragraph 5, why does Eaton lie about not liking Mamie?
3. In paragraph 14, Eaton says that "the white blood in our veins fights valiantly for the Chinese half of us." What does she mean by that?
4. Comment on the different reactions of Eaton's parents to their children's struggles with other children. Which (if either) is the better reaction? Explain.
5. Describe Eaton's personality as a child.
6. Why do you think "a bird on the wing" is Eaton's "emblem of happiness" (paragraph 32)?
7. As a child, why does Eaton develop such an interest in China and the Chinese rather than in the English and England? What does she learn from all of her reading?
8. Discuss the event with her employer, Mr. K. (paragraphs 51–65).
9. What strategies do the Eurasians in California use to get by?
10. Discuss Eaton's assertion that she has "no nationality" and that "[i]ndividuality is more than nationality" (paragraph 100).

☐ *Outward Exploration: Writing*

1. In the second paragraph, Eaton says that her mother has forgotten that eventful day when Eaton first learned "that I was something different and apart from other children." Write an essay about a significant event in your life which a parent or some participant in the event has forgotten. Make the event vivid for your readers. In addition, explore the possible reasons why that person has forgotten the event and your reactions to his or her forgetting.
2. One question that recurs throughout this essay is "Why did people from two nationalities or races marry and have children?" Beneath the question is the anguish of the children who resulted from that marriage (not only Eaton but the children of the Chinese scholar and his American wife). Such marriages are much more common today than at the end of the nineteenth century when Eaton grew

up. Have the experiences of the children of such marriages changed? Do research to find the answers, and perhaps interview a friend whose parents are different nationalities (or religions or whatever).

3. Throughout the essay, Eaton is dogged by the question of her race. What exactly is *race,* anyway? Write an essay exploring the concept of *race.* Do library research. Consider other texts in this book as well, such as those by Harriet Jacobs, Frederick Douglass, and Kate Chopin.

4. Write an essay arguing either for or against Eaton's belief and hope that someday most of the world will be Eurasian (paragraph 45). Would that be a desirable situation? Why or why not? Perhaps Eaton really wants *all* the races and nationalities (not just European and Asian) to intermarry and create one single race. Would such a mixture be a desirable situation? Why or why not?

5. Drawing on your personal experiences, write an essay either illustrating or denying Eaton's idea that "[i]ndividuality is more than nationality." You might do some research to discover other people's definitions of *individuality* and *nationality.*

The Wretched of the Hearth

BARBARA EHRENREICH

☐ *Inward Exploration*

If you have ever watched the television sitcom Roseanne, *write at least one paragraph conveying your impressions of the show. If you have never seen* Roseanne, *write a paragraph about any other television sitcom you have seen. What makes it succeed or fail? What is success for a television sitcom anyway?*

"Roseanne" the sitcom, which was inspired by Barr the standup   1
comic, is a radical departure simply for featuring blue-collar Americans—and for depicting them as something other than half-witted
greasers and low-life louts. The working class does not usually get much
of a role in the American entertainment spectacle. In the seventies mumbling, muscular blue-collar males (*Rocky, The Deer Hunter, Saturday
Night Fever*) enjoyed a brief modishness on the screen, while Archie
Bunker, the consummate blue-collar bigot, raved away on the tube. But
even these grossly stereotyped images vanished in the eighties, as the
spectacle narrowed in on the brie-and-chardonnay class. Other than
"Roseanne," I can find only one sitcom that deals consistently with the
sub-yuppie condition: "Married . . . with children," a relentlessly nasty
portrayal of a shoe salesman and his cognitively disabled family members. There may even be others, but sociological zeal has not sufficed to
get me past the opening sequences of "Major Dad," "Full House" or
"Doogie Howser."

Not that "Roseanne" is free of class stereotyping. The Connors
must bear part of the psychic burden imposed on all working-class
people by their economic and occupational betters. . . . They indulge in
a manic physicality that would be unthinkable among the more controlled and genteel Huxtables. They maintain a traditional, low-fiber
diet of white bread and macaroni. They are not above a fart joke.

Still, in "Roseanne" I am willing to forgive the stereotypes as markers designed to remind us of where we are: in the home of a construction
worker and his minimum-wage wife. Without the reminders, we might
not be aware of how thoroughly the deeper prejudices of the professional class are being challenged. Roseanne's fictional husband Dan
(played by the irresistibly cuddly John Goodman) drinks domestic beer
and dedicates Sundays to football; but far from being a Bunkeresque
boor, he looks to this feminist like the fabled "sensitive man" we have
all been pining for. He treats his rotund wife like a sex goddess. He picks

up on small cues signaling emotional distress. He helps with homework. And when Roseanne works overtime, he cooks, cleans, and rides herd on the kids without any of the piteous whining we have come to expect from upscale males in their rare, and lavishly documented, encounters with soiled Pampers.

Roseanne Connor has her own way of defying the stereotypes. Variously employed as a fast-food operative, factory worker, a bartender, and a telephone salesperson, her real dream is to be a writer. When her twelve-year-old daughter Darlene (brilliantly played by Sara Gilbert) balks at a poetry-writing assignment, Roseanne gives her a little talking-to involving Sylvia Plath. "She inspired quite a few women, including *moi*." In another episode, a middle-aged friend thanks Roseanne for inspiring her to dump her chauvinist husband and go to college. We have come a long way from the dithering, cowering Edith Bunker.

Most of the time the Connors do the usual sitcom things. They have the little domestic misunderstandings that can be patched up in twenty-four minutes with wisecracks and a round of hugs. But "Roseanne" carries working-class verisimilitude into a new and previously taboo dimension—the workplace. In the world of employment, Roseanne knows exactly where she stands: "All the good power jobs are taken. Vanna turns the letters. Leona's got hotels. Margaret's running England . . . 'Course she's not doing a very good job. . . ." 5

The class conflict continues on other fronts. In one episode, Roseanne arrives late for an appointment with Darlene's history teacher, because she has been forced to work overtime at Wellman. The teacher, who is leaning against her desk stretching her quadriceps when Roseanne arrives, wants to postpone the appointment because she has a date to play squash. When Roseanne insists, the teacher tells her that Darlene has been barking in class, "like a dog." This she follows with some psychobabble—on emotional problems and dysfunctional families—that would leave most mothers, whatever their social class, clutched with guilt. Not Roseanne, who calmly informs the yuppie snit that, in the Connor household, everybody barks like dogs.

It is Barr's narrow-eyed cynicism about the family, even more than her class consciousness, that gives "Roseanne" its special frisson. Archie Bunker got our attention by telling us that we (blacks, Jews, "ethnics," WASPS, etc.) don't really like each other. Barr's message is that even within the family we don't much like each other. We love each other (who else do we have?); but The Family, with its impacted emotions, its lopsided division of labor, and its ancient system of age-graded humiliations, just doesn't work. Or rather, it doesn't work unless the contradictions are smoothed out with irony and the hostilities are periodically blown off as humor. Coming from mom, rather than from a jaded teen-ager or a bystander dad, this is scary news indeed. . . .

On the one hand, she presents the family as a zone of intimacy and support, well worth defending against the forces of capitalism, which drive both mothers and fathers out of the home, scratching around for paychecks. On the other hand, the family is hardly a haven, especially of its grown-up females. It is marred from within by—among other things—the patriarchal division of leisure, which makes dad and the kids the "consumers" of mom's cooking, cleaning, nurturing, and (increasingly) her earnings. Mom's job is to keep the whole thing together—to see that the mortgage payments are made, to fend off the viperish teenagers, to find the missing green sock—but mom is no longer interested in being a human sacrifice on the altar of "pro-family values." She's been down to the feminist bookstore; she's been reading Sylvia Plath.

This is a bleak and radical vision. Not given to didacticism, Barr offers no programmatic ways out. Surely, we are led to conclude, pay equity would help, along with child care, and so on. But Barr leaves us hankering for a quality of change that goes beyond mere reform: for a world in which even the lowliest among us—the hash-slinger, the sock-finder, the factory hand—will be recognized as the poet she truly is.

☐ *Outward Exploration: Discussion*

1. Why does Ehrenreich view *Roseanne* as a radical departure from earlier television comedies?
2. Why does Ehrenreich use the term *brie-and-chardonnay class?*
3. What stereotypes still exist in *Roseanne?*
4. In what ways does the husband transcend the stereotypical blue-collar worker and husband?
5. Why does Ehrenreich mention *The Bill Cosby Show, Married . . . with children,* and *All in the Family?*
6. Explain this essay's title.

☐ *Outward Exploration: Writing*

1. Select a visual text—either a television series or a movie or a play. Then, following Ehrenreich's lead, analyze and explore that visual text. Compare and contrast it with other, similar texts. Explore your own reactions to the visual text and its sources.
2. Humor is a very tricky subject. It is also a fascinating subject. Select two or three humorous texts that you know well (they might be essays in this book, or short stories, or movies, or a combination). Compare and contrast them. What techniques and qualities do they have in common? Which are unique to one particular work? Then do some library research on humor and comedy. Using those insights and your own observations of these humorous texts, write an essay exploring the concept of *humor.*

Selections from
Poor Richard's Almanack

BENJAMIN FRANKLIN

☐ *Inward Exploration*

For comfort or advice, most of us turn to some maxims, proverbs, aphorisms, or adages—in short, pithy sayings that state succinctly a general truth or fundamental principle or rule of conduct. For instance, when facing a separation from a person with whom we are romantically involved, we might invoke the adage that "absence makes the heart grow fonder." If we are worried about the relationship or simply cynical in general, we might fall back on "out of sight, out of mind." Make a list of pithy sayings that you know. Select one of them and write a paragraph explaining how your experience has proven that it is true (or false).

Light purse, heavy heart.   1733   *1*
He's a fool that makes his doctor his heir.
Love well, whip well.
Hunger never saw bad bread.
Fools make feasts, and wise men eat 'em.   *5*
He that lies down with dogs, shall rise up with fleas.
He is ill clothed, who is bare of virtue.
There is no little enemy.

Without justice courage is weak.   1734
Where there's marriage without love, there will be love   *10*
    without marriage.
Do good to thy friend to keep him, to thy enemy to gain him.
He that cannot obey, cannot command.
Marry your son when you will, but your daughter when
    you can.
Approve not of him who commends all you say.   1735   *15*
Necessity never made a good bargain.
Be slow in chusing a friend, slower in changing.
Three may keep a secret, if two of them are dead.
Deny self for self's sake.
To be humble to superiors is duty, to equals courtesy, to   *20*
    inferiors nobleness.

Fish and visitors stink in three days.   1736
Do not do that which you would not have known.
Bargaining has neither friends nor relations.
Now I've a sheep and a cow, every body bids me good morrow.   *25*
God helps them that help themselves.
He that speaks much, is much mistaken.
God heals, and the doctor takes the fees.

There are no ugly loves, nor handsome prisons.   1737
Three good meals a day is bad living.   *30*

Who has deceiv'd thee so oft as thyself?   1738
Read much, but not many books.
Let thy vices die before thee.

He that falls in love with himself, will have no rivals.   1739
Sin is not hurtful because it is forbidden, but it is forbidden   *35*
    because it's hurtful.

An empty bag cannot stand upright.   1740

Learn of the skilful: he that teaches himself, hath a fool
    for his master.   1741

Death takes no bribes.   1742   *40*

An old man in a house is a good sign.   1744
Fear God, and your enemies will fear you.

He's a fool that cannot conceal his wisdom.   1745
Many complain of their memory, few of their judgment.

When the well's dry, we know the worth of water.   1746   *45*
The sting of a reproach is the truth of it.

Write injuries in dust, benefits in marble.   1747

Nine men in *ten* are suicides.   1749

A man in a passion rides a mad horse.

He is a governor that governs his passions, and he is a servant   *50*
    that serves them.   1750
Sorrow is good for nothing but sin.

Calamity and prosperity are the touchstones of integrity.   1752
Generous minds are all of kin.

Haste makes waste.   1753   *55*

The doors of wisdom are never shut.   1755

The way to be safe, is never to be secure.   1757

❏ *Outward Exploration: Discussion*

1. Comment on Franklin's ideas about love.
2. Comment on Franklin's ideas about friendship.
3. Comment on Franklin's political ideas.
4. Comment on Franklin's vision of human nature.
5. Comment on Franklin's moral advice.
6. Comment on Franklin's religious ideas.

❏ *Outward Exploration: Writing*

1. Using these selections from *Poor Richard's Almanack* (or more if you like), write an essay exploring Franklin's vision of humankind and of the world.
2. The pithy saying is a popular form of literature. Compare and contrast Franklin's sayings with those of some other writer (for instance, Ambrose Bierce or William Blake). You might consider such things as their structure, style, subject matter, or tone.
3. Select one of Franklin's maxims that seems to speak particularly to you. After explaining its implications, show how it relates to your personal experience.
4. Select several of Franklin's related maxims that seem to speak particularly to you. After explaining their implications, show how they relate to your personal experience.

The Objects of My Invention

ABBY FRUCHT

📖 *Inward Exploration*

List at least five objects which are significant to you in some way. Select one object and write at least one paragraph which describes the object in detail and, in the process, also suggests its significance.

Or, select an object. Then select an emotion. Write at least one paragraph which describes the object in detail and, in the process, also suggests that emotion.

Fiction writers, always on the lookout for their own peculiar truths, must first create a world in which revelation is possible. When a writer opens an imagined cupboard in the corner of an imagined room, when she drops evidence into the pocket of some character's blue jeans, when she fills a town, a forest, a face with details, she searches for details with life, with personality, with influence.

Concrete objects influence the best of stories. They have *impact*—a word that has to do with motion, with kinetic activity. When one object strikes another, it puts the second object in motion. And when the second object strikes a third, it does the same thing—knocking the third object over, skewing it, throwing it off course. When an author writes a piece of fiction, she imagines that its details are billiard balls or dominoes, and then endows even the most apparently mundane of them with the properties of an eight ball or the energy of that first flick of a finger.

Details, in fiction, are not mere embellishment; they are catalysts for action, for emotional drama. So, for instance, if a character picks up a bottle, the author takes care to describe that bottle and her character's precise, intimate grip on it in such a way that something might happen. What's in the bottle? Is there anything in there that doesn't belong? Will the character swallow it, spit it out, choke on it, spill a little down the corner of his chin? Will he drop the bottle, throw it, break it, blow into it? Does he see himself reflected in it? Does he see somebody else reflected in it? Will what he sees make him more thirsty than he is already? Does he see his own desperation surfacing in the bottle? Does he see hunger? Does he see yearning? When describing that bottle, the writer makes it a bottle that has possibilities. Perhaps it might show up later in her story, on some neglected child's windowsill with furtive secrets blown into it—or maybe broken on the sidewalk, all ready to be run over by somebody's converted school bus. Then perhaps the bus's tire will go flat and the driver will step out into the dark night, and who knows what might happen, all because of that bottle.

I'm not suggesting the author must know all there is to know about the bottle the second she puts it on the page. But I am suggesting that she puts it there in such a way that it has a kind of presence, however slight; agency, however slight; effect, however slight.

When you think about it, the idea of a still life is kind of a joke, 5 because life is not still. It has a way of influencing even the most unassuming things. In her 1978 interview in *The Paris Review*'s "Writers at Work" series, Joan Didion talks about a jewel worn by one of her characters: "I hadn't planned that emerald in 'Common Prayer' to recur the way it does. It was just something I thought Charlotte might have, but as I went along the emerald got very useful. I kept taking that emerald one step further. By the end of the novel the emerald is almost the narrative. I had a good time with that emerald."

You might gain a better understanding of the process by which a simple, ordinary object may be handled as a generator of narrative by looking at a few passages from James Baldwin's novel *Giovanni's Room*. The setting is the interior of a bar in Paris in the 1950's. The narrator is a young American just beginning to recognize and examine his own homosexuality. Jacques is a friend, Giovanni is the bartender:

"Then I realized that I would have to pay, for this round anyway; it was impossible to tug Jacques's sleeve for the money as though I were his ward. I coughed and put my 10,000-franc note on the bar.

"'You are rich,' said Giovanni, and set my drink before me.

"'But no. No. I simply have no change.'

"He grinned. I could not tell whether he grinned because he thought 10 I was lying or because he knew I was telling the truth. In silence he took the bill and rang it up and carefully counted out my change on the bar before me. Then he filled his glass and went back to his original position at the cash register. I felt a tightening in my chest."

Of interest here is the 10,000-franc note, the equivalent these days of about $500. Surely Baldwin could have provided his narrator with a 20-franc note, enough for a couple of beers. But the tension here is heightened simply because, instead of paying for the beers with a smaller note, the narrator pays with a very large one. This is a story about homosexuality, and the sly Giovanni is an object of some speculation among the patrons at the bar. All of a sudden, out of nowhere, a bit of drama finds its way between the lines of the scene featuring him and the narrator, introducing the beginnings of an erotic exchange around which the entire novel will ultimately revolve.

Any writer of fiction is necessarily involved in the creation of a flexible, responsive world, a world whose natural, physical and psychological laws might shift and even crack a little in order to accommodate the demands of a story. But in order for those shifts and cracks to have grace, the smallest parts of their world must be mobile at the start. Every time a writer creates a detail that has life and potential, she gives herself the option of reshaping reality.

When I talk about reshaping reality, I'm not talking about creating something like Disney's *Beauty and the Beast;* I'm not concerned with inventing, say, a singing, dancing, little-boy teacup who squeals every time someone drops a cube of sugar inside him. He's cute, but I don't want him. Still, that movie has the right idea, as do a lot of children's books that include an animated environment. What children's books or films do is introduce the notion that a teacup might act upon the circumstances of the larger, surrounding story. The teacup, in other words, exercises a kind of will. When writers talk about the human players in their novels, they often say things like: "She just walked right out of the marriage. I couldn't stop her. She had a will of her own!" That's fine (although debatable). But writers should say the same things about the teacups, the eyeglasses, the dollar bills, the spoons.

How is a world made flexible? How are the parts made mobile and responsive? How might a spoon in a still life suddenly clatter to the floor or contain, in its tarnish, remnants of the lipstick of a woman who died 20 months earlier? Is it done with mirrors? Is it done with light? With composition? With imagery? With epiphany? Well, close. But, to be exact, it's done with language. With words. When a writer writes a novel or a story, she doesn't look with her eyes, she looks with her words. She doesn't listen with her ears, she listens with her words. She doesn't touch with her fingers, she touches with her words.

Once an object is indisputably present, it can become, in turn, 15 unpredictable. A magician cannot make a rabbit disappear unless every whisker of the rabbit is there in the first place. It's the same way with writing fiction. Only an author who looks at each part of the world of her story closely, probingly, insistently, stubbornly, will discern its secrets. What's more, if she brings to this inspection a vision inspired by the larger themes of her story, then the object of her gaze might eventually generate a circumstance that advances those themes. Is she writing a love story? Well, if she looks at her spoon with love, then perhaps she will discover those traces of lipstick. Is she writing a ghost story? Then if she drinks her tea with trepidation, maybe she will discover, reflected up at her from the bottom of the cup, a little white-nightgowned infant with circles under its eyes.

Writers are accustomed to looking at people this way too. Here's a portrait of a man from Alfred Chester's story "In Praise of Vespasian." I'm impressed by how the language of its gaze fluctuates between the objective and the subjective:

"Though I liked Joaquin, I was never really easy in his presence; the fiber of him seemed somehow always to be quaking; he was too intense, too fragilely built. . . . But he was good-looking, nearly beautiful, and today, thinking of his face, I remember the proud well-shaped bone under it, the pronounced mortality, over which the glowing skin was pulled taut."

What can we intuit about the narrator when we read that Joaquin is "too intense"? And what can we intuit about the narrative's themes when we read that Joaquin's face exhibits "pronounced mortality"? There's real texture in these words, real flexibility. And so the description of Joaquin is kinetic, full of psychological potential. Chester's story is teeming with this kind of language. It is, in fact, animated by it. Here are some examples:

"The air is gray and smells of cold lamb."

"Alone, and with no distractions, he sets off across Paris, on foot   20
once again, having left his bus money in the sink of the urinal."

"A hand has come under the partition—a too white, too fine, too hairy, too naked English hand."

It is important to examine the word choices in these passages. Each time Chester put his pen to paper, he was faced with a choice. Why, for instance, did the man drop his bus money in the sink of the urinal instead of placing it in his new lover's hand or buying that lover a bouquet of flowers? A story about a man forced to walk across the city because he has spent his bus money on a bouquet of roses would be remarkably different from a story in which a man is forced to walk across the city because he has scattered his few coins in the grime of a public lavatory. Instead of the roses' perfume, the stench of the urinal, along with the sordidness of the act of payment for sex, infuses the atmosphere of the narrative.

Later in the same story, having made his way through Paris, the protagonist tries unsuccessfully to arrange a sexual encounter in a restroom. The two men are shut up in side-by-side booths; the partition between them is constructed so that all that is visible to one man is the other man's feet and an occasional "too white" hand. One of the men is wearing heavy black boots, the other is in sandals. Chester writes: "And among it all he believes he can hear the black boots crying down to the sandals with a despair that pierces and grieves him."

In the space of a single brief observation, Chester's language constructs a metaphor for the kind of troubled sexuality that concerns his story—the masculine alongside the feminine, the submissive alongside the dominant. In place of two sets of ordinary shoes, the boots and the sandals become instruments of great emotion and suspense.

The other day, while at work on a new novel, I felt mired in ambi-   25
guity. After 25 pages, my main character seemed generic and obtuse, annoyingly inscrutable. I knew what she did, but I didn't know why. I

knew what attracted her, but I didn't know what frightened her. In other words, I didn't know her secrets. My job, then, was to give her the opportunity to reveal them to me. (This seems to be what people mean when they insist that characters have lives and wills of their own. That's not really true. It's a trick of words, of camouflage, that writers like to play on themselves.)

In order to give my character some secrets, I had to set her world in motion. I resolved to burn down part of the bed and breakfast where she lived and worked. After a while, I decided to start a fire in the pantry. It seemed clear to me, too, that something or someone would die in the fire, but I didn't know what or who. Experimentally, I sacrificed a couple of goldfish—then, oddly enough, a batch of yogurt culture.

I became interested in the burned-up yogurt for several reasons. To begin with, yogurt is a sensual thing, yet it's also an ordinary food of which most readers know the taste and feel. The very familiarity of its slippery whiteness would save me from having to use a lot of time and effort describing it. I would be free to move on to more interesting concerns—that is, the qualities that made this particular yogurt different from other yogurt. Then it occurred to me that the existence of the yogurt might allow me to introduce into the narrative something having to do with the female reproductive tract, which might figure somehow in the book's theme of sexual desire. So I phoned a friend who used to make her own yogurt, looked through a couple of cookbooks, and re-read the portion of "Our Bodies, Ourselves" that advises an application of yogurt for the cure of yeast infections.

I decided that my character had been carting around this particular yogurt culture for 16 years, that she had, in fact, been nurturing it, and that she included dollops of it in all her pies, stews, soups and pastries. Its destruction awoke in her an inexplicable grief. That grief made her nervous; she didn't want to be the kind of person who might be reduced to tears over a batch of acidophilus. She didn't want to be the kind of person who would have to think of herself, from then on, as lonely. She had always reveled in her solitude; now it was suspect. That was her first big secret, and it has since led to others, awakened by details like off-key harmonicas and unwrapped nuggets of hard candy. There remains a locket, in the glove compartment of my character's boyfriend's station wagon. She hasn't touched it yet, so I don't know what's in it or what will happen as a result of its being opened.

But I do know that it will somehow matter to the story, and it will teach me something new about my heroine. Even the dullest objects, graced by the peculiar specificity of the language that describes them, can surprise, delight and mystify. These objects can radiate. They can communicate. To the solitary fiction writer (or reader), even a wayward, discarded teaspoon can provide good company. This is not to say that you should content yourself with the friendship of a spoon—only that if you follow one around for a couple of pages, you might find yourself in places you never before imagined.

☐ *Outward Exploration: Discussion*

1. According to Frucht, how can concrete objects help writers?
2. What benefit is to be gained for you as an essayist from reading a piece about writing fiction?
3. How does the following sentence apply to you as an essayist: "Only an author who looks at each part of the world of her story closely, probingly, insistently, stubbornly, will discern its secrets"?

☐ *Outward Exploration: Writing*

1. List the objects that were or that could have been "on the scene" in an essay that you wrote earlier or which you are in the process of writing now. Select one of those objects and write a detailed description of it. Does the object connect in some way to the point of your essay? Does it reveal a point you hadn't noticed before? You might revise the earlier essay and deepen it with such attention to object. In this case, you should write a short essay explaining the process and depth of the changes and attach it to the essay proper.
2. Several of the essays in this text have used objects in revealing ways. Select two or three such essays, and explore their techniques and methods for using and revealing objects. Compare those to the ones Frucht discusses in this essay. What conclusions can you draw? What lessons (if any) have you learned?

Madonna: Plantation Mistress or Soul Sister?

BELL HOOKS

❏ *Inward Exploration*

Write at least one paragraph about singer and actress Madonna. Explain your feelings about her music, her videos, and her movies. What does she represent in American society?

> Subversion is contextual, historical, and above all social. No matter how exciting the "destabilizing" potential of texts, bodily or otherwise, whether those texts are subversive or recuperative or both or neither cannot be determined by abstraction from actual social practice.
>
> —SUSAN BORDO

White women "stars" like Madonna, Sandra Bernhard, and many others publicly name their interest in, and appropriation of, black culture as yet another sign of their radical chic. Intimacy with that "nasty" blackness good white girls stay away from is what they seek. To white and other nonblack consumers, this gives them a special flavor, an added spice. After all it is a very recent historical phenomenon for any white girl to be able to get some mileage out of flaunting her fascination and envy of blackness. The thing about envy is that it is always ready to destroy, erase, take over, and consume the desired object. That's exactly what Madonna attempts to do when she appropriates and commodifies aspects of black culture. Needless to say this kind of fascination is a threat. It endangers. Perhaps that is why so many of the grown black women I spoke with about Madonna had no interest in her as a cultural icon and said things like, "The bitch can't even sing." It was only among young black females that I could find die-hard Madonna fans. Though I often admire and, yes at times, even envy Madonna because she has created a cultural space where she can invent and reinvent herself and receive public affirmation and material reward, I do not consider myself a Madonna fan.

Once I read an interview with Madonna where she talked about her envy of black culture, where she stated that she wanted to be black as a child. It is a sign of white privilege to be able to "see" blackness and black culture from a standpoint where only the rich culture of opposition black people have created in resistance marks and defines us. Such a perspective enables one to ignore white supremacist domination and the hurt it inflicts via oppression, exploitation, and everyday wounds and pains. White folks who do not see black pain never really understand the complexity of black pleasure. And it is no wonder then that when they attempt to imitate the joy in living which they see as the "essence" of soul and blackness, their cultural productions may have an air of sham and falseness that may titillate and even move white audiences yet leave many black folks cold.

Needless to say, if Madonna had to depend on masses of black women to maintain her status as cultural icon she would have been dethroned some time ago. Many of the black women I spoke with expressed intense disgust and hatred of Madonna. Most did not respond to my cautious attempts to suggest that underlying those negative feelings might lurk feelings of envy, and dare I say it, desire. No black woman I talked to declared that she wanted to "be Madonna." Yet we have only to look at the number of black women entertainers/stars (Tina Turner, Aretha Franklin, Donna Summer, Vanessa Williams, Yo-Yo, etc.) who gain greater crossover recognition when they demonstrate that, like Madonna, they too, have a healthy dose of "blonde ambition." Clearly their careers have been influenced by Madonna's choices and strategies.

For masses of black women, the political reality that underlies Madonna's and our recognition that this is a society where "blondes" not only "have more fun" but where they are more likely to succeed in any endeavor is white supremacy and racism. We cannot see Madonna's change in hair color as being merely a question of aesthetic choice. I agree with Julie Burchill in her critical work *Girls on Film,* when she reminds us: "What does it say about racial purity that the best blondes have all been brunettes (Harlow, Monroe, Bardot)? I think it says that we are not as white as we think. I think it says that Pure is a Bore." I also know that it is the expressed desire of the nonblonde Other for those characteristics that are seen as the quintessential markers of racial aesthetic superiority that perpetuate and uphold white supremacy. In this sense Madonna has much in common with the masses of black women who suffer from internalized racism and are forever terrorized by a standard of beauty they feel they can never truly embody.

Like many black women who have stood outside the culture's fascination with the blonde beauty and who have only been able to reach it through imitation and artifice, Madonna often recalls that she was a working-class white girl who saw herself as ugly, as outside the mainstream beauty standard. And indeed what some of us like about her is the way she deconstructs the myth of "natural" white girl beauty by exposing the extent to which it can be and is usually artificially constructed and maintained. She mocks the conventional racist-defined beauty ideal even as she rigorously strives to embody it. Given her obsession with exposing the reality that the ideal female beauty in this society can be attained by artifice and social construction, it should come as no surprise that many of her fans are gay men, and that the majority of nonwhite men, particularly black men, are among that group. Jennie Livingston's film *Paris Is Burning* suggests that many black gay men, especially queens/divas, are as equally driven as Madonna by "blonde ambition." Madonna never lets her audience forget that whatever "look" she acquires is attained by hard work—"it ain't natural." And as Burchill comments in her chapter "Homosexual Girls":

> I have a friend who drives a cab and looks like a Marlboro Man but at night is the second best Jean Harlow I have ever seen. He summed up the kind of film star he adores, brutally and brilliantly, when he said, "I like actresses who look as if they've spent hours putting themselves together—and even then they don't look right."

Certainly no one, not even die-hard Madonna fans, ever insists that her beauty is not attained by skillful artifice. And indeed, a major point of the documentary film *Truth or Dare: In Bed With Madonna* was to demonstrate the amount of work that goes into the construction of her image. Yet when the chips are down, the image Madonna most exploits is that of the quintessential "white girl." To maintain that image she must always position herself as an outsider in relation to black culture. It is that position of outsider that enables her to colonize and appropriate black experience for her own opportunistic ends even as she attempts to mask her acts of racist aggression as affirmation. And no other group sees that as clearly as black females in this society. For we have always known that the socially constructed image of innocent white womanhood relies on the continued production of the racist/sexist sexual myth that black women are not innocent and never can be. Since we are coded always as "fallen" women in the racist cultural iconography we can never, as can Madonna, publicly "work" the image of ourselves as innocent female daring to be bad. Mainstream culture always reads the black female body as sign of sexual experience. In part, many black women who are disgusted by Madonna's flaunting of sexual experience are enraged because the very image of sexual agency that she is able to project and affirm with material gain has been the stick this society has used to justify its continued beating and assault on the black female body. The vast majority of black women in the United States, more concerned with projecting images of respectability than with the idea of female sexual agency and transgression, do not often feel we have the "freedom" to act in rebellious ways in regards to sexuality without being punished. We have only to contrast the life story of Tina Turner with that of Madonna to see the different connotations "wild" sexual agency has when it is asserted by a black female. Being represented publicly as an active sexual being has only recently enabled Turner to gain control over her life and career. For years the public image of aggressive sexual agency Turner projected belied the degree to which she was sexually abused and exploited privately. She was also materially exploited. Madonna's career could not be all that it is if there were no Tina Turner and yet, unlike her cohort Sandra Bernhard, Madonna never articulates the cultural debt she owes black females.

In her most recent appropriations of blackness, Madonna almost always imitates phallic black masculinity. Although I read many articles which talked about her appropriating male codes, no critic seems to have noticed her emphasis on black male experience. In his *Playboy* profile, "Playgirl of the Western World," Michael Kelly describes Madonna's crotch grabbing as "an eloquent visual put-down of male phallic pride." He points out that she worked with choreographer Vince Paterson to perfect the gesture. Even though Kelly tells readers that Madonna was consciously imitating Michael Jackson, he does not contextualize his interpretation of the gesture to include this act of appropriation from black male culture. And in that specific context the groin grabbing gesture is an assertion of pride and phallic domination that usually takes place in an all-male context. Madonna's imitation of this gesture could just as easily be read as an expression of envy.

Throughout [many] of her autobiographical interviews runs a thread of expressed desire to possess the power she perceives men have. Madonna may hate the phallus, but she longs to possess its power. She is always first and foremost in competition with men to see who has the biggest penis. She longs to assert phallic power, and like every other group in this white supremacist society, she clearly sees black men as embodying a quality of maleness that eludes white men. Hence they are often the group of men she most seeks to imitate, taunting white males with her own version of "black masculinity." When it comes to entertainment rivals, Madonna clearly perceives black male stars like Prince and Michael Jackson to be the standard against which she must measure herself and that she ultimately hopes to transcend.

Fascinated yet envious of black style, Madonna appropriates black culture in ways that mock and undermine, making her presentation one that upstages. This is most evident in the video "Like a Prayer." Though I read numerous articles that discussed public outrage at this video, none focused on the issue of race. No article called attention to the fact that Madonna flaunts her sexual agency by suggesting that she is breaking the ties that bind her as a white girl to white patriarchy, and establishing ties with black men. She, however, and not black men, does the choosing. The message is directed at white men. It suggests that they only labeled black men rapists for fear that white girls would choose black partners over them. Cultural critics commenting on the video did not seem at all interested in exploring the reasons Madonna chooses a black cultural backdrop for this video, i.e., black church and religious experience. Clearly, it was this backdrop that added to the video's controversy.

In her commentary in the *Washington Post,* "Madonna: Yuppie God- 10
dess," Brooke Masters writes: "Most descriptions of the controversial video focus on its Catholic imagery: Madonna kisses a black saint, and develops Christ-like markings on her hands. However, the video is also a feminist fairy tale. Sleeping Beauty and Snow White waited for their princes to come along, Madonna finds her own man and wakes him up." Notice that this writer completely overlooks the issue of race and gender. That Madonna's chosen prince was a black man is in part what made the representation potentially shocking and provocative to a white supremacist audience. Yet her attempt to exploit and transgress traditional racial taboos was rarely commented on. Instead critics concentrated on whether or not she was violating taboos regarding religion and representation.

In the United States, Catholicism is most often seen as a religion that has [few] or no black followers and Madonna's video certainly perpetuates this stereotype with its juxtaposition of images of black non-Catholic representations with the image of the black saint. Given the importance of religious experience and liberation theology in black life, Madonna's use of this imagery seemed particularly offensive. For she made black characters act in complicity with her as she aggressively flaunted her critique of Catholic manners, her attack on organized religion. Yet, no black voices that I know of came forward in print calling attention to the fact that the realm of the sacred that is mocked in this film is black religious experience, or that this appropriative "use" of that experience was offensive to many black folk. Looking at the video with a group of students in my class on the politics of sexuality where we critically analyze the way race and representations of blackness are used to sell products, we discussed the way in which black people in the video are caricatures reflecting stereotypes. They appear grotesque. The only role black females have in this video is to catch (i.e., rescue) the "angelic" Madonna when she is "falling." This is just a contemporary casting of the black female as Mammy. Made to serve as supportive backdrop for Madonna's drama, black characters in "Like a Prayer" remind one of those early Hollywood depictions of singing black slaves in the great plantation movies or those Shirley Temple films where Bojangles was trotted out to dance with Miss Shirley and spice up her act. Audiences were not supposed to be enamored of Bojangles, they were supposed to see just what a special little old white girl Shirley really was. In her own way Madonna is a modern day Shirley Temple. Certainly her expressed affinity with black culture enhances her value.

Eager to see the documentary *Truth or Dare* because it promised to focus on Madonna's transgressive sexual persona, which I find interesting,

I was angered by her visual representations of her domination over not white men (certainly not over Warren Beatty or Alek Keshishian), but people of color and white working-class women. I was too angered by this to appreciate other aspects of the film I might have enjoyed. In *Truth or Dare* Madonna clearly revealed that she can only think of exerting power along very traditional, white supremacist, capitalistic, patriarchal lines. That she made people who were dependent on her for their immediate livelihood submit to her will was neither charming nor seductive to me or the other black folks that I spoke with who saw the film. We thought it tragically ironic that Madonna would choose as her dance partner a black male with dyed blonde hair. Perhaps had he appeared less like a white-identified black male consumed by "blonde ambition" he might have upstaged her. Instead he was positioned as a mirror, into which Madonna and her audience could look and see only a reflection of herself and the worship of "whiteness" she embodies—that white supremacist culture wants everyone to embody. Madonna used her power to ensure that he and the other nonwhite women and men who worked for her, as well as some of the white subordinates, would all serve as the backdrop to her white-girl-makes-good-drama. Joking about the film with other black folks, we commented that Madonna must have searched long and hard to find a black female that was not a good dancer, one who would not deflect attention away from her. And it is telling that when the film directly reflects something other than a positive image of Madonna, the camera highlights the rage this black female dancer was suppressing. It surfaces when the "subordinates" have time off and are "relaxing."

As with most Madonna videos, when critics talk about this film they tend to ignore race. Yet no viewer can look at this film and not think about race and representation without engaging in forms of denial. After choosing a cast of characters from marginalized groups— nonwhite folks, heterosexual and gay, and gay white folks—Madonna publicly describes them as "emotional cripples." And of course in the context of the film this description seems borne out by the way they allow her to dominate, exploit, and humiliate them. Those Madonna fans who are determined to see her as politically progressive might ask themselves why it is she completely endorses those racist/sexist/classist stereotypes that almost always attempt to portray marginalized groups as "defective." Let's face it, by doing this, Madonna is not breaking with any white supremacist, patriarchal status quo; she is endorsing and perpetuating it.

Some of us do not find it hip or cute for Madonna to brag that she has a "fascistic side," a side well documented in the film. Well, we did not see any of her cute little fascism in action when it was Warren Beatty calling her out in the film. No, there the image of Madonna was the little woman who grins and bears it. No, her "somebody's got to be in charge side," as she names it, was most expressed in her interaction with those representatives from marginalized groups who are most often victimized by the powerful. Why is it there is little or no discussion of Madonna as racist or sexist in her relation to other women? Would audiences be charmed by some rich white male entertainer telling us he must "play father" and oversee the actions of the less powerful, especially women and men of color? So why did so many people find it cute when Madonna asserted that she dominates the interracial casts of gay and heterosexual folks in her film because they are crippled and she "like[s] to play mother." No, this was not a display of feminist power, this was the same old phallic nonsense with white pussy at the center. And many of us watching were not simply unmoved—we were outraged.

Perhaps it is a sign of a collective feeling of powerlessness that many   *15* black, nonwhite, and white viewers of this film who were disturbed by the display of racism, sexism, and heterosexism (yes, it's possible to hire gay people, support AIDS projects, and still be biased in the direction of phallic patriarchal heterosexuality) in *Truth or Dare* have said so little. Sometimes it is difficult to find words to make a critique when we find ourselves attracted by some aspect of a performer's act and disturbed by others, or when a performer shows more interest in promoting progressive social causes than is customary. We may see that performer as above critique. Or we may feel our critique will in no way intervene on the worship of them as a cultural icon.

To say nothing, however, is to be complicit with the very forces of domination that make "blonde ambition" necessary to Madonna's success. Tragically, all that is transgressive and potentially empowering to feminist women and men about Madonna's work may be undermined by all that it contains that is reactionary and in no way unconventional or new. It is often the conservative elements in her work converging with the status quo that have the most powerful impact. For example: Given the rampant homophobia in this society and the concomitant heterosexist voyeuristic obsession with gay life-styles, to what extent does Madonna progressively seek to challenge this if she insists on primarily representing gays as in some way emotionally handicapped or defective? Or when Madonna responds to the critique that she exploits gay men by cavalierly stating: "What does exploitation mean? . . . In a revolution, some people have to get hurt. To get people to change, you have to turn the table over. Some dishes get broken."

I can only say this doesn't sound like liberation to me. Perhaps when Madonna explores those memories of her white working-class childhood in a troubled family in a way that enables her to understand intimately the politics of exploitation, domination, and submission, she will have a deeper connection with oppositional black culture. If and when this radical critical self-interrogation takes place, she will have the power to create new and different cultural productions, work that will be truly transgressive—acts of resistance that transform rather than simply seduce.

❑ *Outward Exploration: Discussion*

1. What was your image of Madonna before you read this essay?
2. Why does hooks say that Madonna is a white supremacist and racist? Do you agree? Why or why not?
3. According to hooks, what is the significance of Madonna's changing hair color?
4. According to hooks, why are black women particularly attuned to Madonna's attempts to "mask her acts of racist aggression as affirmation"?
5. Why do black women feel less free to act rebelliously about sexuality?
6. Explain hooks's analysis of the video *Like a Prayer.* Do you agree?
7. What does hooks see in *Truth or Dare?*

❑ *Outward Exploration: Writing*

1. Write an essay that responds to hooks's analysis and charges.
2. Select some other popular icon and examine him or her in a way similar to the approach hooks uses.
3. Even well-meaning people can often have attitudes and perform actions which are, ultimately, harmful to those they are trying to help. Take an instance from your own experience (for example, an event that occurred to you or a text such as a video or movie or book) and explore it using a technique similar to hooks's.
4. Following hooks's lead, analyze the works of some other artist in music, painting, books, theater, or dance. Look for the social and political underpinnings of that work.

from *Incidents in the Life of a Slave Girl*

HARRIET JACOBS

❏ *Inward Exploration*

Write at least one paragraph explaining what you imagine being a slave would be like.

During the first years of my service in Dr. Flint's family, I was accustomed to share some indulgences with the children of my mistress. Though this seemed to me no more than right, I was grateful for it, and tried to merit the kindness by the faithful discharge of my duties. But I now entered on my fifteenth year—a sad epoch in the life of a slave girl. My master began to whisper foul words in my ear. Young as I was, I could not remain ignorant of their import. I tried to treat them with indifference or contempt. The master's age, my extreme youth, and the fear that his conduct would be reported to my grandmother, made him bear this treatment for many months. He was a crafty man, and resorted to many means to accomplish his purposes. Sometimes he had stormy, terrific° ways, that made his victims tremble; sometimes he assumed a gentleness that he thought must surely subdue. Of the two, I preferred his stormy moods, although they left me trembling. He tried his utmost to corrupt the pure principles my grandmother had instilled. He peopled my young mind with unclean images, such as only a vile monster could think of. I turned from him with disgust and hatred. But he was my master. I was compelled to live under the same roof with him—where I saw a man forty years my senior daily violating the most sacred commandments of nature. He told me I was his property; that I must be subject to his will in all things. My soul revolted against the mean tyranny. But where could I turn for protection? No matter whether the slave girl be as black as ebony or as fair as her mistress. In either case, there is no shadow of law to protect her from insult, from violence, or even from death; all these are inflicted by fiends who bear the shape of men. The mistress, who ought to protect the helpless victim, has no other feelings towards her but those of jealousy and rage. The degradation, the wrongs, the vices, that grow out of slavery, are more than I

——————
terrific: terrifying

can describe. They are greater than you would willingly believe. Surely, if you credited one half the truths that are told you concerning the helpless millions suffering in this cruel bondage, you at the north would not help to tighten the yoke. You surely would refuse to do for the master, on your own soil, the mean and cruel work which trained bloodhounds and the lowest class of whites do for him at the south.

Every where the years bring to all enough of sin and sorrow; but in slavery the very dawn of life is darkened by these shadows. Even the little child, who is accustomed to wait on her mistress and her children, will learn, before she is twelve years old, why it is that her mistress hates such and such a one among the slaves. Perhaps the child's own mother is among those hated ones. She listens to violent outbreaks of jealous passion, and cannot help understanding what is the cause. She will become prematurely knowing in evil things. Soon she will learn to tremble when she hears her master's footfall. She will be compelled to realize that she is no longer a child. If God has bestowed beauty upon her, it will prove her greatest curse. That which commands admiration in the white woman only hastens the degradation of the female slave. I know that some are too much brutalized by slavery to feel the humiliation of their position; but many slaves feel it most acutely, and shrink from the memory of it. I cannot tell how much I suffered in the presence of these wrongs, nor how I am still pained by the retrospect. My master met me at every turn, reminding me that I belonged to him, and swearing by heaven and earth that he would compel me to submit to him. If I went out for a breath of fresh air, after a day of unwearied toil, his footsteps dogged me. If I knelt by my mother's grave, his dark shadow fell on me even there. The light heart which nature had given me became heavy with sad forebodings. The other slaves in my master's house noticed the change. Many of them pitied me; but none dared to ask the cause. They had no need to inquire. They knew too well the guilty practices under that roof; and they were aware that to speak of them was an offence that never went unpunished.

I longed for some one to confide in. I would have given the world to have laid my head on my grandmother's faithful bosom, and told her all my troubles. But Dr. Flint swore he would kill me, if I was not as silent as the grave. Then, although my grandmother was all in all to me, I feared her as well as loved her. I had been accustomed to look up to her with a respect bordering upon awe. I was very young, and felt shamefaced about telling her such impure things, especially as I knew her to be very strict on such subjects. Moreover, she was a woman of a high spirit. She was usually very quiet in her demeanor; but if her indignation was once roused, it was not very easily quelled. I had been told that she once chased a white gentleman with a loaded pistol, because he insulted one of her daughters. I dreaded the consequences of a violent outbreak; and both pride and fear kept me silent. But though I did not confide in my grandmother, and even evaded her vigilant watchfulness and inquiry, her presence in the neighborhood was some protection to me. Though she had been a slave, Dr. Flint was afraid of her. He dreaded her scorching rebukes. Moreover, she was known and patronized by many people; and he did not wish to have his villainy made public. It was lucky for me that I did not live on a distant plantation, but in a town not so large that the inhabitants were ignorant of each other's affairs. Bad as are the laws and customs in a slaveholding community, the doctor, as a professional man, deemed it prudent to keep up some outward show of decency.

O, what days and nights of fear and sorrow that man caused me! Reader, it is not to awaken sympathy for myself that I am telling you truthfully what I suffered in slavery. I do it to kindle a flame of compassion in your hearts for my sisters who are still in bondage, suffering as I once suffered.

I once saw two beautiful children playing together. One was a fair 5 white child; the other was her slave, and also her sister. When I saw them embracing each other, and heard their joyous laughter, I turned sadly away from the lovely sight. I foresaw the inevitable blight that would fall on the little slave's heart. I knew how soon her laughter would be changed to sighs. The fair child grew up to be a still fairer woman. From childhood to womanhood her pathway was blooming with flowers, and overarched by a sunny sky. Scarcely one day of her life had been clouded when the sun rose on her happy bridal morning.

How had those years dealt with her slave sister, the little playmate of her childhood? She, also, was very beautiful; but the flowers and sunshine of love were not for her. She drank the cup of sin, and shame, and misery, whereof her persecuted race are compelled to drink.

In view of those things, why are ye silent, ye free men and women of the north? Why do your tongues falter in maintenance of the right? Would that I had more ability! But my heart is so full, and my pen is so weak! There are noble men and women who plead for us, striving to help those who cannot help themselves. God bless them! God give them strength and courage to go on! God bless those, every where, who are laboring to advance the cause of humanity!

▢ *Outward Exploration: Discussion*

1. Why doesn't Dr. Flint simply rape Jacobs?
2. What approaches does Dr. Flint use to convince her to do his will?
3. At the end of paragraph 1, what does Jacobs ask Northerners to avoid?
4. According to Jacobs, what is a slave girl's greatest curse?
5. Why didn't Jacobs simply tell her grandmother?

6. According to Jacobs, what is her reason for telling her readers about her experiences?

7. What is the effect of the direct address to readers in the last paragraph?

☐ *Outward Exploration: Writing*

1. Write an essay that compares and contrasts Jacobs's essay with the selection from Frederick Douglass's *Narrative of the Life of Frederick Douglass, Written by Himself.*

2. Use an event or a series of events from your own life to support a call to action on some issue that you care about.

3. Explore Jacobs's text in terms of what Toni Morrison says in "The Site of Memory."

4. Read all of *Incidents in the Life of a Slave Girl* or some other slave narrative and write an essay exploring the text.

The Site of Memory

Toni Morrison

❏ *Inward Exploration*

Write at least one paragraph about your process of writing. Be as specific as possible about how you recognize a topic as being worth exploring.

My inclusion in a series of talks on autobiography and memoir is   *1*
not entirely a misalliance. Although it's probably true that a fiction
writer thinks of his or her work as alien in that company, what I have to
say may suggest why I'm not completely out of place here. For one
thing, I might throw into relief the differences between self-recollection
(memoir) and fiction, and also some of the similarities—the places
where those two crafts embrace and where that embrace is symbiotic.

But the authenticity of my presence here lies in the fact that a very
large part of my own literary heritage is the autobiography. In this country the print origins of black literature (as distinguished from the oral
origins) were slave narratives. These book-length narratives (autobiographies, recollections, memoirs), of which well over a hundred were
published, are familiar texts to historians and students of black history.
They range from the adventure-packed life of Olaudah Equiano's *The
Interesting Narrative of the Life of Olaudah Equiano, or Gustavus Vassa, the
African, Written by Himself* (1769) to the quiet desperation of *Incidents in
the Life of a Slave Girl: Written by Herself* (1861), in which Harriet Jacobs
("Linda Brent") records hiding for seven years in a room too small to
stand up in; from the political savvy of Frederick Douglass's *Narrative of
the Life of Frederick Douglass, an American Slave, Written by Himself* (1845)
to the subtlety and modesty of Henry Bibb, whose voice, in *Life and
Adventures of Henry Bibb, an American Slave, Written by Himself* (1849), is
surrounded by ("loaded with" is a better phrase) documents attesting to
its authenticity. Bibb is careful to note that his formal schooling (three
weeks) was short, but that he was "educated in the school of adversity,
whips, and chains." Born in Kentucky, he put aside his plans to escape
in order to marry. But when he learned that he was the father of a slave
and watched the degradation of his wife and child, he reactivated those
plans.

Whatever the style and circumstances of these narratives, they were
written to say principally two things. One: "This is my historical life—
my singular, special example that is personal, but that also represents

the race." Two: "I write this text to persuade other people—you, the reader, who is probably not black—that we are human beings worthy of God's grace and the immediate abandonment of slavery." With these two missions in mind, the narratives were clearly pointed.

In Equiano's account, the purpose is quite up-front. Born in 1745 near the Niger River and captured at the age of ten, he survived the Middle Passage, American plantation slavery, wars in Canada and the Mediterranean; learned navigation and clerking from a Quaker named Robert King, and bought his freedom at twenty-one. He lived as a free servant, traveling widely and living most of his latter life in England. Here he is speaking to the British without equivocation: "I hope to have the satisfaction of seeing the renovation of liberty and justice resting on the British government. . . . I hope and expect the attention of gentlemen of power. . . . May the time come—at least the speculation is to me pleasing—when the sable people shall gratefully commemorate the auspicious era of extensive freedom." With typically eighteenth-century reticence he records his singular and representative life for one purpose: to change things. In fact, he and his co-authors *did* change things. Their works gave fuel to the fires that abolitionists were setting everywhere.

More difficult was getting the fair appraisal of literary critics. The 5 writings of church martyrs and confessors are and were read for the eloquence of their message as well as their experience of redemption, but the American slaves' autobiographical narratives were frequently scorned as "biased," "inflammatory" and "improbable." These attacks are particularly difficult to understand in view of the fact that it was extremely important, as you can imagine, for the writers of these narratives to appear as objective as possible—not to offend the reader by being too angry, or by showing too much outrage, or by calling the reader names. As recently as 1966, Paul Edwards, who edited and abridged Equiano's story, praises the narrative for its refusal to be "inflammatory."

"As a rule," Edwards writes, "he [Equiano] puts no emotional pressure on the reader other than that which the situation itself contains—his language does not strain after our sympathy, but expects it to be given naturally and at the proper time. This quiet avoidance of emotional display produces many of the best passages in the book." Similarly, an 1836 review of Charles Bell's *Life and Adventures of a Fugitive Slave,* which appeared in the "Quarterly Anti-Slavery Magazine," praised Bell's account for its objectivity. "We rejoice in the book the more, because it is not a partisan work. . . . It broaches no theory in regard to [slavery], nor proposes any mode or time of emancipation."

As determined as these black writers were to persuade the reader of the evil of slavery, they also complimented him by assuming his nobility of heart and his high-mindedness. They tried to summon up his finer nature in order to encourage him to employ it. They knew that their readers were the people who could make a difference in terminating slavery. Their stories—of brutality, adversity and deliverance—had great popularity in spite of critical hostility in many quarters and patronizing sympathy in others. There was a time when the hunger for "slave stories" was difficult to quiet, as sales figures show. Douglass's *Narrative* sold five thousand copies in four months; by 1847 it had sold eleven thousand copies. Equiano's book had thirty-six editions between 1789 and 1850. Moses Roper's book had ten editions from 1837 to 1856; William Wells Brown's was reprinted four times in its first year. Solomon Northrop's book sold twenty-seven thousand copies before two years had passed. A book by Josiah Henson (argued by some to be the model for the "Tom" of Harriet Beecher Stowe's *Uncle Tom's Cabin*) had a pre-publication sale of five thousand.

In addition to using their own lives to expose the horrors of slavery, they had a companion motive for their efforts. The prohibition against teaching a slave to read and write (which in many Southern states carried severe punishment) and against a slave's learning to read and write had to be scuttled at all costs. These writers knew that literacy was power. Voting, after all, was inextricably connected to the ability to read; literacy was a way of assuming and proving the "humanity" that the Constitution denied them. That is why the narratives carry the subtitle "written by himself," or "herself," and include introductions and prefaces by white sympathizers to authenticate them. Other narratives, "edited by" such well-known anti-slavery figures as Lydia Maria Child and John Greenleaf Whittier, contain prefaces to assure the reader how little editing was needed. A literate slave was supposed to be a contradiction in terms.

One has to remember that the climate in which they wrote reflected not only the Age of Enlightenment but its twin, born at the same time, the Age of Scientific Racism. David Hume, Immanuel Kant and Thomas Jefferson, to mention only a few, had documented their conclusions that blacks were incapable of intelligence. Frederick Douglass knew otherwise, and he wrote refutations of what Jefferson said in "Notes on the State of Virginia": "Never yet could I find that a black had uttered a thought above the level of plain narration, never see even an elementary trait of painting or sculpture." A sentence that I have always thought ought to be engraved at the door to the Rockefeller Collection of African Art. Hegel, in 1813, had said that Africans had no "history " and couldn't write in modern languages. Kant disregarded a perceptive observation by a black man by saying, "This fellow was quite black from head to foot, a clear proof that what he said was stupid."

Yet no slave society in the history of the world wrote more—or   *10* more thoughtfully—about its own enslavement. The milieu, however, dictated the purpose and the style. The narratives are instructive, moral and obviously representative. Some of them are patterned after the sentimental novel that was in vogue at the time. But whatever the level of eloquence or the form, popular taste discouraged the writers from dwelling too long or too carefully on the more sordid details of their experience. Whenever there was an unusually violent incident, or a scatological one, or something "excessive," one finds the writer taking refuge in the literary conventions of the day. "I was left in a state of distraction not to be described" (Equiano). "But let us now leave the rough usage of the field . . . and turn our attention to the less repulsive slave life as it existed in the house of my childhood" (Douglass). "I am not about to harrow the feelings of my readers by a terrific representation of the untold horrors of that fearful system of oppression. . . . It is not my purpose to descend deeply into the dark and noisome caverns of the hell of slavery" (Henry Box Brown).

Over and over, the writers pull the narrative up short with a phrase such as, "But let us drop a veil over these proceedings too terrible to relate." In shaping the experience to make it palatable to those who were in a position to alleviate it, they were silent about many things, and they "forgot" many other things. There was a careful selection of the instances that they would record and a careful rendering of those that they chose to describe. Lydia Maria Child identified the problem in her introduction to "Linda Brent's" tale of sexual abuse: "I am well aware that many will accuse me of indecorum for presenting these pages to the public; for the experiences of this intelligent and much-injured woman belong to a class which some call delicate subjects, and others indelicate. This peculiar phase of Slavery has generally been kept veiled; but the public ought to be made acquainted with its monstrous features, and I am willing to take the responsibility of presenting them with the veil drawn [aside]."

But most importantly—at least for me—there was no mention of their interior life.

For me—a writer in the last quarter of the twentieth century, not much more than a hundred years after Emancipation, a writer who is black and a woman—the exercise is very different. My job becomes how to rip that veil drawn over "proceedings too terrible to relate." The exercise is also critical for any person who is black, or who belongs to any marginalized category, for, historically, we were seldom invited to participate in the discourse even when we were its topic.

Moving that veil aside requires, therefore, certain things. First of all, I must trust my own recollections. I must also depend on the recollections of others. Thus memory weighs heavily in what I write, in how I begin and in what I find to be significant. Zora Neale Hurston said, "Like the dead-seeming cold rocks, I have memories within that came out of the material that went to make me." These "memories within" are the subsoil of my work. But memories and recollections won't give me total access to the unwritten interior life of these people. Only the act of the imagination can help me.

If writing is thinking and discovery and selection and order and   15
meaning, it is also awe and reverence and mystery and magic. I suppose
I could dispense with the last four if I were not so deadly serious about
fidelity in the milieu out of which I write and in which my ancestors
actually lived. Infidelity to that milieu—the absence of the interior life,
the deliberate excising of it from the records that the slaves themselves
told—is precisely the problem in the discourse that proceeded without
us. How I gain access to that interior life is what drives me and is the
part of this talk which both distinguishes my fiction from autobiographical strategies and which also embraces certain autobiographical
strategies. It's a kind of literary archeology: on the basis of some information and a little bit of guesswork you journey to a site to see what
remains were left behind and to reconstruct the world that these remains
imply. What makes it fiction is the nature of the imaginative act: my
reliance on the image—on the remains—in addition to recollection, to
yield up a kind of a truth. By "image," of course, I don't mean "symbol"; I simply mean "picture" and the feelings that accompany the
picture.

Fiction, by definition, is distinct from fact. Presumably it's the product of imagination—invention—and it claims the freedom to dispense
with "what really happened," or where it really happened, or when it
really happened, and nothing in it needs to be publicly verifiable, although much in it can be verified. By contrast, the scholarship of the
biographer and the literary critic seems to us only trustworthy when the
events of fiction can be traced to some publicly verifiable fact. It's the
research of the "Oh, yes, this is where he or she got it from" school,
which gets its own credibility from excavating the credibility of the
sources of the imagination, not the nature of the imagination.

The work that I do frequently falls, in the minds of most people,
into that realm of fiction called fantastic, or mythic, or magical, or unbelievable. I'm not comfortable with these labels. I consider that my
single gravest responsibility (in spite of that magic) is not to lie. When I
hear someone say, "Truth is stranger than fiction," I think that old chest-
nut is truer than we know, because it doesn't say that truth is truer than
fiction; just that it's stranger, meaning that it's odd. It may be excessive,
it may be more interesting, but the important thing is that it's random—and fiction is not random.

Therefore the crucial distinction for me is not the difference between
fact and fiction, but the distinction between fact and truth. Because facts
can exist without human intelligence, but truth cannot. So if I'm looking to find and expose a truth about the interior life of people who didn't
write it (which doesn't mean that they didn't have it); if I'm trying to fill
in the blanks that the slave narratives left—to part the veil that was
so frequently drawn, to implement the stories that I heard—then the
approach that's most productive and most trustworthy for me is the

recollection that moves from the image to the text. Not from the text to the image.

Simone de Beauvoir, in *A Very Easy Death,* says, "I don't know why I was so shocked by my mother's death." When she heard her mother's name being called at the funeral by the priest, she says, "Emotion seized me by the throat. . . . 'Françoise de Beauvoir': the words brought her to life; they summed up her history, from birth to marriage to widowhood to the grave. Françoise de Beauvoir—that retiring woman, so rarely named, became an *important person.*" The book becomes an exploration both into her own grief and into the images in which the grief lay buried.

Unlike Mme. de Beauvoir, Frederick Douglass asks the reader's patience for spending about half a page on the death of his grandmother— easily the most profound loss he had suffered—and he apologizes by saying, in effect, "It really was very important to me. I hope you aren't bored by my indulgence." He makes no attempt to explore that death: its images or its meaning. His narrative is as close to factual as he can make it, which leaves no room for subjective speculation. James Baldwin, on the other hand, in *Notes of a Native Son,* says, in recording his father's life and his own relationship to his father, "All of my father's Biblical texts and songs, which I had decided were meaningless, were ranged before me at his death like empty bottles, waiting to hold the meaning which life would give them for me." And then his text fills those bottles. Like Simone de Beauvoir, he moves from the event to the image that it left. My route is the reverse: the image comes first and tells me what the "memory" is about.

I can't tell you how I felt when my father died. But I was able to write *Song of Solomon* and imagine, not him, and not his specific interior life, but the world that he inhabited and the private or interior life of the people in it. And I can't tell you how I felt reading to my grandmother while she was turning over and over in her bed (because she was dying, and she was not comfortable), but I could try to reconstruct the world that she lived in. And I have suspected, more often than not, that I *know* more than she did, that I *know* more than my grandfather and my great-grandmother did, but I also know that I'm no wiser than they were. And whenever I have tried earnestly to diminish their vision and prove to myself that I know more, and when I have tried to speculate on their interior life and match it up with my own, I have been overwhelmed every time by the richness of theirs compared to my own. Like Frederick Douglass talking about his grandmother, and James Baldwin talking about his father, and Simone de Beauvoir talking about her mother, these people are my access to me; they are my entrance into my own interior life. Which is why the images that float around them—the remains, so to speak, at the archeological site—surface first, and they surface so vividly and so compellingly that I acknowledge

20

them as my route to a reconstruction of a world, to an exploration of an interior life that was not written and to the revelation of a kind of truth.

So the nature of my research begins with something as ineffable and as flexible as a dimly recalled figure, the corner of a room, a voice. I began to write my second book, which was called *Sula,* because of my preoccupation with a picture of a woman and the way in which I heard her name pronounced. Her name was Hannah, and I think she was a friend of my mother's. I don't remember seeing her very much, but what I do remember is the color around her—a kind of violet, a suffusion of something violet—and her eyes, which appeared to be half closed. But what I remember most is how the women said her name: how they said "Hannah Peace" and smiled to themselves, and there was some secret about her that they knew, which they didn't talk about, at least not in my hearing, but it seemed *loaded* in the way in which they said her name. And I suspected that she was a little bit of an outlaw but that they approved in some way.

And then, thinking about their relationship to her and the way in which they talked about her, the way in which they articulated her name, made me think about friendship between women. What is it that they forgive each other for? And what it is that is unforgivable in the world of women. I don't want to know any more about Miss Hannah Peace, and I'm not going to ask my mother who she really was and what did she do and what were you laughing about and why were you smiling? Because my experience when I do this with my mother is so crushing: she will give you *the* most pedestrian information you ever heard, and I would like to keep all of my remains and my images intact in their mystery when I begin. Later I will get to the facts. That way I can explore two worlds—the actual and the possible.

What I want to do this evening is to track an image from picture to meaning to text—a journey which appears in the novel that I'm writing now, which is called *Beloved.*

I'm trying to write a particular kind of scene, and I see corn on   *25* the cob. To "see" corn on the cob doesn't mean that it suddenly hovers; it only means that it keeps coming back. And in trying to figure out "What is all this corn doing?" I discover what it *is* doing.

I see the house where I grew up in Lorain, Ohio. My parents had a garden some distance away from our house, and they didn't welcome me and my sister there, when we were young, because we were not able to distinguish between the things that they wanted to grow and the things that they didn't, so we were not able to hoe, or weed, until much later.

I see them walking, together, away from me. I'm looking at their backs and what they're carrying in their arms: their tools, and maybe a peck basket. Sometimes when they walk away from me they hold hands, and they go to this other place in the garden. They have to cross some railroad tracks to get there.

I also am aware that my mother and father sleep at odd hours because my father works many jobs and works at night. And these naps are times of pleasure for me and my sister because nobody's giving us chores, or telling us what to do, or nagging us in any way. In addition to which, there is some feeling of pleasure in them that I'm only vaguely aware of. They're very rested when they take these naps.

And later on in the summer we have an opportunity to eat corn, which is the one plant that I can distinguish from the others, and which is the harvest that I like the best; the others are the food that no child likes—the collards, the okra, the strong, violent vegetables that I would give a great deal for now. But I do like the corn because it's sweet, and because we all sit down to eat it, and it's finger food, and it's hot, and it's even good cold, and there are neighbors in, and there are uncles in, and it's easy, and it's nice.

The picture of the corn and the nimbus of emotion surrounding it   30
became a powerful one in the manuscript I'm now completing.

Authors arrive at text and subtext in thousands of ways, learning each time they begin anew how to recognize a valuable idea and how to render the texture that accompanies, reveals or displays it to its best advantage. The process by which this is accomplished is endlessly fascinating to me. I have always thought that as an editor for twenty years I understood writers better than their most careful critics, because in examining the manuscript in each of its subsequent stages I knew the author's process, how his or her mind worked, what was effortless, what took time, where the "solution" to a problem came from. The end result—the book—was all that the critic had to go on.

Still, for me, that was the least important aspect of the work. Because, no matter how "fictional" the account of these writers, or how much it was a product of invention, the act of imagination is bound up with memory. You know, they straightened out the Mississippi River in places, to make room for houses and livable acreage. Occasionally the river floods these places. "Floods" is the word they use, but in fact it is not flooding; it is remembering. Remembering where it used to be. All water has a perfect memory and is forever trying to get back to where it was. Writers are like that: remembering where we were, what valley we ran through, what the banks were like, the light that was there and the route back to our original place. It is emotional memory—what the nerves and the skin remember as well as how it appeared. And a rush of imagination is our "flooding."

Along with personal recollection, the matrix of the work I do is the wish to extend, fill in and complement slave autobiographical narratives. But only the matrix. What comes of all that is dictated by other concerns, not least among them the novel's own integrity. Still, like water, I remember where I was before I was "straightened out."

❑ *Outward Exploration: Discussion*

1. According to Morrison, what two things were the slave narratives written to say?

2. Why did the writers of the slave narratives refrain from showing their anger and from verbally attacking their white readers?

3. In addition to exposing the horrors of slavery, what else did the slave narratives do?

4. What is the contrast between the way the writers of slave narratives and Morrison see their task as writers?

5. What is Morrison's definition of writing?

6. What does Morrison mean when she says that some writers move "from the event to the image that it left" (paragraph 20)? What implication does this idea have for you as a writer?

7. Rather than the difference between fact and fiction, what does Morrison consider to be the crucial distinction?

8. Explain Morrison's water image at the end of the essay.

❑ *Outward Exploration: Writing*

1. Return to some "site of memory" that seems significant to you and do some literary archaeology of your own. Write an essay about what you find there in your past or about the process of recovering a memory, or write an essay that combines both.

2. If you have particular knowledge about a group of texts as Morrison does about slave narratives, use that expertise and write an essay that reveals something about those texts and about you.

3. Morrison gives us a positive vision of memory. Write an essay that explains your own sense of memory.

Love Me or Leave Me

BHARATI MUKHERJEE

❑ *Inward Exploration*

Make a list of texts (for example, movies, songs, television series, books) which have influenced the way you view the world and understand yourself. Select one text from the list and write at least one paragraph explaining what that impact was.

I first saw America when I was twenty. Outdoors, even in New 1 York City, the air must have been lambent with summertime the day that my seventeen-year-old sister and I flew into Idlewild, but inside the terminal, waiting in a long, nervous line of foreign students and tourists to be questioned by suspicious Immigration and Naturalization Service officials, the light felt interrogation-harsh.

"Let's go back home," my sister said. She was a veteran shuttler between India and the United States, having already put in a fall semester as a sophomore at Vassar College, and having rushed back, homesick, at Christmas.

We didn't turn around and get on an Air India plane that summer afternoon because we didn't want to disappoint our father. Coming to school in the States had been his idea, not ours. We stayed in line and had our visas and chest X-rays checked by an official who was amused that I was headed for the University of Iowa.

"Know how to find Iowa on the map?" the man asked me. And when I lied, yes, he laughed, "Hell, I don't," and wished me good luck.

My sister got homesick again that winter, desperately enough to be 5 sent back to India.

"It must be hard for you, too," my father wrote in each of his thrice-weekly letters. "But be brave. And before you know it, the program will be over." Meanwhile, he was interviewing Bengali Brahmin bachelors in order to find me the perfect groom.

The truth, which I couldn't share with my family, was that I was happier in Iowa City than in Calcutta. It was that time in my life when every song and film about love seemed to speak directly to me. I fell in love with, and married, a man who happened to be an American citizen, and scrapped all plans for ever going back to live in India.

If I had gone to graduate school in Paris or London, I might just as easily have fallen in love with a Frenchman or a Briton and made my life over very differently than I have in America. But in my family, my father, a very successful businessman, a devout Brahmin, and a benevolent patriarch who made all decisions, was also a contradictory man. He had no son; thus his financial empire could not be passed on. He wanted education and independence for his three daughters. (When would-be husbands later demanded dowries, he answered, "My daughters are all educated women. That is worth more than all the gold I could give them.") He was a progressive man in a traditional context; he saw in Doris Day an empowered woman.

He sent us to America, a country he himself had not seen, instead of to Europe, where he had been a happy graduate student, because he was in love with the world of Doris Day and all MGM musicals. He never spoke of "the United States." It was always "America." To him America was a realistic-looking facade on an MGM backlot, where fantasies about young women achieving fulfillment and power could be acted out as they couldn't in tradition-bound Calcutta.

My father never missed Doris Day at the Metro Cinema on Chowringhee Avenue. He would call my sisters and me from his office on Thursdays—which was our day off from school, a neo-colonial establishment run by Irish nuns for Calcutta's most proper girls—to say that he had rearranged his schedule so that he could accompany us to the matinee show.   *10*

Though he savored every Doris Day film, even *Please Don't Eat the Daisies* and *Pillow Talk,* his favorite was *The Man Who Knew Too Much.* On jerky drives through the crowded city, in between yelling at the chauffeur to be more cautious and at the two bodyguards cramped in the back of our conspicuously large Dodge station wagon to be more alert for bomb-tossing, acid-splashing, communism-inspired thugs, he would sing "Que Será, Será." "What Will Be, Will Be" became for him more a mantra than a song; it synthesized a New World pleasure in risk taking with a fatalistic Hindu acceptance of disastrous outcomes.

The marvel that was my father's love for Doris Day will become clearer if I tell you that the neighborhoods we had to drive through to get from our home or from my father's pharmaceutical factory on the outskirts of the city to the Metro Cinema in midtown roiled with the fecund despair of the destitute and the permanently displaced. The Calcutta of the fifties—the Calcutta of my childhood—should have been heady with post-Independence hope and vitality. Certainly politicians promised every Indian boom times. But what choked the streets was the human debris from famines and religious riots. Even an oversheltered, overprivileged child like me was toughened enough by Old World cynicism (which, in those days, I accepted as a synonym for wisdom) to cut through jingoistic nation-building slogans. Though at school the nuns assured us that prayer would quickly bring Mr. Stalin and his Calcutta admirers to their senses, we could see and smell the "blood-dimmed tide" surging at our horizon. In that transitional decade, when preparations to flee the city seemed cowardly and prayer little more than escapism, Doris Day was an abstraction for democracy. A person with gumption—any person, even a ten-cents-a-dance taxi dancer like Ruth Etting—could turn her grim life around. The handicaps of caste, class, and gender could be overcome.

Doris Day was a physical curiosity. I don't think I'd ever come across a woman so tall, so big. And in those days, the only blond hair I expected to see was the Technicolor-bright cap of it on her Cinemascope-sized head. Most enforcers of the Raj—people who might have had natural or bleached yellow hair, British corporate executives and civil servants, for instance, the lighter-skinned Eurasians, even many of the Iraqi and Syrian Jews whom we'd thought of as "Europeans"—had left just before or just after 1947, when India became a sovereign nation. The bedtime stories my mother told me had been about teen-age Bengali freedom fighters rather than the traditional ones about gods fighting shape-changing demons.

I had thrilled to my mother's stories about schoolgirls raiding police arsenals or hiding pistols in dormitories. Fan worship of a British film star would have seemed to me treasonous regression. Doris Day, with her mighty shoulders and toothy smile, a woman who said exactly what was on her mind and said it in a nearly incomprehensible American accent with stereophonic loudness, was all right to love precisely because she was American. (In my neo-colonial school I had been forced to study British and European history, not the history of the United States and its various involvements, and so was slow to catch the ironies of undeclared imperialism.)

Brought up as I was to accept rather than to protest decisions made   15
for me, Doris Day grew into an icon of spunk.

My father may have been in Europe on a business trip when *Love Me or Leave Me* finally came to Calcutta. Or perhaps he had seen the trailer for it the week before and decided that the Doris Day who sang "Que Será, Será"—*his* Doris Day—had to be kept separate from the gritty Doris Day who cocked a hip in a black sheath dress and burned the screen with "Ten Cents a Dance." Perhaps he saw the film on his own and decided that he had to protect us from the sex and sleaze it revealed about adult life just ahead. In any case, this was the only Doris Day film I didn't see or talk over with him.

Ten of us convent-school friends went to see it the evening our Overseas Cambridge School Leaving Certificate Examinations were over. I was fifteen. In three weeks I would start college as a sophomore. That I should be sneaking into my first "adults only" film that evening seemed deliciously symbolic.

I try not to think now how we must have appeared to the street people and beggars outside the Metro Cinema or how we might have appeared to Charles Vidor, the director, if he had seen us being chaperoned by servants from cars to the movie theater. We were ten adventurous but shockable young ladies dressed in our mothers' evening saris, with hair pinned up in elaborate chignons and smelling of sandalwood soap and jasmine. I remember I wore a peach-colored French chiffon sparkling with sequins.

I also remember that I walked into the theater (which always smelled of musty velvet drapes) expecting to be titillated, and that I walked out convinced I'd been uplifted.

What *could* I have discovered in a story about an obscure chorine in   20
Chicago who meets a crooked nightclub owner and allows him to help her become a singing star even though it means denying or delaying true love? That the world was a rough place in which to be a poor woman with talent but without protection.

Early in the film, when Ruth Etting had to wear skimpy, spangled chorus-line costumes and put up with the teasing of less ambitious chorus girls ("Oh, I forgot. You're different. You're going places"), I identified with her totally. I, too, intended to go places, be somebody.

"You don't have to do a thing!" I mimicked her telling off Marty Snyder, played by James Cagney, my second-most-favorite screen villain. (James Mason was the first.) "I'll get it for myself!"

"It" was my own desire to be a writer and touch people with my novels.

I'd started my first novel at age nine and had published several first-person stories about Roman gladiators and Napoleon in local English-language magazines. But I was careful to hide from the nuns and from relatives and friends the forcefulness of my need for self-expression. They tolerated my "gift for the pen" (the mother superior's phrase) only because they regarded fiction writing as a womanly accomplishment, on a par with flower arranging or playing a musical instrument.

The Doris Day of *Love Me or Leave Me* sent me subliminal mes-   25
sages. When she pleaded with James Cagney to let her sing in bigger clubs in cities out of his reach, she pleaded for me. And when she begged, "I have to work. Don't you understand? I've got to. It's all I've got," I substituted "write" for "work." In Marty's admonition, "You're going to work here so you don't get so big," I heard my own community's censure of women who didn't accept their place.

Though my world was silken with privilege, I would have to choose, like Ruth Etting, between paralysis and ambition, between protection and pain.

My parents and the parents of my friends were nominally patrons of the arts in that they bought or were given tickets to events such as the premiere of Jean Renoir's *The River* (set in Bengal) or charity performances by the Moral Rearmament Society, but they knew no writers or filmmakers. They didn't attend screenings at the foreign-film club founded by Satyajit Ray. Like them, I hadn't heard of *film noir* at the time, and I certainly hadn't known of screenwriter Daniel Fuchs, let alone read his proletariat novels about Brooklyn Jews. I must have missed the neo-*noir* significance of the first shot of Marty "The Gimp" Snyder standing in shadow outside a garishly lit dance hall, lusting after a spirited blond goddess. I had to have missed the odd resonance of Marty's mumbled "Mazel tov!" as Ruth, "Chicago's Sweetheart," went off to give her first star performance. How could I have caught the ethnic ambiguity of Snyder as a last name? Or that Fuchs's Chicago was not that different from Brooklyn? What I did instead was to Bengalize Fuchs's Chicago-Brooklyn, just as I had, before the age of ten, Bengalized the alien societies of my favorite Tolstoy, Dostoyevsky, and Gorky novels.

I accepted, more readily perhaps than I should have, that Charles Vidor's film was about Ruth Etting. Ruth was its hero, Marty its villain. But even the huge and wholesome Doris Day couldn't quite sanitize her character's moral ambiguities. For a decade the nuns had forced on us an annual course titled "Moral Science" in which they presented right and wrong with absolute clarity. But there on the Metro Cinema screen (from which I learned more about the world outside than from the school-approved Victorian and Edwardian novels) was virtuous Doris Day assuring me through song that "I can be good, I can be bad / It all depends on you . . . ," that it was not at all unethical for the Woman as Artist to lie and cheat and use men on the way to stardom.

With one song she reduced the stern, solid truths of Moral Science to fictions. She guaranteed us women who fancied ourselves talented extraordinary absolution.

"I've tried it without help," she explains to Johnny, her piano-   *30* playing faithful admirer, as she breaks a date. "I didn't mind it being hard. I just minded that it didn't work." And off she goes for a night of salacious fun with corrupt and ill-mannered Marty, who can pack her shows with his applauding friends.

The nuns had taught us that what mattered was how we played the game and not whether we won or lost. And my Hindu parents had taught us that after the householder phase of material comforts and family devotions we must prepare for phases of self-abnegation. But Doris Day, the oracle of the silver screen, busted those old truths in one evening. The end justified the means.

Doris Day's Ruth Etting was a woman whose virtue was not assailed by her manipulativeness with men. (I think now that if Rita Hayworth had played the role I might have been totally unsettled by Etting's self-justifications; I didn't see a Rita Hayworth film until years later.) The trouble was that I couldn't stop worrying about the walk-on chorines, the fatigued women in soiled leotards and snagged stockings. They may have had more talent than Ruth, but they were less calculating. The first time Marty Snyder visited her in her dressing room, Ruth had pegged him as a powerful man and seized rather promptly his offer of protection. She'd rejected a lifetime of cheap pick-ups. She was, as Marty might say, a smart cookie.

I did believe her when she declared, "I'm not a tramp!" Marty was accustomed to picking up whores, not artists who were having to pay the bills with taxi dancing, women he could get his faithful buddy, Georgie, to throw back into mean streets with a tip or a pat on the rump. Her sense of self-worth had been established within the first few minutes of screen time; even as a starving rookie taxi dancer, she'd kicked the letch who for his ten cents had groped when he should only have danced.

The woman artist combined smart-cookie-ness with integrity and innocence. I watched, amazed, as Ruth's self-righteous morality triumphed over Marty's street codes on the larger-than-life screen.

Marty himself was an ambiguous villain. In fact, he was more a raw   35
force than a villain. In his crooked, dog-eat-dog world, his crook's-eye view made sense.

"I couldn't handle those people with kid gloves." That was Marty's convincing self-defense. "It's push or get pushed."

How could I fault him for initially assuming that Ruth shared his moral environment? When Ruth refused to weekend with him in Florida as payment for his having gotten her a big singing gig in his Chicago nightclub, he sized her up as a smart cookie holding out for more. "Ah, I get it," he rationalized. "She thinks it's a line . . . I say Miami, and she thinks it'll be Atlantic City."

I just couldn't summon up hate for him.

So he was a crook; so what? My schoolfriends and I—Calcutta's small, elite band of missionary-educated postcolonial adolescents, brought up on too much Oscar Wilde and Somerset Maugham—confused mordant wit and cynicism with sophistication. I persuaded myself that Marty was, in fact, an incompetent in the world of serious crime.

Marty won me over with his enthusiasm. How could I dislike a man   40
who used "You've got a very excellent personality" as his line to a dancer in a dingy dressing room?

Like my father, an optimist, Marty could say lines like "You want to know what your trouble is, girlie? You got no faith in human nature," and mean it.

Marty trying to control his wife didn't shock me. In traditional, patriarchal Hindu families like mine, men commanded and women obeyed; to love was to protect. I understood that Marty slapping Ruth was Hollywood—not Hindu—shorthand for deplorable behavior and that Hollywood would deliver Marty his comeuppance.

To me, Marty was a bewildered, lovesick fool; a man of strength brought low by bravado or hubris. (At fifteen I could declaim soliloquies from Shakespeare, Racine, and Sophocles, and regularly used words like "hubris" and "catharsis.") Marty was a man who bullied and bossed because he lacked self-confidence. Without Ruth's total dependence on him, he became nothing. He was the guy from the wrong side of the tracks, the thug, the loner, who had built himself a fortune but not an identity and confidence. In his life the question "Who *are* you?" and the answer "They think I'm nothing" recurred with sinister regularity.

How could I know then—coming from an overdetermined, confident hierarchical culture in which everyone knew the most minute detail of everyone else's life, in which a family name revealed caste and region—that the ambiguously named, mysteriously unrooted Marty Snyder was, in his splendor, his power, his pathetic hollowness, an American archetype? And that the reading of such ambiguity, from the stagnant steadiness of the Calcutta upper classes, could be alluring?

Marty's crime was love, the kind of monstrously possessive,   45
Othello-like love that turned the beloved into chattel. It was not that different and no more overwhelming than the love I both cherished and hoped to escape. In Marty's "Didn't I do wonders for her?" guilt made me imagine I was hearing a patriarch's lament.

By the time Doris Day finally sang "Love Me or Leave Me," I knew what the future held. Things would work out for me as a writer as long as I rejected both the Johnnys and the Martys. The Martys, the tiny tough guys with limps, were all trouble; they charged you up with unseemly passion and got you to break rules, take calamitous risks. The patient, long-suffering Johnnys appealed to your modesty and goodness; they shamed you into working hard, following rules, and waiting for a payoff that was more likely to be self-righteous liberty than stardom.

There was a cost. There was always a cost. Ruth didn't know or couldn't admit that cost to herself. She hadn't *asked* Marty for "breaks." Marty had sensed her wants. He'd given; she'd grabbed.

That cynical lesson cut deep. As I left the Metro Cinema that winter night and drove through a city awaiting Marxist revolution, I hoped that when I started my life over on an MGM backlot made up to look like America, I'd retain enough of the worldliness of my Calcutta youth to be more honest with myself than Ruth had been.

📖 Outward Exploration: Discussion

1. Why does Mukherjee begin her essay with her arrival in the United States instead of beginning chronologically with her childhood?
2. How does she make a transition to her childhood from that opening?
3. How did his life in Calcutta in the 1950s influence the way her father viewed Doris Day movies?
4. Describe Mukherjee's education.
5. What was the effect of the school's not offering American history? What does the term "undeclared imperialism" mean?

6. Beginning with paragraph 16, Mukherjee analyzes *Love Me or Leave Me* in great detail. Discuss the elements of her analysis and how they became personally significant for her.

7. Comment on Mukherjee's movie-derived insight in paragraph 46—the two types of men, their control over women, and her resolve to avoid both types.

8. What did Mukherjee learn from *Love Me or Leave Me?* How does that influence the way you understand the essay's last paragraph? Explain.

❏ *Outward Exploration: Writing*

Select a text which has influenced the way you view the world and understand yourself. Analyze that text with the same kind of depth and insight as Mukherjee does, explaining what its impact has been on you.

At Home in the Parliament
of Whores

P. J. O'ROURKE

❏ *Inward Exploration*

Make a list of all the adjectives that come to mind when you see the term "New England town meeting." Then make a list of adjectives that you think describe the "federal government."

Hundreds of miles from the ambitions and deceits of Washington   1
there is a little town in New Hampshire where I live. This town is
tucked under the arm of an impressive mountain and is surrounded by
resplendent gauds of foliage in the autumn and wreathed in downy cov-
erlets of snow all winter long. Delicate spires of colonial church steeples
nick the cloud-chased New England sky, and a pellucid trout stream
rolls and chuckles in the shadow of the old woolen mill, now a historical landmark. A mere fifty-one hundred souls make their home here.
There's not a stop light or a parking meter to be seen. The whole town
could be a Norman Rockwell painting come to life if Norman Rockwell
had been better at depicting towns that have convenience stores on half
the street corners and are filled with pseudo–Cape Cod tract houses,
each with a snowmobile for sale in its front yard.

Still, my little town—let's call it Blatherboro—is as decent a place
as you will find in America. In 1989 the Blatherboro Police Department
received twenty-nine reports of lost property. In the meantime, town
residents turned fifty-nine items of lost property in to the police. The
citizens of Blatherboro are decent to the point of defying arithmetic.

The citizens of Blatherboro are also employed. Virtually no one in
the town is out of work or stays that way long. The town welfare officer, a very practical lady, has been known to come by people's houses
early in the morning and *take* them job hunting. Only sixty-three Blatherboro households required any charity in 1989, and that charity was, as
the word indicates, charity. The $21,000 that the town spent on public
assistance was all supplied by private donations.

Blatherboro's residents are educated and sensible—literate enough
to support three local weekly newspapers and sensitive enough to their
neighbors' feelings to make sure that no very juicy news appears in any
of the three. They are a calm, law-abiding lot. Shootings, stabbings,
rapes and so forth are unheard of in Blatherboro (though there is a cer-

tain amount of discreet wife beating and child abuse, especially during the midwinter doldrums). The last murder of any note took place in 1919 and is still discussed with indignation.

Blatherboro is a nice town, but not so nice as to be eerie. The people   5
of Blatherboro are good people but not dreadfully good. Blatherboro is an uncommonly comfortable place for comfortably common people, like me, to live. It is the economy section of Beulah.

The government of Blatherboro is as homey and reasonable as Blatherboro itself. There is a traditional New England town meeting held once a year. Here the business of democracy is disposed of in one sitting. And here I go to do my civic duty and help dispose of it.

There is nothing at all of a Rockwell painting to a real New England town meeting, and nothing of a Robert Frost poem either. "Whose woods these are I think I know. . . ." Hah. Whose woods are whose everybody knows exactly, and everybody knows who got them rezoned for a shopping mall and who couldn't get the financing to begin construction and why it was he couldn't get it. And you'd hardly use our town meeting as a calendar photograph. It's held in the high-school gym, a windowless space barely large enough for full-court basketball, redolent of damp socks and painted two-tone yellow in the two worst tones of yellow ever seen except in terminal jaundice.

This political arena is filled with folding metal chairs of an ingeniously uncomfortable design. The front rows of the folding chairs are occupied by elderly know-it-alls in lime-green blazers—business executives who retired (much to the relief of their respective businesses, no doubt) and moved to Blatherboro to reside in their summer homes year-round. These former items of corporate deadwood spend most of their day basking in the warm glow of New Hampshire tax policy. (New Hampshire tax policy is to not have any taxes—there is no state or local income tax and no sales tax either.) And the rest of the time they devote to thinking up great ideas and swell notions for improving everything in Blatherboro, especially the efficiency of its government.

Sitting in the back rows of the folding chairs and standing around the gymnasium walls are the Blatherboro natives, ranging in type from deer-poaching swamp Yankees to frayed Emersonian Brahmins and including a large number of working-stiff French Canadians. The natives live in fear that the improvements in efficiency proposed by the blowhard retirees will send the one tax New Hampshire does have, the town property tax, soaring. This property tax keeps soaring anyway, despite the fact that every single person at the town meeting has a plan to reduce taxes.

The Blatherboro selectmen (who are the equivalent of city council-   10
men, except this isn't a city and there's no council) and the Blatherboro town manager sit at a folding table facing the earnest crowd, and the town moderator stands behind a podium and calls on people. Members

of the local Boy Scout troop carry microphones to the orators in the audience, and a combination of bad PA system and typical gym acoustics produces a voice of the people that is more *pox* than *vox populi*.

Despite the minimal nature of Blatherboro town government and, indeed, the minimal nature of Blatherboro, and despite the goodwill, good sense and good New England parsimony of Blatherboro's residents, the result of the annual town meeting is always a stupid and expensive mess.

Much of the stupidity is common to all government. There are certain subjects about which people are incurable boneheads. Humans apparently cannot rationally consider what constitutes a danger to humanity or how likely any given danger is to occur. Thus, Blatherboro has fifteen police officers—the same ratio of police to population as New York City. The annual Blatherboro police budget is $425,000. This in a town that, in 1989, had 520 crimes, of which 155 were minor incidents of teenage vandalism. The cost of police protection against the remaining 365 more or less serious malefactions was $1,164 each—more than the damage caused by any of them.

On the other hand, almost everything in Blatherboro is built out of wood. Half the town is too rural to have fire hydrants, and a lot of the town is too cheap to have smoke detectors. Every home has a fireplace, most have wood stoves and quite a few have wood-burning furnaces, so that in March 1989, for example, there were three chimney fires in four days. But the Blatherboro Fire Department is a completely volunteer organization with an annual budget of less than $50,000.

People are also very stupid about what makes people smart. The local school system, which serves Blatherboro and the nearby town of Quaintford, isn't very bad. But it isn't any good either. The Blatherboro–Quaintford School District Annual Report expounds at length on "competency-based programs," "whole-language instruction" and "curriculum coordination" and devotes a dozen pages to discussing "budget objectives" and listing the various administrators, speech pathologists, special-education consultants and so forth that are thought necessary to modern education. But nowhere does the annual report remark on the fact that the high school's ninth grade has 124 students, while the high school's tenth grade—whose denizens are of legal age to leave school—has 79. This is a 36-percent drop-out rate, about the same as the drop-out rate in most inner-city slums.

The Blatherboro–Quaintford schools have only a total of 1,488   15
students, kindergarten through twelfth grade, yet there is a complete school-district office with a staff of fifteen people, including a superintendent of schools, an assistant superintendent and a business administrator. And there are an additional twenty-eight principals, assistant principals, counselors, aides and other people who don't actually teach anything on the school-system payroll.

Blatherboro's annual per-student spending is over $5,000—almost three times the national average for state college tuitions. If Blatherboro's parents and taxpayers were as serious about education as they—and every other parent and taxpayer in America—always say they are, they could gather the youngsters into miniature academies of perhaps fifteen students each and hire $75,000-per-year private tutors to teach them. In the academic-infested groves of New England, $75,000 would hire a fine tutor. Alternatively, Blatherboro students could be packed off to the local Catholic schools, where they'd get a better education—and a good, sharp rap on the knuckles if they showed any need for counseling—for less than half the price.

City planning is also beyond Blatherboro's ken. The town has a Planning Board, a Board of Adjustment, a building inspector, a Conservation Commission and a Historic District Commission, and the place still looks like hell. Of course, there are patches of twee and precious prerevolutionary beauty, as there are in all old New England towns. Sections of Blatherboro are so overrun with white clapboard and green shutters that if a man were to unzip his fly in these parts of town, the Historic District Commission would probably make him put green shutters on either side of that, too. But the rest of the place looks like every other piece of overpaved, cheap-jack, fake-front highway sprawl in the nation. I don't happen to mind this sprawl myself, at least not in theory, because in theory I'm a private-property strict constructionist. But I do mind all the boards and commissions and employees of the town wasting my money failing to prevent it.

Besides the ordinary and general kinds of idiocy, the Blatherboro Town Meeting also deals in some witlessness specific (but no doubt not unique) to Blatherboro.

The retired blowhards had gotten together with the Blatherboro elected officials, the members of the Chamber of Commerce and all the other people in town whose method of torturing their neighbors is good citizenship and decided that the town offices were too small. Too small for what was not explained, though the selectmen gave an elaborate presentation, complete with slide show, detailing just how much too small. The proposed solution was to sell the snug and handsome little town hall that sits on the Blatherboro common and sell the Mayberry RFD storefront police department down the street and buy an empty factory building out on the east side of town and put everybody in there. This would cost $1.3 million but would, it was said, save the town money in the long term.

The Town Flake stood up to speak. He is an old and addled gentleman with hair in long, white tangles—WASP dreadlocks. He's been making a complete and utter pest of himself at town meetings for over thirty years. He owns his own mimeograph machine and runs off reams of smudgy philippics accusing town government of incompetence and

20

waste. He knows all the regulations in *Robert's Rules of Order* and uses them until he has to be shushed by the moderator or shouted down by the townspeople. And he is always and invariably right on every issue. "Save money in the long term! Save money in the long term!" said the Town Flake with high scorn. "Government's always full of ideas to *save money in the long term.* Just why is it that government never has a single, solitary idea about saving money *now?*" The Town Flake was shushed by the moderator.

A very old lady wanted to know, if we were going to sell the town office, were we also going to sell the World War I monument on the common? It was patiently explained to her that monuments (or commons either) don't get sold. Whereupon another even older lady asked, if the town office got sold, did the World War I monument go with it? The question would come up twice again in the debate.

Someone else wanted to know why a factory couldn't go in the factory building—and provide jobs and pay taxes. To which the selectmen replied that the economy's a bit slow in New England these days, and no business is likely to buy the factory.

"Well, if no business is likely to buy the factory, who the heck is going to buy the town hall and the police station?" hollered the Town Flake.

The arguments continued for two hours. And these arguments were, in their effect, much more persuasive against democracy than for buying the factory or keeping the town hall. It is remarkable, on close inspection, what a lousy way to get things done democracy is. Not that democracy necessarily makes the wrong decisions. Private enterprise can do this with equal or greater ease. But in a democracy the decision-making process must be listened to. The great thing about the invisible hand of the market is not that it's invisible but that it's silent.

Buying a factory to put the town government in was at last voted   25
down, 241 to 207.

Debate now moved to whether the town should spend $1.7 million to build a new water tank.

The Town Flake pointed out that one reason the tank would be so expensive is that the town intended to build it in a valley with pumps instead of on a hill with gravity. He was shushed by the moderator.

New Hampshire is—with the exception of tropical rain forests (which I hear won't be around much longer anyway)—the wettest place on earth. When the snow melts in spring, there's not a basement in the state that you can't launch a boat in. A summer day without rain is considered something to tell your grandchildren about. You cannot walk half a mile in a straight line anywhere in New Hampshire without drowning in a stream, lake, beaver pond or somebody's flooded cellar. Yet the town of Blatherboro was running out of water. This was a stupidity beyond the range of local talents. Anything as astonishingly dumb as this must have the federal government involved in it somehow. And, indeed, it did. Congress had passed the Safe Drinking Water Act of 1982, which assumed that people in small towns were too far removed from Senate subcommittee hearings and presidential fact-finding commissions to know whether their drinking water was safe. Federal law now mandates that all water taken from surface sources in small towns everywhere must be filtered and chlorinated whether it needs to be or not.

So Blatherboro is obliged to build an entire new water system. The $1.7-million water tank is the first step in a three-phase construction program that will eventually cost the town $6.2 million. Never mind that that's enough money to drill a nice, new, clean, private artesian well for every household in town.

The only thing more depressing than democracy at work is democracy not allowed to. The debate on the water tank had just begun when the town's attorney pointed out that if Blatherboro didn't comply with federal water regulations, the town would be fined $25,000 per day. The water tank was approved by a grudging 251 to 108.

Next was an article "To authorize the Board of Selectmen . . . to apply for, accept and expend any and all Federal or State grants, gifts or funds that may become available during the ensuing year." This was passed overwhelmingly, as well it might have been, with loud shouts of "Aye!"

There followed an hour-long argument about whether to close a small section of the old town road. The blowhard retirees claimed that the road should be closed because the town natives liked to run their four-wheel-drive vehicles through there at all hours of the night, and the town natives argued that the road should be kept open because they liked to run their four-wheel-drive vehicles through there at all hours of the night. The natives won on a voice vote by being able to yell "nay" louder with no teeth than the retirees could yell "aye" with false ones. After that the $4-million town-government operating budget was passed with no debate whatsoever, the reasoning being that the thing had already been debated at public Budget Committee hearings, although no one had attended them. There was one "nay" from the Town Flake.

With these mundane matters out of the way, it was time for the real gist of the town meeting, the big fight everybody was waiting for, the keen excitement and high drama of quarreling about sewers.

It really is impossible to overstate the tedium of government. As boring as civics classes were back in high school, they were a bacchanal compared with civics itself. The next six hours of the Blatherboro Town Meeting were devoted to bickering about whether the Department of Public Works should have exclusive authority to approve sewer-line hookups. Of course, I have used the words *quarrel, fight* and even *bicker* in a strictly poetic sense. I doubt that in the course of the evening's long and brutal fray so much as a voice was raised. A town meeting is tedious with that amazing and inexplicable tedium of a large number of people behaving themselves in public. It is the opposite of a mob or a riot, the flip side of human collective behavior. Taking part in a New England town meeting is like being a cell in a plant.

Nevertheless, there were very strong feelings about effluvian mat-   35
ters in Blatherboro. An article was proposed that, if passed, would re-
quire that a special town meeting be convened to approve any expansion of the town sewer system costing more than $50,000. The idea was not to save money on sewers. User fees and hookup charges already reim-burse the town for all sewer costs. The purpose of the proposal was, instead, to control growth. Every commercial, industrial or housing de-velopment of any size would need to be approved by the town as a whole or wind up swimming in its own waste. Specifically, this article was aimed at stopping a golf course and condominium complex already under construction on the west side of town. The golf-course developer had been punctilious in meeting the town's Planning Board, Board of Adjustment, Conservation Commission and Historic District Commis-sion requirements and in obeying all applicable state and federal laws. The golf-course and condo-complex owner had needed to obtain forty-seven permits from eleven different government agencies in order to start building his golf course and condo complex. But he had done so. An all-sewage special town meeting was the last possible way to stop the guys in plaid pants and kiltie shoes.

As I mentioned before, I hold private-property rights to be sa-cred—in theory. Which is like saying I'm rich—in Bulgaria. In theory we're all lots of things: good, kind and, above all, consistent. I hold private-property rights to be sacred in theory, but in practice I had thrown in with the anti-golf-course faction.

To be fair, we weren't opposed to the golf course for any Pals-of-the-Animals, Eco-Stalinist reasons. Most of us play golf. We didn't have any cutesy-artsy objections to seeing trees cut down. It's a lot easier to shoot a deer on a 350-yard par four fairway than it is in the deep woods. And we weren't opposed to growth itself—in theory. But the sad truth of local government, like the sad truth of national government, is that people are no longer an asset. Humans do not benefit the modern state. Total 1989 Blatherboro town expenditure—including the town's share of county government and school-system costs—was $9.5 million, or about $1,860 per person. Almost all this money was raised through property taxes and automobile registration fees. A typical new family moving to Blatherboro, with a mom, dad and two kids (for families still come in that configuration in New Hampshire), would be buying a town-house condominium with a tax-assessed value of $100,000. The current property tax rate on that condominium is $2,860 a year. If the new family owns two late-model cars, registration fees (which are based on the blue-book value of the automobile) would be about $340. Add in a few miscellaneous levies and charges, and the new family ends up contributing approximately $3,500 per annum to the Blatherboro town coffers. But that is almost $4,000 less than what the town will spend on these people. A family of four must own at least a quarter of a million dollars worth of property to carry its own weight in the Blatherboro town budget.

Theory is important, sure, but it shouldn't get between a man and his wallet. You can't serve theory for dinner. People have a *theoretical* right to do what they want with their property, and people have a *theoretical* right to move into my town. *But . . .*

It was at this moment, in the middle of the Blatherboro sewer debate, that I achieved enlightenment about government. I had a dominion epiphany. I reached regime satori. The whole town meeting was suddenly illuminated by the pure, strong radiance of truth (a considerable improvement over the fluorescent tubes).

It wasn't mere disillusionment that I experienced. Government isn't   *40* a good way to solve problems; I already knew that. And I'd been to Washington and seen for myself that government is concerned mostly with self-perpetuation and is subject to fantastic ideas about its own capabilities. I understood that government is wasteful of the nation's resources, immune to common sense and subject to pressure from every half-organized bouquet of assholes. I had observed, in person, government solemnity in debate of ridiculous issues and frivolity in execution of serious duties. I was fully aware that government is distrustful of and disrespectful toward average Americans while being easily gulled by Americans with money, influence or fame. What I hadn't realized was *government is morally wrong.*

The whole idea of our government is this: If enough people get together and act in concert, they can take something and not pay for it. And here, in small-town New Hampshire, in this veritable world's capital of probity, we were about to commit just such a theft. If we could collect sufficient votes in favor of special town meetings about sewers, we could make a golf course and condominium complex disappear for free. We were going to use our suffrage to steal a fellow citizen's property rights. We weren't even going to take the manly risk of holding him up at gunpoint.

Not that there's anything wrong with our limiting growth. If we Blatherboro residents don't want a golf course and condominium complex, we can go buy that land and not build them. Of course, to buy the land, we'd have to borrow money from the bank, and to pay the bank loan, we'd have to do something profitable with the land, something like . . . build a golf course and condominium complex. Well, at least that would be constructive. We would be adding something—if only golf—to the sum of civilization's accomplishments. Better to build a golf course right through the middle of Redwood National Park and condominiums on top of the Lincoln Memorial than to sit in council gorging on the liberties of others, gobbling their material substance, eating freedom.

What we were trying to do with our legislation in the Blatherboro Town Meeting was wanton, cheap and greedy—a sluttish thing. This should come as no surprise. Authority has always attracted the lowest elements in the human race. All through history mankind has been bullied by scum. Those who lord it over their fellows and toss commands in every direction and would boss the grass in the meadow about which way to bend in the wind are the most depraved kind of prostitutes. They will submit to any indignity, perform any vile act, do anything to achieve power. The worst off-sloughings of the planet are the ingredients of sovereignty. Every government is a parliament of whores.

The trouble is, in a democracy the whores are us.

☐ *Outward Exploration: Discussion*

1. In your own words, describe the Blatherboro that we see in paragraphs 1–5.
2. What effect does O'Rourke's use of statistics achieve in paragraphs 12 and 13?
3. What are his objections to the local school system? How right is he?
4. List some of the comic devices O'Rourke uses.
5. Describe the tone of this essay. Justify your response.
6. Discuss O'Rourke's attitude toward the "Town Flake."
7. What is O'Rourke's attitude toward democracy?
8. What is his ultimate insight, the epiphany he gains at the town meeting?
9. This essay ends a book of essays about the federal government. The book's title, *Parliament of Whores: A Lone Humorist Attempts to Explain the Entire U.S. Government,* suggests O'Rourke's vision of himself (a humorist), and the book's title is explained in paragraphs 43 and 44 of this essay. Discuss this essay as an argument—how effectively does O'Rourke make his case about government? What points does he make particularly well? Which seem weak? What are his assumptions about government and about human nature? Ultimately, does he convince you that his ideas about government are correct?

❑ *Outward Exploration: Writing*

1. Write an essay in response to O'Rourke. In addition to pointing out areas where you believe he is wrong and providing evidence to support your claims, make a case supporting your own vision of democracy. Feel free to quote from a variety of sources.

2. Using O'Rourke's essay as a model, write a satiric exploratory essay about a subject that you know a great deal about.

Shooting an Elephant

George Orwell

☐ *Inward Exploration*

Write at least one paragraph discussing imperialism. *If you are not sure what this term means, check a dictionary or an encyclopedia.*

In Moulmein, in lower Burma, I was hated by large numbers of   *1*
people—the only time in my life that I have been important enough for
this to happen to me. I was sub-divisional police officer of the town,
and in an aimless, petty kind of way anti-European feeling was very
bitter. No one had the guts to raise a riot, but if a European woman
went through the bazaars alone somebody would probably spit betel
juice over her dress. As a police officer I was an obvious target and was
baited whenever it seemed safe to do so. When a nimble Burman tripped
me up on the football field and the referee (another Burman) looked the
other way, the crowd yelled with hideous laughter. This happened more
than once. In the end the sneering yellow faces of young men that met
me everywhere, the insults hooted after me when I was at a safe distance, got badly on my nerves. The young Buddhist priests were the
worst of all. There were several thousands of them in the town and none
of them seemed to have anything to do except stand on street corners
and jeer at Europeans.

All this was perplexing and upsetting. For at that time I had already
made up my mind that imperialism was an evil thing and the sooner I
chucked up my job and got out of it the better. Theoretically—and
secretly, of course—I was all for the Burmese and all against their op-
pressors, the British. As for the job I was doing, I hated it more bitterly
than I can perhaps make clear. In a job like that you see the dirty work
of Empire at close quarters. The wretched prisoners huddling in the
stinking cages of the lock-ups, the gray, cowed faces of the long-term
convicts, the scarred buttocks of the men who had been flogged with
bamboos—all these oppressed me with an intolerable sense of guilt. But
I could get nothing into perspective. I was young and ill educated and I
had had to think out my problems in the utter silence that is imposed on
every Englishman in the East. I did not even know that the British Empire is dying, still less did I know that it is a great deal better than the
younger empires that are going to supplant it. All I knew was that I was
stuck between my hatred of the empire I served and my rage against the
evil-spirited little beasts who tried to make my job impossible. With one

part of my mind I thought of the British Raj as an unbreakable tyranny, as something clamped down, in *saecula saeculorum,* upon the will of prostrate peoples; with another part I thought that the greatest joy in the world would be to drive a bayonet into a Buddhist priest's guts. Feelings like these are the normal by-products of imperialism; ask any Anglo-Indian official, if you can catch him off duty.

One day something happened which in a roundabout way was enlightening. It was a tiny incident in itself; but it gave me a better glimpse than I had had before of the real nature of imperialism—the real motives for which despotic governments act. Early one morning the sub-inspector at a police station the other end of the town rang me up on the 'phone and said that an elephant was ravaging the bazaar. Would I please come and do something about it? I did not know what I could do, but I wanted to see what was happening and I got on to a pony and started out. I took my rifle, an old .44 Winchester and much too small to kill an elephant, but I thought the noise might be useful *in terrorem.* Various Burmans stopped me on the way and told me about the elephant's doings. It was not, of course, a wild elephant, but a tame one which had gone "must." It had been chained up, as tame elephants always are when their attack of "must" is due, but on the previous night it had broken its chain and escaped. Its mahout, the only person who could manage it when it was in that state, had set out in pursuit, but had taken the wrong direction and was now twelve hours' journey away, and in the morning the elephant had suddenly reappeared in the town. The Burmese population had no weapons and were quite helpless against it. It had already destroyed somebody's bamboo hut, killed a cow and raided some fruit-stalls and devoured the stock; also it had met the municipal rubbish van and, when the driver jumped out and took to his heels, had turned the van over and inflicted violences upon it.

The Burmese sub-inspector and some Indian constables were waiting for me in the quarter where the elephant had been seen. It was a very poor quarter, a labyrinth of squalid bamboo huts, thatched with palm-leaf, winding all over a steep hillside. I remember that it was a cloudy, stuffy morning at the beginning of the rains. We began questioning the people as to where the elephant had gone and, as usual, failed to get any definite information. That is invariably the case in the East; a story always sounds clear enough at a distance, but the nearer you get to the scene of events the vaguer it becomes. Some of the people said that the elephant had gone in one direction, some said that he had gone in another, some professed not even to have heard of any elephant. I had almost made up my mind that the whole story was a pack of lies, when we heard yells a little distance away. There was a loud, scandalized cry of "Go away, child! Go away this instant!" and an old woman with a switch in her hand came round the corner of a hut, violently shooing away a crowd of naked children. Some more women followed, clicking their tongues and exclaiming; evidently there was something that the children ought not to have seen. I rounded the hut and saw a man's dead body sprawling in the mud. He was an Indian, a black Dravidian coolie, almost naked, and he could not have been dead many minutes. The people said that the elephant had come suddenly upon him round the corner of the hut, caught him with its trunk, put its foot on his back and ground him into the earth. This was the rainy season and the ground was soft, and his face had scored a trench a foot deep and a couple of yards long. He was lying on his belly with arms crucified and head sharply twisted to one side. His face was coated with mud, the eyes wide open, the teeth bared and grinning with an expression of unendurable agony. (Never tell me, by the way, that the dead look peaceful. Most of the corpses I have seen looked devilish.) The friction of the great beast's foot had stripped the skin from his back as neatly as one skins a rabbit. As soon as I saw the dead man I sent an orderly to a friend's house nearby to borrow an elephant rifle. I had already sent back the pony, not wanting it to go mad with fright and throw me if it smelt the elephant.

The orderly came back in a few minutes with a rifle and five car- 5 tridges, and meanwhile some Burmans had arrived and told us that the elephant was in the paddy fields below, only a few hundred yards away. As I started forward practically the whole population of the quarter flocked out of the houses and followed me. They had seen the rifle and were all shouting excitedly that I was going to shoot the elephant. They had not shown much interest in the elephant when he was merely ravaging their homes, but it was different now that he was going to be shot. It was a bit of fun to them, as it would be to an English crowd; besides they wanted the meat. It made me vaguely uneasy. I had no intention of shooting the elephant—I had merely sent for the rifle to defend myself if necessary—and it is always unnerving to have a crowd following you. I marched down the hill, looking and feeling a fool, with the rifle over my shoulder and an ever-growing army of people jostling at my heels. At the bottom, when you got away from the huts, there was a metalled road and beyond that a miry waste of paddy fields a thousand yards across, not yet ploughed but soggy from the first rains and dotted with coarse grass. The elephant was standing eight yards from the road, his left side toward us. He took not the slightest notice of the crowd's approach. He was tearing up bunches of grass, beating them against his knees to clean them, and stuffing them into his mouth.

I had halted on the road. As soon as I saw the elephant I knew with perfect certainty that I ought not to shoot him. It is a serious matter to shoot a working elephant—it is comparable to destroying a huge and costly piece of machinery—and obviously one ought not to do it if it can possibly be avoided. And at that distance, peacefully eating, the elephant looked no more dangerous than a cow. I thought then and I think now that his attack of "must" was already passing off; in which case he would merely wander harmlessly about until the mahout came back and caught him. Moreover, I did not in the least want to shoot him. I decided that I would watch him for a little while to make sure that he did not turn savage again, and then go home.

But at that moment I glanced round at the crowd that had followed me. It was an immense crowd, two thousand at the least and growing every minute. It blocked the road for a long distance on either side. I looked at the sea of yellow faces above the garish clothes—faces all happy and excited over this bit of fun, all certain that the elephant was going to be shot. They were watching me as they would watch a conjurer about to perform a trick. They did not like me, but with the magical rifle in my hands I was momentarily worth watching. And suddenly I realized that I should have to shoot the elephant after all. The people expected it of me and I had got to do it; I could feel their two thousand wills pressing me forward, irresistibly. And it was at this moment, as I stood there with the rifle in my hands, that I first grasped the hollowness, the futility of the white man's dominion in the East. Here was I, the white man with his gun, standing in front of the unarmed native crowd—seemingly the leading actor of the piece; but in reality I was only an absurd puppet pushed to and fro by the will of these yellow faces behind. I perceived in this moment that when the white man turns tyrant it is his own freedom that he destroys. He becomes a sort of hollow, posing dummy, the conventionalized figure of a sahib. For it is the condition of his rule that he shall spend his life in trying to impress the "natives," and so in every crisis he has got to do what the "natives" expect of him. He wears a mask, and his face grows to fit it. I had got to shoot the elephant. I had committed myself to doing it when I sent for the rifle. A sahib has got to act like a sahib; he has got to appear resolute, to know his own mind and do definite things. To come all that way, rifle in hand, with two thousand people marching at my heels, and then to trail feebly away, having done nothing—no, that was impossible. The crowd would laugh at me. And my whole life, every white man's life in the East, was one long struggle not to be laughed at.

But I did not want to shoot the elephant. I watched him beating his bunch of grass against his knees with that preoccupied grandmotherly air that elephants have. It seemed to me that it would be murder to shoot him. At that age I was not squeamish about killing animals, but I had never shot an elephant and never wanted to. (Somehow it always seems worse to kill a *large* animal.) Besides, there was the beast's owner to be considered. Alive, the elephant was worth at least a hundred pounds; dead, he would only be worth the value of his tusks, five pounds, possibly. But I had got to act quickly. I turned to some experienced-looking Burmans who had been there when we arrived, and asked them how the elephant had been behaving. They all said the same thing: he took no notice of you if you left him alone, but he might charge if you went too close to him.

It was perfectly clear to me what I ought to do. I ought to walk up to within, say, twenty-five yards of the elephant and test his behavior. If he charged, I could shoot; if he took no notice of me, it would be safe to leave him until the mahout came back. But also I knew that I was going to do no such thing. I was a poor shot with a rifle and the ground was soft mud into which one would sink at every step. If the elephant charged and I missed him, I should have about as much chance as a toad under a steam-roller. But even then I was not thinking particularly of my own skin, only of the watchful yellow faces behind. For at that moment, with the crowd watching me, I was not afraid in the ordinary sense, as I would have been if I had been alone. A white man mustn't be frightened in front of "natives"; and so, in general, he isn't frightened. The sole thought in my mind was that if anything went wrong those two thousand Burmans would see me pursued, caught, trampled on, and reduced to a grinning corpse like that Indian up the hill. And if that happened it was quite probable that some of them would laugh. That would never do. There was only one alternative. I shoved the cartridges into the magazine and lay down on the road to get a better aim.

The crowd grew very still, and a deep, low, happy sigh, as of people   10
who see the theater curtain go up at last, breathed from innumerable throats. They were going to have their bit of fun after all. The rifle was a beautiful German thing with crosshair sights. I did not then know that in shooting an elephant one would shoot to cut an imaginary bar running from ear-hole to ear-hole. I ought, therefore, as the elephant was sideways on, to have aimed straight at his ear-hole; actually I aimed several inches in front of this, thinking the brain would be further forward.

When I pulled the trigger I did not hear the bang or feel the kick—one never does when a shot goes home—but I heard the devilish roar of glee that went up from the crowd. In that instant, in too short a time, one would have thought, even for the bullet to get there, a mysterious terrible change had come over the elephant. He neither stirred, nor fell, but every line of his body had altered. He looked suddenly stricken, shrunken, immensely old, as though the frightful impact of the bullet had paralyzed him without knocking him down. At last, after what seemed a long time—it might have been five seconds, I dare say—he sagged flabbily to his knees. His mouth slobbered. An enormous senility seemed to have settled upon him. One could have imagined him thousands of years old. I fired again into the same spot. At the second shot he did not collapse but climbed with desperate slowness to his feet and stood weakly upright, with legs sagging and head drooping. I fired a third time. That was the shot that did for him. You could see the agony of it jolt his whole body and knock the last remnant of strength from his legs. But in falling he seemed for a moment to rise, for as his hind legs collapsed beneath him he seemed to tower upward like a huge rock toppling, his trunk reaching skyward like a tree. He trumpeted, for the first and only time. And then down he came, his belly toward me, with a crash that seemed to shake the ground even where I lay.

I got up. The Burmans were already racing past me across the mud. It was obvious that the elephant would never rise again, but he was not dead. He was breathing very rhythmically with long rattling gasps, his great mound of a side painfully rising and falling. His mouth was wide open—I could see far down into caverns of pale pink throat. I waited a long time for him to die, but his breathing did not weaken. Finally I fired my two remaining shots into the spot where I thought his heart must be. The thick blood welled out of him like red velvet, but still he did not die. His body did not even jerk when the shots hit him, the tortured breathing continued without a pause. He was dying, very slowly and in great agony, but in some world remote from me where not even a bullet could damage him further. I felt that I had got to put an end to that dreadful noise. It seemed dreadful to see the great beast lying there, powerless to move and yet powerless to die, and not even to be able to finish him. I sent back for my small rifle and poured shot after shot into his heart and down his throat. They seemed to make no impression. The tortured gasps continued as steadily as the ticking of a clock.

In the end I could not stand it any longer and went away. I heard later that it took him half an hour to die. Burmans were bringing dahs and baskets even before I left, and I was told they had stripped his body almost to the bones by the afternoon.

Afterward, of course, there were endless discussions about the shooting of the elephant. The owner was furious, but he was only an Indian and could do nothing. Besides, legally I had done the right thing, for a mad elephant has to be killed, like a mad dog, if its owner fails to control it. Among the Europeans opinion was divided. The older men said I was right, the younger men said it was a damn shame to shoot an elephant for killing a coolie, because an elephant was worth more than any damn Coringhee coolie. And afterward I was very glad that the coolie had been killed; it put me legally in the right and it gave me a sufficient pretext for shooting the elephant. I often wondered whether any of the others grasped that I had done it solely to avoid looking a fool.

☐ Outward Exploration: Discussion

1. According to Orwell's first two paragraphs, what were conditions like in Burma at the time of this event?

2. Have you ever been in a similar situation—in other words, doing a

job or performing a task of which you did not approve on moral (or some other) grounds? If so, what were your feelings? Given the situation, does Orwell react normally? Explain.

3. Explain Orwell's complicated feelings expressed in paragraph 2.

4. Point out where and how Orwell moves from establishing the background context to beginning to narrate the major event in the essay.

5. Point out vivid details which Orwell uses to help "put us on the scene."

6. Why were the Burmese so interested once Orwell sent for the rifle?

7. Why is Orwell made uneasy by their interest?

8. Comment on the techniques Orwell uses in paragraph 7 to reveal the pressure building up on him to shoot the elephant.

9. What insights into imperialism does Orwell gain?

10. What other courses of action does Orwell consider? Why does he reject them?

11. Point out particularly effective pieces of description in paragraphs 11 and 12.

12. Comment on the ironic revelations about the imperial attitude displayed in the essay's last paragraph.

❏ *Outward Exploration: Writing*

1. Have you ever been in a situation where you did something you did not want to do simply because you felt great pressure from either your peers or people to whom you felt yourself superior? If so, write an essay exploring that event. Look at the psychological dynamics involved in the pressure. Feel free to refer to Orwell's experience as a comparison or contrast to your own.

2. *Power* has been the topic of several pieces in this book—for example, George Orwell's "A Hanging," Bruno Bettelheim's "The Ignored Lesson of Anne Frank," and Tobias Wolff's "On Being a Real Westerner." Write an essay exploring the concept of *power*. You might consult some outside sources in addition to the essays in this book.

3. A concept related to power but somewhat different is *leadership*. Write an essay exploring the concept of *leadership*. Consider some of the following issues: What qualities make a great (or effective) leader? Is a great leader always an effective leader? Is an effective leader always a great one? Why do people follow some people and not others? Are some people born followers? Draw on your experiences of local leaders (student politicians, leaders of clubs and

teams, administrators) as well as on state, national, and military leaders for examples. You might consult outside sources.

4. Another concept related to power is *tyranny*. If you have had personal experience with tyranny or a tyrant on some level (for example, the school bully), write an essay exploring the concept. Use concepts from Orwell's essay, but feel free to consult outside sources for more insights.

Being a Jr.

RAFAEL A. SUAREZ, JR.

☐ *Inward Exploration*

Write at least one paragraph exploring your thoughts about the idea of some-one's being named "junior."

There is a photograph in my parents' house in Brooklyn which   *1*
never fails to grab a gaze as I pass by. It was taken in 1958, on the beach in Jacksonville, Florida. My father, trim, smiling, tan, holds his first-born, a little over a year old. That's me. On that sunny day in Florida my sailor father is a few months past his twentieth birthday. I think of myself at twenty, a senior in college living in my first apartment, and laugh at the idea of my having had a child at that age.

My father looks happy in the photo. I look happy, too. Today I have a face something like his, a body much like his, and a name *exactly* like his. Exactly the same, except for two letters and a period on my birth certificate, diploma, driver's license and credit cards: Jr. At the risk of sounding a little syrupy, I'd say his name is one of the nicest things my father has ever given me. Rafael is one of the seven archangels, and he is known as God's healer for his role in restoring the sight of Tobit in that Apocryphal book. Thus Angel, my father's middle name, and mine, is fitting.

There are hundreds, perhaps thousands of names for men. There are plenty of other names in my own family that would have worked per-fectly well. My brothers got them. My father and mother could have given me a different middle name. Then I would have been named for my father, but not a Jr.

When friends first see my byline, or look over my shoulder as I sign a register, and they see the "Jr." at the end, there are several reactions. "I wouldn't like that," said one. "I like having my *own* name." Some men say, "You're a junior? Me too!"

Only men get to say that, because only men get to be juniors.   *5*
Women with feminized versions of their fathers' names don't get a legal tag to reflect the fact and neither do women named for their mothers. Besides, the attitudes that go with having "junior children" seem to be more closely associated with boys than girls. Though customs are changing, carrying on the family name is still something done by boys and very effectively done by "juniors."

In addition to the sexual exclusivity of juniorism, there is a cultural one. Though there is no religious reason for it, Eastern European Ashkenazic Jews will not name children for their fathers or mothers, except in the unlikely event that the father is dead at a boy's birth. There are exceptions to this generalization, but none of the guys with whom I played ball at the Jewish Community House in Bensonhurst were juniors. Most of my Jewish buddies are carrying a dead relative's initials around, or some rough English cognate of a Hebrew name. It seems a shame that not only dad but *all* of the living are excluded from the thrill of having a namesake.

I'm happy with my name, and I like being a junior, but there is a down side. Mail meant for me still somehow ends up at my father's house. When I still lived at home I got half my mail "pre-opened." I can still remember the look on my father's face when my friends on the phone, asking for me and getting him, would launch into personal conversation. Family members finally got into the habit of asking "junior or senior?" when callers weren't specific enough.

In the world of juniors, I was one of the lucky ones. I was never called "Junior" as a nickname. I knew one Junior for years without ever knowing his real name. He and many other Juniors will tell you that Junior is their real name and sign it that way on a greeting card or a letter. These are the guys people probably have in mind when they ask me if I have a fragile sense of identity because of my juniorhood.

Identity is not a problem. In addition to being me, I get the privilege of having my name attached to something longer-lived than just me. When I introduce myself, I don't say "My name is . . ." or "I am called . . ." I say "I am Rafael." The difference is important, because a name doesn't only tell people what to call you, it tells them who you are.

I often think about my life as being not only a gift from my parents   10
to me, but as being a gift from me to them. It must be a special gift for my father, since we have the same name. I think of the kick he probably gets when he sees my byline in a magazine or newspaper, or when he sees my name, *our* name, under my face when I report on television. He loves my brothers and is proud of them. But it can't be the same as seeing his name, his son's name, in a prominent place.

Of the three brothers, am I the most like my father? Maybe. I think that when I was named for my father, the intention was that my name not be simply a utile thing, not be just a handy sound to summon a boy when the garbage needs to be taken down. When a child is named, it is an attempt to define the child. And my definition is my father. I thank my parents for their vote of confidence, and I hope I live up to my name.

Still, there are complications of juniorhood, and they don't end at the age of majority or when a boy moves away from home. I will be a junior until the day I die, no matter how long my father lives. If I ever have a son, he can be named for me, but he can't be "Jr." We would have to begin the numbers game, which somehow doesn't have the intimacy of "Sr." and "Jr." This theoretical manchild would have "3d" (pronounced "the third") at the end of his name, and I'm not sure how I feel about that. My wife says, unequivocally, "No way." A friend suggested that the resulting name would be a "little too Waspy." But I don't think Rafael Angel Suarez 3d has to worry about being too Waspy.

☐ *Outward Exploration: Discussion*

1. Why does the author begin his essay by discussing the photograph of his father?

2. What are your feelings about parents naming their sons "junior"? If you aren't a "junior," would you like to be? Should there be an equivalent term for daughters who have their mothers' exact names? Why or why not?

3. Does your religious or ethnic or family group have particular customs about naming children? Explain.

☐ *Outward Exploration: Writing*

1. Write an essay explaining the tradition for naming children in your family (or ethnic or religious group). Explore its impact on you. For instance, would you like to change the name you have? Why or why not?

2. According to the author, "When a child is named, it is an attempt to define the child." Assuming that is true, how did your parents attempt to define you? What characteristics and personality traits did your name suggest to them? What traits does it suggest to you? Why?

3. Assume that you can change your name (both first and last if you like) to any name you wish. What name(s) would you choose? Why? Write an essay exploring the sources of that particular name's associations for you.

A Modest Proposal

JONATHAN SWIFT

For Preventing the Children of Poor People in *Ireland,* from Being a Burden to Their Parents or Country; and for Making Them Beneficial to the Public.

It is a melancholy object to those, who walk through this great   1
town, or travel in the country; when they see the streets, the roads, and cabin-doors crowded with beggars of the female sex, followed by three, four, or six children, all in rags, and importuning every passenger for an alms. These mothers, instead of being able to work for their honest livelihood, are forced to employ all their time in strolling to beg sustenance for their helpless infants; who, as they grow up, either turn thieves for want of work; or leave their dear native country, to fight for the Pretender in Spain, or sell themselves to the Barbados.

I think it is agreed by all parties, that this prodigious number of children in the arms, or on the backs, or at the heels of their mothers, and frequently of their fathers, is in the present deplorable state of the kingdom, a very great additional grievance; and therefore, whoever could find out a fair, cheap, and easy method of making these children sound and useful members of the Commonwealth, would deserve so well of the public, as to have his statue set up for a preserver of the nation.

But my intention is very far from being confined to provide only for the children of professed beggars: it is of a much greater extent, and shall take in the whole number of infants at a certain age, who are born of parents, in effect as little able to support them, as those who demand our charity in the streets.

As to my own part, having turned my thoughts for many years, upon this important subject, and maturely weighed the several schemes of other projectors, I have always found them grossly mistaken in their computation. It is true a child, just dropped from its dam, may be supported by her milk, for a solar year with little other nourishment; at most not above the value of two shillings; which the mother may certainly get or the value in scraps, by her lawful occupation of begging: and, it is exactly at one year old, that I propose to provide for them in such a manner, as, instead of being a charge upon their parents, or the parish, or wanting food and raiment for the rest of their lives; they shall, on the contrary, contribute to the feeding, and partly to the clothing, of many thousands.

There is likewise another great advantage in my scheme, that it will prevent those voluntary abortions, and that horrid practice of women murdering their bastard children; alas! too frequent among us; sacrificing the poor innocent babes, I doubt, more to avoid the expense than the shame; which would move tears and pity in the most savage and inhuman breast.

The number of souls in Ireland being usually reckoned one million and a half; of these I calculate there may be about two hundred thousand couples whose wives are breeders; from which number I subtract thirty thousand couples, who are able to maintain their own children; although I apprehend there cannot be so many, under the present distresses of the kingdom; but this being granted, there will remain an hundred and seventy thousand breeders. I again subtract fifty thousand, for those women who miscarry, or whose children die by accident, or disease, within the year. There only remain an hundred and twenty thousand children of poor parents, annually born: the question therefore is, how this number shall be reared, and provided for? Which, as I have already said, under the present situation of affairs, is utterly impossible, by all the methods hitherto proposed: for we can neither employ them in handicraft or agriculture; we neither build houses, (I mean in the country) nor cultivate land: they can very seldom pick up a livelihood by stealing until they arrive at six years old; except where they are of towardly parts; although, I confess, they learn the rudiments much earlier; during which time, they can, however, be properly looked upon only as probationers; as I have been informed by a principal gentleman in the country of Cavan, who protested to me, that he never knew above one or two instances under the age of six, even in a part of the kingdom so renowned for the quickest proficiency in that art.

I am assured by our merchants, that a boy or a girl before twelve years old, is no saleable commodity; and even when they come to this age, they will not yield above three pounds, or three pounds and half a crown at most, on the Exchange; which cannot turn to account either to the parents or the kingdom; the charge of nutriment and rags, having been at least four times that value.

I shall now therefore humbly propose my own thoughts; which I hope will not be liable to the least objection.

I have been assured by a very knowing American of my acquaintance in London; that a young healthy child, well nursed, is, at a year old, a most delicious, nourishing, and wholesome food; whether stewed, roasted, baked, or boiled; and I make no doubt, that it will equally serve in a fricassee, or ragout.

I do therefore humbly offer it to public consideration, that of the hundred and twenty thousand children, already computed, twenty thousand may be reserved for breed; whereof only one fourth part to be males; which is more than we allow to sheep, black cattle, or swine; and my reason is, that these children are seldom the fruits of marriage, a circumstance not much regarded by our savages; therefore, one male will be sufficient to serve four females. That the remaining hundred thousand, may, at a year old, be offered in sale to the persons of quality and fortune, through the kingdom; always advising the mother to let them suck plentifully in the last month, so as to render them plump, and fat for a good table. A child will make two dishes at an entertainment for friends; and when the family dines alone, the fore or hind quarter will make a reasonable dish; and seasoned with a little pepper or salt, will be very good boiled on the fourth day, especially in winter.

I have reckoned upon a medium, that a child just born will weigh twelve pounds; and in a solar year, if tolerably nursed, increaseth to twenty eight pounds.

I grant this food will be somewhat dear, and therefore very proper for landlords; who, as they have already devoured most of the parents, seem to have the best title to the children.

Infants' flesh will be in season throughout the year; but more plentiful in March, and a little before and after: for we are told by a grave author, an eminent French physician, that fish being a prolific diet, there are more children born in Roman Catholic countries about nine months after Lent, than at any other season: therefore reckoning a year after Lent, the markets will be more glutted than usual; because the number of Popish infants, is, at least, three to one in this kingdom; and therefore it will have one other collateral advantage by lessening the number of Papists among us.

I have already computed the charge of nursing a beggar's child (in which list I reckon all cottagers, labourers, and four-fifths of the farmers) to be about two shillings per annum, rags included; and I believe no gentleman would repine to give ten shillings for the carcass of a good fat child; which, as I have said, will make four dishes of excellent nutritive meat, when he hath only some particular friend, or his own family, to dine with him. Thus the squire will learn to be a good landlord, and grow popular among his tenants; the mother will have eight shillings net profit, and be fit for work until she produceth another child.

Those who are more thrifty (as I must confess the times require) may flay the carcass; the skin of which, artificially dressed, will make admirable gloves for ladies, and summer boots for fine gentlemen.

As to our city of Dublin; shambles may be appointed for this purpose, in the most convenient parts of it; and butchers we may be assured will not be wanting; although I rather recommend buying the children alive, and dressing them hot from the knife, as we do roasting pigs.

A very worthy person, a true lover of his country, and whose virtues I highly esteem, was lately pleased, in discoursing on this matter, to offer a refinement upon my scheme. He said, that many gentlemen of this kingdom, having of late destroyed their deer; he conceived, that the want of venison might be well supplied by the bodies of young lads and maidens, not exceeding fourteen years of age, nor under twelve; so great a number of both sexes in every county being now ready to starve, for want of work and service: and these to be disposed of by their parents, if alive, or otherwise by their nearest relations. But with due deference to so excellent a friend, and so deserving a patriot, I cannot be altogether in his sentiments. For as to the males, my American acquaintance assured me from frequent experience, that their flesh was generally tough and lean, like that of our schoolboys, by continual exercise, and their taste disagreeable; and to fatten them would not answer the charge. Then, as to the females, it would, I think, with humble submission, be a loss to the public, because they soon would become breeders themselves: and besides it is not improbable, that some scrupulous people might be apt to censure such a practice (although indeed very unjustly) as a little bordering upon cruelty; which, I confess, hath always been with me the strongest objection against any project, how wellsoever intended.

But in order to justify my friend; he confessed, that this expedient was put into his head by the famous Salmanaazor, a native of the island Formosa, who came from thence to London, above twenty years ago, and in conversation told my friend, that in his country, when any young person happened to be put to death, the executioner sold the carcass to persons of quality, as a prime dainty; and that, in his time, the body of a plump girl of fifteen, who was crucified for an attempt to poison the emperor, was sold to his imperial Majesty's prime minister of state, and other great mandarins of the court, in joints from the gibbet, at four hundred crowns. Neither indeed can I deny, that if the same use were made of several plump young girls in this town, who, without one single groat to the fortunes, cannot stir abroad without a chair, and appear at the playhouse, and assemblies in foreign fineries, which they never will pay for; the kingdom would not be the worse.

Some persons of a desponding spirit are in great concern about that vast number of poor people, who are aged, diseased, or maimed; and I have been desired to employ my thoughts what course may be taken, to ease the nation of so grievous an encumbrance. But I am not in the least pain upon that matter; because it is very well known, that they are every day dying, and rotting, by cold and famine, and filth, and vermin, as fast as can be reasonably expected. And as the younger labourers, they are now in almost as hopeful a condition: they cannot get work, and consequently pine away for want of nourishment, to a degree, that if at any time they are accidentally hired to common labor, they have not strength to perform it; and thus the country, and themselves, are in a fair way of being soon delivered from the evils to come.

I have too long digressed; and therefore shall return to my subject. *20* I think the advantages by the proposal which I have made, are obvious, and many, as well as of the highest importance.

For, first, as I have already observed, it would greatly lessen the number of Papists, with whom we are yearly overrun; being the principal breeders of the nation, as well as our most dangerous enemies; and who stay at home on purpose, with a design to deliver the kingdom to the Pretender; hoping to take their advantage by the absence of so many good Protestants, who have chosen rather to leave their country, than stay at home, and pay tithes against their conscience, to an idolatrous Episcopal curate.

Secondly, the poorer tenants will have something valuable of their own, which, by law, may be made liable to distress, and help to pay their landlord's rent; their corn and cattle being already seized, and money a thing unknown.

Thirdly, whereas the maintenance of an hundred thousand children, from two years old, and upwards, cannot be computed at less than ten shillings a piece per annum, the nation's stock will be thereby increased fifty thousand pounds per annum; besides the profit of a new dish, introduced to the tables of all gentlemen of fortune in the kingdom, who have any refinement in taste; and the money will circulate among ourselves, the goods being entirely of our own growth and manufacture.

Fourthly, the constant breeders, besides the gain of eight shillings sterling per annum, by the sale of their children, will be rid of the charge of maintaining them after the first year.

Fifthly, this food would likewise bring great custom to taverns, *25* where the vintners will certainly be so prudent, as to produce the best receipts for dressing it to perfection; and consequently, have their houses frequented by all the fine gentlemen, who justly value themselves upon their knowledge in good eating; and a skillful cook, who understands how to oblige his guests, will contrive to make it as expensive as they please.

Sixthly, this would be a great inducement to marriage, which all wise nations have either encouraged by rewards, or enforced by laws and penalties. It would increase the care and tenderness of mothers towards their children, when they were sure of a settlement for life, to the poor babes, provided in some sort by the public, to their annual profit instead of expense. We should soon see an honest emulation among the married women, which of them could bring the fattest child to the market. Men would become as fond of their wives, during the time of their pregnancy, as they are now of their mares in foal, their cows in calf, or sows when they are ready to farrow; nor offer to beat or kick them, (as it is too frequent a practice) for fear of a miscarriage.

Many other advantages might be enumerated. For instance, the addition of some thousand carcasses in our exportation of barrelled beef: the propagation of swines' flesh, and improvement in the art of making good bacon; so much wanted among us by the great destruction of pigs, too frequent at our tables, and are no way comparable in taste, or magnificence, to a well-grown fat yearling child; which roasted whole, will make a considerable figure at a Lord Mayor's feast, or any other public entertainment. But this, and many others, I omit; being studious of brevity.

Supposing that one thousand families in this city, would be constant customers for infants' flesh; besides others who might have it at merry meetings, particularly weddings and christenings; I compute that Dublin would take off, annually, about twenty thousand carcasses; and the rest of the kingdom (where probably they will be sold somewhat cheaper) the remaining eighty thousand.

I can think of no one objection, that will possibly be raised against this proposal; unless it should be urged, that the number of people will be thereby much lessened in the kingdom. This I freely own; and it was indeed one principal design in offering it to the world. I desire the reader will observe, that I calculate my remedy for this one individual kingdom of Ireland, and for no other that ever was, is, or I think can be upon earth. Therefore, let no man talk to me of other expedients: *of taxing our absentees at five shillings a pound: of using neither clothes, nor household furniture except what is of our own growth and manufacture: of utterly rejecting the materials and instruments that promote foreign luxury: of curing the expensiveness of pride, vanity, idleness, and gaming in our women: of introducing a vein of parsimony, prudence and temperance: of learning to love our country, wherein we differ even from* Laplanders, *and the inhabitants of* Topinamboo: *of quitting our animosities, and factions; nor act any longer like the* Jews, *who were murdering one another at the very moment their city was taken: of being a little cautious not to sell our country and consciences for nothing; of teaching landlords to have, at least, one degree of mercy towards their tenants.* Lastly, *of putting a spirit of honesty, industry, and skill into our shopkeepers; who, if a resolution could now be taken to buy only our native goods, would immediately unite to cheat and exact upon us in the price, the measure, and the goodness; nor could ever yet be brought to make one fair proposal of just dealing, though often and earnestly invited to it.*

Therefore I repeat, let no man talk to me of these and the like expedients; 'till he hath, at least, a glimpse of hope, that there will ever be some hearty and sincere attempt to put them in practice. *30*

But, as to myself; having been wearied out for many years with offering vain, idle, visionary thoughts; and at length utterly despairing of success, I fortunately fell upon this proposal; which, as it is wholly new, so it hath something solid and real, of no expense, and little trouble, full in our own power; and whereby we can incur no danger in disobliging England: for, this kind of commodity will not bear expor-

tation; the flesh being of too tender a consistency, to admit a long continuance in salt; *although, perhaps, I could name a country, which would be
glad to eat up our whole nation without it.*

After all, I am not so violently bent upon my own opinion, as to
reject any offer proposed by wise men, which shall be found equally
innocent, cheap, easy, and effectual. But before something of that kind
shall be advanced, in contradiction to my scheme, and offering a better;
I desire the author, or authors, will be pleased maturely to consider two
points. First, as things now stand, how they will be able to find food
and raiment, for a hundred thousand useless mouths and backs? And
secondly, there being a round million of creatures in human figure,
throughout this kingdom; whose whole subsistence, put into a common
stock, would leave them in debt two millions of pounds sterling; adding
those, who are beggars by profession, to the bulk of farmers, cottagers,
and laborers, with their wives and children, who are beggars in effect; I
desire those politicians, who dislike my overture, and may perhaps be
so bold to attempt an answer, that they will first ask the parents of these
mortals, whether they would not, at this day, think it a great happiness
to have been sold for food at a year old, in the manner I prescribe; and
thereby have avoided such a perpetual scene of misfortunes, as they have
since gone through; by the oppression of landlords; the impossibility of
paying rent, without money or trade; the want of common sustenance,
with neither house nor clothes, to cover them from the inclemencies of
weather; and the most inevitable prospect of entailing the like, or greater
miseries upon their breed for ever.

I profess, in the sincerity of my heart, that I have not the least personal interest, in endeavoring to promote this necessary work; having
no other motive than the public good of my country, by advancing
our trade, providing for infants, relieving the poor, and giving some
pleasure to the rich. I have no children, by which I can propose to get
a single penny; the youngest being nine years old, and my wife past
childbearing.

☐ *Outward Exploration: Discussion*

1. What is the speaker's stated goal in the essay?
2. What picture does this essay indirectly paint of the economy and
   living conditions in Ireland?
3. What exactly is his plan?
4. What are the advantages of the speaker's plan?
5. Why does he reject his friend's plan to hunt teenagers?
6. What is the speaker's attitude toward the Irish? Give evidence to
   support your answer.
7. What is the speaker's attitude toward Americans?

8. At times Swift's speaker sounds a lot like modern politicians when they discuss their plans in general terms. Point out instances in the essay and from current events which support this idea.

9. Explain the speaker's tone as he gives the details of his plan (paragraphs 9–16).

10. What aspects of the essay give the illusion that the speaker is logical?

11. What are the real solutions that Swift (as opposed to his speaker) wants to see enacted?

12. Why doesn't Swift simply write an argument detailing and supporting these real solutions?

13. Discuss the essay's title.

14. Discuss the methods that Swift uses to make his real point about the Irish situation.

▢ Outward Exploration: Writing

1. Write an essay that analyzes "A Modest Proposal." In the process, you might evaluate its effectiveness as an argument.

2. Write an essay discussing the conditions in Ireland during Swift's lifetime. To write such an essay, you will have to do research. In the essay, you should compare what you learn from other sources with Swift's version of the facts. Would the real solutions he suggested have addressed at least some of the sources of Ireland's problems? Explain. Your essay might end up being an argument for different solutions or a defense of his solutions.

3. One of the powerful aspects of Swift's essay is his indirect exposure of the British assumption that the Irish were less than human. In "Am I Blue?" Alice Walker discovers that even assuming that animals are "only animals" is incorrect. Write an essay exploring the similarities and differences between the two essays. In the process, you will probably have to define the concept of *animal* very carefully and fully

4. Another powerful aspect of Swift's essay is his speaker's inability to get at the root of the problem. Instead of exploring ways to remedy the causes of the poverty (for example, lack of jobs, excessive taxation, absentee landlords), the speaker invents a method of eliminating many of the poor people. Permanently. Do you see shortsighted and misguided approaches to social problems in our world today? Pick a modern problem (for example, crime, prisons, health-care costs, drugs, welfare, misuse of scientific discoveries, sexual abuse). Do some research about the nature of the problem and possible solutions. Step back from the problem to think about its deeper causes. Then write an essay in which you create a persona

similar to Swift's—someone who manufactures a creative solution that does not deal with the causes of the problem. Make the solution outrageous (so that your readers will know you are actually advocating the opposite solution) but also *logical and believable given the assumptions of your speaker.*

5. Follow the directions in the preceding suggestion, but instead of creating a Swiftian speaker, write the argument in a straightforward manner. State your real solution and give evidence to support it.

6. The greatest justification for the speaker's plan in "A Modest Proposal" is economic. Consider his economic arguments carefully. Then do some research about a current government plan which has also promised economic advantages. Compare and contrast the promises. Then consider the current plan from the human point of view. In other words, ignoring economic promises and evidence, what are the human ramifications of the plan? Who will suffer or be hurt by the plan? What assumptions are being made by the creators of the plan? Write an essay arguing that the plan is seriously flawed because it has failed to take into account the human factor or arguing that despite the effect on certain segments of the population the plan should still be adopted. You might write this as a serious, straightforward argument or you might create a persona like Swift's.

Fenimore Cooper's Literary Offenses

MARK TWAIN

◻ *Inward Exploration*

If you are familiar with any of the works of James Fenimore Cooper, write a paragraph explaining your impressions of them. If you are not familiar with his works, make a list of the requirements of a good story: For example, what things must a story have and what must it avoid in order to be enjoyable or literary?

> *The Pathfinder* and *The Deerslayer* stand at the head of Cooper's novels as artistic creations. There are others of his works which contain parts as perfect as are to be found in these, and scenes even more thrilling. Not one can be compared with either of them as a finished whole.
>
> The defects in both of these tales are comparatively slight. They were pure works of art.
>
> —PROF. LOUNSBURY

> The five tales reveal an extraordinary fulness of invention.
> . . . One of the very greatest characters in fiction, "Natty Bumppo." . . .
>
> The craft of the woodsman, the tricks of the trapper, all the delicate art of the forest, were familiar to Cooper from his youth up.
>
> —PROF. BRANDER MATTHEWS

> Cooper is the greatest artist in the domain of romantic fiction yet produced by America.
>
> —WILKIE COLLINS

It seems to me that it was far from right for the Professor of English   1
Literature in Yale, the Professor of English Literature in Columbia, and Wilkie Collins, to deliver opinions on Cooper's literature without having read some of it. It would have been much more decorous to keep silent and let persons talk who have read Cooper.

Cooper's art has some defects. In one place in *Deerslayer,* and in the restricted space of two-thirds of a page, Cooper has scored 114 offences against literary art out of a possible 115. It breaks the record.

There are nineteen rules governing literary art in the domain of romantic fiction—some say twenty-two. In *Deerslayer* Cooper violated eighteen of them. These eighteen require:

1. That a tale shall accomplish something and arrive somewhere. But the *Deerslayer* tale accomplishes nothing and arrives in the air.

2. They require that the episodes of a tale shall be necessary parts of the tale, and shall help to develop it. But as the *Deerslayer* tale is not a tale, and accomplishes nothing and arrives nowhere, the episodes have no rightful place in the work, since there was nothing for them to develop.

3. They require that the personages in a tale shall be alive, except in the case of corpses, and that always the reader shall be able to tell the corpses from the others. But this detail has often been overlooked in the *Deerslayer* tale.

4. They require that the personages in a tale, both dead and alive, shall exhibit a sufficient excuse for being there. But this detail also has been overlooked in the *Deerslayer* tale.

5. They require that when the personages of a tale deal in conversation, the talk shall sound like human talk, and be talk such as human beings would be likely to talk in the given circumstances, and have a discoverable meaning, also a discoverable purpose, and a show of relevancy, and remain in the neighborhood of the subject in hand, and be interesting to the reader, and help out the tale, and stop when the people cannot think of anything more to say. But this requirement has been ignored from the beginning of the *Deerslayer* tale to the end of it.

6. They require that when the author describes the character of a personage in his tale, the conduct and conversation of that personage shall justify said description. But this law gets little or no attention in the *Deerslayer* tale, as "Natty Bumppo's" case will amply prove.

7. They require that when a personage talks like an illustrated, gilt-edged, tree-calf, hand tooled, seven-dollar Friendship's Offering in the beginning of a paragraph, he shall not talk like a negro minstrel in the end of it. But this rule is flung down and danced upon in the *Deerslayer* tale.

8. They require that crass stupidities shall not be played upon the reader as "the craft of the woodsman, the delicate art of the forest," by either the author or the people in the tale. But this rule is persistently violated in the *Deerslayer* tale.

9. They require that the personages of a tale shall confine themselves to possibilities and let miracles alone; or, if they venture a miracle, the author must so plausibly set it forth as to make it look possible and reasonable. But these rules are not respected in the *Deerslayer* tale.

10. They require that the author shall make the reader feel a deep

interest in the personages of his tale and in their fate; and that he shall make the reader love the good people in the tale and hate the bad ones. But the reader of the *Deerslayer* tale dislikes the good people in it, is indifferent to the others, and wishes they would all get drowned together.

11. They require that the characters in a tale shall be so clearly defined that the reader can tell beforehand what each will do in a given emergency. But in the *Deerslayer* tale this rule is vacated.

In addition to these large rules there are some little ones. These re-   *15*
quire that the author shall

12. *Say* what he is proposing to say, nor merely come near it.

13. Use the right word, not its second cousin.

14. Eschew surplusage.

15. Not omit necessary details.

16. Avoid slovenliness of form.   *20*

17. Use good grammar.

18. Employ a simple and straightforward style.

Even these seven are coldly and persistently violated in the *Deerslayer* tale.

Cooper's gift in the way of invention was not a rich endowment; but such as it was he liked to work it, he was pleased with the effects, and indeed he did some quite sweet things with it. In his little box of stage properties he kept six or eight cunning devices, tricks, artifices for his savages and woodsmen to deceive and circumvent each other with, and he was never so happy as when he was working these innocent things and seeing them go. A favorite one was to make a moccasined person tread in the tracks of the moccasined enemy, and thus hide his own trail. Cooper wore out barrels and barrels of moccasins in working that trick. Another stage-property that he pulled out of his box pretty frequently was his broken twig. He prized his broken twig above all the rest of his effects, and worked it the hardest. It is a restful chapter in any book of his when somebody doesn't step on a dry twig and alarm all the reds and whites for two hundred yards around. Every time a Cooper person is in peril, and absolute silence is worth four dollars a minute, he is sure to step on a dry twig. There may be a hundred handier things to step on, but that wouldn't satisfy Cooper. Cooper requires him to turn out and find a dry twig; and if he can't do it, go and borrow one. In fact the Leather Stocking Series ought to have been called the Broken Twig Series.

I am sorry there is not room to put in a few dozen instances of the   *25*
delicate art of the forest, as practiced by Natty Bumppo and some of the

other Cooperian experts. Perhaps we may venture two or three samples. Cooper was a sailor—a naval officer; yet he gravely tells us how a vessel, driving toward a lee shore in a gale, is steered for a particular spot by her skipper because he knows of an *undertow* there which will hold her back against the gale and save her. For just pure woodcraft, or sailor-craft, or whatever it is, isn't that neat? For several years Cooper was daily in the society of artillery, and he ought to have noticed that when a cannon ball strikes the ground it either buries itself or skips a hundred feet or so; skips again a hundred feet or so—and so on, till it finally gets tired and rolls. Now in one place he loses some "females"—as he always calls women—in the edge of a wood near a plain at night in a fog, on purpose to give Bumppo a chance to show off the delicate art of the forest before the reader. These mislaid people are hunting for a fort. They hear a cannon-blast, and a cannon-ball presently comes rolling into the wood and stops at their feet. To the females this suggests nothing. The case is very different with the admirable Bumppo. I wish I may never know peace again if he doesn't strike out promptly and *follow the track* of that cannon-ball across the plain through the dense fog and find the fort. Isn't it a daisy? If Cooper had any real knowledge of Nature's ways of doing things, he had a most delicate art in concealing the fact. For instance: one of his acute Indian experts, Chingachgook (pronounced Chicago, I think), has lost the trail of a person he is tracking through the forest. Apparently that trail is hopelessly lost. Neither you nor I could ever have guessed out the way to find it. It was very different with Chicago. Chicago was not stumped for long. He turned a running stream out of its course, and there, in the slush in its old bed, were that person's moccasin-tracks. The current did not wash them away, as it would have done in all other like cases—no, even the eternal laws of Nature have to vacate when Cooper wants to put up a delicate job of woodcraft on the reader.

We must be a little wary when Brander Matthews tells us that Cooper's books "reveal an extraordinary fulness of invention." As a rule, I am quite willing to accept Brander Matthews's literary judgments and applaud his lucid and graceful phrasing of them; but that particular statement needs to be taken with a few tons of salt. Bless your heart, Cooper hadn't any more invention than a horse; and I don't mean a high-class horse, either; I mean a clothes-horse. It would be very difficult to find a really clever "situation" in Cooper's books; and still more difficult to find one of any kind which he has failed to render absurd by his handling of it. Look at the episodes of "the caves;" and at the celebrated scuffle between Maqua and those others on the table-land a few days later; and at Hurry Harry's queer water-transit from the castle to the ark, and at Deerslayer's half hour with his first corpse; and at the quarrel between Hurry Harry and Deerslayer later; and at—but choose for yourself; you can't go amiss.

If Cooper had been an observer, his inventive faculty would have worked better, not more interestingly, but more rationally, more plausibly. Cooper's proudest creations in the way of "situations" suffer noticeably from the absence of the observer's protecting gift. Cooper's eye was splendidly inaccurate. Cooper seldom saw anything correctly. He saw nearly all things as through a glass eye, darkly. Of course a man who cannot see the commonest little everyday matters accurately is working at a disadvantage when he is constructing a "situation." In the *Deerslayer* tale Cooper has a stream which is fifty feet wide, where it flows out of a lake; it presently narrows to twenty as it meanders along for no given reason, and yet, when a stream acts like that it ought to be required to explain itself. Fourteen pages later the width of the brook's outlet from the lake has suddenly shrunk thirty feet, and become "the narrowest part of the stream." This shrinkage is not accounted for. The stream has bends in it, a sure indication that it has alluvial banks, and cuts them; yet these bends are only thirty and fifty feet long. If Cooper had been a nice and punctilious observer he would have noticed that the bends were oftener nine hundred feet long than short of it.

Cooper made the exit of that stream fifty feet wide in the first place, for no particular reason; in the second place, he narrowed it to less than twenty to accommodate some Indians. He bends a "sapling" to the form of an arch over this narrow passage, and conceals six Indians in its foliage. They are "laying" for a settler's scow or ark which is coming up the stream on its way to the lake; it is being hauled against the still current by a rope whose stationary end is anchored in the lake; its rate of progress cannot be more than a mile an hour. Cooper describes the ark, but pretty obscurely. In the matter of dimensions "it was little more than a modern canal boat." Let us guess, then, that it was about 140 feet long. It was of "greater breadth than common." Let us guess, then, that it was about sixteen feet wide. This leviathan had been prowling down bends where it had only two feet of space to spare on each side. We cannot too much admire this miracle. A low-roofed log dwelling occupies "two-third's of the ark's length"—a dwelling ninety feet long and sixteen feet wide, let us say—a kind of vestibule train. The dwelling has two rooms—each forty-five feet long and sixteen feet wide, let us guess. One of them is the bed-room of the Hutter girls, Judith and Hetty; the other is the parlor, in the day time, at night it is papa's bed chamber. The ark is arriving at the stream's exit, now, whose width has been reduced to less than twenty feet to accommodate the Indians—say to eighteen. There is a foot to spare on each side of the boat. Did the Indians notice that there was going to be a tight squeeze there? Did they notice that they could make money by climbing down out of that arched sapling and just stepping aboard when the ark scraped by? No; other Indians would have noticed these things, but Cooper's Indians never notice anything. Cooper thinks they are marvelous creatures for noticing, but he was almost always in error about his Indians. There was seldom a sane one among them.

The ark is 140 feet long; the dwelling is 90 feet long. The idea of the Indians is to drop softly and secretly from the arched sapling to the dwelling as the ark creeps along under it at the rate of a mile an hour, and butcher the family. It will take the ark a minute and a half to pass under. It will take the 90-foot dwelling a minute to pass under. Now, then, what did the six Indians do? It would take you thirty years to guess, and even then you would have to give it up, I believe. Therefore, I will tell you what the Indians did. Their chief, a person of quite extraordinary intellect for a Cooper Indian, warily watched the canal boat as it squeezed along under him, and when he had got his calculations fined down to exactly the right shade, as he judged, he let go and dropped. And *missed the house!* That is actually what he did. He missed the house, and landed in the stern of the scow. It was not much of a fall, yet it knocked him silly. He lay there unconscious. If the house had been 97 feet long, he would have made the trip. The fault was Cooper's, not his. The error lay in the construction of the house. Cooper was no architect.

There still remained in the roost five Indians. The boat has passed under and is now out of their reach. Let me explain what the five did— you would not be able to reason it out for yourself. No. 1 jumped for the boat, but fell in the water astern of it. Then No. 2 jumped for the boat, but fell in the water still further astern of it. Then No. 3 jumped for the boat, and fell a good way astern of it. Then No. 4 jumped for the boat, and fell in the water *away* astern. Then even No. 5 made a jump for the boat—for he was a Cooper Indian. In the matter of intellect, the difference between a Cooper Indian and the Indian that stands in front of the cigar shop is not spacious. The scow episode is really a sublime burst of invention; but it does not thrill, because the inaccuracy of the details throws a sort of air of fictitiousness and general improbability over it. This comes of Cooper's inadequacy as an observer.

The reader will find some examples of Cooper's high talent for inaccurate observation in the account of the shooting match in *The Pathfinder*. "A common wrought nail was driven lightly into the target, its head having been first touched with paint." The color of the paint is not stated—an important omission, but Cooper deals freely in important omissions. No, after all, it was not an important omission; for this nail head is a *hundred yards* from the marksman and could not be seen by them at that distance no matter what its color might be. How far can the best eyes see a common house fly? A hundred yards? It is quite impossible. Very well, eyes that cannot see a house fly that is a hundred yards away cannot see an ordinary nail head at that distance, for the size of the two objects is the same. It takes a keen eye to see a fly or a nail head at fifty yards—one hundred and fifty feet. Can the reader do it?

30

The nail was lightly driven, its head painted, and game called. Then the Cooper miracles began. The bullet of the first marksman chipped an edge of the nail head; the next man's bullet drove the nail a little way into the target—and removed all the paint. Haven't the miracles gone far enough now? Not to suit Cooper; for the purpose of this whole scheme is to show off his prodigy, Deerslayer-Hawkeye-Long-Rifle-Leather-Stocking-Pathfinder-Bumppo before the ladies.

> "Be all ready to clench it, boys!" cried out Pathfinder, stepping into his friend's tracks the instant they were vacant. "Never mind a new nail; I can see that, though the paint is gone, and what I can see, I can hit at a hundred yards, though it were only a mosquito's eye. Be ready to clench!"
>
> The rifle cracked, the bullet sped its way and the head of the nail was buried in the wood, covered by the piece of flattened lead.

There, you see, is a man who could hunt flies with a rifle, and command a ducal salary in a Wild West show to-day, if we had him back with us.

The recorded feat is certainly surprising, just as it stands; but it is not surprising enough for Cooper. Cooper adds a touch. He has made Pathfinder do this miracle with another man's rifle, and not only that, but Pathfinder did not have even the advantage of loading it himself. He had everything against him, and yet he made that impossible shot, and not only made it, but did it with absolute confidence, saying, "Be ready to clench." Now a person like that would have undertaken that same feat with a brickbat, and with Cooper to help he would have achieved it, too.

Pathfinder showed off handsomely that day before the ladies. His 35 very first feat was a thing which no Wild West show can touch. He was standing with the group of marksmen, observing—a hundred yards from the target, mind: one Jasper raised his rifle and drove the centre of the bull's-eye. Then the quartermaster fired. The target exhibited no result this time. There was a laugh. "It's a dead miss," said Major Lundie. Pathfinder waited an impressive moment or two, then said in that calm, indifferent, know-it-all way of his, "No, Major—he has covered Jasper's bullet, as will be seen if any one will take the trouble to examine the target."

Wasn't it remarkable! How *could* he see that little pellet fly through the air and enter that distant bullet-hole? Yet that is what he did; for nothing is impossible to a Cooper person. Did any of those people have any deep-seated doubts about this thing? No; for that would imply sanity, and these were all Cooper people.

> The respect for Pathfinder's skill and for his *quickness and accuracy of sight* (the italics are mine) was so profound and general, that the instant he made this declaration the spectators began to dis-

trust their own opinions, and a dozen rushed to the target in order to ascertain the fact. There, sure enough, it was found that the quartermaster's bullet had gone through the hole made by Jasper's, and that, too, so accurately as to require a minute examination to be certain of the circumstances, which, however, was soon established by discovering one bullet over the other in the stump against which the target was placed.

They made a "minute" examination; but never mind, how could they know that there were two bullets in that hole without digging the latest one out? for neither probe nor eyesight could prove the presence of any more than one bullet. Did they dig? No; as we shall see. It is the Pathfinder's turn now; he steps out before the ladies, takes aim, and fires.

But alas! here is a disappointment; an incredible, an unimaginable disappointment—for the target's aspect is unchanged; there is nothing there but that same old bullet hole!

"If one dared to hint at such a thing," cried Major Duncan, "I should say that the Pathfinder has also missed the target."

As nobody had missed it yet, the "also" was not necessary; but never mind about that, for the Pathfinder is going to speak.

"No, no, Major," said he, confidently, "that *would* be a risky declaration. I didn't load the piece, and can't say what was in it, but if it was lead, you will find the bullet driving down those of the Quartermaster and Jasper, else is not my name Pathfinder."

A shout from the target announced the truth of this assertion.

Is the miracle sufficient as it stands? Not for Cooper. The Pathfinder 40 speaks again, as he "now slowly advances towards the stage occupied by the females:"

"That's not all, boys, that's not all; if you find the target touched at all. I'll own to a miss. The Quartermaster cut the wood, but you'll find no wood cut by that last messenger."

The miracle is at last complete. He knew—doubtless *saw*—at the distance of a hundred yards—that his bullet had passed into the hole *without fraying the edges*. There were now three bullets in that one hole—three bullets imbedded processionally in the body of the stump back of the target. Everybody knew this—somehow or other—and yet nobody had dug any of them out to make sure. Cooper is not a close observer, but he is interesting. He is certainly always that, no matter what happens. And he is more interesting when he is not noticing what he is about than when he is. This is a considerable merit.

The conversations in the Cooper books have a curious sound in our modern ears. To believe that such talk really even came out of people's mouths would be to believe that there was a time when time was of no value to a person who thought he had something to say; when a man's mouth was a rolling-mill, and busied itself all day long in turning four-foot pigs of thought into thirty-foot bars of conversational railroad iron by attenuation; when subjects were seldom faithfully stuck to, but the talk wandered all around and arrived nowhere; when conversations consisted mainly of irrelevances, with here and there a relevancy, a relevancy with an embarrassed look, as not being able to explain how it got there.

Cooper was certainly not a master in the construction of dialogue. Inaccurate observation defeated him here as it defeated him in so many other enterprises of his. He even failed to notice that the man who talks corrupt English six days in the week must and will talk it on the seventh, and can't help himself. In the *Deerslayer* story he lets Deerslayer talk the showiest kind of book talk sometimes, and at other times the basest of base dialects. For instance, when someone asks him if he has a sweetheart, and if so, where she abides, this is his majestic answer:

> "She's in the forest—hanging from the boughs of the trees, in a soft rain—in the dew on the open grass—the clouds that float about in the blue heavens—the birds that sing in the woods—the sweet springs where I slake my thirst—and in all the other glorious gifts that come from God's Providence!"

And he preceded that, a little before, with this:

> "It consarns me as all things that touches a fri'nd consarns a fri'nd."

And this is another of his remarks: 45

> "If I was Injin born, now, I might tell of this, or carry in the scalp and boast of the expl'ite afore the whole tribe; or if my inimy had only been a bear"—and so on.

We cannot imagine such a thing as a veteran Scotch Commander-in-Chief comporting himself in the field like a windy melodramatic actor, but Cooper could. On one occasion Alice and Cora were being chased by the French through a fog in the neighborhood of their father's fort:

> "*Point de quartier aux coquins!*" cried an eager pursuer, who seemed to direct the operations of the enemy.
>
>   "Stand firm and be ready, my gallant 60ths!" suddenly exclaimed a voice above them; "wait to see the enemy; fire low, and sweep the glacis."
>
>   "Father! father!" exclaimed a piercing cry from out the mist; "it is I! Alice! thy own Elsie! spare, O! save your daughters!"
>
>   "Hold!" shouted the former speaker, in the awful tones of

parental agony, the sound reaching even to the woods, and rolling back in solemn echo. "'Tis she! God has restored me my
children! Throw open the sally-port; to the field, 60ths, to the
field; pull not a trigger, lest ye kill my lambs! Drive off these
dogs of France with your steel."

Cooper's word-sense was singularly dull. When a person has a poor
ear for music he will flat and sharp right along without knowing it. He
keeps near the tune, but it is *not* the tune. When a person has a poor ear
for words, the result is a literary flatting and sharping; you perceive what
he is intending to say, but you also perceive that he doesn't *say* it. This
is Cooper. He was not a word-musician. His ear was satisfied with the
approximate word. I will furnish some circumstantial evidence in support of this charge. My instances are gathered from half a dozen pages
of the tale called *Deerslayer*. He uses "verbal," for "oral"; "precision,"
for "facility"; "phenomena," for "marvels"; "necessary," for "predetermined"; "unsophisticated," for "primitive"; "preparation," for "ex-
pectancy"; "rebuked," for "subdued"; "dependent on," for "resulting
from"; "fact," for "condition"; "fact," for "conjecture"; "precaution,"
for "caution"; "explain," for "determine"; "mortified," for "disappointed"; "meretricious," for "factitious"; "materially," for "considerably"; "decreasing," for "deepening"; "increasing," for "disappearing";
"embedded," for "enclosed"; "treacherous," for "hostile"; "stood,"
for "stopped"; "softened," for "replaced"; "rejoined," for "remarked";
"situation," for "condition"; "different," for "differing"; "insensible,"
for "unsentient"; "brevity," for "celerity"; "distrusted," for "suspicious"; "mental imbecility," for "imbecility"; "eyes," for "sight";
"counteracting," for "opposing"; "funeral obsequies," for "obsequies."

There have been daring people in the world who claimed that Cooper could write English, but they are all dead now—all dead but Lounsbury. I don't remember that Lounsbury makes the claim in so many
words, still he makes it, for he says that *Deerslayer* is a "pure work of
art." Pure, in that connection, means faultless—faultless in all details—
and language is a detail. If Mr. Lounsbury had only compared Cooper's
English with the English which he writes himself—but it is plain that
he didn't; and so it is likely that he imagines until this day that Cooper's
is as clean and compact as his own. Now I feel sure, deep down in my
heart, that Cooper wrote about the poorest English that exists in our
language, and that the English of *Deerslayer* is the very worst than even
Cooper ever wrote.

I may be mistaken, but it does seem to me that *Deerslayer* is not a
work of art in any sense; it does seem to me that it is destitute of every
detail that goes to the making of a work of art; in truth, it seems to me
that *Deerslayer* is just simply a literary *delirium tremens*.

A work of art? It has no invention; it has no order, system, se-   *50*
quence, or result, it has no lifelikeness, no thrill, no stir, no seeming of

reality; its characters are confusedly drawn, and by their acts and words they prove that they are not the sort of people the author claims that they are; its humor is pathetic; its pathos is funny; its conversations are—oh! indescribable; its love-scenes odious; its English a crime against the language.

Counting these out, what is left is Art. I think we must all admit that.

Outward Exploration: Discussion

1. Discuss some of the rules of literary art that Twain lists in his essay. Which ones are still valid? Which ones seem either out-of-date or simply wrong? Explain.
2. Why does Twain begin his essay with quotations from three literary experts?
3. What is Twain's major criticism of those critics? What is the implication of his criticism?
4. Why does Twain object to Cooper's having "six or eight cunning devices, tricks, artifices for his savages and woodsmen to deceive and circumvent each other with"?
5. Discuss Twain's devices for mocking Cooper.
6. What are Twain's objections to the river episode?
7. What are Twain's objections to the shooting episode?
8. In the next-to-last paragraph, Twain gives a negative summary of art. Rephrase it so that you have Twain's definition of art. How does this definition match up against the rules at the beginning of the essay?
9. How fair is Twain's criticism of Cooper? Explain.

Outward Exploration: Writing

1. Make up your own list of rules of what is required for a text to be considered a successful piece of literary fiction (it can include whatever rules of Twain's you agree with as well as some of your own). Then write an essay evaluating some work of fiction. For example, you apply your rules to one of the stories in this book, or to some short story or novel or play that you have read for another class or on your own.
2. Make up your own list of rules for any kind of text (for example, a movie, a television series, a painting, a building). Then apply those rules to one particular text. For instance, you might write rules for a successful science fiction or horror movie, or for a successful comedy.

3. Write an essay in which you apply Twain's rules to some other text. For instance, how well does Nathaniel Hawthorne's "Young Goodman Brown" fare when evaluated in terms of Twain's rules? How does that evaluation compare to your responses to the story itself? Or use those rules to judge a movie or television show. For example, how well would a television show like *Star Trek: The Next Generation* or a movie series like *Indiana Jones* fare when judged by such rules? Compare what the rules compel you to say about the text with your own responses and critical judgment of that text. If your judgment varies from that which the rules lead you to conclude, what other rules are influencing your judgment? Ultimately, the point of this essay will be to evaluate Twain's rules (for example, you might find that his rules are useful or somewhat useful or totally misguided).

4. Create your own criteria for anything (for instance, a successful meal, a successful college course, a successful vacation). Write an essay using those criteria to evaluate one specific example. The essay may be either humorous or serious.

5. Read a selection from Cooper and then write a rebuttal of Twain's essay.

6. For a research project, you might read passages from several books which suggest criteria for writing fiction. For example, using their indices, you might locate passages in several books that deal with plot structure or point of view or dialogue or some other element of fiction. Compare and contrast the advice they give, then apply whatever criteria seem appropriate to some literary text.

   There are really two types of books about fiction writing. There are many books which suggest formulae for writing stories and novels "that sell." These books tend to be prescriptive and not very useful to those who wish to be serious writers. They might, however, be good sources of rules for this assignment. The other type of book tries to help writers find and direct their creative spark in imaginative ways. These books are useful in that they focus on creating original fiction rather than on churning out an imitation of the current best-selling writer. Some such books include Carol Bly's *The Passionate, Accurate Story* (Milkweed Editions, 1990), John Braine's *Writing a Novel* (McGraw-Hill, 1975), Dorothea Brande's *Becoming a Writer* (J. P. Tarcher, 1981), Annie Dillard's *The Writing Life* (Harper and Row, 1989) and *Living by Fiction* (Harper and Row, 1982), E. M. Forster's *Aspects of the Novel* (Harcourt Brace and Company, 1956), John Gardner's *The Art of Fiction: Notes on Craft for Young Writers* (Alfred A. Knopf, 1984) and *Becoming a Novelist* (Harper and Row, 1983), Rust Hills's *Writing in General and the Short Story in Particular* (Bantam, 1979), Jerome Stern's *Making Shapely Fiction* (Norton, 1991). If you are interested in becoming a fiction writer, these are the kinds of books you should read.

Chinese Puzzle

GRACE MING-YEE WAI

☐ *Inward Exploration*

Write at least one paragraph describing the influence of some adult on your life (for example, your mother or father, an uncle, aunt, or teacher).

I am a first generation Chinese-American woman educated in both   1
private and public American schools. I grew up in the mid-South city
of Memphis, Tennessee, where there were very few other Asian families. We lived in the South, I realized after my teens, primarily for economic reasons. Although there were more Asians in cities such as New
York, Los Angeles, or San Francisco, it would have been very expensive
to live in those cities, and our grocery store would have had much more
competition. My parents immigrated to the United States from Hong
Kong before I was born, for a better life for themselves and their children. Neither had a college education, but both emphasized hard work
and the importance of education. Like all parents, they hoped their children would be fortunate enough to receive a quality education that
would provide future opportunity and financial security.

My sister, brother, and I have been lucky to receive an education
and all of us have reached or are near our goals, but not without pain
and sacrifices. When I was 10 years old, my father was shot and killed
while being robbed for $26 in change. He was the favorite son of seven
living children. He took in one of my cousins from Hong Kong so she
could study nursing. My youngest uncle was the only one of their
generation to become a professional, primarily because he was lucky
enough to have the opportunity to go to dental school at the University
of Tennessee in Memphis.

Dad owned a small grocery store in a poor neighborhood. My parents worked more than 12 hours a day, seven days a week. We lived
above the store in five rooms and one bathroom. At different times, my
grandmother, three uncles, an aunt and her two sons also lived with us.
My brother, sister and I had a maid who came six days a week to take
care of us. I became very attached to her and cried on her day off. I still
send Willie Christmas cards every year.

My father had a fierce temper. Whenever something upset him a
little, he yelled a lot, so my brother, sister, and I shuddered at the
thought of angering him. His bark was worse than his bite, however.

He was also very fair. He loved us all very much. He and Mom worked hard for us, for the family. Family meant everything.

Since Mom and Dad worked so much, there was not much time for us kids. We occasionally went to Shoney's for a hamburger. It was a big treat to pat the statue of Big Boy on the stomach upon entering and exiting the restaurant. Dad took me to the dog track once because I wanted to go with him. I think I just wanted very much to have him for myself since he was always helping other people and working in the store with Mom.

I was the first to go to school because I was the oldest child. When I was four years old, I went to prekindergarten at a small, private, Episcopal school. On my first day, Dad drove me to the door, but he would not take me to my class. I knew where my class was located because we visited earlier to meet my teachers. My heart was pounding with a force I did not know my little body had when I jumped out of the car, and I know fear was evident on my face, but Dad didn't budge. I asked, "Daddy, aren't you coming with me?" He replied, "No, Grace, you know where your class is and who your teachers are. You can go by yourself." He was teaching me to be self-sufficient at four. Still, it must have been difficult for him to watch his firstborn walk alone into a world of which he would not have a part. It was my first day of independence.

I clearly remember my sixth birthday because Dad was in the hospital with pneumonia. He was working so hard he paid very little attention to his health. As a result, he spent almost the entire summer before I entered first grade in the hospital. Mom visited him nightly. On my birthday I was allowed to see him. I have memories of sitting happily in the lobby of the hospital talking to the nurses, telling them with a big smile that I was going to see my dad because it was my birthday. I couldn't wait to see him because children under 12 were not allowed to visit patients, so I had not seen him in a long time. When I entered his hospital room, I saw tubes inserted into his nose and needles stuck in his arm. He was very, very thin. I was frightened and wanted to cry, but I was determined to have a good visit. So I stayed for a while, and he wished me a happy birthday. When it was time to go, I kissed him good-bye and waited until I left his room to cry.

In first grade, I lived with my grandparents because a public elementary school was just across the street. My father bought the house for my grandparents with plans for us three children to attend Levi Elementary School since it was close and convenient. My brother and sister stayed with my parents because Nancy was only four, and Robert was in kindergarten at my old school which was near the store. I felt very isolated and alone in that great big house away from my immediate family.

I learned from my father while in first grade one valuable lesson that still affects me now: never be afraid to ask questions. I was very self-conscious and timid in school. My grades were falling. My father asked me: "How are you going to learn if you don't ask questions?" Even then, when I was six years of age, he tried to make me realize the importance of taking initiative in school. He made me realize improving in school was up to me because he could not be with me all the time.

In those days, my grandmother took care of me. She had moved to   *10* America when I was three years old to be with my youngest uncle when he came to go to college. My grandfather joined us three years later. Every morning my grandmother got me dressed and made my breakfast. While I sat at the dining room table, she combed and brushed my hair to prepare me for school. She spoke no English, so we conversed in Cantonese. Every day after school, I called the store to talk to my mother. I really missed being with my parents, brother, and sister and looked forward to their weekly visits. Of course, only one parent visited at a time because someone had to be at the store. I was very jealous that Robert and Nancy were able to stay with my parents.

After school, my grandfather liked to see what I learned that day. It was always a treat to show him the new words I was taught to write in school. Every night I rewrote all the new words for him. He always smiled with approval. Sometimes he helped me with my mathematics. My grandfather played with numbers a lot and actually had an abacus on his desk, which he used daily.

My grandmother did not read or write English. I was learning material she would never understand. She was my caretaker. She cooked and cleaned the house. She fed and bathed me. Neither of my grandparents worked. At that time, they were in their mid-sixties. They had no desire to learn the culture of the new land. Their livelihood depended upon my father, and they were happy merely to be near their children's families.

In the summer, my sister and brother joined me at our grandparents' house. We played a lot more since we had a yard. At the store, we stayed upstairs mostly. When summer was over, I was alone with my grandparents again. That year, in second grade, I was often chased around by Albert, a little black boy in my class. He would try to kiss me. Other children were fascinated by my straight black hair, and would constantly try to touch it. I was jeered at by other children for being Chinese, for having squinty eyes and a flat nose. I was almost ashamed of being Chinese, and being so young I did not understand it at all. I had grown up around other blacks who had frequented our store. Many were my friends, but in school I was having trouble—with black and white children. There were no other Chinese children in my school.

I refrained from telling my parents about Albert because earlier in the school year, I had been hit on the head during recess by a classmate with a baseball bat and had to have stitches. My father told me I should not have been playing so recklessly in school. But one day, in my attempt to hide from Albert, I fell and scraped both knees badly. The principal found me and told me that I should tell my teacher if he did it again. After the next episode, I told my teacher, but made the mistake of embarrassing myself by telling in front of the class. What hurt even more was the fact that my teacher did not do anything about it. Finally, I decided I must tell my parents. I think I feared they would think I had done something wrong, that it was my fault—that perhaps I provoked the boy. I also feared my father's temper.

First I told my mother, and she encouraged me to tell my dad about it. He would make the final decision. I sighed and then proceeded to creep upstairs where he was taking a nap and sat outside their bedroom. When my father awoke, fearfully, I told him about what was happening to me in school. Dad was so understanding. To my relief, he was calm and collected, not angry. He asked me what I wanted to do. He asked if I would like to go to the private school my brother and sister attended. Would I! I was so happy. Yes! I wanted to go back to school with Robert and Nancy! That meant, also, that I would be moving back to the store to live with my parents.

I realize now that Dad was very angry. Not at me, but angry with the teachers and the principal of my elementary school for ignoring my distress. He took me out of Levi in the middle of the year. I feel for the people Dad dealt with to get me out of school. I imagine he probably went there red-faced and smoking with anger to fill out the necessary paperwork. It is funny, though, how Dad let me feel I made the decision to leave Levi.

My father was a loving and devoted son to my grandparents. He made sure they were happy and comfortable. He wanted them with us so he was assured of their well-being. My grandfather had fallen ill when I was around seven years old. The doctors thought he had cancer. Twenty years ago, that meant certain death. The night the diagnosis was given, I was alone with my parents after the store was closed. Dad was crying. I was frightened because I had never before seen him cry. Taking off his glasses and looking at me with red, teary eyes and unmistakable pain, he asked me, "Do you love your Ye-Ye?" It was difficult to speak to him when he seemed so vulnerable, but with all the courage I could muster and tears welling up in my eyes, I answered, "Yes." Mom was behind Dad comforting him. At seven years of age, I was learning what it is to love your parents, and I was learning even Dads cry. Thankfully, my grandfather's cancer went into remission after treatment.

When Dad caught wind of the fact that I was doing poorly on my multiplication tables in third grade, he drilled me nightly in the back of the store where he stood behind the meat counter. I remember sweating and feeling extremely apprehensive and fearful of his wrath if I answered incorrectly. I quickly learned my multiplication tables inside out.

On the day he died, Dad came to my grandparents' house where my brother, sister, and I were staying for Thanksgiving weekend. He planned to go car-shopping with his older brother. I went along with them. We had lunch at Shoney's afterward, at my suggestion, of course.

I did not care about car-shopping. I just wanted to spend time with Dad, even if we were with my uncle. I chattered away while we had lunch. When we returned to my grandparents' house, he took a nap in my bedroom before going back to work at the store. I was to wake him in an hour. Upon leaving, he picked me up for a big hug and kiss good-bye. I had my arms around his neck and my head on his shoulder. He told me to be good before putting me down. I did not know it would be the last time I would see him alive.

Later, in the afternoon, I heard my grandfather making dozens of   20
phone calls, saying with grief and shock: "Ah, Davey say joh loh, Davey say joh loh!" meaning, "Davey's dead, Davey's dead!" I couldn't believe his words and rushed to tell my sister and brother, who responded with disbelief and dismay. They thought I was lying to them, playing a cruel trick on them. Later, when we had heard the grown-ups talking and were in fact sure Dad was killed, the three of us went up to our favorite spot in the attic where we cried and cried and hugged one another. We were in the way of the adults. They did not know how to talk to us, nor would they answer our questions. We only had each other for comfort.

My aunts and uncles from various parts of the country left their families to rush to Memphis the day Dad was shot. We had a full house of people who came by to bring food, to pay respects. It was very late in the evening before all but family were left in our house. It seemed peaceful once again. My best friend brought a plant the next day. We were both at a loss for words—we did not need them. It was enough just to see her.

The next day, there was an article in the newspaper about what happened. My aunt said it did not do my father justice. The robber was never caught by the police. In fact, the police later found the bag of change lying in an alley nearby. My mom's reaction was calm as she told me, "Even if they find him, it won't bring your daddy back, Grace."

The day of my father's funeral was rainy and cold. There was a long procession of cars on the way to the cemetery. My father was well respected by others in the community and had many friends. My grandmother did not attend the funeral. As long as I knew her, she never once set foot in a hospital, nor did she go to funerals. My grandfather also elected not to attend, but as the hearse passed by their house, he ran out, down the long walkway to the gate with a black raincoat held above his head. He wished to open the coffin to see his son one more time, but it was nailed shut. It was only possible for him to touch the casket.

All my teachers and the principal of our school attended Dad's funeral. Willie was there too. We were all crying when they came to see us. Later, my best friend told me the teachers didn't think we would be returning to school for a while. They were surprised to find us in class the following day. My friends did not know how to react to me, and in homeroom, my teacher asked, in front of everyone, if I was okay. I was not okay. I was in pain, but what could I do? I lost my father. He was never coming back. I tried to be strong, and looking down at my desk, I said, "Yes, I'm okay."

We were so young: Robert eight, and Nancy seven. Now we are grown adults. I wonder what it would have been like if Dad were living during our developing years. I suspect I would be a very different person. I am very much a feminist and a professional now. I don't think he would have allowed me to move 1,000 miles from home to live on my own after college. I probably would not have been allowed to participate in many things such as dating, parties, and school activities if he were alive during my adolescence, for he was extremely strict.

We visited his gravesite every year on his birthday, on the anniversary of his death, and on holidays such as New Year's and Christmas. Following my grandmother's Asian traditions, we brought incense to burn at the gravesite, and food: a bowl of rice, fruit, a main dish for his spirit to eat. We also burned special paper, which my grandmother stated represented money for Dad to spend in the afterlife. We did these things for her since she would not go to the cemetery. Following American tradition, we also brought flowers. When the incense was lit, the money burning, and the food set out with chopsticks along with tea and sometimes scotch (he had to have something to drink as well as utensils!), we took turns paying our respects by bowing to the headstone three times and silently told his spirit whatever we wanted to tell him, whatever was on our minds. When done, we bowed again three times to bid farewell until the next time.

I write this now because it is more than 14 years since my father's death. I think about how fast those 14 years have gone by and all the changes and growing that have taken place. I wonder if he is proud of me now. I wonder what I would be like today if he were alive. Even though I only had him in the first 10 years of my life, I know there is much of him in me. I have his temperament, his strictness, and his self-righteous nature. I have his sense of fairness, generosity, and loyalty. He taught me much in those first 10 years. There are also scars from his death because my family did not talk about our loss. We took the blow and went on with life.

In the last four years, I have also lost both grandparents. They are buried with my father. One day, my mother and uncles will join them. Whenever I return to Memphis to visit family and friends, I also go to the cemetery to visit my father and grandparents. I don't follow all the traditions my grandmother so treasured, but I do carry incense and flowers with me. I still bow and have my talk with each. Those are always peaceful and contemplative moments. Sometimes I drive by the old store, the old house, and the private elementary school to relive some of my past.

Death does not get easier. The people I love will not be with me forever. That hurts. Death, however, is a part of life we all face at some point. Nevertheless, it is a comfort to me to believe that after death, those I love go somewhere nice and comfortable. My grandmother always wished to return as a bird—to fly over the earth—soaring and free. I hope she made it.

❏ Outward Exploration: Discussion

1. Describe the personality of Wai's father.
2. Why did she have to live with her grandparents for a while?
3. What was her experience in school?
4. Explain Wai's relationship with her father.
5. What was the long-term effect of her father's death?

❏ Outward Exploration: Writing

1. Write an essay about an important or cataclysmic event in your life.
2. Write an essay about a particular family member who has had a significant impact on your life.
3. Wai speculates about what her life would have been like if her father had lived, and she concludes that it might have been very different and perhaps not as pleasing. Following her lead in that section of her essay, write an essay of your own in which you speculate about "what if X had never happened."
4. Write an essay exploring your concept of *death*.
5. Write an essay analyzing the similarities and differences between the father–child relationship as revealed in Wai's essay and one other that deals with fathers (for example, James Baldwin's "Notes of a Native Son" or Raymond Carver's "My Father's Life").

Glossary

Accommodation The process of letting your readers know that you understand "where they are coming from," that you understand their assumptions, their beliefs, and their concerns about whatever your essay's subject is. Accommodation is particularly crucial in arguments since most readers will be closed to your ideas unless they first see that you understand their position.

Active voice A term signifying the active relationship between the subject and the verb in a sentence. When a verb is in the active voice, its subject acts. For example: "Elly scored the basket." *Elly* is the subject and performs the action of scoring. See *passive voice.*

Adage A traditional saying, usually a succinct statement that expresses a basic truth or practical precept.

Analogy An extended comparison between two similar but unrelated items which uses the familiar or the simpler to explain the unfamiliar or more complex (for example, John Donne says that two lovers parting is similar to a virtuous man's dying and taking leave of his soul).

Analysis A process of thought by which a whole is divided into its parts in order to study the individual parts and how they connect to make that whole.

Aphorism A brief statement of a truth or an opinion; an *adage.*

Argue The process of putting forth reasons for and against an idea or a proposition. It is the attempt to prove by reasoning and by giving evidence to support an idea or a proposition.

Argument A mode of expository writing that features *logical* support of an idea or a proposition and, often, a logical attack on the opposite idea or proposition (for example, an argument in favor of gun control would probably also attack the reasons offered by those opposing gun control). As with the other forms of expository writing, argument may be the major mode of a complete essay, or it may be included as part of an essay whose major thrust is *narration, exposition,* or *description.*

Cause and effect One of the classical methods for exploring a subject. You explain why something happened or what its results were.

Claim An assertion about the nature of things. It is the idea or proposition that you are trying to prove in an *argument.* For example: "Grading should be abolished and all courses should be pass/fail."

Clause A group of words having both a subject and a verb.

Coherence A clear relationship between sentences within a paragraph, between paragraphs within a section, and between sections within an essay.

Communication The conscious attempt to convey information and ideas to an audience (as far as this book is concerned, the major mode for communicating is writing). The term implies your making conscious decisions as a writer—for example, selecting words and phrasings which will accurately suggest the meaning you wish. Communication can be direct, indirect, explicit, or implicit. With exploratory essays, as with all essays, the primary mode of communication should be direct and explicit. Exploratory essays, however, have an implicit component as well and may use symbolism, evocative language, and emotional appeals to suggest some of their meanings. The major point of an exploratory essay, however, should usually be made explicit.

Comparison and contrast A rhetorical strategy that involves noting the significant similarities and differences between two or more items. Usually you should use this method to accomplish one of three goals: (1) to show that two seemingly very similar items are actually significantly different (for example, the economic plans of two Democratic presidential candidates); (2) to show that two seemingly very different items are actually very similar (for example, the economic plans of the Democratic and Republican presidential candidates); or (3) to prove that one item is superior to another (for example, the Democratic candidate's economic plan is more realistic or efficient than that of the Republican candidate).

Compound sentence Two or more *independent (or main) clauses* that are joined into one unit. The previous sentence is not an example of a compound sentence, but the sentence you are now reading is a compound sentence.

Compound–complex sentence A unit that features at least *one independent (or main) clause* and at least *one dependent (or subordinate) clause*. Because this is a dependent clause followed by an independent clause, this is a compound–complex sentence.

Concession In argumentation, the process of admitting that the opposition's argument has some merit, although you should try to convey the following impression to your readers when possible: "My opponents are right that x, but x is less significant than they think because . . . ." See *refutation*.

Connotation The set of associations and implications that make up our general sense of a word beyond its literal definition. See *denotation*.

Controversy Any issue about which intelligent, educated, fair-minded people can disagree and argue logically.

Definition A rhetorical strategy in which you explain the essential meaning or nature of a thing.

Denotation The dictionary definition of a word's literal meaning; the most specific and direct meaning of a word. See *connotation*.

Dependent (or subordinate) clause A group of words having a subject and a verb and starting with a subordinating conjunction such as *although, after,* and *because.*

Description A rhetorical strategy in which you focus on your sensory experience of a subject (in other words, what you see, hear, smell, touch, and taste). As with the other forms of expository writing, description may be the major mode of a complete essay, or it may be included as part of an essay whose major thrust is *argument, exposition,* or *narration.*

Dialogue The exchange of information or ideas between two or more people in a literary text.

Distance A metaphor based on physical distance which suggests the amount of space between when the event occurred and when you write about that event. There are two major kinds of distance in exploratory writing: temporal distance and emotional distance. *Temporal distance* refers to the amount of time separating you from the actual event—did it occur yesterday, last month, five years ago? Usually, the more time separating you from the event, the better your chance of seeing many aspects of the event's *internal significance.* Similarly, the more time separating your revising a draft from the time you originally wrote that draft, the better chance you have of seeing its flaws and gaps. *Emotional distance* has no direct correlation with temporal distance, although common sense suggests that sometimes they are linked. Emotional distance is the difference between your original emotions and your emotions now as you look back on the event. In other words, if you can express in your draft *only* the emotions you felt during the event, you have not effectively explored the event and do not yet see deeply enough into its internal significance. More emotional distance is necessary. For example, it is the difference between saying "Karen's reaction made me angry" and "Karen's reaction made me angry because it threatened my belief in our forever relationship."

Distancing words Verbs of remembering, feeling, thinking. Because they report rather than dramatize, they often prevent your readers from directly experiencing the emotions and thoughts in your essay.

Draft Any version of an essay (or document) before its final version.

Dramatization Derived from the word *drama* and closely related to *narration,* this term literally means the act of making something like a drama or play on stage. In other words, rather than *summarizing* or *telling* what happened, the writer helps readers see the scene, smell the odors, taste the tastes, hear the dialogue and sounds, and feel the textures that were present during an event. In short, the writer creates the illusion that the readers are "on the scene" rather than hearing a report about the event. This is accomplished by using vivid language to provide many specific details. Most narrative essays require a mixture of dramatizing and telling to convey their points clearly.

Evidence Any kind of data which are used to prove something.

Evidence includes expert testimony, logical demonstrations, statistics, facts, and pertinent personal experiences.

Exploratory essay A form of nonfiction prose writing which features the examination of a subject with the additional purpose of revealing something about the writer's intellectual, emotional, and philosophical makeup. Included in its definition are the familiar essay, the literary essay, and the personal essay. The exploratory essay has more latitude than traditional academic essays in the way the subject is examined and in the essay's structure itself.

Exposition A mode of nonfiction writing whose main goal is explanation. As with the other forms of expository writing, exposition may be the major mode of a complete essay, or it may be included as part of an essay whose major thrust is *argument, narration,* or *description.*

External significance The importance or meaning of such things as events or beliefs to your lifestyle. For instance, all of the following are examples that have external significance: your job, your marital status, the number and kinds of possessions you can own, the locations where you live and work, and changes in any of those. External significance can be profound in terms of your everyday life (for example, losing a job, winning the lottery), but may or may not have much *internal significance.* In exploratory essays (as opposed, perhaps, to autobiographical essays), external significance should never be the point of the essay nor the reason for writing it.

Familiar essay A type of exploratory essay; the writer's friendly attitude and tone toward the reader, a "commonplace" subject matter, and an informal and at times almost conversational mode of expression are its major features.

Fast-write The first draft that you write of your essay. You should write it quickly, focusing only on putting the ideas into words, the words into sentences, the sentences into paragraphs, the paragraphs into a coherent order. Ignore the finer points of style and punctuation. The fast-write is comparable to an artist's rough sketch—it reveals what goes where and in what proportion. After it is finished, you begin the process of revising and improving.

Figurative language This is the imaginative use of words (for example, *imagery, similes,* and *metaphors*).

Free modifier Usually a *participial phrase* that adds information and can either begin or end a sentence. For example: "*Seeing* the disconnected hose dangling from the water filter, he realized the reason why the swimming pool was empty. He took the filter's motor to the repair shop, *carrying* it in one hand and *swearing* at it for being broken during the hottest week of the summer."

Global significance The importance that your essay's topic (for example, an event or a concept) has for your readers. Usually this importance should be pointed out explicitly, but it may be simply suggested. Global significance can often be suggested by references to the works of other writers, by references to famous people, and by allusions to fictional characters. If you point out how most people would react to a particular situation and then explain how you reacted, you will have established global significance for your readers. If your essay is about sibling relationships but your reader is an only child, what is the essay's global significance for him or her? Perhaps it gives the reader insight into family dynamics or into forces that mold the personalities of people that he or she might interact with every day (for example, knowing the "middle-child syndrome" might help the reader understand a friend or co-worker's recent outburst). When reading published essays, it is a good idea to identify their global significance for you.

Illusion of spontaneity The reader's erroneous belief that a piece of writing has flowed effortlessly from the writer's pen. This appearance of ease and immediacy is actually a carefully crafted effect.

Imagery Imaginative representation using sensory evidence.

Implied metaphor A figure of speech in which two unlike items are compared indirectly by your using terms associated with one item to describe the other. For example: "The man chewed his lips as his nose twitched rapidly to sniff the air." The two items in the previous sentence are a man and a rabbit, but the rabbit is implied rather than mentioned explicitly.

Independent (or main) clause A group of words having a subject and a verb and capable of standing on its own as a complete thought. This sentence is an independent clause.

Inner self The essence of each of us as a person. It is the collection of hopes, fears, and beliefs that gives us a sense of our identity and our self-image. The inner self is our sense of who we are after all the superficial and not-so-superficial role-playing is over and after all pretense has been removed. It is our core identity.

Internal significance The psychological, spiritual, emotional, or intellectual importance or meaning of anything (such as an event, a concept, or a belief) for you the writer. No matter how insignificant a thing might be in terms of your lifestyle (losing a dime, forgetting a friend's birthday), it may have profound importance to your *inner self*. Internal significance is often contrasted with *external significance*.

Interpretation The act of explicitly explaining the meaning of a text. Using information from the text itself (its structure, its details) as well as extra-textual information such as the text's historical context and its genre, readers construct a sense of what the text is suggesting.

Literary essay The type of exploratory essay which places greater emphasis on the essay itself as a crafted artifact rather than as a simple deliverer of messages, as well as on the greater use of "literary" devices such as dialogue, description of scene, dramatic heightening, and figurative language.

Logic A mode of reasoning, a way of understanding that relies on clearly stated principles. Often it uses *claims, evidence* or data, and *warrants* to come to a conclusion.

Maxim A succinct statement of a general truth or fundamental principle or rule of conduct.

Metaphor A figure of speech which implies a connection between two unlike items. For example: "The man is a rabbit."

Modern edited English The term used to name the form of English which is used in academic and professional settings. It features academically accepted usage, correct spelling, grammar, and punctuation. It normally avoids slang and colloquialisms.

Narration The form of expository writing whose purpose is to recount an event or a series of events (see also *description, argument,* and *exposition*). It frequently employs many of the techniques of fiction, such as vivid description, *dialogue, figurative language,* and *dramatization.* Although narration often features chronological order, it may use flashbacks. It may begin or end with an explicit statement of the event's significance, or that significance may remain implicit. As with the other forms of expository writing, narration may be the major mode of a complete essay, or it may be included as part of an essay whose major thrust is argument or exposition or description.

Official subject In exploratory writing, the topic that shares the spotlight with the writer. The official subject is explained, illustrated, or proven and, in the process, you the writer are also revealed.

Participial phrase A group of words that contains either a present or past *participle* plus its object or complement and perhaps some modifiers. It functions as an adjective and thus modifies a noun or a pronoun. For example: "*Smiling and waving to the crowd,* the candidate tripped on his way to the podium."

Participle A verb form that can be used in a verb phrase (was *thinking*) or as an adjective (*flashing* light). Present participles usually end in -*ing* while most regular past participles end in -*ed* (irregular past participles usually end in -*n, -en, -t*). Here are some examples: *running, promised, been, arisen, meant.*

Passive voice One of the possible relationships between the subject and its verb. The subject receives the action of the verb instead of performing the action (as in the *active voice*). For example: "Don *was dropped* from the team."

Persona A representation of the self, a mask or an identity that you assume in order to emphasize some aspect of your personality and downplay or even hide other aspects. These masks may be social, psychological, literary, or cultural.

Personal essay The form of exploratory essay whose major purpose is the revelation of the writer's self—opinions, emotions, beliefs, life experiences.

Personal experience A term that refers to every book you have ever read, everything you have ever seen on television and in the movies, every song lyric you have ever listened to, every conversation you have ever overheard, every family story ever told to you, every adventure recounted to you by family or friends or strangers, every thought you have ever had, every attitude you have ever held, every observation you have ever made, every fantasy you have ever had, every dream that you remember. There are five categories of personal experience: events you have participated in, events you have witnessed, mental occurrences such as thoughts or fantasies, attitudes such as assumptions or beliefs, any external information (facts or opinions) that you have acquired from any source including television, movies, conversations, books, songs, lectures.

Personal significance The importance that your essay's topic (for example, an event or a concept) has to your *inner self.* Usually this importance should be pointed out explicitly, but it may be simply suggested.

Personal subject Any topic which you write about in order to reveal something about your personality, your thoughts, your beliefs, and your life experiences. They are the topics that you might discuss with acquaintances, friends, religious leaders, or therapists. Although you might feel an initial resistance (either emotional or psychological) to writing about such a topic, such resistance should fade as you write. This concept is contrasted with *private subject.* The designations *personal* and *private* are subjective evaluations on the part of you (the writer), and as such might change from time to time (usually private subjects become personal subjects).

Pithy saying A general term that refers to *adages, aphorisms, maxims,* and *proverbs*—all of which are succinct statements of a general truth or fundamental principle or rule of conduct.

Prewriting The first step in the writing process. It includes anything that you do before writing the first draft (the *fast-write*). Prewriting includes all the idea-generating techniques discussed in Chapter 1 as well as talking to your friends about the topic, researching it, and planning.

Private subjects Topics you cannot bring yourself to write about for readers. For your whole life, such subjects can stay where they are, hidden and safe. They may simply be too private to explore in front of an audience. As your confidence in particular readers grows, however, you might discover that what was once a private subject has become a *personal subject.* In other words, the designation *private subject* is not unchangeable; it depends on your comfort level with examining a particular topic and with particular readers.

Proverb A succinct statement that expresses a basic truth or practical precept. Because the Old Testament has a book called "Proverbs," the term now might have a religious suggestion in some people's minds.

Questioning A technique for expanding ideas in your essays. After each statement or assertion in your draft, ask yourself questions about it and write out the answers, thus increasing your content and expanding your ideas. Questions are listed in Chapter 10.

Refutation The process of giving evidence or a logical demonstration to prove that an argument is false or flawed. See *concession.*

Resumptive modifier A phrase that usually comes at the end of a sentence. It begins with the repetition of a key noun or verb from the sentence and then adds extra information. For example: "Angelo *sang* his favorite song for her, *sang* it with more feeling than he had ever sung it before."

Revision The process by which you see anew your ideas and the essay which expresses them. During the revision process, you should focus on deepening the essay's content, making it more accessible to your particular audience, making the ideas more coherent and unified, and polishing the style as much as possible.

Rhetorical situation The potential interaction among the writer, the reader, and the text (in this case, your essay). The rhetorical situation includes three major questions: What is your purpose for writing this particular essay? Who are your readers? What are their expectations and levels of knowledge about your topic? In other words, as writer you must try to discover the most effective way to make your essay achieve your purpose. That purpose will almost always include conveying information and impressions to your readers. At times it might also include persuading your readers to consider or to believe particular ideas or causing them to feel certain emotions.

Scene The setting where an event occurs.

Self-expression Although this term can refer to anything you do as a writer to "talk to yourself" about a topic, it usually refers to a journal entry or a first draft—in other words, it refers to the first time you tell yourself what you know about the topic. Because you are expressing yourself to discover what you know and what you think about the topic, you need not be concerned with communication with other readers. You are both writer and reader, so your goal in self-expression is to get the ideas into words and into some kind of order. Self-expression always comes before you consider the *rhetorical situation* or the act of *communication* with readers.

Sentence fragment Anything that is not a complete sentence even though it is set up as though it were (for example, it begins with a capital letter and ends with a period). Because such fragments can be confusing. What you just read is an example of a fragment.

Sexist language Language which assumes one gender is dominant.

Showing Although a nontechnical term, *showing* is a useful concept, particularly for those writing narration. Taken from the theory of fiction writing which values dramatization and enactment over **exposition** and **summary,** *showing* is the act of providing specific details in vivid language to create the illusion that readers can see, hear, smell, touch, and taste elements of the scene depicted. Showing is the act of **dramatizing** a scene rather than merely reporting it. For example, instead of reporting that "Alex and Ramona danced," a writer might show the event: "Alex continued to circle around the ever-moving Ramona, displaying his athletic ability with jumps and splits and spins as Ramona twirled gracefully in a narrow space, the center of Alex's circle. When the music changed to a waltz, Alex swept her into his arms and executed eight perfect turns around the floor." Most exploratory essays about events require a mixture of showing and **telling.**

Simile A figure of speech in which a comparison between two unlike objects is made explicit by the use of a word such as *like* or *as*. For example: "The man sniffed the air like a rabbit."

Simple sentence One main (or independent) clause that may have various types of modifiers but no other clauses. This, for example, is a simple sentence—one subject, one verb.

Split perspective Refers to the fact that you have two different views of any event: the emotions and thoughts that occurred to you during the event (called the **you-then** perspective) and the emotions and thoughts that occur to you as you write about that event and your former self (called the **you-now** perspective). For a discussion of the implications of the split perspective, see Chapter 3.

Stereotype A generalization about some group (for example, human beings, Californians, Democrats, older brothers, mothers-in-law) based perhaps on observations of a few individuals within that group, observations that are then erroneously expanded to include all members of the group. Thus a stereotype is always a simplification (and often can be totally incorrect for all but the one or two individuals within the group who were originally observed). Nevertheless, stereotypes can be useful *as a starting place* when you consider yourself or a concept (for instance, *fathering*).

Style The quality of language and characteristic habits of thought which distinguish your writing from anyone else's. In other words, style is the way you select and arrange words, sentences, and paragraphs to convey your thoughts.

Suitcase word or phrase Any vague or general word or group of words which may hold a great deal of meaning for you the writer but whose meaning cannot be intuitively understood by your readers.

Summary The presentation of a body of material or an event in a condensed form in order to highlight or reveal its essence. Usually details, supporting evidence, quotations, and dialogue are eliminated or merely referred to in passing.

Summative modifier A phrase that usually comes at the end of a sentence. It uses one word to summarize the earlier parts of the sentence and then provides additional information. For example: "In one year the company lost two ships and a government contract, financial *catastrophes* from which it could never recover."

Synonym A word that has a similar or nearly the same meaning as another word.

Telling A nontechnical term that is usually paired with *showing,* often in the advice "show, don't tell." It is the act of explaining and reporting an event rather than *dramatizing* or showing it. For instance, "Tyrone and Sarah discussed the project" would normally be perceived as an act of telling, whereas giving readers the actual dialogue between Tyrone and Sarah would be considered showing. Telling is particularly useful for four tasks: (1) making meaning and significance explicit, (2) briefly reporting unimportant details, (3) moving from one *scene* to another, (4) commenting on the events or the people involved.

Text Anything created to communicate with others—for example, novels, short stories, poems, letters, advertisements, plays (both written and staged versions), and films. The term also includes such things as sculpture and architecture. In short, anything that is made by humans to communicate with others is a text.

Time marker Any word or phrase or piece of information that lets your readers know how a section or an event of your essay relates temporally to the other sections or events. Time markers include such words as *then, afterwards, meanwhile,* and *before.* Time markers also include pieces of information such as *when I was five years old, in 1989,* and *after my grandfather's birthday.*

Transitional words The explicit words and phrases that signal the exact connection between their ideas.

Vantage points A number of different ways of considering yourself. For example, you might think about yourself from the human-level vantage point, or from the gender vantage point, or from the educational vantage point. By focusing on only one such aspect of yourself at a time, you can learn more about yourself than if you try to think about your entire self all at once.

Warrant Any assumption or a general principle that underlies an argument and establishes the relevance of the evidence to the claim.

Wordiness An affliction of style in which the writer uses more words than are necessary to convey the meaning.

Writing to discover The underlying *private* purpose of exploratory writing—to learn something new about yourself as you write. What you discover may or may not be revealed in your final draft of the essay. That decision depends on you and your relationship to your readers. The *public* purpose of exploratory writing is to reveal something about your inner self to your readers.

Writing process The preparations and actions which you take as you create an essay. Often discussed as a four-step process (prewriting, drafting, revising, editing), writers actually move back and forth throughout the process, for example, stopping in the middle of revising to prewrite.

You-now Your thoughts, attitudes, feelings, and beliefs in the present moment (as you write) about an event and about the ***you-then***. Often the you-now has a more detached attitude and a broader vision of the subject and its context than the you-then. Because the you-now knows the long-term outcome and effects, you are better able to judge the event's personal significance. See also ***split perspective.***

You-then Your thoughts, attitudes, feelings, and beliefs *at the time* of the event your essay recounts. See ***you-now*** and ***split perspective.***

About the Authors of the Readings

Woody Allen (b. 1935) is one of America's leading humorists and film directors (*Annie Hall, Interiors,* and *Hannah and Her Sisters*). His essays and stories have been collected in *Getting Even, Without Feathers,* and *Side Effects.*

Maya Angelou (b. 1928) is a poet, teacher, singer, dancer, actor, writer-producer, and civil-rights leader. In addition to her poetry, Angelou is noted for her autobiographical prose, including *I Know Why the Caged Bird Sings.*

Francis Bacon (1561–1626) held several high offices during the reign of Queen Elizabeth I, including lord high chancellor of England. He wrote primarily about philosophy and science. His *Essays* (1597) were extremely popular during his lifetime, and his *Novum Organum* (1620) attempted to replace Aristotelian logic.

James Baldwin (1924–1987) was a major American writer of the twentieth century, writing novels, plays, and essays. His works include *Going to Meet the Man* (short stories); two plays, *Blues for Mister Charlie* and *The Amen Corner;* six novels, including *Go Tell It On the Mountain* and *Just Above My Head;* and several volumes of personal essays, including *Notes of a Native Son, Nobody Knows My Name,* and *The Fire Next Time.*

Dave Barry is a Pulitzer Prize–winning syndicated columnist at the *Miami Herald* and the author of several books, including *Dave Barry's Greatest Hits, Dave Barry Turns 40,* and *Dave Barry Talks Back.*

Bruno Bettelheim (1903–1990) was a renowned psychoanalyst who explored the behavior of emotionally disturbed children. A student of Sigmund Freud and a survivor of Nazi concentration camps, Bettelheim looked at the "extreme situations" posed by modern life. His works include *Surviving, The Informed Heart: Autonomy in a Mass Age, Love Is Not Enough, The Children of Dream,* and a study of the psychological effects of fairy tales entitled *The Uses of Enchantment* (winner of a National Book Award).

Ambrose Bierce (1842–?) was the son of a poor Ohio farmer; he became a journalist after serving with the Union army during the Civil War. His cynical and at times nihilistic outlook led to his nickname "Bitter Bierce." He wrote numerous short stories and newspaper columns. In 1913 he disappeared in revolutionary-torn Mexico and was never heard from again. Among his works are *In The Midst of Life, Can Such Things Be?* and *The Devil's Dictionary.*

William Blake (1757–1827) was an English poet and painter. He is considered a forerunner of the English Romantic movement. His works include *Songs of Innocence* and *Songs of Experience* (both collections of lyrics) and the Prophetic Books such as *The Marriage of Heaven and Hell.*

Anne Bradstreet (1612?–1672) was one of the first American poets in Puritan New England. After having unusually broad educational opportunities in England as a child, she married and emigrated with other Puritans to Massachusetts. The mother of eight children, she wrote poetry that moved beyond the conventional public verse to more personal poems.

Raymond Carver (1938–1989) was one of the most influential short-story writers of the late twentieth-century. Before his death from lung cancer, he published six collections of short stories, including *Will You Please Be Quiet, Please, What We Talk About When We Talk About Love,* and *Cathedral,* along with many poems. Carver studied creative writing with John Gardner and then passed his insights along to many younger writers, including Jay McInerney. Among his many awards were a Guggenheim Fellowship (1977–78) and an NEA Award in Fiction (1979).

Lorna Dee Cervantes (b. 1959) is a California native of Mexican descent. In 1974 she founded Mango Publications, which features the works of Chicano writers. Her first book of poetry is *Emplumada.*

Sucheng Chan (b. 1941) teaches history at the University of California, Santa Barbara. Her works include *Asian Americans: An Interpretative History* and *The Bittersweet Soil: The Chinese in California Agriculture, 1860–1910.*

Kate Chopin (1851–1904) grew up in a wealthy Catholic family in St. Louis and married a French-Creole businessman from Louisiana. At the age of 39, she began a writing career that ultimately produced 95 stories, 2 novels, 1 play, and 8 essays of literary criticism. Her most famous work is *The Awakening.*

Stephen Crane (1871–1900) was born in New Jersey and in his brief life managed to publish 5 novels, 2 volumes of poetry, and more than 300 sketches, stories, and reports. A journalist by trade, Crane is most famous for his ironic poetry and for his novels, particularly *Maggie: A Girl of the Streets* and *The Red Badge of Courage.*

Joan Didion (b. 1934) is a political journalist, a novelist, and an essayist. Her works include novels such as *Play It As It Lays* and *The Book of Common Prayer,* and essay volumes such as *Miami, Slouching towards Bethlehem,* and *The White Album.*

Annie Dillard (b. 1945) has written *Tickets for the Prayer Wheel* (poetry), *Living by Fiction* (literary theory), *The Living* (novel), and *An American Childhood* (autobiography, winner of an American Book Award). She is best known for her essay collections, including *Teaching a Stone to Talk* and the Pulitzer Prize–winning *Pilgrim at Tinker Creek.* Among her awards are the New York Presswomen's Award for Excellence (1975), an NEA Fellowship (1980–81), and a Guggenheim Fellowship (1985–86).

Frederick Douglass (1818–1895) was born in slavery in Maryland. In 1838 he escaped to the North and became one of the most articulate advocates of abolition and women's rights of the period. He lectured extensively and wrote several books, including *Narrative of the Life of Frederick Douglass, Written by Himself* and *My Bondage and My Freedom*.

Gerald Early (b. 1952) is a professor of African American studies at Washington University. He is the author of *Tuxedo Junction: Essays on American Culture*. A contributor to several journals such as *Antaeus* and the *Hudson Review*, he has edited two recent essay collections, namely, *The Afro-American Essay and Its Cultural Content from Polemics to Pulpit* and *Lure and Loathing: Essays on Race, Identity, and the Ambivalence of Assimilation*. He has received awards from CCLM-General Electric and the Whitting Foundation.

Charles Alexander Eastman (1858–1939) was a Santee Sioux born in Minnesota. After completing his medical degree at Boston University, he took a post as the government physician at Pine Ridge reservation where he witnessed the events surrounding the massacre at Wounded Knee. He became a well-known writer in his own day and was admired for his apparent ability to adapt to white American culture. Among his works are *Indian Boyhood, Old Indian Days, From Deep Woods to Civilization*, and *The Soul of the Indian*.

Edith Maud Eaton (1865–1914) was the second child of a Chinese woman and an Englishman. Eaton embraced her Chinese heritage and faced a great deal of discrimination. Writing under the pseudonym of Sui Sin Far, she was the first person of Chinese heritage to write in defense of the Chinese in America. Her stories were collected in *Mrs. Spring's Fragrance*.

Barbara Ehrenreich frequently writes on issues of concern to women for a variety of publications such as *Ms.* and *The New Republic*. Her books include *The Worst Years of Our Lives: Irreverent Notes from a Decade, Fear of Falling: The Inner Life of the Middle Class*, and the novel *Kipper's Game*.

Nora Ephron (b. 1941) has been on the staff of *New York* and *Esquire* as well as contributing articles to many other publications. Her works include *Wallflower at the Orgy, Crazy Salad, Scribble, Scribble: Notes on the Media*, and the novel *Heartburn*. She has written several screenplays, including *When Harry Met Sally* and *Sleepless in Seattle*.

Jean Ervin has published essays and stories in a number of journals including *Iowa Woman*. Her books include *The Twin Cities Perceived: A Study in Words and Drawings*.

Benjamin Franklin (1706–1790) was born in Boston and became one of the major figures in early American history. He was a politician, a diplomat, a statesman, an inventor, a printer, a publisher, an economist, a scientist, and a writer. His works include *Poor Richard's Almanack* and *The Autobiography of Benjamin Franklin*.

Abby Frucht has written several novels, including *Snap, Licorice,* and *Are You Mine?*

Susan Glaspell (1876–1948) was a feminist, fiction writer, and playwright from Iowa. She helped to found the Provincetown Players and wrote such plays as *Suppressed Desires, Bernice,* and *Alison's House* (winner of a Pulitzer Prize).

Rose Del Castillo Guilbault is a columnist on Hispanic issues, an associate editor at Pacific News Service, and director of editorials and public affairs at a San Francisco television station.

Joy Harjo (b. 1951) is a Native American poet from Oklahoma. Her poetry collections include *The Last Song* and *She Had Some Horses.*

Nathaniel Hawthorne (1804–1869) is one of the great American writers of the nineteenth century. Author of *The Scarlet Letter* and *The House of Seven Gables* as well as many short stories, Hawthorne explored the darker side of Romanticism and of the human heart.

Garrett Kaoru Hongo (b. 1951) is one of the most prolific and accomplished contemporary Asian American poets. A native of Hawaii, he grew up in California. Presently he is the poetry editor of the *Missouri Review.* His works include *Yellow Light* and *The River of Heaven.*

bell hooks (b. 1952) is the pseudonym for Gloria Watkins, a professor in the departments of English and Women's Studies at Oberlin College and a regular contributor to *Zeta Magazine.* Her books include *And There We Slept: Poems, Ain't I a Woman: Black Women and Feminism, Feminist Theory from Margin to Center, Talking Back: Thinking Feminist, Thinking Black,* and *Black Looks: Race and Representation.*

Janette Turner Hospital was born in Australia and now spends her time in Canada, Massachusetts, and Australia. Her novels include *The Tiger and the Pit, Borderline, Dislocations,* and *The Last Magician.* She won Canada's Seal Award for *The Ivory Swing.*

Zora Neale Hurston (1901?–1960) was born in Florida. She became a collector of African American folk tales—*Mules and Men*—and one of the most significant voices of the Harlem Renaissance. She is best known now for her novel *Their Eyes Were Watching God.*

Molly Ivins was born and raised in Texas. A journalist for over twenty years, Ivins has written for many national magazines as well as for the *Texas Observer, Time,* and the *New York Times.* She writes a nationally syndicated column for the *Fort Worth Star.* Her works include *Molly Ivins Can't Say That, Can She?*

Harriet Jacobs (1813?–1897) was born a slave in North Carolina. Taught to read and write by her first mistress who died when Jacobs was eleven, she became the property of a three-year-old girl whose father (called Dr. Flint in the autobiography but actually Dr. James Norcom) relentlessly harrassed her sexually. Trying to avoid his advances, she ultimately became the mistress of another white man and had two children by him, but Norcom refused to stop. Finally

Jacobs hid for several years in a tiny garret above her grandmother's shed in order to avoid his advances. In 1842 she fled to the North where abolitionist friends finally bought her freedom for $300 and she began working as a nurse for Mrs. Bruce (actually Cornelia Grinnell Willis). She wrote *Incidents in the Life of a Slave Girl* under the pseudonym Linda Brent. In addition to exploring Jacobs's thoughts and feelings, the book helped to broaden the genre of the slave narrative to include the experiences of African American women.

Maxine Hong Kingston (b. 1940) is the author of *The Woman Warrior: Memoirs of a Childhood Among Ghosts* (winner of the National Book Critics Circle Award for nonfiction), *China Men* (winner of the American Book Award), and *Tripmaster Monkey—His Fake Book*. Among her awards are an NEA Writing Fellowship (1980) and a Guggenheim Fellowship (1981).

Edward Koch served as democratic mayor of New York City from 1978 to 1990. He is the author of *Mayor: An Autobiography* written with William Rauch.

Tato Laviera (b. 1951) is a poet and playwright who was born in Puerto Rico and has lived in New York City since 1960. His works include *La Carreta Made a U-Turn, Olú Clemente, Enclave,* and *AmerRícan*.

Alan Lightman (b. 1948) was born and grew up in Tennessee. He has taught astronomy and physics at Harvard and has been a staff member of the Smithsonian Astrophysical Observatory in Cambridge. He was the 1991 chairman of the high energy astrophysics division of the American Astronomy Society. He is currently the director of the Program in Writing and Humanistic Studies at MIT. His poetry won the Rhysling Award (1983), and he has written numerous scientific articles. His books include *Time Travel and Papa Joe's Pipe, Ancient Light: Our Changing View of the Universe, Time for the Stars: Astronomy in the 1990s, Origins: The Lives and Worlds of Modern Cosmologists, A Modern Day Yankee in a Connecticut Court and Other Essays on Science,* and *Einstein's Dream* (a novel).

Jack London (1876–1916) was born in San Francisco. After trying several jobs (including sailor, electrician, and gold miner), he settled on writing as a way of achieving some stability in his life. Among his primary works are *The Call of the Wild, Martin Eden,* and *White Fang*.

Barry Lopez (b. 1945), a resident of rural Oregon for the past 20 years, is author of several nonfiction books such as *Arctic Dreams, Of Wolves and Men,* and *Crossing Open Ground* and of several collections of fiction including *Winter Count* and *River Notes*. He is a contributing editor to *Harper's* and the *North American Review*. Among other honors, he has received the John Burroughs Medal and the American Book Award.

Nancy Mairs (b. 1943) is a writer of poems, short stories, articles, and essays. After graduating from Wheaton College (Norton, Massachusetts), Mairs went on to become a teacher and a writer. Mairs has turned her bouts with depression and the fact that she has multiple sclerosis into an opportunity to explore herself and others more deeply. Her works include *Plaintext: Deciphering a Woman's Life, Remembering the Bone House: An Erotics of Space and Place, Carnal Acts,* and *Ordinary Time: Cycles in Marriage, Faith, and Renewal.* She was a William P. Sloan Fellow in nonfiction (1984) and received the Western States Book Award in 1984.

Jay McInerney is a resident of New York City. His novels include *Bright Lights, Big City,* and *Ransom.*

N. Scott Momaday (b. 1934) is a Native American born on a Kiowa reservation in Oklahoma. His works include two volumes of poetry (*Angel of Geese* and *The Gourd Dancer*), an autobiography (*Names: A Memoir*), and novels (*The Ancient Child* and *House Made of Dawn,* which won a Pulitzer Prize). He has also written a book of Kiowa tribal legends—*The Way to Rainy Mountain.* He has taught at several universities including the University of California at Berkeley, Stanford University, and the University of Arizona. Among his awards are an Academy of American Poets Prize and a Guggenheim Fellowship.

Toni Morrison (b. 1931) is an Ohio native who graduated from Howard and Cornell Universities. Since 1965 she has served as an editor with Random House while writing on her own. Her novels include *The Bluest Eye, Sula, Song of Solomon, Tar Baby, Beloved, Jazz,* and *Playing in the Dark: Whiteness and the Literary Imagination.* Among her awards are the Pulitzer Prize, the Robert F. Kennedy Book Award, and the Melcher Book Award.

Bharati Mukherjee (b. 1940), a native of Calcutta, India, emigrated to Canada and then to the United States where she earned graduate and postgraduate degrees. She has published short stories (*Darkness, The Middleman and Other Stories,* winner of the 1988 National Book Critics Circle Award) and novels (*The Tiger's Daughter, Wife, Jasmine*). With her husband, Clark Blaise, she has co-authored two nonfiction books, *Days and Nights in Calcutta* and *The Sorrow and the Terror: The Haunting Legacy of the Air India Tragedy.*

Gloria Naylor (b. 1950), a New York City native, has written on race issues for such publications as the *New York Times* and *Life* magazine and has been a visiting professor and writer-in-residence at several universities. Her novel *The Women of Brewster Place* explores the lives of several African American women and won the American Book Award for the best first novel. Other novels include *Linden Hills* and *Mama Day.* Her nonfiction has been published in *Centennial.*

Kesaya E. Noda (b. 1950) was born in California and raised in New Hampshire. Her first book, *The Yamato Colony,* is a history of the California community where her family grew up.

Joyce Carol Oates (b. 1938) is one of the most productive literary writers of the twentieth century. She has published over 40 books including novels and collections of short stories, essays, and criticism. Her novel *Them* (1970) won a National Book Award. Her works include *Wonderland, The Raven's Wing, New Heaven, New Earth, With Shuddering Fall, You Must Remember This,* and *Bellefleur.* She has also won an O. Henry Prize and a Guggenheim Fellowship. She and her husband, Raymond Smith, run the Ontario Review Press and publish *The Ontario Review.*

P. J. O'Rourke (b. 1947) was born in Ohio. He began writing for *National Lampoon* in 1973 and is now foreign affairs desk chief for *Rolling Stone.* Among his works are *Modern Manners, The Bachelor Home Companion, Give War a Chance: Eyewitness Accounts of Mankind's Struggle Against Tyranny, Injustice, and Alcohol-Free Beer,* and *Parliament of Whores.*

George Orwell (1903–1950) was born Eric Blair in Bengal, India, the son of a colonial administrator. His most famous novels are *Animal Farm* and *Nineteen Eighty-Four,* and his essays are among the most often anthologized.

Scott Russell Sanders (b. 1945) has written in a number of genres including historical novels, science fiction, mainstream fiction, folk tales, children's stories, and essays. He has been a columnist for the *Chicago-Sun Times* and a professor of English at Indiana University. Among his awards are a Woodrow Wilson Fellowship (1976–78) and an NEA Fellowship (1983–84). His works include *Secrets of the Universe* and *The Paradise of Bombs,* which won the Associated Writing Programs Award for Creative Nonfiction.

Leslie Marmon Silko (b. 1948) was born in New Mexico. Her heritage includes Languna Pueblo, Mexican, and Caucasian. Her works include *Languna Woman: Poems,* the novels *Ceremony* and *Almanac of the Dead,* and a collection of short stories titled *Storyteller.*

Stevie Smith (1902–1971) was born Florence Margaret Smith in England. After working in a London publisher's office, she devoted her time to writing poetry and novels and to broadcasting for the BBC. Her books include *Collected Poems* and *Some Are More Human Than Others.*

Cathy Song (1955) was born in Hawaii, daughter of a Chinese mother and a Korean father. Her collections include *Picture Bride* (which won the Yale Younger Poets Award) and *Frameless Windows, Squares of Light.*

Gary Soto (b. 1952) is a noted Mexican American writer. He has published eight collections of poetry, including *Black Hair, Home Course* *in Religion,* and *The Elements of San Joaquin,* which won the U.S. Award of the International Poetry Forum. His autobiographical collection, *Living Up the Street,* won the American Book Award. He has also received the Andrew Carnegie Medal, a Guggenheim Foundation Fellowship, and two NEA Fellowships.

Sue Standing (b. 1952) was born in Salt Lake City and grew up in Seattle. She is director of the writing/literature major at Wheaton College (Massachusetts). Her collections of poetry include *Deception Pass, Amphibious Weather,* and *Gravida.* Among her awards are an NEA Fellowship (1984) and a Bunting Fellowship (1978–79).

Gloria Steinem (b. 1934) is one of America's best known feminists. She was a co-founder and editor of *Ms.* magazine and has been an effective lecturer and fund-raiser for the women's movement. Her books include *Outrageous Acts and Everyday Rebellions* and *Revolution from Within: A Book of Self-Esteem.*

Rafael Suarez, Jr., is a television reporter who lives in Chicago.

Jonathan Swift (1667–1745) was born and educated in Dublin and moved to England in 1689 to serve as secretary to Sir William Temple before returning to Ireland. He wrote brilliant political journalism and satire. In 1713 he was appointed dean of St. Patrick's in Dublin as reward for service to the Tories. Among his works are *The Battle of the Books* and *A Tale of a Tub.*

Lewis Thomas (b. 1913) is a physician, medical researcher, and essayist. He has been a researcher and administrator at such places as Tulane University and Yale University Medical School. He was president and chancellor of Memorial Sloan-Kettering Cancer Center. His works include *The Lives of a Cell: Notes of a Biology-Watcher, The Medusa and the Snail,* and *The Youngest Science: Notes of a Medicine-Watcher.*

Henry David Thoreau (1817–1862) is arguably the American Romantic who has had the greatest influence on the twentieth century, primarily through *Walden,* a work of philosophy and literature.

Mark Twain (1835–1910) is one of America's most famous humorists. Born Samuel Clemens, he adopted the pseudonym of Mark Twain and created a career as a satirist, journalist, novelist, and orator. Among his works are *Adventures of Huckleberry Finn* and *The Adventures of Tom Sawyer.*

Luisa Valenzuela (b. 1938) is an Argentinean novelist and short-story writer whose works include *Strange Things Happen Here, The Lizard's Tale,* and *Open Door.*

Tino Villanueva (b. 1941) is a poet and painter who was born in Texas. Currently a preceptor in Spanish at Boston University, he is the founder of *Imagine: International Chicano Poetry Journal.* His works include *Hay Otra Voz Poems, Shaking Off the Dark, Crónica de Mis Anos Peores,* and *Scene from the Movie GIANT,* which won an American Book Award.

Grace Ming-Yee Wai, a first-generation Chinese American, was raised in Memphis, Tennessee.

Alice Walker (b. 1944) was the eighth and youngest child of African American sharecroppers in Georgia. A poet, novelist, short-story writer, and essayist, she has taught at several colleges and universities. Among her works are the essay collections called *In Search of Our Mothers' Gardens* and *Living By the Word* and novels such as *The Temple of My Familiar* and *The Color Purple,* winner of both the Pulitzer Prize and the American Book Award. Among her awards are a Rosenthal Award (1973) and a Guggenheim Foundation Award (1979).

Elwyn Brooks White (1899–1985) came to prominence as a contributor to the *New Yorker* and *Harper's.* His collections include *Every Day Is Saturday, One Man's Meat,* and *Essays.* Such works as *Charlotte's Web,* a children's classic, demonstrate his versatility. Among his many awards are the American Academy of Arts and Letters Gold Medal (1960), a Presidential Medal of Freedom (1963), and a National Medal for Literature (1971).

Joy Williams (b. 1944) is a Massachusetts native who is a novelist, short story writer, and essayist. Among her awards are an NEA (1973), a Wallace Stegner Fellowship at Stanford University (1974–75), and a Guggenheim Fellowship (1974). Her works include the novels *State of Grace* and *The Changeling.*

Tobias Wolff has written several books including *This Boy's Life, In the Garden of the North American Martyrs,* and *The Barracks Thief.*

Virginia Woolf (1882–1941) is one of the most important writers of the twentieth century. Innovative and profound, she helped create modern literature as we know it. Her novels include *Mrs. Dalloway* (1925), *To the Lighthouse* (1927), and *The Waves* (1931). Her nonfiction includes *A Room of One's Own* and *The Common Reader.*

Acknowledgments

WOODY ALLEN, "Random Reflections of a Second-Rate Mind," from *Tikkun,* 1990. Copyright © 1990 by Woody Allen. "My Speech to the Graduates," from *Side Effects.* Copyright © 1980 by Woody Allen. Reprinted by permission of Random House, Inc.

MAYA ANGELOU, "My Uncle Willie," from *I Know Why the Caged Bird Sings* by Maya Angelou. Copyright © 1969 by Maya Angelou. Reprinted by permission of Random House, Inc.

JAMES BALDWIN, excerpt from *Notes of a Native Son* by James Baldwin. Copyright © 1955, renewed 1983 by James Baldwin. Reprinted by permission of Beacon Press.

DAVE BARRY, "Daze of Wine and Roses," from *Dave Barry's Greatest Hits* by Dave Barry. Copyright © 1988 by Dave Barry. Reprinted by permission of Crown Publishers, Inc.

BRUNO BETTELHEIM, "The Ignored Lesson of Anne Frank," from *Surviving and Other Essays.* Copyright © 1979 by Bruno Bettelheim and Trude Bettelheim as Trustees. Reprinted by permission of Alfred A. Knopf, Inc.

RAYMOND CARVER, "My Father's Life," from *Esquire,* 1984. Copyright © 1991 by Tess Gallagher. Reprinted by permission of International Creative Management, Inc.

LORNA DEE CERVANTES, "Poem for the Young White Man Who Asked Me How I, an Intelligent, Well-Read Person, Could Believe in the War between Races," from *Emplumada* by Lorna Dee Cervantes, by permission of the University of Pittsburgh Press. Copyright © 1981 by Lorna Dee Cervantes.

SUCHENG CHAN, "You're Short, Besides!" from *Making Waves* by Asian Women United. Copyright © 1989 by Asian Women United. Reprinted by permission of Beacon Press.

JOAN DIDION, "Why I Write," copyright © 1976 by Joan Didion. First published in "The New York Times Book Review." Reprinted by permission of Wallace Literary Agency.

ANNIE DILLARD, "Seeing," from *Pilgrim at Tinker Creek* by Annie Dillard. Copyright © 1974 by Annie Dillard. Reprinted by permission of HarperCollins Publishers, Inc. "Living Like Weasels," from *Teaching a Stone to Talk* by Annie Dillard. Copyright © 1982 by Annie Dillard. Reprinted by permission of HarperCollins Publishers, Inc.

GERALD EARLY, Introduction to *Tuxedo Junction,* copyright © 1989 by Gerald Early. Published by The Ecco Press. Reprinted by permission.

BARBARA EHRENREICH, "The Wretched of the Hearth," from *The New Republic,* April 2, 1990. Reprinted by permission of the author.

NORA EPHRON, "A Few Words about Breasts," from *Crazy Salad.* Copyright © 1972 by Nora Ephron. Reprinted by permission of International Creative Management, Inc.

JEAN ERVIN, "Afterthoughts," first published in *Iowa Woman.* Copyright © 1992 by Iowa Woman Endeavors. Reprinted by permission of the author. This essay also appeared in *Best American Essays 1993.*

ABBY FRUCHT, "The Objects of My Invention," from *The New York Times,* April 11, 1993. Copyright © 1993 by The New York Times Company. Reprinted by permission.

SUSAN GLASPELL, *Trifles.* Reprinted by permission of Dodd, Mead & Company, Inc., from *Plays* by Susan Glaspell. Copyright © 1920 by Dodd, Mead & Company, Inc. Copyright renewed 1948 by Susan Glaspell.

ROSE DEL CASTILLO GUILBAULT, "Americanization is Tough on 'Macho'," from *This World*, August 20, 1989. Reprinted by permission of the author.

JOY HARJO, "The Woman Hanging from the Thirteenth Floor Window," from *She Had Some Horses* by Joy Harjo. Copyright © 1983 by Joy Harjo. Used by permission of the publisher, Thunder's Mouth Press.

GARRETT KAORU HONGO, "Off from Swing Shift," from *Yellow Light*. Copyright © 1982 by Garrett Kaoru Hongo, Wesleyan University Press. Reprinted by permission of University Press of New England.

BELL HOOKS, "Madonna: Plantation Mistress or Soul Sister?" from *Black Looks: Race and Representation* by bell hooks. Reprinted by permission of South End Press.

JANETTE TURNER HOSPITAL, "The Dark Wood," from *Dislocations* by Janette Turner Hospital. Copyright © 1987 by the author, published by Louisiana State University Press. Used with permission.

ZORA NEALE HURSTON, "How It Feels to Be Colored Me," from *I Love Myself When I Am Laughing*. Reprinted by permission of the Estate of Zora Neale Hurston.

MOLLY IVINS, "The Perils and Pitfalls of Reporting in the Lone Star State," from *Molly Ivins Can't Say That, Can She?* by Molly Ivins. Copyright © 1991 by Molly Ivins. Reprinted by permission of Random House, Inc.

MAXINE HONG KINGSTON, "Photograph of My Parents," from *The Woman Warrior*. Copyright © 1975, 1976 by Maxine Hong Kingston. Reprinted by permission of Alfred A. Knopf, Inc.

EDWARD I. KOCH, "Death and Justice: How Capital Punishment Affirms Life," from *The New Republic*, April 15, 1985. Copyright © 1985, The New Republic, Inc. Reprinted by permission of The New Republic.

TATO LAVIERA, "Latero Story," reprinted with permission from the publisher of *Mainstream Ethics* (Houston: Arte Publico Press–University of Houston, 1988).

ALAN P. LIGHTMAN, "Students and Teachers," from *Time Travel and Papa Joe's Pipe* by Alan P. Lightman. Reprinted with the permission of Scribner's, an imprint of Simon & Schuster. Text copyright © 1984 Alan P. Lightman.

BARRY LOPEZ, "The Stone Horse," from *Crossing Open Ground* by Barry Lopez. Copyright © 1978, 1979, 1980, 1981, 1982, 1983, 1984, 1985, 1986, 1988 by Barry Lopez. Reprinted by permission of Sterling Lord Literistic, Inc.

NANCY MAIRS, "On Being a Cripple" and "On Being Raised by a Daughter," from *Plaintext* by Nancy Mairs, University of Arizona Press. Copyright © 1986, 1992 by Nancy Mairs.

JAY MCINERNEY, "Raymond Carver, Mentor," from *The New York Times*, August 6, 1989. Copyright © 1989 by The New York Times Company. Reprinted by permission.

GRACE MING-YEE WAI, "Chinese Puzzle," from *Ms.* Magazine. Reprinted by permission of *Ms.* Magazine. Copyright © 1988.

N. SCOTT MOMADAY, "My Horse and I," from *The Names* by N. Scott Momaday. Copyright © 1987 by N. Scott Momaday. Reprinted by permission of the author.

TONI MORRISON, "The Site of Memory," from *Inventing the Truth*, published by Houghton Mifflin. Copyright © 1987 by Toni Morrison. Reprinted by permission of International Creative Management, Inc.

BHARATI MUKHERJEE, "Love Me or Leave Me," copyright © by Bharati Mukherjee. Reprinted by permission of the author.

GLORIA NAYLOR, "Mommy, What Does 'Nigger' Mean?" from "Hers" column, February 20, 1986, in *The New York Times*. Copyright © 1986 by The New York Times Company. Reprinted by permission.

KESAYA E. NODA, "Growing Up Asian in America," from *Making Waves* by Asian Women United. Copyright © 1989 by Asian Women United. Reprinted by permission of Beacon Press.

JOY WILLIAMS, "Save the Whales, Screw the Shrimp," in *Esquire,* 1989. Copyright © 1989 by Joy Williams. Reprinted by permission of International Creative Management, Inc.

TOBIAS WOLFF, "On Being a Real Westerner," from *This Boy's Life: A Memoir* by Tobias Wolff. Copyright © 1989 by Tobias Wolff. Used by permission of Grove/Atlantic, Inc.

VIRGINIA WOOLF, "The Death of the Moth" from *The Death of the Moth and Other Essays* by Virginia Woolf. Copyright © 1942 by Harcourt Brace & Company and renewed 1970 by Marjorie T. Parsons, Executrix. Reprinted by permission of the publisher.

Index of Authors and Titles

A

Afterthoughts, JEAN ERVIN, 220

Against Nature, JOYCE CAROL OATES, 470

ALLEN, WOODY
  My Speech to the Graduates, 633
  Random Reflections of a Second-Rate Mind, 464

Am I Blue? ALICE WALKER, 453

Americanization Is Tough on "Macho," ROSE DEL CASTILLO GUILBAULT, 352

ANGELOU, MAYA, My Uncle Willie, 216

At Home in the Parliament of Whores, P. J. O'ROURKE, 728

B

BACON, FRANCIS, The Four Idols, 430

BALDWIN, JAMES, Notes of a Native Son, 247

BARRY, DAVE, Daze of Wine and Roses, 637

Beauty: When the Other Dancer Is the Self, ALICE WALKER, 190

Being a Jr., RAFAEL A. SUAREZ, JR., 746

BETTELHEIM, BRUNO, The Ignored Lesson of Anne Frank, 369

BIERCE, AMBROSE, Selections from The Devil's Dictionary, 365

BLAKE, WILLIAM, Proverbs of Hell, 641

BRADSTREET, ANNE, To My Dear Children, 644

C

CARVER, RAYMOND, My Father's Life, 231

Censors, The, LUISA VALENZUELA, 549

CERVANTES, LORNA DEE, Poem for the Young White Man Who Asked Me How I, An Intelligent, Well-Read Person, Could Believe in the War Between Races, 565

CHAN, SUCHENG, "You're Short, Besides!" 650

Chinese Puzzle, GRACE MING-YEE WAI, 770

CHOPIN, KATE, Desirée's Baby, 509

CRANE, STEPHEN, Five Short Poems, 568

D

Dark Wood, The, JANETTE TURNER HOSPITAL, 527

Daze of Wine and Roses, DAVE BARRY, 637

Death and Justice: How Capital Punishment Affirms Life, EDWARD I. KOCH, 458

Death of the Moth, The, VIRGINIA WOOLF, 399

Désirée's Baby, KATE CHOPIN, 509

Devil's Dictionary, The, Selections from, AMBROSE BIERCE, 365

DIDION, JOAN, Why I Write, 33

DILLARD, ANNIE
  Living Like Weasels, 414
  Seeing, 60

DOUGLASS, FREDERICK, from Narrative of the Life of Frederick Douglass, Written by Himself, 658

E

EARLY, GERALD, Introduction to Tuxedo Junction, 127

EASTMAN, CHARLES ALEXANDER, The Ghost Dance War, 666

EATON, EDITH MAUD (SUI SIN FAR), Leaves from the Mental Portfolio of an Eurasian, 674

EHRENREICH, BARBARA, The Wretched of the Hearth, 687

EPHRON, NORA, A Few Words about Breasts, 106

ERVIN, JEAN, Afterthoughts, 220

Essayist and the Essay, The, E. B. WHITE, 30

F

Fenimore Cooper's Literary Offenses, MARK TWAIN, 758

Few Words about Breasts, A, NORA EPHRON, 106

Five Short Poems, STEPHEN CRANE, 568

Four Idols, The, FRANCIS BACON, 430

FRANKLIN, BENJAMIN, Selections from Poor Richard's Almanack, 690

FRUCHT, ABBY, The Objects of My Invention, 693

G

Ghost Dance War, The, CHARLES ALEXANDER EASTMAN, 666

GLASPELL, SUSAN, Trifles, 552

Growing Up Asian in America, KESAYA E. NODA, 94

GUILBAULT, ROSE DEL CASTILLO, Americanization Is Tough on "Macho," 352

H

Hanging, A, GEORGE ORWELL, *165*

HARJO, JOY, The Woman Hanging from the Thirteenth Floor Window, *571*

HAWTHORNE, NATHANIEL, Young Goodman Brown, *515*

HONGO, GARRETT, Off from Swing Shift, *574*

HOOKS, BELL, Madonna: Plantation Mistress or Soul Sister? *699*

Hopper's Women, SUE STANDING, *582*

HOSPITAL, JANETTE TURNER, The Dark Wood, *527*

How It Feels to Be Colored Me, ZORA NEALE HURSTON, *102*

HURSTON, ZORA NEALE, How It Feels to Be Colored Me, *102*

I

Ignored Lesson of Anne Frank, The, BRUNO BETTELHEIM, *369*

Incidents in the Life of a Slave Girl, from, HARRIET JACOBS, *707*

Introduction to *Tuxedo Junction,* GERALD EARLY, *127*

IVINS, MOLLY, The Perils and Pitfalls of Reporting in the Lone Star State, *403*

J

JACOBS, HARRIET, from *Incidents in the Life of a Slave Girl,* *707*

K

KINGSTON, MAXINE HONG, Photographs of My Parents, *287*

KOCH, EDWARD I., Death and Justice: How Capital Punishment Affirms Life, *458*

L

Language and Literature from a Pueblo Indian Perspective, LESLIE MARMON SILKO, *52*

Latero Story, TATO LAVIERA, *576*

LAVIERA, TATO, Latero Story, *576*

Leaves from the Mental Portfolio of an Eurasian, EDITH MAUD EATON (SUI SIN FAR), *674*

LIGHTMAN, ALAN, Students and Teachers, *296*

Like Mexicans, GARY SOTO, *291*

Living Like Weasels, ANNIE DILLARD, *414*

LONDON, JACK, To Build a Fire, *535*

LOPEZ, BARRY, The Stone Horse, *174*

Love Me or Leave Me, BHARATI MUKHERJEE, *720*

M

Madonna: Plantation Mistress or Soul Sister? BELL HOOKS, *699*

MAIRS, NANCY, On Being a Cripple, *115*

MAIRS, NANCY, On Being Raised by a Daughter, *307*

MCINERNEY, JAY, Raymond Carver, Mentor, *240*

Modest Proposal, A, JONATHAN SWIFT, *749*

MOMADAY, N. SCOTT, My Horse and I, *302*

"Mommy, What Does 'Nigger' Mean?" GLORIA NAYLOR, *348*

MORRISON, TONI, The Site of Memory, *711*

MUKHERJEE, BHARATI, Love Me or Leave Me, *720*

My Father's Life, RAYMOND CARVER, *231*

My Horse and I, N. SCOTT MOMADAY, *302*

My Speech to the Graduates, WOODY ALLEN, *633*

My Uncle Willie, MAYA ANGELOU, *216*

N

Narrative of the Life of Frederick Douglass, Written by Himself, from, FREDERICK DOUGLASS, *658*

NAYLOR, GLORIA, "Mommy, What Does 'Nigger' Mean?" *348*

NODA, KESAYA E., Growing Up Asian in America, *94*

Notes of a Native Son, JAMES BALDWIN, *247*

O

O'ROURKE, P. J., At Home in the Parliament of Whores, *728*

OATES, JOYCE CAROL, Against Nature, *470*

Objects of My Invention, The, ABBY FRUCHT, *693*

Off from Swing Shift, GARRETT HONGO, *574*

On Being a Cripple, NANCY MAIRS, *115*

On Being a Real Westerner, TOBIAS WOLFF, *161*

On Being Raised by a Daughter, NANCY MAIRS, *307*

On Natural Death, LEWIS THOMAS, *362*

On the Decay of the Art of Lying,
MARK TWAIN, *356*
Once More to the Lake, E. B. WHITE,
183
ORWELL, GEORGE
A Hanging, *165*
Shooting an Elephant, *738*

P
Perils and Pitfalls of Reporting in the
Lone Star State, The, MOLLY IVINS,
403
Photographs of My Parents, MAXINE
HONG KINGSTON, *287*
Poem for the Young White Man Who
Asked Me How I, An Intelligent,
Well-Read Person, Could Believe in
the War Between Races, LORNA DEE
CERVANTES, *565*
Poor Richard's Almanack, Selections
from, BENJAMIN FRANKLIN, *690*
Proverbs of Hell, WILLIAM BLAKE, *641*

R
Random Reflections of a Second-Rate
Mind, WOODY ALLEN, *464*
Raymond Carver, Mentor, JAY
MCINERNEY, *240*

S
SANDERS, SCOTT RUSSELL, The Singular
First Person, *40*
Save the Whales, Screw the Shrimp,
JOY WILLIAMS, *478*
Scene from the Movie *GIANT,* TINO
VILLANUEVA, *584*
Seeing, ANNIE DILLARD, *60*
Shooting an Elephant, GEORGE ORWELL,
738
SILKO, LESLIE MARMON, Language and
Literature from a Pueblo Indian
Perspective, *52*
Singular First Person, The, SCOTT
RUSSELL SANDERS, *40*
Site of Memory, The, TONI MORRISON,
711
SMITH, STEVIE, The Weak Monk, *579*
SONG, CATHY, The Youngest Daughter,
580
SOTO, GARY, Like Mexicans, *291*
STANDING, SUE, Hopper's Women, *582*
STEINEM, GLORIA, Unlearning Romance,
320
Stone Horse, The, BARRY LOPEZ, *174*

Students and Teachers, ALAN LIGHTMAN,
296
SUAREZ, RAFAEL A., JR., Being a Jr., *746*
SWIFT, JONATHAN, A Modest Proposal,
749

T
THOMAS, LEWIS, On Natural Death, *362*
THOREAU, HENRY DAVID
The War of the Ants, *170*
Where I Lived, and What I Lived
For, *419*
To Build a Fire, JACK LONDON, *535*
To My Dear Children, ANNE
BRADSTREET, *644*
Trifles, SUSAN GLASPELL, *552*
TWAIN, MARK
Fenimore Cooper's Literary Offenses,
758
On the Decay of the Art of Lying,
356
Was the World Made for Man? *394*

U
Unlearning Romance, GLORIA STEINEM,
320

V
VALENZUELA, LUISA, The Censors, *549*
VILLANUEVA, TINO, Scene from the
Movie *GIANT, 584*

W
WAI, GRACE MING-YEE, Chinese Puzzle,
770
WALKER, ALICE
Am I Blue? *453*
Beauty: When the Other Dancer Is
the Self, *190*
War of the Ants, The, HENRY DAVID
THOREAU, *170*
Was the World Made for Man? MARK
TWAIN, *394*
Weak Monk, The, STEVIE SMITH, *579*
Where I Lived, and What I Lived For,
HENRY DAVID THOREAU, *419*
WHITE, E. B.
Once More to the Lake, *183*
The Essayist and the Essay, *30*
Why I Write, JOAN DIDION, *33*
WILLIAMS, JOY, Save the Whales, Screw
the Shrimp, *478*
WOLFF, TOBIAS, On Being a Real
Westerner, *161*

Woman Hanging from the Thirteenth Floor Window, The, JOY HARJO, *571*

WOOLF, VIRGINIA, The Death of the Moth, *399*

Wretched of the Hearth, The, BARBARA EHRENREICH, *687*

Y

"You're Short, Besides!" SUCHENG CHAN, *650*

Young Goodman Brown, NATHANIEL HAWTHORNE, *515*

Youngest Daughter, The, CATHY SONG, *580*